CSS
The Definitive Guide

Other resources from O'Reilly

Related titles

HTML & XHTML: The
   Definitive Guide

JavaScript: The Definitive
   Guide

Learning JavaScript

Dynamic HTML: The
   Definitive Reference

JavaScript & DHTML
   Cookbook™

Web Design in a Nutshell

oreilly.com

oreilly.com is more than a complete catalog of O'Reilly books. You'll also find links to news, events, articles, weblogs, sample chapters, and code examples.

oreillynet.com is the essential portal for developers interested in open and emerging technologies, including new platforms, programming languages, and operating systems.

Conferences

O'Reilly brings diverse innovators together to nurture the ideas that spark revolutionary industries. We specialize in documenting the latest tools and systems, translating the innovator's knowledge into useful skills for those in the trenches. Visit *conferences.oreilly.com* for our upcoming events.

Safari Bookshelf (*safari.oreilly.com*) is the premier online reference library for programmers and IT professionals. Conduct searches across more than 1,000 books. Subscribers can zero in on answers to time-critical questions in a matter of seconds. Read the books on your Bookshelf from cover to cover or simply flip to the page you need. Try it today for free.

THIRD EDITION

CSS
The Definitive Guide

Eric A. Meyer

O'REILLY®

Beijing · Cambridge · Farnham · Köln · Paris · Sebastopol · Taipei · Tokyo

CSS: The Definitive Guide, Third Edition

by Eric A. Meyer

Copyright © 2007, 2004, 2000 O'Reilly Media, Inc. All rights reserved.
Printed in the United States of America.

Published by O'Reilly Media, Inc., 1005 Gravenstein Highway North, Sebastopol, CA 95472.

O'Reilly books may be purchased for educational, business, or sales promotional use. Online editions are also available for most titles (*safari.oreilly.com*). For more information, contact our corporate/institutional sales department: (800) 998-9938 or *corporate@oreilly.com*.

Editor: Tatiana Apandi
Production Editor: Rachel Monaghan
Copyeditor: Rachel Monaghan
Proofreader: Laurel R.T. Ruma

Indexer: Reg Aubry
Cover Designer: Karen Montgomery
Interior Designer: David Futato
Illustrators: Robert Romano and Jessamyn Read

Printing History:

May 2000:	First Edition.
March 2004:	Second Edition.
November 2006:	Third Edition.

 This book uses RepKover™, a durable and flexible lay-flat binding.

ISBN-10: 0-596-52733-0
ISBN-13: 978-0-596-52733-4
[C] [1/08]

To my wife and daughter
and all the joys they bring me.

Table of Contents

Preface

If you are a web designer or document author interested in sophisticated page styling, improved accessibility, and saving time and effort, this book is for you. All you really need before starting the book is a decent knowledge of HTML 4.0. The better you know HTML, of course, the better prepared you'll be. You will need to know very little else to follow this book.

This third edition of *CSS: The Definitive Guide* covers CSS2 and CSS2.1 (up through the 11 April 2006 Working Draft), the latter of which is, in many ways, a clarification of the first. While some CSS3 modules have reached Candidate Recommendation status as of this writing, I have chosen not to cover them in this edition (with the exception of some CSS3 selectors). I made this decision because implementation of these modules is still incomplete or nonexistent. I feel it's important to keep the book focused on currently supported and well-understood levels of CSS, and to leave any future capabilities for future editions.

Conventions Used in This Book

The following typographical conventions are used in this book:

Italic

> Indicates new terms, URLs, variables in text, user-defined files and directories, commands, file extensions, filenames, directory or folder names, and UNC pathnames.

`Constant width`

> Indicates command-line computer output, code examples, Registry keys, and keyboard accelerators.

`Constant width bold`

> Indicates user input in examples.

`Constant width italic`

> Indicates variables in examples and in Registry keys. It is also used to indicate variables or user-defined elements within italic text (such as pathnames or filenames). For instance, in the path *\Windows\username*, replace username with your name.

This icon signifies a tip, suggestion, or general note.

This icon indicates a warning or caution.

Property Conventions

Throughout this book, there are boxes that break down a given CSS property. These have been reproduced practically verbatim from the CSS specifications, but some explanation of the syntax is in order.

Throughout, the allowed values for each property are listed with the following syntax:

Value: [<length> | thick | thin]{1,4}
Value: [<family-name> ,]* <family-name>
Value: <url>? <color> [/ <color>]?
Value: <url> || <color>

Any words between "<" and ">" give a type of value or a reference to another property. For example, the property font will accept values that actually belong to the property font-family. This is denoted by the text <font-family>. Any words presented in constant width are keywords that must appear literally, without quotes. The forward slash (/) and the comma (,) must also be used literally.

Several keywords strung together means that all of them must occur in the given order. For example, help me means that the property must use those keywords in that exact order.

If a vertical bar separates alternatives (X | Y), then any one of them must occur. A vertical double bar (X || Y) means that X, Y, or both must occur, but they may appear in any order. Brackets ([...]) are for grouping things together. Juxtaposition is stronger than the double bar, and the double bar is stronger than the bar. Thus "V W | X || Y Z" is equivalent to "[V W] | [X || [Y Z]]".

Every word or bracketed group may be followed by one of the following modifiers:

- An asterisk (*) indicates that the preceding value or bracketed group is repeated zero or more times. Thus, bucket* means that the word bucket can be used any number of times, including zero. There is no upper limit defined on the number of times it can be used.

- A plus (+) indicates that the preceding value or bracketed group is repeated one or more times. Thus, mop+ means that the word mop must be used at least once, and potentially many more times.

- A question mark (?) indicates that the preceding value or bracketed group is optional. For example, [pine tree]? means that the words pine tree need not be used (although they must appear in that exact order if they are used).

- A pair of numbers in curly braces ({M,N}) indicates that the preceding value or bracketed group is repeated at least M and at most N times. For example, ha{1,3} means that there can be one, two, or three instances of the word ha.

Some examples follow:

give || me || liberty
> At least one of the three words must be used, and they can be used in any order. For example, give liberty, give me, liberty me give, and give me liberty are all valid.

[I | am]? the || walrus
> Either the word I or am may be used, but not both, and use of either is optional. In addition, either the or walrus, or both, must follow in any order. Thus, you could construct I the walrus, am walrus the, am the, I walrus, walrus the, and so forth.

koo+ ka-choo
> One or more instances of koo must be followed by ka-choo. Therefore, koo koo ka-choo, koo koo koo ka-choo, and koo ka-choo are all legal. The number of koos is potentially infinite, although there are bound to be implementation-specific limits.

I really{1,4}? [love | hate] [Microsoft | Netscape | Opera | Safari]
> This is the all-purpose web designer's opinion expresser. This example can be interpreted as I love Netscape, I really love Microsoft, and similar expressions. Anywhere from zero to four reallys may be used. You also get to pick between love and hate, even though only love was shown in this example.

[[Alpha || Baker || Cray],]{2,3} and Delphi
> This is a potentially long and complicated expression. One possible result would be Alpha, Cray, and Delphi. The comma is placed because of its position within the nested bracket groups.

Using Code Examples

This book is here to help you get your job done. In general, you may use the code in this book in your programs and documentation. You do not need to contact us for permission unless you're reproducing a significant portion of the code. For example, writing a program that uses several chunks of code from this book does not require permission. Selling or distributing a CD-ROM of examples from O'Reilly books does require permission. Answering a question by citing this book and quoting example code does not require permission. Incorporating a significant amount of example code from this book into your product's documentation does require permission.

We appreciate, but do not require, attribution. An attribution usually includes the title, author, publisher, and ISBN. For example: "*CSS: The Definitive Guide*, Third Edition, by Eric A. Meyer. Copyright 2007 O'Reilly Media, Inc., 978-0-596-52733-4."

If you feel your use of code examples falls outside fair use or the permission given above, feel free to contact us at *permissions@oreilly.com*.

How to Contact Us

We at O'Reilly have tested and verified the information in this book to the best of our ability, but you may find that features have changed (or even that we have made mistakes!). Please let us know about any errors you find, as well as your suggestions for future editions, by writing to:

> O'Reilly Media, Inc.
> 1005 Gravenstein Highway North
> Sebastopol, CA 95472
> 800-998-9938 (in the United States or Canada)
> 707-829-0515 (international or local)
> 707-829-0104 (fax)

There is a web page for this book, which lists errata, examples, or any additional information. You can access this page at:

> *http://www.oreilly.com/catalog/csstdg3*

To comment or ask technical questions about this book, send email to:

> *bookquestions@oreilly.com*

For more information about books, conferences, Resource Centers, and the O'Reilly Network, see the O'Reilly web site at:

> *http://www.oreilly.com*

Safari® Enabled

 When you see a Safari® Enabled icon on the cover of your favorite technology book, that means the book is available online through the O'Reilly Network Safari Bookshelf.

Safari offers a solution that's better than e-books. It's a virtual library that lets you easily search thousands of top tech books, cut and paste code samples, download chapters, and find quick answers when you need the most accurate, current information. Try it for free at *http://safari.oreilly.com*.

Acknowledgments

I'd like to take a moment to thank the people who have backed me up during the long process of getting this book to its readers.

First, I'd like to thank everyone at O'Reilly for all they've done over the years, giving me my break into publishing and continuing to give me the opportunity to produce a book that matters. For this third edition, I'd like to thank Tatiana Apandi for her good humor, patience, and understanding as I played chicken with my deadlines.

I'd also like to thank most profoundly my technical reviewers. For the first edition, that was David Baron and Ian Hickson, with additional input from Bert Bos and Håkon Lie. The second edition was reviewed by Tantek Çelik and Ian Hickson. The fine folks who performed technical review on the third edition, the one you hold in your hands, were Darrell Austin, Liza Daly, and Neil Lee. All lent their considerable expertise and insight, keeping me honest and up-to-date on the latest changes in CSS as well as taking me to task for sloppy descriptions and muddled explanations. None of the editions, least of all this one, could have been as good as it is without their collective efforts, but of course whatever errors you find in the text are my fault, not theirs. That's kind of a cliché, I know, but it's true nonetheless.

Similarly, I'd like to thank everyone who pointed out errata that needed to be addressed. I may not have always been good about sending back email right away, but I read all of your questions and concerns and, when needed, made corrections. The continued feedback and constructive criticism will only help the book get better, as it always has.

There are a few personal acknowledgments to make as well.

To the staff of WRUW, 91.1 FM Cleveland, thank you for nine years of support, great music, and straight-out fun. Maybe one day I'll bring Big Band back to your airwaves, and maybe not; but either way, keep on keepin' on.

To Jeffrey Zeldman, thanks for being a great colleague and partner; and to the whole Zeldman family, thanks for being such wonderful friends.

To "Auntie" Molly, thanks for always being who you are.

To "Uncle" Jim, thanks for everything, both professionally and personally. It's no exaggeration to say I wouldn't be where I am without your influence, and our lives would be a good deal poorer without you around.

To the Bread and Soup Crew—Jim, Genevieve, Jim, Gini, Ferrett, Jen, Jenn, and Molly—thanks for all your superb cooking and tasty conversation.

To my extended family, thank you as always for your love and support.

To anyone I should have thanked, but didn't: my apologies. And my thanks.

And to my wife and daughter, more thanks than I can ever express for making my days richer than I have any right to expect, and for showering me with more love than I could ever hope to repay. Though I'll keep trying, of course.

—Eric A. Meyer
Cleveland Heights, Ohio
1 August 2006

CHAPTER 1

CSS and Documents

Cascading Style Sheets (CSS) are a powerful way to affect the presentation of a document or a collection of documents. Obviously, CSS is basically useless without a document of some sort, since it would have no content to present. Of course, the definition of "document" is extremely broad. For example, Mozilla and related browsers use CSS to affect the presentation of the browser chrome itself. Still, without the content of the chrome—buttons, address inputs, dialog boxes, windows, and so on—there would be no need for CSS (or any other presentational information).

The Web's Fall from Grace

Back in the dimly remembered, early years of the Web (1990–1993), HTML was a fairly lean language. It was composed almost entirely of structural elements that were useful for describing things like paragraphs, hyperlinks, lists, and headings. It had nothing even remotely approaching tables, frames, or the complex markup we assume is necessary to create web pages. HTML was originally intended to be a structural markup language, used to describe the various parts of a document; very little was said about how those parts should be displayed. The language wasn't concerned with appearance—it was just a clean little markup scheme.

Then came Mosaic.

Suddenly, the power of the World Wide Web was obvious to almost anyone who spent more than 10 minutes playing with it. Jumping from one document to another was no more difficult than pointing the cursor at a specially colored bit of text, or even an image, and clicking the mouse. Even better, text and images could be displayed together, and all you needed to create a page was a plain-text editor. It was free, it was open, and it was cool.

Web sites began to spring up everywhere. There were personal journals, university sites, corporate sites, and more. As the number of sites increased, so did the demand for new HTML elements that would each perform a specific function. Authors started demanding that they be able to make text boldfaced or italicized.

At the time, HTML wasn't equipped to handle those sorts of desires. You could declare a bit of text to be emphasized, but that wasn't necessarily the same as being italicized—it could be boldfaced instead, or even normal text with a different color, depending on the user's browser and preferences. There was nothing to ensure that what the author created was what the reader would see.

As a result of these pressures, markup elements like `<FONT>` and `<BIG>` started to creep into the language. Suddenly, a structural language started to become presentational.

What a Mess

Years later, we have inherited the problems of this haphazard process. Large parts of HTML 3.2 and HTML 4.0, for example, were devoted to presentational considerations. The ability to color and size text through the font element, to apply background colors and images to documents and tables, to use table attributes (such as cellspacing), and to make text blink on and off are all the legacy of the original cries for "more control!"

For an example of the mess in action, take a quick glance at almost any corporate web site's markup. The sheer amount of markup in comparison to actual useful information is astonishing. Even worse, for most sites, the markup is almost entirely comprised of tables and font elements, neither of which conveys any real semantic meaning as to what's being presented. From a structural standpoint, these pages are little better than random strings of letters.

For example, let's assume that for page titles, an author uses font elements instead of heading elements like h1:

```
<font size="+3" face="Helvetica" color="red">Page Title</font>
```

Structurally speaking, the font tag has no meaning. This makes the document far less useful. What good is a font tag to a speech-synthesis browser, for example? If an author uses heading elements instead of font elements, though, the speaking browser can use a certain speaking style to read the text. With the font tag, the browser has no way to know that the text is any different from other text.

Why do authors run roughshod over structure and meaning this way? Because they want readers to see the page as they designed it. To use structural HTML markup is to give up a lot of control over a page's appearance, and it certainly doesn't allow for the kind of densely packed page designs that have become so popular over the years. But consider the following problems with such an approach:

- Unstructured pages make content indexing inordinately difficult. A truly powerful search engine would allow users to search only page titles, or only section headings within pages, or only paragraph text, or perhaps only those paragraphs that are marked as important. To accomplish such a feat, however, the page contents must be contained within some sort of structural markup—exactly the sort of markup most pages lack. Google, for example, does pay attention to markup structure when indexing pages, so a structural page will increase your Google rank.

- Lack of structure reduces accessibility. Imagine that you are blind and rely on a speech-synthesis browser to search the Web. Which would you prefer: a structured page that lets your browser read only section headings so that you can choose which section you'd like to hear more about; or a page that is so lacking in structure that your browser is forced to read the entire thing with no indication of what's a heading, what's a paragraph, and what's important? Let's return to Google—the search engine is, in effect, the world's most active blind user, with millions of friends who accept its every suggestion about where to surf and shop.

- Advanced page presentation is possible only with some sort of document structure. Imagine a page in which only the section headings are shown, with an arrow next to each. The user can decide which section heading applies to him and click on it, thus revealing the text of that section.

- Structured markup is easier to maintain. How many times have you spent several minutes hunting through someone else's HTML (or even your own) in search of the one little error that's messing up your page in one browser or another? How much time have you spent writing nested tables and font elements, only to get a sidebar with white hyperlinks in it? How many linebreak elements have you inserted trying to get exactly the right separation between a title and the following text? By using structural markup, you can clean up your code and make it easier to find what you're looking for.

Granted, a fully structured document is a little plain. Due to that one single fact, a hundred arguments in favor of structural markup won't sway a marketing department from using the type of HTML that was so prevalent at the end of the 20th century, and which persists even today. What we need is a way to combine structural markup with attractive page presentation.

CSS to the Rescue

Of course, the problem of polluting HTML with presentational markup was not lost on the World Wide Web Consortium (W3C), which began searching for a quick solution. In 1995, the consortium started publicizing a work-in-progress called CSS. By 1996, it had become a full Recommendation, with the same weight as HTML itself. Here's why.

Rich Styling

In the first place, CSS allows for much richer document appearances than HTML ever allowed, even at the height of its presentational fervor. CSS lets you set colors on text and in the background of any element; permits the creation of borders around any element, as well as the increase or decrease of the space around them; lets you change the way text is capitalized, decorated (e.g., underlining), spaced, and even whether it is displayed at all; and allows you to accomplish many other effects.

Take, for example, the first (and main) heading on a page, which is usually the title of the page itself. The proper markup is:

```
<h1>Leaping Above The Water</h1>
```

Now, suppose you want this title to be dark red, use a certain font, be italicized and underlined, and have a yellow background. To do all of that with HTML, you'd have to put the h1 into a table and load it up with a ton of other elements like font and U. With CSS, all you need is one rule:

```
h1 {color: maroon; font: italic 2em Times, serif; text-decoration: underline;
    background: yellow;}
```

That's it. As you can see, everything you did in HTML can be done in CSS. There's no need to confine yourself to only those things HTML can do, however:

```
h1 {color: maroon; font: italic 2em Times, serif; text-decoration: underline;
    background: yellow url(titlebg.png) repeat-x;
    border: 1px solid red; margin-bottom: 0; padding: 5px;}
```

You now have an image in the background of the h1 that is only repeated horizontally, and a border around it, separated from the text by at least five pixels. You've also removed the margin (blank space) from the bottom of the element. These are feats that HTML can't even come close to matching—and that's just a taste of what CSS can do.

Ease of Use

If the depth of CSS doesn't convince you, then perhaps this will: style sheets can drastically reduce a web author's workload.

First, style sheets centralize the commands for certain visual effects in one handy place, instead of scattering them throughout the document. As an example, let's say you want all of the h2 headings in a document to be purple. Using HTML, the way to do this would be to put a font tag in every heading, like so:

```
<h2><font color="purple">This is purple!</font></h2>
```

This must be done for every heading of level two. If you have 40 headings in your document, you have to insert 40 font elements throughout, one for each heading! That's a lot of work for one little effect.

Let's assume that you've gone ahead and put in all those font elements. You're done, you're happy—and then you decide (or your boss decides for you) that those h2 headings should really be dark green, not purple. Now you have to go back and fix every single one of those font elements. Sure, you might be able to find-and-replace, as long as headings are the only purple text in your document. If you've put other purple font elements in your document, then you *can't* find-and-replace because you'd affect those, too.

It would be much better to have a single rule instead:

```
h2 {color: purple;}
```

Not only is this faster to type, but it's easier to change. If you do switch from purple to dark green, all you have to change is that one rule.

Let's go back to the highly styled h1 element from the previous section:

```
h1 {color: maroon; font: italic 2em Times, serif; text-decoration: underline;
    background: yellow;}
```

This may look like it's worse to write than HTML, but consider a case where you have a page with about a dozen h2 elements that should look the same as the h1. How much markup will be required for those 12 h2 elements? A lot. On the other hand, with CSS, all you need to do is this:

```
h1, h2 {color: maroon; font: italic 2em Times, serif; text-decoration: underline;
        background: yellow;}
```

Now the styles apply to both h1 and h2 elements, with just three extra keystrokes.

If you want to change the way h1 and h2 elements look, the advantages of CSS are even more striking. Consider how long it would take to change the HTML markup for an h1 and 12 h2 elements, compared to changing the previous styles to this:

```
h1, h2 {color: navy; font: bold 2em Helvetica, sans-serif;
        text-decoration: underline overline; background: silver;}
```

If the two approaches were timed on a stopwatch, I'm betting the CSS-savvy author would easily beat the HTML jockey.

In addition, most CSS rules are collected into one location in the document. It is possible to scatter them throughout the document by grouping them into associated styles or individual elements, but it's usually far more efficient to place all of your styles into a single style sheet. This lets you create (or change) the appearance of an entire document in one place.

Using Your Styles on Multiple Pages

But wait—there's more! Not only can you centralize all of the style information for a page in one place, but you can also create a style sheet that can then be applied to multiple pages. This is accomplished by a process in which a style sheet is saved to its own document and then imported by any page for use with that document. Using this capability, you can quickly create a consistent look for an entire web site. All you have to do is link the single style sheet to all of the documents on your web site. Then, if you ever want to change the look of your site's pages, you need only edit a single file and the change will be propagated throughout the entire server—automatically!

Consider a site where all of the headings are gray on a white background. They get this color from a style sheet that says:

```
h1, h2, h3, h4, h5, h6 {color: gray; background: white;}
```

Now let's say this site has 700 pages, each of which uses the style sheet that says the headings should be gray. At some point, the site's webmaster decides that the headings should be white on a gray background. So she edits the style sheet to say:

```
h1, h2, h3, h4, h5, h6 {color: white; background: gray;}
```

Then she saves the style sheet to disk and the change is made. That sure beats having to edit 700 pages to enclose every heading in a table and a font tag, doesn't it?

Cascading

That's not all! CSS also makes provisions for conflicting rules; these provisions are collectively referred to as the *cascade*. For instance, take the previous scenario in which you import a single style sheet into several web pages. Now inject a set of pages that share many of the same styles, but also include specialized rules that apply only to them. You can create another style sheet that is imported into those pages, in addition to the already existing style sheet, or you could just place the special styles into the pages that need them.

For example, on one page out of the 700, you might want headings to be yellow on dark blue instead of white on gray. In that single document, then, you could insert this rule:

```
h1, h2, h3, h4, h5, h6 {color: yellow; background: blue;}
```

Thanks to the cascade, this rule will override the imported rule for white-on-gray headings. By understanding the cascade rules and using them to your advantage, you can create highly sophisticated sheets that can be changed easily and come together to give your pages a professional look.

The power of the cascade is not confined to the author. Web surfers (or *readers*) can, in some browsers, create their own style sheets (called *reader style sheets*, obviously enough) that will cascade with the author's styles as well as the styles used by the browser. Thus, a reader who is colorblind could create a style that makes hyperlinks stand out:

```
a:link, a:visited {color: white; background: black;}
```

A reader style sheet can contain almost anything: a directive to make text large enough to read if the user has impaired vision, rules to remove images for faster reading and browsing, and even styles to place the user's favorite picture in the background of every document. (This isn't recommended, of course, but it is possible.) This lets readers customize their web experience without having to turn off all of the author's styles.

Between importing, cascading, and its variety of effects, CSS is a wonderful tool for any author or reader.

Compact File Size

Besides the visual power of CSS and its ability to empower both author and reader, there is something else about it that your readers will like. It can help keep document sizes as small as possible, thereby speeding download times. How? As I've mentioned, a lot of pages have used tables and font elements to achieve nifty visual effects. Unfortunately, both of these methods create additional HTML markup that drives up the file sizes. By grouping visual style information into central areas and representing those rules using a fairly compact syntax, you can remove the font elements and other bits of the usual tag soup. Thus, CSS can keep your load times low and your reader satisfaction high.

Preparing for the Future

HTML, as I pointed out earlier, is a structural language, while CSS is its complement: a stylistic language. Recognizing this, the W3C, the body that debates and approves standards for the Web, is beginning to remove stylistic elements from HTML. The reasoning for this move is that style sheets can be used to create the effects that certain HTML elements now provide, so who needs them?

Thus, the XHTML specification has a number of elements that are deprecated—that is, they are in the process of being phased out of the language altogether. Eventually, they will be marked as obsolete, which means that browsers will be neither required nor encouraged to support them. Among the deprecated elements are <font>, <basefont>, <u>, <strike>, <s>, and <center>. With the advent of style sheets, none of these elements are necessary. And there may be more elements deprecated as time goes by.

As if that weren't enough, there is the possibility that HTML will be gradually replaced by the *Extensible Markup Language* (*XML*). XML is much more complicated than HTML, but it is also far more powerful and flexible. Despite this, XML does not provide any way to declare style elements such as <i> or <center>. Instead, it is quite probable that XML documents will rely on style sheets to determine their appearance. While the style sheets used with XML may not be CSS, they will probably be whatever follows CSS and very closely resemble it. Therefore, learning CSS now gives authors a big advantage when the time comes to make the jump to an XML-based web.

So, to get started, it's very important to understand how CSS and document structures relate to each other. It's possible to use CSS to affect document presentation in a very profound way, but there are also limits to what you can do. Let's start by exploring some basic terminology.

Elements

Elements are the basis of document structure. In HTML, the most common elements are easily recognizable, such as p, table, span, a, and div. Every single element in a document plays a part in its presentation. In CSS terms, at least as of CSS2.1, that means each element generates a box that contains the element's content.

Replaced and Nonreplaced Elements

Although CSS depends on elements, not all elements are created equally. For example, images and paragraphs are not the same type of element, nor are span and div. In CSS, elements generally take two forms: replaced and nonreplaced. The two types are explored in detail in Chapter 7, which covers the particulars of the box model, but I'll address them briefly here.

Replaced elements

Replaced elements are those where the element's content is replaced by something that is not directly represented by document content. The most familiar XHTML example is the img element, which is replaced by an image file external to the document itself. In fact, img has no actual content, as you can see by considering a simple example:

```
<img src="howdy.gif" />
```

This markup fragment contains no actual content—only an element name and an attribute. The element presents nothing unless you point it to some external content (in this case, an image specified by the src attribute). The input element is also replaced by a radio button, checkbox, or text input box, depending on its type. Replaced elements also generate boxes in their display.

Nonreplaced elements

The majority of HTML and XHTML elements are *nonreplaced elements*. This means that their content is presented by the user agent (generally a browser) inside a box generated by the element itself. For example, hi there is a nonreplaced element, and the text "hi there" will be displayed by the user agent. This is true of paragraphs, headings, table cells, lists, and almost everything else in XHTML.

Element Display Roles

In addition to replaced and nonreplaced elements, CSS2.1 uses two other basic types of elements: *block-level* and *inline-level*. These types will be more familiar to authors who have spent time with HTML or XHTML markup and its display in web browsers; the elements are illustrated in Figure 1-1.

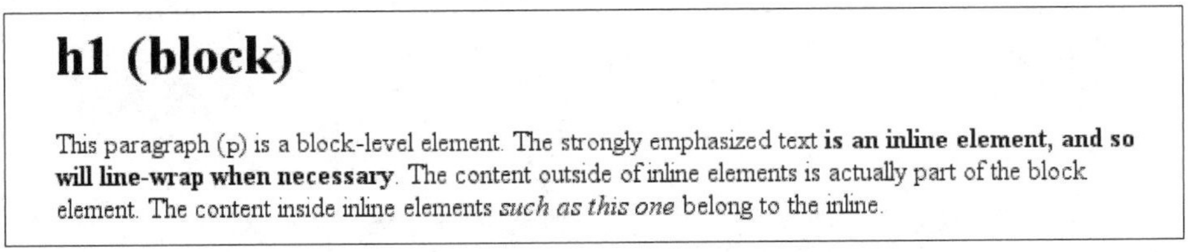

h1 (block)

This paragraph (p) is a block-level element. The strongly emphasized text **is an inline element, and so will line-wrap when necessary**. The content outside of inline elements is actually part of the block element. The content inside inline elements *such as this one* belong to the inline.

Figure 1-1. Block- and inline-level elements in an XHTML document

Block-level elements

Block-level elements generate an element box that (by default) fills its parent element's content area and cannot have other elements at its sides. In other words, it generates "breaks" before and after the element box. The most familiar block elements from HTML are p and div. Replaced elements can be block-level elements, but they usually are not.

List items are a special case of block-level elements. In addition to behaving in a manner consistent with other block elements, they generate a marker—typically a bullet for unordered lists and a number for ordered lists—that is "attached" to the element box. Except for the presence of this marker, list items are in all other ways identical to other block elements.

Inline-level elements

Inline-level elements generate an element box within a line of text and do not break up the flow of that line. The best inline element example is the a element in XHTML. Other candidates are strong and em. These elements do not generate a "break" before or after themselves, so they can appear within the content of another element without disrupting its display.

Note that while the names "block" and "inline" share a great deal in common with block- and inline-level elements in XHTML, there is an important difference. In HTML and XHTML, block-level elements cannot descend from inline-level elements. In CSS, there is no restriction on how display roles can be nested within each other.

To see how this works, let's consider a CSS property, display.

You may have noticed that there are a lot of values, only three of which I've even come close to mentioning: block, inline, and list-item. We're not going to explore the others now, mostly because they are covered in some detail in Chapter 2 and Chapter 7.

For the moment, let's just concentrate on block and inline. Consider the following markup:

```
<body>
<p>This is a paragraph with <em>an inline element</em> within it.</p>
</body>
```

display

Values:	none | inline | block | inline-block | list-item | run-in | table | inline-table | table-row-group | table-header-group | table-footer-group | table-row | table-column-group | table-column | table-cell | table-caption | inherit
Initial value:	inline
Applies to:	All elements
Inherited:	No
Computed value:	Varies for floated, positioned, and root elements (see CSS2.1, section 9.7); otherwise, as specified

Here we have two block elements (body and p) and an inline element (em). According to the XHTML specification, em can descend from p, but the reverse is not true. Typically, the XHTML hierarchy works out such that inlines can descend from blocks, but not the other way around.

CSS, on the other hand, has no such restrictions. You can leave the markup as it is but change the display roles of the two elements like this:

```
p {display: inline;}
em {display: block;}
```

This causes the elements to generate a block box inside an inline box. This is perfectly legal and violates no specification. The only problem would be if you tried to reverse the nesting of the elements:

```
<em><p>This is a paragraph improperly enclosed by an inline element.</p></em>
```

No matter what you do to the display roles via CSS, this is not legal in XHTML.

While changing the display roles of elements can be useful in XHTML documents, it becomes downright critical for XML documents. An XML document is unlikely to have any inherent display roles, so it's up to the author to define them. For example, you might wonder how to lay out the following snippet of XML:

```
<book>
 <maintitle>Cascading Style Sheets: The Definitive Guide</maintitle>
 <subtitle>Second Edition</subtitle>
 <author>Eric A. Meyer</author>
 <publisher>O'Reilly and Associates</publisher>
 <pubdate>2004</pubdate>
 <isbn>blahblahblah</isbn>
</book>
<book>
 <maintitle>CSS2 Pocket Reference</maintitle>
 <author>Eric A. Meyer</author>
 <publisher>O'Reilly and Associates</publisher>
```

```
<pubdate>2004</pubdate>
<isbn>blahblahblah</isbn>
</book>
```

Since the default value of `display` is `inline`, the content would be rendered as inline text by default, as illustrated in Figure 1-2. This isn't a terribly useful display.

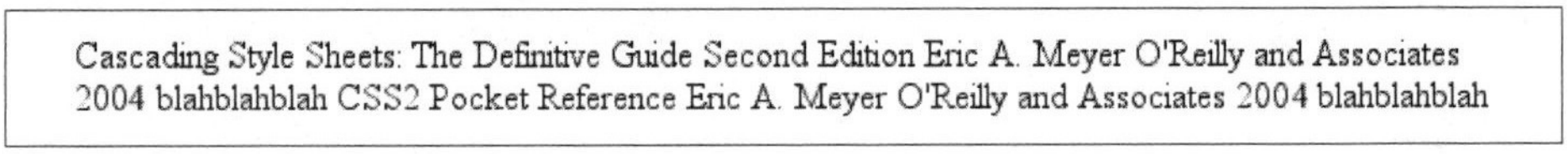

Cascading Style Sheets: The Definitive Guide Second Edition Eric A. Meyer O'Reilly and Associates 2004 blahblahblah CSS2 Pocket Reference Eric A. Meyer O'Reilly and Associates 2004 blahblahblah

Figure 1-2. Default display of an XML document

You can define the basics of the layout with `display`:

```
book, maintitle, subtitle, author, isbn {display: block;}
publisher, pubdate {display: inline;}
```

You've now set five of the seven elements to be block and two to be inline. This means each of the block elements will be treated much as `div` is treated in XHTML, and the two inlines will be treated in a manner similar to `span`.

This fundamental ability to affect display roles makes CSS highly useful in a variety of situations. You could take the preceding rules as a starting point, add a number of other styles, and get the result shown in Figure 1-3.

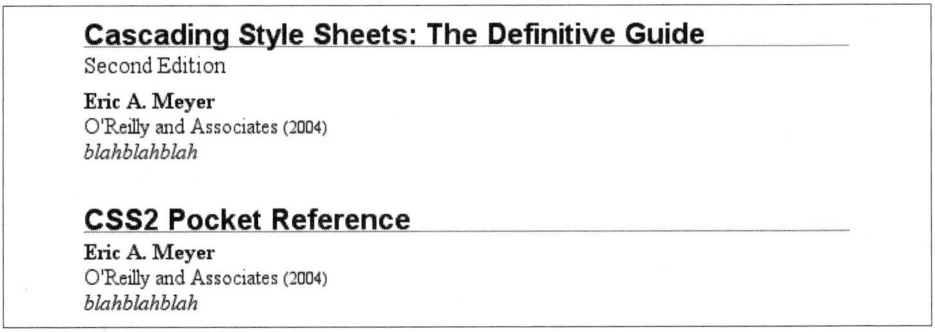

Cascading Style Sheets: The Definitive Guide
Second Edition

Eric A. Meyer
O'Reilly and Associates (2004)
blahblahblah

CSS2 Pocket Reference
Eric A. Meyer
O'Reilly and Associates (2004)
blahblahblah

Figure 1-3. Styled display of an XML document

Throughout the rest of this book, we'll explore the various properties and values that allow presentation like this. First, though, we need to look at how one can associate CSS with a document. After all, without tying the two together, there's no way for the CSS to affect the document. We'll explore this in an XHTML setting since it's the most familiar.

Bringing CSS and XHTML Together

I've mentioned that HTML and XHTML documents have an inherent structure, and that's a point worth repeating. In fact, that's part of the problem with web pages of old: too many of us forgot that documents are supposed to have an internal structure, which is altogether different than a visual structure. In our rush to create the coolest-looking pages on the Web, we bent, warped, and generally ignored the idea that pages should contain information with some structural meaning.

That structure is an inherent part of the relationship between XHTML and CSS; without the structure, there couldn't be a relationship at all. To understand it better, let's look at an example XHTML document and break it down by pieces:

```html
<html>
<head>
<title>Eric's World of Waffles</title>
<link rel="stylesheet" type="text/css" href="sheet1.css" media="all" />
<style type="text/css">
@import url(sheet2.css);
h1 {color: maroon;}
body {background: yellow;}
/* These are my styles! Yay! */
</style>
</head>
<body>
<h1>Waffles!</h1>
<p style="color: gray;">The most wonderful of all breakfast foods is
the waffle--a ridged and cratered slab of home-cooked, fluffy goodness
that makes every child's heart soar with joy. And they're so easy to make!
Just a simple waffle-maker and some batter, and you're ready for a morning
of aromatic ecstasy!
</p>
</body>
</html>
```

This markup is shown in Figure 1-4.

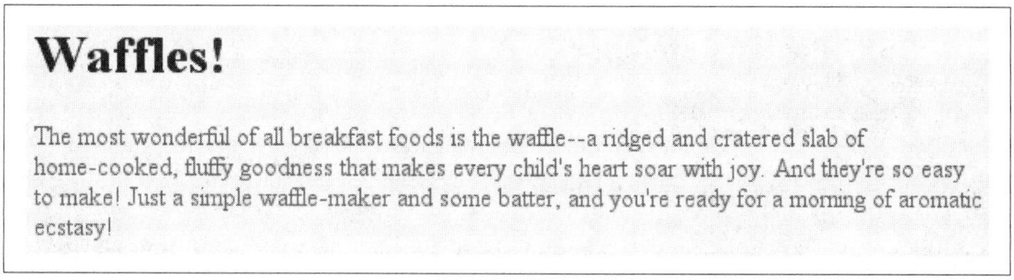

Waffles!

The most wonderful of all breakfast foods is the waffle--a ridged and cratered slab of home-cooked, fluffy goodness that makes every child's heart soar with joy. And they're so easy to make! Just a simple waffle-maker and some batter, and you're ready for a morning of aromatic ecstasy!

Figure 1-4. A simple document

Now, let's examine the various ways this document connects to CSS.

The link Tag

First, consider the use of the link tag:

```html
<link rel="stylesheet" type="text/css" href="sheet1.css" media="all" />
```

The link tag is a little-regarded but nonetheless perfectly valid tag that has been hanging around the HTML specification for years, just waiting to be put to good use.

Its basic purpose is to allow HTML authors to associate other documents with the document containing the link tag. CSS uses it to link style sheets to the document; in Figure 1-5, a style sheet called *sheet1.css* is linked to the document.

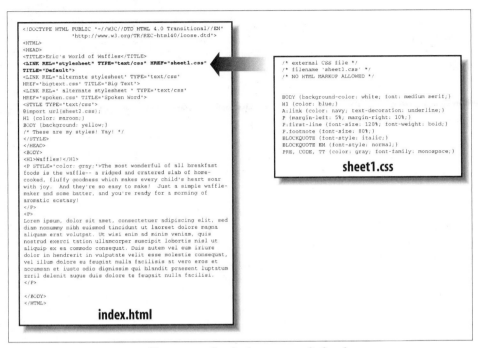

Figure 1-5. A representation of how external style sheets are applied to documents

These style sheets, which are not part of the HTML document but are still used by it, are referred to as *external style sheets*. This is because they're style sheets that are external to the HTML document. (Go figure.)

To successfully load an external style sheet, link must be placed inside the head element but may not be placed inside any other element, rather like title. This will cause the web browser to locate and load the style sheet and use whatever styles it contains to render the HTML document in the manner shown in Figure 1-5.

And what is the format of an external style sheet? It's simply a list of rules, just like those we saw in the previous section and in the example XHTML document, but in this case, the rules are saved into their own file. Just remember that no XHTML or any other markup language can be included in the style sheet—only style rules. Here are the contents of an external style sheet:

```
h1 {color: red;}
h2 {color: maroon; background: white;}
h3 {color: white; background: black;
  font: medium Helvetica;}
```

That's all there is to it—no HTML markup or comments at all, just plain-and-simple style declarations. These are saved into a plain-text file and are usually given an extension of *.css*, as in *sheet1.css*.

 An external style sheet cannot contain any document markup at all, only CSS rules and CSS comments, both of which are explained later in the chapter. The presence of markup in an external style sheet can cause some or all of it to be ignored.

The filename extension is not required, but some older browsers won't recognize the file as containing a style sheet unless it actually ends with *.css*, even if you *do* include the correct type of text/css in the link element. In fact, some web servers won't hand over a file as text/css unless its filename ends with *.css*, though that can usually be fixed by changing the server's configuration files.

Attributes

For the rest of the link tag, the attributes and values are fairly straightforward. rel stands for "relation," and in this case, the relation is stylesheet. type is always set to text/css. This value describes the type of data that will be loaded using the link tag. That way, the web browser knows that the style sheet is a CSS style sheet, a fact that will determine how the browser deals with the data it imports. After all, there may be other style languages used in the future, so it's important to declare which language you're using.

Next, we find the href attribute. The value of this attribute is the URL of your style sheet. This URL can be either absolute or relative, depending on what works for you. In our example, of course, the URL is relative. It just as easily could have been something like http://www.meyerweb.com/sheet1.css.

Finally, we have a media attribute. The value used in this case, all, means that the style sheet should be applied in all presentation media. CSS2 defines a number of allowed values for this attribute:

all
　　Use in all presentational media.

aural
　　Use in speech synthesizers, screen readers, and other audio renderings of the document.

braille
　　Use when rendering the document with a Braille device.

embossed
　　Use when printing with a Braille printing device.

handheld

> Use on handheld devices like personal digital assistants or web-enabled cell phones.

print

> Use when printing the document for sighted users and also when displaying a "print preview" of the document.

projection

> Use in a projection medium, such as a digital projector used to present a slideshow when delivering a speech.

screen

> Use when presenting the document in a screen medium like a desktop computer monitor. All web browsers running on such systems are screen-medium user agents.

tty

> Use when delivering the document in a fixed-pitch environment like teletype printers.

tv

> Use when the document is being presented on a television.

The majority of these media types are not supported by any current web browser. The three most widely supported ones are all, screen, and print. As of this writing, Opera also supports projection, which allows a document to be presented as a slideshow.

You can use a style sheet in more than one medium by providing a comma-separated list of the media in which it applies. Thus, for example, you can use a linked style sheet in both screen and projection media:

```
<link rel="stylesheet" type="text/css" href="visual-sheet.css"
    media="screen, projection" />
```

Note that there can be more than one linked style sheet associated with a document. In these cases, only those link tags with a rel of stylesheet will be used in the initial display of the document. Thus, if you wanted to link two style sheets named *basic.css* and *splash.css*, it would look like this:

```
<link rel="stylesheet" type="text/css" href="basic.css" />
<link rel="stylesheet" type="text/css" href="splash.css" />
```

This will cause the browser to load both style sheets, combine the rules from each, and apply them all to the document. (We'll see exactly how the sheets are combined in Chapter 3, but for now, let's just accept that they're combined.) For example:

```
<link rel="stylesheet" type="text/css" href="basic.css" />
<link rel="stylesheet" type="text/css" href="splash.css" />

<p class="a1">This paragraph will be gray only if styles from the
stylesheet 'basic.css' are applied.</p>
<p class="b1">This paragraph will be gray only if styles from the
stylesheet 'splash.css' are applied.</p>
```

The one attribute that is not in your example markup, but could be, is the `title` attribute. This attribute is not often used, but it could become important in the future and, if used improperly, can have unexpected effects. Why? We will explore that in the next section.

Alternate style sheets

It's also possible to define *alternate style sheets*. These are defined by making the value of the `rel` attribute `alternate stylesheet`, and they are used in document presentation only if selected by the user.

Should a browser be able to use alternate style sheets, it will use the values of the `link` elements' `title` attributes to generate a list of style alternatives. So you could write the following:

```
<link rel="stylesheet" type="text/css"
    href="sheet1.css" title="Default" />
<link rel="alternate stylesheet" type="text/css"
    href="bigtext.css" title="Big Text" />
<link rel="alternate stylesheet" type="text/css"
    href="zany.css" title="Crazy colors!" />
```

Users could then pick the style they want to use, and the browser would switch from the first one (labeled "Default" in this case) to whichever the user picked. Figure 1-6 shows one way in which this selection mechanism is accomplished.

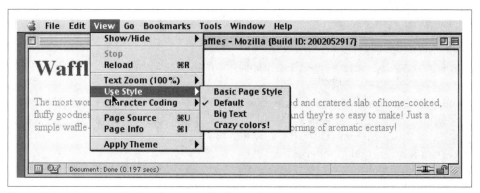

Figure 1-6. A browser offering alternate style sheet selection

 Alternate style sheets are supported in most Gecko-based browsers like Mozilla and Netscape 6+, and in Opera 7. They can be supported in Internet Explorer through the use of JavaScript but are not natively supported by those browsers.

It is also possible to group alternate style sheets together by giving them the same `title` value. Thus, you make it possible for the user to pick a different presentation for your site in both screen and print media. For example:

```
<link rel="stylesheet" type="text/css"
   href="sheet1.css" title="Default" media="screen" />
<link rel="stylesheet" type="text/css"
   href="print-sheet1.css" title="Default" media="print" />
<link rel="alternate stylesheet" type="text/css"
   href="bigtext.css" title="Big Text" media="screen" />
<link rel="alternate stylesheet" type="text/css"
   href="print-bigtext.css" title="Big Text" media="print" />
```

If a user selects "Big Text" from the alternate style sheet selection mechanism in a conforming user agent, then *bigtext.css* will be used to style the document in the screen medium, and *print-bigtext.css* will be used in the print medium. Neither *sheet1.css* nor *print-sheet1.css* will be used in any medium.

Why is that? Because if you give a link with a rel of stylesheet a title, then you are designating that style sheet as a *preferred style sheet*. This means that its use is preferred to alternate style sheets, and it will be used when the document is first displayed. Once you select an alternate style sheet, however, the preferred style sheet will *not* be used.

Furthermore, if you designate a number of style sheets as preferred, then all but one of them will be ignored. Consider:

```
<link rel="stylesheet" type="text/css"
   href="sheet1.css" title="Default layout" />
<link rel="stylesheet" type="text/css"
   href="sheet2.css" title="Default text sizes" />
<link rel="stylesheet" type="text/css"
   href="sheet3.css" title="Default colors" />
```

All three link elements now refer to preferred style sheets, thanks to the presence of a title attribute on all three, but only one of them will actually be used in that manner. The other two will be ignored completely. Which two? There's no way to be certain, as neither HTML nor XHTML provide a method of determining which preferred style sheets should be ignored or which should be used.

If you simply don't give a style sheet a title, then it becomes a *persistent style sheet* and is always used in the display of the document. Often, this is exactly what an author wants.

The style Element

The style element is one way to include a style sheet, and it appears in the document itself:

```
<style type="text/css">
```

style should always use the attribute type; in the case of a CSS document, the correct value is "text/css", just as it was with the link element.

The style element should always start with <style type="text/css">, as shown in the preceding example. This is followed by one or more styles and is finished with a closing `</style>` tag. It is also possible to give the style element a media attribute, with the same allowed values as previously discussed for linked style sheets.

The styles between the opening and closing style tags are referred to as the *document style sheet*, or the *embedded style sheet* since this style sheet is embedded within the document. It will contain many of the styles that will apply to the document, but it can also contain multiple links to external style sheets using the @import directive.

The @import Directive

Now we'll discuss the stuff that is found inside the style tag. First, we have something very similar to link: the @import directive:

```
@import url(sheet2.css);
```

Just like link, @import can be used to direct the web browser to load an external style sheet and use its styles in the rendering of the HTML document. The only major difference is in the actual syntax and placement of the command. As you can see, @import is found inside the style container. It must be placed there, before the other CSS rules, otherwise it won't work at all. Consider this example:

```
<style type="text/css">
@import url(styles.css); /* @import comes first */
h1 {color: gray;}
</style>
```

Like link, there can be more than one @import statement in a document. Unlike link, however, the style sheets of every @import directive will be loaded and used; there is no way to designate alternate style sheets with @import. So, given the following markup:

```
@import url(sheet2.css);
@import url(blueworld.css);
@import url(zany.css);
```

all three external style sheets will be loaded, and all of their style rules will be used in the display of the document.

 Many older browsers cannot process varying forms of the @import directive. This fact can actually be used to one's advantage in "hiding" styles from these browsers. For more details, see *http://w3development.de/css/hide_css_from_browsers*.

As with link, you can restrict imported style sheets to one or more media by listing the media to which it should be applied after the style sheet's URL:

```
@import url(sheet2.css) all;
@import url(blueworld.css) screen;
@import url(zany.css) projection, print;
```

`@import` can be highly useful if you have an external style sheet that needs to use the styles found in other external style sheets. Since external style sheets cannot contain any document markup, the `link` element can't be used—but `@import` can. Therefore, you might have an external style sheet that contains the following:

```
@import url(http://example.org/library/layout.css);
@import url(basic-text.css);
@import url(printer.css) print;
body {color: red;}
h1 {color: blue;}
```

Well, maybe not those exact styles, but you get the idea. Note the use of both absolute and relative URLs in the previous example. Either URL form can be used, just as with `link`.

Note also that the `@import` directives appear at the beginning of the style sheet, as they did in our example document. CSS requires the `@import` directive to come before any other rules in a style sheet. An `@import` that comes after other rules (e.g., `body {color: red;}`) will be ignored by conforming user agents.

 Internet Explorer for Windows does not ignore any `@import` directive, even those that come after other rules. Since other browsers do ignore improperly placed `@import` directives, it is easy to mistakenly place the `@import` directive incorrectly and thus alter the display in other browsers.

Actual Style Rules

After the `@import` statement in our example, we find some ordinary style rules. What they mean doesn't actually matter for this discussion, although you can probably guess that they set `h1` elements to be maroon and `body` elements to have a yellow background:

```
h1 {color: maroon;}
body {background: yellow;}
```

Styles such as these comprise the bulk of any embedded style sheet—simple and complex, short and long. Rarely will you have a document where the `style` element does not contain any rules.

Backward accessibility

For those of you concerned about making your documents accessible to older browsers, there is an important warning to consider. You're probably aware that browsers ignore tags they don't recognize; for example, if a web page contains a `blooper` tag, browsers will completely ignore the tag because it isn't one they recognize.

The same is true with style sheets. If a browser does not recognize `<style>` and `</style>`, it will ignore them altogether. However, the declarations within those tags will not necessarily be ignored because they look like ordinary text as far as the browser is concerned. So your style declarations will appear at the top of your page! (Of course, the browser should ignore the text because it isn't part of the body element, but this is never the case.)

To combat this problem, it is recommended that you enclose your declarations in a comment tag. In the example given here, the beginning of the comment tag appears just after the opening style tag, and the end of the comment appears just before the closing style tag:

```
<style type="text/css"><!--
@import url(sheet2.css);
h1 {color: maroon;}
body {background: yellow;}
--></style>
```

This should cause older browsers to completely ignore the declarations as well as the style tags because HTML comments are not displayed. Meanwhile, those browsers that understand CSS will still be able to read the style sheet.

CSS Comments

CSS also allows for comments. These are very similar to C/C++ comments in that they are surrounded by /* and */:

```
/* This is a CSS1 comment */
```

Comments can span multiple lines, just as in C++:

```
/* This is a CSS1 comment, and it
can be several lines long without
any problem whatsoever. */
```

It's important to remember that CSS comments cannot be nested. So, for example, this would not be correct:

```
/* This is a comment, in which we find
 another comment, which is WRONG
   /* Another comment */
 and back to the first comment */
```

However, it's hardly ever desirable to nest comments, so this limitation is no big deal.

 One way to create "nested" comments accidentally is to temporarily comment out a large block of a style sheet that already contains a comment. Since CSS doesn't permit nested comments, the "outside" comment will end where the "inside" comment ends.

If you wish to place comments on the same line as markup, then you need to be careful about how you place them. For example, this is the correct way to do it:

```
h1 {color: gray;}    /* This CSS comment is several lines */
h2 {color: silver;} /* long, but since it is alongside */
p {color: white;}    /* actual styles, each line needs to */
pre {color: gray;}   /* be wrapped in comment markers. */
```

Given this example, if each line isn't marked off, then most of the style sheet will become part of the comment and thus will not work:

```
h1 {color: gray;}    /* This CSS comment is several lines
h2 {color: silver;}  long, but since it is not wrapped
p {color: white;}     in comment markers, the last three
pre {color: gray;}    styles are part of the comment. */
```

In this example, only the first rule (h1 {color: gray;}) will be applied to the document. The rest of the rules, as part of the comment, are ignored by the browser's rendering engine.

Moving on with the example, you see some more CSS information actually found inside an XHTML tag!

Inline Styles

For cases where you want to simply assign a few styles to one individual element, without the need for embedded or external style sheets, employ the HTML attribute style to set an *inline style*:

```
<p style="color: gray;">The most wonderful of all breakfast foods is
the waffle--a ridged and cratered slab of home-cooked, fluffy goodness...
</p>
```

The style attribute can be associated with any HTML tag whatsoever, except for those tags that are found outside of body (head or title, for instance).

The syntax of a style attribute is fairly ordinary. In fact, it looks very much like the declarations found in the style container, except here the curly braces are replaced by double quotation marks. So <p style="color: maroon; background: yellow;"> will set the text color to be maroon and the background to be yellow *for that paragraph only*. No other part of the document will be affected by this declaration.

Note that you can only place a declaration block, not an entire style sheet, inside an inline style attribute. Therefore, you can't put an @import into a style attribute, nor can you include any complete rules. The only thing you can put into the value of a style attribute is what might go between the curly braces of a rule.

Use of the style attribute is not generally recommended. Indeed, it is marked as deprecated by XHTML 1.1 and is very unlikely to appear in XML languages other than XHTML. Some of the primary advantages of CSS—the ability to organize centralized styles that control an entire document's appearance or the appearance of all documents on a web server—are negated when you place styles into a style attribute. In many ways, inline styles are not much better than the font tag, although they do have a good deal more flexibility.

Summary

With CSS, it is possible to completely change the way elements are presented by a user agent. This can be executed at a basic level with the `display` property, and in a different way by associating style sheets with a document. The user will never know whether this is done via an external or embedded style sheet, or even with an inline style. The real importance of external style sheets is the way in which they allow authors to put all of a site's presentation information in one place, and point all of the documents to that place. This not only makes site updates and maintenance a breeze, but it helps to save bandwidth since all of the presentation is removed from documents.

To make the most of the power of CSS, authors need to know how to associate a set of styles with the elements in a document. To fully understand how CSS can do all of this, authors need a firm grasp of the way CSS selects pieces of a document for styling, which is the subject of the next chapter.

CHAPTER 2

Selectors

One of the primary advantages of CSS—particularly to designers—is its ability to easily apply a set of styles to all elements of the same type. Unimpressed? Consider this: by editing a single line of CSS, you can change the colors of all your headings. Don't like the blue you're using? Change that one line of code, and they can all be purple, yellow, maroon, or any other color you desire. That lets you, the designer, focus on design, rather than grunt work. The next time you're in a meeting and someone wants to see headings with a different shade of green, just edit your style and hit Reload. *Voilà!* The results are accomplished in seconds and there for everyone to see.

Of course, CSS can't solve all your problems—you can't use it to change the color of your GIFs, for example—but it can make some global changes much easier. So let's begin with selectors and structure.

Basic Rules

As I've stated, a central feature of CSS is its ability to apply certain rules to an entire set of element types in a document. For example, let's say that you want to make the text of all h2 elements appear gray. Using old-school HTML, you'd have to do this by inserting `<FONT COLOR="gray">...</FONT>` tags in all your h2 elements:

```
<h2><font color="gray">This is h2 text</font></h2>
```

Obviously, this is a tedious process if your document contains a lot of h2 elements. Worse, if you later decide that you want all those h2s to be green instead of gray, you'd have to start the manual tagging all over again.

CSS allows you to create rules that are simple to change, edit, and apply to all the text elements you define (the next section will explain how these rules work). For example, simply write this rule once to make all your h2 elements gray:

```
h2 {color: gray;}
```

If you want to change all h2 text to another color—say, silver—simply alter the rule:

```
h2 {color: silver;}
```

Rule Structure

To illustrate the concept of rules in more detail, let's break down the structure.

Each rule has two fundamental parts, the *selector* and the *declaration block*. The declaration block is composed of one or more *declarations*, and each declaration is a pairing of a *property* and a *value*. Every style sheet is made up of a series of rules. Figure 2-1 shows the parts of a rule.

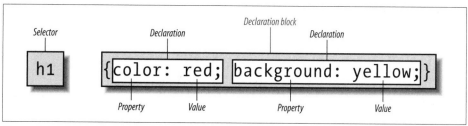

Figure 2-1. The structure of a rule

The selector, shown on the left side of the rule, defines which piece of the document will be affected. In Figure 2-1, h1 elements are selected. If the selector were p, then all p (paragraph) elements would be selected.

The right side of the rule contains the declaration block, which is made up of one or more declarations. Each declaration is a combination of a CSS property and a value of that property. In Figure 2-1, the declaration block contains two declarations. The first states that this rule will cause parts of the document to have a color of red, and the second states that part of the document will have a background of yellow. So, all of the h1 elements in the document (defined by the selector) will be styled in red text with a yellow background.

Element Selectors

A selector is most often an HTML element, but not always. For example, if a CSS file contains styles for an XML document, a selector might look something like this:

```
QUOTE {color: gray;}
BIB {color: red;}
BOOKTITLE {color: purple;}
MYElement {color: red;}
```

In other words, the elements of the document serve as the most basic selectors. In XML, a selector could be anything, since XML allows for the creation of new markup languages that can have just about anything as an element name. If you're styling an HTML document, on the other hand, the selector will generally be one of the many HTML elements such as p, h3, em, a, or even html itself. For example:

```
html {color: black;}
h1 {color: gray;}
h2 {color: silver;}
```

The results of this style sheet are shown in Figure 2-2.

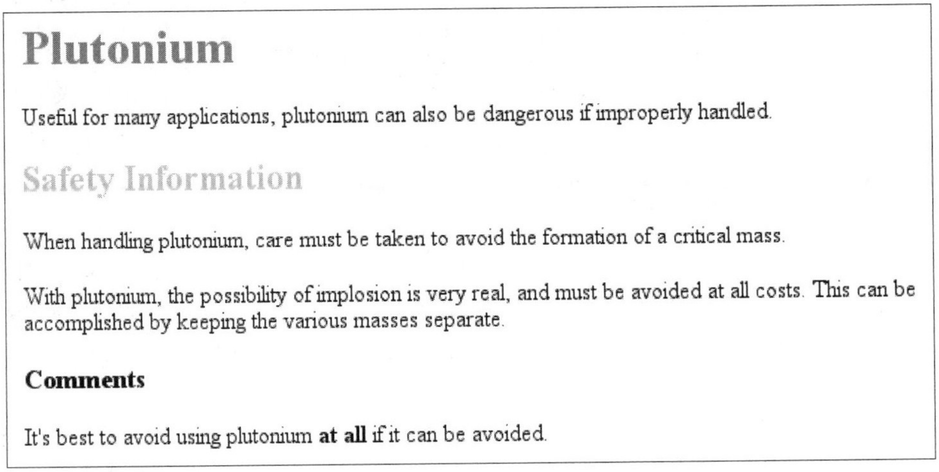

Plutonium

Useful for many applications, plutonium can also be dangerous if improperly handled.

Safety Information

When handling plutonium, care must be taken to avoid the formation of a critical mass.

With plutonium, the possibility of implosion is very real, and must be avoided at all costs. This can be accomplished by keeping the various masses separate.

Comments

It's best to avoid using plutonium **at all** if it can be avoided.

Figure 2-2. Simple styling of a simple document

Once you've globally applied styles directly to elements, you can shift those styles from one element to another. Let's say you decide that the paragraph text, not the h1 elements, in Figure 2-2 should be gray. No problem. Simply change the h1 selector to p:

```
html {color: black;}
p {color: gray;}
h2 {color: silver;}
```

The results are shown in Figure 2-3.

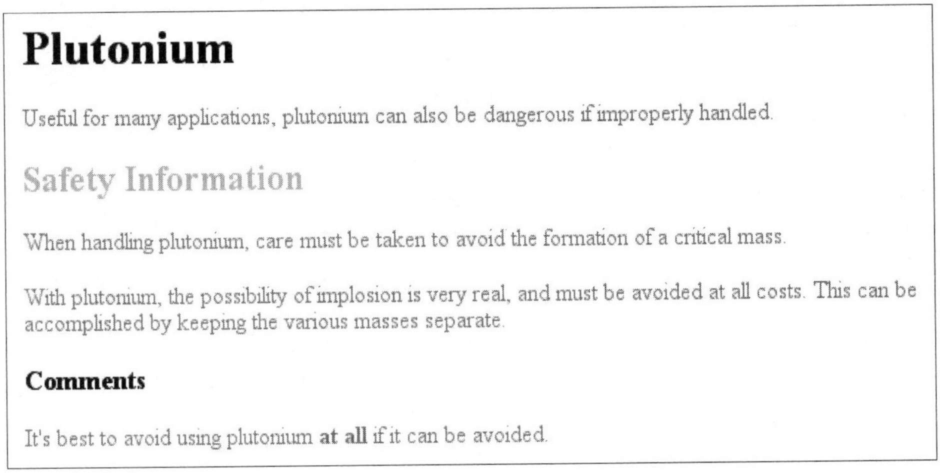

Plutonium

Useful for many applications, plutonium can also be dangerous if improperly handled.

Safety Information

When handling plutonium, care must be taken to avoid the formation of a critical mass.

With plutonium, the possibility of implosion is very real, and must be avoided at all costs. This can be accomplished by keeping the various masses separate.

Comments

It's best to avoid using plutonium **at all** if it can be avoided.

Figure 2-3. Moving a style from one element to another

Declarations and Keywords

The declaration block contains one or more declarations. A declaration is always formatted as a property followed by a colon and then a *value* followed by a semicolon. The colon and semicolon can be followed by zero or more spaces. In nearly all cases, a value is either a single keyword or a space-separated list of one or more keywords that are permitted for that property. If you use either an incorrect property or value in a declaration, the whole thing will be ignored. Thus, the following two declarations would fail:

```
brain-size: 2cm;  /* unknown property */
color: ultraviolet;  /* unknown value */
```

In an instance where you can use more than one keyword for a property's value, the keywords are usually separated by spaces. Not every property can accept multiple keywords, but many, such as the font property, can. Let's say you want to define medium-sized Helvetica for paragraph text, as illustrated in Figure 2-4.

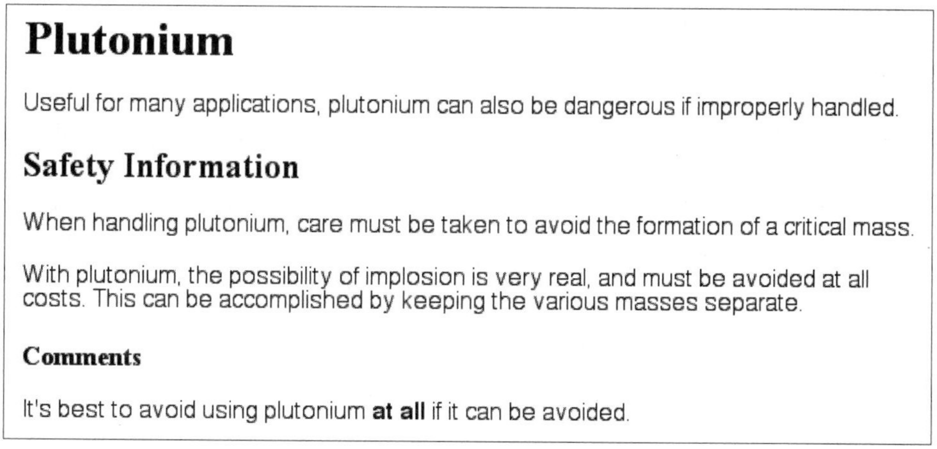

Plutonium

Useful for many applications, plutonium can also be dangerous if improperly handled.

Safety Information

When handling plutonium, care must be taken to avoid the formation of a critical mass.

With plutonium, the possibility of implosion is very real, and must be avoided at all costs. This can be accomplished by keeping the various masses separate.

Comments

It's best to avoid using plutonium **at all** if it can be avoided.

Figure 2-4. The results of a property value with multiple keywords

The rule would read as follows:

```
p {font: medium Helvetica;}
```

Note the space between medium and Helvetica, each of which is a keyword (the first is the font's size and the second is the actual font name). The space allows the user agent to distinguish between the two keywords and apply them correctly. The semicolon indicates that the declaration has been concluded.

These space-separated words are referred to as keywords because, taken together, they form the value of the property in question. For instance, consider the following fictional rule:

```
rainbow: red orange yellow green blue indigo violet;
```

There is no such property as rainbow, of course, and two of the colors used aren't valid either, but the example is useful for illustrative purposes. The value of rainbow is red orange yellow green blue indigo violet, and the seven keywords add up to a single, unique value. We can redefine the value for rainbow as follows:

```
rainbow: infrared red orange yellow green blue indigo violet ultraviolet;
```

Now we have a new value for rainbow composed of nine keywords instead of seven. Although the name of the two values is the same, they are as unique and different as zero and one.

 As we've seen, CSS keywords are separated by spaces—except in one instance. In the CSS property font, there is exactly one place where a forward slash (/) can be used to separate two specific keywords. Here's an example:

```
h2 {font: large/150% sans-serif;}
```

The slash separates the keywords that set the element's font size and line height. This is the only place the slash is allowed to appear in the font declaration. All of the other keywords allowed for font are separated by spaces.

Those are the basics of simple declarations, but they can get much more complex. The next section begins to show you just how powerful CSS can be.

Grouping

So far, we've learned fairly simple techniques for applying a single style to a single selector. But what if you want the same style to apply to multiple elements? If that's the case, you'll want to use more than one selector or apply more than one style to an element or group of elements.

Grouping Selectors

Let's say you want h2 elements and paragraphs to have gray text. The easiest way to accomplish this is to use the following declaration:

```
h2, p {color: gray;}
```

By placing the h2 and p selectors on the left side of the rule and separating them with a comma, you've defined a rule where the style on the right (color: gray;) applies to the elements referenced by both selectors. The comma tells the browser that there are two different selectors involved in the rule. Leaving out the comma would give the rule a completely different meaning, which we'll explore later in "Descendant Selectors."

There are really no limits on how many selectors you can group together. For example, if you want to display a large number of elements in gray, you might use something like the following rule:

```
body, table, th, td, h1, h2, h3, h4, p, pre, strong, em, b, i {color: gray;}
```

Grouping allows an author to drastically compact certain types of style assignments, which makes for a shorter style sheet. The following alternatives produce exactly the same result, but it's pretty obvious which one is easier to type:

```
h1 {color: purple;}
h2 {color: purple;}
h3 {color: purple;}
h4 {color: purple;}
h5 {color: purple;}
h6 {color: purple;}


h1, h2, h3, h4, h5, h6 {color: purple;}
```

Grouping allows for some interesting choices. For example, all of the groups of rules in the following example are equivalent—each merely shows a different way of grouping both selectors and declarations:

```
/* group 1 */
h1 {color: silver; background: white;}
h2 {color: silver; background: gray;}
h3 {color: white; background: gray;}
h4 {color: silver; background: white;}
b {color: gray; background: white;}

/* group 2 */
h1, h2, h4 {color: silver;}
h2, h3 {background: gray;}
h1, h4, b {background: white;}
h3 {color: white;}
b {color: gray;}

/* group 3 */
h1, h4 {color: silver; background: white;}
h2 {color: silver;}
h3 {color: white;}
h2, h3 {background: gray;}
b {color: gray; background: white;}
```

Any of these will yield the result shown in Figure 2-5. (These styles use grouped declarations, which are explained in the upcoming section, "Grouping Declarations.")

The universal selector

CSS2 introduced a new simple selector called the *universal selector*, displayed as an asterisk (*). This selector matches any element at all, much like a wildcard. For example, to make every single element in a document red, you would write:

```
* {color: red;}
```

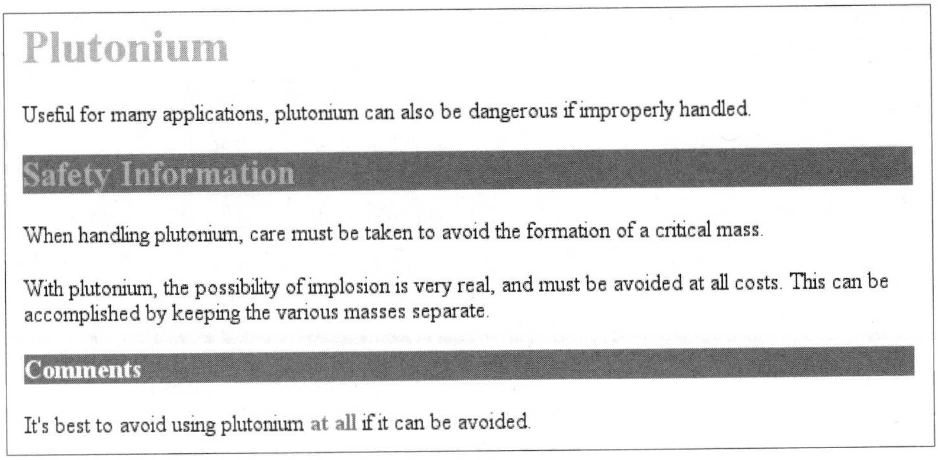

Plutonium

Useful for many applications, plutonium can also be dangerous if improperly handled.

Safety Information

When handling plutonium, care must be taken to avoid the formation of a critical mass.

With plutonium, the possibility of implosion is very real, and must be avoided at all costs. This can be accomplished by keeping the various masses separate.

Comments

It's best to avoid using plutonium **at all** if it can be avoided.

Figure 2-5. The result of equivalent style sheets

This declaration is equivalent to a grouped selector that lists every single element contained within the document. The universal selector lets you assign the color value red to every element in the document in one efficient stroke. Beware, however: although the universal selector is convenient, it can have unintended consequences, which I'll discuss in the next chapter.

Grouping Declarations

Since you can group selectors together into a single rule, it follows that you can also group declarations. Assume that you want all h1 elements to appear in purple, 18-pixel-high Helvetica text on an aqua background (and you don't mind blinding your readers). You could write your styles like this:

```
h1 {font: 18px Helvetica;}
h1 {color: purple;}
h1 {background: aqua;}
```

But this method is inefficient; imagine creating such a list for an element that will carry 10 or 15 styles! Instead, you can group your declarations together:

```
h1 {font: 18px Helvetica; color: purple; background: aqua;}
```

This will have exactly the same effect as the three-line style sheet just shown.

Note that using semicolons at the end of each declaration is crucial when you're grouping them. Browsers ignore whitespace in style sheets, and the user agent must rely on correct syntax to parse the style sheet. You can fearlessly format styles like the following:

```
h1 {
  font: 18px Helvetica;
  color: purple;
  background: aqua;
}
```

If the second semicolon is omitted, however, the user agent will interpret the style sheet as follows:

```
h1 {
  font: 18px Helvetica;
  color: purple  background: aqua;
}
```

Because `background:` is not a valid value for `color`, and because `color` can be given only one keyword, a user agent will ignore the `color` declaration (including the `background:` aqua part) entirely. It might render `h1`s as purple text without an aqua background, but more likely, you won't even get purple `h1`s. Instead, they will be the default color (which is usually black) with no background at all. (The declaration `font: 18px Helvetica` will still take effect since it was correctly terminated with a semicolon.)

 Although it is not technically necessary to follow the last declaration of a rule with a semicolon, it is generally good practice to do so. First, it will keep you in the habit of terminating your declarations with semicolons, the lack of which is one of the most common causes of rendering errors. Second, if you decide to add another declaration to a rule, you won't have to worry about forgetting to insert an extra semicolon. Finally, some older browsers such as Internet Explorer 3.x have a greater tendency to become confused if the semicolon is left off the final declaration in a rule. Avoid all these problems—always follow a declaration with a semicolon, wherever the rule appears.

As with selector grouping, declaration grouping is a convenient way to keep your style sheets short, expressive, and easy to maintain.

Grouping Everything

You now know that you can group selectors, and you can group declarations. By combining both kinds of grouping in single rules, you can define very complex styles using only a few statements. Now, what if you want to assign some complex styles to all the headings in a document, and you want the same styles to be applied to all of them? Here's how to do it:

```
h1, h2, h3, h4, h5, h6 {color: gray; background: white; padding: 0.5em;
  border: 1px solid black; font-family: Charcoal, sans-serif;}
```

You've grouped the selectors, so the styles on the right side of the rule will be applied to all the headings listed, and grouping the declarations means that all of the listed styles will be applied to the selectors on the left side of the rule. The result of this rule is shown in Figure 2-6.

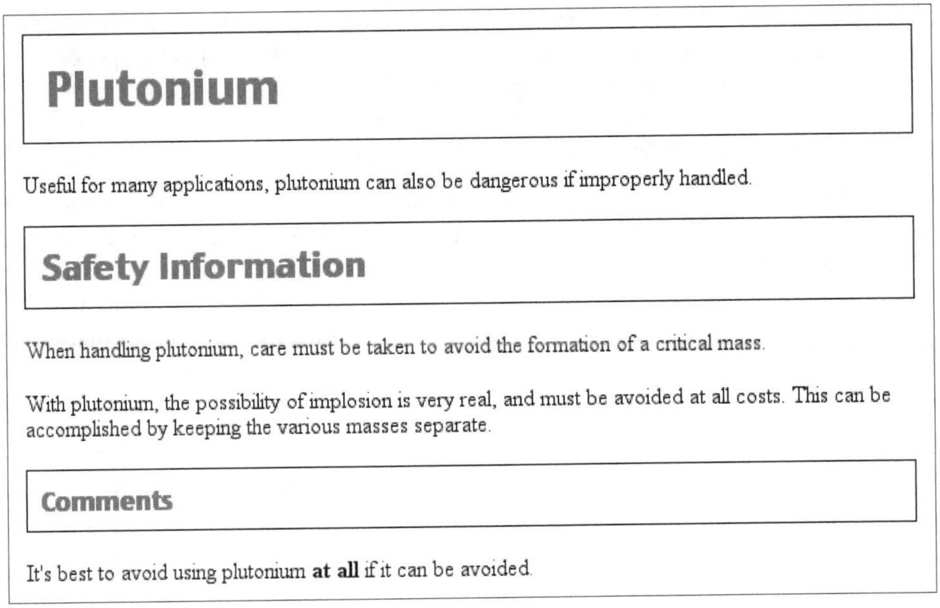

Plutonium

Useful for many applications, plutonium can also be dangerous if improperly handled.

Safety Information

When handling plutonium, care must be taken to avoid the formation of a critical mass.

With plutonium, the possibility of implosion is very real, and must be avoided at all costs. This can be accomplished by keeping the various masses separate.

Comments

It's best to avoid using plutonium **at all** if it can be avoided.

Figure 2-6. Grouping both selectors and rules

This approach is preferable to the drawn-out alternative, which would begin with something like this:

```
h1 {color: gray;}
h2 {color: gray;}
h3 {color: gray;}
h4 {color: gray;}
h5 {color: gray;}
h6 {color: gray;}
h1 {background: white;}
h2 {background: white;}
h3 {background: white;}
```

and continue for many lines. You *can* write out your styles the long way, but I wouldn't recommend it—editing them would be as tedious as using font tags everywhere!

It's possible to add even more expression to selectors and to apply styles in a way that cuts across elements in favor of types of information. Of course, to get something so powerful, you'll have to do a little work in return, but it's well worth it.

Class and ID Selectors

So far, we've been grouping selectors and declarations together in a variety of ways, but the selectors we've been using are still simple ones that refer only to document elements. They're fine up to a point, but there are times when you need something a little more specialized.

In addition to raw document elements, there are two other types of selectors: *class selectors* and *ID selectors*, which let you assign styles in a way that is independent of document elements. These selectors can be used on their own or in conjunction with element selectors. However, they work only if you've marked up your document appropriately, so using them generally involves a little forethought and planning.

For example, say you're drafting a document that discusses ways of handling plutonium. The document contains various warnings about safely dealing with such a dangerous substance. You want each warning to appear in boldface text so that it will stand out. However, you don't know which elements these warnings will be. Some warnings could be entire paragraphs, while others could be a single item within a lengthy list or a small section of text. So, you can't define a rule using simple selectors of any kind. Suppose you tried this route:

```
p {font-weight: bold;}
```

All paragraphs would be bold, not just those that contain warnings. You need a way to select only the text that contains warnings, or more precisely, a way to select only those elements that are warnings. How do you do it? You apply styles to parts of the document that have been marked in a certain way, independent of the elements involved, by using class selectors.

Class Selectors

The most common way to apply styles without worrying about the elements involved is to use class selectors. Before you can use them, however, you need to modify your actual document markup so that the class selectors will work. Enter the class attribute:

```
<p class="warning">When handling plutonium, care must be taken to avoid
the formation of a critical mass.</p>
<p>With plutonium, <span class="warning">the possibility of implosion is
very real, and must be avoided at all costs</span>. This can be accomplished
by keeping the various masses separate.</p>
```

To associate the styles of a class selector with an element, you must assign a class attribute to the appropriate value. In the previous code, a class value of warning was assigned to two elements: the first paragraph and the span element in the second paragraph.

All you need now is a way to apply styles to these classed elements. In HTML documents, you can use a very compact notation where the name of a class is preceded by a period (.) and can be joined with a simple selector:

```
*.warning {font-weight: bold;}
```

When combined with the example markup shown earlier, this simple rule has the effect shown in Figure 2-7. That is, the style of font-weight: bold will be applied to every element (thanks to the presence of the universal selector) that carries a class attribute with a value of warning.

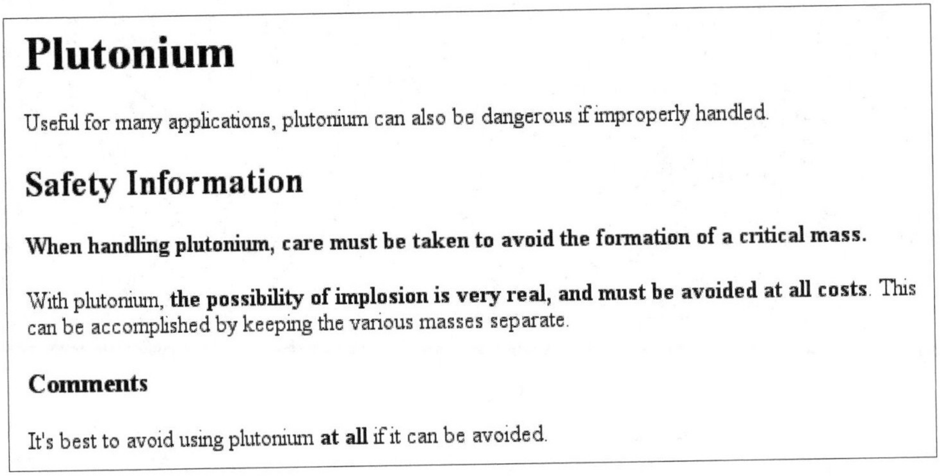

Plutonium

Useful for many applications, plutonium can also be dangerous if improperly handled.

Safety Information

When handling plutonium, care must be taken to avoid the formation of a critical mass.

With plutonium, **the possibility of implosion is very real, and must be avoided at all costs**. This can be accomplished by keeping the various masses separate.

Comments

It's best to avoid using plutonium **at all** if it can be avoided.

Figure 2-7. Using a class selector

As you can see, the class selector works by directly referencing a value that will be found in the class attribute of an element. This reference is *always* preceded by a period (.), which marks it as a class selector. The period helps keep the class selector separate from anything with which it might be combined—such as an element selector. For example, you may want boldface text only when an entire paragraph is a warning:

```
p.warning {font-weight: bold;}
```

The selector now matches any p elements that have a class attribute containing the word warning, but no other elements of any kind, classed or otherwise. The selector p.warning translates to: "Any paragraph whose class attribute contains the word warning." Since the span element is not a paragraph, the rule's selector doesn't match it, and it won't be converted to bold text.

If you did want to assign different styles to the span element, you could use the selector span.warning:

```
p.warning {font-weight: bold;}
span.warning {font-style: italic;}
```

In this case, the warning paragraph is boldfaced, while the warning span is italicized. Each rule applies only to a specific type of element/class combination, so it does not leak over to other elements.

Another option is to use a combination of a general class selector and an element-specific class selector to make the styles even more useful, as in the following markup:

```
.warning {font-style: italic;}
span.warning {font-weight: bold;}
```

The results are shown in Figure 2-8.

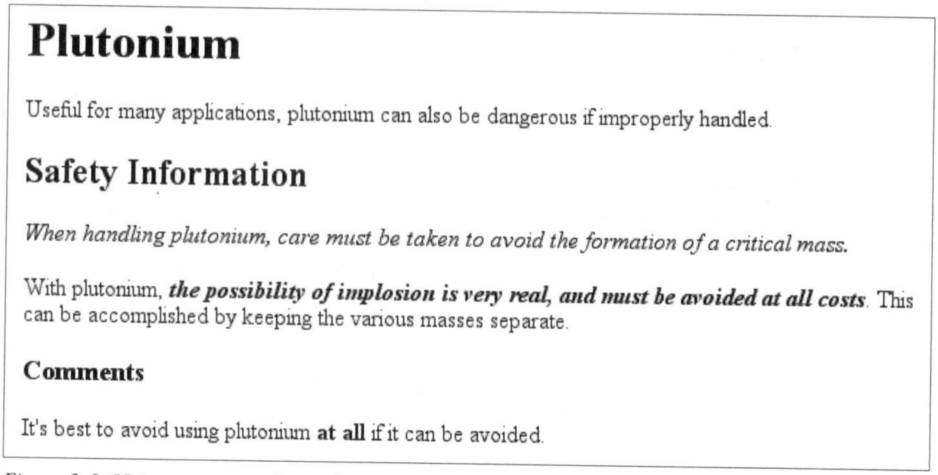

Plutonium

Useful for many applications, plutonium can also be dangerous if improperly handled.

Safety Information

When handling plutonium, care must be taken to avoid the formation of a critical mass.

*With plutonium, **the possibility of implosion is very real, and must be avoided at all costs**. This can be accomplished by keeping the various masses separate.*

Comments

It's best to avoid using plutonium **at all** if it can be avoided.

Figure 2-8. Using generic and specific selectors to combine styles

In this situation, any warning text will be italicized, but only the text within a span element and text with a class of warning will be boldfaced and italicized.

Notice the format of the general class selector in the previous example: it's simply a class name preceded by a period without any element name. In cases where you only want to select all elements that share a class name, you can omit the universal selector from a class selector without any ill effects.

Multiple Classes

In the previous section, we dealt with class values that contained a single word. In HTML, it's possible to have a space-separated list of words in a single class value. For example, if you want to mark a particular element as being both urgent and a warning, you could write:

```
<p class="urgent warning">When handling plutonium, care must be taken to
avoid the formation of a critical mass.</p>
<p>With plutonium, <span class="warning">the possibility of implosion is
very real, and must be avoided at all costs</span>. This can be accomplished
by keeping the various masses separate.</p>
```

The order of the words doesn't actually matter; warning urgent would also suffice.

Now let's say you want all elements with a class of warning to be boldface, those with a class of urgent to be italic, and those elements with both values to have a silver background. This would be written as follows:

```
.warning {font-weight: bold;}
.urgent {font-style: italic;}
.warning.urgent {background: silver;}
```

By chaining two class selectors together, you can select only those elements that have both class names, in any order. As you can see, the HTML source contains class="urgent warning" but the CSS selector is written .warning.urgent. Regardless, the rule will still cause the "When handling plutonium…" paragraph to have a silver background, as illustrated in Figure 2-9.

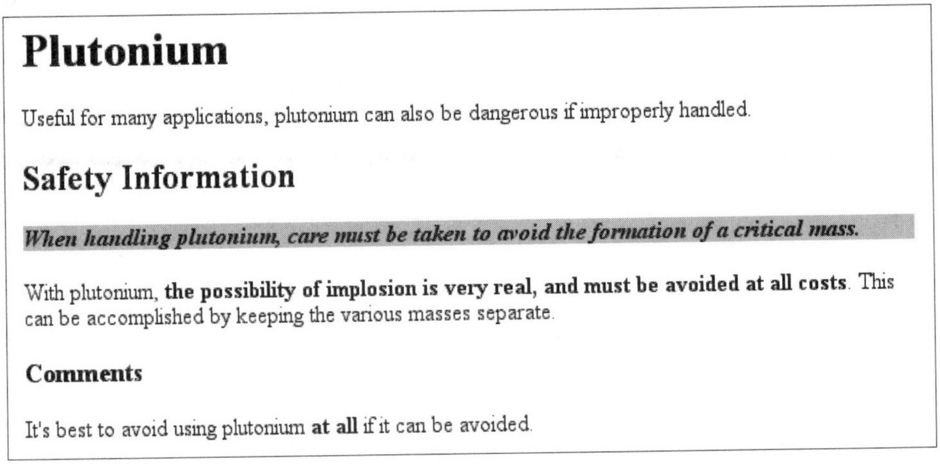

Plutonium

Useful for many applications, plutonium can also be dangerous if improperly handled.

Safety Information

When handling plutonium, care must be taken to avoid the formation of a critical mass.

With plutonium, **the possibility of implosion is very real, and must be avoided at all costs**. This can be accomplished by keeping the various masses separate.

Comments

It's best to avoid using plutonium **at all** if it can be avoided.

Figure 2-9. Selecting elements with multiple class names

If a multiple class selector contains a name that is not in the space-separated list, then the match will fail. Consider the following rule:

```
p.warning.help {background: red;}
```

As you would expect, the selector will match only those p elements with a class containing the words warning and help. Therefore, it will not match a p element with just the words warning and urgent in its class attribute. It would, however, match the following:

```
<p class="urgent warning help">Help me!</p>
```

 In versions previous to IE7, Internet Explorer for both platforms has problems with correctly handling multiple class selectors. In these older versions, although you can select a single class name out of a list, selecting based on multiple names in a list does not work properly. Thus, p.warning would work as expected, but p.warning.help would match any p elements that have a class attribute with the word help because it comes last in the selector. If you wrote p.help.warning, then older versions of Explorer would match any p elements that have warning in their class value, whether or not help appears in the same value.

ID Selectors

In some ways, ID selectors are similar to class selectors, but there are a few crucial differences. First, ID selectors are preceded by an octothorpe (#)—also known as a pound sign, hash mark, or tic-tac-toe board—instead of a period. Thus, you might see a rule like this one:

```
*#first-para {font-weight: bold;}
```

This rule applies boldface text to any element whose id attribute has a value of first-para.

The second difference is that instead of referencing values of the class attribute, ID selectors refer, unsurprisingly, to values found in id attributes. Here's an example of an ID selector in action:

```
*#lead-para {font-weight: bold;}

<p id="lead-para">This paragraph will be boldfaced.</p>
<p>This paragraph will NOT be bold.</p>
```

Note that the value lead-para could have been assigned to any element within the document. In this particular case, it is applied to the first paragraph, but you could have applied it just as easily to the second or third paragraph.

As with class selectors, it is possible to omit the universal selector from an ID selector. In the previous example, you could also have written:

```
#lead-para {font-weight: bold;}
```

The effect of this selector would be the same.

Deciding Between Class and ID

You may assign classes to any number of elements, as demonstrated earlier; the class name warning was applied to both a p and a span element, and it could have been applied to many more elements. IDs, on the other hand, are used once, and only once, within an HTML document. Therefore, if you have an element with an id value of lead-para, no other element in that document can have an id value of lead-para.

 In the real world, browsers don't usually check for the uniqueness of IDs in HTML, which means that if you sprinkle an HTML document with several elements, all of which have the same value for their ID attributes, you'll probably get the same styles applied to each. This is incorrect behavior, but it happens anyway. Having more than one of the same ID value in a document also makes DOM scripting more difficult, since functions like getElementById() depend on there being one, and only one, element with a given ID value.

Unlike class selectors, ID selectors can't be combined, since ID attributes do not permit a space-separated list of words.

On a purely syntactical level, the dot-class notation (e.g., .warning) is not guaranteed to work for XML documents. As of this writing, the dot-class notation works in HTML, SVG, and MathML, and it may well be permitted in future languages, but it's up to each language's specification to decide that. The hash-ID notation (e.g., #lead) will work in any document language that has an attribute that enforces uniqueness within a document. Uniqueness can be enforced with an attribute called id, or indeed anything else, as long as the attribute's contents are defined to be unique within the document.

Another difference between class and id names is that IDs carry more weight when you're trying to determine which styles should be applied to a given element. I'll explain this in greater detail in the next chapter.

As with classes, IDs can also be selected independently of an element. There may be circumstances in which you know that a certain ID value will appear in a document, but you don't know the element on which it will appear (as in the plutonium-handling warnings), so you'll want to declare standalone ID selectors. For example, you may know that in any given document, there will be an element with an ID value of mostImportant. You don't know whether that most important thing will be a paragraph, a short phrase, a list item, or a section heading. You know only that it will exist in each document, occur in an arbitrary element, and appear no more than once. In that case, you would write a rule like this:

```
#mostImportant {color: red; background: yellow;}
```

This rule would match any of the following elements (which, as I noted before, should *not* appear together in the same document because they all have the same ID value):

```
<h1 id="mostImportant">This is important!</h1>
<em id="mostImportant">This is important!</em>
<ul id="mostImportant">This is important!</ul>
```

Also note that class and ID selectors may be case-sensitive, depending on the document language. HTML and XHTML define class and ID values to be case-sensitive, so the capitalization of your class and ID values must match that found in your documents. Thus, in the following pairing of CSS and HTML, the element will not be boldfaced:

```
p.criticalInfo {font-weight: bold;}

<p class="criticalinfo">Don't look down.</p>
```

Because of the change in case for the letter *i*, the selector will not match the element shown.

 Some older browsers did not treat class and ID names as case-sensitive, but all browsers current as of this writing enforce case sensitivity.

Attribute Selectors

When it comes to both class and ID selectors, what you're really doing is selecting values of attributes. The syntax used in the previous two sections is particular to HTML, SVG, and MathML documents (as of this writing). In other markup languages, these class and ID selectors may not be available. To address this situation, CSS2 introduced *attribute selectors*, which can be used to select elements based on their attributes and the values of those attributes. There are four types of attribute selectors.

 Attribute selectors are supported by Safari, Opera, and all Gecko-based browsers, but not by Internet Explorer up through IE5/Mac and IE6/Win. IE7 fully supports all CSS2.1 attribute selectors, as well as a few CSS3 attribute selectors, which are covered in this section.

Simple Attribute Selection

If you want to select elements that have a certain attribute, regardless of that attribute's value, you can use a simple attribute selector. For example, to select all h1 elements that have a class attribute with any value and make their text silver, write:

```
h1[class] {color: silver;}
```

So, given the following markup:

```
<h1 class="hoopla">Hello</h1>
<h1 class="severe">Serenity</h1>
<h1 class="fancy">Fooling</h1>
```

you get the result shown in Figure 2-10.

Hello

Serenity

Fooling

Figure 2-10. Selecting elements based on their attributes

This strategy is very useful in XML documents, as XML languages tend to have element and attribute names that are very specific to their purpose. Consider an XML language that is used to describe planets of the solar system (we'll call it PlanetML). If you want to select all planet elements with a moons attribute and make them bold-face, thus calling attention to any planet that has moons, you would write:

```
planet[moons] {font-weight: bold;}
```

This would cause the text of the second and third elements in the following markup fragment to be boldfaced, but not the first:

```
<planet>Venus</planet>
<planet moons="1">Earth</planet>
<planet moons="2">Mars</planet>
```

In HTML documents, you can use this feature in a number of creative ways. For example, you could style all images that have an alt attribute, thus highlighting those images that are correctly formed:

```
img[alt] {border: 3px solid red;}
```

(This particular example is useful more for diagnostic purposes—that is, determining whether images are indeed correctly formed—than for design purposes.)

If you wanted to boldface any element that includes title information, which most browsers display as a "tool tip" when a cursor hovers over the element, you could write:

```
*[title] {font-weight: bold;}
```

Similarly, you could style only those anchors (a elements) that have an href attribute.

It is also possible to select based on the presence of more than one attribute. You do this simply by chaining the attribute selectors together. For example, to boldface the text of any HTML hyperlink that has both an href and a title attribute, you would write:

```
a[href][title] {font-weight: bold;}
```

This would boldface the first link in the following markup, but not the second or third:

```
<a href="http://www.w3.org/" title="W3C Home">W3C</a><br />
<a href="http://www.webstandards.org">Standards Info</a><br />
<a title="Not a link">dead.letter</a>
```

Selection Based on Exact Attribute Value

In addition to selecting elements with attributes, you can further narrow the selection process to encompass only those elements whose attributes are a certain value. For example, let's say you want to boldface any hyperlink that points to a certain document on the web server. This would look something like:

```
a[href="http://www.css-discuss.org/about.html"] {font-weight: bold;}
```

Any attribute and value combination can be specified for any element. However, if that exact combination does not appear in the document, then the selector won't match anything. Again, XML languages can benefit from this approach to styling. Let's return to our PlanetML example. Suppose you want to select only those planet elements that have a value of 1 for the attribute moons:

```
planet[moons="1"] {font-weight: bold;}
```

This would boldface the text of the second element in the following markup fragment, but not the first or third:

```
<planet>Venus</planet>
<planet moons="1">Earth</planet>
<planet moons="2">Mars</planet>
```

As with attribute selection, you can chain together multiple attribute-value selectors to select a single document. For example, to double the size of the text of any HTML hyperlink that has both an href with a value of http://www.w3.org/ and a title attribute with a value of W3C Home, you would write:

```
a[href="http://www.w3.org/"][title="W3C Home"] {font-size: 200%;}
```

This would double the text size of the first link in the following markup, but not the second or third:

```
<a href="http://www.w3.org/" title="W3C Home">W3C</a><br />
<a href="http://www.webstandards.org"
  title="Web Standards Organization">Standards Info</a><br />
<a href="http://www.example.org/" title="W3C Home">dead.link</a>
```

The results are shown in Figure 2-11.

Figure 2-11. Selecting elements based on attributes and their values

Note that this format requires an exact match for the attribute's value. Matching becomes an issue when the form encounters values that can in turn contain a space-separated list of values (e.g., the HTML attribute class). For example, consider the following markup fragment:

```
<planet type="barren rocky">Mercury</planet>
```

The only way to match this element based on its exact attribute value is to write:

```
planet[type="barren rocky"] {font-weight: bold;}
```

If you were to write planet[type="barren"], the rule would not match the example markup and thus would fail. This is true even for the class attribute in HTML. Consider the following:

```
<p class="urgent warning">When handling plutonium, care must be taken to
avoid the formation of a critical mass.</p>
```

To select this element based on its exact attribute value, you would have to write:

```
p[class="urgent warning"] {font-weight: bold;}
```

This is *not* equivalent to the dot-class notation covered earlier, as we will discuss in the next section. Instead, it selects any p element whose class attribute has *exactly* the value urgent warning, with the words in that order and a single space between them. It's effectively an exact string match.

Also, be aware that ID selectors and attribute selectors that target the id attribute are not precisely the same. In other words, there is a subtle but crucial difference between h1#page-title and h1[id="page-title"]. This difference is explained in the next chapter.

Selection Based on Partial Attribute Values

For any attribute that accepts a space-separated list of words, it is possible to select based on the presence of any one of those words. The classic example in HTML is the class attribute, which can accept one or more words as its value. Consider our usual example text:

```
<p class="urgent warning">When handling plutonium, care must be taken to
avoid the formation of a critical mass.</p>
```

Let's say you want to select elements whose class attribute contains the word warning. You can do this with an attribute selector:

```
p[class~="warning"] {font-weight: bold;}
```

Note the presence of the tilde (~) in the selector. It is the key to selection based on the presence of a space-separated word within the attribute's value. If you omit the tilde, you would have an exact-value matching requirement, as discussed in the previous section.

This selector construct is equivalent to the dot-class notation discussed earlier. Thus, p.warning and p[class~="warning"] are equivalent when applied to HTML documents. Here's an example that is an HTML version of the "PlanetML" markup seen earlier:

```
<span class="barren rocky">Mercury</planet>
<span class=" cloudy barren">Venus</planet>
<span class="life-bearing cloudy">Earth</planet>
```

To italicize all elements with the word barren in their class attribute, you write:

```
span[class~="barren"] {font-style: italic;}
```

This rule's selector will match the first two elements in the example markup and thus italicize their text, as shown in Figure 2-12. This is the same result we would expect from writing span.barren {font-style: italic;}.

Mercury Venus Earth

Figure 2-12. Selecting elements based on portions of attribute values

So why bother with the tilde-equals attribute selector in HTML? Because it can be used for any attribute, not just class. For example, you might have a document that contains a number of images, only some of which are figures. You can use a partial-value attribute selector aimed at the title text to select only those figures:

```
img[title~="Figure"] {border: 1px solid gray;}
```

This rule will select any image whose title text contains the word Figure. Therefore, as long as all your figures have title text that looks something like "Figure 4. A bald-headed elder statesman," this rule will match those images. For that matter, the selector img[title~="Figure"] will also match a title attribute with the value "How To Figure Out Who's In Charge." Any image that does not have a title attribute, or whose title value doesn't contain the word "Figure," won't be matched.

The even more advanced CSS Selectors module, which was released well after CSS2 was completed, contains a few more partial-value attribute selectors (or, as the specification calls them, "substring matching attribute selectors"). Since these are supported in many modern browsers, including IE7, we'll cover them quickly in Table 2-1.

Table 2-1. Substring matching attribute selectors

Type	Description
[foo^="bar"]	Selects any element with an attribute foo whose value begins with "bar".
[foo$="bar"]	Selects any element with an attribute foo whose value ends with "bar".
[foo*="bar"]	Selects any element with an attribute foo whose value contains the substring "bar".

Thus, given the following rules and markup, we would get the result shown in Figure 2-13.

```
span[class*="cloud"] {font-style: italic;}
span[class^="bar"] {background: silver;}
span[class$="y"] {font-weight: bold;}

<span class="barren rocky">Mercury</span>
<span class="cloudy barren">Venus</span>
<span class="life-bearing cloudy">Earth</span>
```

Mercury *Venus* ***Earth***

Figure 2-13. Selecting elements based on substrings within attribute values

The first of the three rules matches any span element whose class attribute contains the substring cloud, so both "cloudy" planets are matched. The second rule matches any span element whose class attribute starts with the substring bar, so the only match is Mercury, whose class value is barren rocky. Venus is not matched because the bar in barren comes later in its class value, not at the beginning. Finally, the third rule matches any span element whose class attribute ends with the substring y, so Mercury and Earth both are picked. Venus is again left out in the cold, since the end of its class value is not y.

As you can imagine, there are many useful applications for such selectors. As an example, suppose you wanted to specially style any links to the O'Reilly Media web site. Instead of classing them all and writing styles based on that class, you could simply write the following rule:

```
a[href*="oreilly.com"] {font-weight: bold;}
```

And, of course, you aren't confined to the class and href attributes. Any attribute is up for grabs here. title, alt, src, id... you name it, you can style based on its value or some part thereof. The following rule draws attention to any spacer GIF in an old-school table layout (plus any other image with the string "space" in its URL):

```
img[src*="space"] {border: 5px solid red;}
```

 As of this writing, support for these substring selectors is confined to Safari, Gecko-based browsers, Opera, and IE7/Win.

A Particular Attribute Selection Type

The last type of attribute selector, the particular attribute selector, is easier to show than it is to describe. Consider the following rule:

```
*[lang|="en"] {color: white;}
```

This rule will select any element whose lang attribute is equal to en or begins with en-. Therefore, the first three elements in the following example markup would be selected, but the last two would not:

```
<h1 lang="en">Hello!</h1>
<p lang="en-us">Greetings!</p>
<div lang="en-au">G'day!</div>
<p lang="fr">Bonjour!</p>
<h4 lang="cy-en">Jrooana!</h4>
```

In general, the form [att|="val"] can be used for any attribute and its values. Let's say you have a series of figures in an HTML document, each of which has a filename like *figure-1.gif* and *figure-3.jpg*. You can match all of these images using the following selector:

```
img[src|="figure"] {border: 1px solid gray;}
```

The most common use for this type of attribute selector is to match language values, as demonstrated later in this chapter.

Using Document Structure

As I've mentioned before, CSS is powerful because it uses the structure of HTML documents to determine appropriate styles and how to apply them. That's only part of the story since it implies that such determinations are the only way CSS uses document structure. Structure plays a much larger role in the way styles are applied to a document. Let's take a moment to discuss structure before moving on to more powerful forms of selection.

Understanding the Parent-Child Relationship

To understand the relationship between selectors and documents, you need to once again examine how documents are structured. Consider this very simple HTML document:

```
<html>
<head>
 <base href="http://www.meerkat.web/">
 <title>Meerkat Central</title>
</head>
<body>
 <h1>Meerkat <em>Central</em></h1>
 <p>
 Welcome to Meerkat <em>Central</em>, the <strong>best meerkat web site
 on <a href="inet.html">the <em>entire</em> Internet</a></strong>!</p>
 <ul>
  <li>We offer:
   <ul>
    <li><strong>Detailed information</strong> on how to adopt a meerkat</li>
    <li>Tips for living with a meerkat</li>
    <li><em>Fun</em> things to do with a meerkat, including:
     <ol>
      <li>Playing fetch</li>
      <li>Digging for food</li>
      <li>Hide and seek</li>
     </ol>
    </li>
   </ul>
  </li>
  <li>...and so much more!</li>
 </ul>
 <p>
 Questions? <a href="mailto:suricate@meerkat.web">Contact us!</a>
 </p>
</body>
</html>
```

Much of the power of CSS is based on the *parent-child relationship* of elements. HTML documents (actually, most structured documents of any kind) are based on a hierarchy of elements, which is visible in the "tree" view of the document (see

Figure 2-14). In this hierarchy, each element fits somewhere into the overall structure of the document. Every element in the document is either the *parent* or the *child* of another element, and it's often both.

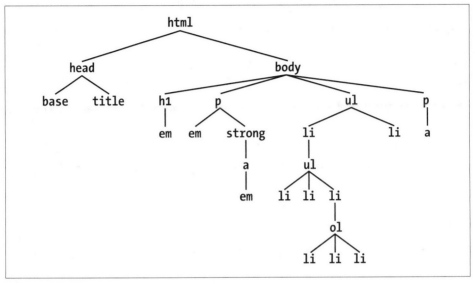

Figure 2-14. A document tree structure

An element is said to be the parent of another element if it appears directly above that element in the document hierarchy. For example, in Figure 2-14, the first p element is parent to the em and strong elements, while strong is parent to an anchor element, which is itself parent to another em element. Conversely, an element is the child of another element if it is directly beneath the other element. Thus, the anchor element in Figure 2-14 is a child of the strong element, which is in turn child to the p element, and so on.

The terms parent and child are specific applications of the terms *ancestor* and *descendant*. There is a difference between them: in the tree view, if an element is exactly one level above another, then they have a parent-child relationship. If the path from one element to another continues through two or more levels, the elements have an ancestor-descendant relationship, but not a parent-child relationship. (Of course, a child is also a descendant, and a parent is an ancestor.) In Figure 2-14, the first ul element is parent to two li elements, but the first ul is also the ancestor of every element descended from its li element, all the way down to the most deeply nested li elements.

Also, in Figure 2-14, there is an anchor that is a child of strong, but also a descendant of paragraph, body, and html elements. The body element is an ancestor of everything that the browser will display by default, and the html element is ancestor to the entire document. For this reason, the html element is also called the *root element*.

Descendant Selectors

The first benefit of understanding this model is the ability to define *descendant selectors* (also known as *contextual selectors*). Defining descendant selectors is the act of creating rules that operate in certain structural circumstances but not others. As an example, let's say you want to style only those em elements that are descended from h1 elements. You could put a class attribute on every em element found within an h1, but that's almost as time-consuming as using the font tag. It's obviously far more efficient to declare rules that match only em elements that are found inside h1 elements.

To do so, write the following:

```
h1 em {color: gray;}
```

This rule will make gray any text in an em element that is the descendant of an h1 element. Other em text, such as that found in a paragraph or a block quote, will not be selected by this rule. Figure 2-15 makes this clear.

Meerkat *Central*

Figure 2-15. Selecting an element based on its context

In a descendant selector, the selector side of a rule is composed of two or more space-separated selectors. The space between the selectors is an example of a *combinator*. Each space combinator can be translated as "found within," "which is part of," or "that is a descendant of," but only if you read the selector right to left. Thus, h1 em can be translated as, "Any em element that is a descendant of an h1 element." (To read the selector left to right, you might phrase it something like, "Any h1 that contains an em will have the following styles applied to the em.")

You aren't limited to two selectors, of course. For example:

```
ul ol ul em {color: gray;}
```

In this case, as Figure 2-16 shows, any emphasized text that is part of an unordered list that is part of an ordered list that is itself part of an unordered list (yes, this is correct) will be gray. This is obviously a very specific selection criterion.

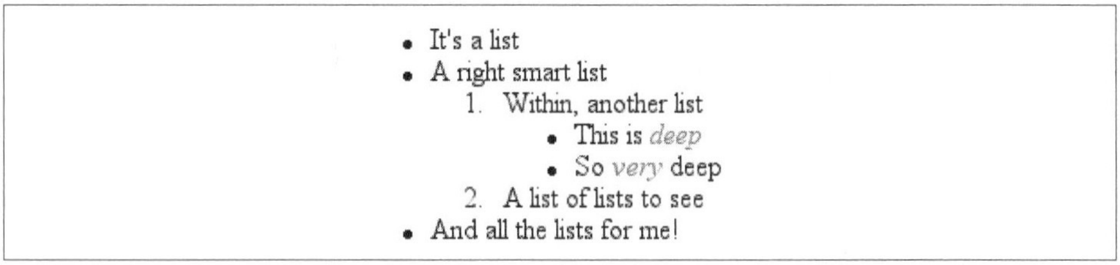

- It's a list
- A right smart list
  1. Within, another list
     - This is *deep*
     - So *very* deep
  2. A list of lists to see
- And all the lists for me!

Figure 2-16. A very specific descendant selector

Descendant selectors can be extremely powerful. They make possible what could never be done in HTML—at least not without oodles of font tags. Let's consider a common example. Assume you have a document with a sidebar and a main area. The sidebar has a blue background, the main area has a white background, and both areas include lists of links. You can't set all links to be blue because they'd be impossible to read in the sidebar.

The solution: descendant selectors. In this case, you give the table cell that contains your sidebar a class of `sidebar`, and assign the main area a class of `main`. Then, you write styles like this:

```
td.sidebar {background: blue;}
td.main {background: white;}
td.sidebar a:link {color: white;}
td.main a:link {color: blue;}
```

Figure 2-17 shows the result.

Figure 2-17. Using descendant selectors to apply different styles to the same type of element

`:link` refers to links to resources that haven't been visited. We'll talk about it in detail later in this chapter.

Here's another example: let's say that you want gray to be the text color of any b (boldface) element that is part of a `blockquote`, and also for any bold text that is found in a normal paragraph:

```
blockquote b, p b {color: gray;}
```

The result is that the text within b elements that are descended from paragraphs or block quotes will be gray.

One overlooked aspect of descendant selectors is that the degree of separation between two elements can be practically infinite. For example, if you write ul em, that syntax will select any em element descended from a ul element, no matter how deeply nested the em may be. Thus, ul em would select the em element in the following markup:

```
<ul>
<li>List item 1
<ol>
<li>List item 1-1</li>
<li>List item 1-2</li>
<li>List item 1-3
```

```
<ol>
<li>List item 1-3-1</li>
<li>List item <em>1-3-2</em></li>
<li>List item 1-3-3</li>
</ol></li>
<li>List item 1-4</li>
</ol></li>
</ul>
```

Selecting Children

In some cases, you don't want to select an arbitrarily descended element; rather, you want to narrow your range to select an element that is a child of another element. You might, for example, want to select a strong element only if it is a child (as opposed to a descendant) of an h1 element. To do this, you use the child combinator, which is the greater-than symbol (>):

```
h1 > strong {color: red;}
```

This rule will make red the strong element shown in the first h1 below, but not the second:

```
<h1>This is <strong>very</strong> important.</h1>
<h1>This is <em>really <strong>very</strong></em> important.</h1>
```

Read right to left, the selector h1 > strong translates as "selects any strong element that is a child of an h1 element." The child combinator is optionally surrounded by whitespace. Thus, h1 > strong, h1> strong, and h1>strong are all equivalent. You can use or omit whitespace as you wish.

When viewing the document as a tree structure, it's easy to see that a child selector restricts its matches to elements that are directly connected in the tree. Figure 2-18 shows part of a document tree.

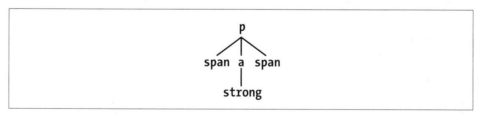

Figure 2-18. A document tree fragment

In this tree fragment, you can easily pick out parent-child relationships. For example, the a element is parent to the strong, but it is child to the p element. You could match elements in this fragment with the selectors p > a and a > strong, but not p > strong, since the strong is a descendant of the p but not its child.

You can also combine descendant and child combinations in the same selector. Thus, `table.summary td > p` will select any p element that is a child of a td element that is itself descended from a table element that has a class attribute containing the word summary.

Selecting Adjacent Sibling Elements

Let's say you want to style the paragraph immediately after a heading or give a special margin to a list that immediately follows a paragraph. To select an element that immediately follows another element with the same parent, you use the *adjacent-sibling combinator*, represented as a plus symbol (+). As with the child combinator, the symbol can be surrounded by whitespace at the author's discretion.

To remove the top margin from a paragraph immediately following an h1 element, write:

```
h1 + p {margin-top: 0;}
```

The selector is read as, "selects any paragraph that immediately follows an h1 element that shares a parent with the p element."

To visualize how this selector works, it is easiest to once again consider a fragment of a document tree, shown in Figure 2-19.

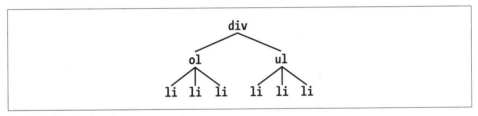

Figure 2-19. Another document tree fragment

In this fragment, a pair of lists descends from a div element, one ordered and the other not, each containing three list items. Each list is an adjacent sibling, and the list items themselves are also adjacent siblings. However, the list items from the first list are *not* siblings of the second, since the two sets of list items do not share the same parent element. (At best, they're cousins.)

Remember that you can select the second of two adjacent siblings only with a single combinator. Thus, if you write `li + li {font-weight: bold;}`, only the second and third items in each list will be boldfaced. The first list items will be unaffected, as illustrated in Figure 2-20.

To work properly, CSS requires that the two elements appear in "source order." In our example, an ol element is followed by a ul element. This allows you to select the second element with `ol + ul`, but you cannot select the first using the same syntax. For `ul + ol` to match, an ordered list must immediately follow an unordered list.

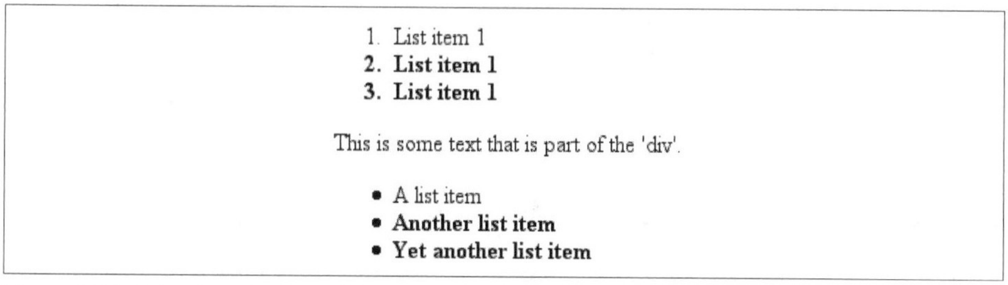

> 1. List item 1
> **2. List item 1**
> **3. List item 1**
>
> This is some text that is part of the 'div'.
>
> - A list item
> - **Another list item**
> - **Yet another list item**

Figure 2-20. Selecting adjacent siblings

In addition, text content between two elements does not prevent the adjacent-sibling combinator from working. Consider this markup fragment, whose tree view would be the same as that shown in Figure 2-19:

```
<div>
<ol>
<li>List item 1</li>
<li>List item 1</li>
<li>List item 1</li>
</ol>
This is some text that is part of the 'div'.
<ul>
<li>A list item</li>
<li>Another list item</li>
<li>Yet another list item</li>
</ul>
</div>
```

Even though there is text between the two lists, you can still match the second list with the selector ol + ul. That's because the intervening text is not contained with a sibling element, but is instead part of the parent div. If you wrapped that text in a paragraph element, it would then prevent ol + ul from matching the second list. Instead, you might have to write something like ol + p + ul.

As the following example illustrates, the adjacent-sibling combinator can be used in conjunction with other combinators:

```
html > body table + ul{margin-top: 1.5em;}
```

The selector translates as "selects any ul element that immediately follows a sibling table element that is descended from a body element that is itself a child of an html element."

 Internet Explorer for Windows through IE6 does not support child and adjacent-sibling selectors. IE7 supports both.

Pseudo-Classes and Pseudo-Elements

Things get really interesting with *pseudo-class selectors* and *pseudo-element selectors*. These selectors let you assign styles to structures that don't necessarily exist in the document, or to phantom classes that are inferred by the state of certain elements, or even by the state of the document itself. In other words, the styles are applied to pieces of a document based on something other than the structure of the document, and in a way that cannot be precisely deduced simply by studying the document's markup.

It may sound like I'm applying styles at random, but I'm not. Instead, I'm applying styles based on somewhat ephemeral conditions that can't be predicted in advance. However, the circumstances under which the styles will appear are, in fact, well-defined. Think of it this way: during a sporting event, whenever the home team scores, the crowd will cheer. You don't know exactly when during a game the team will score, but when it does, the crowd will cheer, just as predicted. The fact that you can't predict the moment of the cause doesn't make the effect any less expected.

Pseudo-Class Selectors

Let's begin by examining pseudo-class selectors since they're better supported by browsers and are therefore more widely used.

Consider the anchor element (a), which, in HTML and XHTML, establishes a link from one document to another. Anchors are always anchors, of course, but some anchors refer to pages that have already been visited, while others refer to pages that have yet to be visited. You can't tell the difference by simply looking at the HTML markup, because in the markup, all anchors look the same. The only way to tell which links have been visited is by comparing the links in a document to the user's browser history. So, there are actually two basic types of anchors: visited and unvisited. These types are known as *pseudo-classes,* and the selectors that use them are called *pseudo-class selectors*.

To better understand these classes and selectors, consider how browsers behave with regard to links. The Mosaic convention designated that links to pages you hadn't visited were blue, and links to already visited pages were red (the red became purple in succeeding browsers such as Internet Explorer). So, if you could insert classes into anchors, such that any already visited anchor would have a class of, say, "visited," then you could write a style to make such anchors red:

```
a.visited {color: red;}

<a href="http://www.w3.org/" class="visited">W3C Web site</a>
```

However, such an approach requires that the classes on anchors change every time you visit a new page, which is a little silly. Instead, CSS defines pseudo-classes that make the anchors to visited pages act as though they have classes of "visited":

```
a:visited {color: red;}
```

Now, any anchor that points to a visited page will be red, and you don't even have to add class attributes to any of the anchors. Note the colon (:) in the rule. The colon separating the a and the visited is the calling card of a pseudo-class or pseudo-element. All pseudo-class and -element keywords are preceded by a colon.

Link pseudo-classes

CSS2.1 defines two pseudo-classes that apply only to hyperlinks. In HTML and XHTML 1.0 and 1.1, these are any a elements with an href attribute; in XML languages, they're any elements that act as links to another resource. Table 2-2 describes these two pseudo-classes.

Table 2-2. Link pseudo-classes

Name	Description
:link	Refers to any anchor that is a hyperlink (i.e., has an href attribute) and points to an address that has not been visited. Note that some browsers may incorrectly interpret :link to refer to any hyperlink, visited or unvisited.
:visited	Refers to any anchor that is a hyperlink to an already visited address.

The first of the pseudo-classes in Table 2-1 may seem a bit redundant. After all, if an anchor hasn't been visited, then it must be unvisited, right? If that's the case, all we should need is the following:

```
a {color: blue;}
a:visited {color: red;}
```

Although this format seems reasonable, it's actually not quite enough. The first of the rules shown here applies not only to unvisited links, but also to target anchors such as this one:

```
<a name="section4">4. The Lives of Meerkats</a>
```

The resulting text would be blue because the a element will match the rule a {color: blue;}, as shown above. Therefore, to avoid applying your link styles to target anchors, use the :link pseudo-class:

```
a:link {color: blue;}    /* unvisited links are blue */
a:visited {color: red;}   /* visited links are red */
```

As you may have already realized, the :link and :visited pseudo-class selectors are functionally equivalent to the body attributes link and vlink. Assume that an author wants all anchors to unvisited pages to be purple and anchors to visited pages to be silver. In HTML 3.2, this could be specified as follows:

```
<body link="purple" vlink="silver">
```

In CSS, the same effect would be accomplished with:

```
a:link {color: purple;}
a:visited {color: silver;}
```

In the case of the CSS pseudo-classes, of course, you can apply more than just colors. Let's say you want visited links to be italicized and to have, in addition to their silver color, a strikethrough line, as shown in Figure 2-21.

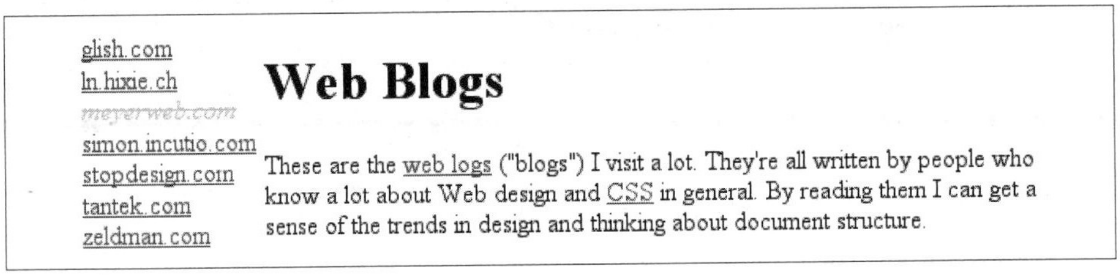

Figure 2-21. Applying multiple styles to a visited link

This is simply done with the following styles:

```
a:visited {color: silver; text-decoration: line-through; font-style: italic;}
```

This is a good place to revisit class selectors and show how they can be combined with pseudo-classes. For example, let's say you want to change the color of links that point outside your own site. If you assign a class to each of these anchors, it's easy:

```
<a href="http://www.mysite.net/">My home page</a>
<a href="http://www.site.net/" class="external">Another home page</a>
```

To apply different styles to the external link, all you need is a rule like this:

```
a.external:link, a.external:visited {color: maroon;}
```

This rule will make the second anchor in the preceding markup maroon, while the first anchor will remain the default color for hyperlinks (usually blue).

The same general syntax is used for ID selectors as well:

```
a#footer-copyright:link{font-weight: bold;}
a#footer-copyright:visited {font-weight: normal;}
```

Although :link and :visited are very useful, they're also static—they typically don't change the styling of a document after its initial display. Other pseudo-classes that aren't quite so static are available in CSS2.1; we'll review them next.

Dynamic pseudo-classes

CSS2.1 defines three pseudo-classes that can change a document's appearance as a result of user behavior. These dynamic pseudo-classes have traditionally been used to style hyperlinks, but the possibilities are much wider. Table 2-3 describes these pseudo-classes.

Table 2-3. Dynamic pseudo-classes

Name	Description
`:focus`	Refers to any element that currently has the input focus—i.e., can accept keyboard input or be activated in some way.
`:hover`	Refers to any element over which the mouse pointer is placed—e.g., a hyperlink over which the mouse pointer is hovering.
`:active`	Refers to any element that has been activated by user input—e.g., a hyperlink on which a user clicks during the time the mouse button is held down.

As with `:link` and `:visited`, these pseudo-classes are most familiar in the context of hyperlinks. Many web pages have styles that look like this:

```
a:link {color: navy;}
a:visited {color: gray;}
a:hover {color: red;}
a:active {color: yellow;}
```

The first two rules use static pseudo-classes, and the last two employ dynamic pseudo-classes. `:active` is analogous to the `alink` attribute in HTML 3.2, although, as before, you can apply color changes and any style you like to active links.

> The order of the pseudo-classes is more important than it might seem at first. The usual recommendation is "link-visited-hover-active," although this has been modified to "link-visited-focus-hover-active." The next chapter explains why this particular ordering is important and discusses several reasons you might choose to change or even ignore the recommended ordering.

Notice that the dynamic pseudo-classes can be applied to any element, which is good since it's often useful to apply dynamic styles to elements that aren't links. For example, using this markup:

```
input:focus {background: silver; font-weight: bold;}
```

you could highlight a form element that is ready to accept keyboard input, as shown in Figure 2-22.

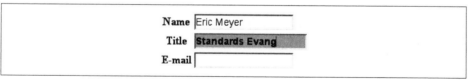

Figure 2-22. Highlighting a form element that has focus

You can also perform some rather odd feats by applying dynamic pseudo-classes to arbitrary elements. You might decide to give users a "highlight" effect by way of the following:

```
body *:hover {background: yellow;}
```

This rule will cause any element that's descended from the body element to display a yellow background when it's in a hover state. Headings, paragraphs, lists, tables, images, and anything else found inside the body will be changed to have a yellow background. You could also change the font, put a border around the element being hovered, or alter anything else the browser will allow.

 Internet Explorer for Windows through IE6 does not permit dynamic pseudo-classes to select any elements other than hyperlinks. IE7 added support for :hover on any element, but not :focus styles for form elements.

Real-world issues with dynamic styling

Dynamic pseudo-classes present some interesting issues and peculiarities. For example, it's possible to set visited and unvisited links to one font size and make hovered links a larger size, as shown in Figure 2-23:

```
a:link, a:visited {font-size: 13px;}
a:hover {font-size: 20px;}
```

glish.com
ln.hixie.ch
meyerweb.com

Web Blogs

simon.incutip.com
stopdesign.com
tantek.com
zeldman.com

These are the web logs ("blogs") I visit a lot. They're all written by people who know a lot about Web design and CSS in general. By reading them I can get a sense of the trends in design and thinking about document structure.

Figure 2-23. Changing layout with dynamic pseudo-classes

As you can see, the user agent increases the size of the anchor while the mouse pointer hovers over it. A user agent that supports this behavior must redraw the document while an anchor is in hover state, which could force a reflow of all the content that follows the link.

However, the CSS specifications state that user agents are not required to redraw a document once it's been rendered for initial display, so you can't absolutely rely on your intended effect taking place. I strongly recommend that you avoid designs that depend on such behavior.

Selecting a first child

Another static pseudo-class, `:first-child`, is used to select elements that are the first children of other elements. This particular pseudo-class is easily misunderstood, so an extended example is in order. Consider the following markup:

```
<div>
<p>These are the necessary steps:</p>
<ul>
<li>Insert key</li>
<li>Turn key <strong>clockwise</strong></li>
<li>Push accelerator</li>
</ul>
<p>
Do <em>not</em> push the brake at the same time as the accelerator.
</p>
</div>
```

In this example, the elements that are first children are the first p, the first li, and the strong and em elements. Given the following two rules:

```
p:first-child {font-weight: bold;}
li:first-child {text-transform: uppercase;}
```

you get the result shown in Figure 2-24.

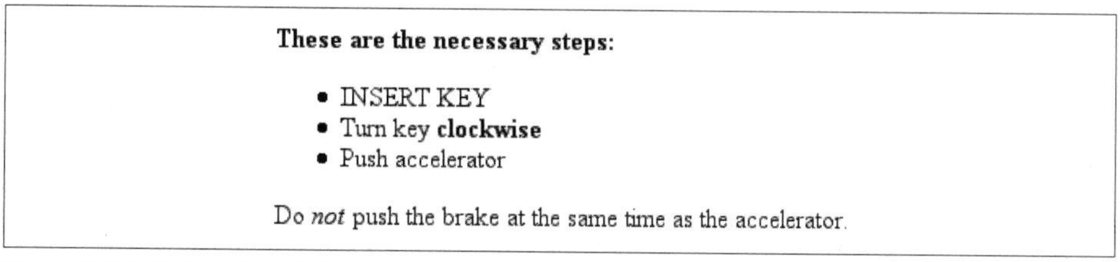

These are the necessary steps:

- INSERT KEY
- Turn key **clockwise**
- Push accelerator

Do *not* push the brake at the same time as the accelerator.

Figure 2-24. Styling first children

The first rule boldfaces any p element that is the first child of another element. The second rule uppercases any li element that is the first child of another element (which, in HTML, must be either an ol or a ul element).

The most common error is to assume that a selector like `p:first-child` will select the first child of a p element. However, remember the nature of pseudo-classes, which is to attach a sort of phantom class to the element associated with the pseudo-class. If you were to add actual classes to the markup, it would look like this:

```
<div>
<p class="first-child">These are the necessary steps:</p>
<ul>
<li class="first-child">Insert key</li>
<li>Turn key <strong class="first-child">clockwise</strong></li>
<li>Push accelerator</li>
</ul>
```

```
<p>
Do <em class="first-child">not</em> push the brake at the same time as the
accelerator.
</p>
</div>
```

Therefore, if you want to select those em elements that are the first children of another element, you write em:first-child. This selector allows you to, for example, style the first item in a list, the first paragraph of a div, or the first td in a table row.

 Internet Explorer for Windows through IE6 does not support :first-child, but IE7 does.

Selecting based on language

For situations where you want to select an element based on its language, you can use the :lang( ) pseudo-class. In terms of its matching patterns, the :lang( ) pseudo-class is exactly like the |= attribute selector. For example, to italicize any element in French, you would write:

```
*:lang(fr) {font-style: italic;}
```

The primary difference between the pseudo-selector and the attribute selector is that the language information can be derived from a number of sources, some of which are outside the element itself. As CSS2.1 states:

> In HTML, the language is determined by a combination of the lang attribute, the META element, and possibly by information from the protocol (such as HTTP headers). XML uses an attribute called xml:lang, and there may be other document language-specific methods for determining the language.

Therefore, the pseudo-class is a bit more robust than the attribute selector and is probably a better choice in most cases where language-specific styling is needed.

Combining pseudo-classes

With CSS2.1, you can combine pseudo-classes in the same selector. For example, you can make unvisited links red when they're hovered, but visited links maroon when *they're* hovered:

```
a:link:hover {color: red;}
a:visited:hover {color: maroon;}
```

The order you specify doesn't actually matter; you could also write a:hover:link to the same effect as a:link:hover. It's also possible to assign separate hover styles to unvisited and visited links that are in another language—for example, German:

```
a:link:hover:lang(de) {color: gray;}
a:visited:hover:lang(de) {color: silver;}
```

Be careful not to combine mutually exclusive pseudo-classes. For example, a link cannot be both visited and unvisited, so `a:link:visited` doesn't make any sense. User agents will most likely ignore such a selector and thus effectively ignore the entire rule, although this cannot be guaranteed, as different browsers will have different error-handling behaviors.

 Internet Explorer for Windows through IE6 does not correctly recognize combined pseudo-classes. As with class-value combinations, it will pay attention to the last of the combined pseudo-classes. Thus, given `a:link:hover`, older versions of IE/Win will pay attention to the `:hover` but not the `:link` portion of the selector. IE7 does not suffer from this limitation; it correctly handles combined pseudo-classes.

Pseudo-Element Selectors

Much as pseudo-classes assign phantom classes to anchors, pseudo-elements insert fictional elements into a document in order to achieve certain effects. Four pseudo-elements are defined in CSS2.1: styling the first letter, styling the first line, and styling before and after elements.

Styling the first letter

The first pseudo-element styles the first letter, and only that letter, of a block-level element:

```
p:first-letter {color: red;}
```

This rule causes the first letter of every paragraph to be colored red. Alternatively, you could make the first letter of each h2 twice as big as the rest of the heading:

```
h2:first-letter {font-size: 200%;}
```

The result of this rule is illustrated in Figure 2-25.

> # This is an h2 element

Figure 2-25. The :first-letter pseudo-element in action

As I mentioned, this rule effectively causes the user agent to respond to a fictional element that encloses the first letter of each h2. It would look something like this:

```
<h2><h2:first-letter>T</h2:first-letter>his is an h2 element</h2>
```

The `:first-letter` styles are applied only to the contents of the fictional element shown in the example. This `<h2:first-letter>` element does *not* appear in the document source. Instead, its existence is constructed on the fly by the user agent and is used to apply the `:first-letter` style(s) to the appropriate block of text. In other words, `<h2:first-letter>` is a pseudo-element. Remember, you don't have to add any new tags. The user agent will do it for you.

Styling the first line

Similarly, `:first-line` can be used to affect the first line of text in an element. For example, you could make the first line of each paragraph in a document purple:

```
p:first-line {color: purple;}
```

In Figure 2-26, the style is applied to the first displayed line of text in each paragraph. This is true no matter how wide or narrow the display region is. If the first line contains only the first five words of the paragraph, then only those five words will be purple. If the first line contains the first 30 words of the element, then all 30 will be purple.

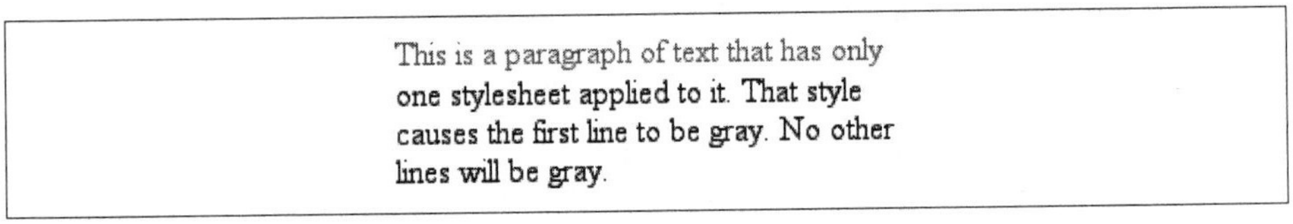

This is a paragraph of text that has only
one stylesheet applied to it. That style
causes the first line to be gray. No other
lines will be gray.

Figure 2-26. The :first-line pseudo-element in action

Because the text from "This" to "only" should be purple, the user agent employs a fictional markup that looks something like this:

```
<p><p:first-line>This is a paragraph of text that has only</p:first-line>
one stylesheet applied to it. That style
causes the first line to be purple. No other ...
```

If the first line of text were edited to include only the first seven words of the paragraph, then the fictional `</p:first-line>` would move back and occur just after the word "that."

Restrictions on :first-letter and :first-line

In CSS2, the `:first-letter` and `:first-line` pseudo-elements can be applied only to block-level elements such as headings or paragraphs and not to inline-level elements such as hyperlinks. In CSS2.1, `:first-letter` applies to all elements. There are also limits on the CSS properties that may be applied to `:first-line` and `:first-letter`. Table 2-4 displays the limits.

Table 2-4. Properties permitted on pseudo-elements

:first-letter	:first-line
All font properties	All font properties
color	color
All background properties	All background properties
All margin properties	word-spacing
All padding properties	letter-spacing
All border properties	text-decoration

Table 2-4. Properties permitted on pseudo-elements (continued)

:first-letter	:first-line
text-decoration	vertical-align
vertical-align (if float is set to none)	text-transform
text-transform	line-height
line-height	clear (CSS2 only; removed in CSS2.1)
float	text-shadow (CSS2 only)
letter-spacing (added in CSS2.1)	
word-spacing (added in CSS2.1)	
clear (CSS2 only; removed in CSS2.1)	
text-shadow (CSS2 only)	

In addition, all pseudo-elements must be placed at the very end of the selector in which they appear. Therefore, it would not be legal to write p:first-line em since the pseudo-element comes before the subject of the selector (the subject is the last element listed). The same rule applies to the other two pseudo-elements CSS2.1 defines.

Style before and after elements

Let's say you want to preface every h2 element with a pair of silver square brackets as a typographical effect:

```
h2:before {content: "]]"; color: silver;}
```

CSS2.1 lets you insert *generated content*, and then style it directly using the pseudo-elements :before and :after. Figure 2-27 illustrates an example.

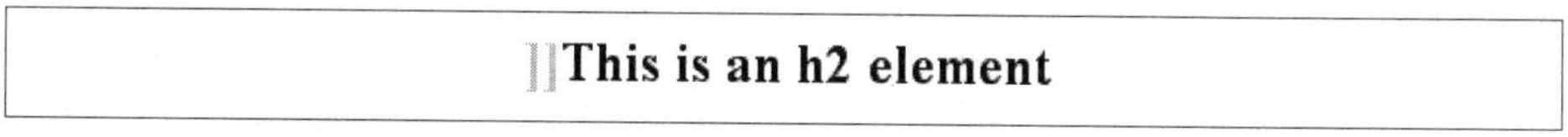

‖This is an h2 element

Figure 2-27. Inserting content before an element

The pseudo-element is used to insert the generated content and to style it. To place content after an element, use the pseudo-element :after. You could end your documents with an appropriate finish:

```
body:after {content: "  The End.";}
```

Generated content is a separate subject, and the entire topic (including more detail on :before and :after) is covered more thoroughly in Chapter 12.

Summary

By using selectors based on the document's language, authors can create CSS rules that apply to a large number of similar elements just as easily as they can construct rules that apply in very narrow circumstances. The ability to group together both selectors and rules keeps style sheets compact and flexible, which incidentally leads to smaller file sizes and faster download times.

Selectors are the one thing that user agents usually must get right because the inability to correctly interpret selectors pretty much prevents a user agent from using CSS at all. On the flip side, it's crucial for authors to correctly write selectors because errors can prevent the user agent from applying the styles as intended. An integral part of correctly understanding selectors and how they can be combined is a strong grasp of how selectors relate to document structure and how mechanisms—such as inheritance and the cascade itself—come into play when determining how an element will be styled. This is the subject of the next chapter.

CHAPTER 3

Structure and the Cascade

Chapter 2 shows how document structure and CSS selectors allow you to apply a wide variety of styles to elements. Knowing that every valid document generates a structural tree, you can create selectors that target elements based on their ancestors, attributes, sibling elements, and more. The structural tree is what allows selectors to function and is also central to a similarly crucial aspect of CSS: inheritance.

Inheritance is the mechanism by which some property values are passed on from an element to its descendants. When determining which values should apply to an element, a user agent must consider not only inheritance but also the specificity of the declarations, as well as the origin of the declarations themselves. This process of consideration is what's known as the *cascade*. We will explore the interrelation between these three mechanisms—specificity, inheritance, and the cascade—in this chapter.

Above all, regardless of how abstract things may seem, keep going! Your perseverance will be rewarded.

Specificity

You know from Chapter 2 that you can select elements using a wide variety of means. In fact, it's possible that the same element could be selected by two or more rules, each with its own selector. Let's consider the following three pairs of rules. Assume that each pair will match the same element:

```
h1 {color: red;}
body h1 {color: green;}

h2.grape {color: purple;}
h2 {color: silver;}

html > body table tr[id="totals"] td ul > li {color: maroon;}
li#answer {color: navy;}
```

Obviously, only one of the two rules in each pair can win out, since the matched elements can be only one color or the other. How do you know which one will win?

The answer is found in the *specificity* of each selector. For every rule, the user agent evaluates the specificity of the selector and attaches it to each declaration in the rule. When an element has two or more conflicting property declarations, the one with the highest specificity will win out.

 This isn't the whole story in terms of conflict resolution. In fact, all style conflict resolution is handled by the cascade, which has its own section later in this chapter.

A selector's specificity is determined by the components of the selector itself. A specificity value is expressed in four parts, like this: 0,0,0,0. The actual specificity of a selector is determined as follows:

- For every ID attribute value given in the selector, add 0,1,0,0.
- For every class attribute value, attribute selection, or pseudo-class given in the selection, add 0,0,1,0.
- For every element and pseudo-element given in the selector, add 0,0,0,1. CSS2 contradicted itself as to whether pseudo-elements had any specificity at all, but CSS2.1 makes it clear that they do, and this is where they belong.
- Combinators and the universal selector do not contribute anything to the specificity (more on these values later).

For example, the following rules' selectors result in the indicated specificities:

```
h1 {color: red;}  /* specificity = 0,0,0,1 */
p em {color: purple;}  /* specificity = 0,0,0,2 */
.grape {color: purple;}  /* specificity = 0,0,1,0 */
*.bright {color: yellow;}  /* specificity = 0,0,1,0 */
p.bright em.dark {color: maroon;}  /* specificity = 0,0,2,2 */
#id216 {color: blue;}  /* specificity = 0,1,0,0 */
div#sidebar *[href] {color: silver;}  /* specificity = 0,1,1,1 */
```

Given a case where an em element is matched by both the second and fifth rules in the example above, that element will be maroon because the fifth rule's specificity outweighs the second's.

As an exercise, let's return to the pairs of rules from earlier in the section and fill in the specificities:

```
h1 {color: red;}  /* 0,0,0,1 */
body h1 {color: green;}  /* 0,0,0,2  (winner)*/

h2.grape {color: purple;}  /* 0,0,1,1 (winner) */
h2 {color: silver;}  /* 0,0,0,1 */

html > body table tr[id="totals"] td ul > li {color: maroon;}  /* 0,0,1,7 */
li#answer {color: navy;}  /* 0,1,0,1  (winner) */
```

You've indicated the winning rule in each pair; in each case, it's because the specificity is higher. Notice how they're sorted. In the second pair, the selector h2.grape wins because it has an extra 1: 0,0,1,1 beats out 0,0,0,1. In the third pair, the second rule wins because 0,1,0,1 wins out over 0,0,1,7. In fact, the specificity value 0,0,1,0 will win out over the value 0,0,0,13.

This happens because the values are sorted from left to right. A specificity of 1,0,0,0 will win out over any specificity that begins with a 0, no matter what the rest of the numbers might be. So 0,1,0,1 wins over 0,0,1,7 because the 1 in the first value's second position beats out the second 0 in the second value.

Declarations and Specificity

Once the specificity of a selector has been determined, the value will be conferred on all of its associated declarations. Consider this rule:

```
h1 {color: silver; background: black;}
```

For specificity purposes, the user agent must treat the rule as if it were "ungrouped" into separate rules. Thus, the previous example would become:

```
h1 {color: silver;}
h1 {background: black;}
```

Both have a specificity of 0,0,0,1, and that's the value conferred on each declaration. The same splitting-up process happens with a grouped selector as well. Given the rule:

```
h1, h2.section {color: silver; background: black;}
```

the user agent treats it as follows:

```
h1 {color: silver;}  /* 0,0,0,1 */
h1 {background: black;}  /* 0,0,0,1 */
h2.section {color: silver;}  /* 0,0,1,1 */
h2.section {background: black;}  /* 0,0,1,1 */
```

This becomes important in situations where multiple rules match the same element and where some declarations clash. For example, consider these rules:

```
h1 + p {color: black; font-style: italic;}  /* 0,0,0,2 */
p {color: gray; background: white; font-style: normal;}  /* 0,0,0,1 */
*.aside {color: black; background: silver;}  /* 0,0,1,0 */
```

When applied to the following markup, the content will be rendered as shown in Figure 3-1:

```
<h1>Greetings!</h1>
<p class="aside">
It's a fine way to start a day, don't you think?
</p>
<p>
There are many ways to greet a person, but the words are not as important as the act
of greeting itself.
</p>
<h1>Salutations!</h1>
```

```
<p>
There is nothing finer than a hearty welcome from one's fellow man.
</p>
<p class="aside">
Although a thick and juicy hamburger with bacon and mushrooms runs a close second.
</p>
```

Greetings!

It's a fine way to start a day, don't you think?

There are many ways to greet a person, but the words are not so important as the act of greeting itself

Salutations!

There is nothing finer than a hearty welcome from one's fellow man.

Although a thick and juicy hamburger with bacon and mushrooms runs a close second

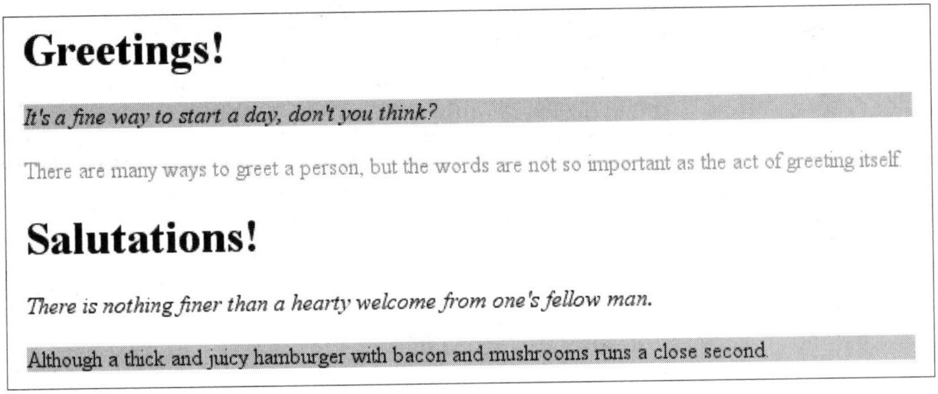

Figure 3-1. How different rules affect a document

In every case, the user agent determines which rules match an element, calculates all of the associated declarations and their specificities, determines which ones win out, and then applies the winners to the element to get the styled result. These machinations must be performed on every element, selector, and declaration. Fortunately, the user agent does it all automatically. This behavior is an important component of the cascade, which we will discuss later in this chapter.

Universal Selector Specificity

As mentioned earlier, the universal selector does not contribute to the specificity of a selector. In other words, it has a specificity of 0,0,0,0, which is different than having no specificity (as we'll discuss in "Inheritance"). Therefore, given the following two rules, a paragraph descended from a div will be black, but all other elements will be gray:

```
div p {color: black;}  /* 0,0,0,2 */
* {color: gray;}  /* 0,0,0,0 */
```

As you might expect, this means that the specificity of a selector that contains a universal selector along with other selectors is not changed by the presence of the universal selector. The following two selectors have exactly the same specificity:

```
div p  /* 0,0,0,2 */
body * strong  /* 0,0,0,2 */
```

Combinators, by comparison, have no specificity at all—not even zero specificity. Thus, they have no impact on a selector's overall specificity.

ID and Attribute Selector Specificity

It's important to note the difference in specificity between an ID selector and an attribute selector that targets an id attribute. Returning to the third pair of rules in the example code, we find:

```
html > body table tr[id="totals"] td ul > li {color: maroon;}  /* 0,0,1,7 */
li#answer {color: navy;}  /* 0,1,0,1  (winner) */
```

The ID selector (#answer) in the second rule contributes 0,1,0,0 to the overall specificity of the selector. In the first rule, however, the attribute selector ([id="totals"]) contributes 0,0,1,0 to the overall specificity. Thus, given the following rules, the element with an id of meadow will be green:

```
#meadow {color: green;}  /* 0,1,0,0 */
*[id="meadow"] {color: red;}  /* 0,0,1,0 */
```

Inline Style Specificity

So far, we've seen specificities that begin with a zero, so you may be wondering why it's there at all. As it happens, that first zero is reserved for inline style declarations, which trump any other declaration's specificity. Consider the following rule and markup fragment:

```
h1 {color: red;}
```

```
<h1 style="color: green;">The Meadow Party</h1>
```

Given that the rule is applied to the h1 element, you would still probably expect the text of the h1 to be green. This is what happens in CSS2.1, and it happens because every inline declaration has a specificity of 1,0,0,0.

This means that even elements with id attributes that match a rule will obey the inline style declaration. Let's modify the previous example to include an id:

```
h1#meadow {color: red;}
```

```
<h1 id="meadow" style="color: green;">The Meadow Party</h1>
```

Thanks to the inline declaration's specificity, the text of the h1 element will still be green.

> The primacy of inline style declarations is new to CSS2.1, and it exists to capture the state of web browser behavior at the time CSS2.1 was written. In CSS2, the specificity of an inline style declaration was 1,0,0 (CSS2 specificities had three values, not four). In other words, it had the same specificity as an ID selector, which would have easily overridden inline styles.

Importance

Sometimes, a declaration is so important that it outweighs all other considerations. CSS2.1 calls these *important declarations* (for obvious reasons) and lets you mark them by inserting !important just before the terminating semicolon in a declaration:

```
p.dark {color: #333 !important; background: white;}
```

Here, the color value of #333 is marked !important, whereas the background value of white is not. If you wish to mark both declarations as important, each declaration will need its own !important marker:

```
p.dark {color: #333 !important; background: white !important;}
```

You must place !important correctly, or the declaration may be invalidated. !important *always* goes at the end of the declaration, just before the semicolon. This placement is especially important—no pun intended—when it comes to properties that allow values containing multiple keywords, such as font:

```
p.light {color: yellow; font: smaller Times, serif !important;}
```

If !important were placed anywhere else in the font declaration, the entire declaration would likely be invalidated and none of its styles applied.

Declarations that are marked !important do not have a special specificity value, but are instead considered separately from nonimportant declarations. In effect, all !important declarations are grouped together, and specificity conflicts are resolved relative to each other. Similarly, all nonimportant declarations are considered together, with property conflicts resolved using specificity. In any case where an important and a nonimportant declaration conflict, the important declaration *always* wins.

Figure 3-2 illustrates the result of the following rules and markup fragment:

```
h1 {font-style: italic; color: gray !important;}
.title {color: black; background: silver;}
* {background: black !important;}

<h1 class="title">NightWing</h1>
```

Figure 3-2. Important rules always win

Important declarations and their handling are discussed in more detail in "The Cascade" later in this chapter.

Inheritance

As important as specificity may be to understanding how declarations are applied to a document, another key concept is inheritance. Inheritance is the mechanism by which styles are applied not only to a specified element, but also to its descendants. If a color is applied to an h1 element, for example, then that color is applied to all text in the h1, even the text enclosed within child elements of that h1:

```
h1 {color: gray;}
```

```
<h1>Meerkat <em>Central</em></h1>
```

Both the ordinary h1 text and the em text are colored gray because the em element inherits the value of color. If property values could not be inherited by descendant elements, the em text would be black, not gray, and you'd have to color that element separately.

Inheritance also works well with unordered lists. Let's say you apply a style of color: gray; for ul elements:

```
ul {color: gray;}
```

You expect that a style that is applied to a ul will also be applied to its list items, and to any content of those list items. Thanks to inheritance, that's exactly what happens, as Figure 3-3 demonstrates.

- Oh, don't you wish
- That you could be a fish
- And swim along with me
- Underneath the sea

1. Strap on some fins
2. Adjust your mask
3. Dive in!

Figure 3-3. Inheritance of styles

It's easier to see how inheritance works by turning to a tree diagram of a document. Figure 3-4 shows the tree diagram for a very simple document containing two lists: one unordered and the other ordered.

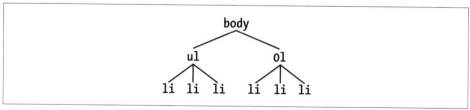

Figure 3-4. A simple tree diagram

When the declaration color: gray; is applied to the ul element, that element takes on that declaration. The value is then propagated down the tree to the descendant elements and continues on until there are no more descendants to inherit the value. Values are *never* propagated upward; that is, an element never passes values up to its ancestors.

 There is an exception to the upward propagation rule in HTML: background styles applied to the body element can be passed to the html element, which is the document's root element and therefore defines its canvas.

Inheritance is one of those things about CSS that is so basic that you almost never think about it unless you have to. However, you should still keep a few things in mind.

First, note that some properties are not inherited—generally as a result of simple common sense. For example, the property border (which is used to set borders on elements) does not inherit. A quick glance at Figure 3-5 reveals why this is the case. If borders were inherited, documents would become much more cluttered—unless the author took the extra effort to turn off the inherited borders.

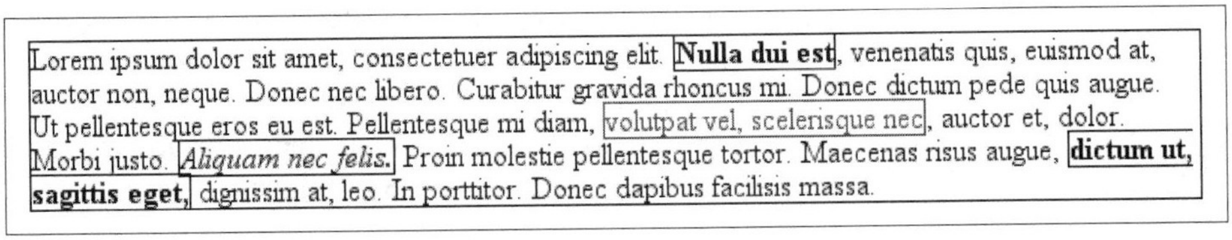

Lorem ipsum dolor sit amet, consectetuer adipiscing elit. **Nulla dui est**, venenatis quis, euismod at, auctor non, neque. Donec nec libero. Curabitur gravida rhoncus mi. Donec dictum pede quis augue. Ut pellentesque eros eu est. Pellentesque mi diam, volutpat vel, scelerisque nec, auctor et, dolor. Morbi justo. *Aliquam nec felis.* Proin molestie pellentesque tortor. Maecenas risus augue, **dictum ut, sagittis eget,** dignissim at, leo. In porttitor. Donec dapibus facilisis massa.

Figure 3-5. Why borders aren't inherited

As it happens, most of the box-model properties—including margins, padding, backgrounds, and borders—are not inherited for the same reason. After all, you wouldn't want all of the links in a paragraph to inherit a 30-pixel left margin from their parent element!

Inherited values have no specificity at all, not even zero specificity. This seems like an academic distinction until you work through the consequences of the lack of inherited specificity. Consider the following rules and markup fragment and compare them to the result shown in Figure 3-6:

```
* {color: gray;}
h1#page-title {color: black;}

<h1 id="page-title">Meerkat <em>Central</em></h1>
<p>
Welcome to the best place on the web for meerkat information!
</p>
```

Meerkat *Central*

Welcome to the best place on the Web for meerkat information!

Figure 3-6. Zero specificity defeats no specificity

Inherit the Bugs

Due to problems in various browser implementations, an author cannot rely on inheritance to operate as expected in all circumstances. For example, Navigator 4 (and, to a lesser extent, Explorer 4 and 5) does not inherit styles into tables. Thus, the following rule would result in a document with smaller text everywhere outside of tables:

```
body {font-size: 0.8em;}
```

This is not correct behavior under CSS, but it does exist, so authors have historically resorted to tricks such as:

```
body, table, th, td {font-size: 0.8em;}
```

This is more likely, although still not guaranteed, to achieve the desired effect in buggy browsers.

Unfortunately, the above "fix" leads to an even worse problem in browsers that do implement inheritance correctly, such as IE6/Win, IE5/Mac, Netscape 6+, and others. In those browsers, you will end up with text inside a table cell that is 41 percent of the size of the user's default font size setting. It is often more dangerous to attempt to work around inheritance bugs in old browsers than it is to write correct CSS for updated browsers.

Since the universal selector applies to all elements and has zero specificity, its color declaration's value of gray wins out over the inherited value of black, which has no specificity at all. Therefore, the em element is rendered gray instead of black.

This example vividly illustrates one of the potential problems of using the universal selector indiscriminately. Because it can match any element, the universal selector often has the effect of short-circuiting inheritance. This can be worked around, but it's usually more sensible to avoid the problem in the first place by not using the universal selector indiscriminately.

The complete lack of specificity for inherited values is not a trivial point. For example, assume that a style sheet has been written such that all text in a "toolbar" is to be white on black:

```
#toolbar {color: white; background: black;}
```

This will work as long as the element with an id of toolbar contains nothing but plain text. If, however, the text within this element is all hyperlinks (a elements), then the user agent's styles for hyperlinks will take over. In a web browser, this means they'll likely be colored blue, since the browser's style sheet probably contains an entry like this:

```
a:link {color: blue;}
```

To overcome this problem, you must declare:

```
#toolbar {color: white; background: black;}
#toolbar a:link {color: white;}
```

By targeting the rule directly to the a elements within the toolbar, you'll get the result shown in Figure 3-7.

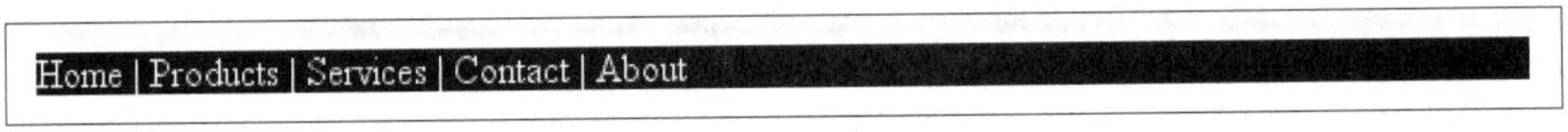

Figure 3-7. Directly assigning styles to the relevant elements

The Cascade

Throughout this chapter, we've skirted one rather important issue: what happens when two rules of equal specificity apply to the same element? How does the browser resolve the conflict? For example, say you have the following rules:

```
h1 {color: red;}
h1 {color: blue;}
```

Which one wins? Both have a specificity of 0,0,0,1, so they have equal weight and should both apply. That simply can't be the case because the element can't be both red and blue. But which will it be?

Finally, the name "Cascading Style Sheets" makes some sense. CSS is based on a method of causing styles to cascade together, which is made possible by combining inheritance and specificity. The cascade rules for CSS2.1 are simple enough:

1. Find all rules that contain a selector that matches a given element.

2. Sort by explicit weight all declarations applying to the element. Those rules marked !important are given higher weight than those that are not. Sort by origin all declarations applying to a given element. There are three origins: author, reader, and user agent. Under normal circumstances, the author's styles win out over the reader's styles. !important reader styles are stronger than any other styles, including !important author styles. Both author and reader styles override the user agent's default styles.

3. Sort by specificity all declarations applying to a given element. Those elements with a higher specificity have more weight than those with lower specificity.

4. Sort by order all declarations applying to a given element. The later a declaration appears in the style sheet or document, the more weight it is given. Declarations that appear in an imported style sheet are considered to come before all declarations within the style sheet that imports them.

To be perfectly clear about how this all works, let's consider three examples that illustrate the last three of the four cascade rules.

Sorting by Weight and Origin

Under the second rule, if two rules apply to an element, and one is marked !important, the important rule wins out:

```
p {color: gray !important;}
```

```
<p style="color: black;">Well, <em>hello</em> there!</p>
```

Despite the fact that there is a color assigned in the style attribute of the paragraph, the !important rule wins out, and the paragraph is gray. This gray is inherited by the em element as well.

Furthermore, the origin of a rule is considered. If an element is matched by normal-weight styles in both the author's style sheet and the reader's style sheet, then the author's styles are used. For example, assume that the following styles come from the indicated origins:

```
p em {color: black;}    /* author's style sheet */
```

```
p em {color: yellow;}   /* reader's style sheet */
```

In this case, emphasized text within paragraphs is colored black, not yellow, because normal-weight author styles win out over normal-weight reader styles. However, if both rules are marked !important, the situation changes:

```
p em {color: black !important;}    /* author's style sheet */
```

```
p em {color: yellow !important;}   /* reader's style sheet */
```

Now the emphasized text in paragraphs will be yellow, not black.

As it happens, the user agent's default styles—which are often influenced by the user preferences—are figured into this step. The default style declarations are the least influential of all. Therefore, if an author-defined rule applies to anchors (e.g., declaring them to be white), then this rule overrides the user agent's defaults.

To sum up, there are five levels to consider in terms of declaration weight. In order of most to least weight, these are:

1. Reader important declarations
2. Author important declarations
3. Author normal declarations
4. Reader normal declarations
5. User agent declarations

Authors typically need to worry about only the first four weight levels, since any-thing declared will win out over the user agent styles.

Sorting by Specificity

According to the third rule, if conflicting declarations apply to an element and they all have the same weight, they should be sorted by specificity, with the most specific declaration winning out. For example:

```
p#bright {color: silver;}
p {color: black;}

<p id="bright">Well, hello there!</p>
```

Given the rules shown, the text of the paragraph will be silver, as illustrated in Figure 3-8. Why? Because the specificity of p#bright (0,1,0,1) overrode the specific-ity of p (0,0,0,1), even though the latter rule comes later in the style sheet.

Well, hello there!

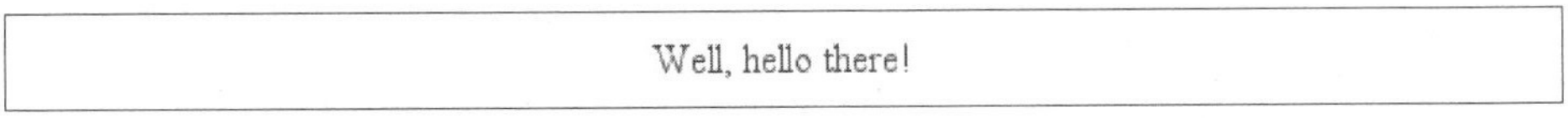

Figure 3-8. Higher specificity wins out over lower specificity

Sorting by Order

Finally, under the fourth rule, if two rules have exactly the same weight, origin, and specificity, then the one that occurs later in the style sheet wins out. Therefore, let's return to our earlier example, where we find the following two rules in the docu-ment's style sheet:

```
h1 {color: red;}
h1 {color: blue;}
```

Because its rule comes later in the style sheet, the value of color for all h1 elements in the document will be blue, not red. Any rule that is contained in the document with a higher weight than the imported rule wins out. This is true even if the rule is part of the document's style sheet and not part of an element's style attribute. Consider the following:

```
p em {color: purple;}  /* from imported style sheet */

p em {color: gray;}    /* rule contained within the document */
```

In this case, the second rule shown will win out over the imported rule because it is a part of the document's style sheet.

For the purposes of this rule, styles specified in the style attribute of an element are considered to be at the end of the document's style sheet, which places them after all other rules. However, this is a largely academic point, since inline style declarations have a higher specificity than any style sheet selector in CSS2.1.

Remember that in CSS2, inline style declarations have a specificity equal to ID selectors. In a CSS2 (but not CSS2.1) user agent, `style` attribute declarations are considered to appear at the end of the document's style sheet and are sorted by weight, origin, specificity, and order as with any other declaration in the style sheet.

Order sorting is the reason behind the often-recommended ordering of link styles. The recommendation is that you array your link styles in the order link-visited-hover-active, or LVHA, like this:

```
:link {color: blue;}
:visited {color: purple;}
:hover {color: red;}
:active {color: orange;}
```

Thanks to the information in this chapter, you now know that the specificity of all of these selectors is the same: `0,0,1,0`. Because they all have the same weight, origin, and specificity, the last one that matches an element will win out. An unvisited link that is being "clicked" is matched by three of the rules—`:link`, `:hover`, and `:active`—so the last one of those three declared will win out. Given the LVHA ordering, `:active` will win, which is likely what the author intended.

Assume for a moment that you decide to ignore the common ordering and alphabetize your link styles instead. This would yield:

```
:active {color: orange;}
:hover {color: red;}
:link {color: blue;}
:visited {color: purple;}
```

Given this ordering, no link would ever show `:hover` or `:active` styles because the `:link` and `:visited` rules come after the other two. Every link must be either visited or unvisited, so those styles will always override the `:hover` rule.

Let's consider a variation on the LVHA order that an author might want to use. In this ordering, only unvisited links will get a hover style; visited links do not. Both visited and unvisited links will get an active style:

```
:link {color: blue;}
:hover {color: red;}
:visited {color: purple;}
:active {color: orange;}
```

Of course, sometimes such conflicts arise when all the states attempt to set the same property. If each state styles a different property, then the order does not matter. In the following case, the link styles could be given in any order and would still function:

```
:link {font-weight: bold;}
:visited {font-style: italic;}
:hover {color: red;}
:active {background: yellow;}
```

You may also have realized that the order of the :link and :visited styles doesn't matter. You could order the styles LVHA or VLHA with no ill effect. However, LVHA tends to be preferred because it was recommended in the CSS2 specification and also because the mnemonic "LoVe—HA!" gained rather wide currency. (There's some bitterness out there, apparently.)

The ability to chain pseudo-classes together eliminates these worries. The following could be listed in any order without any negative effects:

```
:link {color: blue;}
:visited {color: purple;}
:link:hover {color: red;}
:visited:hover {color: gray;}
```

Because each rule applies to a unique set of link states, they do not conflict. Therefore, changing their order will not change the styling of the document. The last two rules do have the same specificity, but that doesn't matter. A hovered unvisited link will not be matched by the rule regarding hovered visited links, and vice versa. If we were to add active-state styles, then order would start to matter again. Consider:

```
:link {color: blue;}
:visited {color: purple;}
:link:hover {color: red;}
:visited:hover {color: gray;}
:link:active {color: orange;}
:visited:active {color: silver;}
```

If the active styles were moved before the hover styles, they would be ignored. Again, this would happen due to specificity conflicts. The conflicts could be avoided by adding more pseudo-classes to the chains, like this:

```
:link:hover:active {color: orange;}
:visited:hover:active {color: silver;}
```

Chained pseudo-classes, which lessen worries about specificity and ordering, would be used much more often if Internet Explorer had historically supported them. (See Chapter 2 for more information on this subject.)

Non-CSS Presentational Hints

It is possible that a document will contain presentational hints that are not CSS—e.g., the font element. Non-CSS hints are treated as if they have a specificity of 0 and appear at the *beginning* of the author's style sheet. Such presentation hints will be overridden by any author or reader styles, but not by the user agent's styles.

Summary

Perhaps the most fundamental aspect of Cascading Style Sheets is the cascade itself—the process by which conflicting declarations are sorted out and from which the final document presentation is determined. Integral to this process is the specificity of selectors and their associated declarations, and the mechanism of inheritance.

In the next chapter, we will look at the many types of units that are used to give property values their meaning. Once we have completed that discussion, the fundamentals will be out of the way, and you'll be ready to learn about the properties used to style documents.

CHAPTER 4

Values and Units

In this chapter, we'll tackle the elements that are the basis for almost everything you can do with CSS: the *units* that affect the colors, distances, and sizes of a whole host of properties. Without units, you couldn't declare that a paragraph should be purple, or that an image should have 10 pixels of blank space around it, or that a heading's text should be a certain size. By understanding the concepts put forth here, you'll be able to learn and use the rest of CSS much more quickly.

Numbers

There are two types of numbers in CSS: *integers* ("whole" numbers) and *reals* (fractional numbers). These number types serve primarily as the basis for other value types, but, in a few instances, raw numbers can be used as a value for a property.

In CSS2.1, a real number is defined as an integer that is optionally followed by a decimal and fractional numbers. Therefore, the following are all valid number values: 15.5, -270.00004, and 5. Both integers and reals may be either positive or negative, although properties can (and often do) restrict the range of numbers they will accept.

Percentages

A *percentage value* is a calculated real number followed by a percentage sign (%). Percentage values are nearly always relative to another value, which can be anything, including the value of another property of the same element, a value inherited from the parent element, or a value of an ancestor element. Any property that accepts percentage values will define any restrictions on the range of allowed percentage values, and will also define the degree to which the percentage is relatively calculated.

Color

One of the first questions every starting web author asks is, "How do I set colors on my page?" Under HTML, you have two choices: you could use one of a small number of colors with names, such as red or purple, or employ a vaguely cryptic method using hexadecimal codes. Both of these methods for describing colors remain in CSS, along with some other—and, I think, more intuitive—methods.

Named Colors

Assuming that you're content to pick from a small, basic set of colors, the easiest method is simply to use the name of the color you want. CSS calls these color choices, logically enough, *named colors*.

Contrary to what some browser makers might have you believe, you have a limited palette of valid named-color keywords. For example, you're not going to be able to choose "mother-of-pearl" because it isn't a defined color. As of CSS2.1, the CSS specification defines 17 color names. These are the 16 colors defined in HTML 4.01 plus orange:

aqua	fuchsia	lime	olive	red	white
black	gray	maroon	orange	silver	yellow
blue	green	navy	purple	teal	

So, let's say you want all first-level headings to be maroon. The best declaration would be:

```
h1 {color: maroon;}
```

Simple and straightforward, isn't it? Figure 4-1 shows a few more examples:

```
h1 {color: gray;}
h2 {color: silver;}
h3 {color: black;}
```

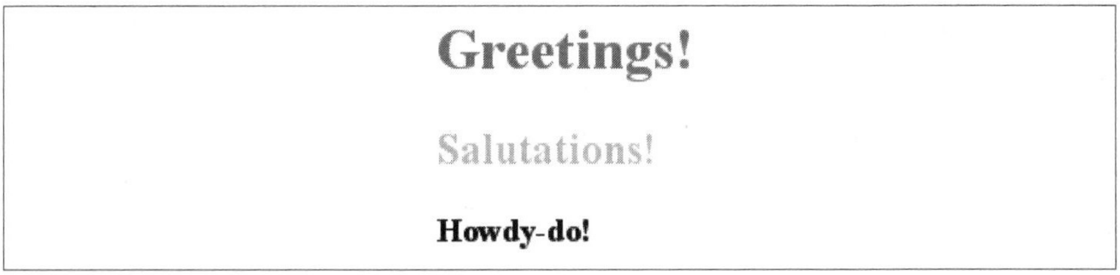

Figure 4-1. Naming colors

Of course, you've probably seen (and maybe even used) color names other than the ones listed earlier. For example, if you specify:

```
h1 {color: lightgreen;}
```

It's likely that all of your h1 elements will indeed turn light green, despite lightgreen not being on the list of named colors in CSS2.1. It works because most web browsers recognize as many as 140 color names, including the standard 17. These extra colors are defined in the CSS3 Color specification, which is not covered in this book. The 17 standard colors (as of this writing) are likely to be more reliable than the longer list of 140 or so colors because the color values for these 17 are defined by CSS2.1. The extended list of 140 colors given in CSS3 is based on the standard X11 RGB values that have been in use for decades, so they are likely to be very well supported.

Fortunately, there are more detailed and precise ways to specify colors in CSS. The advantage is that, with these methods, you can specify any color in the color spectrum, not just 17 (or 140) named colors.

Colors by RGB

Computers create colors by combining different levels of red, green, and blue, a combination that is often referred to as *RGB color*. In fact, if you were to open up an old CRT computer monitor and dig far enough into the projection tube, you would discover three "guns." (I don't recommend trying to find the guns, though, if you're worried about voiding the monitor's warranty.) These guns shoot out electron beams at varying intensities at each point on the screen. Then, the brightness of each beam combines at those points on your screen, forming all of the colors you see. Each point is known as a *pixel*, which is a term we'll return to later in this chapter. Even though most monitors these days don't use electron guns, their color output is still based on RGB mixtures.

Given the way colors are created on a monitor, it makes sense that you should have direct access to those colors, determining your own mixture of the three for maximum control. That solution is complex, but possible, and the payoffs are worth it because there are very few limits on which colors you can produce. There are four ways to affect color in this manner.

Functional RGB colors

There are two color value types that use *functional RGB notation* as opposed to hexadecimal notation. The generic syntax for this type of color value is rgb(color), where color is expressed using a triplet of either percentages or integers. The percentage values can be in the range 0%–100%, and the integers can be in the range 0–255.

Thus, to specify white and black, respectively, using percentage notation, the values would be:

```
rgb(100%,100%,100%)
rgb(0%,0%,0%)
```

Using the integer-triplet notation, the same colors would be represented as:

```
rgb(255,255,255)
rgb(0,0,0)
```

Assume you want your h1 elements to be a shade of red that lies between the values for red and maroon. red is equivalent to rgb(100%,0%,0%), whereas maroon is equal to (50%,0%,0%). To get a color between those two, you might try this:

```
h1 {color: rgb(75%,0%,0%);}
```

This makes the red component of the color lighter than maroon, but darker than red. If, on the other hand, you want to create a pale red color, you would raise the green and blue levels:

```
h1 {color: rgb(75%,50%,50%);}
```

The closest equivalent color using integer-triplet notation is:

```
h1 {color: rgb(191,127,127);}
```

The easiest way to visualize how these values correspond to color is to create a table of gray values. Besides, grayscale printing is all we can afford for this book, so that's what we'll do in Figure 4-2:

```
p.one {color: rgb(0%,0%,0%);}
p.two {color: rgb(20%,20%,20%);}
p.three {color: rgb(40%,40%,40%);}
p.four {color: rgb(60%,60%,60%);}
p.five {color: rgb(80%,80%,80%);}
p.six {color: rgb(0,0,0);}
p.seven {color: rgb(51,51,51);}
p.eight {color: rgb(102,102,102);}
p.nine {color: rgb(153,153,153);}
p.ten {color: rgb(204,204,204);}
```

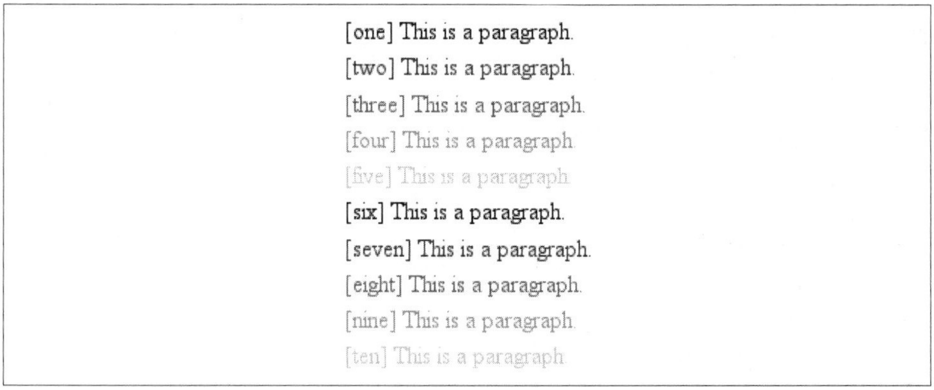

Figure 4-2. Text set in shades of gray

Of course, since we're dealing in shades of gray, all three RGB values are the same in each statement. If any one of them were different from the others, then a color would start to emerge. If, for example, rgb(50%,50%,50%) were modified to be rgb(50%,50%,60%), the result would be a medium-dark color with just a hint of blue.

It is possible to use fractional numbers in percentage notation. You might, for some reason, want to specify that a color be exactly 25.5 percent red, 40 percent green, and 98.6 percent blue:

```
h2 {color: rgb(25.5%,40%,98.6%);}
```

A user agent that ignores the decimal points (and some do) should round the value to the nearest integer, resulting in a declared value of `rgb(26%,40%,99%)`. In integer triplets, of course, you are limited to integers.

Values that fall outside the allowed range for each notation are "clipped" to the nearest range edge, meaning that a value that is greater than 100% or less than 0% will default to those allowed extremes. Thus, the following declarations would be treated as if they were the values indicated in the comments:

```
P.one {color: rgb(300%,4200%,110%);}   /*  100%,100%,100%  */
P.two {color: rgb(0%,-40%,-5000%);}    /*  0%,0%,0%  */
p.three {color: rgb(42,444,-13);}    /* 42,255,0  */
```

Conversion between percentages and integers may seem arbitrary, but there's no need to guess at the integer you want—there's a simple formula for calculating them. If you know the percentages for each of the RGB levels you want, then you need only apply them to the number 255 to get the resulting values. Let's say you have a color of 25 percent red, 37.5 percent green, and 60 percent blue. Multiply each of these percentages by 255, and you get 63.75, 95.625, and 153. Round these values to the nearest integers, and *voilà*: `rgb(64,96,153)`.

Of course, if you already know the percentage values, there isn't much point in converting them into integers. Integer notation is more useful for people who use programs such as Photoshop, which can display integer values in the "Info" dialog, or for those who are so familiar with the technical details of color generation that they normally think in values of 0–255. Then again, such people are probably more familiar with thinking in hexadecimal notation, which is our next topic.

Hexadecimal RGB colors

CSS allows you to define a color using the same hexadecimal color notation so familiar to HTML web authors:

```
h1 {color: #FF0000;}   /* set H1s to red */
h2 {color: #903BC0;}   /* set H2s to a dusky purple */
h3 {color: #000000;}   /* set H3s to black */
h4 {color: #808080;}   /* set H4s to medium gray */
```

Computers have been using "hex notation" for quite some time now, and programmers are typically either trained in its use or pick it up through experience. Their familiarity with hexadecimal notation likely led to its use in setting colors in old-school HTML. The practice was simply carried over to CSS.

Here's how it works: by stringing together three hexadecimal numbers in the range 00 through FF, you can set a color. The generic syntax for this notation is #RRGGBB. Note that there are no spaces, commas, or other separators between the three numbers.

Hexadecimal notation is mathematically equivalent to the integer-pair notation discussed in the previous section. For example, rgb(255,255,255) is precisely equivalent to #FFFFFF, and rgb(51,102,128) is the same as #336680. Feel free to use whichever notation you prefer—it will be rendered identically by most user agents. If you have a calculator that converts between decimal and hexadecimal, making the jump from one to the other should be pretty simple.

For hexadecimal numbers that are composed of three matched pairs of digits, CSS permits a shortened notation. The generic syntax of this notation is #RGB:

```
h1 {color: #000;}   /* set H1s to black */
h2 {color: #666;}   /* set H2s to dark gray */
h3 {color: #FFF;}   /* set H3s to white */
```

As you can see from the markup, there are only three digits in each color value. However, since hexadecimal numbers between 00 and FF need two digits each, and you have only three total digits, how does this method work?

The answer is that the browser takes each digit and replicates it. Therefore, #F00 is equivalent to #FF0000, #6FA would be the same as #66FFAA, and #FFF would come out #FFFFFF, which is the same as white. Obviously, not every color can be represented in this manner. Medium gray, for example, would be written in standard hexadecimal notation as #808080. This cannot be expressed in shorthand; the closest equivalent would be #888, which is the same as #888888.

Bringing the colors together

Table 4-1 presents an overview of some of the colors we've discussed. These color keywords might not be recognized by browsers and, therefore, they should be defined with either RGB or hex-pair values (just to be safe). In addition, there are some shortened hexadecimal values that do not appear at all. In these cases, the longer (six-digit) values cannot be shortened because they do not replicate. For example, the value #880 expands to #888800, not #808000 (otherwise known as olive). Therefore, there is no shortened version of #808000, and the appropriate entry in the table is blank.

Table 4-1. Color equivalents

Color	Percentage	Numeric	Hexadecimal	Short hex
red	rgb(100%,0%,0%)	rgb(255,0,0)	#FF0000	#F00
orange	rgb(100%,40%,0%)	rgb(255,102,0)	#FF6600	#F60
yellow	rgb(100%,100%,0%)	rgb(255,255,0)	#FFFF00	#FF0
green	rgb(0%,50%,0%)	rgb(0,128,0)	#008000	
blue	rgb(0%,0%,100%)	rgb(0,0,255)	#0000FF	#00F

Table 4-1. Color equivalents (continued)

Color	Percentage	Numeric	Hexadecimal	Short hex
aqua	rgb(0%,100%,100%)	rgb(0,255,255)	#00FFFF	#0FF
black	rgb(0%,0%,0%)	rgb(0,0,0)	#000000	#000
fuchsia	rgb(100%,0%,100%)	rgb(255,0,255)	#FF00FF	#F0F
gray	rgb(50%,50%,50%)	rgb(128,128,128)	#808080	
lime	rgb(0%,100%,0%)	rgb(0,255,0)	#00FF00	#0F0
maroon	rgb(50%,0%,0%)	rgb(128,0,0)	#800000	
navy	rgb(0%,0%,50%)	rgb(0,0,128)	#000080	
olive	rgb(50%,50%,0%)	rgb(128,128,0)	#808000	
purple	rgb(50%,0%,50%)	rgb(128,0,128)	#800080	
silver	rgb(75%,75%,75%)	rgb(192,192,192)	#C0C0C0	
teal	rgb(0%,50%,50%)	rgb(0,128,128)	#008080	
white	rgb(100%,100%,100%)	rgb(255,255,255)	#FFFFFF	#FFF

Web-safe colors

The "web-safe" colors are those colors that generally avoid dithering on 256-color computer systems. Web-safe colors can be expressed in multiples of the RGB values 20% and 51, and the corresponding hex-pair value 33. Also, 0% or 0 is a safe value. So, if you use RGB percentages, make all three values either 0% or a number divisible by 20—for example, rgb(40%,100%,80%) or rgb(60%,0%,0%). If you use RGB values on the 0–255 scale, the values should be either 0 or divisible by 51, as in rgb(0,204,153) or rgb(255,0,102).

With hexadecimal notation, any triplet that uses the values 00, 33, 66, 99, CC, and FF is considered to be web-safe. Examples are #669933, #00CC66, and #FF00FF. This means the shorthand hex values that are web-safe are 0, 3, 6, 9, C, and F; therefore, #693, #0C6, and #F0F are examples of web-safe colors.

Length Units

Many CSS properties, such as margins, depend on length measurements to properly display various page elements. It's no surprise, then, that there are a number of ways to measure length in CSS.

All length units can be expressed as either positive or negative numbers followed by a label (although some properties will accept only positive numbers). You can also use real numbers—that is, numbers with decimal fractions, such as 10.5 or 4.561. All length units are followed by a two-letter abbreviation that represents the actual unit of length being specified, such as in (inches) or pt (points). The only exception to this rule is a length of 0 (zero), which need not be followed by a unit.

These length units are divided into two types: *absolute length units* and *relative length units*.

Absolute Length Units

We'll start with absolute units because they're easiest to understand, despite the fact that they're almost unusable in web design. The five types of absolute units are as follows:

Inches (in)

> As you might expect, this notation refers to the inches you'd find on a ruler in the United States. (The fact that this unit is in the specification, even though almost the entire world uses the metric system, is an interesting insight into the pervasiveness of U.S. interests on the Internet—but let's not get into virtual sociopolitical theory right now.)

Centimeters (cm)

> Refers to the centimeters that you'd find on rulers the world over. There are 2.54 centimeters to an inch, and one centimeter equals 0.394 inches.

Millimeters (mm)

> For those Americans who are metric-challenged, there are 10 millimeters to a centimeter, so an inch equals 25.4 millimeters, and a millimeter equals 0.0394 inches.

Points (pt)

> Points are standard typographical measurements that have been used by printers and typesetters for decades and by word-processing programs for many years. Traditionally, there are 72 points to an inch (points were defined before widespread use of the metric system). Therefore, the capital letters of text set to 12 points should be one-sixth of an inch tall. For example, p {font-size: 18pt;} is equivalent to p {font-size: 0.25in;}.

Picas (pc)

> Picas are another typographical term. A pica is equivalent to 12 points, which means there are 6 picas to an inch. As just shown, the capital letters of text set to 1 pica should be one-sixth of an inch tall. For example, p {font-size: 1.5pc;} would set text to the same size as the example declarations found in the definition of points.

Of course, these units are really useful only if the browser knows all the details of the monitor on which your page is displayed, the printer you're using, or whatever other user agent might apply. On a web browser, display is affected by the size of the monitor and the resolution to which the monitor is set—and there isn't much that you, as the author, can do about these factors. You can only hope that, if nothing else, the measurements will be consistent in relation to each other—that is, that a setting of 1.0in will be twice as large as 0.5in, as shown in Figure 4-3.

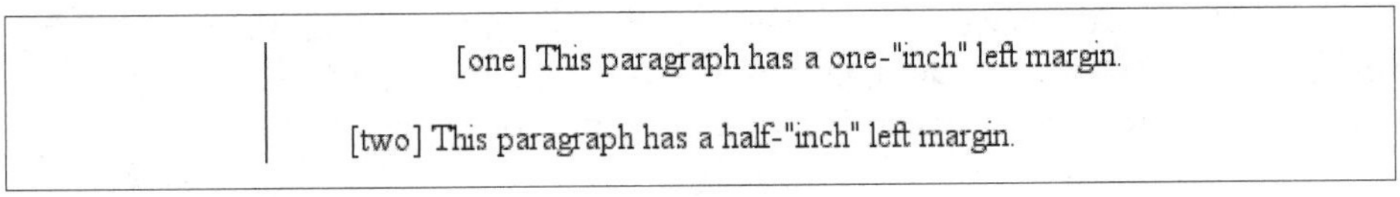

[one] This paragraph has a one-"inch" left margin.

[two] This paragraph has a half-"inch" left margin.

Figure 4-3. Setting absolute-length left margins

Working with absolute lengths

If a monitor's resolution is set to 1,024 pixels wide by 768 pixels tall, its screen size is exactly 14.22 inches wide by 10.67 inches tall, and it is filled entirely by the display area, then each pixel will be 1/72 of an inch wide and tall. As you might guess, this scenario is a very, very rare occurrence (have you ever seen a monitor with those dimensions?). So, on most monitors, the actual number of pixels per inch (ppi) is higher than 72—sometimes much higher, up to 120 ppi and beyond.

As a Windows user, you might be able to set your display driver to make the display of elements correspond correctly to real-world measurements. To try, click Start → Settings → Control Panel. In the Control Panel, double-click Display. Click the Settings tab, and click Advanced to reveal a dialog box (which may differ on each PC). You should see a section labeled Font Size; select Other, and then hold a ruler up to the screen and move the slider until the onscreen ruler matches the physical ruler. Click OK until you're free of dialog boxes, and you're set.

If you're a Mac Classic user, there's no place to set this information in the operating system—the Mac Classic OS (that is, any version previous to OS X) makes an assumption about the relationship between on-screen pixels and absolute measurements by declaring your monitor to have 72 pixels to the inch. This assumption is totally wrong, but it's built into the operating system, and therefore pretty much unavoidable. As a result, on many Classic Mac-based web browsers, any point value will be equivalent to the same length in pixels: 24pt text will be 24 pixels tall, and 8pt text will be 8 pixels tall. This is, unfortunately, slightly too small to be legible. Figure 4-4 illustrates the problem.

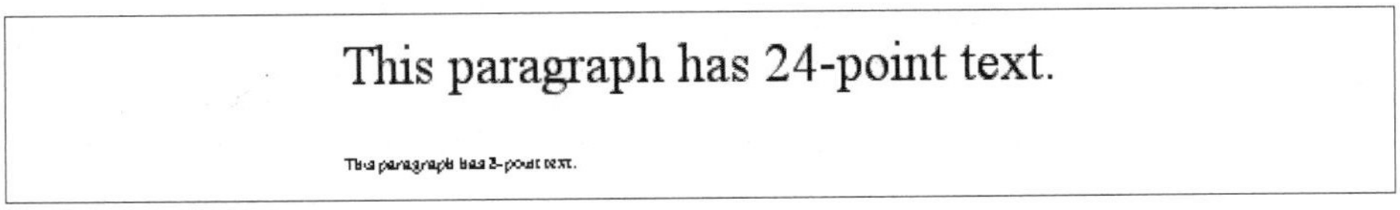

This paragraph has 24-point text.

This paragraph has 8-point text.

Figure 4-4. Teensy text makes for difficult reading

In OS X, the built-in assumed ppi value is closer to Windows: 96ppi. This doesn't make it any more correct, but it's at least consistent with Windows machines.

The Classic Mac display problem is an excellent example of why points should be strenuously avoided when designing for the Web. Ems, percentages, and even pixels are all preferable to points where browser display is concerned.

 Beginning with Internet Explorer 5 for Macintosh and Gecko-based browsers such as Netscape 6+, the browser itself contains a preference setting for setting ppi values. You can pick the standard Macintosh ratio of 72ppi, the common Windows ratio of 96ppi, or a value that matches your monitor's ppi ratio. This last option works similarly to the Windows setting just described, where you use a sliding scale to compare to a ruler and thus get an exact match between your monitor and physical-world distances.

Despite all we've seen, let's make the highly suspect assumption that your computer knows enough about its display system to accurately reproduce real-world measurements. In that case, you could make sure every paragraph has a top margin of half an inch by declaring p {margin-top: 0.5in;}. Regardless of font size or any other circumstances, a paragraph will have a half-inch top margin.

Absolute units are much more useful in defining style sheets for printed documents, where measuring things in terms of inches, points, and picas is common. As you've seen, attempting to use absolute measurements in web design is perilous at best, so let's turn to some more useful units of measure.

Relative Length Units

Relative units are so called because they are measured in relation to other things. The actual (or absolute) distance they measure can change due to factors beyond their control, such as screen resolution, the width of the viewing area, the user's preference settings, and a whole host of other things. In addition, for some relative units, their size is almost always relative to the element that uses them and will thus change from element to element.

There are three relative length units: em, ex, and px. The first two stand for "em-height" and "x-height," which are common typographical measurements; however, in CSS, they have meanings you might not expect if you are familiar with typography. The last type of length is px, which stands for "pixels." A pixel is one of the dots you can see on your computer's monitor if you look closely enough. This value is defined as relative because it depends on the resolution of the display device, a subject we'll soon cover.

em and ex units

First, however, let's consider em and ex. In CSS, one "em" is defined to be the value of font-size for a given font. If the font-size of an element is 14 pixels, then for that element, 1em is equal to 14 pixels.

Obviously, this value can change from element to element. For example, let's say you have an h1 with a font size of 24 pixels, an h2 element with a font size of 18 pixels, and a paragraph with a font size of 12 pixels. If you set the left margin of all three at 1em, they will have left margins of 24 pixels, 18 pixels, and 12 pixels, respectively:

```
h1 {font-size: 24px;}
h2 {font-size: 18px;}
p {font-size: 12px;}
h1, h2, p {margin-left: 1em;}
small {font-size: 0.8em;}

<h1>Left margin = <small>24 pixels</small></h1>
<h2>Left margin = <small>18 pixels</small></h2>
<p>Left margin = <small>12 pixels</small></p>
```

When setting the size of the font, on the other hand, the value of em is relative to the font size of the parent element, as illustrated by Figure 4-5.

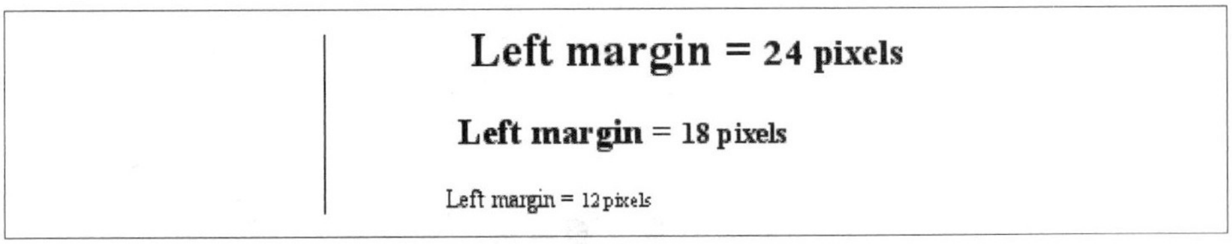

Figure 4-5. Using em for margins and font sizing

ex, on the other hand, refers to the height of a lowercase *x* in the font being used. Therefore, if you have two paragraphs in which the text is 24 points in size, but each paragraph uses a different font, then the value of ex could be different for each paragraph. This is because different fonts have different heights for *x*, as you can see in Figure 4-6. Even though the examples use 24-point text—and therefore, each example's em value is 24 points—the x-height for each is different.

Practical issues with em and ex

Of course, everything I've just explained is completely theoretical. I've outlined what is *supposed* to happen, but in practice, many user agents get their value for ex by taking the value of em and dividing it in half. Why? Apparently, most fonts don't have the value of their ex height built-in, and it's a very difficult thing to compute. Since most fonts have lowercase letters that are about half as tall as uppercase letters, it's a convenient fiction to assume that 1ex is equivalent to 0.5em.

A few browsers, including Internet Explorer 5 for Mac, actually attempt to determine the x-height of a given font by internally rendering a lowercase *x* and counting pixels to determine its height compared to that of the font-size value used to create the character. This is not a perfect method, but it's much better than simply making 1ex equal to 0.5em. We CSS practitioners can hope that, as time goes on, more user agents will start using real values for ex and the half-em shortcut will fade into the past.

Figure 4-6. Varying x-heights

Pixel lengths

On the face of things, pixels are straightforward. If you look at a monitor closely enough, you can see that it's broken up into a grid of tiny little boxes. Each box is a pixel. If you define an element to be a certain number of pixels tall and wide, as in the following markup:

```
<p>
The following image is 20 pixels tall and wide: <img src="test.gif"
  style="width: 20px; height: 20px;" alt="" />
</p>
```

then it follows that the element will be that many monitor elements tall and wide, as shown in Figure 4-7.

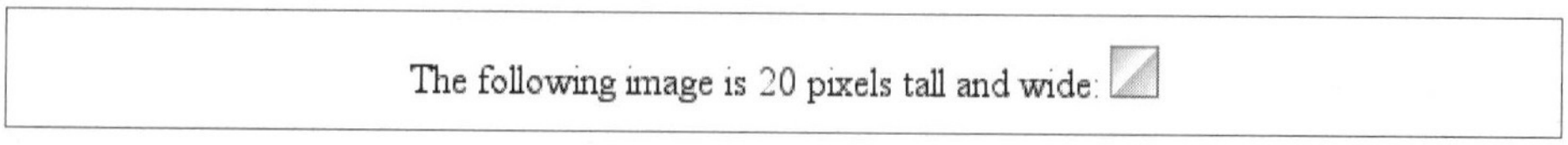

The following image is 20 pixels tall and wide:

Figure 4-7. Using pixel lengths

Unfortunately, there is a potential drawback to using pixels. If you set font sizes in pixels, then users of Internet Explorer for Windows previous to IE7 cannot resize the text using the Text Size menu in their browser. This can be a problem if your text is too small for a user to comfortably read. If you use more flexible measurements, such as em, the user can resize text. (If you're exceedingly protective of your design, you might call *that* a drawback, of course.)

On the other hand, pixel measurements are perfect for expressing the size of images, which are already a certain number of pixels tall and wide. In fact, the only time you would not want pixels to express image size is if you want them scaled along with the size of the text. This is an admirable and occasionally useful approach, and one that would really make sense if you were using vector-based images instead of pixel-based images. (With the adoption of Scalable Vector Graphics, look for more on this in the future.)

Pixel theory

So why are pixels defined as relative lengths? I've explained that the tiny boxes of color in a monitor are pixels. However, how many of those boxes equals one inch? This may seem like a non sequitur, but bear with me for a moment.

In its discussion of pixels, the CSS specification recommends that in cases where a display type is significantly different than 96ppi, user agents should scale pixel measurements to a "reference pixel." CSS2 recommended 90ppi as the reference pixel, but CSS2.1 recommends 96ppi—a measurement common to Windows machines and adopted by modern Macintosh browsers such as Safari.

In general, if you declare something like font-size: 18px, a web browser will almost certainly use actual pixels on your monitor—after all, they're already there—but with other display devices, like printers, the user agent will have to rescale pixel lengths to something more sensible. In other words, the printing code has to figure out how many dots there are in a pixel, and to do so, it may use the 96ppi reference pixel.

 One example of problems with pixel measurements can be found in an early CSS1 implementation. In Internet Explorer 3.x, when a document was printed, IE3 assumed that 18px was the same as 18 dots, which on a 600dpi printer works out to be 18/600, or 3/100, of an inch—or, if you prefer, .03in. That's pretty small text!

Because of this potential for rescaling, pixels are defined as a relative unit of measurement, even though, in web design, they behave much like absolute units.

What to do?

Given all the issues involved, the best measurements to use are probably the relative measurements, most especially em, and also px when appropriate. Because ex is, in most currently used browsers, basically a fractional measurement of em, it's not all that useful for the time being. If more user agents support real x-height measurements, ex might come into its own. In general, ems are more flexible because they scale with font sizes, so elements and element separation will stay more consistent.

Other element aspects may be more amenable to the use of pixels, such as borders or the positioning of elements. It all depends on the situation. For example, in designs that traditionally use spacer GIFs to separate pieces of a design, pixel-length margins will produce an identical effect. Converting that separation distance to ems would allow the design to grow or shrink as the text size changes—which might or might not be a good thing.

URLs

If you've written web pages, you're obviously familiar with URLs (or, in CSS2.1, URIs). Whenever you need to refer to one—as in the @import statement, which is used when importing an external style sheet—the general format is:

```
url(protocol://server/pathname)
```

This example defines what is known as an *absolute URL*. By absolute, I mean a URL that will work no matter where (or rather, in what page) it's found, because it defines an absolute location in web space. Let's say that you have a server called *www.waffles.org*. On that server, there is a directory called pix, and in this directory is an image *waffle22.gif*. In this case, the absolute URL of that image would be:

```
http://www.waffles.org/pix/waffle22.gif
```

This URL is valid no matter where it is found, whether the page that contains it is located on the server *www.waffles.org* or *web.pancakes.com*.

The other type of URL is a *relative URL*, so named because it specifies a location that is relative to the document that uses it. If you're referring to a relative location, such as a file in the same directory as your web page, then the general format is:

```
url(pathname)
```

This works only if the image is on the same server as the page that contains the URL. For argument's sake, assume that you have a web page located at *http://www.waffles.org/syrup.html* and that you want the image *waffle22.gif* to appear on this page. In that case, the URL would be:

```
pix/waffle22.gif
```

This path works because the web browser knows that it should start with the place it found the web document and then add the relative URL. In this case, the pathname *pix/waffle22.gif* added to the server name *http://www.waffles.org* equals *http://www.waffles.org/pix/waffle22.gif*. You can almost always use an absolute URL in place of a relative URL; it doesn't matter which you use, as long as it defines a valid location.

In CSS, relative URLs are relative to the style sheet itself, not to the HTML document that uses the style sheet. For example, you may have an external style sheet that imports another style sheet. If you use a relative URL to import the second style sheet, it must be relative to the first style sheet. As an example, consider an HTML document at *http://www.waffles.org/toppings/tips.html*, which has a link to the style sheet *http://www.waffles.org/styles/basic.css*:

```
<link rel="stylesheet" type="text/css"
    href="http://www.waffles.org/styles/basic.css">
```

Inside the file *basic.css* is an @import statement referring to another style sheet:

```
@import url(special/toppings.css);
```

This @import will cause the browser to look for the style sheet at *http://www.waffles.org/styles/special/toppings.css*, not at *http://www.waffles.org/toppings/special/toppings.css*. If you have a style sheet at the latter location, then the @import in *basic.css* should read:

```
@import url(http://www.waffles.org/toppings/special/toppings.css);
```

 Netscape Navigator 4 interprets relative URLs in relation to the HTML document, not the style sheet. If you have a lot of NN4.x visitors or want to make sure NN4.x can find all of your style sheets and background images, it's generally easiest to make all of your URLs absolute, since Navigator handles those correctly.

Note that there cannot be a space between the url and the opening parenthesis:

```
body {background: url(http://www.pix.web/picture1.jpg);}   /* correct */
body {background: url (images/picture2.jpg);}          /* INCORRECT */
```

If the space isn't omitted, the entire declaration will be invalidated and thus ignored.

Keywords

For those times when a value needs to be described with a word of some kind, there are keywords. A very common example is the keyword none, which is distinct from 0 (zero). Thus, to remove the underline from links in an HTML document, you would write:

```
a:link, a:visited {text-decoration: none;}
```

Similarly, if you want to force underlines on the links, then you would use the keyword underline.

If a property accepts keywords, then its keywords will be defined only for the scope of that property. If two properties use the same word as a keyword, the behavior of the keyword for one property will not be shared with the other. As an example, normal, as defined for letter-spacing, means something very different than the normal defined for font-style.

inherit

There is one keyword that is shared by all properties in CSS2.1: inherit. inherit makes the value of a property the same as the value of its parent element. In most cases, you don't need to specify inheritance, since most properties inherit naturally; however, inherit can still be very useful.

For example, consider the following styles and markup:

```
#toolbar {background: blue; color: white;}

<div id="toolbar">
<a href="one.html">One</a> | <a href="two.html">Two</a> |
<a href="three.html">Three</a>
</div>
```

The div itself will have a blue background and a white foreground, but the links will be styled according to the browser's preference settings. They'll most likely end up as blue text on a blue background, with white vertical bars between them.

You could write a rule that explicitly sets the links in the "toolbar" to be white, but you can make things a little more robust by using inherit. You simply add the following rule to the style sheet:

```
#toolbar a {color: inherit;}
```

This will cause the links to use the inherited value of color in place of the user agent's default styles. Ordinarily, directly assigned styles override inherited styles, but inherit can reverse that behavior.

CSS2 Units

In addition to what we've covered in CSS2.1, CSS2 contains a few extra units, all of which are concerned with aural style sheets (employed by those browsers that are capable of speech). These units were not included in CSS2.1, but since they may be part of future versions of CSS, we'll briefly discuss them here:

Angle values

Used to define the position from which a given sound should originate. There are three types of angles: degrees (deg), grads (grad), and radians (rad). For example, a right angle could be declared as 90deg, 100grad, or 1.57rad; in each case, the values are translated into degrees in the range 0 through 360. This is also true of negative values, which are allowed. The measurement –90deg is the same as 270deg.

Time values

Used to specify delays between speaking elements. They can be expressed as either milliseconds (ms) or seconds (s). Thus, 100ms and 0.1s are equivalent. Time values cannot be negative, as CSS is designed to avoid paradoxes.

Frequency values

Used to declare a given frequency for the sounds that speaking browsers can produce. Frequency values can be expressed as hertz (Hz) or megahertz (MHz) and cannot be negative. The values' labels are case-insensitive, so 10MHz and 10Mhz are equivalent.

The only user agent known to support any of these values at this writing is *Emacspeak*, an aural style sheets implementation. See Chapter 14 for details on aural styles.

In addition to these values, there is also an old friend with a new name. A *URI* is a *Uniform Resource Identifier*, which is sort of another name for a Uniform Resource Locator (URL). Both the CSS2 and CSS2.1 specifications require that URIs be declared with the form url(...), so there is no practical change.

Summary

Units and values cover a wide spectrum of areas, from length units to special keywords that describe effects (such as underline) to color units to the location of files (such as images). For the most part, units are the one area that user agents get almost totally correct, but it's those few little bugs and quirks that can get you. Navigator 4.x's failure to interpret relative URLs correctly, for example, has bedeviled many authors and led to an overreliance on absolute URLs. Colors are another area where user agents almost always do well, except for a few little quirks here and there. The vagaries of length units, however, far from being bugs, are an interesting problem for any author to tackle.

These units all have their advantages and drawbacks, depending upon the circumstances in which they're used. We've already seen some of these circumstances, and their nuances will be discussed in the rest of the book, beginning with the CSS properties that describe ways to alter how text is displayed.

CHAPTER 5

Fonts

As the authors of the CSS specification clearly recognized, font selection is a popular (and crucial) feature. After all, how many pages are littered with dozens, or even hundreds, of <FONT FACE="...">` tags? In fact, the beginning of the "Font Properties" section of the specification begins with the sentence, "Setting font properties will be among the most common uses of style sheets."

Despite that importance, however, there currently isn't a way to ensure consistent font use on the Web because there isn't a uniform way of describing fonts and variants of fonts. For example, the fonts Times, Times New Roman, and TimesNR may be similar or even the same, but how would a user agent know that? An author might specify "TimesNR" in a document, but what happens when a user views the document without that particular font installed? Even if Times New Roman is installed, the user agent has no way to know that the two are effectively interchangeable. And if you're hoping to force a certain font on a reader, forget it.

Although CSS2 defined facilities for downloadable fonts, they weren't well implemented by web browsers, and a reader could always refuse to download fonts for performance reasons. CSS does *not* provide ultimate control over fonts any more than a word processor does; when someone else loads a Microsoft Office document you have created, its display will depend on that person's installed fonts. If she doesn't have the same fonts you do, then the document will look different. This is also true of documents designed using CSS.

The problem of font naming becomes especially confusing once you enter the realm of font variants, such as bold or italic text. Most people know what italic text looks like, but few can explain how it's different from slanted text, even though there are differences. "Slanted" is not the only other term for italic-style text, either—for example, you'll find *oblique, incline* (or *inclined*), *cursive*, and *kursiv*, among others. Thus, one font may have a variant called something like TimesItalic, whereas another uses something like GeorgiaOblique. Although the two may be effectively equivalent as the "italic form" of each font, they are labeled quite differently. Similarly, the font variant terms *bold, black,* and *heavy* may or may not mean the same thing.

CSS attempts to provide some resolution mechanisms for all of these font questions, although it cannot provide a complete solution. The most complicated parts of font handling in CSS are font-family matching and font-weight matching, with font-size calculations running a close third. The font aspects addressed by CSS are font styles, such as italics, and font variants, such as small caps; these are much more straightforward, relatively speaking. These various aspects of font styling are all brought together in a single property, font, which we'll discuss later in this chapter. First, let's discuss font families, since they're the most basic step in choosing the right font for your document.

Font Families

Although there are, as discussed earlier, a number of ways to label what is effectively the same font, CSS makes a valiant attempt to help user agents sort out the mess. After all, what we think of as a "font" may be composed of many variations to describe boldfacing, italic text, and so forth. For example, you're probably familiar with the font Times. However, Times is actually a combination of many variants, including TimesRegular, TimesBold, TimesItalic, TimesOblique, TimesBoldItalic, TimesBoldOblique, and so on. Each of these variants of Times is an actual *font face*, but Times, as we usually think of it, is a combination of all these variant faces. In other words, Times is actually a *font family*, not just a single font, even though most of us think about fonts as being single entities.

In addition to each specific font family such as Times, Verdana, Helvetica, or Arial, CSS defines five generic font families:

Serif fonts
> These fonts are proportional and have serifs. A font is proportional if all characters in the font have different widths due to their various sizes. For example, a lowercase *i* and a lowercase *m* are different widths. (This book's paragraph font is proportional, for example.) Serifs are the decorations on the ends of strokes within each character, such as little lines at the top and bottom of a lowercase *l*, or at the bottom of each leg of an uppercase *A*. Examples of serif fonts are Times, Georgia, and New Century Schoolbook.

Sans-serif fonts
> These fonts are proportional and do not have serifs. Examples of sans-serif fonts are Helvetica, Geneva, Verdana, Arial, and Univers.

Monospace fonts
> Monospace fonts are not proportional. These generally are used to emulate typewritten text, the output from an old dot-matrix printer, or an even older video-display terminal. In these fonts, each character is exactly the same width as all the others, so a lowercase *i* is the same width as a lowercase *m*. These fonts may or may not have serifs. If a font has uniform character widths, it is classified as monospace, regardless of the presence of serifs. Examples of monospace fonts are Courier, Courier New, and Andale Mono.

Cursive fonts

> These fonts attempt to emulate human handwriting. Usually, they are composed largely of curves and have stroke decorations that exceed those found in serif fonts. For example, an uppercase *A* might have a small curl at the bottom of its left leg or be composed entirely of swashes and curls. Examples of cursive fonts are Zapf Chancery, Author, and Comic Sans.

Fantasy fonts

> Such fonts are not really defined by any single characteristic other than our inability to easily classify them in one of the other families. A few such fonts are Western, Woodblock, and Klingon.

In theory, every font family a user could install will fall into one of these generic families. In practice, this may not be the case, but the exceptions (if any) are likely to be few and far between.

Using Generic Font Families

You can employ any of these families in a document by using the property `font-family`.

font-family	
Values:	[[<family-name> | <generic-family>],]* [<family-name> | <generic-family>] | inherit
Initial value:	User agent-specific
Applies to:	All elements
Inherited:	Yes
Computed value:	As specified

If you want a document to use a sans-serif font, but you do not particularly care which one, then the appropriate declaration would be this:

```
body {font-family: sans-serif;}
```

This will cause the user agent to pick a sans-serif font family (such as Helvetica) and apply it to the body element. Thanks to inheritance, the same font choice will be applied to all the elements that descend from the body—unless a more specific selector overrides it, of course.

Using nothing more than these generic families, an author can create a fairly sophisticated style sheet. The following rule set is illustrated in Figure 5-1:

```
body {font-family: serif;}
h1, h2, h3, h4 {font-family: sans-serif;}
code, pre, tt, span.input {font-family: monospace;}
p.signature {font-family: cursive;}
```

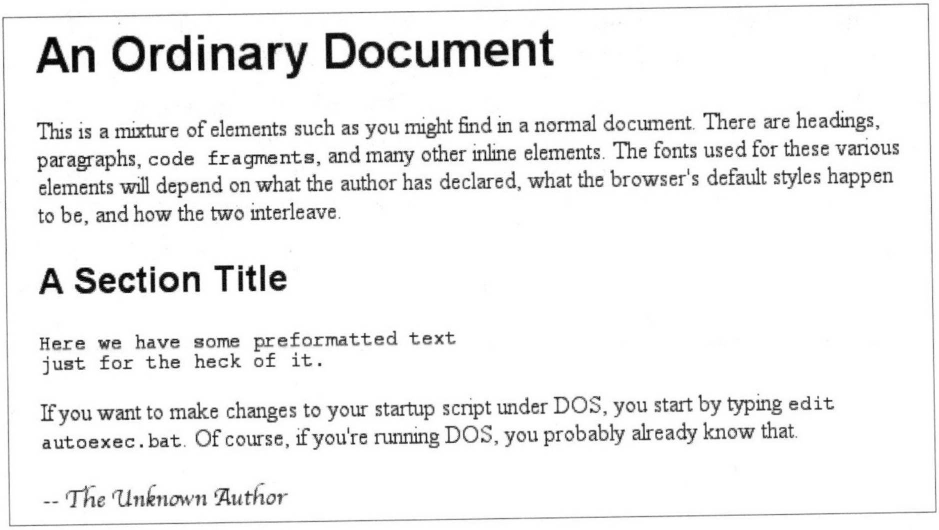

An Ordinary Document

This is a mixture of elements such as you might find in a normal document. There are headings, paragraphs, code fragments, and many other inline elements. The fonts used for these various elements will depend on what the author has declared, what the browser's default styles happen to be, and how the two interleave.

A Section Title

```
Here we have some preformatted text
just for the heck of it.
```

If you want to make changes to your startup script under DOS, you start by typing `edit autoexec.bat`. Of course, if you're running DOS, you probably already know that.

-- *The Unknown Author*

Figure 5-1. Various font families

Thus, most of the document will be in a serif font such as Times, including all paragraphs except those that have a `class` of `signature`, which will instead be rendered in a cursive font such as Author. Headings 1 through 4 will be in sans-serif font like Helvetica, while the elements code, pre, tt, and span.input will be in a monospace font like Courier—which, coincidentally, is how most of these elements are usually presented in this book.

Specifying a Font Family

An author may, on the other hand, have more specific preferences for which font to use in the display of a document or element. In a similar vein, a user may want to create a user style sheet that defines the exact fonts that are used in the display of all documents. In either case, font-family is still the property to use.

Assume for the moment that all h1s should use Georgia as their font. The simplest rule for this would be the following:

```
h1 {font-family: Georgia;}
```

This will cause the user agent displaying the document to use Georgia for all h1s, as shown in Figure 5-2.

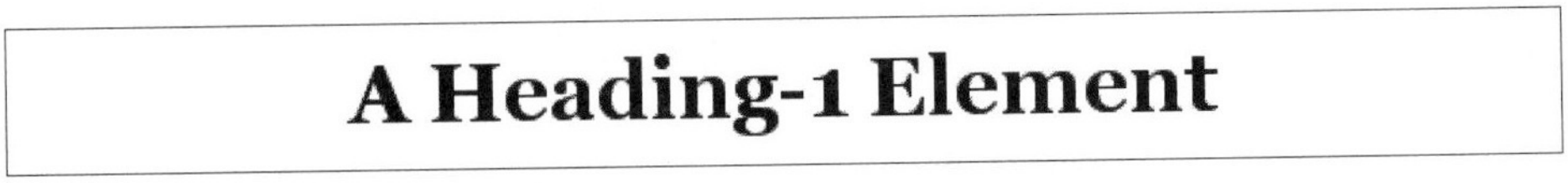

A Heading-1 Element

Figure 5-2. An h1 element using Georgia

Of course, this rule assumes that the user agent has Georgia available for use. If it doesn't, the user agent will be unable to use the rule at all. It won't ignore the rule, but if it can't find a font called "Georgia," it can't do anything but display h1 elements using the user agent's default font.

All is not lost, however. By combining specific font names with generic font families, you can create documents that come out, if not exact, at least close to your intentions. To continue the previous example, the following markup tells a user agent to use Georgia if it's available, and to use another serif font if it's not.

```
h1 {font-family: Georgia, serif;}
```

If a reader doesn't have Georgia installed but does have Times, the user agent might use Times for h1 elements. Even though Times isn't an exact match to Georgia, it's probably close enough.

For this reason, I strongly encourage you to always provide a generic family as part of any font-family rule. By doing so, you provide a fallback mechanism that lets user agents pick an alternative when they can't provide an exact font match. Such a backup measure is especially helpful since, in a cross-platform environment, there is no way to know who has which fonts installed. Sure, every Windows machine in the world may have Arial and Times New Roman installed, but some Macintoshes (particularly older ones) don't, and the same is probably true of Unix machines. Conversely, while MarkerFelt and Charcoal are common to all recent Macintoshes, it's unlikely that Windows and Unix users will have either font installed, and it is even less likely that they'll have both. Here are a few more examples:

```
h1 {font-family: Arial, sans-serif;}
h2 {font-family: Charcoal, sans-serif;}
p {font-family: TimesNR, serif;}
address {font-family: Chicago, sans-serif;}
```

If you're familiar with fonts, you might have a number of similar fonts in mind for displaying a given element. Let's say that you want all paragraphs in a document to be displayed using Times, but you would also accept TimesNR, Georgia, New Century Schoolbook, and New York (all of which are serif fonts). First, decide the order of preference for these fonts, and then string them together with commas:

```
p {font-family: Times, TimesNR, 'New Century Schoolbook', Georgia,
    'New York', serif;}
```

Based on this list, a user agent will look for the fonts in the order they're listed. If none of the listed fonts are available, then it will simply pick a serif font that is available.

Using quotation marks

You may have noticed the presence of single quotes in the previous example, which we haven't seen before. Quotation marks are needed in a font-family declaration only if a font name has one or more spaces in it, such as New York, or if the font name includes symbols such as # or $. In both cases, the entire font name should be enclosed in quotation marks to keep the user agent from getting confused about what the name really is. (You might think the commas would suffice, but they don't.) Thus, a font called Karrank% should probably be quoted:

```
h2 {font-family: Wedgie, 'Karrank%', Klingon, fantasy;}
```

If you leave off the quotation marks, there is a chance that user agents will ignore that particular font name altogether, although they'll still process the rest of the rule. Note that the quoting of a font name containing a symbol is not actually required by the CSS2.1 specification. Instead, it's recommended, which is as close to describing "best practices" as the CSS specification ever really gets. Similarly, it is recommended that you quote a font name containing spaces. As it turns out, the only required quotation is for font names that match accepted keywords. Thus, if you call for a font whose actual name is "cursive," you'll need to quote it.

Obviously, font names that use a single word—one that doesn't conflict with any of the keywords for `font-family`—need not be quoted, and generic family names (serif, monospace, etc.) should never be quoted when they refer to the actual generic families. If you quote a generic name, then the user agent will assume that you are asking for a specific font with that name (for example, "serif"), not a generic family.

As for which quotation marks to use, both single and double quotes are acceptable. Remember that if you place a `font-family` rule in a style attribute, you'll need to use whichever quotes you didn't use for the attribute itself. Therefore, if you use double quotes to enclose the `font-family` rule, then you'll have to use single quotes within the rule, as in the following markup:

```
p {font-family: sans-serif;}  /* sets paragraphs to sans-serif by default */

<!-- the next example is correct (uses single-quotes) -->
<p style="font-family: 'New Century Schoolbook', Times, serif;">...</p>

<!-- the next example is NOT correct (uses double-quotes) -->
<p style="font-family: "New Century Schoolbook", Times, serif;">...</p>
```

If you use double quotes in such a circumstance, they interfere with the attribute syntax, as you can see in Figure 5-3.

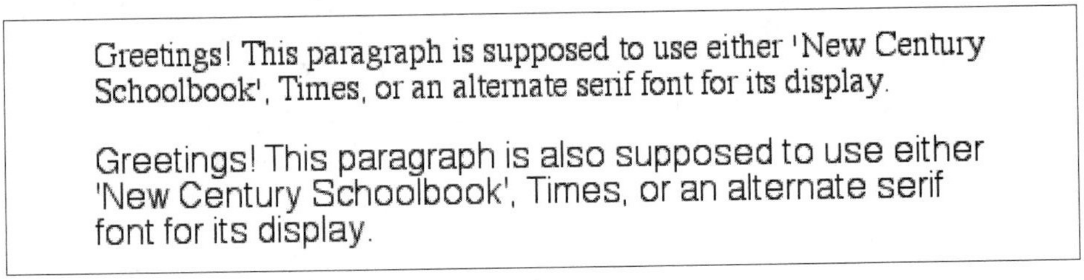

Greetings! This paragraph is supposed to use either 'New Century Schoolbook', Times, or an alternate serif font for its display.

Greetings! This paragraph is also supposed to use either 'New Century Schoolbook', Times, or an alternate serif font for its display.

Figure 5-3. The perils of incorrect quotation marks

Font Weights

Even though you may not realize it, you're already familiar with font weights; bold-faced text is a very common example of an increased font weight. CSS gives you more control over weights, at least in theory, with the property font-weight.

<table>
<tr><td colspan="2" align="center">font-weight</td></tr>
<tr><td>Values:</td><td>normal | bold | bolder | lighter | 100 | 200 | 300 | 400 | 500 | 600 | 700 | 800 | 900 | inherit</td></tr>
<tr><td>Initial value:</td><td>normal</td></tr>
<tr><td>Applies to:</td><td>All elements</td></tr>
<tr><td>Inherited:</td><td>Yes</td></tr>
<tr><td>Computed value:</td><td>One of the numeric values (100, etc.), or one of the numeric values plus one of the relative values (bolder or lighter)</td></tr>
</table>

Generally speaking, the heavier a font weight becomes, the darker and "more bold" a font appears. There are a great many ways to label a heavy font face. For example, the font family known as Zurich has a number of variants, such as Zurich Bold, Zurich Black, Zurich UltraBlack, Zurich Light, and Zurich Regular. Each of these uses the same basic font, but each has a different weight.

So let's say that you want to use Zurich for a document, but you'd like to make use of all those different heaviness levels. You could refer to them directly through the font-family property, but you really shouldn't have to do that. Besides, it's no fun having to write a style sheet like this:

```
h1 {font-family: 'Zurich UltraBlack', sans-serif;}
h2 {font-family: 'Zurich Black', sans-serif;}
h3 {font-family: 'Zurich Bold', sans-serif;}
h4, p {font-family: Zurich, sans-serif;}
small {font-family: 'Zurich Light', sans-serif;}
```

Aside from the obvious tedium of writing such a style sheet, it works only if everyone has these fonts installed, and it's a pretty safe bet that most people don't. It would make far more sense to specify a single font family for the whole document and then assign different weights to various elements. You can do this, in theory, using the various values for the property font-weight. This is a fairly obvious font-weight declaration:

```
b {font-weight: bold;}
```

This declaration says, simply, that the b element should be displayed using a boldface font; or, to put it another way, a font that is heavier than the normal font for the document. This is what we're used to, of course, since b does cause text to be boldfaced.

However, what's really happening is that a heavier variant of the font is used for displaying a b element. Thus, if you have a paragraph displayed using Times, and part of it is boldfaced, then there are really two variants of the same font in use: Times and TimesBold. The regular text is displayed using Times, and the boldfaced text is displayed using TimesBold.

How Weights Work

To understand how a user agent determines the heaviness, or weight, of a given font variant, not to mention how weight is inherited, it's easiest to start by talking about the keywords 100 through 900. These number keywords were defined to map to a relatively common feature of font design in which a font is given nine levels of weight. OpenType, for example, employs a numeric scale with nine values. If a font has these weight levels built-in, then the numbers are mapped directly to the predefined levels, with 100 as the lightest variant on the font and 900 as the heaviest.

In fact, there is no intrinsic weight in these numbers. The CSS specification says only that each number corresponds to a weight at least as heavy as the number that precedes it. Thus, 100, 200, 300, and 400 might all map to the same relatively lightweight variant; 500 and 600 could correspond to the same heavier font variant; and 700, 800, and 900 could all produce the same very heavy font variant. As long as no keyword corresponds to a variant that is lighter than the variant assigned to the previous keyword, everything will be all right.

As it happens, these numbers are defined to be equivalent to certain common variant names, not to mention other values for font-weight. 400 is defined to be equivalent to normal, and 700 corresponds to bold. The other numbers do not match up with any other values for font-weight, but they can correspond to common variant names. If there is a font variant labeled something such as "Normal," "Regular," "Roman," or "Book," then it is assigned to the number 400 and any variant with the label "Medium" is assigned to 500. However, if a variant labeled "Medium" is the only variant available, it is *not* assigned to 500 but instead to 400.

A user agent has to do even more work if there are fewer than nine weights in a given font family. In this case, it must fill in the gaps in a predetermined way:

- If the value 500 is unassigned, it is given the same font weight as that assigned to 400.
- If 300 is unassigned, it is given the next variant lighter than 400. If no lighter variant is available, 300 is assigned the same variant as 400. In this case, it will usually be "Normal" or "Medium." This method is also used for 200 and 100.
- If 600 is unassigned, it is given the next variant darker than 400. If no darker variant is available, 600 is assigned the same variant as 500. This method is also used for 700, 800, and 900.

To illustrate this weighting scheme more clearly, let's look at three examples of font weight assignment. In the first example, assume that the font family Karrank% is an OpenType font, so it has nine weights already defined. In this case, the numbers are assigned to each level, and the keywords normal and bold are assigned to the numbers 400 and 700, respectively.

In our second example, consider the font family Zurich, which was discussed near the beginning of this section. Hypothetically, its variants might be assigned numeric values for font-weight, as shown in Table 5-1.

Table 5-1. Hypothetical weight assignments for a specific font family

Font face	Assigned keyword	Assigned number(s)
Zurich Light		100, 200, 300
Zurich Regular	normal	400
Zurich Medium		500
Zurich Bold	bold	600, 700
Zurich Black		800
Zurich UltraBlack		900

The first three number values are assigned to the lightest weight. The "Regular" face gets the keyword normal, as expected, and the number weight 400. Since there is a "Medium" font, it's assigned to the number 500. There is nothing to assign to 600, so it's mapped to the "Bold" font face, which is also the variant to which 700 and bold are assigned. Finally, 800 and 900 are assigned to the "Black" and "UltraBlack" variants, respectively. Note that this last assignment would happen only if those faces had the top two weight levels already assigned. Otherwise, the user agent might ignore them and assign 800 and 900 to the "Bold" face instead, or it might assign them both to one or the other of the "Black" variants.

Finally, let's consider a stripped-down version of Times. In Table 5-2, there are only two weight variants: "TimesRegular" and "TimesBold."

Table 5-2. Hypothetical weight assignments for "Times"

Font face	Assigned keyword	Assigned numbers
TimesRegular	normal	100, 200, 300, 400, 500
TimesBold	bold	600, 700, 800, 900

The assignment of the keywords `normal` and `bold` is straightforward enough, of course. As for the numbers, 100 through 300 are assigned to the "Regular" face because there isn't a lighter face available. 400 is assigned to "Regular" as expected, but what about 500? It is assigned to the "Regular" (or `normal`) face because there isn't a "Medium" face available; thus, it is assigned the same font face as 400. As for the rest, 700 goes with `bold` as always, while 800 and 900, lacking a heavier face, are assigned to the next-lighter face, which is the "Bold" font face. Finally, 600 is assigned to the next-heavier face, which is, of course, the "Bold" face.

`font-weight` is inherited, so if you set a paragraph to be bold:

```
p.one {font-weight: bold;}
```

then all of its children will inherit that boldness, as we see in Figure 5-4.

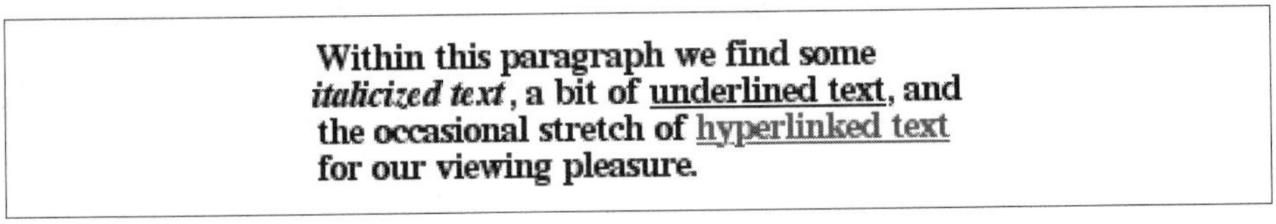

> **Within this paragraph we find some**
> *italicized text*, a bit of <u>underlined text</u>, and
> the occasional stretch of <u>hyperlinked text</u>
> **for our viewing pleasure.**

Figure 5-4. Inherited font-weight

This isn't unusual, but the situation gets interesting when you use the last two values we have to discuss: `bolder` and `lighter`. In general terms, these keywords have the effect you'd anticipate: they make text more or less bold compared to its parent's font weight. First, let's consider `bolder`.

Getting Bolder

If you set an element to have a weight of `bolder`, then the user agent first must determine what `font-weight` value was inherited from the parent element. It then selects the lowest number, which corresponds to a font weight darker than what was inherited. If none is available, then the user agent sets the element's font weight to the next numerical value, unless the value is already 900, in which case the weight remains at 900. Thus, you might encounter the following situations, illustrated in Figure 5-5:

```
p {font-weight: normal;}
p em {font-weight: bolder;}  /* results in bold text, evaluates to '700' */

h1 {font-weight: bold;}
h1 b {font-weight: bolder;}  /* if no bolder face exists, evaluates to '800' */

div {font-weight: 100;} /* assume 'Light' face exists; see explanation */
div strong {font-weight: bolder;} /* results in normal text, weight '400' */
```

In the first example, the user agent moves up the weight ladder from `normal` to `bold`; in numeric terms, it jumps from 400 to 700. In the second example, h1 text is already

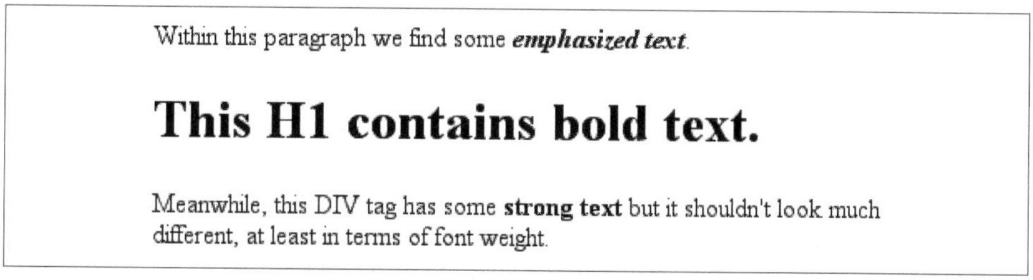

Within this paragraph we find some *emphasized text*.

This H1 contains bold text.

Meanwhile, this DIV tag has some **strong text** but it shouldn't look much different, at least in terms of font weight.

Figure 5-5. Text trying to be bolder

set to bold. If there is no bolder face available, then the user agent sets the weight of b text within an h1 to 800, since that is the next step up from 700 (the numeric equivalent of bold). Since 800 is assigned to the same font face as 700, there is no visible difference between normal h1 text and boldfaced h1 text, but the weights are different nonetheless.

In the last example, paragraphs are set to be the lightest possible font weight, which we assume exists as a "Light" variant. Furthermore, the other faces in this font family are "Regular" and "Bold." Any em text within a paragraph will evaluate to normal since that is the next-heaviest face within the font family. However, what if the only faces in the font are "Regular" and "Bold"? In that case, the declarations would evaluate like this:

```
/*   assume only two faces for this example: 'Regular' and 'Bold'   */
p {font-weight: 100;}   /* looks the same as 'normal' text */
p span {font-weight: bolder;}   /* maps to '700' */
```

As you can see, the weight 100 is assigned to the normal font face, but the value of font-weight is still 100. Thus, any span text that is descended from a p element will inherit the value of 100 and then evaluate to the next-heaviest face, which is the "Bold" face with a numerical weight of 700.

Let's take this one step further and add two more rules, plus some markup, to illustrate how all of this works (see Figure 5-6 for the results):

```
/*   assume only two faces for this example: 'Regular' and 'Bold'   */
p {font-weight: 100;}   /* looks the same as 'normal' text */
p span {font-weight: 400;}   /* so does this */
strong {font-weight: bolder;}   /* even bolder than its parent */
strong b {font-weight: bolder;}   /*bolder still */

<p>
This paragraph contains elements of increasing weight: there is a
<span>span element that contains a <strong>strongly emphasized
element and a <b>boldface element</b></strong></span>.
</p>
```

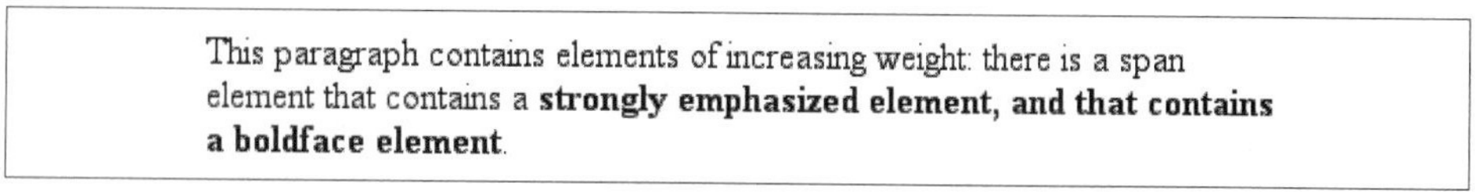

This paragraph contains elements of increasing weight: there is a span element that contains a **strongly emphasized element, and that contains a boldface element**.

Figure 5-6. Moving up the weight scale

In the last two nested elements, the computed value of font-weight is increased because of the liberal use of the keyword bolder. If you were to replace the text in the paragraph with numbers representing the font-weight of each element, you would get the results shown here:

```
<p>
100 <span> 400 <strong> 700 <b> 800 </b></strong></span>.
</p>
```

The first two weight increases are large because they represent jumps from 100 to 400 and from 400 to bold (700). From 700, there is no heavier face, so the user agent simply moves the value of font-weight one notch up the numeric scale (800). Furthermore, if you were to insert a strong element into the b element, it would come out like this:

```
<p>
100 <span> 400 <strong> 700 <b> 800 <strong> 900
</strong></b></strong></span>.
</p>
```

If there were yet another b element inserted into the innermost strong element, its weight would also be 900, since font-weight can never be higher than 900. Assuming that there are only two font faces available, then the text would appear to be either Regular or Bold, as you can see in Figure 5-7:

```
<p>
regular <span> regular <strong> bold <b> bold
<strong> bold </strong></b></strong></span>.
</p>
```

regular regular **bold bold bold** .

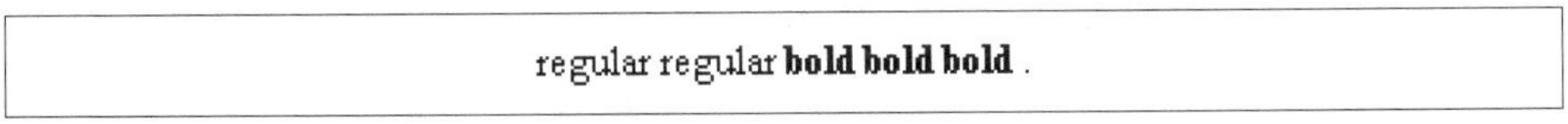

Figure 5-7. Visual weight, with descriptors

Lightening Weights

As you might expect, lighter works in just the same way, except it causes the user agent to move down the weight scale instead of up. With a quick modification of the previous example, you can see this very clearly:

```
/*   assume only two faces for this example: 'Regular' and 'Bold'   */
p {font-weight: 900;}   /* as bold as possible, which will look 'bold' */
p span {font-weight: 700;}   /* this will also be bold */
strong {font-weight: lighter;}   /* lighter than its parent */
b {font-weight: lighter;}   /* lighter still */

<p>
900 <span> 700 <strong> 400 <b> 300 <strong> 200
</strong></b></strong></span>.
</p>
<!-- ...or, to put it another way... -->
```

```
<p>
bold <span> bold <strong> regular <b> regular
<strong> regular </strong></b></strong></span>.
</p>
```

Ignoring the fact that this would be entirely counterintuitive, what you see in Figure 5-8 is that the main paragraph text has a weight of 900. When the strong text is set to be lighter, it evaluates to the next-lighter face, which is the regular face, or 400 (the same as normal) on the numeric scale. The next step down is to 300, which is the same as normal since no lighter faces exist. From there, the user agent can reduce the weight only one numeric step at a time until it reaches 100 (which it doesn't do in the example). The second paragraph shows which text will be bold and which will be regular.

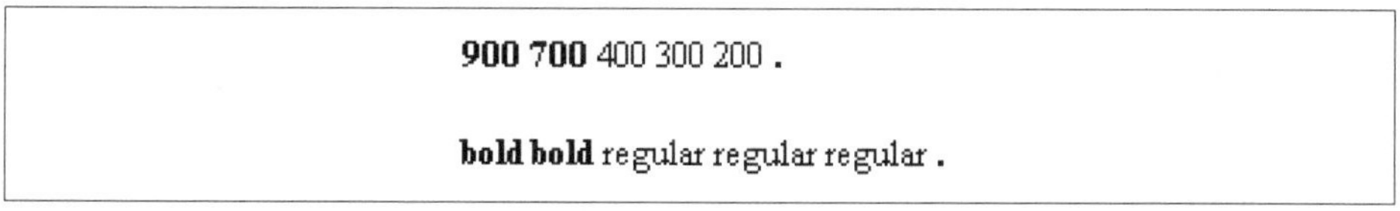

---

900 700 400 300 200 .

bold bold regular regular regular .

Figure 5-8. Making text lighter

Font Size

The methods for determining font size are both very familiar and very different.

font-size

Values:	xx-small | x-small | small | medium | large | x-large | xx-large | smaller | larger | <length> | <percentage> | inherit
Initial value:	medium
Applies to:	All elements
Inherited:	Yes
Percentages:	Calculated with respect to the parent element's font size
Computed value:	An absolute length

In a fashion very similar to the font-weight keywords bolder and lighter, the property font-size has relative-size keywords called larger and smaller. Much like what we saw with relative font weights, these keywords cause the computed value of font-size to move up and down a scale of size values, which you'll need to understand before you can explore larger and smaller. First, though, we need to examine how fonts are sized in the first place.

In fact, the actual relation of the font-size property to what you see rendered is determined by the font's designer. This relationship is set as an *em square* (some call it an *em box*) within the font itself. This em square (and thus the font size) doesn't have to refer to any boundaries established by the characters in a font. Instead, it refers to the distance between baselines when the font is set without any extra leading (line-height in CSS). It is quite possible for fonts to have characters that are taller than the default distance between baselines. For that matter, a font might be defined such that all of its characters are smaller than its em square, as many fonts do. Some hypothetical examples are shown in Figure 5-9.

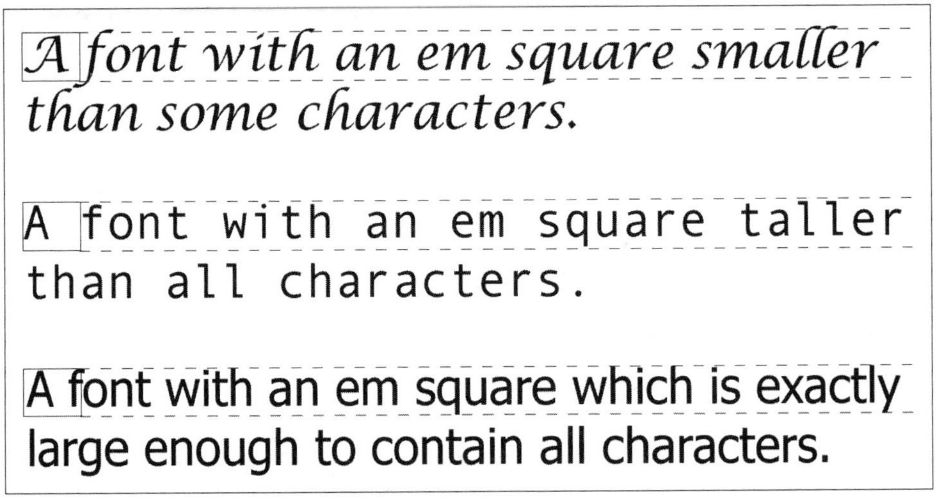

Figure 5-9. Font characters and em squares

Thus, the effect of font-size is to provide a size for the em box of a given font. This does not guarantee that any of the actual displayed characters will be this size.

Absolute Sizes

Having established all of that, we turn now to the absolute-size keywords. There are seven absolute-size values for font-size: xx-small, x-small, small, medium, large, x-large, and xx-large. These are not defined precisely, but are relative to each other, as Figure 5-10 demonstrates:

```
p.one {font-size: xx-small;}
p.two {font-size: x-small;}
p.three {font-size: small;}
p.four {font-size: medium;}
p.five {font-size: large;}
p.six {font-size: x-large;}
p.seven {font-size: xx-large;}
```

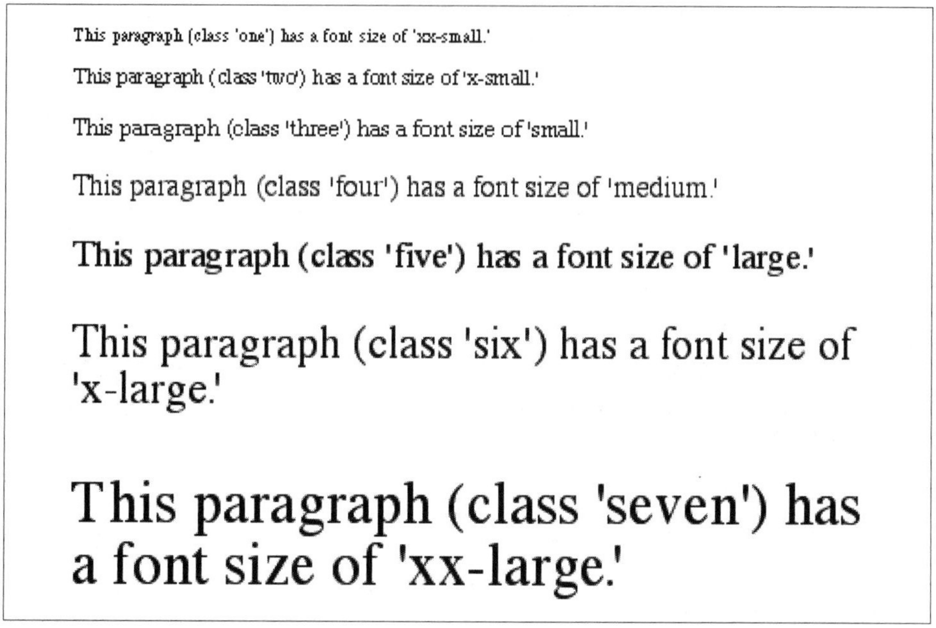

This paragraph (class 'one') has a font size of 'xx-small.'

This paragraph (class 'two') has a font size of 'x-small.'

This paragraph (class 'three') has a font size of 'small.'

This paragraph (class 'four') has a font size of 'medium.'

This paragraph (class 'five') has a font size of 'large.'

This paragraph (class 'six') has a font size of 'x-large.'

This paragraph (class 'seven') has a font size of 'xx-large.'

Figure 5-10. Absolute font sizes

According to the CSS1 specification, the difference (or *scaling factor*) between one absolute size and the next should be about 1.5 going up the ladder, or 0.66 going down. Thus, if medium is the same as 10px, then large should be the same as 15px. On the other hand, the scaling factor does not have to be 1.5; not only might it be different for different user agents, but it was changed to a factor somewhere between 1.0 and 1.2 in CSS2.

Working from the assumption that medium equals 16px, for different scaling factors, we get the absolute sizes shown in Table 5-3. (The following values are approximations, of course.)

Table 5-3. Scaling factors translated to pixels

Keyword	Scaling: 1.5	Scaling: 1.2
xx-small	5px	9px
x-small	7px	11px
small	11px	13px
medium	16px	16px
large	24px	19px
x-large	36px	23px
xx-large	54px	28px

Further complicating the situation is the fact that different user agents have assigned the "default" font size to different absolute keywords. Take the Version 4 browsers as an example: Navigator 4 makes medium the same size as unstyled text, whereas Internet Explorer 4 assumes that small text is equivalent in size to unstyled text. Despite the fact that the default value for font-style is supposed to be medium, IE4's behavior may be wrong, but not quite so wrong as it might first appear.[*] Fortunately, IE6 fixed the problem, at least when the browser is in standards mode, and treats medium as the default.

Relative Sizes

Comparatively speaking, the keywords larger and smaller are simple: they cause the size of an element to be shifted up or down the absolute-size scale, relative to their parent element, using the same scaling factor employed to calculate absolute sizes. In other words, if the browser used a scaling factor of 1.2 for absolute sizes, then it should use the same factor when applying relative-size keywords:

```
p {font-size: medium;}
strong, em {font-size: larger;}

<p>This paragraph element contains <strong>a strong-emphasis element
which itself contains <em>an emphasis element that also contains
<strong>a strong element.</strong></em></strong></p>

<p> medium <strong>large <em> x-large
<strong>xx-large</strong></em></strong></p>
```

Unlike the relative values for weight, the relative-size values are not necessarily constrained to the limits of the absolute-size range. Thus, a font's size can be pushed beyond the sizes for xx-small and xx-large. For example:

```
h1 {font-size: xx-large;}
em {font-size: larger;}

<h1>A Heading with <em>Emphasis</em> added</h1>
<p>This paragraph has some <em>emphasis</em> as well.</p>
```

As you can see in Figure 5-11, the emphasized text in the h1 element is slightly larger than xx-large. The amount of scaling is left up to the user agent, with the scaling factor of 1.2 being preferred. The em text in the paragraph, of course, is shifted one slot up the absolute-size scale (large).

[*] Note that there are seven absolute-size keywords, just as there are seven font sizes (e.g., <font size="5">). Since the typical default font size was historically 3, it makes sense that the third value on the CSS absolute-size keyword list is used to indicate a default font size. Since the third keyword turns out to be small, Explorer behaves accordingly.

> # A Heading with *Emphasis* added
>
> This paragraph has some *emphasis* as well.
>
> # xx-large *xx-large* xx-large
>
> medium *large* medium

Figure 5-11. Relative font sizing at the edges of the absolute sizes

 User agents are not required to increase or decrease font size beyond the limits of the absolute-size keywords.

Percentages and Sizes

In a way, percentage values are very similar to the relative-size keywords. A percentage value is always computed in terms of whatever size is inherited from an element's parent. Percentages, unlike the relative-size keywords, permit much finer control over the computed font size. Consider the following example, illustrated in Figure 5-12:

```
body {font-size: 15px;}
p {font-size: 12px;}
em {font-size: 120%;}
strong {font-size: 135%;}
small, .fnote {font-size: 75%;}

<body>
<p>This paragraph contains both <em>emphasis</em> and <strong>strong
emphasis</strong>, both of which are larger than their parent element.
The <small>small text</small>, on the other hand, is smaller by a quarter.</p>
<p class="fnote">This is a 'footnote' and is smaller than regular text.</p>

<p> 12px <em> 14.4px </em> 12px <strong> 16.2px </strong>  12px
<small> 9px </small> 12px </p>
<p class="fnote"> 10.5px </p>
</body>
```

> This paragraph contains both *emphasis* and **strong emphasis**, both of which are larger than their parent element. The small text, on the other hand, is smaller by a quarter.
>
> This is a 'footnote' and is smaller than regular text.
>
> 12px *14.4px* 12px **16.2px** 12px 9px 12px
>
> 10.5px

Figure 5-12. Throwing percentages into the mix

In this example, the exact pixel size values are shown. In practice, a web browser would very likely round the values off to the nearest whole-number pixel, such as 14px, although advanced user agents may approximate fractional pixels through anti-aliasing or when printing the document. For other font-size values, the browser may (or may not) preserve fractions.

Incidentally, CSS defines the length value em to be equivalent to percentage values, in the sense that 1em is the same as 100% when sizing fonts. Thus, the following would yield identical results (assuming both paragraphs have the same parent element):

```
p.one {font-size: 166%;}
p.two {font-size: 1.6em;}
```

When using em measurements, the same principles apply as with percentages, such as the inheritance of computed sizes, and so forth.

Font Size and Inheritance

Figure 5-12 also demonstrates that, although font-size is inherited in CSS, it is the computed values that are inherited, not percentages. Thus, the value inherited by the strong element is 12px, and this value is modified by the declared value 135% to arrive at 16.2px (which will probably be rounded off to 16px). For the "footnote" paragraph, the percentage is calculated in relation to the font-size value that's inherited from the body element, which is 15px. Multiplying that value by 75% yields 11.25px.

As with the relative-size keywords, percentages are effectively cumulative. Thus, the following markup is displayed as shown in Figure 5-13:

```
p {font-size: 12px;}
em {font-size: 120%;}
strong {font-size: 135%;}

<p>This paragraph contains both<em>emphasis and <strong>strong
emphasis</strong></em>, both of which are larger than the paragraph text. </p>

<p> 12px <em>14.4px <strong> 19.44px </strong></em> 12px  </p>
```

This paragraph contains both *emphasis and **strong emphasis***, both of which are larger than the paragraph text.

12px *14.4px* **19.44px** 12px

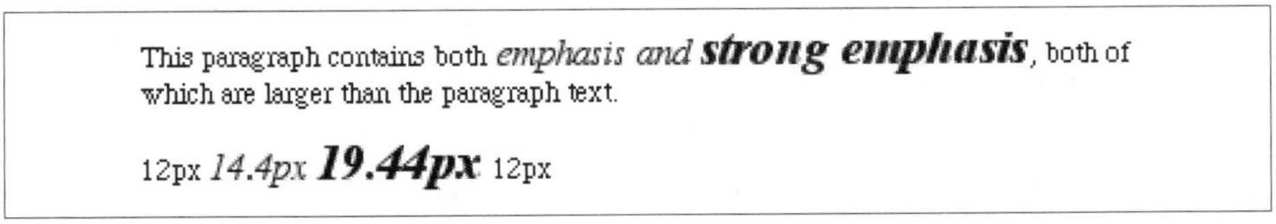

Figure 5-13. The issues of inheritance

The size value for the strong element shown in Figure 5-13 is computed as follows:

$$12 \text{ px} \times 120\% = 14.4\text{px}$$
$$14.4\text{px} \times 135\% = 19.44\text{px} \text{ (possibly rounded to 19px)}$$

There is an alternative scenario, however, in which the final value is slightly different. In this scenario, the user agent rounds off pixel size, and these rounded values are then inherited normally by any child elements. Although this behavior would be incorrect according to the specification, let's assume that the work agent does it. Therefore, you would have:

12px × 120% = 14.4px [14.4px ≈14px]
14px ×135% = 18.9px [18.9px ≈19px]

If one assumes that the user agent is rounding off at each step, then the end result of both this calculation and the previous one is the same: 19 pixels. However, as more and more percentages are multiplied together, the rounding errors will begin to accumulate.

The problem of runaway scaling can go the other direction, too. Consider for a moment a document that is nothing but a series of unordered lists, many of them nested inside other lists. Some of these lists are four nested levels deep. Imagine the effect of the following rule on such a document:

```
ul {font-size: 80%;}
```

Assuming a four-level deep nesting, the most deeply nested unordered list would have a computed font-size value 40.96 percent the size of the parent of the top-level list. Every nested list would have a font size 80 percent as big as its parent list, causing each level to become harder and harder to read. A similar problem can happen if you have a document that uses nested tables for layout. You would then write a rule such as:

```
td {font-size: 0.8em;}
```

Either way, you're likely to end up with a page that's nearly impossible to read.

Using Length Units

The font-size can be set using any of the length values discussed in detail in Chapter 4. All of the following font-size declarations should be equivalent:

```
p.one {font-size: 36pt;}
p.two {font-size: 3pc;}
p.three {font-size: 0.5in;}
p.four {font-size: 1.27cm;}
p.five {font-size: 12.7mm;}
```

The display in Figure 5-14 assumes that the user agent knows how many dots per inch are used in the display medium. Different user agents make different assumptions—some based on the operating system, some based on preferences settings, and some based on the assumptions of the programmer who wrote the user agent. However, the five lines should always be the same size. So, while the result may not exactly match reality (for example, the actual size of p.three may not be half an inch), the measurements should all be consistent with one another.

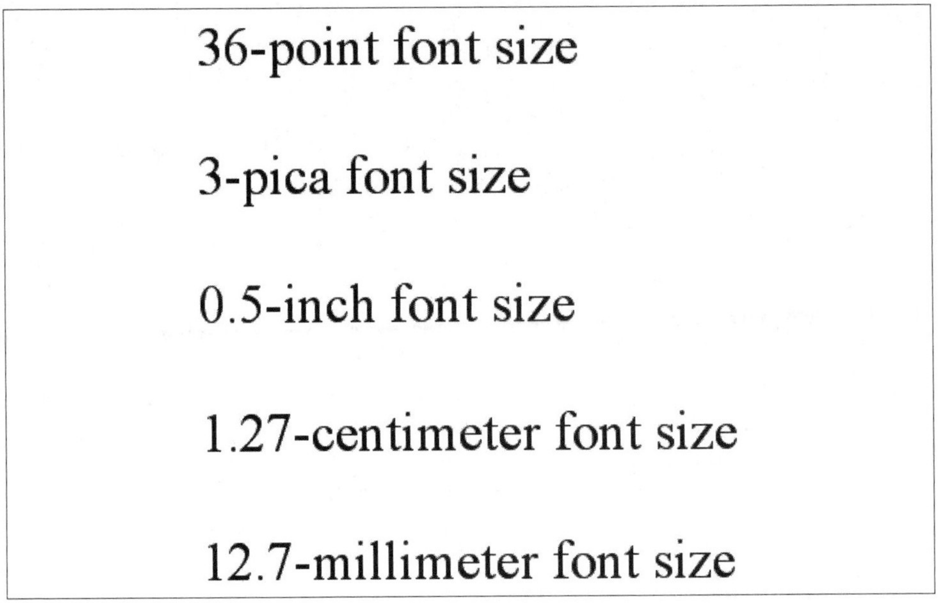

36-point font size

3-pica font size

0.5-inch font size

1.27-centimeter font size

12.7-millimeter font size

Figure 5-14. Various font sizes

There is one more value that is potentially the same as those shown in Figure 5-14, and that's 36px, which would be the same physical distance if the display medium is 72 pixels-per-inch (ppi). However, there are very few monitors with that setting anymore. Most are much higher, in the range of 96ppi to 120ppi. Many very old Macintosh web browsers treat points and pixels as though they are equivalent, so the values 14pt and 14px may look the same on them. This is not, however, the case for Windows and other platforms, including Mac OS X, which is one of the primary reasons why points can be a very difficult measurement to use in document design.

Because of these variations between operating systems, many authors choose to use pixel values for font sizes. This approach is especially attractive when mixing text and images on a web page, since text can (in theory) be set to the same height as graphic elements on the page by declaring font-size: 11px; or something similar, as illustrated by Figure 5-15.

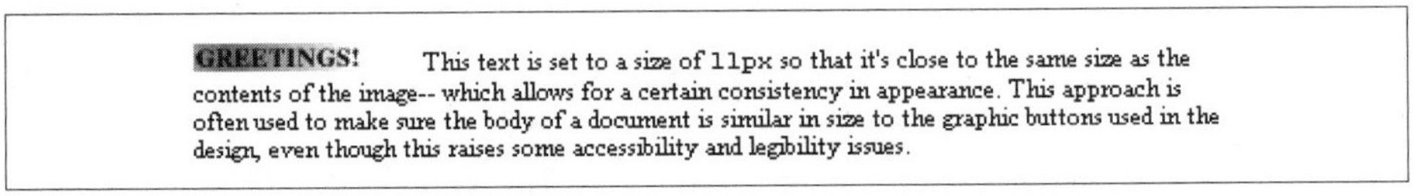

GREETINGS! This text is set to a size of 11px so that it's close to the same size as the contents of the image-- which allows for a certain consistency in appearance. This approach is often used to make sure the body of a document is similar in size to the graphic buttons used in the design, even though this raises some accessibility and legibility issues.

Figure 5-15. Keeping text and graphics in scale with pixel sizes

Using pixel measurements for font-size is certainly one way to get "consistent" results with font-size (and, indeed, with any length at all), but there is a major drawback. Internet Explorer for Windows up through Version 6.0 does not allow users to easily resize text that has been set with pixels. Other browsers, including Mozilla, Netscape 6+, IE5+/Mac, Opera, and even IE7, allow the user to resize text no matter how it's been set. Thus, using pixels to size text is no more of a guarantee that it will stay the same size than is any other method. The other approaches discussed in this chapter, such as keywords and percentages, are a much more robust (and user-friendly) way to go, as they can be used to scale text from the user's default font size.

Styles and Variants

Compared with everything we've covered so far, this section is practically a no-brainer. The properties discussed herein are so straightforward, and the complexities are so minimal, that this discussion will probably come as a great relief. First, we'll talk about font-style, and then move on to font-variant before wrapping up with the font properties.

Fonts with Style

font-style is very simple: it's used to select between normal text, italic text, and oblique text. That's it! The only complication is in recognizing the difference between italic and oblique text and in understanding why browsers don't always give you a choice.

---

font-style

Values:	italic | oblique | normal | inherit
Initial value:	normal
Applies to:	All elements
Inherited:	Yes
Computed value:	As specified

The default value of font-style is, as you can see, normal. This refers to "upright" text, which is probably best described as "text that is not italic or otherwise slanted." The vast majority of text in this book is upright, for instance. That leaves only an explanation of the difference between italic and oblique text. For that, it's easiest to refer to Figure 5-16, which illustrates the differences very clearly.

Basically, italic text is a separate font face, with small changes made to the structure of each letter to account for the altered appearance. This is especially true of serif

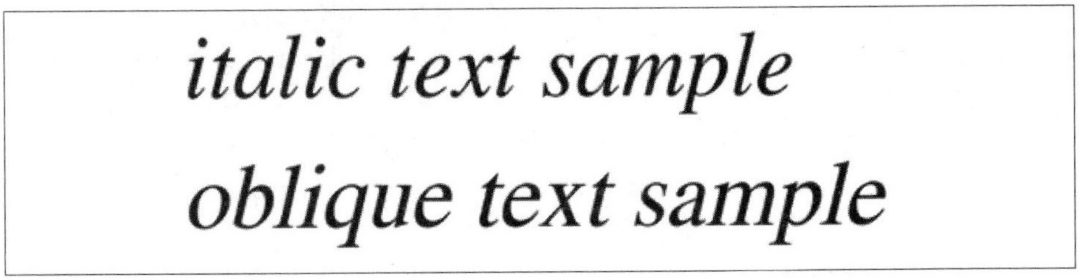

italic text sample

oblique text sample

Figure 5-16. Italic and oblique text in detail

fonts, where, in addition to the fact that the text characters "lean," the serifs may be altered in an italic face. Oblique text, on the other hand, is simply a slanted version of the normal, upright text. Font faces with labels like "Italic," "Cursive," and "Kursiv" are usually mapped to the `italic` keyword, while `oblique` is often assigned faces with labels such as "Oblique," "Slanted," and "Incline."

If you want to make sure that a document uses italic text in familiar ways, you could write a style sheet like this:

```
p {font-style: normal;}
em, i {font-style: italic;}
```

These styles would make paragraphs use an upright font, as usual, and cause the `em` and `i` elements to use an italic font—again, as usual. On the other hand, you might decide that there should be a subtle difference between `em` and `i`:

```
p {font-style: normal;}
em {font-style: oblique;}
i {font-style: italic;}
```

If you look closely at Figure 5-17, you'll see there is no apparent difference between the `em` and `i` elements. In practice, not every font is so sophisticated as to have both an italic face and an oblique face, and even fewer web browsers are sophisticated enough to tell the difference when both faces do exist.

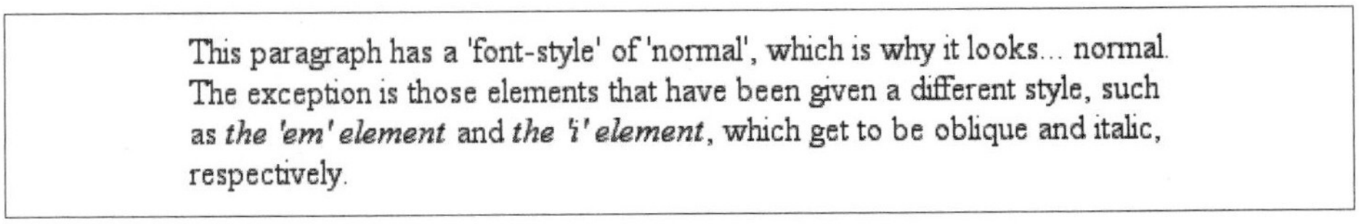

This paragraph has a 'font-style' of 'normal', which is why it looks... normal. The exception is those elements that have been given a different style, such as *the 'em' element* and *the 'i' element*, which get to be oblique and italic, respectively.

Figure 5-17. More font styles

If either of these is the case, then there are a few things that can happen. If there is no "Italic" face, but there is an "Oblique" face, then the latter can be used for the former. If the situation is reversed—an "Italic" face exists, but there is no defined "Oblique" face—the user agent may *not* substitute the former for the latter, according to the specification. Finally, the user agent can simply generate the oblique face by computing a slanted version of the upright font. In fact, this is what most often happens in a digital world, where it's fairly simple to slant a font using a simple computation.

Furthermore, you may find that in some operating systems, a given font that has been declared as `italic` may switch from being italic to oblique depending on the actual size of the font. The display of Times on a Macintosh running the Classic OS (Mac OS 9), for example, is shown in Figure 5-18, and the only difference is a single pixel in size.

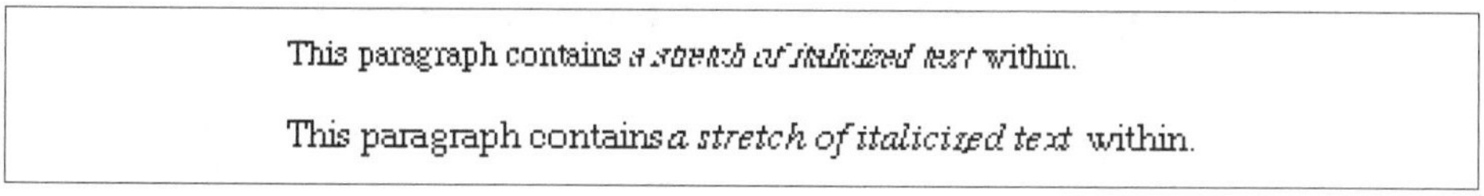

Figure 5-18. Same font, same style, different sizes

There isn't much that can be done about this, unfortunately, except better font handling by operating systems, such as that found in Mac OS X and Windows XP. Usually, the italic and oblique fonts look exactly the same in web browsers.

Still, `font-style` can be useful. For example, it is a common typographic convention that a block quote should be italicized, but that any specially emphasized text within the quote should be upright. To employ this effect, which is illustrated in Figure 5-19, you would use these styles:

```
blockquote {font-style: italic;}
blockquote em, blockquote i {font-style: normal;}
```

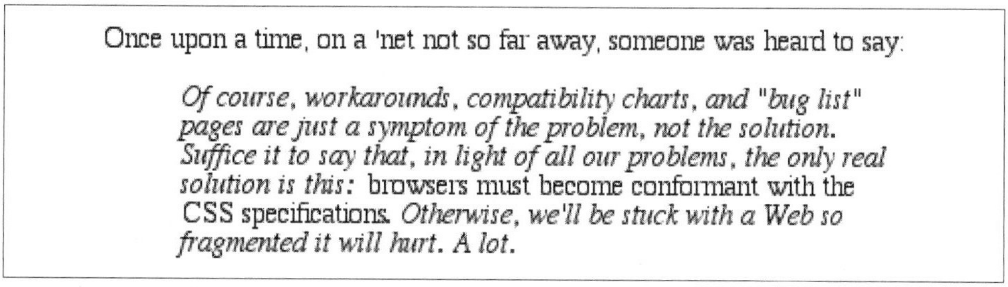

Figure 5-19. Common typographical conventions through CSS

Font Variations

In addition to sizes and styles, fonts can also have variants. CSS offers a way to address one very common variant.

font-variant

Values:	`small-caps` | `normal` | `inherit`
Initial value:	`normal`
Applies to:	All elements
Inherited:	Yes
Computed value:	As specified

As for font-variant, it has only two non-inherit values: the default of normal, which describes ordinary text, and small-caps, which calls for the use of small-caps text. If you aren't familiar with such an effect, IT LOOKS SOMETHING LIKE THIS. Instead of upper- and lowercase letters, a small-caps font employs uppercase letters of different sizes. Thus, you might see something like that shown in Figure 5-20:

```
h1 {font-variant: small-caps;}
h1 code, p {font-variant: normal;}

<h1>The Uses of <code>font-variant</code> On the Web</h1>
<p>
The property <code>font-variant</code> is very interesting...
</p>
```

THE USES OF font-variant ON THE WEB

The property font-variant is very interesting...

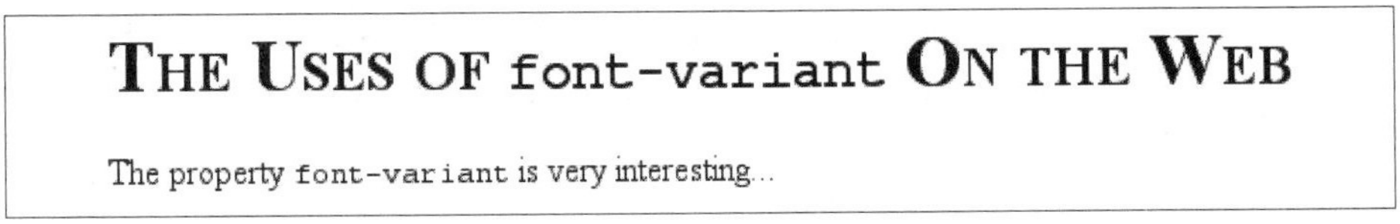

Figure 5-20. The small-caps value in use

As you may notice, in the display of the h1 element, there is a larger uppercase letter wherever an uppercase letter appears in the source and a small uppercase letter wherever there is a lowercase letter in the source. This is very similar to text-transform: uppercase, with the only real difference being that, here, the uppercase letters are of different sizes. However, the reason that small-caps is declared using a font property is that some fonts have a specific small-caps face, which a font property is used to select.

What happens if no such face exists? There are two options provided in the specification. The first is for the user agent to create a small-caps face by scaling uppercase letters on its own. The second is simply to make all letters uppercase and the same size, exactly as if the declaration text-transform: uppercase; had been used instead. This is obviously not an ideal solution, but it is permitted.

> Internet Explorer for Windows took the all-caps route before IE6. Most other browsers display small-caps text when asked to do so.

Stretching and Adjusting Fonts

There are two font properties that appear in CSS2, but not in CSS2.1. They've been dropped from CSS2.1 because, despite being in the specification for years, no browser has bothered to implement either one. The first allows for the horizontal stretching of fonts, and the second allows for intelligent scaling of substituted fonts when the author's first choice is not available. First, let's look at stretching.

As you might expect from the value names, this property is used to make a font's characters fatter or skinnier. It behaves very much like the absolute-size keywords (e.g., xx-large) for the font-size property, with a range of absolute values and two values that let the author alter a font's stretching up or down. For example, an author might decide to stress the text in a strongly emphasized element by stretching the font characters to be wider than their parent element's font characters, as shown in Figure 5-21:

```
strong {font-stretch: wider;}
```

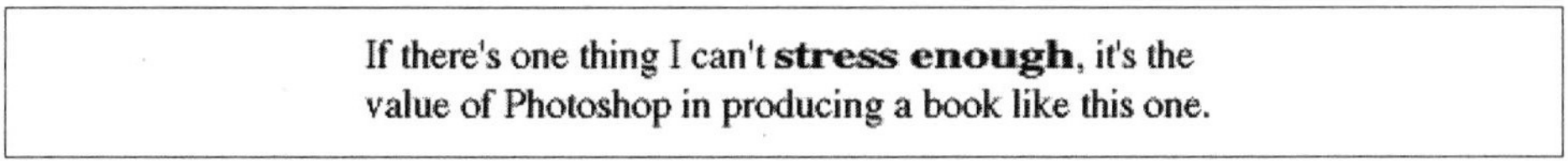

> If there's one thing I can't **stress enough**, it's the
> value of Photoshop in producing a book like this one.

Figure 5-21. Stretching font characters

 Figure 5-21 was altered using Photoshop, since web browsers do not support font-stretch as of this writing.

The similarly unimplemented process of adjusting font size is a little more complicated.

The goal of this property is to preserve legibility when the font used is not the author's first choice. Because of the differences in font appearance, one font may be legible at a certain size, while another font at the same size is difficult or impossible to read.

The factors that influence a font's legibility are its size and its x-height. The number that results from dividing the x-height by the font-size is referred to as the *aspect value*. Fonts with higher aspect values tend to be legible as the font's size is reduced; conversely, fonts with low aspect values become illegible more quickly.

A good example is to compare the common fonts Verdana and Times. Consider Figure 5-22 and the following markup, which shows both fonts at a font-size of 10px:

```
p {font-size: 10px;}
p.cl1 {font-family: Verdana, sans-serif;}
p.cl2 {font-family: Times, serif; }
```

Donec ut magna. Aliquam erat volutpat. Cum sociis natoque penatibus et magnis dis parturient montes, nascetur ridiculus mus. Nulla facilisi. Aenean mattis,.dui et ullamcorper ornare, erat est sodales mi, non blandit sem ipsum quis justo. Nulla tincidunt.

Quisque et orci nec lacus hendrerit fringilla. Sed quam nibh, elementum et, scelerisque a, aliquam vestibulum, sapien. Etiam commodo auctor sapien. Pellentesque tincidunt lacus nec quam. Integer sit amet neque vel eros interdum ornare. Sed consequat.

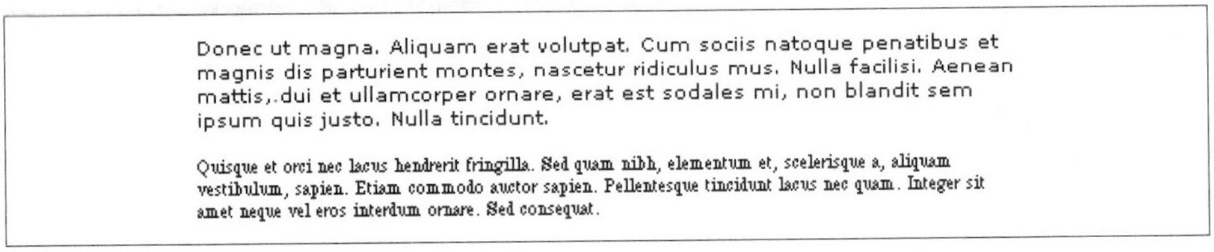

Figure 5-22. Comparing Verdana and Times

The text in Times is much harder to read than the Verdana text. This is partly due to the limitations of pixel-based display, but it is also because Times simply becomes harder to read at smaller font sizes.

As it turns out, the ratio of x-height to character size in Verdana is 0.58, whereas in Times it is 0.46. What you can do in this case is declare the aspect value of Verdana, and the user agent will adjust the size of the text that's actually used. This is accomplished using the formula:

Declared font-size × (font-size-adjust value ÷ aspect value of available font) = Adjusted font-size

So, in a situation where Times is used instead of Verdana, the adjustment is as follows:

10px × (0.58 ÷ 0.46) = 12.6px

which leads to the result shown in Figure 5-23:

```
p {font: 10px Verdana, sans-serif; font-size-adjust: 0.58;}
p.cl1 {font-family: Times, serif; }
```

Donec ut magna. Aliquam erat volutpat. Cum sociis natoque penatibus et magnis dis parturient montes, nascetur ridiculus mus. Nulla facilisi. Aenean mattis, dui et ullamcorper ornare, erat est sodales mi, non blandit sem ipsum quis justo. Nulla tincidunt.

Quisque et orci nec lacus hendrerit fringilla. Sed quam nibh, elementum et, scelerisque a, aliquam vestibulum, sapien. Etiam commodo auctor sapien. Pellentesque tincidunt lacus nec quam. Integer sit amet neque vel eros interdum ornare. Sed consequat.

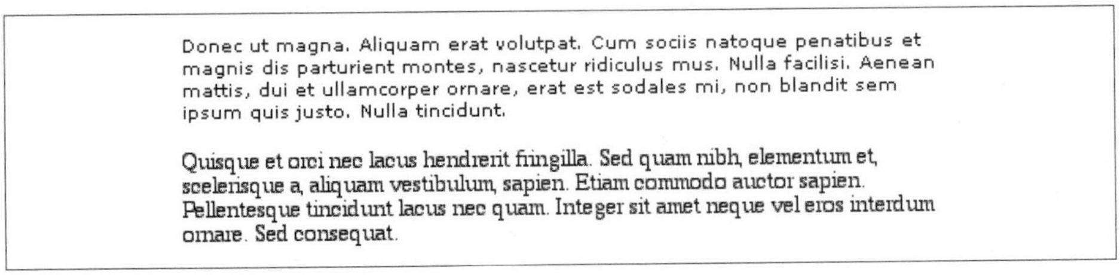

Figure 5-23. Adjusting Times

Figure 5-23 was altered using Photoshop, since very few web browsers support font-size-adjust as of this writing.

Of course, to allow a user agent to intelligently make size adjustments, you have to know the aspect value of your first-choice font. There is no way in CSS2 to simply get the value from the font, and many fonts may not have the information available in the first place.

The font Property

All of these properties are very sophisticated, of course, but using them all could get a little tedious:

```
h1 {font-family: Verdana, Helvetica, Arial, sans-serif; font-size: 30px;
    font-weight: 900; font-style: italic; font-variant: small-caps;}
h2 {font-family: Verdana, Helvetica, Arial, sans-serif; font-size: 24px;
    font-weight: bold; font-style: italic; font-variant: normal;}
```

Some of this problem could be solved by grouping selectors, but wouldn't it be easier to combine everything into a single property? Enter font, which is the shorthand property for all the other font properties (and a little more besides).

font	
Values:	[[<font-style> || <font-variant> || <font-weight>]? <font-size> [/ <line-height>]? <font-family>] | caption | icon | menu | message-box | small-caption | status-bar | inherit
Initial value:	Refer to individual properties
Applies to:	All elements
Inherited:	Yes
Percentages:	Calculated with respect to the parent element for <font-size> and with respect to the element's <font-size> for <line-height>
Computed value:	See individual properties (font-style, etc.)

Generally speaking, a font declaration can have any one value from each of the listed font properties, or else a "system font" value (described in the section "Using System Fonts"). Therefore, the preceding example could be shortened as follows:

```
h1 {font: italic 900 small-caps 30px Verdana, Helvetica, Arial, sans-serif;}
h2 {font: bold normal italic 24px Verdana, Helvetica, Arial, sans-serif;}
```

and have exactly the same effect (illustrated by Figure 5-24).

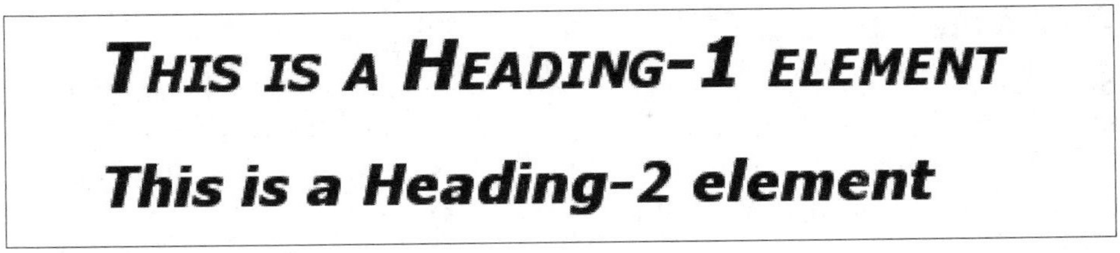

THIS IS A HEADING-1 ELEMENT

This is a Heading-2 element

Figure 5-24. Typical font rules

I say that the styles "could be" shortened in this way because there are a few other possibilities, thanks to the relatively loose way in which font can be written. If you look closely at the preceding example, you'll see that the first three values don't occur in the same order. In the h1 rule, the first three values are the values for font-style, font-weight, and font-variant, in that order, whereas in the second, they're ordered font-weight, font-variant, and font-style. There is nothing wrong here because these three can be written in any order. Furthermore, if any of them has a value of normal, that can be left out altogether. Therefore, the following rules are equivalent to the previous example:

```
h1 {font: italic 900 small-caps 30px Verdana, Helvetica, Arial, sans-serif;}
h2 {font: bold italic 24px Verdana, Helvetica, Arial, sans-serif;}
```

In this example, the value of normal was left out of the h2 rule, but the effect is exactly the same as in the preceding example.

It's important to realize, however, that this free-for-all situation applies only to the first three values of font. The last two are much stricter in their behavior. Not only must font-size and font-family appear in that order as the last two values in the declaration, but both must always be present in a font declaration. Period, end of story. If either is left out, then the entire rule will be invalidated and very likely ignored completely by a user agent. Thus, the following rules will get you the result shown in Figure 5-25:

```
h1 {font: normal normal italic 30px sans-serif;}   /*no problem here */
h2 {font: 1.5em sans-serif;}    /* also fine; omitted values set to 'normal' */
h3 {font: sans-serif;}   /* INVALID--no 'font-size' provided */
h4 {font: lighter 14px;}   /* INVALID--no 'font-family' provided */
```

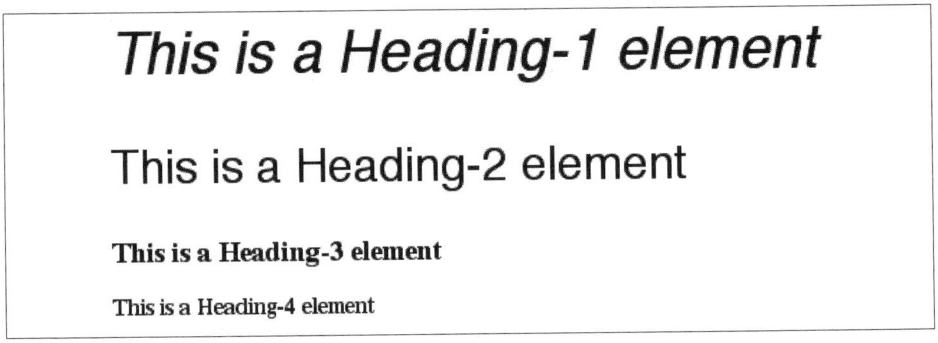

This is a Heading-1 element

This is a Heading-2 element

This is a Heading-3 element

This is a Heading-4 element

Figure 5-25. The necessity of both size and family

Adding the Line Height

So far, we've treated font as though it has only five values, which isn't quite true. It is also possible to set the line-height using font, despite that fact that line-height is a text property, not a font property. It's done as a sort of addition to the font-size value, separated from it by a forward slash (/):

```
body {font-size: 12px;}
h2 {font: bold italic 200%/1.2 Verdana, Helvetica, Arial, sans-serif;}
```

These rules, demonstrated in Figure 5-26, set all h2 elements to be bold and italic (using face for one of the sans-serif font families), set the font-size to 24px (twice the body's size), and set the line-height to 30px.

This is a Heading-2 element that has had a 'line-height' of '1.2' set for it.

Figure 5-26. Adding line height to the mix

This addition of a value for line-height is entirely optional, just as the first three font values are. If you do include a line-height, remember that the font-size always comes before line-height, never after, and the two are always separated by a slash.

This may seem repetitive, but it's one of the most common errors made by CSS authors, so I can't say it enough: the required values for font are font-size and font-family, in that order. Everything else is strictly optional.

 line-height is discussed in the next chapter.

Using Shorthands Properly

It is important to remember that font, being a shorthand property, can act in unexpected ways if you are careless with its use. Consider the following rules, which are illustrated in Figure 5-27:

```
h1, h2, h3 {font: italic small-caps 250% sans-serif;}
h2 {font: 200% sans-serif;}
h3 {font-size: 150%;}

<h1>This is an h1 element</h1>
<h2>This is an h2 element</h2>
<h3>This is an h3 element</h3>
```

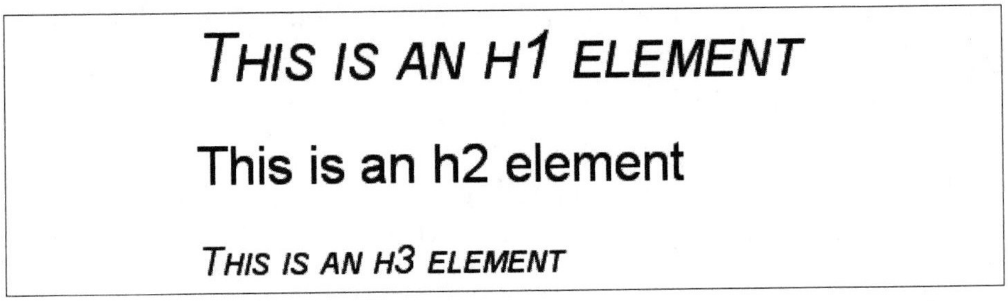

Figure 5-27. Shorthand changes

Did you notice that the h2 element is neither italicized nor small-capped, and that none of the elements are boldfaced? This is the correct behavior. When the shorthand property font is used, any omitted values are reset to their defaults. Thus, the previous example could be written as follows and still be exactly equivalent:

```
h1, h2, h3 {font: italic normal small-caps 250% sans-serif;}
h2 {font: normal normal normal 200% sans-serif;}
h3 {font-size: 150%;}
```

This sets the h2 element's font style and variant to normal, and the font-weight of all three elements to normal. This is the expected behavior of shorthand properties. The h3 does not suffer the same fate as the h2 because you used the property font-size, which is not a shorthand property and therefore affects only its own value.

Using System Fonts

In situations where you want to make a web page "blend in" with the user's operating system, the system font values of font come in very handy. These are used to take the font size, family, weight, style, and variant of elements of the operating system, and apply them to an element. The values are as follows:

caption
> Used for captioned controls, such as buttons

icon
> Used to label icons

menu
> Used in menus—that is, drop-down menus and menu lists

message-box
> Used in dialog boxes

small-caption
> Used for labeling small controls

status-bar
> Used in window status bars

For example, you might want to set the font of a button to be the same as that of the buttons found in the operating system. For example:

```
button {font: caption;}
```

With these values, it is possible to create web-based applications that look very much like applications native to the user's operating system.

Note that system fonts may only be set as a whole; that is, the font family, size, weight, style, etc., are all set together. Therefore, the button text from our previous example will look exactly the same as button text in the operating system, whether or not the size matches any of the content around the button. You can, however, alter the individual values once the system font has been set. Thus, the following rule will make sure the button's font is the same size as its parent element's font:

```
button {font: caption; font-size: 1em;}
```

If you call for a system font and no such font exists on the user's machine, the user agent may try to find an approximation, such as reducing the size of the caption font to arrive at the small-caption font. If no such approximation is possible, then the user agent should use a default font of its own. If it can find a system font but can't read all of its values, then it should use the default value. For example, a user agent may be able to find a status-bar font but not get any information about whether the font is small-caps. In that case, the user agent will use the value normal for the small-caps property.

 User interface styles are discussed in more detail in Chapter 13.

Font Matching

As we've seen, CSS allows for the matching of font families, weights, and variants. This is all accomplished through font matching, which is a vaguely complicated procedure. Understanding it is important for authors who want to help user agents make good font selections when displaying their documents. I left it for the end of the chapter because it's not really necessary to understand how the font properties work, and some readers will probably want to skip this part and go on to the next chapter. If you're still interested, here's how font matching works.

1. The user agent creates, or otherwise accesses, a database of font properties. This database lists the various CSS properties of all of the fonts to which the user agent has access. Typically, this will be all fonts installed on the machine, although there could be others (for example, the user agent could have its own built-in fonts). If the user agent encounters two identical fonts, it will simply ignore one of them.

2. The user agent takes apart an element to which font properties have been applied and constructs a list of font properties necessary for the display of that element. Based on that list, the user agent makes an initial choice of a font family to use in

displaying the element. If there is a complete match, then the user agent can use that font. Otherwise, it needs to do a little more work.

    a. A font is first matched against the font-style. The keyword italic is matched by any font that is labeled as either "italic" or "oblique." If neither is available, then the match fails.

    b. The next match attempt is on font-variant. Any font that is not labeled "small-caps" is assumed to be normal. A font can be matched to small-caps by any font that is labeled as "small-caps," by any font that allows the synthesis of a small-caps style, or by any font where lowercase letters are replaced by uppercase letters.

    c. The next match is to font-weight, which can never fail thanks to the way font-weight is handled in CSS (explained earlier in the chapter).

    d. Then, font-size is tackled. This must be matched within a certain tolerance, but that tolerance is defined by the user agent. Thus, one user agent might allow matching within a 20 percent margin of error, whereas another might allow only 10 percent differences between the size specified and the size that is actually used.

3. If there was no font match in Step 2, the user agent looks for alternate fonts within the same font family. If it finds any, then it repeats Step 2 for that font.

4. Assuming a generic match has been found, but it doesn't contain everything needed to display a given element—the font is missing the copyright symbol, for instance—then the user agent goes back to Step 3, which entails a search for another alternate font and another trip through Step 2.

5. Finally, if no match has been made and all alternate fonts have been tried, then the user agent selects the default font for the given generic font family and does the best it can to display the element correctly.

The whole process is long and tedious, but it helps to understand how user agents pick the fonts they do. For example, you might specify the use of Times or any other serif font in a document:

```
body {font-family: Times, serif;}
```

For each element, the user agent should examine the characters in that element and determine whether Times can provide characters to match. In most cases, it can do so with no problem. Assume, however, that a Chinese character has been placed in the middle of a paragraph. Times has nothing that can match this character, so the user agent has to work around the character or look for another font that can fulfill the needs of displaying that element. Of course, any Western font is highly unlikely to contain Chinese characters, but should one exist (let's call it AsiaTimes), the user agent could use it in the display of that one element—or simply for the single character. Thus, the whole paragraph might be displayed using AsiaTimes, or everything in the paragraph might be in Times except for the single Chinese character, which is displayed in AsiaTimes.

Font-Face Rules

CSS2 introduced a way to exert much greater control over font matching through an @font-face rule. Since no web browsers had fully implemented this rule as of spring 2003, @font-face was removed from CSS2.1. I will not spend much time on it, as the aspects of this rule are very complicated and could probably fill a chapter (or a book!) of their own.

There are four ways to arrive at a font to be used in the document. We'll look briefly at each, since future versions of CSS may use this mechanism, and most SVG renderers at least partially support the font-face matching described in CSS2. If you are in a situation where you need to implement @font-face, please refer to the CSS2 specification, or whatever the latest version of CSS might be (such as the CSS3 Web Fonts module); the following descriptions are incomplete at best.

Font-name matching

To match the font name, the user agent uses an available font that has the same family name as the requested font. The font's appearance and metrics might not be the same. This is the method described earlier in this section.

Intelligent font matching

In this case, the user agent uses an available font that is the closest match in appearance to the requested font. The two may not match exactly, but they should be as close as possible.

The information used to match the two fonts includes the kind of font (text or symbol), nature of serifs, weight, cap height, x-height, ascent, descent, slant, and so on. For example, an author could request that a certain font be as close as possible to a certain slant by writing:

```
@font-face {font-style: normal; font-family: "Times"; slope: -5;}
```

It would then be up to the user agent to find a serif normal (upright) font with a slope as close to five degrees to the right as possible, if Times does not fit the bill. There are a great many font aspects described in CSS2, all of which can be used to drive the matching process in a user agent that supports them.

Font synthesis

It's also possible that a user agent would choose to actually generate, on the fly, a font whose appearance and metrics match the description given in the @font-face rule. CSS2 has this to say about the process:

In this case, the user agent creates a font that is not only a close match in appearance, but also matches the metrics of the requested font. The synthesizing information includes the matching information and typically requires more accurate values for the parameters than are used for some matching schemes. In particular, synthesis requires accurate width metrics and character to glyph substitution and position information if all the layout characteristics of the specified font are to be preserved.

If this makes sense to you, then you probably don't need my help to explain it. If not, you probably won't ever need to worry about it.

Font download

In this approach, the user agent may download a remote font for use in the document. To declare a font for downloading, you might write something like this:

```
@font-face {font-family: "Scarborough Fair";
    src: url(http://www.example.com/fonts/ps/scarborough.ps);}
```

You could then use that font throughout the document.

Even in a user agent that permits font downloading, it may take some time to retrieve the font file (such files can be quite large), which would delay the rendering of the document or at least delay the final rendering.

Summary

Although authors cannot count on a specific font being used in a document, they can very easily specify generic font families to be used. This particular behavior is very well supported, since any user agent that didn't let authors (or even readers) assign fonts would quickly find itself out of favor.

As for the other areas of font manipulation, support varies. Changing the size of fonts usually works well, but 20th-century implementations ranged from frustratingly simplistic to very nearly correct in this area. The frustration for authors is usually not the way in which font sizing is supported, but rather, in how a unit they want to use (points) can yield very different results in different media, or even in different operating systems and user agents. The dangers of using points are many, and using length units for web design is generally not a good idea. Percentages, em units, and ex units are usually best for changing font sizes, since these scale very well in all common display environments.

The other frustration is likely the continued lack of a mechanism to specify fonts for downloading and use in a document. This means that authors are still dependent on the fonts available to the user, and therefore, they cannot predict what appearance that text will take.

Speaking of styling text, there are ways to do it that don't involve fonts, which the next chapter will address.

CHAPTER 6

Text Properties

Sure, a lot of web design involves picking the right colors and getting the coolest look for your pages, but when it comes right down to it, you probably spend more of your time worrying about where text will go and how it will look. Such concerns gave rise to HTML tags such as <FONT> and <CENTER>, which allow you some measure of control over the appearance and placement of text.

Because text is so important, there are many CSS properties that affect it in one way or another. What is the difference between text and fonts? Simply, text is the content, and fonts are used to display that content. Using text properties, you can affect the position of text in relation to the rest of the line, superscript it, underline it, and change the capitalization. You can even simulate, to a limited degree, the use of a typewriter's Tab key.

Indentation and Horizontal Alignment

Let's start with a discussion of how you can affect the horizontal positioning of text within a line. Think of these basic actions as the same types of steps you might take to create a newsletter or write a report.

Indenting Text

Indenting the first line of a paragraph on a web page is one of the most sought-after text-formatting effects. (Eliminating the blank line between paragraphs, which is discussed in Chapter 7, is a close second.) Some sites create the illusion of indented text by placing a small transparent image before the first letter in a paragraph, which shoves over the text. Other sites use the utterly nonstandard SPACER tag. Thanks to CSS, there's a better way to indent text, called text-indent.

Using text-indent, the first line of any element can be indented by a given length—even if that length is negative. The most common use for this property is, of course, to indent the first line of paragraphs:

```
p {text-indent: 3em;}
```

text-indent

Values:	\<length\> | \<percentage\> | `inherit`
Initial value:	0
Applies to:	Block-level elements
Inherited:	Yes
Percentages:	Refer to the width of the containing block
Computed value:	For percentage values, as specified; for length values, the absolute length

This rule will cause the first line of any paragraph to be indented three ems, as shown in Figure 6-1.

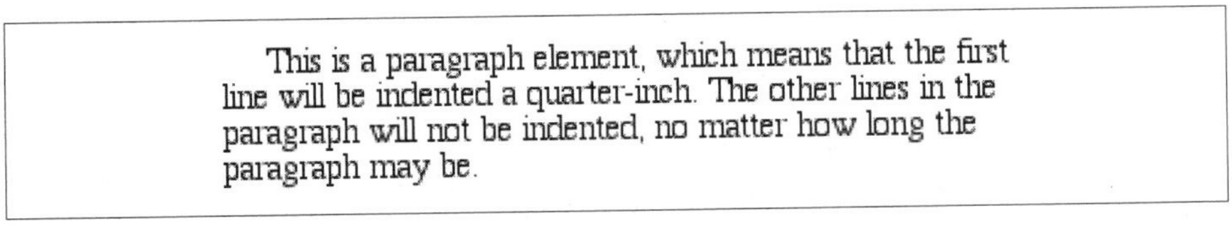

This is a paragraph element, which means that the first line will be indented a quarter-inch. The other lines in the paragraph will not be indented, no matter how long the paragraph may be.

Figure 6-1. Text indenting

In general, you can apply `text-indent` to any block-level element. You can't apply it to inline elements or on replaced elements such as images. However, if you have an image within the first line of a block-level element, like a paragraph, it will be shifted over with the rest of the text in the line.

If you want to "indent" the first line of an inline element, you can create the effect with left padding or margin.

You can also set negative values for `text-indent`, a technique that leads to a number of interesting effects. The most common use is a "hanging indent," where the first line hangs out to the left of the rest of the element:

```
p {text-indent: -4em;}
```

Be careful when setting a negative value for `text-indent`: the first three words ("This is a") may be chopped off by the left edge of the browser window. To avoid display problems, I recommend you use a margin or some padding to accommodate the negative indentation:

```
p {text-indent: -4em; padding-left: 4em;}
```

Negative indents can, however, be used to your advantage. Consider the following example, demonstrated in Figure 6-2, which adds a floated image to the mix:

```
p.hang {text-indent: -25px;}

<img src="star.gif" style="width: 60px; height: 60px;
float: left;" alt="An image of a five-pointed star."/>
<p class="hang"> This paragraph has a negatively indented first
line, which overlaps the floated image that precedes the text.  Subsequent
lines do not overlap the image, since they are not indented in any way.</p>
```

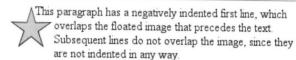

Figure 6-2. A floated image and negative text indenting

A variety of interesting designs can be achieved using this simple technique.

Any unit of length, including percentage values, may be used with text-indent. In the following case, the percentage refers to the width of the parent element of the element being indented. In other words, if you set the indent value to 10%, the first line of an affected element will be indented by 10 percent of its parent element's width, as shown in Figure 6-3:

```
div {width: 400px;}
p {text-indent: 10%;}

<div>
<p>This paragraph is contained inside a DIV, which is 400px wide, so the
first line of the paragraph is indented 40px (400 * 10% = 40).  This is
because percentages are computed with respect to the width of the element.</p>
</div>
```

This paragraph is contained inside a DIV that is 400px wide, so the first line of the paragraph is indented 40px (400 * 10% = 40). This is because percentages are computed with respect to the width of the element.

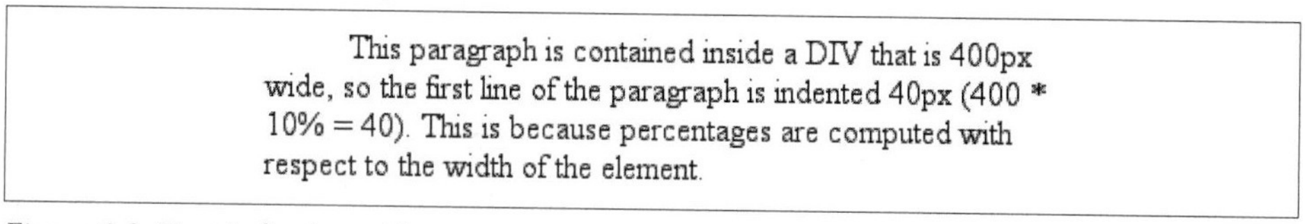

Figure 6-3. Text indenting with percentages

Note that this indentation only applies to the first line of an element, even if you insert line breaks. The interesting part about text-indent is that because it's inherited, it can have unexpected effects. For example, consider the following markup, which is illustrated in Figure 6-4:

```
div#outer {width: 500px;}
div#inner {text-indent: 10%;}
p {width: 200px;}
```

```
<div id="outer">
<div id="inner">
This first line of the DIV is indented by 50 pixels.
<p>
This paragraph is 200px wide, and the first line of the paragraph
is indented 50px.  This is because computed values for 'text-indent'
are inherited, instead of the declared values.
</p>
</div>
</div>
```

> This first line of the DIV is indented by 50 pixels.
>
> This paragraph is 200px
> wide, and the first line of the
> paragraph is indented 50px. This
> is because computed values for
> 'text-indent' are inherited, instead
> of the declared values.

Figure 6-4. Inherited text indenting

In versions of CSS prior to 2.1, text-indent always inherited the computed value, not the declared value.

Horizontal Alignment

Even more basic than text-indent is the property text-align, which affects how the lines of text in an element are aligned with respect to one another. The first three values are pretty straightforward, but the fourth and fifth have a few complexities.

text-align

CSS2.1 values:	left | center | right | justify | inherit
CSS2 values:	left | center | right | justify | <string> | inherit
Initial value:	User agent-specific; may also depend on writing direction
Applies to:	Block-level elements
Inherited:	Yes
Computed value:	As specified
Note:	CSS2 included a <string> value that was dropped from CSS2.1 due to a lack of implementation

The quickest way to understand how these values work is to examine Figure 6-5.

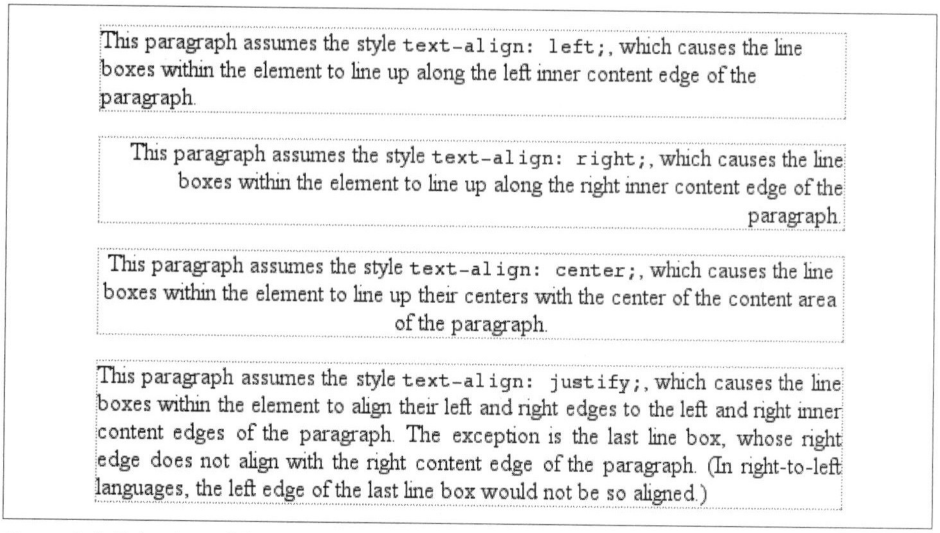

This paragraph assumes the style text-align: left;, which causes the line boxes within the element to line up along the left inner content edge of the paragraph.

This paragraph assumes the style text-align: right;, which causes the line boxes within the element to line up along the right inner content edge of the paragraph.

This paragraph assumes the style text-align: center;, which causes the line boxes within the element to line up their centers with the center of the content area of the paragraph.

This paragraph assumes the style text-align: justify;, which causes the line boxes within the element to align their left and right edges to the left and right inner content edges of the paragraph. The exception is the last line box, whose right edge does not align with the right content edge of the paragraph. (In right-to-left languages, the left edge of the last line box would not be so aligned.)

Figure 6-5. Behaviors of the text-align property

Obviously, the values left, right, and center cause the text within elements to be aligned exactly as described. Because text-align applies only to block-level elements, such as paragraphs, there's no way to center an anchor within its line without aligning the rest of the line (nor would you want to, since that would likely cause text overlap).

For Western languages, which are read from left to right, the default value of text-align is left. The text aligns on the left margin and has a ragged right margin (otherwise known as "left-to-right" text). Languages such as Hebrew and Arabic default to right since they are read right to left. As expected, center causes each line of text to be centered within the element.

 Centering block-level or table elements is accomplished by properly setting the left and right margins on those elements. See Chapter 7 for details.

Although you may be tempted to believe that text-align: center is the same as the <CENTER> element, it's actually quite different. <CENTER> affected not only text, but also centered whole elements, such as tables. text-align does not control the alignment of elements, only their inline content. Figure 6-5 illustrates this clearly. The actual elements are not shifted from one side to the other. Only the text within them is affected.

 One of the more pernicious bugs in IE/Win up through IE6 is that it actually does treat text-align: center as if it were the <CENTER> element, and centers elements as well as text. This does not happen in standards mode in IE6 and later, but it persists in IE5.x and earlier.

The last horizontal alignment property is justify, which raises some issues of its own. In justified text, both ends of a line of text are placed at the inner edge of the parent element, as Figure 6-6 shows. Then, the spacing between words and letters is adjusted so that each line is precisely the same length. Justified text is common in the print world (for example, in this book), but under CSS, a few extra considerations come into play.

> This is a paragraph of justified text. Notice that the spacing between words, or even between individual letters, depends greatly on the number of words in each line. Intraword and intracharacter spacing is adjusted to create the justification effect, so it can effectively override values for properties such as **word-spacing** and **letter-spacing**.

Figure 6-6. Justified text

The user agent—not CSS—determines how justified text should be stretched to fill the space between the left and right edges of the parent. Some browsers, for example, might add extra space only between words, while others might distribute the extra space between letters (although the CSS specification specifically states that "user agents may not further increase or decrease the inter-character space" if the property letter-spacing has been assigned a length value). Other user agents may reduce space on some lines, thus mashing the text together a bit more than usual. All of these possibilities will affect the appearance of an element, and may even change its height, depending on how many lines of text result from the user agent's justification choices.

CSS also doesn't specify how hyphenation should be handled.* Most justified text uses hyphenation to break long words across two lines, thus reducing the space between words and improving the appearance of lines. However, since CSS defines no hyphenation behavior, user agents are unlikely to perform any automatic hyphenation. As a result, justified text looks much less attractive under CSS than it does in print, especially when elements become so narrow that only a few words can fit on each line. You can still use narrow design elements, of course, but be aware of the drawbacks.

---

* Hyphenation is not described in CSS because different languages have different hyphenation rules. Rather than try to concoct a set of rules that would most likely be incomplete, the specification simply avoids the problem.

Vertical Alignment

Now that we've covered horizontal alignment, let's move on to vertical alignment. Since the construction of lines is covered in much more detail in Chapter 7, I'll just stick to a quick overview here.

The Height of Lines

The line-height property refers to the distance between the baselines of lines of text rather than the size of the font, and it determines the amount by which the height of each element's box is increased or decreased. In the most basic cases, specifying line-height is a way to increase (or decrease) the vertical space between lines of text, but this is a misleadingly simple way of looking at how line-height works. line-height controls the *leading*, which is the extra space between lines of text above and beyond the font's size. In other words, the difference between the value of line-height and the size of the font is the leading.

<table>
<tr><td colspan="2" align="center">line-height</td></tr>
<tr><td>Values:</td><td><length> | <percentage> | <number> | normal | inherit</td></tr>
<tr><td>Initial value:</td><td>normal</td></tr>
<tr><td>Applies to:</td><td>All elements (but see text regarding replaced and block-level elements)</td></tr>
<tr><td>Inherited:</td><td>Yes</td></tr>
<tr><td>Percentages:</td><td>Relative to the font size of the element</td></tr>
<tr><td>Computed value:</td><td>For length and percentage values, the absolute value; otherwise, as specified</td></tr>
</table>

When applied to a block-level element, line-height defines the minimum distance between text baselines within that element. Note that it defines a minimum, not an absolute value, and baselines of text can wind up being pushed further apart than the value of line-height. line-height does not affect layout for replaced elements, but it still applies to them. (This subtle mystery is explained in Chapter 7.)

Constructing a line

Every element in a line of text generates a *content area*, which is determined by the size of the font. This content area in turn generates an *inline box* that is, in the absence of any other factors, exactly equal to the content area. The leading generated by line-height is one of the factors that increases or decreases the height of each inline box.

To determine the leading for a given element, simply subtract the computed value of font-size from the computed value of line-height. That value is the total amount of leading. And remember, it can be a negative number. The leading is then divided in half, and each half-leading is applied to the top and bottom of the content area. The result is the inline box for that element.

As an example, let's say the font-size (and therefore the content area) is 14 pixels tall, and the line-height is computed to 18 pixels. The difference (four pixels) is divided in half, and each half is applied to the top and bottom of the content area. This creates an inline box that is 18 pixels tall, with 2 extra pixels above and below the content area. This sounds like a roundabout way to describe how line-height works, but there are excellent reasons for the description.

Once all of the inline boxes have been generated for a given line of content, they are then considered in the construction of the line box. A line box is exactly as tall as needed to enclose the top of the tallest inline box and the bottom of the lowest inline box. Figure 6-7 shows a diagram of this process.

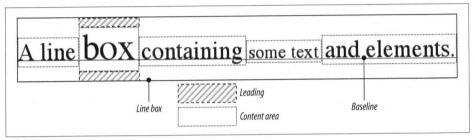

Figure 6-7. Line box diagram

Assigning values to line-height

Let's now consider the possible values of line-height. If you use the default value of normal, the user agent must calculate the vertical space between lines. Values can vary by user agent, but they're generally 1.2 times the size of the font, which makes line boxes taller than the value of font-size for a given element.

Most values are simple length measures (e.g., 18px or 2em). Be aware that even if you use a valid length measurement, such as 4cm, the browser (or the operating system) may be using an incorrect metric for real-world measurements, so the line height may not show up as exactly four centimeters on your monitor. For more details, see Chapter 4.

em, ex, and percentage values are calculated with respect to the font-size of the element. The markup is relatively straightforward, and the results are shown in Figure 6-8:

```
body {line-height: 14px; font-size: 13px;}
p.cl1 {line-height: 1.5em;}
p.cl2 {font-size: 10px; line-height: 150%;}
p.cl3 {line-height: 0.33in;}
```

```
<p>This paragraph inherits a 'line-height' of 14px from the body, as well as
a 'font-size' of 13px.</p>
<p class="cl1">This paragraph has a 'line-height' of 19.5px(13 * 1.5), so
it will have slightly more line-height than usual.</p>
<p class="cl2">This paragraph has a 'line-height' of 15px (10 * 150%), so
it will have slightly more line-height than usual.</p>
<p class="cl3">This paragraph has a 'line-height' of 0.33in, so it will have
slightly more line-height than usual.</p>
```

This paragraph inherits a 'line-height' of 14px from the body, as well as a 'font-size' of 13px.

This paragraph has a 'line-height' of 21px(14 * 1.5), so it will have slightly more line-height than usual.

This paragraph has a 'line-height' of 15px (10 * 150%), so it will have slightly more line-height than usual.

This paragraph has a 'line-height' of 0.33in, so it will have slightly more line-height than usual.

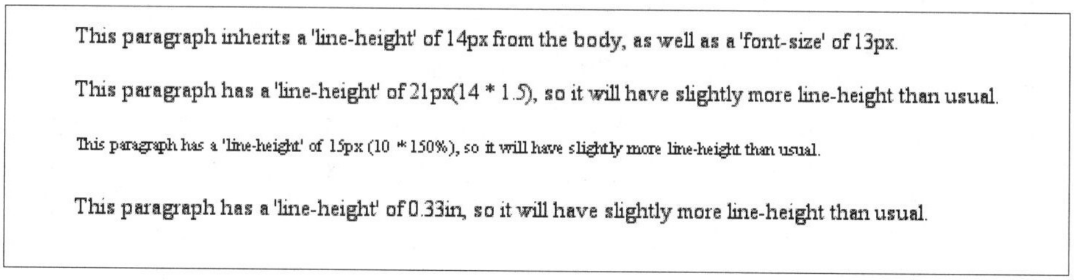

Figure 6-8. Simple calculations with the line-height property

Line height and inheritance

When the line-height is inherited by one block-level element from another, things get a bit trickier. line-height values inherit from the parent element as computed from the parent, not the child. The results of the following markup are shown in Figure 6-9. It probably wasn't what the author had in mind:

```
body {font-size: 10px;}
div {line-height: 1em;}  /* computes to '10px' */
p {font-size: 18px;}

<div>
<p>This paragraph's 'font-size' is 18px, but the inherited 'line-height'
value is only 10px.  This may cause the lines of text to overlap each
other by a small amount.</p>
</div>
```

This paragraph's 'font-size' is 18px, but the inherited 'line-height' value is only 10px. This may cause the lines of text to overlap each other by a small amount.

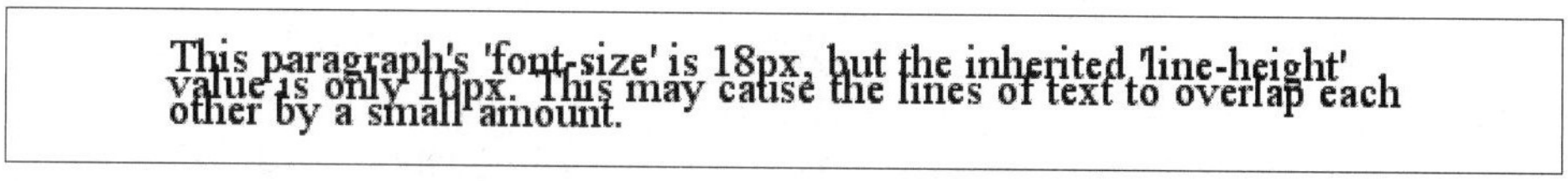

Figure 6-9. Small line-height, large font-size, slight problem

Why are the lines so close together? Because the computed line-height value of 10px was inherited by the paragraph from its parent div. One solution to the small line-height problem depicted in Figure 6-9 is to set an explicit line-height for every element, but that's not very practical. A better alternative is to specify a number, which actually sets a scaling factor:

```
body {font-size: 10px;}
div {line-height: 1;}
p {font-size: 18px;}
```

When you specify a number, you cause the scaling factor to be an inherited value instead of a computed value. The number will be applied to the element and all of its child elements, so that each element has a `line-height` calculated with respect to its own `font-size` (see Figure 6-10):

```
div {line-height: 1.5;}
p {font-size: 18px;}

<div>
<p>This paragraph's 'font-size' is 18px, and since the 'line-height'
set for the parent div is 1.5, the 'line-height' for this paragraph
is 27px (18 * 1.5).</p>
</div>
```

> **This paragraph's 'font-size' is 18px, and since the 'line-height' set for the parent div is 1.5, the 'line-height' for this paragraph is 27px (18 * 1.5).**

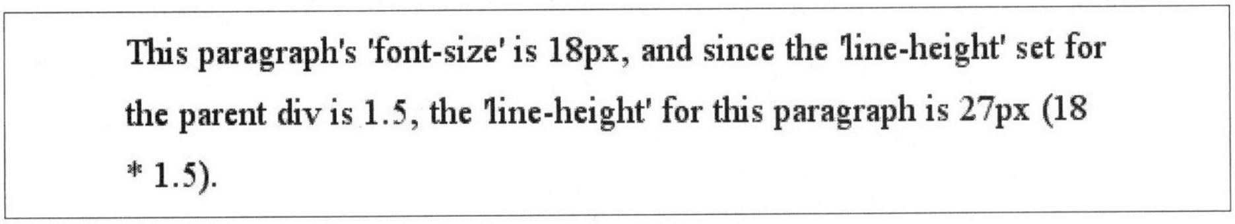

Figure 6-10. Using line-height factors to overcome inheritance problems

Though it seems like `line-height` distributes extra space both above and below each line of text, it actually adds (or subtracts) a certain amount from the top and bottom of an inline element's content area to create an inline box. Assume that the default `font-size` of a paragraph is 12pt and consider the following:

```
p {line-height: 16pt;}
```

Since the "inherent" line height of 12-point text is 12 points, the preceding rule will place an extra 4 points of space around each line of text in the paragraph. This extra amount is divided in two, with half going above each line and the other half below. You now have 16 points between the baselines, which is an indirect result of how the extra space is apportioned.

If you specify the value `inherit`, then the element will use the computed value for its parent element. This isn't really any different than allowing the value to inherit naturally, except in terms of specificity and cascade resolution. See Chapter 3 for details on these topics.

Now that you have a basic grasp of how lines are constructed, let's talk about vertically aligning elements relative to the line box.

Vertically Aligning Text

If you've ever used the elements `sup` and `sub` (the superscript and subscript elements), or used an image with markup such as `<img src="foo.gif" align="middle">`, then you've done some rudimentary vertical alignment. In CSS, the `vertical-align` property applies only to inline elements and replaced elements such as images and form inputs. `vertical-align` is not an inherited property.

vertical-align

Values:	baseline | sub | super | top | text-top | middle | bottom | text-bottom | \<percentage> | \<length> | inherit
Initial value:	baseline
Applies to:	Inline elements and table cells
Inherited:	No
Percentages:	Refer to the value of line-height for the element
Computed value:	For percentage and length values, the absolute length; otherwise, as specified
Note:	When applied to table cells, only the values baseline, top, middle, and bottom are recognized

vertical-align accepts any one of eight keywords, a percentage value, or a length value. The keywords are a mix of the familiar and unfamiliar: baseline (the default value), sub, super, bottom, text-bottom, middle, top, and text-top. We'll examine how each keyword works in relation to inline elements.

 Remember: vertical-align does *not* affect the alignment of content within a block-level element. You can, however, use it to affect the vertical alignment of elements within table cells. See Chapter 11 for details.

Baseline alignment

vertical-align: baseline forces the baseline of an element to align with the baseline of its parent. Browsers, for the most part, do this anyway, since you'd obviously expect the bottoms of all text elements in a line to be aligned.

If a vertically aligned element doesn't have a baseline—that is, if it's an image, a form input, or another replaced element—then the bottom of the element is aligned with the baseline of its parent, as Figure 6-11 shows:

```
img {vertical-align: baseline;}

<p>The image found in this paragraph <img src="dot.gif" alt="A dot" /> has its
bottom edge aligned with the baseline of the text in the paragraph.</p>
```

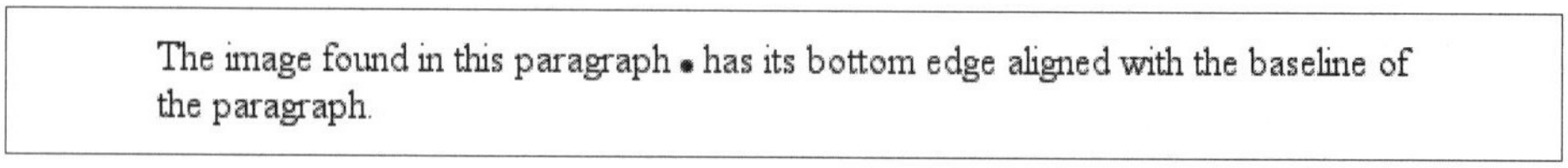

The image found in this paragraph • has its bottom edge aligned with the baseline of the paragraph.

Figure 6-11. Baseline alignment of an image

This alignment rule is important because it causes some web browsers to always put a replaced element's bottom edge on the baseline, even if there is no other text in the line. For example, let's say you have an image in a table cell all by itself. The image may actually be on a baseline, but in some browsers, the space below the baseline causes a gap to appear beneath the image. Other browsers will "shrink-wrap" the image with the table cell, and no gap will appear. The gap behavior is correct, according to the CSS Working Group, despite its lack of appeal to most authors.

 See my article "Images, Tables, and Mysterious Gaps" at *http://developer.mozilla.org/en/docs/Images,_Tables,_and_Mysterious_Gaps* for a more detailed explanation of gap behavior and ways to work around it. Chapter 7 also covers this aspect of inline layout in more detail.

Superscripting and subscripting

The declaration `vertical-align: sub` causes an element to be subscripted, meaning that its baseline (or bottom, if it's a replaced element) is lowered with respect to its parent's baseline. The specification doesn't define the distance the element is lowered, so it may vary depending on the user agent.

`super` is the opposite of `sub`; it raises the element's baseline (or bottom of a replaced element) with respect to the parent's baseline. Again, the distance the text is raised depends on the user agent.

Note that the values `sub` and `super` do *not* change the element's font size, so subscripted or superscripted text will not become smaller (or larger). Instead, any text in the sub- or superscripted element should be, by default, the same size as text in the parent element, as illustrated by Figure 6-12:

```
span.raise {vertical-align: super;}
span.lower {vertical-align: sub;}

<p>This paragraph contains <span class="raise">superscripted</span>
and <span class="lower">subscripted</span> text.</P>
```

This paragraph contains superscripted and subscripted text.

Figure 6-12. Superscript and subscript alignment

 If you wish to make super- or subscripted text smaller than the text of its parent element, you can do so using the property `font-size`, which is covered in Chapter 5.

Bottom feeding

vertical-align: bottom aligns the bottom of the element's inline box with the bottom of the line box. For example, the following markup results in Figure 6-13:

```
.feeder {vertical-align: bottom;}

<p>This paragraph, as you can see quite clearly, contains
a <img src="tall.gif" alt="tall" class="feeder" /> image and
a <img src="short.gif" alt="short" class="feeder" /> image,
and then some text that is not tall.</p>
```

This paragraph, as you can see quite clearly,
contains a image and a image, and then
some text that is not tall.

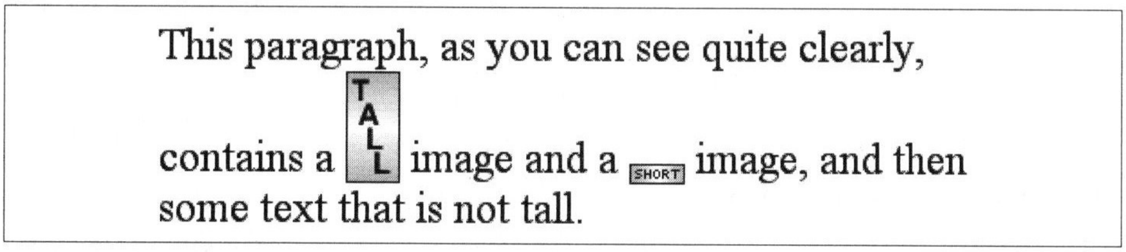

Figure 6-13. Bottom alignment

The second line of the paragraph in Figure 6-13 contains two inline elements, whose bottom edges are aligned with each other. They're also below the baseline of the text.

vertical-align: text-bottom refers to the bottom of the text in the line. For the purposes of this value, replaced elements, or any other kinds of non-text elements, are ignored. Instead, a "default" text box is considered. This default box is derived from the font-size of the parent element. The bottom of the aligned element's inline box is then aligned with the bottom of the default text box. Thus, given the following markup, you get a result like the one shown in Figure 6-14:

```
img.tbot {vertical-align: text-bottom;}

<p>Here: a <img src="tall.gif" style="vertical-align: middle;" alt="tall" />
image, and then a <img src="short.gif" class="tbot" alt="short" /> image.</p>
```

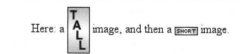

Figure 6-14. Text-bottom alignment

Getting on top

Employing vertical-align: top has the opposite effect of bottom. Likewise, vertical-align: text-top is the reverse of text-bottom. Figure 6-15 shows how the following markup would be rendered:

```
.up {vertical-align: top;}
.textup {vertical-align: text-top;}
```

```
<p>Here: a <img src="tall.gif" alt="tall image"> tall image, and then
<span class="up">some text</span> that's been vertically aligned.</p>
<p>Here: a <img src="tall.gif" class="textup" alt="tall"> image that's been
vertically aligned, and then a <img src="short.gif" class="textup" alt="short" />
image that's similarly aligned.</p>
```

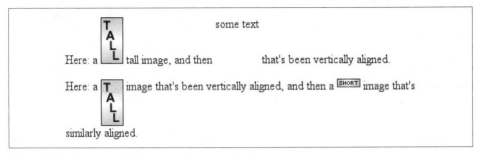

Figure 6-15. Aligning with the top and text-top of a line

Of course, the exact position of this alignment will depend on which elements are in the line, how tall they are, and the size of the parent element's font.

In the middle

There's the value middle, which is usually (but not always) applied to images. It does not have the exact effect you might assume given its name. middle aligns the middle of an inline element's box with a point that is 0.5ex above the baseline of the parent element, where 1ex is defined relative to the font-size for the parent element. Figure 6-16 shows this in more detail.

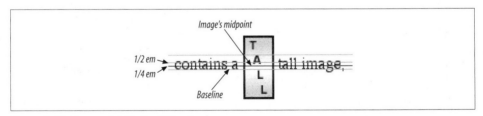

Figure 6-16. Precise detail of middle alignment

Since most user agents treat 1ex as one-half em, middle usually aligns the vertical midpoint of an element with a point one-quarter em above the parent's baseline. Don't rely on this happening, however, since some user agents actually calculate the exact x-height for each element. (See Chapter 5 for more details on x-height.)

Percentages

Percentages don't let you simulate align="middle" for images. Instead, setting a percentage value for vertical-align raises or lowers the baseline of the element (or the bottom edge of a replaced element) by the amount declared, with respect to the parent's baseline. (The percentage you specify is calculated as a percentage of line-height for the element, *not* its parent.) Positive percentage values raise the element, and negative values lower it. Depending on how the text is raised or lowered, it can appear to be placed in adjacent lines, as shown in Figure 6-17, so take care when using percentage values:

```
sub {vertical-align: -100%;}
sup {vertical-align: 100%;}

<p>We can either <sup>soar to new heights</sup> or, instead,
<sub>sink into despair...</sub></p>
```

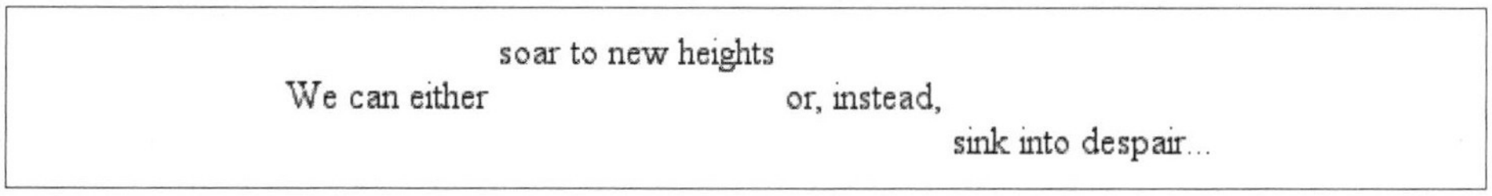

Figure 6-17. Percentages and fun effects

Let's consider percentage values in more detail. Assume the following:

```
<div style="font-size: 14px; line-height: 18px;">
I felt that, if nothing else, I deserved a
<span style="vertical-align: 50%;">raise</span> for my efforts.
</div>
```

The 50%-aligned span element has its baseline raised nine pixels, which is half of the element's inherited line-height value of 18px, *not* seven pixels.

Length alignment

Finally, let's consider vertical alignment with a specific length. vertical-align is very straightforward: it shifts an element up or down by the declared distance. Thus, vertical-align: 5px; will shift an element upward five pixels from its unaligned placement. Negative length values shift the element downward. This simple form of alignment did not exist in CSS1, but it was added in CSS2.

It's important to realize that vertically aligned text does not become part of another line, nor does it overlap text in other lines. Consider Figure 6-18, in which some vertically aligned text appears in the middle of a paragraph.

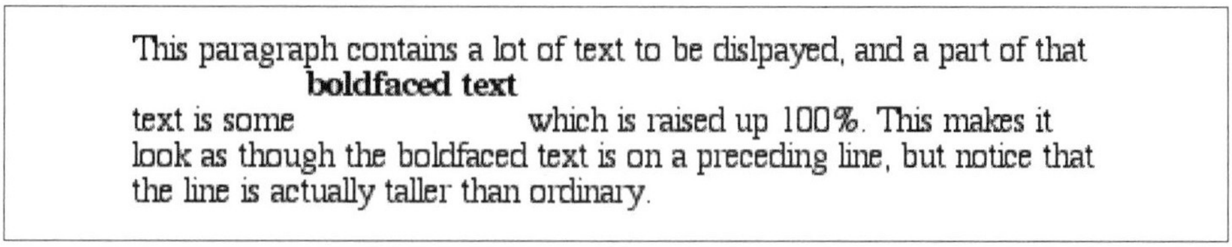

Figure 6-18. Vertical alignments can cause lines to get taller

As you can see, any vertically aligned element can affect the height of the line. Recall the description of a line box, which is exactly as tall as necessary to enclose the top of the tallest inline box and the bottom of the lowest inline box. This includes inline boxes that have been shifted up or down by vertical alignment.

Word Spacing and Letter Spacing

Now that we've dealt with alignment, let's look at manipulating word and letter spacing. As usual, these properties have some nonintuitive issues.

Word Spacing

The word-spacing property accepts a positive or negative length. This length is *added* to the standard space between words. In effect, word-spacing is used to *modify* inter-word spacing. Therefore, the default value of normal is the same as setting a value of zero (0).

<table>
<tr><td colspan="2" align="center">**word-spacing**</td></tr>
<tr><td>Values:</td><td><length> | normal | inherit</td></tr>
<tr><td>Initial value:</td><td>normal</td></tr>
<tr><td>Applies to:</td><td>All elements</td></tr>
<tr><td>Inherited:</td><td>Yes</td></tr>
<tr><td>Computed value:</td><td>For normal, the absolute length 0; otherwise, the absolute length</td></tr>
</table>

If you supply a positive length value, then the space between words will increase. Setting a negative value for word-spacing brings words closer together:

```
p.spread {word-spacing: 0.5em;}
p.tight {word-spacing: -0.5em;}
p.base {word-spacing: normal;}
p.norm {word-spacing: 0;}

<p class="spread">The spaces between words in this paragraph will be increased
  by 0.5em.</p>
<p class="tight">The spaces between words in this paragraph will be decreased
  by 0.5em.</p>
<p class="base">The spaces between words in this paragraph will be normal.</p>
<p class="norm">The spaces between words in this paragraph will be normal.</p>
```

Manipulating these settings has the effect shown in Figure 6-19.

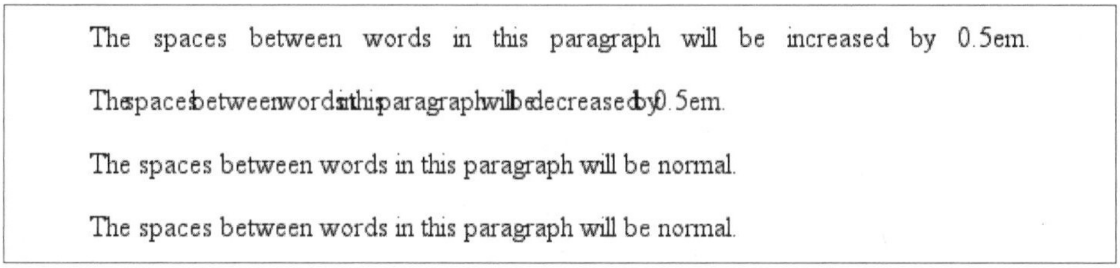

The spaces between words in this paragraph will be increased by 0.5em.

Thespacebetweenwordsinthisparagraphwilbedecreasedby0.5em.

The spaces between words in this paragraph will be normal.

The spaces between words in this paragraph will be normal.

Figure 6-19. Changing the space between words

So far, I haven't actually given you a precise definition of "word." In the simplest CSS terms, a "word" is any string of nonwhitespace characters that is surrounded by whitespace of some kind. This definition has no real semantic meaning; it simply assumes that a document contains words surrounded by one or more whitespace characters. A CSS-aware user agent cannot be expected to decide what is a valid word in a given language and what isn't. This definition, such as it is, means word-spacing is unlikely to work in any languages that employ pictographs, or non-Roman writing styles. The property allows you to create very unreadable documents, as Figure 6-20 makes clear. Use word-spacing with care.

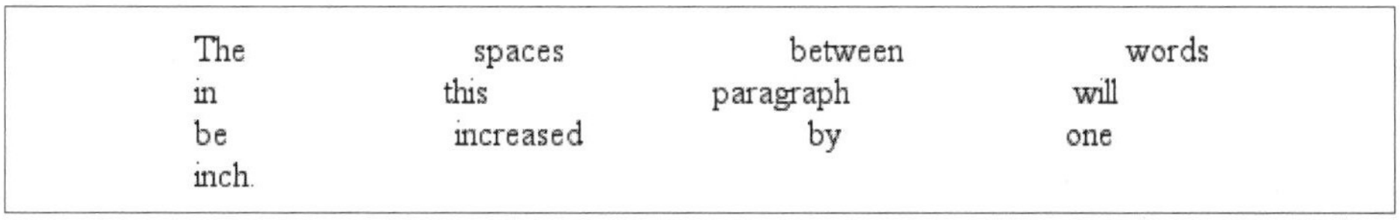

The	spaces	between	words
in	this	paragraph	will
be	increased	by	one
inch.			

Figure 6-20. Really wide word spacing

Letter Spacing

Many of the issues you encounter with word-spacing also occur with letter-spacing. The only real difference between the two is that letter-spacing modifies the space between characters, or letters.

letter-spacing

Values:	<length> | normal | inherit
Initial value:	normal
Applies to:	All elements
Inherited:	Yes
Computed value:	For length values, the absolute length; otherwise, normal

As with the word-spacing property, the permitted values of letter-spacing include any length. The default keyword is normal (making it the same as letter-spacing: 0). Any length value you enter will increase or decrease the space between letters by that amount. Figure 6-21 shows the results of the following markup:

```
p {letter-spacing: 0;}    /* identical to 'normal' */
p.spacious {letter-spacing: 0.25em;}
p.tight {letter-spacing: -0.25em;}

<p>The letters in this paragraph are spaced as normal.</p>
<p class="spacious">The letters in this paragraph are spread out a bit.</p>
<p class="tight">The letters in this paragraph are a bit smashed together.</p>
```

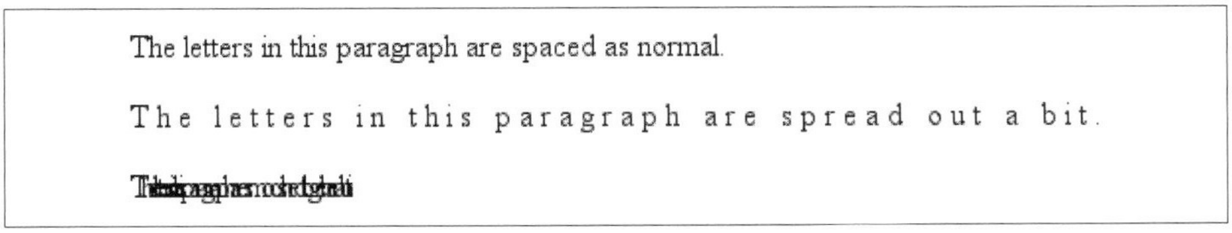

The letters in this paragraph are spaced as normal.

The letters in this paragraph are spread out a bit.

Thisiparagraphmodetightah

Figure 6-21. Various kinds of letter spacing

Using letter-spacing to increase emphasis is a time-honored technique. You might write the following declaration and get an effect like the one shown in Figure 6-22:

```
strong {letter-spacing: 0.2em;}

<p>This paragraph contains <strong>strongly emphasized text</strong>
that is spread out for extra emphasis.</p>
```

This paragraph contains **s t r o n g l y e m p h a s i z e d t e x t** that is spread out for extra emphasis.

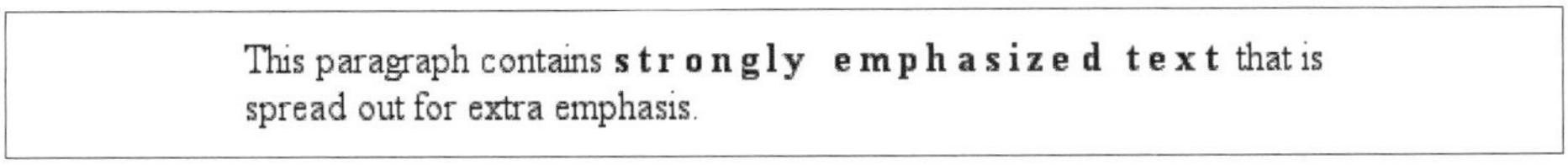

Figure 6-22. Using letter-spacing to increase emphasis

Spacing and Alignment

The value of word-spacing may be influenced by the value of the property text-align. If an element is justified, the spaces between letters and words may be altered to fit the text along the full width of the line. This may in turn alter the spacing declared by the author with word-spacing. If a length value is assigned to letter-spacing, then it cannot be changed by text-align, but if the value of letter-spacing is normal, then inter-character spacing may be changed in order to justify the text. CSS does not specify how the spacing should be calculated, so user agents simply fill it in.

As usual, the child of an element inherits the computed value of that element. You cannot define a scaling factor for word-spacing or letter-spacing to be inherited in place of the computed value (as is the case with line-height). As a result, you may run into problems such as those shown in Figure 6-23:

```
p {letter-spacing: 0.25em; font-size: 20px;}
small {font-size: 50%;}

<p>This spacious paragraph features <small>tiny text that is just
as spacious</small>, even though the author probably wanted the
spacing to be in proportion to the size of the text.</p>
```

This spacious paragraph features tiny text that is just as spacious, even though the author probably wanted the spacing to be in proportion to the size of the text.

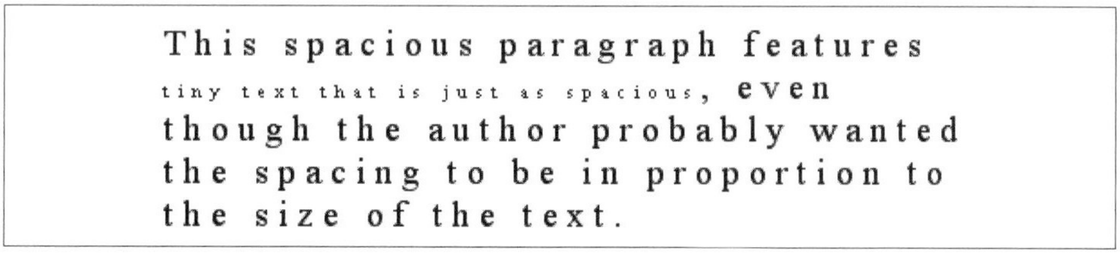

Figure 6-23. Inherited letter spacing

The only way to achieve letter spacing that's in proportion to the size of the text is to set it explicitly, as follows:

```
p {letter-spacing: 0.25em;}
small {font-size: 50%; letter-spacing: 0.25em;}
```

Text Transformation

Now let's look at ways to manipulate the capitalization of text using the property text-transform.

text-transform

Values:	uppercase | lowercase | capitalize | none | inherit
Initial value:	none
Applies to:	All elements
Inherited:	Yes
Computed value:	As specified

The default value none leaves the text alone and uses whatever capitalization exists in the source document. As their names imply, uppercase and lowercase convert text into all upper- or lowercase characters. Finally, capitalize capitalizes only the first letter of each word. Figure 6-24 illustrates each of these settings in a variety of ways:

```
h1 {text-transform: capitalize;}
strong {text-transform: uppercase;}
p.cummings {text-transform: lowercase;}
p.raw {text-transform: none;}

<h1>The heading-one at the beginninG</h1>
<p>
```

```
By default, text is displayed in the capitalization it has in the source
document, but <strong>it is possible to change this</strong> using
the property 'text-transform'.
</p>
<p class="cummings">
For example, one could Create TEXT such as might have been Written by
the late Poet e.e.cummings.
</p>
<p class="raw">
If you feel the need to Explicitly Declare the transformation of text
to be 'none', that can be done as well.
</p>
```

The Heading-one At The BeginninG

By default, text is displayed in the capitalization it has in the source document, but **IT
IS POSSIBLE TO CHANGE THIS** using the property 'text-transform'.

for example, one could create text such as might have been written by the late poet
e.e.cummings.

If you feel the need to Explicitly Declare the transformation of text to be 'none', that
can be done as well.

Figure 6-24. Various kinds of text transformation

Different user agents may have different ways of deciding where words begin and, as
a result, which letters are capitalized. For example, the text "heading-one" in the h1
element, shown in Figure 6-24, could be rendered in one of two ways: "Heading-
one" or "Heading-One." CSS does not say which is correct, so either is possible.

You probably also noticed that the last letter in the h1 element in Figure 6-24 is still
uppercase. This is correct: when applying a text-transform of capitalize, CSS only
requires user agents to make sure the first letter of each word is capitalized. They can
ignore the rest of the word.

As a property, text-transform may seem minor, but it's very useful if you suddenly
decide to capitalize all your h1 elements. Instead of individually changing the content
of all your h1 elements, you can just use text-transform to make the change for you:

```
h1 {text-transform: uppercase;}

<h1>This is an H1 element</h1>
```

The advantages of using text-transform are twofold. First, you only need to write a
single rule to make this change, rather than changing the h1 itself. Second, if you
decide later to switch from all capitals back to initial capitals, the change is even easier, as Figure 6-25 shows:

```
h1 {text-transform: capitalize;}

<h1>This is an H1 element</h1>
```

This Is An H1 Element

Figure 6-25. Transforming an H1 element

Text Decoration

Next we come to text-decoration, which is a fascinating property that offers a whole truckload of interesting behaviors.

<table>
<tr><td colspan="2" align="center">text-decoration</td></tr>
<tr><td>Values:</td><td>none | [underline || overline || line-through || blink] | inherit</td></tr>
<tr><td>Initial value:</td><td>none</td></tr>
<tr><td>Applies to:</td><td>All elements</td></tr>
<tr><td>Inherited:</td><td>No</td></tr>
<tr><td>Computed value:</td><td>As specified</td></tr>
</table>

As you might expect, underline causes an element to be underlined, just like the U element in HTML. overline causes the opposite effect—drawing a line across the top of the text. The value line-through draws a line straight through the middle of the text, which is also known as *strikethrough text* and is equivalent to the S and strike elements in HTML. blink causes the text to blink on and off, just like the much-maligned blink tag supported by Netscape. Figure 6-26 shows examples of each of these values:

```
p.emph {text-decoration: underline;}
p.topper {text-decoration: overline;}
p.old {text-decoration: line-through;}
p.annoy {text-decoration: blink;}
p.plain {text-decoration: none;}
```

 It's impossible to show the effect of blink in print, of course, but it's easy enough to imagine (perhaps all too easy). Incidentally, user agents are not required to support blink, and as of this writing, Internet Explorer never has.

The value none turns off any decoration that might otherwise have been applied to an element. Usually, undecorated text is the default appearance, but not always. For example, links are usually underlined by default. If you want to suppress the underlining of hyperlinks, you can use the following CSS rule to do so:

```
a {text-decoration: none;}
```

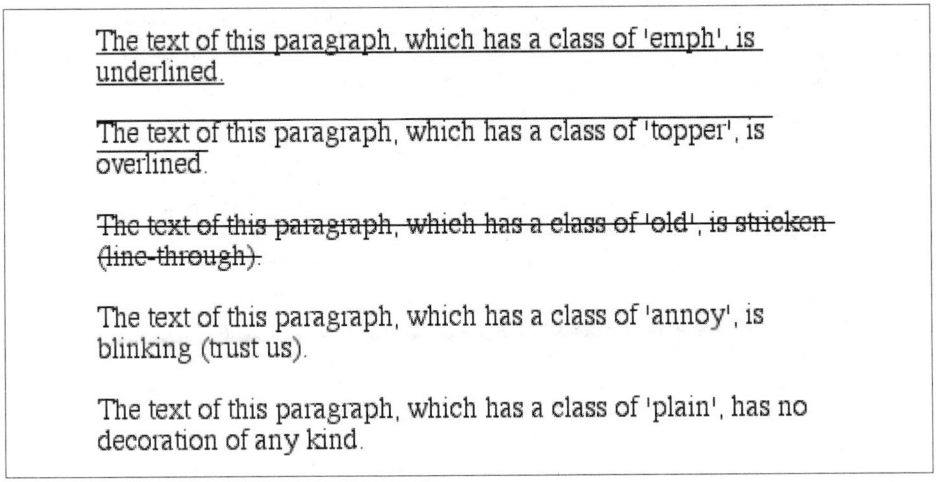

The text of this paragraph, which has a class of 'emph', is underlined.

The text of this paragraph, which has a class of 'topper', is overlined.

~~The text of this paragraph, which has a class of 'old', is stricken (line-through).~~

The text of this paragraph, which has a class of 'annoy', is blinking (trust us).

The text of this paragraph, which has a class of 'plain', has no decoration of any kind.

Figure 6-26. Various kinds of text decoration

If you explicitly turn off link underlining with this sort of rule, the only visual difference between the anchors and normal text will be their color (at least by default, though there's no ironclad guarantee that there will be a difference in their colors).

 Although I personally don't have a problem with it, many users are annoyed when they realize you've turned off link underlining. It's a matter of opinion, so let your own tastes be your guide, but remember: if your link colors aren't sufficiently different from normal text, users may have a hard time finding hyperlinks in your documents.

You can also combine decorations in a single rule. If you want all hyperlinks to be both underlined and overlined, the rule is:

```
a:link, a:visited {text-decoration: underline overline;}
```

Be careful, though: if you have two different decorations matched to the same element, the value of the rule that wins out will completely replace the value of the loser. Consider:

```
h2.stricken {text-decoration: line-through;}
h2 {text-decoration: underline overline;}
```

Given these rules, any h2 element with a class of stricken will have only a line-through decoration. The underline and overline decorations are lost, since shorthand values replace one another instead of accumulating.

Weird Decorations

Now, let's look into the unusual side of text-decoration. The first oddity is that text-decoration is *not* inherited. No inheritance implies that any decoration lines drawn with the text—under, over, or through it—will be the same color as the parent element. This is true even if the descendant elements are a different color, as depicted in Figure 6-27:

```
p {text-decoration: underline; color: black;}
strong {color: gray;}

<p>This paragraph, which is black and has a black underline, also contains
<strong>strongly emphasized text</strong> which has the black underline
beneath it as well.</p>
```

This paragraph, which is black and has a black underline, also contains strongly emphasized text which has the black underline beneath it as well.

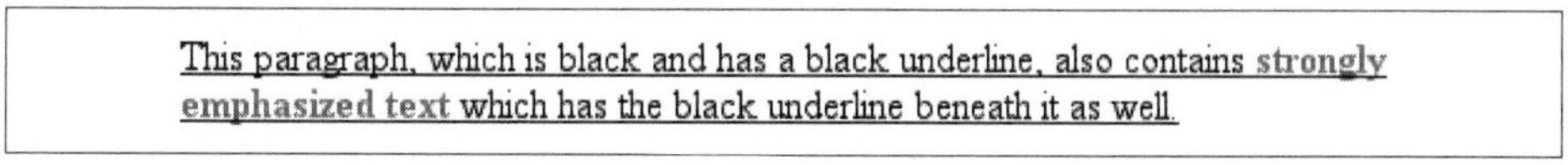

Figure 6-27. Color consistency in underlines

Why is this so? Because the value of text-decoration is not inherited, the strong element assumes a default value of none. Therefore, the strong element has *no* underline. Now, there is very clearly a line under the strong element, so it seems silly to say that it has none. Nevertheless, it doesn't. What you see under the strong element is the paragraph's underline, which is effectively "spanning" the strong element. You can see it more clearly if you alter the styles for the boldface element, like this:

```
p {text-decoration: underline; color: black;}
strong {color: gray; text-decoration: none;}

<p>This paragraph, which is black and has a black underline, also contains
<strong>strongly emphasized text</strong> which has the black underline beneath it as
well.</p>
```

The result is identical to the one shown in Figure 6-27, since all you've done is to explicitly declare what was already the case. In other words, there is no way to turn off underlining (or overlining or a line-through) generated by a parent element.

When text-decoration is combined with vertical-align, even stranger things can happen. Figure 6-28 shows one of these oddities. Since the sup element has no decoration of its own, but it is elevated within an overlined element, the overline cuts through the middle of the sup element:

```
p {text-decoration: overline; font-size: 12pt;}
sup {vertical-align: 50%; font-size: 12pt;}
```

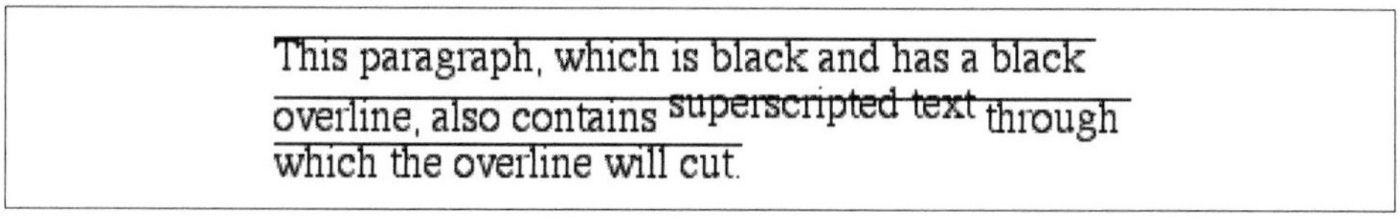

This paragraph, which is black and has a black overline, also contains superscripted text through which the overline will cut.

Figure 6-28. Correct, although strange, decorative behavior

By now you may be vowing never to use text decorations because of all the problems they could create. In fact, I've given you the simplest possible outcomes since we've explored only the way things *should* work according to the specification. In reality, some web browsers do turn off underlining in child elements, even though they aren't supposed to. The reason browsers violate the specification is simple enough: author expectations. Consider this markup:

```
p {text-decoration: underline; color: black;}
strong {color: silver; text-decoration: none;}

<p>This paragraph, which is black and has a black underline, also contains
<strong>boldfaced text</strong> which does not have black underline
beneath it.</p>
```

Figure 6-29 shows the display in a web browser that has switched off the underlining for the strong element.

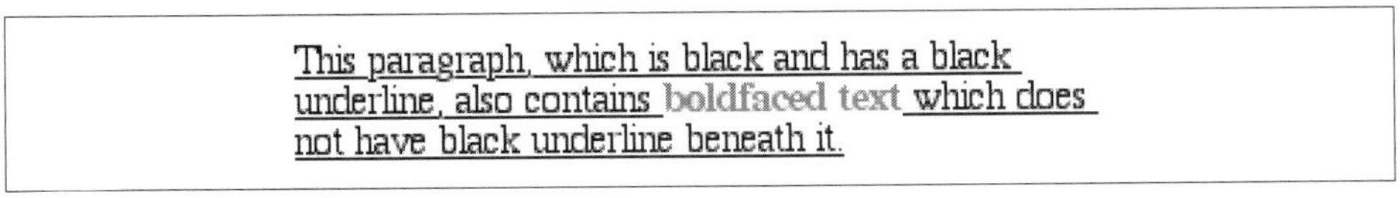

This paragraph, which is black and has a black underline, also contains boldfaced text which does not have black underline beneath it.

Figure 6-29. How some browsers really behave

The caveat here is that many browsers *do* follow the specification, and future versions of existing browsers (or any other user agents) might one day follow the specification precisely. If you depend on using none to suppress decorations, it's important to realize that it may come back to haunt you in the future, or even cause you problems in the present. Then again, future versions of CSS may include the means to turn off decorations without using none incorrectly, so maybe there's hope.

There is a way to change the color of a decoration without violating the specification. As you'll recall, setting a text decoration on an element means that the entire element has the same color decoration, even if there are child elements of different colors. To match the decoration color with an element, you must explicitly declare its decoration, as follows:

```
p {text-decoration: underline; color: black;}
strong {color: silver; text-decoration: underline;}

<p>This paragraph, which is black and has a black underline, also contains
<strong>strongly emphasized text</strong> which has the black underline
beneath it as well, but whose gray underline overlays the black underline
of its parent.</p>
```

In Figure 6-30, the strong element is set to be gray and to have an underline. The gray underline visually "overwrites" the parent's black underline, so the decoration's color matches the color of the strong element.

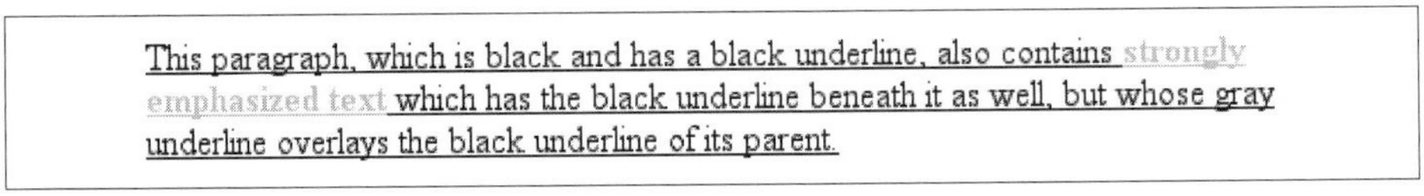

This paragraph, which is black and has a black underline, also contains strongly emphasized text which has the black underline beneath it as well, but whose gray underline overlays the black underline of its parent.

Figure 6-30. Overcoming the default behavior of underlines

Text Shadows

CSS2 includes a property for adding drop shadows to text, but this property did not make it into CSS2.1 because no browser had implemented full support for it by the time CSS2.1 was completed. When you consider the effort necessary to make a web browser determine the outlines of text in an element and then compute one or more shadows—all of which would have to blend together without overlapping the text itself—the lack of drop shadows in the specification is perhaps understandable.

---

text-shadow

Values:	none | [<color> || <length> <length> <length>? ,]* [<color> || <length> <length> <length>?] | inherit
Initial value:	none
Applies to:	All elements
Inherited:	No

The obvious default is to not have a drop shadow for text. Otherwise, it's theoretically possible to define one or more shadows. Each shadow is defined by a color and three length values. The color sets the shadow's color, of course, so it's possible to define green, purple, or even white shadows.

The first two length values determine the offset distance of the shadow from the text, and the optional third length value defines the "blur radius" for the shadow. To define a green shadow offset five pixels to the right and half an em down from the text, with no blurring, you would write:

```
text-shadow: green 5px 0.5em;
```

Negative lengths cause the shadow to be offset to the left and upward from the original text.

The blur radius is defined as the distance from the shadow's outline to the edge of the blurring effect. A radius of two pixels would result in blurring that fills the space between the shadow's outline and the edge of the blurring. The exact blurring method is not defined, so different user agents might employ different effects. As an example, the following styles might be rendered something like Figure 6-31:

```
p.cl1 {color: black; text-shadow: silver 2px 2px 2px;}
p.cl2 {color: white; text-shadow: 0 0 4px black;}
p.cl3 {color: black; text-shadow: 1em 1em 5px gray, -1em -1em silver;}
```

> Keep your eye on the shadows. They move when you aren't watching.
>
> I run between the shadows — some are phantoms, some are real.
>
> Slipping through the dark streets and the echoes and the shadows...
> Slipping through the dark streets and the echoes and the shadows...
> Slipping through the dark streets and the echoes and the shadows...

Figure 6-31. Dropping shadows all over

 Figure 6-31 was produced using Photoshop, since web browsers do not support `text-shadow` as of this writing.

Handling Whitespace

Now that we've covered a variety of ways to style the text, let's talk about the property `white-space`, which affects the user agent's handling of space, newline, and tab characters within the document source.

---

white-space

Values:	`normal` | `nowrap` | `pre` | `pre-wrap` | `pre-line` | `inherit`
Initial value:	`normal`
Applies to:	All elements (CSS2.1); block-level elements (CSS1 and CSS2)
Inherited:	No
Computed value:	As specified

Using this property, you can affect how a browser treats the whitespace between words and lines of text. To a certain extent, default XHTML handling already does this: it collapses any whitespace down to a single space. So given the following markup, the rendering in a web browser would show only one space between each word and ignore the linefeed in the elements.

```
<p>This    paragraph   has      many
    spaces         in it.</p>
```

You can explicitly set this default behavior with the following declaration:

```
p {white-space: normal;}
```

This rule tells the browser to do as browsers have always done: discard extra whitespace. Given this value, linefeed characters (carriage returns) are converted into spaces, and any sequence of more than one space in a row is converted to a single space.

Should you set white-space to pre, however, the whitespace in an affected element is treated as though the elements were XHTML pre elements; whitespace is *not* ignored, as shown in Figure 6-32:

```
p {white-space: pre;}

<p>This    paragraph   has     many
      spaces          in it.</p>
```

This   paragraph has   many
         spaces   in it.

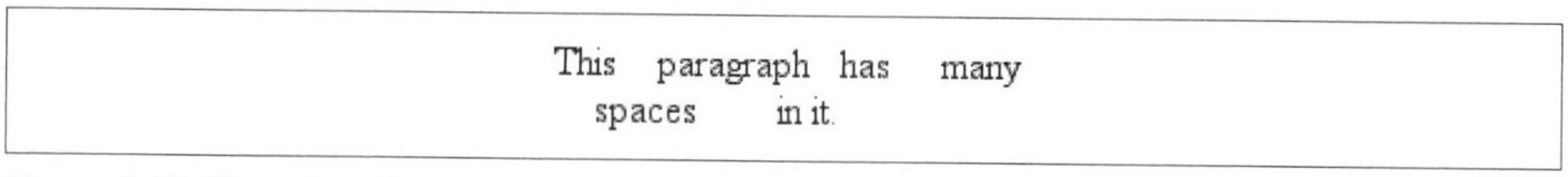

Figure 6-32. Honoring the spaces in markup

With a white-space value of pre, the browser will pay attention to extra spaces and even carriage returns. In this respect, and in this respect alone, any element can be made to act like a pre element.

The opposite value is nowrap, which prevents text from wrapping within an element, except wherever you use a br element. Using nowrap in CSS is much like setting a table cell not to wrap in HTML 4 with <td nowrap>, except the white-space value can be applied to any element. The effects of the following markup are shown in Figure 6-33:

```
<p style="white-space: nowrap;">This paragraph is not allowed to wrap,
which means that the only way to end a line is to insert a line-break
element.  If no such element is inserted, then the line will go forever,
forcing the user to scroll horizontally to read whatever can't be
initially displayed <br/>in the browser window.</p>
```

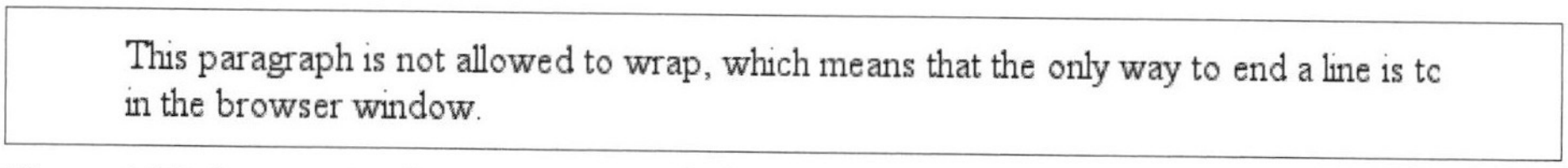

This paragraph is not allowed to wrap, which means that the only way to end a line is to
in the browser window.

Figure 6-33. Suppressing line wrapping with the white-space property

You can actually use white-space to replace the nowrap attribute on table cells:

```
td {white-space: nowrap;}

<table><tr>
<td>The contents of this cell are not wrapped.</td>
<td>Neither are the contents of this cell.</td>
<td>Nor this one, or any after it, or any other cell in this table.</td>
<td>CSS prevents any wrapping from happening.</td>
</tr></table>
```

CSS2.1 introduced the values pre-wrap and pre-line, which were absent in earlier versions of CSS. The effect of these values is to allow authors to better control whitespace handling.

If an element is set to pre-wrap, then text within that element has whitespace sequences preserved, but text lines are wrapped normally. With this value, line-breaks in the source and those that are generated are also honored. pre-line is the opposite of pre-wrap and causes whitespace sequences to collapse as in normal text but honors new lines. For example, consider the following markup, which is illustrated in Figure 6-34:

```
<p style="white-space: pre-wrap;">
This paragraph     has a great    many    s p a c e s    within  its textual
   content,  but their    preservation    will    not    prevent   line
      wrapping or line breaking.
</p>
<p style="white-space: pre-line;">
This paragraph     has a great    many    s p a c e s    within  its textual
   content,  but their collapse  will    not    prevent   line
      wrapping or line breaking.
</p>
```

This paragraph   has a great many   s p a c e s within its textual
content, but their   preservation   will   not   prevent   line
wrapping or line breaking.

This paragraph has a great many s p a c e s within its textual
content, but their collapse will not prevent line
wrapping or line breaking.

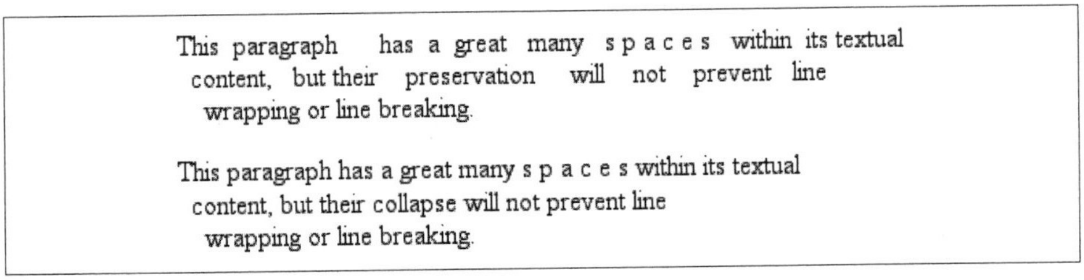

Figure 6-34. Two different ways to handle whitespace

Table 6-1 summarizes the behaviors of white-space properties.

Table 6-1. white-space properties

Value	Whitespace	Linefeeds	Auto line wrapping
pre-line	Collapsed	Honored	Allowed
normal	Collapsed	Ignored	Allowed
nowrap	Collapsed	Ignored	Prevented
pre	Preserved	Honored	Prevented
pre-wrap	Preserved	Honored	Allowed

Text Direction

If you're reading this book in English or any number of other languages, then you're reading the text left to right and top to bottom, which is the flow direction of English. Not every language runs this way, though. There are many right-to-left languages such as Hebrew and Arabic, and CSS2 introduced a property to describe their directionality.

direction

Values:	`ltr` | `rtl` | `inherit`
Initial value:	`ltr`
Applies to:	All elements
Inherited:	Yes
Computed value:	As specified

The `direction` property affects the writing direction of text in a block-level element, the direction of table column layout, the direction in which content horizontally overflows its element box, and the position of the last line of a fully justified element. For inline elements, direction applies only if the property `unicode-bidi` is set to either `embed` or `bidi-override`. (See below for a description of `unicode-bidi`.)

 Before CSS3, CSS included no provisions in the specification for top-to-bottom languages. As of this writing, the CSS3 Text Module is a Candidate Recommendation, and it addresses this point with a new property called `writing-mode`.

Although `ltr` is the default, it is expected that if a browser is displaying right-to-left text, the value will be changed to `rtl`. Thus, a browser might carry an internal rule stating something like the following:

```
*:lang(ar), *:lang(he) {direction: rtl;}
```

The real rule would be longer and encompass all right-to-left languages, not just Arabic and Hebrew, but it illustrates the point. While CSS attempts to address writing direction, Unicode has a much more robust method for handling directionality. With the property `unicode-bidi`, CSS authors can take advantage of some of Unicode's capabilities.

unicode-bidi

Values:	`normal` | `embed` | `bidi-override` | `inherit`
Initial value:	`normal`
Applies to:	All elements
Inherited:	No
Computed value:	As specified

Here we'll simply quote the value descriptions from the CSS2.1 specification, which do a good job of capturing the essence of each value:

normal

>The element does not open an additional level of embedding with respect to the bidirectional algorithm. For inline-level elements, implicit reordering works across element boundaries.

embed

>If the element is inline-level, this value opens an additional level of embedding with respect to the bidirectional algorithm. The direction of this embedding level is given by the direction property. Inside the element, reordering is done implicitly. This corresponds to adding an LRE (U+202A; for direction: ltr) or an RLE (U+202B; for direction: rtl) at the start of the element and a PDF (U+202C) at the end of the element.

bidi-override

>This creates an override for inline-level elements. For block-level elements, this creates an override for inline-level descendants not within another block. This means that, inside the element, reordering is strictly in sequence according to the direction property; the implicit part of the bidirectional algorithm is ignored. This corresponds to adding an LRO (U+202D; for direction: ltr) or RLO (U+202E; for direction: rtl) at the start of the element and a PDF (U+202C) at the end of the element.

Summary

Even without altering the font in use, there are many ways to change the appearance of text. There are classic effects such as underlining, of course, but CSS also enables you to draw lines over text or through it, change the amount of space between words and letters, indent the first line of a paragraph (or other block-level element), align text to the left or right, and much more. You can even alter the amount of space between lines of text, although this operation is unexpectedly complicated and covered in more detail in Chapter 7.

These behaviors are all relatively well supported, or else not supported at all. Full justification of text is a major one that is not well supported, and most user agents released during the 20th century exhibited bugs in the text decoration and vertical alignment, as well as line-height calculations. On the other hand, word and letter spacing almost always work correctly when they're supported, and text indentation has manifested only a few very small bugs. The same is true of the ability to alter capitalization, which is usually supported correctly.

At a few points in this chapter, I mentioned that the layout of lines was a more complicated process than presented. The next chapter covers details of that process and a great deal more.

CHAPTER 7

Basic Visual Formatting

In the previous chapters, we covered a great deal of practical information on how CSS handles text and fonts in a document. In this chapter, we'll look at the theoretical side of visual rendering, answering many of the questions we skipped earlier in the interest of addressing how CSS is implemented.

Why is it necessary to spend an entire chapter on the theoretical underpinnings of visual rendering in CSS? The answer is that with a model as open and powerful as that contained within CSS, no book could hope to cover every possible way of combining properties and effects. You will obviously go on to discover new ways of using CSS for your own document effects.

In the course of exploring CSS, you may encounter seemingly strange behaviors in user agents. With a thorough grasp of how the visual rendering model works in CSS, you'll be able to determine whether a behavior is a correct (though unexpected) consequence of the rendering engine CSS defines, or whether you've stumbled across a bug that needs to be reported.

Basic Boxes

CSS assumes that every element generates one or more rectangular boxes, called *element boxes*. (Future versions of the specification may allow for nonrectangular boxes, but for now everything is rectangular.) Each element box has a *content area* at its core. The content area is surrounded by optional amounts of padding, borders, and margins. These items are considered optional because they could all be set to a width of zero, effectively removing them from the element box. An example content area is shown in Figure 7-1, along with the surrounding regions of padding, border, and margins.

Each of the margins, borders, and padding can be set using various properties, such as `margin-left` or `border-bottom`. The content's background—a color or tiled image, for example—is also applied to the padding. The margins are always transparent, revealing the background of any parent elements. Padding cannot be a negative value, but margins can. We'll explore the effects of negative margins later in this chapter.

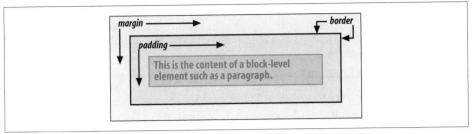

Figure 7-1. The content area and its surroundings

Borders are generated using defined styles, such as solid or inset, and their colors are set using the border-color property. If no color is set, then the border takes on the foreground color of the element's content. For example, if the text of a paragraph is white, then any borders around that paragraph will be white unless the author explicitly declares a different border color. If a border style has gaps of some type, then the element's background is visible through those gaps. In other words, the border has the same background as the content and padding. Finally, the width of a border can never be negative.

 The various components of an element box can be affected by a number of properties, such as width or border-right. Many of these properties will be used in this chapter, even though we haven't discussed them yet. The actual property definitions are given in Chapter 8, which builds on the concepts set forth in this chapter.

You will, however, find differences in how various types of elements are formatted. Block-level elements are treated differently than inline-level elements, while floated and positioned elements have their own ways of behaving.

The Containing Block

Every element is laid out with respect to its containing block; in a very real way, the containing block is the "layout context" for an element. CSS2.1 defines a series of rules for determining an element's containing block. I'll cover only those rules that pertain to the concepts covered in this chapter and leave the rest for future chapters.

For an element in the normal, Western-style flow of text, the containing block is formed by the *content edge* of the nearest block-level, table cell, or inline-block ancestor box. Consider the following markup:

```
<body>
 <div>
  <p>This is a paragraph.</p>
 </div>
</body>
```

In this very simple example, the containing block for the p element is the div element, as that is the closest ancestor element that is block-level, a table cell, or inline-block (in this case, it's a block box). Similarly, the div's containing block is the body. Thus, the layout of the p is dependent on the layout of the div, which is in turn dependent on the layout of the body.

You don't need to worry about inline elements since the way they are laid out doesn't depend directly on containing blocks. We'll talk about them later in the chapter.

A Quick Refresher

Let's quickly review the kinds of elements we'll be discussing, as well as some important terms that are needed to follow the explanations in this chapter:

Normal flow
> The left-to-right, top-to-bottom rendering of text in Western languages and the familiar text layout of traditional HTML documents. Note that the flow direction may be changed in non-Western languages. Most elements are in the normal flow, and the only way for an element to leave it is to be floated or positioned (covered in Chapter 10). Remember, the discussions in this chapter cover only elements in the normal flow.

Nonreplaced element
> An element whose content is contained within the document. For example, a paragraph is a nonreplaced element because its textual content is found within the element itself.

Replaced element
> An element that serves as a placeholder for something else. The classic example of a replaced element is the img element, which simply points to an image file that is then inserted into the document's flow at the point where the img element itself is found. Most form elements are also replaced (e.g., <input type="radio">).

Block-level element
> An element such as a paragraph, heading, or a div. These elements generate "new lines" both before and after their boxes when in the normal flow, so that block-level elements in the normal flow stack vertically. An element can be made to generate a block-level box by declaring display: block.

Inline element
> An element such as strong or span. These elements do not generate "line breaks" before or after themselves, and they are descendants of a block-level element. You can cause an element to generate an inline-level box by declaring display: inline.

Root element
> The element at the top of the document tree. In HTML documents, this is the element html. In XML documents, it can be whatever the language permits.

Block-Level Elements

Block-level elements can behave in both predictable and surprising ways. The handling of element placement along the horizontal and vertical axes can differ, for example. To fully understand how block-level elements are handled, you must clearly understand a number of boundaries and areas. They are shown in detail in Figure 7-2.

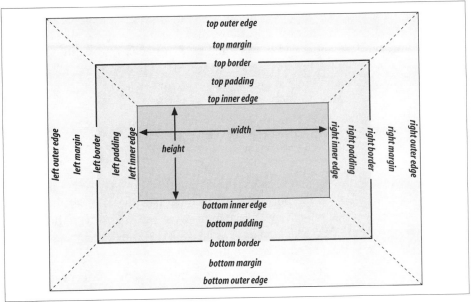

Figure 7-2. The complete box model

In general, the `width` of an element is defined as the distance from the left inner edge to the right inner edge, and the `height` is the distance from the inner top to the inner bottom. Both of these properties can be applied to an element.

The various widths, heights, padding, and margins combine to determine how a document is laid out. In most cases, the height and width of the document are automatically determined by the browser and are based on the available display region and other factors. Under CSS, of course, you can assert more direct control over the way elements are sized and displayed. You can select different effects for horizontal and vertical layouts, so we'll tackle them separately.

Horizontal Formatting

Horizontal formatting is often more complex than you'd think. Part of the complexity has to do with how `width` affects the width of the content area, *not* the entire visible element box. Consider the following example:

```
<p style="width: 200px;">wideness?</p>
```

This line of code will make the paragraph's content 200 pixels wide. If you gave the element a background, this would be quite obvious. However, any padding, borders, or margins you specify are *added* to the width value. Suppose you do this:

```
<p style="width: 200px; padding: 10px; margin: 20px;">wideness?</p>
```

The visible element box is now 220 pixels wide since you've added 10 pixels of padding to the right and left of the content. The margins will now extend another 20 pixels to both sides for an overall element box width of 260 pixels.

Understanding the hidden additions to width is critical. Most users think that width refers to the width of the visible element box, and that if they declare an element to have padding, borders, and a width, the value they supply for the width will be the distance from the outer left border edge to the outer right border edge. *This is not the case in CSS.* Keep this fact firmly in mind to avoid confusion later.

 As of this writing, the Box Model module of CSS includes proposals for ways to let authors choose whether width refers to the content width or the visible box width.

Almost as simple is the rule that says that the sum of the horizontal components of a block-level element box in the normal flow always equals the width of the parent. Take two paragraphs within a div whose margins have been set to 1em. The content width (the value of width) of the paragraph, plus its left and right padding, borders, and margins, always add up to the width of the div's content area.

Let's say the width of the div is 30em, making the sum total of the content width, padding, borders, and margins of each paragraph 30em. In Figure 7-3, the "blank" space around the paragraphs is actually their margins. If the div had any padding, there would be even more blank space, but that isn't the case here. I'll discuss padding soon.

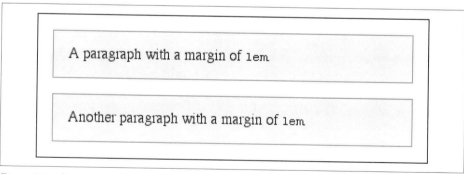

Figure 7-3. Element boxes are as wide as their parent element's width

Horizontal properties

The "seven properties" of horizontal formatting are: margin-left, border-left, padding-left, width, padding-right, border-right, and margin-right. These properties, which are diagrammed in Figure 7-4, relate to the horizontal layout of block-level boxes.

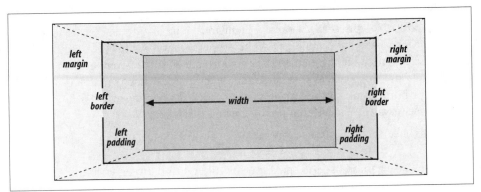

Figure 7-4. The "seven properties" of horizontal formatting

The values of these seven properties must add up to the width of the element's containing block, which is usually the value of width for a block element's parent (since block-level elements nearly always have block-level elements for parents).

Of these seven properties, only three may be set to auto: the width of the element's content and the left and right margins. The remaining properties must be set either to specific values or default to a width of zero. Figure 7-5 shows which parts of the box can take a value of auto and which cannot.

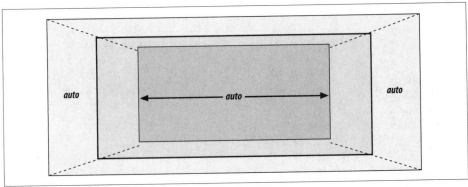

Figure 7-5. Horizontal properties that can be set to auto

width must either be set to auto or a nonnegative value of some type. When you do use auto in horizontal formatting, different effects can result.

CSS allows browsers to set a minimum value for width; this is the value below which a block-level element's width cannot drop. The value of this minimum can vary between browsers, as it is not defined in the specification.

Using auto

If you set width, margin-left, or margin-right to a value of auto, and give the remaining two properties specific values, then the property that is set to auto determines the length required to make the element box's width equal to the parent element's width. In other words, let's say the sum of the seven properties must equal 400 pixels, no padding or borders are set, the right margin and width are set to 100px, and the left margin is set to auto. The left margin will be 200 pixels wide:

```
p {margin-left: auto; margin-right: 100px;
   width: 100px;}   /* 'auto' left margin evaluates to 200px */
```

In a sense, auto can be used to make up the difference between everything else and the required total. However, what if all three of these properties are set to 100px and none of them are set to auto?

In the case where all three properties are set to something other than auto—or, in CSS terminology, when these formatting properties have been overconstrained—then margin-right is *always* forced to be auto. This means that if both margins and the width are set to 100px, then the user agent will reset the right margin to auto. The right margin's width will then be set according to the rule that one auto value "fills in" the distance needed to make the element's overall width equal that of its containing block. Figure 7-6 shows the result of the following markup:

```
p {margin-left: 100px; margin-right: 100px;
   width: 100px;}   /* right margin forced to be 200px */
```

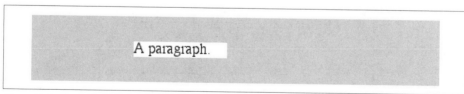

Figure 7-6. Overriding the margin-right setting

margin-right is forced to be auto only for left-to-right languages such as English. In right-to-left languages, everything is reversed, so margin-left is forced to be auto, not margin-right.

If both margins are set explicitly, and width is set to auto, then the value of width will be set to whatever value is needed to reach the required total (which is the content width of the parent element). The results of the following markup are shown in Figure 7-7:

```
p {margin-left: 100px; margin-right: 100px; width: auto;}
```

> A paragraph.

Figure 7-7. Automatic width

The case shown in Figure 7-7 is the most common since it is equivalent to setting the margins and not declaring anything for the width. The result of the following markup is exactly the same as that shown in Figure 7-7:

```
p {margin-left: 100px; margin-right: 100px;} /* same as before */
```

More than one auto

Now let's see what happens when two of the three properties (width, margin-left, or margin-right) are set to auto. If both margins are set to auto, as shown in the code below, then they are set to equal lengths, thus centering the element within its parent, as you can see in Figure 7-8:

```
p {width: 100px; margin-left: auto; margin-right: auto;}
```

> A paragraph.

Figure 7-8. Setting an explicit width

Setting both margins to equal lengths is the correct way to center elements, as opposed to using text-align. (text-align applies only to the inline content of a block-level element, so setting an element to have a text-align of center shouldn't center it.)

 In practice, only browsers released after February 1999 correctly handle auto margin centering, and not all of them get it completely right. Those that do not handle auto margins correctly behave in inconsistent ways, but the safest bet is to assume that outdated browsers will reset both margins to zero.

Another way of sizing elements is to set one of the margins and the width to auto. The margin set to auto is reduced to zero:

```
p {margin-left: auto; margin-right: 100px;
   width: auto;}  /* left margin evaluates to 0 */
```

The width is then set to the value necessary to make the element fill its containing block.

Finally, what happens when all three properties are set to auto? The answer is simple: both margins are set to zero, and the width is made as wide as possible. This result is the same as the default situation, when no values are explicitly declared for margins or the width. In such a case, the margins default to zero and the width defaults to auto.

Note that since horizontal margins do not collapse, the padding, borders, and margins of a parent element can affect its children. The effect is indirect in that the margins (and so on) of an element can induce an offset for child elements. The results of the following markup are shown in Figure 7-9:

```
div {padding: 30px; background: silver;}
p {margin: 20px; padding: 0; background: white;}
```

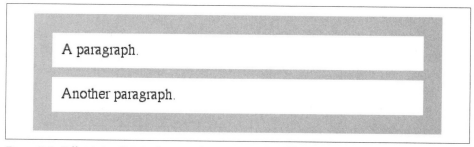

Figure 7-9. Offset is implicit in the parent's margins and padding

Negative margins

So far, this probably all seems rather straightforward, and you may be wondering why I said things could be complicated. There's another side to margins: the negative side. That's right, it's possible to set negative values for margins. Doing so results in some interesting effects, assuming that the user agent supports negative margins at all.

 According to the CSS specification, user agents are not required to fully support negative margins. It says: "Negative values for margin properties are allowed, but there may be implementation-specific limits." As of this writing, there are few, if any, such limits in current browsers.

Remember that the total of the seven horizontal properties always equals the width of the parent element. As long as all properties are zero or greater, an element can never be wider than its parent's content area. However, consider the following markup, depicted in Figure 7-10:

```
div {width: 400px; border: 3px solid black;}
p.wide {margin-left: 10px; width: auto; margin-right: -50px; }
```

Yes, indeed, the child element is wider than its parent! This is mathematically correct:

$$10px + 0 + 0 + 440px + 0 + 0 - 50px = 400px$$

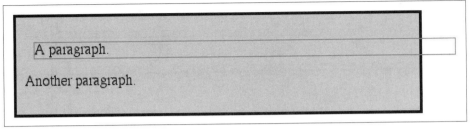

Figure 7-10. Wider children through negative margins

The 440px is the evaluation of width: auto, which is the number needed to balance out the rest of the values in the equation. Even though it leads to a child element sticking out of its parent, the specification hasn't been violated because the values of the seven properties add up to the required total. It's a semantic dodge, but it's valid behavior.

Now, let's add some borders to the mix:

```
div {width: 400px; border: 3px solid black;}
p.wide {margin-left: 10px; width: auto; margin-right: -50px;
  border: 3px solid gray;}
```

The resulting change will be a reduction in the evaluated width of width:

$$10px + 3px + 0 + 434px + 0 + 3px - 50px = 400px$$

If you were to introduce padding, then the value of width would drop even more.

Conversely, it's possible to have auto right margins evaluate to negative amounts. If the values of other properties force the right margin to be negative in order to satisfy the requirement that elements be no wider than their containing block, then that's what will happen. Consider:

```
div {width: 400px; border: 3px solid black;}
p.wide {margin-left: 10px; width: 500px; margin-right: auto;
  border: 3px solid gray;}
```

The equation will work out like this:

$$10px + 3px + 0 + 500px + 0 + 3px - 116px = 400px$$

The right margin will evaluate to -116px. Even if you'd given it another value, this would be the case because of the rule stipulating that if an element's dimensions are overconstrained, the right margin is reset to whatever is needed to make the numbers work out correctly (except in right-to-left languages, where the left margin would be overruled).

Let's consider another example, illustrated in Figure 7-11, where the left margin is set to be negative:

```
div {width: 400px; border: 3px solid black;}
p.wide {margin-left: -50px; width: auto; margin-right: 10px;
  border: 3px solid gray;}
```

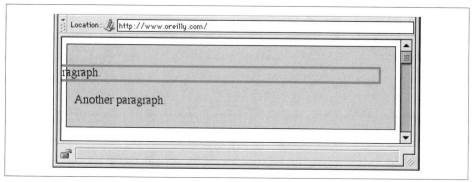

Figure 7-11. Setting a negative left margin

With a negative left margin, not only does the paragraph spill beyond the borders of the div, but it also spills beyond the edge of the browser window itself!

 Remember that padding, borders, and content widths (and heights) can never be negative. Only margins can be less than zero.

Percentages

When it comes to percentage values for the width, padding, and margins, the same basic rules apply. It doesn't really matter whether the values are declared with lengths or percentages.

Percentages can be very useful. Suppose you want an element's content to be two-thirds the width of its containing block, the right and left padding to be 5 percent each, the left margin to be 5 percent, and the right margin to take up the slack. That would be written something like:

```
<p style="width: 67%; padding-right: 5%; padding-left: 5%; margin-right: auto;
margin-left: 5%;">playing percentages</p>
```

The right margin would evaluate to 18 percent (100% − 67% − 5% − 5% − 5%) of the width of the containing block.

Mixing percentages and length units can be tricky, however. Consider the following example:

```
<p style="width: 67%; padding-right: 2em; padding-left: 2em; margin-right: auto;
margin-left: 5em;">mixed lengths</p>
```

In this case, the element's box can be defined like this:

5em + 0 + 2em + 67% + 2em + 0 + auto = containing block width

In order for the right margin's width to evaluate to zero, the element's containing block must be `27.272727em` wide (with the content area of the element being `18.272727em` wide). Any wider than that, and the right margin will evaluate to a positive value. Any narrower, and the right margin will be a negative value.

The situation gets even more complicated if you start mixing length values, like this:

```
<p style="width: 67%; padding-right: 15px; padding-left: 10px; margin-right: auto;
margin-left: 5em;">more mixed lengths</p>
```

And, to make things more complex, borders cannot have percentage widths, only lengths. The bottom line is that it's impossible to create a fully flexible element layout based solely on percentages unless you're willing to avoid using borders.

Replaced elements

So far, we've been dealing with the horizontal formatting of nonreplaced block-level elements in the normal flow of text. Replaced block-level elements are a bit simpler to manage. All of the rules for nonreplaced blocks hold true, with one exception: if width is left as auto, then the width of the element is the content's intrinsic width. The image in the following example will be 20 pixels wide because that's the width of the original image:

```
<img src="smile.png" style="display: block; width: auto; margin: 0;">
```

If the actual image were 100 pixels instead, it would be laid out as 100 pixels wide.

It's possible to override this rule by assigning a specific value to width. Suppose you modify the previous example to show the same image three times, each with a different width value:

```
<img src="smile.png" style="display: block; width: 25px; margin: 0;">
<img src="smile.png" style="display: block; width: 50px; margin: 0;">
<img src="smile.png" style="display: block; width: 100px; margin: 0;">
```

This is illustrated in Figure 7-12.

Figure 7-12. Changing replaced element widths

Note that the height of the elements also increases. When a replaced element's width is changed from its intrinsic width, the value of height is scaled to match, unless height has been set to an explicit value of its own. The reverse is also true: if height is set, but width is left as auto, then the width is scaled proportionately to the change in height.

Now that you're thinking about height, let's move on to the vertical formatting of block-level normal-flow elements.

Vertical Formatting

Like horizontal formatting, vertical formatting of block-level elements has its own set of interesting behaviors. The default height of an element is determined by its content. Height is also affected by the width of the content; the skinnier a paragraph becomes, the taller it must be to contain all of the inline content within it.

In CSS, it is possible to set an explicit height on any block-level element. If you do this, the resulting behavior depends on several other factors. Assume that the specified height is greater than that needed to display the content:

```
<p style="height: 10em;">
```

In this case, the extra height has a visual effect somewhat like extra padding. But suppose the height is *less* than what is needed to display the content:

```
<p style="height: 3em;">
```

When that happens, the browser is supposed to provide a means of viewing all content without increasing the height of the element box. The browser may add a scrollbar to the element, as shown in Figure 7-13.

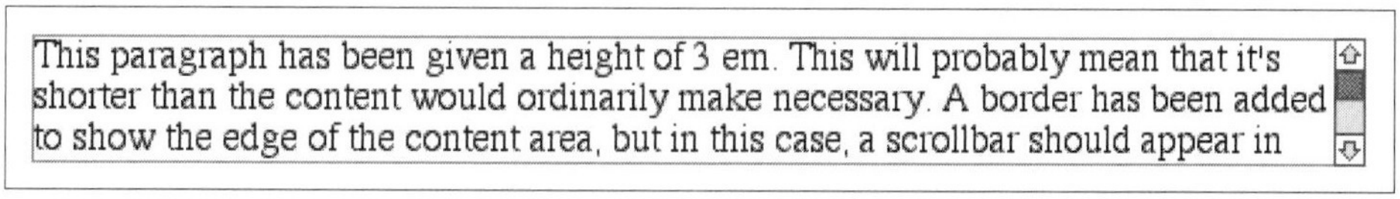

This paragraph has been given a height of 3 em. This will probably mean that it's shorter than the content would ordinarily make necessary. A border has been added to show the edge of the content area, but in this case, a scrollbar should appear in

Figure 7-13. Heights that don't match the element's content height

In a case where the content of an element is taller than the height of its box, the actual behavior of a user agent will depend on the value of (and its support for) the property overflow. This scenario is covered in Chapter 10.

Under CSS1, user agents can ignore any value of height other than auto if an element is not a replaced element (such as an image). In CSS2 and CSS2.1, the value of height cannot be ignored, except in one specific circumstance involving percentage values. We'll talk about that in a moment.

Just as with width, height defines the content area's height, not the height of the visible element box. Any padding, borders, or margins on the top or bottom of the element box are *added* to the value for height.

Vertical properties

As was the case with horizontal formatting, vertical formatting also has seven related properties: margin-top, border-top, padding-top, height, padding-bottom, border-bottom, and margin-bottom. These properties are diagrammed in Figure 7-14.

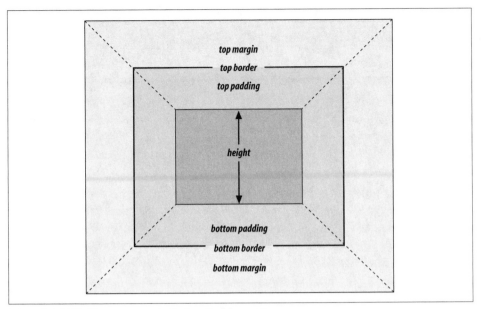

Figure 7-14. The "seven properties" of vertical formatting

The values of these seven properties must equal the height of the element's containing block. This is usually the value of `height` for a block-level element's parent (since block-level elements nearly always have block-level elements for parents).

Only three of these seven properties may be set to `auto`: the `height` of the element's content and the top and bottom margins. The top and bottom padding and borders must be set to specific values or else they default to a width of zero (assuming no `border-style` is declared). If `border-style` has been set, then the width of the borders is set to be the vaguely defined value `medium`. Figure 7-15 provides an illustration for remembering which parts of the box may have a value of `auto` and which may not.

Interestingly, if either `margin-top` or `margin-bottom` is set to `auto` for a block element in the normal flow, it automatically evaluates to 0. A value of 0 unfortunately prevents easy vertical centering of normal-flow elements in their containing blocks. It also means that if you set the top and bottom margins of an element to `auto`, they are effectively reset to 0 and removed from the element box.

 The handling of `auto` top and bottom margins is different for positioned elements. See Chapter 10 for more details.

`height` must be set to `auto` or to a nonnegative value of some type.

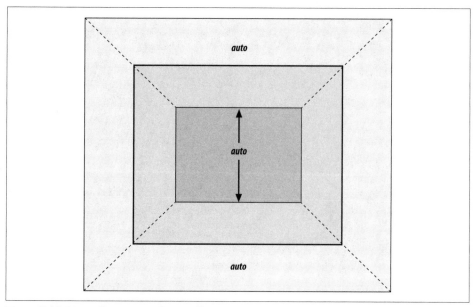

Figure 7-15. Vertical properties that can be set to auto

Percentage heights

You already saw how length-value heights are handled, so let's spend a moment on percentages. If the height of a block-level, normal-flow element is set to a percentage, then that value is taken as a percentage of the height of the containing block. Given the following markup, the resulting paragraph will be 3em tall:

```
<div style="height: 6em;">
 <p style="height: 50%;">Half as tall</p>
</div>
```

Since setting the top and bottom margins to auto will give them zero height, the only way to vertically center the element is to set them both to 25%.

However, in cases where the height of the containing block is not explicitly declared, percentage heights are reset to auto. If you changed the previous example so that the height of the div is auto, the paragraph will now be exactly as tall as the div itself:

```
<div style="height: auto;">
 <p style="height: 50%;">NOT half as tall; height reset to auto</p>
</div>
```

These two possibilities are illustrated in Figure 7-16. (The spaces between the paragraph borders and the div borders are the top and bottom margins on the paragraphs.)

Auto heights

In the simplest case, a block-level, normal-flow element with height: auto is rendered just high enough to enclose the line boxes of its inline content (including text).

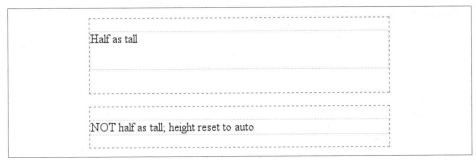

Figure 7-16. Percentage heights in different circumstances

auto height sets a border on a paragraph and assumes no padding—expect the bottom border to go just under the bottom line of text and the top border to go just above the top line of text.

If an auto-height, block-level, normal-flow element has only block-level children, then its default height will be the distance from the top of the topmost block-level child's outer border edge to the bottom of the bottommost block-level child's outer border edge. Therefore, the margins of the child elements will "stick out" of the element that contains them. (This behavior is explained in the next section.) However, if the block-level element has either top or bottom padding, or top or bottom borders, then its height will be the distance from the top of the outer top margin edge of its topmost child to the outer bottom margin edge of its bottommost child:

```
<div style="height: auto; background: silver;">
<p style="margin-top: 2em; margin-bottom: 2em;">A paragraph!</p>
</div>
<div style="height: auto; border-top: 1px solid; border-bottom: 1px solid;
background: silver;">
<p style="margin-top: 2em; margin-bottom: 2em;">Another paragraph!</p>
</div>
```

Both of these behaviors are demonstrated in Figure 7-17.

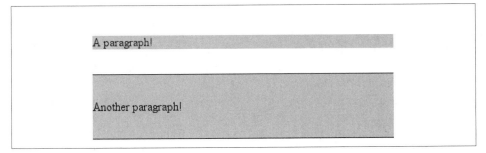

Figure 7-17. Auto heights with block-level children

If you changed the borders to padding in the previous example, the effect on the height of the div would be the same: it would still enclose the paragraph's margins within it.

Collapsing vertical margins

One other important aspect of vertical formatting is the *collapsing* of vertically adjacent margins. Collapsing behavior applies only to margins. Padding and borders, where they exist, are never collapsed by anything.

An unordered list, where list items follow one another, is a perfect example of margin collapsing. Assume that the following is declared for a list that contains five items:

```
li {margin-top: 10px; margin-bottom: 15px;}
```

Each list item has a 10-pixel top margin and a 15-pixel bottom margin. When the list is rendered, however, the distance between adjacent list items is 15 pixels, not 25. This happens because adjacent margins are collapsed along the vertical axis. In other words, the smaller of the two margins is eliminated in favor of the larger. Figure 7-18 shows the difference between collapsed and uncollapsed margins.

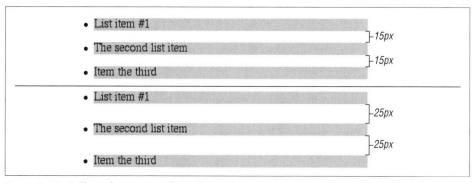

Figure 7-18. Collapsed versus uncollapsed margins

Correctly implemented user agents collapse vertically adjacent margins, as shown in the first list in Figure 7-18, where there are 15-pixel spaces between each list item. The second list shows what would happen if the user agent didn't collapse margins, resulting in 25-pixel spaces between list items.

If you don't like the word "collapse," use "overlap." Although the margins do not really overlap, you can visualize what's happening using the following analogy. Imagine that each element, (for example, a paragraph), is a small piece of paper with the content of the element written on it. Around each piece of paper is some clear plastic, which represents the margins. The first piece of paper (say an h1 piece) is laid down on a canvas. A second piece of paper (a paragraph) is laid down below it and then slid up until the edge of its plastic touches the other paper's edge. If the first piece of paper has half an inch of plastic along its bottom edge, and the second has a third of an inch along its top, then when they slide together, the first piece's plastic edge will touch the top edge of the second piece of paper. The two are now positioned on the canvas, and the plastic attached to the pieces overlaps.

Collapsing also occurs where multiple margins meet, such as at the end of a list. Adding to the earlier example, let's assume the following rules apply:

```
ul {margin-bottom: 15px;}
li {margin-top: 10px; margin-bottom: 20px;}
h1 {margin-top: 28px;}
```

The last item in the list has a bottom margin of 20 pixels, the bottom margin of the ul is 15 pixels, and the top margin of a succeeding h1 is 28 pixels. So once the margins have been collapsed, the distance between the end of the li and the beginning of the h1 is 28 pixels, as shown in Figure 7-19.

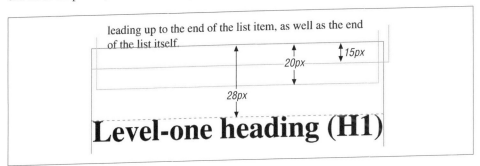

Figure 7-19. Collapsing in detail

Now, recall the examples from the previous section, where the introduction of a border or padding on a containing block caused the margins of its child elements to be contained within it. You can see this behavior by adding a border to the ul element in the previous example:

```
ul {margin-bottom: 15px; border: 1px solid;}
li {margin-top: 10px; margin-bottom: 20px;}
h1 {margin-top: 28px;}
```

With this change, the bottom margin of the li element is now placed inside its parent element (the ul). Therefore, the only margin collapsing that takes place is between the ul and the h1, as illustrated in Figure 7-20.

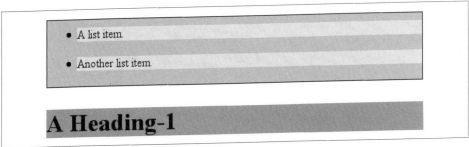

Figure 7-20. Collapsing (or not) with borders added to the mix

Negative margins

Negative margins do have an impact on vertical formatting, and they affect how margins are collapsed. If negative vertical margins are set, then the browser should take the absolute maximum of both margins. The absolute value of the negative margin is then subtracted from the positive margin. In other words, the negative is added to the positive, and the resulting value is the distance between the elements. Figure 7-21 provides two concrete examples.

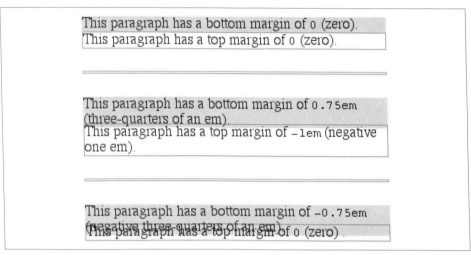

Figure 7-21. Examples of negative vertical margins

Notice the "pulling" effect of negative top and bottom margins. This is really no different from the way that negative horizontal margins cause an element to push outside of its parent. Consider:

```
p.neg {margin-top: -50px; margin-right: 10px;
   margin-left: 10px; margin-bottom: 0;
   border: 3px solid gray;}

<div style="width: 420px; background-color: silver;
   padding: 10px; margin-top: 50px; border: 1px solid;">
<p class="neg">
A paragraph.
</p>
A div.
</div>
```

As you see in Figure 7-22, the paragraph has simply been pulled upward by its negative top margin. Note that the content of the div that follows the paragraph in the markup has also been pulled upward 50 pixels.

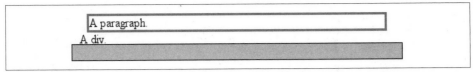

Figure 7-22. The effects of a negative top margin

The negative bottom margin makes the paragraph look like it's been pulled upward. Compare the following markup to the situation depicted in Figure 7-23:

```
p.neg {margin-bottom: -50px; margin-right: 10px;
  margin-left: 10px; margin-top: 0;
  border: 3px solid gray;}

<div style="width: 420px; margin-top: 50px;">
<p class="neg">
A paragraph.
</p>
</div>
<p>
The next paragraph.
</p>
```

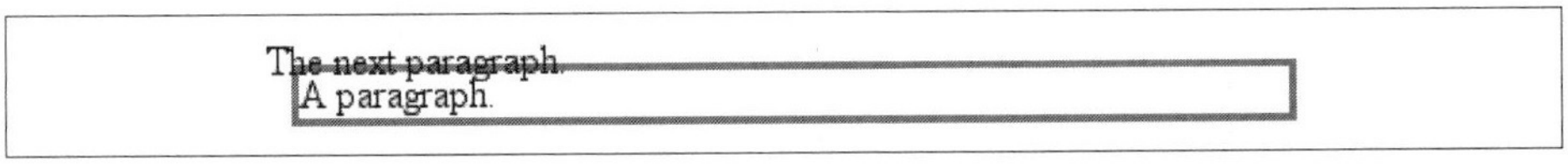

Figure 7-23. The effects of a negative bottom margin

What's really happening in Figure 7-23 is that the elements following the div are placed according to the location of the bottom of the div. As you can see, the end of the div is actually above the visual bottom of its child paragraph. The next element after the div is the appropriate distance from the bottom of the div. This is expected, given the rules you used.

Now let's consider an example where the margins of a list item, an unordered list, and a paragraph are all collapsed. In this case, the unordered list and paragraph are assigned negative margins:

```
li {margin-bottom: 20px;}
ul {margin-bottom: -15px;}
h1 {margin-top: -18px;}
```

The larger of the two negative margins (-18px) is added to the largest positive margin (20px), yielding 20px – 18px = 2px. Thus, there are only two pixels between the bottom of the list item's content and the top of the h1's content, as you can see in Figure 7-24.

One area of unresolved behavior is that if elements overlap each other due to negative margins, it's hard to tell which elements are on top. You may also have noticed

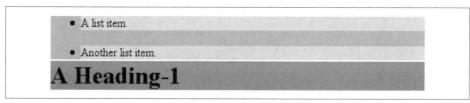

Figure 7-24. Collapsing margins and negative margins, in detail

that none of the examples in this section use background colors. If they did, their content might be overwritten by the background color of a following element. This is expected behavior since browsers usually render elements in order from beginning to end, so a normal-flow element that comes later in the document can be expected to overwrite an earlier element, assuming the two end up overlapping.

List Items

List items have a few special rules of their own. They are typically preceded by a marker, such as a small dot or a number. This marker isn't actually part of the list item's content area, so effects like those illustrated in Figure 7-25 are common.

Figure 7-25. The content of list items

CSS1 says very little about the placement and effects of these markers with regard to a document's layout. CSS2 introduced properties specifically designed to address this issue, such as `marker-offset`. However, changes in thinking and a lack of implementations caused this to be dropped from CSS2.1, and it is likely that future versions of CSS will introduce a different way of defining the distance between the content and the marker. Therefore, the placement of markers is largely beyond the control of authors (at least as of this writing).

> For a more detailed exploration of lists and how they can be styled, see Chapter 12.

The marker attached to a list item element can be either outside the content of the list item or treated as an inline marker at the beginning of the content, depending on the value of the property `list-style-position`. If the marker is brought inside, then the list item will interact with its neighbors exactly like a block-level element, as illustrated in Figure 7-26.

Figure 7-26. Markers inside and outside the list

If the marker stays outside the content, it is placed some distance from the left content edge of the content (in left-to-right languages). No matter how the list's styles are altered, the marker stays the same distance from the content edge. Occasionally, the markers may be pushed outside of the list element itself, as you can see in Figure 7-26.

Inline Elements

After block-level elements, inline elements are the most common. Setting box properties for inline elements takes us into more interesting territory than we've visited so far. Some good examples of inline elements are the em tag and the a tag, both of which are nonreplaced elements, and images, which are replaced elements.

> None of the behavior described in this section applies to table elements. CSS2 introduced new properties and behaviors for handling tables and table content, and these elements behave in ways fairly distinct from either block-level or inline formatting. Table styling is discussed in Chapter 11.

Nonreplaced and replaced elements are treated somewhat differently in the inline context, and we'll look at each in turn as we explore the construction of inline elements.

Line Layout

First, you need to understand how inline content is laid out. It isn't as simple and straightforward as block-level elements, which just generate boxes and usually don't allow anything to coexist with them. By contrast, look *inside* a block-level element, such as a paragraph. You may well ask, "How did all those lines of text get there? What controls their arrangement? How can I affect it?"

To understand how lines are generated, first consider the case of an element containing one very long line of text, as shown in Figure 7-27. Note that you've put a border around the line by wrapping the entire line in a span element and then assigning it a border style:

```
span {border: 1px dashed black;}
```

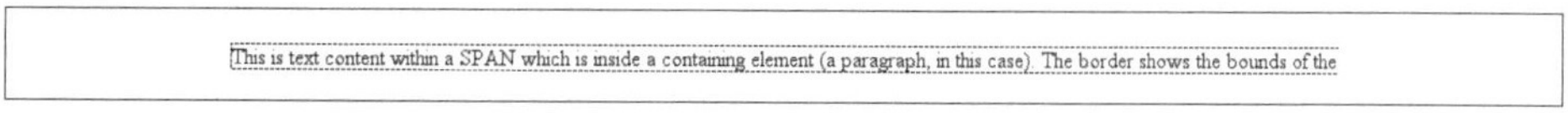

This is text content within a SPAN which is inside a containing element (a paragraph, in this case). The border shows the bounds of the

Figure 7-27. A single-line inline element

Figure 7-27 shows the simplest case of an inline element contained by a block-level element. It's no different, in its own way, than a paragraph with two words in it. The only differences are that, in Figure 7-27, you have a few dozen words and most paragraphs don't contain an explicit inline element such as span.

To get from this simplified state to something more familiar, all you have to do is determine how wide the element should be, and then break up the line so that the resulting pieces will fit into the width of the element. Therefore, we arrive at the state shown in Figure 7-28.

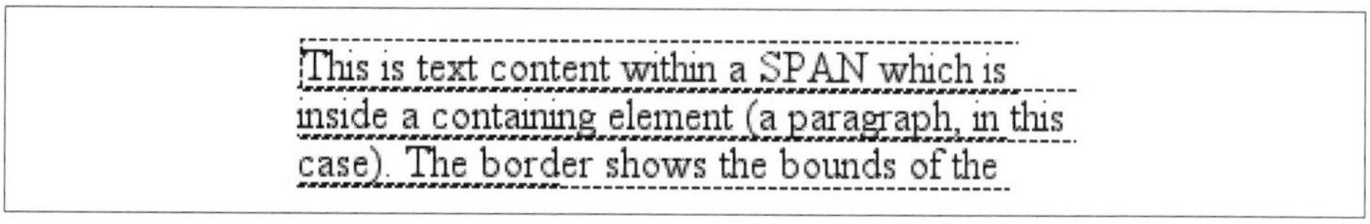

This is text content within a SPAN which is inside a containing element (a paragraph, in this case). The border shows the bounds of the

Figure 7-28. A multiple-line inline element

Nothing has really changed. All you did was take the single line and break it into pieces, and then stack those pieces on top of one another.

In Figure 7-28, the borders for each line of text also happen to coincide with the top and bottom of each line. This is true only because no padding or margin has been set for the inline text. Notice that the borders actually overlap each other slightly; for example, the bottom border of the first line is just below the top border of the second line. This is because the border is actually drawn on the next pixel (assuming you're using a monitor) to the *outside* of each line. Since the lines are touching each other, their borders will overlap, as shown in Figure 7-28.

If you alter the span styles to have a background color, the actual placement of the lines becomes quite clear. Consider Figure 7-29, which contains four paragraphs, each with a different value of text-align and each having the backgrounds of its lines filled in.

As you can see, not every line reaches to the edge of its parent paragraph's content area, which has been denoted with a dotted gray border. For the left-aligned paragraph, the lines are all pushed flush against the left content edge of the paragraph, and each line ends wherever the line is broken. The reverse is true for the right-aligned

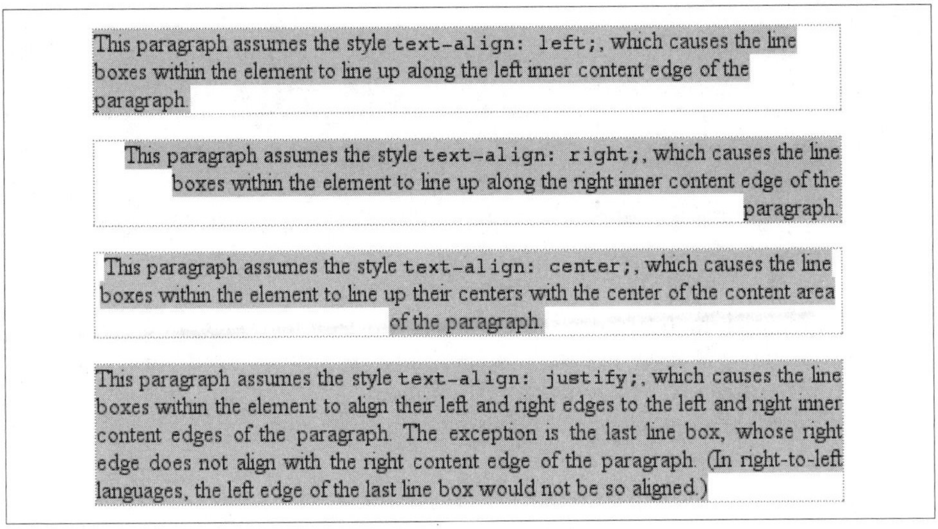

This paragraph assumes the style `text-align: left;`, which causes the line boxes within the element to line up along the left inner content edge of the paragraph.

This paragraph assumes the style `text-align: right;`, which causes the line boxes within the element to line up along the right inner content edge of the paragraph.

This paragraph assumes the style `text-align: center;`, which causes the line boxes within the element to line up their centers with the center of the content area of the paragraph.

This paragraph assumes the style `text-align: justify;`, which causes the line boxes within the element to align their left and right edges to the left and right inner content edges of the paragraph. The exception is the last line box, whose right edge does not align with the right content edge of the paragraph. (In right-to-left languages, the left edge of the last line box would not be so aligned.)

Figure 7-29. Showing lines in different alignments

paragraph. For the centered paragraph, the centers of the lines are aligned with the center of the paragraph. In the last case, where the value of text-align is justify, each line is forced to be as wide as the paragraph's content area, so that the line's edges touch the content edges of the paragraph. The difference between the natural length of the line and the width of the paragraph is made up by altering the spacing between letters and words in each line. Therefore, the value of word-spacing can be overridden when text is justified. (The value of letter-spacing cannot be overridden if it is a length value.)

That pretty well covers how lines are generated in the simplest cases. As you're about to see, however, the inline formatting model is far from simple.

Basic Terms and Concepts

Before we go any further, let's review some basic terms of inline layout, which will be crucial in navigating the following sections:

Anonymous text
> This is any string of characters that is not contained within an inline element. Thus, in the markup <p> I'm so happy!</p>, the sequences " I'm " and " happy!" are anonymous text. Note that the spaces are part of the text since a space is a character like any other.

Em box
> This is defined in the given font, otherwise known as the character box. Actual glyphs can be taller or shorter than their em boxes, as discussed in Chapter 5. In CSS, the value of font-size determines the height of each em box.

Content area

> In nonreplaced elements, the content area can be one of two things, and the CSS2.1 specification allows user agents to choose which one. The content area can be the box described by the em boxes of every character in the element strung together, or it can be the box described by the character glyphs in the element. In this book, I use the em box definition for simplicity's sake. In replaced elements, the content area is the intrinsic height of the element plus any margins, borders, or padding.

Leading

> The leading is the difference between the values of font-size and line-height. This difference is actually divided in half and applied to the top and bottom of the content area. These additions to the content area are called, not surprisingly, half-leading. Leading is applied only to nonreplaced elements.

Inline box

> This is the box described by the addition of the leading to the content area. For nonreplaced elements, the height of the inline box of an element will be exactly equal to the value for line-height. For replaced elements, the height of the inline box of an element will be exactly equal to the content area since leading is not applied to replaced elements.

Line box

> This is the shortest box that bounds the highest and lowest points of the inline boxes that are found in the line. In other words, the top edge of the line box is placed along the top of the highest inline box top, and the bottom of the line box is placed along the bottom of the lowest inline box bottom.

CSS also contains a set of behaviors and useful concepts that emerge from the list of terms and definitions just described:

- The content area is analogous to the content box of a block-level element.
- The background of an inline element is applied to the content area plus any padding.
- Any border on an inline element surrounds the content area plus any padding and borders.
- Padding, borders, and margins on nonreplaced elements have no vertical effect on inline elements or the boxes they generate; that is, they do *not* affect the height of an element's inline box (and thus the line box that contains the element).
- Margins and borders on replaced elements *do* affect the height of the inline box for that element and, by implication, the height of the line box for the line containing the element.

One more thing to note: inline boxes are vertically aligned within the line according to their values for the property vertical-align. I touched on this point in Chapter 6, and this chapter will explain it in more depth.

Before moving on, let's look at a step-by-step process for constructing a line box, which you can use to see how the various pieces of the line fit together to determine its height:

1. Determine the height of the inline box for each element in the line by following these steps:

   a. Find the values of `font-size` and `line-height` for each inline nonreplaced element and any text that is not part of a descendant inline element. Then combine them by subtracting the `font-size` from the `line-height`, which yields the leading for the box. The leading is split in half and applied to the top and bottom of the em boxes.

   b. Find the values of `height`, `margin-top`, `margin-bottom`, `padding-top`, `padding-bottom`, `border-top-width`, and `border-bottom-width` for each replaced element and add them together.

2. For each content area, determine how much of it is above the baseline for the overall line and how much of it is below the baseline. This is not an easy task: you must know the position of the baseline for each element and piece of anonymous text, and the baseline of the line itself; then you must line them all up. In addition, the bottom edge of a replaced element sits on the baseline for the overall line.

3. Determine the vertical offset of any elements that have been given a value for `vertical-align`. This will tell you how far up or down that element's inline box will be moved, and will change how much of the element is above or below the baseline.

4. Now that you know where all of the inline boxes have come to rest, calculate the final line box height. To do so, just add the distance between the baseline and the highest inline box top to the distance between the baseline and the lowest inline box bottom.

Let's consider the whole process in detail, which is key to intelligently styling inline content.

Inline Formatting

As we discussed in Chapter 6, all elements have a `line-height`. This value greatly influences the way inline elements are displayed, so let's give it due attention.

First, let's establish how the height of a line is determined. A line's height (or the height of the line box) is determined by the height of its constituent elements and other content, such as text. It's important to understand that `line-height` actually affects inline elements and other inline content, *not* block-level elements—at least, not directly. You can set a `line-height` value for a block-level element, but the value will have visual impact only if it's applied to inline content within that block-level element. Consider the following empty paragraph, for example:

```
<p style="line-height: 0.25em;"></p>
```

Without content, the paragraph won't have anything to display—you won't see anything. The fact that this paragraph has a line-height of any value—be it 0.25em or 25in—makes no difference without some content to create a line box.

You can certainly set a line-height value for a block-level element and apply that to all of the content within the block, whether or not the content is contained in any inline elements. In a certain sense, then, each line of text contained within a block-level element is its own inline element, whether or not it's surrounded by tags. If you like, picture a fictional tag sequence like this:

```
<p>
<line>This is a paragraph with a number of</line>
<line>lines of text which make up the</line>
<line>contents.</line>
</p>
```

Even though the line tags don't actually exist, the paragraph behaves as if they did—each line of text inherits styles from the paragraph. Therefore, you only bother to create line-height rules for block-level elements so you don't have to explicitly declare a line-height for all of their inline elements, fictional or otherwise.

The fictional line element actually clarifies the behavior that results from setting line-height on a block-level element. According to the CSS specification, declaring line-height on a block-level element sets a *minimum* line-box height for the content of that block-level element. Thus, declaring p.spacious {line-height: 24pt;} means that the minimum height for each line box is 24 points. Technically, content can inherit this line height only if an inline element does so. Most text isn't contained by an inline element. Therefore, if you pretend that each line is contained by the fictional line element, the model works out very nicely.

Inline Nonreplaced Elements

Building on your formatting knowledge, let's move on to the construction of lines containing only nonreplaced elements (or anonymous text). Then, you'll begin to better understand the differences between nonreplaced and replaced elements in inline layout.

Building the boxes

First, for an inline nonreplaced element or piece of anonymous text, the value of font-size determines the height of the content area. If an inline element has a font-size of 15px, then the content area's height is 15 pixels because all of the em boxes in the element are 15 pixels tall, as illustrated in Figure 7-30.

The next thing to consider is the value of line-height for the element, and the difference between it and the value of font-size. If an inline nonreplaced element has a font-size of 15px and a line-height of 21px, the difference is 6 pixels. The user agent splits the six pixels in half and applies half to the top and half to the bottom of the content area, which yields the inline box. This process is illustrated in Figure 7-31.

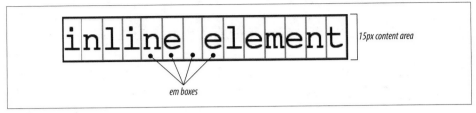

Figure 7-30. em boxes determine content area height

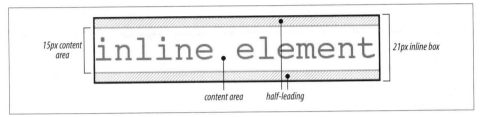

Figure 7-31. Content area plus leading equals inline box

Let's assume that the following is true:

```
<p style="font-size: 12px; line-height: 12px;">
This is text, <em>some of which is emphasized</em>, plus other text<br>
which is <strong style="font-size: 24px;">strongly emphasized</strong>
and which is<br>
larger than the surrounding text.
</p>
```

In this example, most of the text has a font-size of 12px, while the text in one inline nonreplaced element has a size of 24px. However, *all* of the text has a line-height of 12px since line-height is an inherited property. Therefore, the strong element's line-height is also 12px.

Thus, for each piece of text where both the font-size and line-height are 12px, the content height does not change (since the difference between 12px and 12px is zero), so the inline box is 12 pixels high. For the strong text, however, the difference between line-height and font-size is -12px. This is divided in half to determine the half-leading (-6px), and the half-leading is added to both the top and bottom of the content height to arrive at an inline box. Since you're adding a negative number in both cases, the inline box ends up being 12 pixels tall. The 12-pixel inline box is centered vertically within the 24-pixel content height of the element, so the inline box is actually smaller than the content area.

So far, it sounds like you've done the same thing to each bit of text, and all of the inline boxes are the same size, but that's not quite true. The inline boxes in the second line, although they're the same size, don't actually line up because the text is all baseline-aligned (see Figure 7-32).

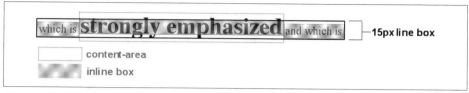

Figure 7-32. Inline boxes within a line

Since inline boxes determine the height of the overall line box, their placement with respect to one another is critical. The line box is defined as the distance from the top of the highest inline box in the line to the bottom of the lowest inline box, and the top of each line box butts up against the bottom of the line box for the preceding line. The result displayed in Figure 7-32 gives you the paragraph shown in Figure 7-33.

Figure 7-33. Line boxes within a paragraph

As you can see in Figure 7-33, the middle line is taller than the other two, but it still isn't big enough to contain all of the text within it. The anonymous text's inline box determines the bottom of the line box, while the top of the strong element's inline box sets the top of the line box. Because that inline box's top is inside the element's content area, the contents of the element spill outside the line box and actually overlap other line boxes. The result is that the lines of text look irregular. Later in the chapter, we'll explore ways to cope with this behavior and methods for achieving consistent baseline spacing.

Vertical alignment

If you change the vertical alignment of the inline boxes, the same height determination principles apply. Suppose that you give the strong element a vertical alignment of 4px:

```
<p style="font-size: 12px; line-height: 12px;">
This is text, <em>some of which is emphasized</em>, plus other text<br>
that is <strong style="font-size: 24px; vertical-align: 4px;">strongly
emphasized</strong> and that is<br>
larger than the surrounding text.
</p>
```

That small change raises the element four pixels, which pushes up both its content area and its inline box. Because the strong element's inline box top was already the highest in the line, this change in vertical alignment also pushes the top of the line box upward by four pixels, as shown in Figure 7-34.

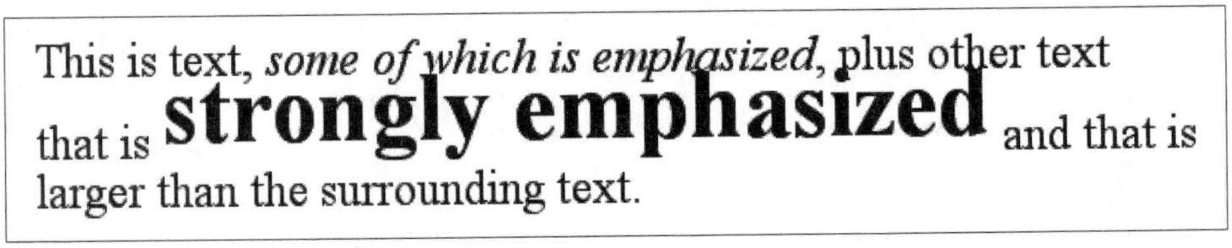

Figure 7-34. Vertical alignment affects line-box height

Let's consider another situation. Here, you have another inline element in the same line as the strong text, and its alignment is other than the baseline:

```
<p style="font-size: 12px; line-height: 12px;">
this is text, <em>some of which is emphasized</em>, plus other text<br>
that is <strong style="font-size: 24px;">strong</strong>
and <span style="vertical-align: top;">tall</span> and that is<br>
larger than the surrounding text.
</p>
```

Now you have the same result as in your earlier example, where the middle line box is taller than the other line boxes. However, notice how the "tall" text is aligned in Figure 7-35.

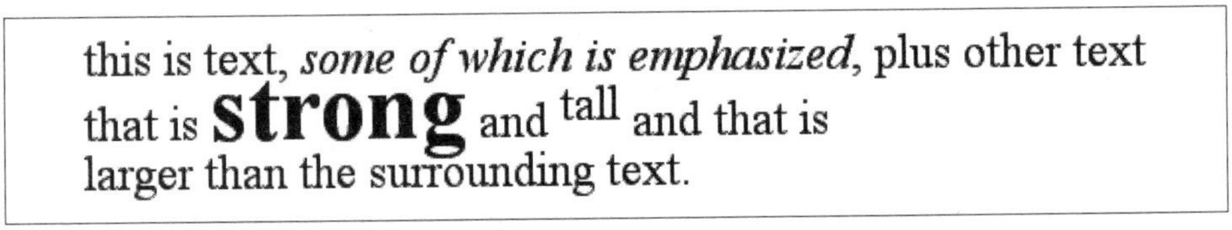

Figure 7-35. Aligning an inline element to the line box

In this case, the top of the "tall" text's inline box is aligned with the top of the line box. Since the "tall" text has equal values for font-size and line-height, the content height and inline box are the same. However, consider this:

```
<p style="font-size: 12px; line-height: 12px;">
This is text, <em>some of which is emphasized</em>, plus other text<br>
that is <strong style="font-size: 24px;">strong</strong>
and <span style="vertical-align: top; line-height: 4px;">tall</span>
and that is<br>
larger than the surrounding text.
</p>
```

Since the line-height for the "tall" text is less than its font-size, the inline box for that element is smaller than its content area. This fact changes the placement of the text itself, since the top of its inline box must be aligned with the top of the line box for its line. Thus, you get the result shown in Figure 7-36.

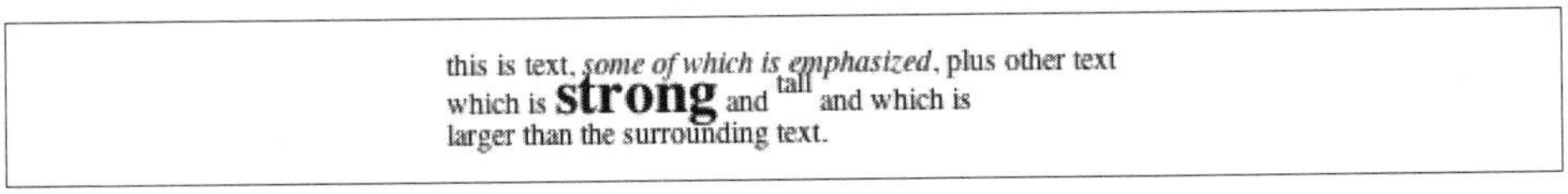

Figure 7-36. Text protruding from the line box (again)

On the other hand, you could set the "tall" text to have a line-height that is actually bigger than its font-size. For example:

```
<p style="font-size: 12px; line-height: 12px;">
This is text, <em>some of which is emphasized</em>, plus other text<br>
that is <strong style="font-size: 24px;">strong</strong>
and <span style="vertical-align: top; line-height: 18px;">tall</span>
and that is<br>
larger than the surrounding text.
</p>
```

Since you've given the "tall" text a line-height of 18px, the difference between line-height and font-size is 6 pixels. The half-leading of 3 pixels is added to the content area and results in an inline box that is 18 pixels tall. The top of this inline box aligns with the top of the line box. Similarly, the value bottom will align the bottom of an inline element's inline box with the bottom of the line box.

In the terms we've been using in this chapter, the effects of the assorted keyword values of vertical-align are:

top

Aligns the top of the element's inline box with the top of the containing line box.

bottom

Aligns the bottom of the element's inline box with the bottom of the containing line box.

text-top

Aligns the top of the element's inline box with the top of the parent's content area.

text-bottom

Aligns the bottom of the element's inline box with the bottom of the parent's content area.

middle

Aligns the vertical midpoint of the element's inline box with a point one-half ex above the baseline of the parent.

super

Moves the content area and inline box of the element upward. The distance is not specified and may vary by user agent.

sub

The same as super, except the element is moved downward instead of upward.

<percentage>

Shifts the element up or down the distance defined by taking the declared percentage of the element's value for line-height.

These values are explained in more detail in Chapter 6.

Managing the line-height

In previous sections, you saw that changing the line-height of an inline element can cause text from one line to overlap another. In each case, though, the changes were made to individual elements. So how can you affect the line-height of elements in a more general way to prevent content from overlapping?

One way is to use the em unit in conjunction with an element whose font-size has changed. For example:

```
p {font-size: 14px; line-height: 1em;}
big {font-size: 250%; line-height: 1em;}

<p>
Not only does this paragraph have "normal" text, but it also<br>
contains a line in which <big>some big text </big> is found.<br>
This large text helps illustrate our point.
</p>
```

By setting a line-height for the big element, you increase the overall height of the line box, providing enough room to display the big element without overlapping any other text and without changing the line-height of all lines in the paragraph. You use a value of 1em so that the line-height for the big element will be set to the same size as big's font-size. Remember, line-height is set in relation to the font-size of the element itself, not the parent element. The results are shown in Figure 7-37.

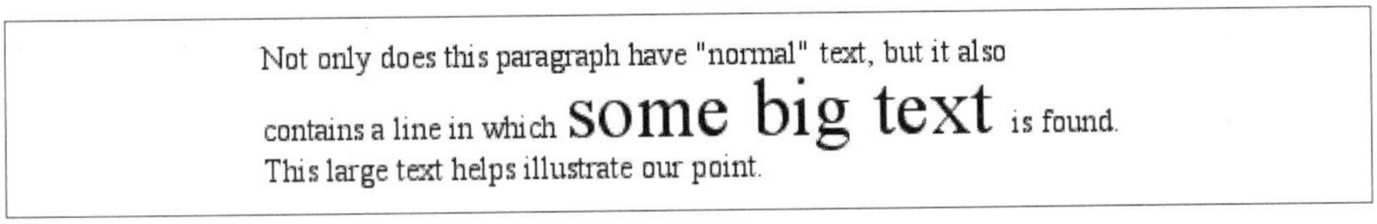

Figure 7-37. Assigning the line-height property to inline elements

Note that the following styles can produce the same result as in Figure 7-37:

```
p {font-size: 14px; line-height: 1;}
big {font-size: 250%;}
```

Unless line-height values are inherited as scaling factors, both the p and big elements would have a line-height of 1. Thus, the height of the inline box would match the height of the content area, just as in Figure 7-37.

Make sure you really understand the previous sections because things will get trickier when you try to add borders. Let's say you want to put five-pixel borders around any hyperlink:

```
a:link {border: 5px solid blue;}
```

If you don't set a large enough line-height to accommodate the border, it will be in danger of overwriting other lines. You could increase the size of the inline box for unvisited links using line-height, as you did for the big element in the earlier example; in this case, you'd just need to make the value of line-height 10 pixels larger than the value of font-size for those links. However, that could be difficult if you don't actually know the size of the font in pixels.

Another solution is to increase the line-height of the paragraph. This will affect every line in the entire element, not just the line in which the bordered hyperlink appears:

```
p {font-size: 14px; line-height: 24px;}
a:link {border: 5px solid blue;}
```

Because there is extra space added above and below each line, the border around the hyperlink doesn't impinge on any other line, as you can see in Figure 7-38.

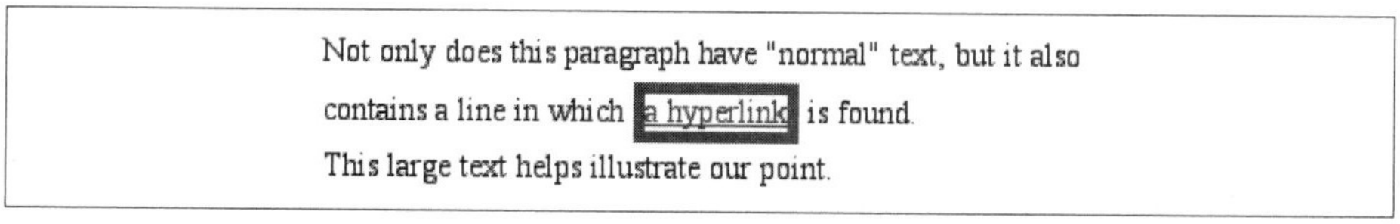

Not only does this paragraph have "normal" text, but it also contains a line in which a hyperlink is found. This large text helps illustrate our point.

Figure 7-38. Increasing line-height to leave room for inline borders

This approach works here, of course, because all of the text is the same size. If there were other elements in the line that changed the height of the line box, your border situation might also change. Consider the following:

```
p {font-size: 14px; line-height: 24px;}
a:link {border: 5px solid blue;}
big {font-size: 150%; line-height: 1.5em;}
```

Given these rules, the height of the inline box of a big element within a paragraph will be 31.5 pixels ($14 \times 1.5 \times 1.5$), and that will also be the height of the line box. To keep baseline spacing consistent, you must make the p element's line-height equal to or greater than 32px.

Baselines and Line Heights

The actual height of each line box depends on the way its component elements line up with one another. This alignment tends to depend very much on where the baseline falls within each element (or piece of anonymous text) because that location determines how their inline boxes are arranged. The placement of the baseline within each em box is different for every font. This information is built into the font files and cannot be altered by any means other than directly editing the font files.

Thus, consistent baseline spacing tends to be more of an art than a science. If you declare all of your font sizes and line heights using a single unit, such as ems, then you have a reliable chance of consistent baseline spacing. If you mix units, however, that feat becomes a great deal more difficult, if not impossible. As of this writing, there are proposals for properties that would let authors enforce consistent baseline spacing regardless of the inline content, which would greatly simplify certain aspects of online typography. None of these proposed properties have been implemented, though, which makes their adoption a distant hope at best.

Scaling line heights

The best way to set line-height, as it turns out, is to use a raw number as the value. This method is the best because the number becomes the scaling factor, and that factor is an inherited, not computed, value. Let's say you want the line-height of all elements in a document to be one-and-a-half times their font-size. You would declare:

```
body {line-height: 1.5;}
```

This scaling factor of 1.5 is passed down from element to element, and, at each level, the factor is used as a multiplier of the font-size of each element. Therefore, the following markup would be displayed as shown in Figure 7-39:

```
p {font-size: 15px; line-height: 1.5;}
small {font-size: 66%;}
big {font-size: 200%;}

<p>This paragraph has a line-height of 1.5 times its font-size. In addition,
any elements within it <small>such as this small element</small> also have
line-heights 1.5 times their font-size...and that includes <big>this big
element right here</big>. By using a scaling factor, line-heights scale
to match the font-size of any element.</p>
```

This paragraph has a line-height of 1.5 times its font-size. In addition, any elements within it such as this small element also have line-heights 1.5 times their font-size...and that includes this big element right here. By using a scaling factor, line-heights scale to match the font-size of any element.

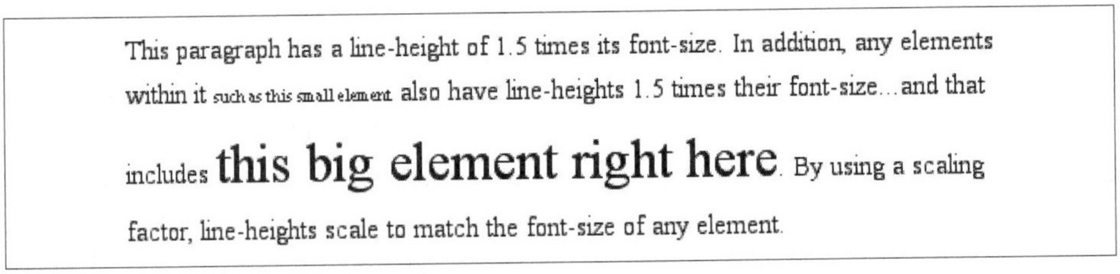

Figure 7-39. Using a scaling factor for line-height

In this example, the line height for the small element turns out to be 15px, and for the big element, it's 45px. (These numbers may seem excessive, but they're consistent with the overall page design.) Of course, if you don't want your big text to generate too much extra leading, you can give it a line-height value, which will override the inherited scaling factor:

```
p {font-size: 15px; line-height: 1.5;}
small {font-size: 66%;}
big {font-size: 200%; line-height: 1em;}
```

Another solution—possibly the simplest of all—is to set the styles such that lines are no taller than absolutely necessary to hold their content. This is where you might use a line-height of 1.0. This value will multiply itself by every font-size to get the same value as the font-size of every element. Thus, for every element, the inline box will be the same as the content area, which means the absolute minimum size necessary is used to contain the content area of each element.

Most fonts still display a little bit of space between the lines of character glyphs because characters are usually smaller than their em boxes. The exception is script ("cursive") fonts, where character glyphs are usually *larger* than their em boxes.

Adding box properties

As you're aware from previous discussions, padding, margins, and borders may all be applied to inline nonreplaced elements. These aspects of the inline element do not influence the height of the line box at all. If you were to apply some borders to a span element without any margins or padding, you'd get results such as those shown in Figure 7-40.

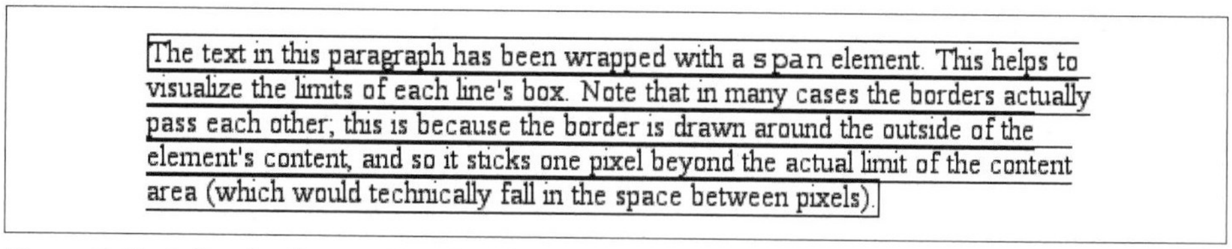

> The text in this paragraph has been wrapped with a span element. This helps to visualize the limits of each line's box. Note that in many cases the borders actually pass each other; this is because the border is drawn around the outside of the element's content, and so it sticks one pixel beyond the actual limit of the content area (which would technically fall in the space between pixels).

Figure 7-40. Inline borders and line-box layout

The border edge of inline elements is controlled by the font-size, not the line-height. In other words, if a span element has a font-size of 12px and a line-height of 36px, its content area is 12px high, and the border will surround that content area.

Alternatively, you can assign padding to the inline element, which will push the borders away from the text itself:

```
span {border: 1px solid black; padding: 4px;}
```

Note that this padding does not alter the actual shape of the content height, so it will not affect the height of the inline box for this element. Similarly, adding borders to an inline element will not affect the way line boxes are generated and laid out, as illustrated in Figure 7-41.

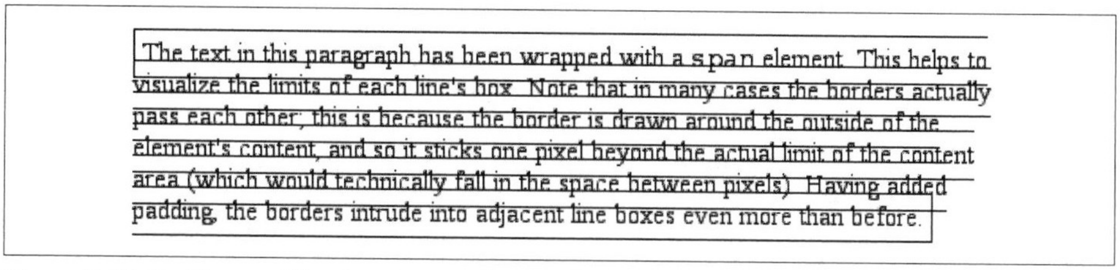

> The text in this paragraph has been wrapped with a span element. This helps to visualize the limits of each line's box. Note that in many cases the borders actually pass each other; this is because the border is drawn around the outside of the element's content, and so it sticks one pixel beyond the actual limit of the content area (which would technically fall in the space between pixels). Having added padding, the borders intrude into adjacent line boxes even more than before.

Figure 7-41. Padding and borders do not alter line height

As for margins, they do not, practically speaking, apply to the top and bottom of an inline non-replaced element, as they don't affect the height of the line box. The ends of the element are another story.

CSS2.1 actually makes margin placement explicit: it defines `margin-top` and `margin-bottom` as applying to all elements except inline nonreplaced elements, instead of simply saying that user agents should ignore top and bottom margins.

Recall the idea that an inline element is basically laid out as a single line and then broken up into pieces. So, if you apply margins to an inline element, those margins will appear at its beginning and end; these are the left and right margins, respectively. Padding also appears at the edges. Thus, although padding and margins (and borders) do not affect line heights, they can still affect the layout of an element's content by pushing text away from its ends. In fact, negative left and right margins can pull text closer to the inline element, or even cause overlap, as Figure 7-42 shows.

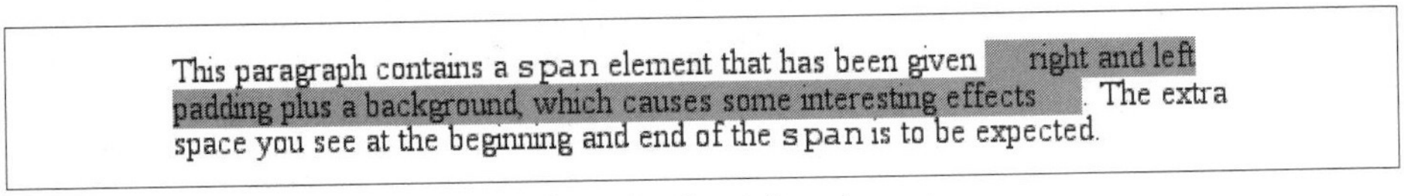

This paragraph contains a span element that has been given right and left
padding plus a background, which causes some interesting effects. The extra
space you see at the beginning and end of the span is to be expected.

Figure 7-42. Padding and margins on the ends of an inline element

Think of an inline element as a strip of paper with some plastic surrounding it. Displaying the inline element on multiple lines is like cutting up the strip into smaller strips. However, no extra plastic is added to each smaller strip. The only plastic is that which was on the strip to begin with, so it appears only at the beginning and end of the original ends of the paper strip (the inline element).

So, what happens when an inline element has a background and enough padding to cause the backgrounds of the lines to overlap? Take the following situation as an example:

```
p {font-size: 15px; line-height: 1em;}
p span {background: #999; padding-top: 10px; padding-bottom: 10px;}
```

All of the text within the `span` element will have a content area that is 15 pixels tall, and you've applied 10 pixels of padding to the top and bottom of each content area. The extra pixels won't increase the height of the line box, which would be fine, except there's a background color. Thus, you get the result shown in Figure 7-43.

iven top
and bottom padding plus a background, which causes some interesting effects. The
overlap you see is to be expected.

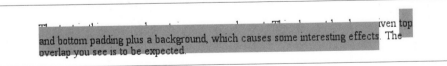

Figure 7-43. Overlapping inline backgrounds

CSS 2.1 explicitly states that the line boxes are drawn in document order: "This will cause the borders on subsequent lines to paint over the borders and text of previous lines." The same principle applies to backgrounds as well, as Figure 7-43 demonstrates. CSS2, on the other hand, allowed user agents "to 'clip' the border and padding areas (i.e., not render them)." Therefore, the results may depend greatly on which specification the user agent follows.

Glyphs Versus Content Area

Even in cases where you try to prevent inline nonreplaced element backgrounds from overlapping, it can still happen, depending on which font is used. The problem lies in the difference between a font's em box and its character glyphs. Most fonts, as it turns out, don't have em boxes whose heights match the character glyphs.

That may sound very abstract, but it has practical consequences. In CSS2.1, we find the following: "The height of the content area should be based on the font, but this specification does not specify how. A user agent may...use the em box or the maximum ascender and descender of the font. (The latter would ensure that glyphs with parts above or below the em box still fall within the content area, but leads to differently sized boxes for different fonts.)"

In other words, the "painting area" of an inline nonreplaced element is left to the user agent. If a user agent takes the em box to be the height of the content area, then the background of an inline nonreplaced element will be equal to the height of the em box (which is the value of font-size). If a user agent uses the maximum ascender and descender of the font, then the background may be taller or shorter than the em box. Therefore, you could give an inline nonreplaced element a line-height of 1em and still have its background overlap the content of other lines.

There is no way to prevent this overlap in CSS2 or CSS2.1, but there are properties proposed for CSS3 that would let the author control the behavior of the user agent. Until these properties are widely implemented, truly precise typography is not possible with CSS.

Inline Replaced Elements

Inline replaced elements, such as images, are assumed to have an intrinsic height and width; for example, an image will be a certain number of pixels high and wide. Therefore, a replaced element with an intrinsic height can cause a line box to become taller than normal. This does *not* change the value of line-height for any element in the line, *including the replaced element itself*. Instead, the line box is simply made tall enough to accommodate the replaced element, plus any box properties. In other words, the entirety of the replaced element—content, margins, borders, and padding—is used to define the element's inline box. The following styles lead to one such example, as shown in Figure 7-44:

```
p {font-size: 15px; line-height: 18px;}
img {height: 30px; margin: 0; padding: 0; border: none;}
```

> The text in this paragraph contains an img element. This element has been given a height that is larger than a typical line box height for this paragraph, which leads to some potentially unwanted consequences. The extra space you see between lines of text is to be expected.

Figure 7-44. Replaced elements can increase the height of the line box but not the value of line-height

Despite all the blank space, the effective value of line-height has not changed for the paragraph or the image itself. line-height simply has no effect on the image's inline box. Because the image in Figure 7-44 has no padding, margins, or borders, its inline box is equivalent to its content area, which is, in this case, 30 pixels tall.

Nonetheless, an inline replaced element still has a value for line-height. Why? In the most common case, it needs the value in order to correctly position the element if it's been vertically aligned. Recall, for example, that percentage values for vertical-align are calculated with respect to an element's line-height. Thus:

```
p {font-size: 15px; line-height: 18px;}
img {vertical-align: 50%;}

<p>The image in this sentence <img src="test.gif" alt="test image">
will be raised 9 pixels.</p>
```

The inherited value of line-height causes the image to be raised nine pixels instead of some other number. Without a value for line-height, it wouldn't be possible to perform percentage-value vertical alignments. The height of the image itself has no relevance when it comes to vertical alignment; the value of line-height is all that matters.

However, for other replaced elements, it might be important to pass on a line-height value to descendant elements within that replaced element. One example is an SVG image, which uses CSS to style any text found within the image.

Adding box properties

After everything else, applying margins, borders, and padding to inline replaced elements almost seems simple.

Padding and borders are applied to replaced elements as usual; padding inserts space around the actual content and the border surrounds the padding. What's unusual about the process is that these two things actually influence the height of the line box because they are part of the inline box of an inline replaced element (unlike inline nonreplaced elements). Consider Figure 7-45, which results from the following styles:

```
img {height: 20px; width: 20px;}
img.one {margin: 0; padding: 0; border: 1px dotted;}
img.two {margin: 5px; padding: 3px; border: 1px solid;}
```

The text in this paragraph contains two img elements. These elements have
been given styles that lead to some potentially unwanted consequences. The
extra space you see between lines of text is to be expected.

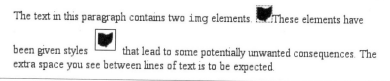

Figure 7-45. Adding padding, borders, and margins to an inline replaced element increases its inline box

Note that the first line box is made tall enough to contain the image, whereas the second is tall enough to contain the image, its padding, and its border.

Margins are also contained within the line box, but they have their own wrinkles. Setting a positive margin is no mystery; it will simply make the inline box of the replaced element taller. Setting negative margins, meanwhile, has a similar effect: it decreases the size of the replaced element's inline box. This is illustrated in Figure 7-46, where you can see that a negative top margin is pulling down the line above the image:

```
img.two {margin-top: -10px;}
```

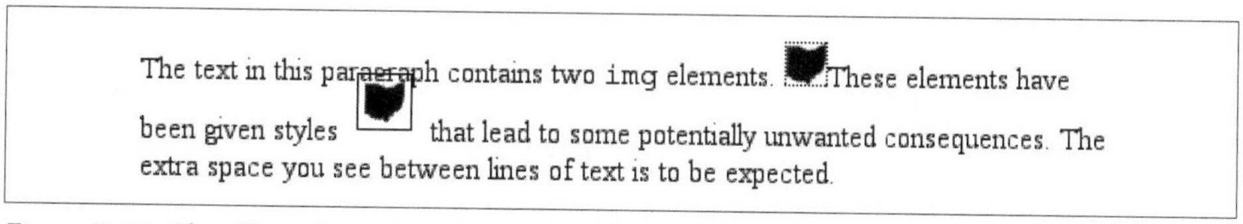

The text in this paragraph contains two img elements. These elements have
been given styles that lead to some potentially unwanted consequences. The
extra space you see between lines of text is to be expected.

Figure 7-46. The effect of negative margins on inline replaced elements

Negative margins operate the same way on block-level elements, of course. In this case, the negative margins make the replaced element's inline box smaller than ordinary. Negative margins are the only way to cause inline replaced elements to bleed into other lines.

Replaced elements and the baseline

You may have noticed by now that, by default, inline replaced elements sit on the baseline. If you add bottom padding, a margin, or a border to the replaced element, the content area will move upward. Replaced elements do not actually have baselines of their own, so the next best thing is to align the bottom of their inline boxes with the baseline. Thus, it is actually the bottom outer margin edge that is aligned with the baseline, as illustrated in Figure 7-47.

This baseline alignment leads to an unexpected (and unwelcome) consequence: an image placed in a table cell all by itself should make the table cell tall enough to contain the line box containing the image. The resizing occurs even if there is no actual

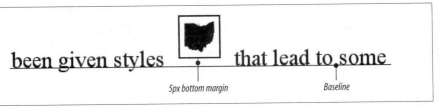

been given styles　that lead to some

5px bottom margin　　　　　　　　　Baseline

Figure 7-47. Inline replaced elements sit on the baseline

text, not even whitespace, in the table cell with the image. Therefore, the common sliced-image and spacer-GIF designs of years past can fall apart quite dramatically in modern browsers. Consider the simplest case:

```
td {font-size: 12px;}
```

```
<td><img src="spacer.gif" height="1" width="10"></td>
```

Under the CSS inline formatting model, the table cell will be 12 pixels tall, with the image sitting on the baseline of the cell. So there might be three pixels of space below the image, and eight above it, although the exact distances would depend on the font family used and the placement of its baseline. This behavior is not confined to images inside table cells; it will also happen in any situation where an inline replaced element is the sole descendant of a block-level or table-cell element. For example, an image inside a div will also sit on the baseline.

 As of this writing, many browsers actually ignore this CSS inline formatting model, but Gecko-based browsers act as the text describes when rendering XHTML and strict HTML documents. See my article "Images, Tables, and Mysterious Gaps" at *http://developer.mozilla.org/en/docs/Images,_Tables,_and_Mysterious_Gaps* for more information.

The most common workaround for such circumstances is simply to make spacer images block-level so that they do not generate a line box. For example:

```
td {font-size: 12px;}
img.block {display: block;}
```

```
<td><img src="spacer.gif" height="1" width="10" class="block"></td>
```

Another possible fix is to make the font-size and line-height of the enclosing table cell 1px, which makes the line box only as tall as the one-pixel image within it.

Here's another interesting effect of inline replaced elements sitting on the baseline: if you apply a negative bottom margin, the element will actually get pulled downward because the bottom of its inline box will be higher than the bottom of its content area. Thus, the following rule would have the result shown in Figure 7-48:

```
p img {margin-bottom: -10px;}
```

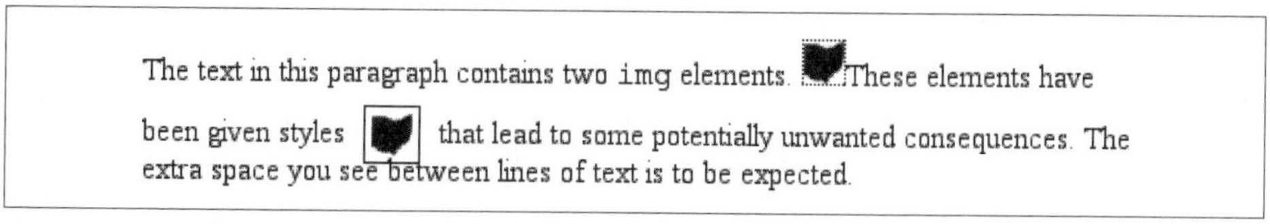

The text in this paragraph contains two img elements. These elements have been given styles that lead to some potentially unwanted consequences. The extra space you see between lines of text is to be expected.

Figure 7-48. Pulling inline replaced elements down with a negative bottom margin

This can easily cause a replaced element to bleed into following lines of text, as Figure 7-48 illustrates.

Some browsers simply place the bottom of the content area on the baseline and ignore any negative bottom margin.

Inline with History

The CSS inline formatting model may seem needlessly complex and, in some ways, even contrary to author expectations. Unfortunately, the complexity is the result of creating a style language that is both backward-compatible with pre-CSS web browsers and also leaves the door open for future expansion into more sophisticated territory—an awkward blend of past and present. It's also the result of making some sensible decisions that avoid one undesirable effect while causing another.

For example, the "spreading apart" of lines of text by image and vertically aligned text owes its roots to the way Mosaic 1.0 behaved. In that browser, any image in a paragraph would simply push open enough space to contain the image. That's a good behavior, since it prevents images from overlapping text in other lines. So when CSS introduced ways to style text and inline elements, its authors endeavored to create a model that did not (by default) cause inline images to overlap other lines of text. However, the same model also meant that a superscript element (sup), for example, would likely also push apart lines of text.

Such effects annoy some authors who want their baselines to be an exact distance apart, but consider the alternative. If line-height forced baselines to be a specified distance apart, you'd easily end up with inline replaced and vertically shifted elements that overlap other lines of text—which would also annoy authors. Fortunately, CSS offers enough power to create your desired effect in one way or another, and the future of CSS holds even more potential.

Altering Element Display

As I mentioned briefly in Chapter 1, you can affect the way a user agent displays by setting a value for the property display. Now that we've taken a close look at visual formatting, let's revisit the display property and discuss two more of its values using concepts from this chapter.

display

Values:	`none` | `inline` | `block` | `inline-block` | `list-item` | `run-in` | `table` | `inline-table` | `table-row-group` | `table-header-group` | `table-footer-group` | `table-row` | `table-column-group` | `table-column` | `table-cell` | `table-caption` | `inherit`
Initial value:	`inline`
Applies to:	All elements
Inherited:	No
Computed value:	Varies for floated, positioned, and root elements (see CSS2.1, section 9.7); otherwise, as specified
Note:	The values `compact` and `marker` appeared in CSS2 but were dropped from CSS2.1 due to a lack of widespread support

We'll ignore the table-related values, since they are covered in Chapter 11, and we'll also ignore the value `list-item` since I deal with lists in detail in Chapter 12. We've spent quite some time discussing `block` and `inline` elements, but let's spend a moment talking about how altering an element's display role can alter layout before we look at `inline-block` and `run-in`.

Changing Roles

When it comes to styling a document, it's obviously handy to be able to change the display role of an element. For example, suppose you have a series of links in a `div` that you'd like to lay out as a vertical sidebar:

```
<div id="navigation">
<a href="index.html">WidgetCo Home</a><a href="products.html">Products</a>
<a href="services.html">Services</a><a href="fun.html">Widgety Fun!</a>
<a href="support.html">Support</a><a href="about.html" id="current">About Us</a>
<a href="contact.html">Contact</a>
</div>
```

You could put all the links into table cells, or wrap each one in its own `div`—or you could just make them all block-level elements, like this:

```
div#navigation a {display: block;}
```

This will make every `a` element within the navigation `div` a block-level element. If you add on a few more styles, you could have a result like that shown in Figure 7-49.

Changing display roles can be useful in cases where you want non-CSS browsers to get the navigation links as inline elements but to lay out the same links as block-level elements. With the links as blocks, you can style them as you would `div` elements, with the advantage that the entire element box becomes part of the link. Thus, if a user's mouse pointer hovers anywhere in the element box, he can then click the link.

Figure 7-49. Changing the display role from inline to block

You may also want to make elements inline. Suppose you have an unordered list of names:

```
<ul id="rollcall">
<li>Bob C.</li>
<li>Marcio G.</li>
<li>Eric M.</li>
<li>Kat M.</li>
<li>Tristan N.</li>
<li>Arun R.</li>
<li>Doron R.</li>
<li>Susie W.</li>
</ul>
```

Given this markup, say you want to make the names into a series of inline names with vertical bars between them (and on each end of the list). The only way to do so is to change their display role. The following rules will have the effect shown in Figure 7-50:

```
#rollcall li {display: inline; border-right: 1px solid; padding: 0 0.33em;}
#rollcall li:first-child {border-left: 1px solid;}
```

| Bob C. | Marcio G. | Eric M. | Kat M. | Tristan N. | Arun R. | Doron R. | Susie W. |

Figure 7-50. Changing the display role from list-item to inline

There are plenty of other ways to use display to your advantage in design. Be creative and see what you can invent!

Be careful to note, however, that you are changing the display role of elements—not changing their inherent nature. In other words, causing a paragraph to generate an inline-level box does *not* turn that paragraph into an inline element. In XHTML, for example, some elements are block while others are inline. (Still others are "flow" elements, but we're ignoring them for the moment.) An inline element can be a descendant of a block element, but the reverse is not true. Thus, while a link can be placed inside a paragraph, a link cannot be wrapped around a paragraph. This will hold true no matter how you style the elements in question. Consider the following markup:

```
<a href="http://www.example.net" style="display: block;">
<p style="display: inline;">this is wrong!</p>
</a>
```

The markup will not validate because the block element (p) is nested inside an inline element (a). The changing of display roles does nothing to change this. display is named such because it affects how the element is displayed, not what kind of element it is.

Inline-Block Elements

As befits the hybrid look of the value name inline-block, inline-block elements are indeed a hybrid of block-level and inline elements. This display value is new in CSS2.1.

An inline-block element relates to other elements and content as an inline box. In other words, it's laid out in a line of text just as an image would be, and, in fact, inline-block elements are formatted within a line as a replaced element. This means the bottom of the inline-block element will rest on the baseline of the text line by default and will not line-break within itself.

Inside the inline-block element, the content is formatted as though the element were block-level. The properties width and height apply to it, as they do to any block-level or inline replaced element, and those properties will increase the height of the line if they are taller than the surrounding content.

Let's consider some example markup that will help make this clearer:

```
<div id="one">
This text is the content of a block-level level element.  Within this
block-level element is another block-level element.  <p>Look, it's a block-level
paragraph.</p>  Here's the rest of the DIV, which is still block-level.
</div>
<div id="two">
This text is the content of a block-level level element.  Within this
block-level element is an inline element.  <p>Look, it's an inline
paragraph.</p>  Here's the rest of the DIV, which is still block-level.
</div>
<div id="three">
This text is the content of a block-level level element.  Within this
block-level element is an inline-block element.  <p>Look, it's an inline-block
paragraph.</p>  Here's the rest of the DIV, which is still block-level.
</div>
```

To this markup, we apply the following rules:

```
div {margin: 1em 0; border: 1px solid;}
p {border: 1px dotted;}
div#one p {display: block; width: 6em; text-align: center;}
div#two p {display: inline; width: 6em; text-align: center;}
div#three p {display: inline-block; width: 6em; text-align: center;}
```

The result of this style sheet is depicted in Figure 7-51.

Notice that in the second div, the inline paragraph is formatted as normal inline content, which means width and text-align are ignored (since they do not apply to inline elements). For the third div, however, the inline-block paragraph honors both

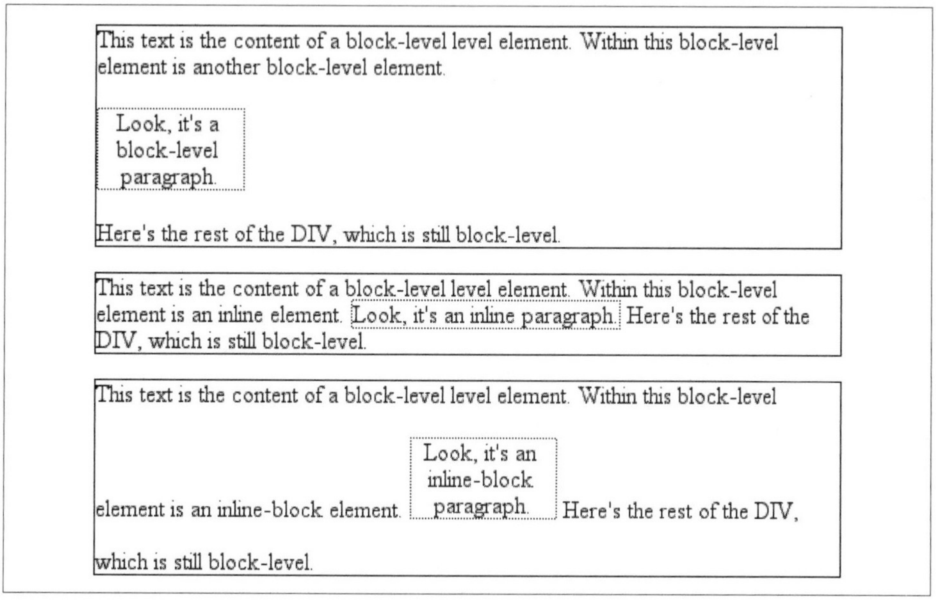

Figure 7-51. The behavior of an inline-block element

properties, since it is formatted as a block-level element. That paragraph also forces its line of text to be much taller, since it affects line height as though it were a replaced element.

If an inline-block element's `width` is not defined or explicitly declared `auto`, the element box will shrink to fit the content. That is, the element box is exactly as wide as necessary to hold the content, and no wider. Inline boxes act the same way, although they can break across lines of text, just as inline-block elements cannot. Thus, the following rule, when applied to the previous markup example:

```
div#three p {display: inline-block; height: 2em;}
```

will create a tall box that's just wide enough to enclose the content, as shown in Figure 7-52.

Inline-block elements can be useful if, for example, you have a set of five hyperlinks that you want to be of equal width within a toolbar. To make them all 20 percent of the width of their parent element, but still leave them inline, declare:

```
#navbar a {display: inline-block; width: 20%;}
```

Run-in Elements

CSS2 introduced the value `run-in`, another interesting block/inline hybrid that can make some block-level elements an inline part of a following element. This ability is

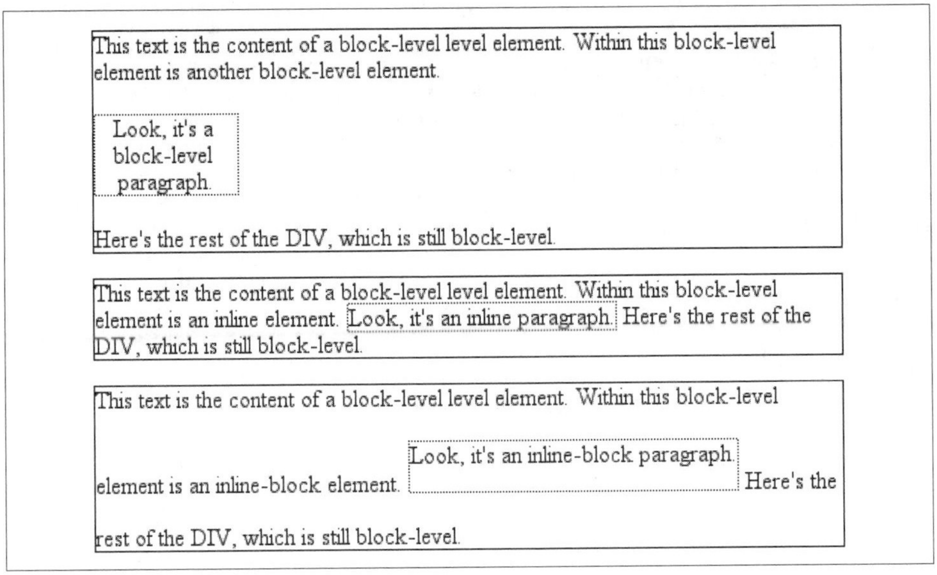

Figure 7-52. Auto-sizing of an inline-block element

useful for certain heading effects that are quite common in print typography, where a heading will appear as part of a paragraph of text.

In CSS, you can make an element run-in simply by changing its display value *and* by making the next element box block-level. Note that I'm talking here about *boxes*, not the elements themselves. In other words, it doesn't matter if an element is block or inline. All that matters is the box that element generates. A strong element set to display: block generates a block-level box; a paragraph set to display: inline generates an inline box.

So, to rephrase: if an element generates a run-in box, and a block box follows that box, then the run-in element will be an inline box at the beginning of the block box. For example:

```
<h3 style="display: run-in; border: 1px dotted; font-size: 125%;
  font-weight: bold;">Run-in Elements</h3>
<p style="border-top: 1px solid black; padding-top: 0.5em;">
Another interesting block/inline hybrid is the value <code>run-in</code>, introduced
in CSS2, which has the ability to take block-level elements and make them an inline
part of a following element. This is useful for certain heading effects that are
quite common in print typography, where a heading will appear as part of a paragraph
of text.
</p>
```

Since the element following the h3 generates a block-level box, the h3 element will be turned into an inline element at the beginning of the p element's content, as illustrated in Figure 7-53.

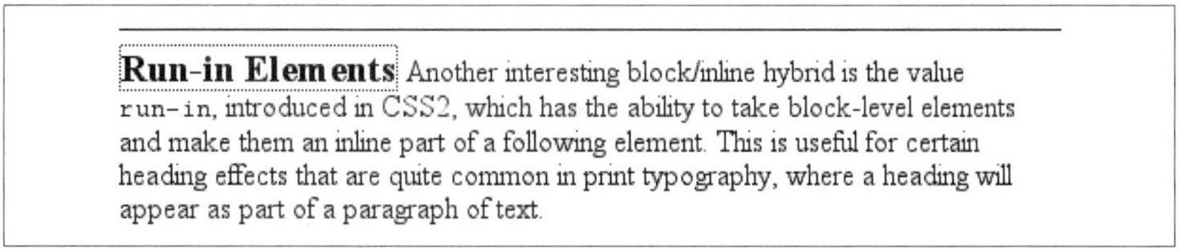

> **Run-in Elements** Another interesting block/inline hybrid is the value
> run-in, introduced in CSS2, which has the ability to take block-level elements
> and make them an inline part of a following element. This is useful for certain
> heading effects that are quite common in print typography, where a heading will
> appear as part of a paragraph of text.

Figure 7-53. Making a heading run-in

Note how the borders of the two elements are placed. The effect of using run-in in this situation is exactly the same as if you'd used this markup instead:

```
<p style="border-top: 1px solid black; padding-top: 0.5em;">
<span style="border: 1px dotted; font-size: 125%; font-weight: bold;">Run-in
Elements</span> Another interesting block/inline hybrid is the value <code>run-in</
code>, introduced in CSS2, which has the ability to take block-level elements and
make them an inline part of a following element. This is useful for certain heading
effects that are quite common in print typography, where a heading will appear as
part of a paragraph of text.
</p>
```

However, there is a slight difference between run-in boxes and the markup example. Even though run-in boxes are formatted as inline boxes within another element, they still inherit properties from their parent element in the document, not the element into which they're placed. Let's extend our example to include an enclosing div and some color:

```
<div style="color: silver;">
<h3 style="display: run-in; border: 1px dotted; font-size: 125%;
  font-weight: bold;">Run-in Elements</h3>
<p style="border-top: 1px solid black; padding-top: 0.5em; color: black;">
Another interesting block/inline hybrid is the value <code>run-in</code>, introduced
in CSS2, which has the ability to take block-level elements and make them an inline
part of a following element.
</p>
%lt;</div>
```

In this situation, the h3 will be silver, not black, as illustrated in Figure 7-54. That's because it inherits the color value from its parent element before it is inserted into the paragraph.

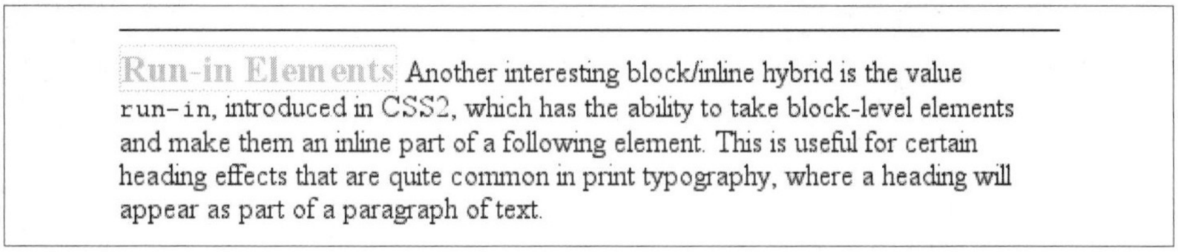

> **Run-in Elements** Another interesting block/inline hybrid is the value
> run-in, introduced in CSS2, which has the ability to take block-level elements
> and make them an inline part of a following element. This is useful for certain
> heading effects that are quite common in print typography, where a heading will
> appear as part of a paragraph of text.

Figure 7-54. Run-in elements inherit from their source parents

The important thing to remember is that run-in will work only if the box after the run-in box is block-level. If it is not, the run-in box itself will be made block-level. Thus, given the following markup, the h3 will remain or even become block-level, since the display value for the table element is (oddly enough) table:

```
<h3 style="display: run-in;">Prices</h3>
<table>
<tr><th>Apples</th><td>$0.59</td></tr>
<tr><th>Peaches</th><td>$0.79</td></tr>
<tr><th>Pumpkin</th><td>$1.29</td></tr>
<tr><th>Pie</th><td>$6.99</td></tr>
</table>
```

It's unlikely that an author would ever apply the value run-in to a naturally inline element, but if this happens, the element will most likely generate a block-level box. For example, the em element in the following markup would become block-level because a block-level box does not follow it:

```
<p>
This is a <em>really</em> odd thing to do, <strong>but</strong> you could do it
if you were so inclined.
</p>
```

 At the time of this writing, very few contemporary browsers offer support for run-in.

Computed values

The computed value of display can change if an element is floated or positioned. It can also change when declared for the root element. In fact, the display, position, and float values interact in interesting ways.

If an element is absolutely positioned, the value of float is set to none. For either floated or absolutely positioned elements, the computed value is determined by the declared value, as shown in Table 7-1.

Table 7-1. Computed display values

Declared value	Computed value
inline-table	table
inline, run-in, table-row-group, table-column, table-column-group, table-header-group, table-footer-group, table-row, table-cell, table-caption, inline-block	block
All others	As specified

In the case of the root element, declaring either of the values inline-table or table results in a computed value of table, whereas declaring none results in the same computed value. All other display values are computed to be block.

Summary

Although some aspects of the CSS formatting model may seem counterintuitive at first, they begin to make sense as you work with them more. In many cases, rules that initially seem nonsensical or even idiotic turn out to prevent bizarre or otherwise undesirable document displays. Block-level elements are in many ways easy to understand, and affecting their layout is typically a simple task. Inline elements, on the other hand, can be tricky to manage, as a number of factors come into play—not least of which is whether the element is replaced or nonreplaced. Now that we've established the underpinnings of document layout, let's turn our attention to how the various layout properties are used. This effort will span several chapters, and we'll start with the most common box properties: padding, borders, and margins.

CHAPTER 8

Padding, Borders, and Margins

If you're like the vast majority of web designers who were working in the late 1990s, your pages all use tables for layout. You design them this way, of course, because tables can be used to create sidebars and to set up a complicated structure for an entire page's appearance. You might even use tables for simpler tasks, like putting text in a colored box with a border. When you think about it, though, you shouldn't need a table for such simple tasks. If you want only a paragraph with a red border and a yellow background, shouldn't creating it be easier than wrapping a single-cell table around it?

The authors of CSS felt it should indeed be easier, so they devoted a great deal of attention to allowing you to define borders for paragraphs, headings, divs, anchors, images—darned near everything a web page can contain. These borders can set an element apart from others, accentuate its appearance, mark certain kinds of data as having been changed, or any number of other things.

CSS also lets you define regions around an element that control how the border is placed in relation to the content and how close other elements can get to that border. Between the content of an element and its border, we find the *padding* of an element, and beyond the border, the *margins*. These properties affect how the entire document is laid out, of course, but more importantly, they very deeply affect the appearance of a given element.

Basic Element Boxes

As we discussed in Chapter 7, all document elements generate a rectangular box called the *element box*, which describes the amount of space that an element occupies in the layout of the document. Therefore, each box influences the position and size of other element boxes. For example, if the first element box in the document is an inch tall, the next box will begin at least an inch below the top of the document. If the first element box is changed to two inches tall, every following element box will shift downward an inch, and the second element box will begin at least two inches below the top of the document, as shown in Figure 8-1.

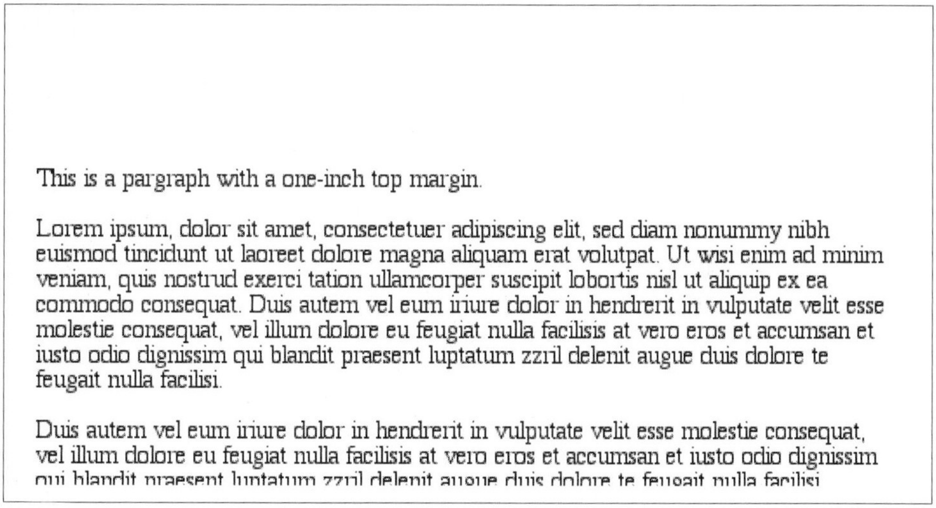

This is a pargraph with a one-inch top margin.

Lorem ipsum, dolor sit amet, consectetuer adipiscing elit, sed diam nonummy nibh euismod tincidunt ut laoreet dolore magna aliquam erat volutpat. Ut wisi enim ad minim veniam, quis nostrud exerci tation ullamcorper suscipit lobortis nisl ut aliquip ex ea commodo consequat. Duis autem vel eum iriure dolor in hendrerit in vulputate velit esse molestie consequat, vel illum dolore eu feugiat nulla facilisis at vero eros et accumsan et iusto odio dignissim qui blandit praesent luptatum zzril delenit augue duis dolore te feugait nulla facilisi.

Duis autem vel eum iriure dolor in hendrerit in vulputate velit esse molestie consequat, vel illum dolore eu feugiat nulla facilisis at vero eros et accumsan et iusto odio dignissim qui blandit praesent luptatum zzril delenit augue duis dolore te feugait nulla facilisi

Figure 8-1. How one element affects all elements

By default, a visually rendered document is composed of a number of rectangular boxes that are distributed such that they don't overlap one another. Also, within certain constraints, these boxes take up as little space as possible, while maintaining a sufficient separation to make clear which content belongs to which element.

 Boxes can overlap if they have been manually positioned, and visual overlap can occur if negative margins are used on normal-flow elements.

To fully understand how margins, padding, and borders are handled, you must clearly understand the box model (also explained in Chapter 7). For reference, I'll include the box model diagram from that chapter (see Figure 8-2).

Width and Height

As Figure 8-2 illustrates, the width of an element is defined as the distance from the left inner edge to the right inner edge, and the height is the distance from the inner top to the inner bottom.

One important note about these two properties: they don't apply to inline nonreplaced elements. For example, if you try to declare a height and width for a hyperlink, CSS-conformant browsers must ignore those declarations. Assume that the following rule applies:

```
a:link {color: red; background: silver; height: 15px; width: 60px;}
```

You'll end up with red links on a silver background whose height and width are determined by the content of the links. They will *not* be 15 pixels tall by 60 pixels wide.

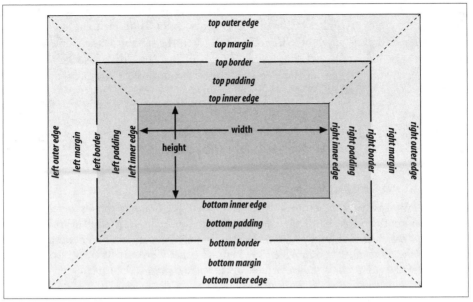

Figure 8-2. The CSS box model

---

width

Values:	<length> | <percentage> | auto | inherit
Initial value:	auto
Applies to:	Block-level and replaced elements
Inherited:	No
Percentages:	Refer to the width of the containing block
Computed value:	For auto and percentage values, as specified; otherwise, an absolute length, unless the property does not apply to the element (then auto)

---

height

Values:	<length> | auto | inherit
Initial value:	auto
Applies to:	Block-level and replaced elements
Inherited:	No
Percentages:	Calculated with respect to the height of the containing block
Computed value:	For auto and percentage values, as specified; otherwise, an absolute length, unless the property does not apply to the element (then auto)

In the course of this chapter, we'll keep the discussion simple by assuming that the height of an element is always calculated automatically. If an element is eight lines long, and each line is an eighth of an inch tall, then the height of the element is one inch. If it's 10 lines tall, then the height is 1.25 inches. In either case, the height is determined by the content of the element, not by the author. It's rarely the case that elements in the normal flow have a set height.

Historical Problems

Prior to Version 6, Internet Explorer for Windows did not act as CSS stipulates with regard to `width` and `height`. The two major differences are:

- IE/Win used `width` and `height` to define the dimensions of the visible element box, not the content of the element box. If you defined an element to have a `width` of 400px, IE/Win would make the distance from the left outer border edge to the right outer border edge 400 pixels. In other words, IE/Win used `width` to describe the total of the element's content area, left and right padding, and left and right border. CSS3 includes proposals to let the author decide what `width` and `height` mean.

- IE/Win applied `width` and `height` to inline nonreplaced elements. For example, if you applied `width` and `height` to a hyperlink, it would be drawn according to the supplied values.

Both of these behaviors were fixed in IE6, but only in "standards" mode. If IE6 renders a document in "quirks" mode, it will still use the previously described behaviors.

Margins Versus Padding

Element boxes provide only small amounts of space between elements. There are three ways to generate additional space around elements: you can add padding, margins, or a combination of padding and margins. Under certain circumstances, the choice doesn't really matter. If an element has a background, however, your decision is already made, because the background will extend into the padding but not the margin.

Thus, the amount of padding and margin you assign to a given element will influence where the background of the element will end. If you set background colors for the elements involved, as illustrated in Figure 8-3, the difference becomes clear. The elements with padding have extra background, as it were, whereas those with margins do not.

In the end, deciding how to set margins and padding is up to the designer, who must weigh the various possibilities against the intended effect and pick the best alternative. To make these choices, of course, it helps to know which properties you can use.

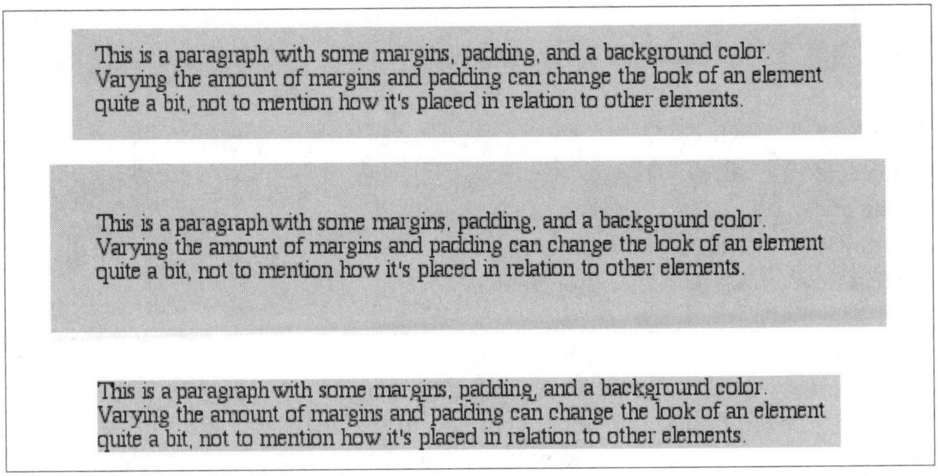

Figure 8-3. Paragraphs with different margins and padding, with backgrounds to illustrate the differences

Margins

The separation between most normal-flow elements occurs because of element margins. Setting a margin creates extra "blank space" around an element. "Blank space" generally refers to an area in which other elements cannot also exist and in which the parent element's background is visible. For example, Figure 8-4 shows the difference between two paragraphs without any margins, and the same two paragraphs with margins.

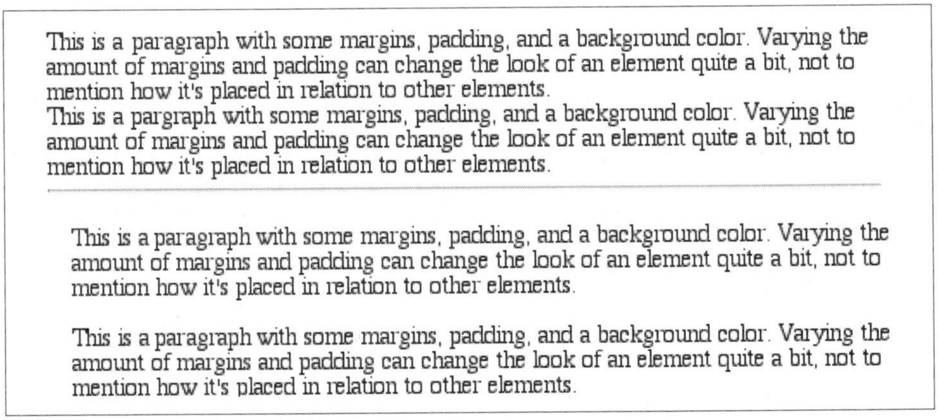

Figure 8-4. Paragraphs with and without margins

The simplest way to set a margin is by using the property `margin`.

	margin	
Values:	[<length> | <percentage> | auto]{1,4} | inherit
Initial value:	Not defined
Applies to:	All elements
Inherited:	No
Percentages:	Refer to the width of the containing block
Computed value:	See individual properties

The effects of setting auto margins were discussed in detail in Chapter 7, so we won't repeat them here. Besides, it's more common to set length values for margins. Suppose you want to set a quarter-inch margin on h1 elements, as illustrated in Figure 8-5. (A background color has been added so you can clearly see the edges of the content area.)

```
h1 {margin: 0.25in; background-color: silver;}
```

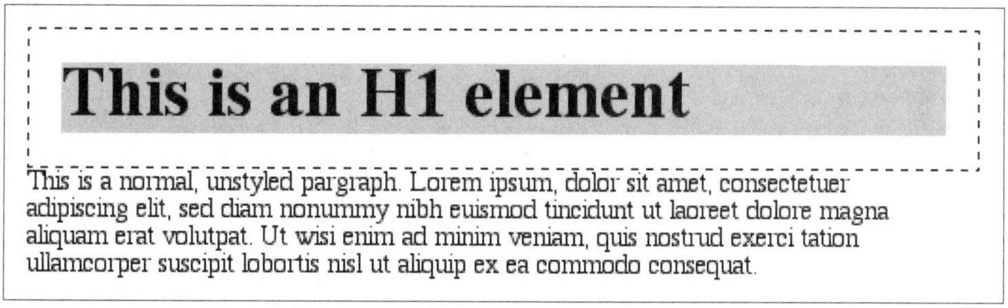

Figure 8-5. Setting a margin for h1 elements

This sets a quarter-inch of blank space on each side of an h1 element. In Figure 8-5, dashed lines represent the blank space, but the lines are purely illustrative and would not actually appear in a web browser.

margin can accept any length of measurement, whether in pixels, inches, millimeters, or ems. However, the default value for margin is effectively 0 (zero), so if you don't declare a value, no margin should appear.

In practice, however, browsers come with preassigned styles for many elements, and margins are no exception. For example, in CSS-enabled browsers, margins generate the "blank line" above and below each paragraph element. Therefore, if you don't declare margins for the p element, the browser may apply some margins on its own. Whatever you declare will override the default styles, of course.

Finally, it's possible to set a percentage value for margin. The details of this value type will be discussed in the upcoming section "Percentages and Margins."

Length Values and Margins

As stated before, any length value can be used in setting the margins of an element. It's simple enough, for example, to apply a 10-pixel whitespace around paragraph elements. The following rule gives paragraphs a silver background and a 10-pixel margin, as shown in Figure 8-6:

```
p {background-color: silver; margin: 10px;}
```

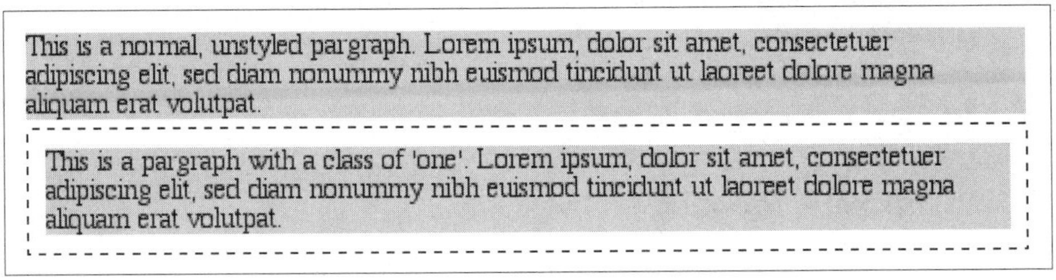

This is a normal, unstyled pargraph. Lorem ipsum, dolor sit amet, consectetuer adipiscing elit, sed diam nonummy nibh euismod tincidunt ut laoreet dolore magna aliquam erat volutpat.

This is a pargraph with a class of 'one'. Lorem ipsum, dolor sit amet, consectetuer adipiscing elit, sed diam nonummy nibh euismod tincidunt ut laoreet dolore magna aliquam erat volutpat.

Figure 8-6. Comparative paragraphs

(Again, the background color helps show the content area, and the dashed lines are for illustrative purposes only.) As Figure 8-6 demonstrates, 10 pixels of space have been added to each side of the content area. The result is somewhat similar to using the hspace and vspace attributes in HTML. In fact, you can use margin to set extra space around an image. Let's say you want one em of space surrounding all images:

```
img {margin: 1em;}
```

That's all it takes.

At times, you might prefer a different amount of space on each side of an element. That's simple as well. If you want all h1 elements to have a top margin of 10 pixels, a right margin of 20 pixels, a bottom margin of 15 pixels, and a left margin of 5 pixels, here's all you need:

```
h1 {margin: 10px 20px 15px 5px;}
```

The order of the values is important, and follows this pattern:

```
margin: top right bottom left
```

A good way to remember this pattern is to keep in mind that the four values go clockwise around the element, starting from the top. The values are *always* applied in this order, so to get the effect you want, you have to arrange them correctly.

 Another easy way to remember the order in which sides must be declared is to keep in mind that getting the sides in the correct order helps you avoid "TRouBLe"—that is, **TRBL**, for "**T**op **R**ight **B**ottom **L**eft."

It's also possible to mix up the types of length value you use. You aren't restricted to using a single length type in a given rule, as shown here:

```
h2 {margin: 14px 5em 0.1in 3ex;}   /* value variety! */
```

Figure 8-7 shows you, with a little extra annotation, the results of this declaration.

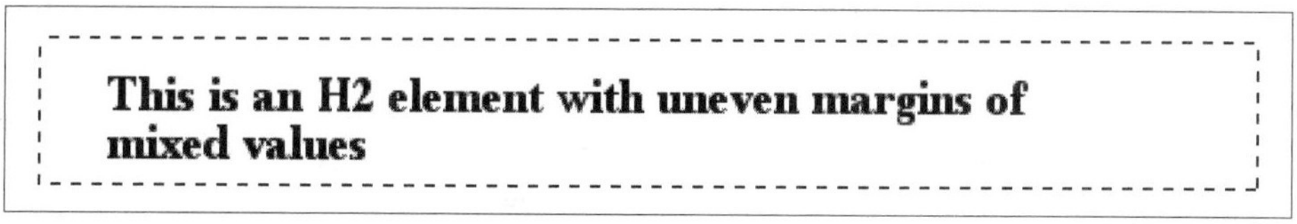

This is an H2 element with uneven margins of mixed values

Figure 8-7. Mixed-value margins

Percentages and Margins

As I mentioned earlier, it's possible to set percentage values for the margins of an element. Percentages are computed in relation to the width of the parent element, so they change if the parent element's width changes in some way. For example, assume the following, which is illustrated in Figure 8-8:

```
p {margin: 10%;}

<div style="width: 200px; border: 1px dotted;">
<p>This paragraph is contained within a DIV that has a width of 200 pixels,
so its margin will be 10% of the width of the paragraph's parent (the DIV).
Given the declared width of 200 pixels, the margin will be 20 pixels on
all sides.</p>
</div>
<div style="width: 100px;  border: 1px dotted;">
<p>This paragraph is contained within a DIV with a width of 100 pixels,
so its margin will still be 10% of the width of the paragraph's parent.
There will, therefore, be half as much margin on this paragraph as that
on the first paragraph.</p>
</div>
```

By contrast, consider the case of elements without a declared width. In such cases, the overall width of the element box (including margins) is dependent on the width of the parent element. This leads to the possibility of "fluid" pages, where the margins of elements enlarge or reduce to match the actual size of the parent element (or display canvas). If you style a document so that its elements use percentage margins, the margins will expand or shrink to fit as the user changes the width of a browser window. The design choice is up to you.

You may have noticed something odd about the paragraphs in Figure 8-8. Not only did their side margins change according to the width of their parent elements, but so did their top and bottom margins. That's the desired behavior in CSS. Refer back to the property definition, and you'll see that percentage values are defined to be relative to the *width* of the parent element. This applies to the top and bottom margins,

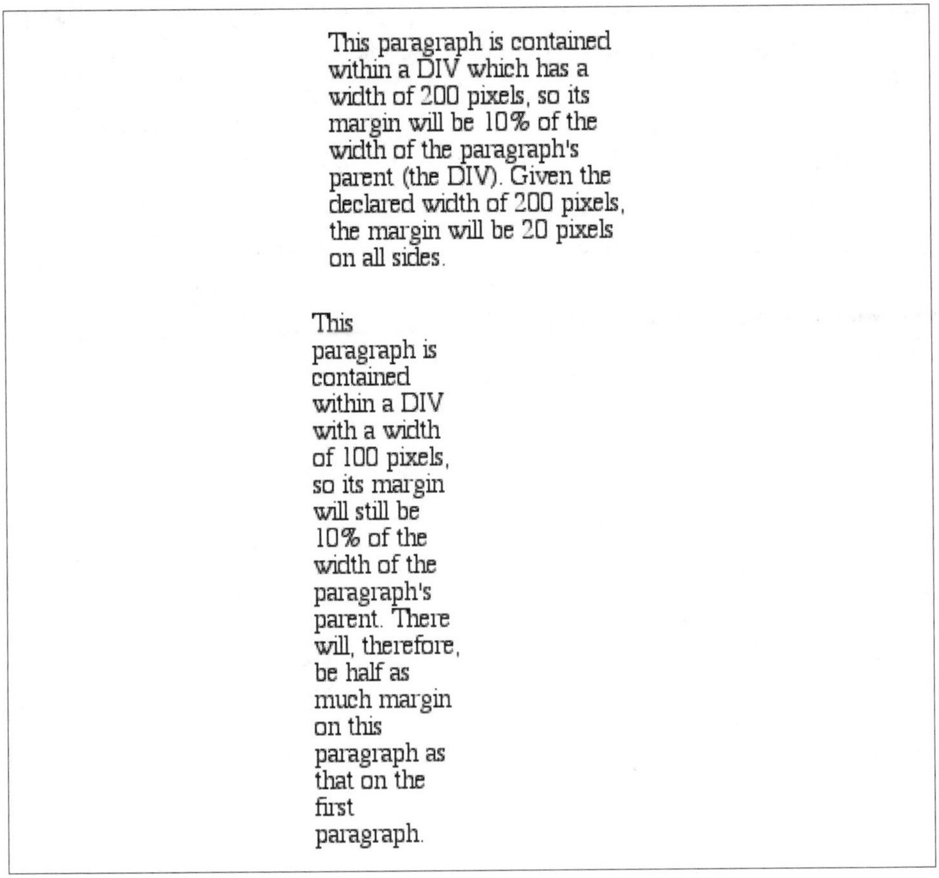

This paragraph is contained within a DIV which has a width of 200 pixels, so its margin will be 10% of the width of the paragraph's parent (the DIV). Given the declared width of 200 pixels, the margin will be 20 pixels on all sides.

This paragraph is contained within a DIV with a width of 100 pixels, so its margin will still be 10% of the width of the paragraph's parent. There will, therefore, be half as much margin on this paragraph as that on the first paragraph.

Figure 8-8. Parent widths and percentages

as well as to the left and right. Thus, given the following styles and markup, the top margin of the paragraph will be 50px:

```
div p {margin-top: 10%;}

<div style="width: 500px;">
<p>This is a paragraph, and its top margin is 10% the width of its parent
element.</p>
</div>
```

If the width of the div changes, the top margin of the paragraph will, too. Seem strange? Consider that most elements in the normal flow are (as we are assuming) as tall as necessary to contain their descendant elements, including margins. If an element's top and bottom margins were a percentage of the parent, an infinite loop could result where the parent's height was increased to accommodate the top and bottom margins, which would then have to increase to match the new height, and so on. Rather than simply ignore percentages for top and bottom margins, the specification authors decided to make it relate to the width of the parent, which does not change based on the width of its descendants.

 The treatment of percentage values for top and bottom margins is different for positioned elements; see Chapter 10 for more details.

It's also possible to mix percentages with length values. Thus, to set h1 elements to have top and bottom margins of one-half em, and side margins that are 10 percent of the width of the browser window, you can declare the following, illustrated in Figure 8-9:

```
h1 {margin: 0.5em 10% 0.5em 10%;}
```

This is an H1 element

This paragraph has no styles. Lorem ipsum, dolor sit amet, consectetuer adipiscing elit, sed diam nonummy nibh euismod tincidunt ut laoreet dolore magna aliquam erat volutpat.

Figure 8-9. Mixed margins

Here, although the top and bottom margins will stay constant in any situation, the side margins will change based on the width of the browser window. Of course, we're assuming that all h1 elements are children of the *body* element and that *body* is as wide as the browser window. Plainly stated, the side margins of h1 elements will be 10 percent of the width of the h1's parent element.

Let's revisit that rule for a moment:

```
h1 {margin: 0.5em 10% 0.5em 10%;}
```

Seems a little redundant, doesn't it? After all, you have to type in the same pair of values twice. Fortunately, CSS offers an easy way to avoid this.

Replicating Values

Sometimes, the values you're entering for margin get a little repetitive:

```
p {margin: 0.25em 1em 0.25em 1em;}
```

You don't have to keep typing in pairs of numbers like this, though. Instead of the preceding rule, try this:

```
p {margin: 0.25em 1em;}
```

These two values are enough to take the place of four. But how? CSS defines a few rules to accommodate fewer than four values for margin. These are:

- If the value for *left* is missing, use the value provided for *right*.
- If the value for *bottom* is missing, use the value provided for *top*.
- If the value for *right* is missing, use the value provided for *top*.

If you prefer a more visual approach, take a look at the diagram shown in Figure 8-10.

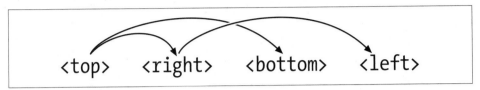

Figure 8-10. Value replication pattern

In other words, if three values are given for margin, the fourth (*left*) is copied from the second (*right*). If two values are given, the fourth is copied from the second, and the third (*bottom*) from the first (*top*). Finally, if only one value is given, the other sides copy that value.

This simple mechanism allows authors to supply only as many values as necessary, as illustrated here:

```
h1 {margin: 0.25em 0 0.5em;} /* same as '0.25em 0 0.5em 0' */
h2 {margin: 0.15em 0.2em;}   /* same as '0.15em 0.2em 0.15em 0.2em' */
p {margin: 0.5em 10px;}      /* same as '0.5em 10px 0.5em 10px' */
p.close {margin: 0.1em;}     /* same as '0.1em 0.1em 0.1em 0.1em' */
```

The method presents a small drawback, which you're bound to encounter eventually. Suppose you want to set the top and left margins for h1 elements to 10 pixels, and the bottom and right margins to 20 pixels. In that case, you have to write the following:

```
h1 {margin: 10px 20px 20px 10px;} /* can't be any shorter */
```

You get what you want, but it takes a while to get it all in. Unfortunately, there is no way to cut down on the number of values needed in such a circumstance. Let's take another example, one where you want all of the margins to be auto—except for the left margin, which should be 3em:

```
h2 {margin: auto auto auto 3em;}
```

Again, you get the effect you want. The problem is that typing auto becomes a little tedious. All you want to do is affect the margin on one side of the element, which leads us to the next topic.

Single-Side Margin Properties

Fortunately, there's a way to assign a value to the margin on a single side of an element. Let's say you only want to set the left margin of h2 elements to 3em. Instead of using the typing-intensive margin, you could take this approach:

```
h2 {margin-left: 3em;}
```

margin-left is one of four properties devoted to setting the margins on each of the four sides of an element box. Their names should come as little surprise.

margin-top, margin-right, margin-bottom, margin-left

Values:	<length> | <percentage> | auto | inherit
Initial value:	0
Applies to:	All elements
Inherited:	No
Percentages:	Refer to the width of the containing block
Computed value:	For percentages, as specified; otherwise, the absolute length

Using any one of these properties lets you set a margin on that side only, without directly affecting any of the other margins.

It's possible to use more than one of these single-side properties in a single rule, for example:

```
h2 {margin-left: 3em; margin-bottom: 2em;
    margin-right: 0; margin-top: 0;
    background: silver;}
```

As you can see in Figure 8-11, the margins are set as you want them. Of course, in this case, it might have been easier to use margin after all:

```
h2 {margin: 0 0 2em 3em;}
```

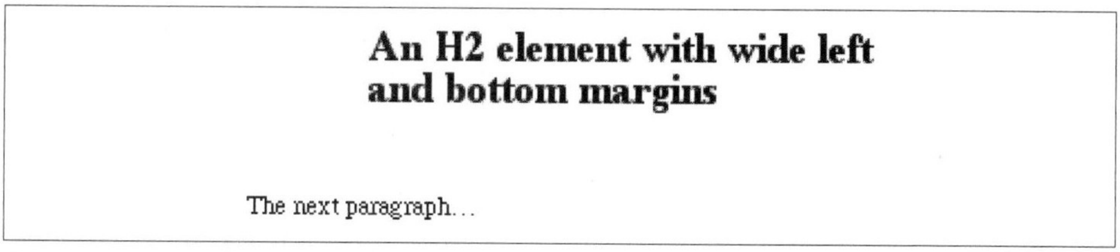

Figure 8-11. *More than one single-side margin*

Whether you use single-side properties or shorthand, you'll get the same result. In general, if you're trying to set margins for more than one side, it's easier to simply use margin. From the standpoint of your document's display, however, it doesn't really matter which approach you use, so choose whichever is easiest for you.

Negative and Collapsed Margins

As was discussed in detail in Chapter 7, it's possible to set negative margins for an element. This can cause the element's box to stick out of its parent or to overlap other elements without violating the box model. Consider these rules, which are illustrated in Figure 8-12:

```
div {border: 1px dotted gray; margin: 1em;}
p {margin: 1em; border: 1px dashed silver;}
p.one {margin:  0 -1em;}
p.two {margin: -1em 0;}
```

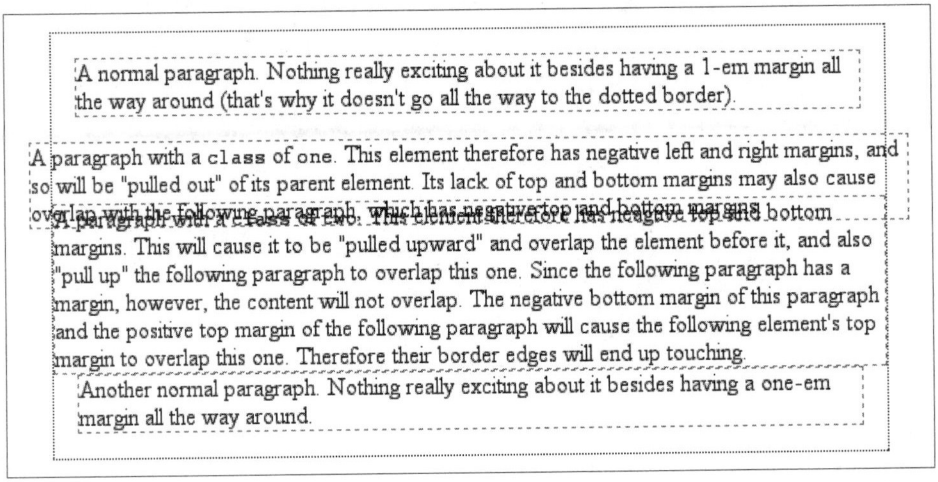

A normal paragraph. Nothing really exciting about it besides having a 1-em margin all the way around (that's why it doesn't go all the way to the dotted border).

A paragraph with a `class` of one. This element therefore has negative left and right margins, and so will be "pulled out" of its parent element. Its lack of top and bottom margins may also cause overlap with the following paragraph, which has negative top and bottom margins. A paragraph with a class of two. This element therefore has negative top and bottom margins. This will cause it to be "pulled upward" and overlap the element before it, and also "pull up" the following paragraph to overlap this one. Since the following paragraph has a margin, however, the content will not overlap. The negative bottom margin of this paragraph and the positive top margin of the following paragraph will cause the following element's top margin to overlap this one. Therefore their border edges will end up touching.

Another normal paragraph. Nothing really exciting about it besides having a one-em margin all the way around.

Figure 8-12. Negative margins in action

In the first case, the math works out such that the paragraph's computed width plus its right and left margins are exactly equal to the width of the parent div. So, the paragraph ends up two ems wider than the parent element without actually being "wider" (from a mathematical point of view). In the second case, the negative top and bottom margins effectively reduce the computed height of the element and move its top and bottom outer edges inward, which is how it ends up overlapping the paragraphs before and after it.

Combining negative and positive margins is actually very useful. For example, you can make a paragraph "punch out" of a parent element by being creative with positive and negative margins, or you can create a Mondrian effect with several overlapping or randomly placed boxes, as shown in Figure 8-13:

```
div {background: silver; border: 1px solid;}
p {margin: 1em;}
p.punch {background: white; margin: 1em -1px 1em 25%;
  border: 1px solid; border-right: none; text-align: center;}
p.mond {background: #333; color: white; margin: 1em 3em -3em -3em;}
```

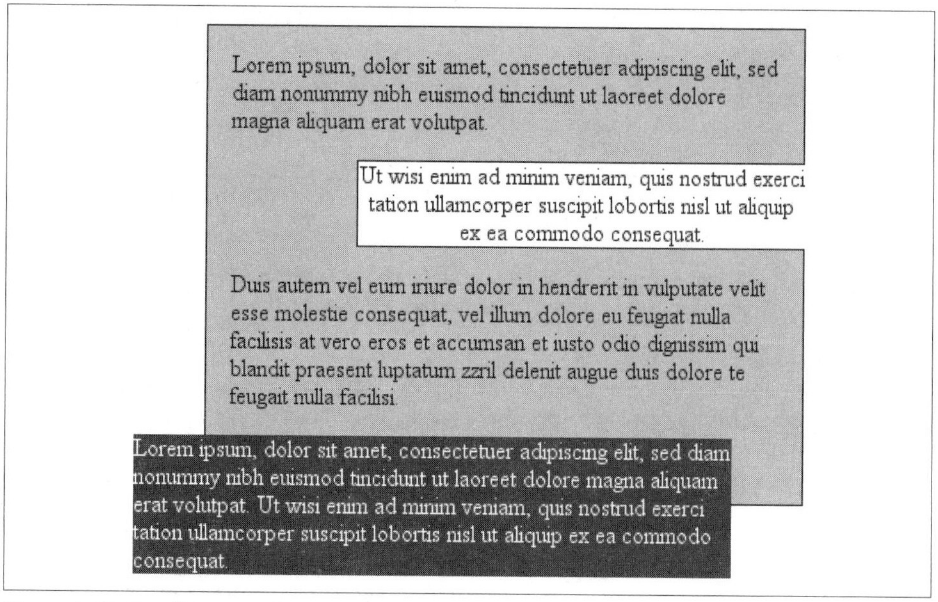

Figure 8-13. Punching out of a parent

Thanks to the negative bottom margin for the "mond" paragraph, the bottom of its parent element is pulled upward, allowing the paragraph to stick out of the bottom of its parent.

Speaking of top and bottom margins, it's also important to remember that vertically adjacent margins in the normal flow will collapse, a topic we covered in the previous chapter. Margin collapsing is at work in practically every document you style. For example, here's a simple rule:

```
p {margin: 15px 0;}
```

This will cause one paragraph to follow another with 15 pixels of "margin space" between them. If margins didn't collapse, there would be 30 pixels of space between two adjacent paragraphs, but that behavior wouldn't be what authors expect.

This does, however, mean that you must be careful about how you style margins. Most likely, you'll want to close up the space between a heading and the following paragraph. Because paragraphs in HTML documents have a top margin, it isn't enough to set the bottom margin for the heading to zero; you must also eliminate the top margin of the paragraph. This is simple to do with CSS2's adjacent-sibling selector:

```
h2 {margin-bottom: 0;}
h2 + p {margin-top: 0;}
```

Unfortunately, browser support for adjacent-sibling selectors is (as of this writing) limited enough that most users will see a 1-em space between the heading and its following paragraph. You can still get the desired effect without using CSS2 selectors, but you'll have to be a little tricky:

```
h2 {margin-bottom: 0;}
p {margin: 0 0 1em;}
```

This will actually remove a top margin from all paragraphs, but since they also all have 1em bottom margins, the desired interparagraph separation will hold, as shown in Figure 8-14.

I'm an H2 and I'm proud!
The paragraphs that follow on will be separated as people expect, but not in the traditional manner: only the bottom margin is used to enforce this separation.

The top margins have been removed. This allows the first paragraph after an h2 (which has had its bottom margin removed) to get up close to the h2 without the use of an adjacent-sibling selector, which some browsers do not support.

Interparagraph spacing. Catch the wave!

Figure 8-14. Intelligently setting margins

This works because the usual 1-em separation between paragraphs is a result of margin collapsing. Thus, if you take away one of those margins—the top margin, in this case—the visual result will be the same as if you'd left the margin in place.

Margins and Inline Elements

Margins can also be applied to inline elements, although the effects are a little different. Let's say you want to set top and bottom margins on strongly emphasized text:

```
strong {margin-top: 25px; margin-bottom: 50px;}
```

This is allowed in the specification, but since you're applying the margins to an inline nonreplaced element, it will have absolutely no effect on the line height. Because margins are effectively transparent, this declaration will have no visual effect whatsoever. This happens because margins on inline nonreplaced elements don't change the line height of an element.

 The only properties that can change the distance between lines containing only text are line-height, font-size, and vertical-align, as described in Chapter 7.

These facts are true only for the top and bottom sides of inline nonreplaced elements; the left and right sides are a different story altogether. We'll start by considering the simple case of a small inline nonreplaced element within a single line. Here, if you set values for the left or right margin, they will be visible, as Figure 8-15 makes clear (so to speak):

```
strong {margin-left: 25px; background: silver;}
```

This paragraph contains **strongly emphasized text** that has been styled as indicated.

Figure 8-15. An inline nonreplaced element with a left margin

Note the extra space between the end of the word just before the inline nonreplaced element and the edge of the inline element's background. You can add that extra space to both ends of the inline if you want:

```
strong {margin: 25px; background: silver;}
```

As expected, Figure 8-16 shows a little extra space on the right and left sides of the inline element, and no extra space above or below it.

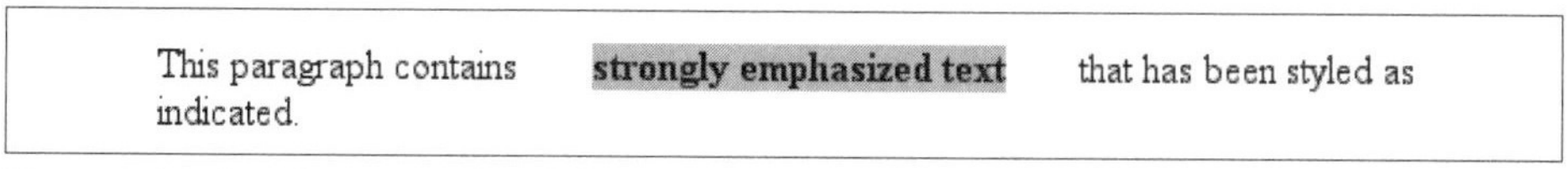

This paragraph contains **strongly emphasized text** that has been styled as indicated.

Figure 8-16. An inline nonreplaced element with a 25-pixel margin

Now, when an inline nonreplaced element stretches across multiple lines, the situation changes a bit. Figure 8-17 demonstrates what happens when an inline nonreplaced element with a margin is displayed across multiple lines:

```
strong {margin: 25px; background: silver;}
```

This paragraph, like the others, contains a small amount of **strongly emphasized text** that has been styled as indicated.

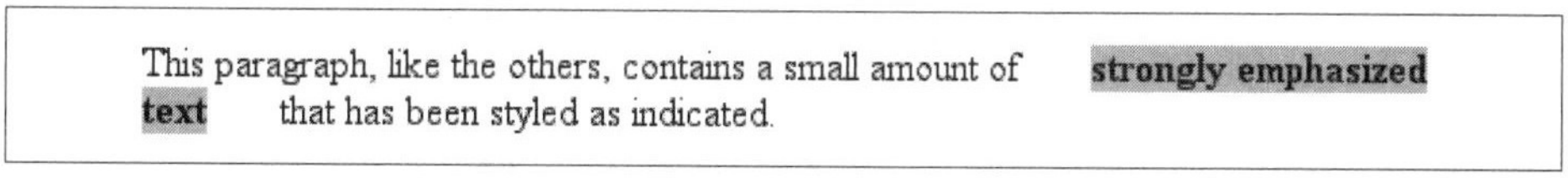

Figure 8-17. An inline nonreplaced element with a 25-pixel margin displayed across two lines of text

The left margin is applied to the beginning of the element and the right margin to the end of it. Margins are *not* applied to the right and left side of each line. Also, you can see that, if not for the margins, the line may have broken after "text" instead of after "strongly emphasized." Margins only affect line breaking by changing the point at which the element's content begins within a line.

The situation gets even more interesting when we apply negative margins to inline nonreplaced elements. The top and bottom of the element aren't affected, and neither are the heights of lines, but the left and right ends of the element can overlap other content, as depicted in Figure 8-18:

```
strong {margin: -25px; background: silver;}
```

This paragraph cont**strongly emphasized text** has been styled as indicated.

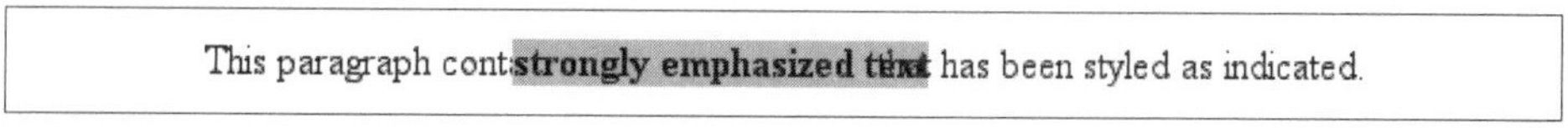

Figure 8-18. An inline nonreplaced element with a negative margin

Replaced elements represent yet another story: margins set for them *do* affect the height of a line, either increasing or reducing it depending on the value for the top and bottom margin. The left and right margins of an inline replaced element act the same as for a nonreplaced element. Figure 8-19 shows a series of different effects on layout from margins set on inline replaced elements.

This paragraph contains a bunch of images in the text `INLINE` . Each one has different margins `INLINE` . Some of these margins are negative, and some are positive `INLINE` . Since replaced element boxes affect line height, the margins on these images can alter the space between baselines `INLINE`. This is to be expected, and is something authors must take into consideratio`INLINE`

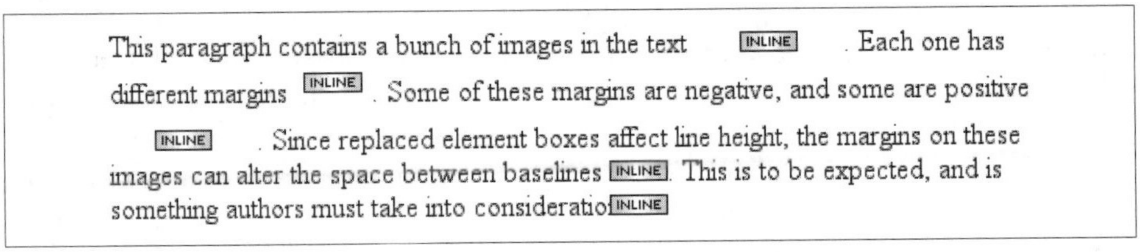

Figure 8-19. Inline replaced elements with differing margin values

Historical Margin Problems

As useful as margins are, a number of problems can arise from their use—all of them centered on Netscape Navigator 4.x (NN4.x), unsurprisingly.

The first hitch is that Navigator 4.x *added* margin rules to its default margins instead of replacing its default values. For example, consider:

```
h1 {margin-bottom: 0;}
p {margin-top: 0;}
```

NN4.x displays the elements with the usual blank space between them because it's adding the zero values to its own default margins. If you want to override this space, you can always use negative margins, such as setting a -1em top margin on the paragraph. The problem with this solution is that it won't work universally. A CSS-conformant browser will then overlap the text, since it replaces the top margin of the paragraph.

The problem gets worse, unfortunately. If you apply margins to inline elements, your layout will more or less shatter. NN4.x assumes that a margin on any element, inline or not, refers to the left edge of the browser window. This is utterly, completely wrong. Unfortunately, if you have a lot of NN4.x visitors, the use of margins on inline elements is a very risky proposition and not one to be taken lightly. Fortunately, it's easy to hide CSS from NN4.x so that you can style your documents without worrying about NN4.x destroying them. Assuming you still worry about the page's appearance in NN4.x, of course.

Borders

Inside the margins of an element are its *borders*. The border of an element is simply one or more lines that surround the content and padding of an element. Thus, the background of the element will stop at the outer border edge, since the background does not extend into the margins, and the border is just inside the margin.

Every border has three aspects: its width, or thickness; its style, or appearance; and its color. The default value for the width of a border is medium, which is not explicitly defined but is usually two pixels. Despite this, the reason you don't usually see borders is that the default style is none, which prevents them from existing. If a border has no style, it doesn't need to exist. (This lack of existence can also reset the width value, but we'll get to that in a little while.)

Finally, the default border color is the foreground color of the element itself. If no color has been declared for the border, it will be the same color as the text of the element. If, on the other hand, an element has no text—let's say it has a table that contains only images—the border color for that table will be the text color of its parent element (due to the fact that color is inherited). That element is likely to be body, div, or another table. Thus, if a table has a border, and the body is its parent, given this rule:

```
body {color: purple;}
```

by default, the border around the table will be purple (assuming the user agent doesn't set a color for tables). Of course, to get that border to appear, you have to do a little work first.

Borders and Backgrounds

The CSS specification strongly implies that the background of an element extends to the outside edge of the border, since it mentions borders being drawn "on top of the background of the element." This is important because some borders are "intermittent"—for example, dotted and dashed borders—and the element's background should appear in the spaces between the visible portions of the border.

When CSS2 was released, it stated that the background extends only into the padding, not the borders. This was later corrected, and CSS2.1 explicitly states that the element's background is the background of the content, padding, and border areas. Most browsers are in agreement with the CSS2.1 definition, although some older browsers may act differently. Background color issues are discussed in more detail in Chapter 9.

Borders with Style

We'll start with border styles, which are the most important aspect of a border—not because they control the appearance of the border (although they certainly do that) but because without a style, there wouldn't be any border at all.

CSS defines 10 distinct non-inherit styles for the property border-style, including the default value of none. The styles are demonstrated in Figure 8-20.

The style value hidden is equivalent to none, except when applied to tables, where it's used for border-conflict resolution. (See Chapter 11 for more details.)

border-style

Values:	[none | hidden | dotted | dashed | solid | double | groove | ridge | inset | outset]{1,4} | inherit
Initial value:	Not defined for shorthand properties
Applies to:	All elements
Inherited:	No
Computed value:	See individual properties (border-top-style, etc.)
Note:	According to CSS1 and CSS2, HTML user agents are only required to support solid and none; the rest of the values (except for hidden) may be interpreted as solid; this restriction was dropped in later drafts of CSS2.1

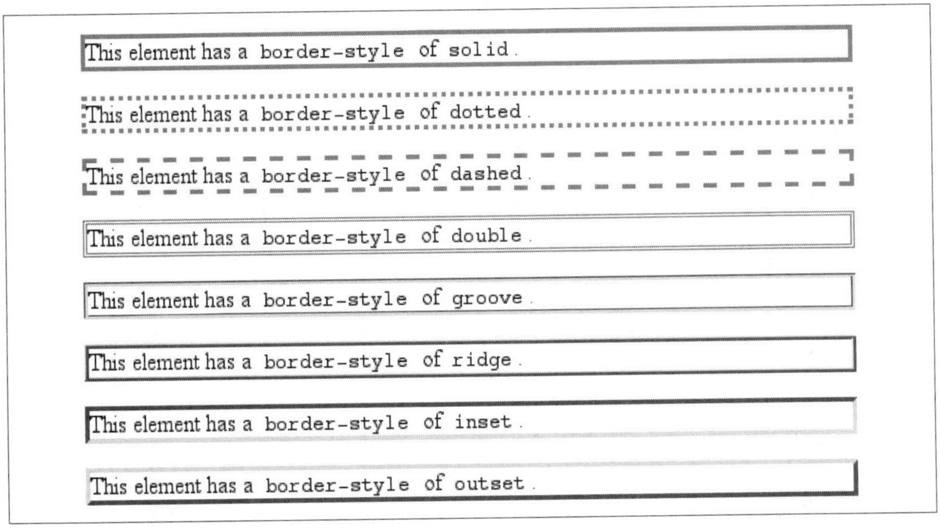

This element has a `border-style` of `solid`.

This element has a `border-style` of `dotted`.

This element has a `border-style` of `dashed`.

This element has a `border-style` of `double`.

This element has a `border-style` of `groove`.

This element has a `border-style` of `ridge`.

This element has a `border-style` of `inset`.

This element has a `border-style` of `outset`.

Figure 8-20. Border styles

The most unpredictable border style is double. It's defined such that the width of the two lines, plus the width of the space between them, is equal to the value of border-width (discussed in the next section). However, the CSS specification doesn't say whether one of the lines should be thicker than the other, or if they should be the same width, or if the space should be thicker or thinner than the lines. All of these things are decided by the user agent, and the author has no way to influence the decision.

All of the borders shown in Figure 8-20 are based on a color value of gray, which makes the visual effects easier to see. The look of a border style is always based in some way on the color of the border, although the exact method may vary between user agents. For example, Figure 8-21 illustrates two different ways of rendering an inset border.

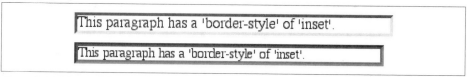

Figure 8-21. Two valid ways of rendering inset

So let's assume you want to define a border style for images that are inside any unvisited hyperlink. You might make them outset, so they have a "raised button" look, as depicted in Figure 8-22:

```
a:link img {border-style: outset;}
```

Figure 8-22. Applying an outset border to a hyperlinked image

Again, the color of the border is based on the element's value for color. In this circumstance, that value is likely to be blue (although it won't show in print) because the image is contained with a hyperlink, and the foreground color of hyperlinks is usually blue. If you so desired, you could change that color to silver, like this:

```
a:link img {border-style: outset; color: silver;}
```

The border will now be based on the light-grayish silver, since that's now the foreground color of the image—even though the image doesn't actually use it, it's still passed on to the border. We'll talk about another way to change border colors later in this chapter.

Multiple styles

It's possible to define more than one style for a given border. For example:

```
p.aside {border-style: solid dashed dotted solid;}
```

The result is a paragraph with a solid top border, a dashed right border, a dotted bottom border, and a solid left border.

Again we see the top-right-bottom-left order of values, just as we saw in our discussion of setting different margins with multiple values. All of the same rules about value replication apply to border styles, as they did with margins and padding. Thus, the following two statements would have the same effect, which is depicted in Figure 8-23:

```
p.new1 {border-style: solid dashed none;}
p.new2 {border-style: solid dashed none dashed;}
```

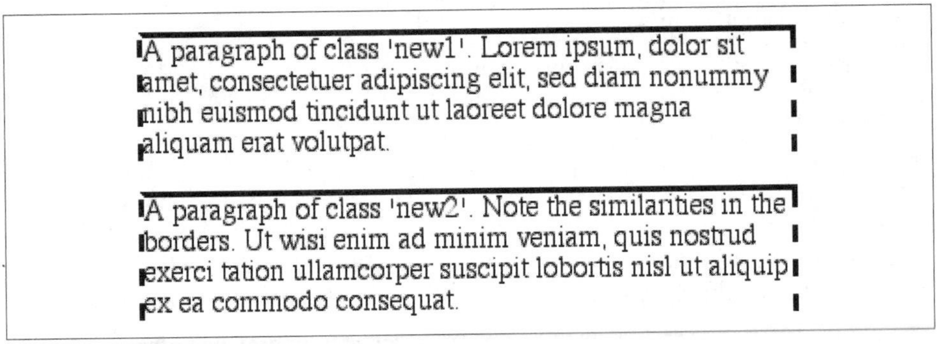

> A paragraph of class 'new1'. Lorem ipsum, dolor sit amet, consectetuer adipiscing elit, sed diam nonummy nibh euismod tincidunt ut laoreet dolore magna aliquam erat volutpat.
>
> A paragraph of class 'new2'. Note the similarities in the borders. Ut wisi enim ad minim veniam, quis nostrud exerci tation ullamcorper suscipit lobortis nisl ut aliquip ex ea commodo consequat.

Figure 8-23. Equivalent style rules

Single-side styles

There may be times when you want to set border styles for just one side of an element box, rather than all four. That's where the single-side border style properties come in.

---

border-top-style, border-right-style, border-bottom-style, border-left-style

Values:	none | hidden | dotted | dashed | solid | double | groove | ridge | inset | outset | inherit
Initial value:	none
Applies to:	All elements
Inherited:	No
Computed value:	As specified

Single-side border style properties are fairly self-explanatory. If you want to change the style for the bottom border, for example, you use `border-bottom-style`.

It's not uncommon to see border used in conjunction with a single-side property. Suppose you want to set a solid border on three sides of a heading, but not have a left border at all, as shown in Figure 8-24.

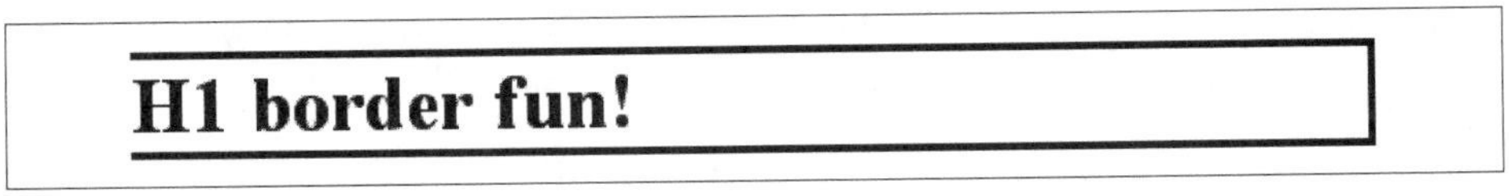

H1 border fun!

Figure 8-24. Removing the left border

There are two equivalent ways to accomplish this:

```
h1 {border-style: solid solid solid none;}
   /* the method above is the same as the one below */
h1 {border-style: solid; border-left-style: none;}
```

What's important to remember is that if you're going to use the second approach, you must place the single-side property after the shorthand, as is usually the case with shorthands. This is because `border-style: solid` is actually a declaration of `border-style: solid solid solid solid`. If you put `border-style-left: none` before the border-style declaration, the shorthand's value will override the single-side value `none`.

You may have noticed that, so far, your border examples have used borders of exactly the same width. This is because you didn't define a width, so it defaulted to a certain value. Next, you'll find out about that default, and much more.

Border Widths

Once you've assigned a border a style, the next step is to give it some width using the property `border-width`.

border-width	
Values:	[thin | medium | thick | <length>]{1,4} | inherit
Initial value:	Not defined for shorthand properties
Applies to:	All elements
Inherited:	No
Computed value:	See individual properties (border-top-style, etc.)

You can also use one of its cousin properties.

border-top-width, border-right-width, border-bottom-width, border-left-width	
Values:	thin | medium | thick | <length> | inherit
Initial value:	medium
Applies to:	All elements
Inherited:	No
Computed value:	Absolute length; 0 if the style of the border is none or hidden

Each of these properties is used to set the width on a specific border side, of course, just as with the margin properties.

 As of CSS2.1, border widths still cannot be given percentage values, which is rather a shame.

There are four ways to assign width to a border: you can give it a length value such as 4px or 0.1em or use one of three keywords. These keywords are thin, medium (the default value), and thick. These keywords don't necessarily correspond to any particular width but are simply defined in relation to one another. According to the specification, thick is always wider than medium, which is in turn always wider than thin.

However, the exact widths are not defined, so one user agent could set them to be equivalent to 5px, 3px, and 2px, while another sets them to be 3px, 2px, and 1px. No matter what width the user agent uses for each keyword, it will be the same throughout the document, regardless of where the border occurs. So, if medium is the same as 2px, then a medium-width border will always be two pixels wide, whether the border surrounds an h1 or a p element. Figure 8-25 illustrates one way to handle these three keywords, as well as how they relate to each other and to the content they surround.

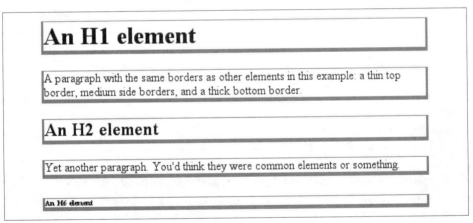

Figure 8-25. The relation of border-width keywords to one another

Let's suppose a paragraph has margins, a background color, and a border style set:

```
p {margin: 5px; background-color: silver;
   border-style: solid;}
```

By default, the border's width is medium. You can change that easily enough:

```
p {margin: 5px; background-color: silver;
   border-style: solid; border-width: thick;}
```

Of course, border widths can be taken to fairly ridiculous extremes, such as setting 50-pixel borders, as depicted in Figure 8-26:

```
p {margin: 5px; background-color: silver;
   border-style: solid; border-width: 50px;}
```

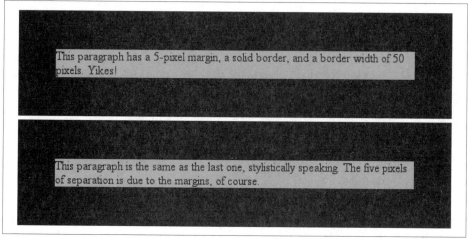

Figure 8-26. Really wide borders

It's also possible to set widths for individual sides, using two familiar methods. The first is to use any of the specific properties mentioned at the beginning of the section, such as `border-bottom-width`. The other way is to use value replication in `border-width`, which is illustrated in Figure 8-27:

```
h1 {border-style: dotted; border-width: thin 0;}
p {border-style: solid; border-width: 15px 2px 7px 4px;}
```

Figure 8-27. Value replication and uneven border widths

No border at all

So far, we've talked only about using a visible border style such as `solid` or `outset`. Let's consider what happens when you set `border-style` to `none`:

```
p {margin: 5px; border-style: none; border-width: 20px;}
```

Even though the border's width is `20px`, the style is set to `none`. In this case, not only does the border's style vanish, so does its width. The border simply ceases to be. Why?

If you'll remember, the terminology used earlier in the chapter was that a border with a style of none does not exist. Those words were chosen very carefully because they help explain what's going on here. Since the border doesn't exist, it can't have any width, so the width is automatically set to 0 (zero), no matter what you try to define. After all, if a drinking glass is empty, you can't really describe it as being half-full of nothing. You can discuss the depth of a glass's contents only if it has actual contents. In the same way, talking about the width of a border makes sense only in the context of a border that exists.

This is important to keep in mind because it's a common mistake to forget to declare a border style. This leads to all kinds of author frustration because, at first glance, the styles appear correct. Given the following rule, though, no h1 element will have a border of any kind, let alone one that's 20 pixels wide:

```
h1 {border-width: 20px;}
```

Since the default value of border-style is none, failing to declare a style is exactly the same as declaring border-style: none. Therefore, if you want a border to appear, you must declare a border style.

Border Colors

Compared to the other aspects of borders, setting the color is pretty easy. CSS uses the single property border-color, which can accept up to four color values at one time.

<table>
<tr><td colspan="2" align="center">**border-color**</td></tr>
<tr><td>Values:</td><td>[<color> | transparent]{1,4} | inherit</td></tr>
<tr><td>Initial value:</td><td>Not defined for shorthand properties</td></tr>
<tr><td>Applies to:</td><td>All elements</td></tr>
<tr><td>Inherited:</td><td>No</td></tr>
<tr><td>Computed value:</td><td>See individual properties (border-top-color, etc.)</td></tr>
</table>

If there are less than four values, value replication takes effect. So if you want h1 elements to have thin black top and bottom borders with thick gray side borders, and medium gray borders around p elements, the following markup will suffice. The result is illustrated in Figure 8-28:

```
h1 {border-style: solid; border-width: thin thick; border-color: black gray;}
p {border-style: solid; border-color: gray;}
```

A single color value will be applied to all four sides, of course, as with the paragraph in the previous example. On the other hand, if you supply four color values, you can

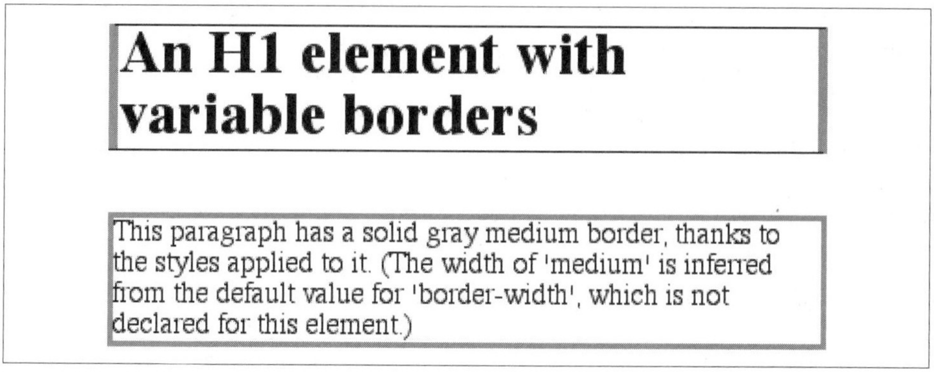

An H1 element with variable borders

This paragraph has a solid gray medium border, thanks to the styles applied to it. (The width of 'medium' is inferred from the default value for 'border-width', which is not declared for this element.)

Figure 8-28. Borders have many aspects

get a different color on each side. Any type of color value can be used, from named colors to hexadecimal and RGB values:

```
p {border-style: solid; border-width: thick;
    border-color: black rgb(25%,25%,25%) #808080 silver;}
```

As I mentioned earlier in the chapter, if you don't declare a color, the default color is the foreground color of the element. Thus, the following declaration will be displayed as shown in Figure 8-29:

```
p.shade1 {border-style: solid; border-width: thick; color: gray;}
p.shade2 {border-style: solid; border-width: thick; color: gray;
    border-color: black;}
```

This paragraph has a solid gray thick border.

This paragraph has a solid black thick border.

Figure 8-29. Border colors based on the element's foreground and the value of the border-color property

The result is that the first paragraph has a gray border, having taken the value gray from the foreground color of the paragraph. The second paragraph, however, has a black border because that color was explicitly assigned using border-color.

There are single-side border-color properties as well. They work in much the same way as the single-side properties for style and width. One way to give headings a solid black border with a solid gray right border is as follows:

```
h1 {border-style: solid; border-color: black; border-right-color: gray;}
```

border-top-color, border-right-color, border-bottom-color, border-left-color

Values:	<color> | transparent | inherit
Initial value:	The value of color for the element
Applies to:	All elements
Inherited:	No
Computed value:	If no value is specified, use the computed value of the property color for the same element; otherwise, as specified

Transparent borders

As you remember, if a border has no style, then it has no width. There are, however, situations where you'll want to create an invisible border. This is where the border color value transparent (introduced in CSS2) comes in. This value is used to create an invisible border that has width.

Let's say you want a set of three links to have borders that are invisible by default, but appear inset when the link is hovered. You can accomplish this by making the borders transparent in the nonhovered case:

```
a:link, a:visited {border-style: solid; border-width: 5px;
   border-color: transparent;}
a:hover {border-color: gray;}
```

This has the effect shown in Figure 8-30.

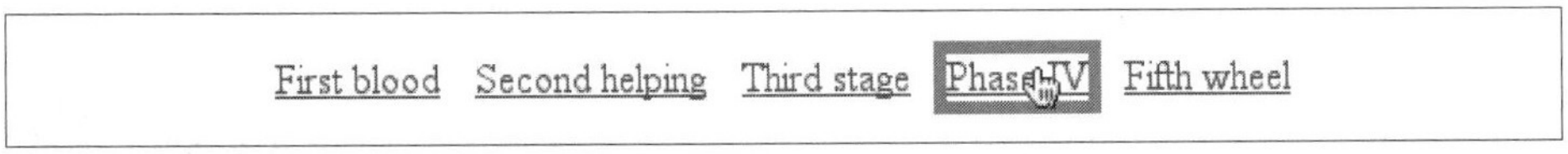

First blood   Second helping   Third stage   Phase IV   Fifth wheel

Figure 8-30. Using transparent borders

In a sense, transparent lets you use borders as if they were extra padding, with the additional benefit of being able to make them visible should you so choose. They act as padding because the background of the element extends into the border area, assuming there is a visible background.

Support for transparent is not present in versions of IE/Win before IE7. In the affected versions, IE will instead base the border color on the element's color value.

Shorthand Border Properties

Unfortunately, shorthand properties such as `border-color` and `border-style` aren't always as helpful as you'd think. For example, you might want to apply a thick, gray, solid border to all `h1` elements, but only along the bottom. If you limit yourself to the properties we've discussed so far, you'll have a hard time applying such a border. Here are two examples:

```
h1 {border-bottom-width: thick;    /* option #1 */
    border-bottom-style: solid;
    border-bottom-color: gray;}

h1 {border-width: 0 0 thick;       /* option #2 */
    border-style: none none solid;
    border-color: gray;}
```

Neither is really convenient, given all the typing involved. Fortunately, there's a better solution:

```
h1 {border-bottom: thick solid gray;}
```

This applies the values to the bottom border alone, as shown in Figure 8-31, leaving the others to their defaults. Since the default border style is `none`, no borders appear on the other three sides of the element.

An H1 element, with a bottom border

Figure 8-31. Setting a bottom border with a shorthand property

As you may have already guessed, there are a total of four such shorthand properties.

---

border-top, border-right, border-bottom, border-left

Values:	[<border-width> || <border-style> || <border-color>] | `inherit`
Initial value:	Not defined for shorthand properties
Applies to:	All elements
Inherited:	No
Computed value:	See individual properties (`border-width`, etc.)

It's possible to use these properties to create some complex borders, such as those shown in Figure 8-32:

```
h1 {border-left: 3px solid gray;
    border-right: black 0.25em dotted;
    border-top: thick silver inset;
    border-bottom: double rgb(33%,33%,33%) 10px;}
```

Figure 8-32. Very complex borders

As you can see, the order of the actual values doesn't really matter. The following three rules yield exactly the same border effect:

```
h1 {border-bottom: 3px solid gray;}
h2 {border-bottom: solid gray 3px;}
h3 {border-bottom: 3px gray solid;}
```

You can also leave out some values and let their defaults kick in, like this:

```
h3 {color: gray; border-bottom: 3px solid;}
```

Since no border color is declared, the default value (the element's foreground) is applied instead. Just remember that if you leave out a border style, the default value of *none* will prevent your border from existing.

By contrast, if you set only a style, you will still get a border. Let's say you simply want a top border style of dashed, and you're willing to let the width default to medium and the color be the same as the text of the element itself. All you need in such a case is the following markup (shown in Figure 8-33):

```
p.roof {border-top: dashed;}
```

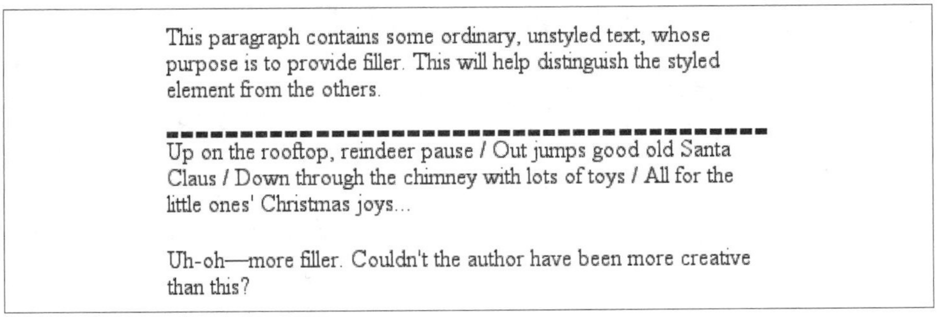

Figure 8-33. Dashing across the top of an element

Another thing to note is that since each of these "border-side" properties apply only to a specific side, there isn't any possibility of value replication—it wouldn't make any sense. There can be only one of each type of value: that is, only one width value, only one color value, and only one border style. So don't try to declare more than one value type:

```
h3 {border-top: thin thick solid purple;}  /* two width values--WRONG */
```

In such a case, the entire statement will be invalid and a user agent would ignore it altogether.

Global Borders

Now, we come to the shortest shorthand border property of all: border.

border	
Values:	[<border-width> || <border-style> || <border-color>]	inherit
Initial value:	Refer to individual properties
Applies to:	All elements
Inherited:	No
Computed value:	As specified

This property has the advantage of being very compact, although that brevity introduces a few limitations. Before we worry about that, let's see how border works. If you want all h1 elements to have a thick, silver border, it's very simple. This declaration would be displayed as shown in Figure 8-34:

```
h1 {border: thick silver solid;}
```

An H1 element with a silver border

Figure 8-34. A really short border declaration

The values are applied to all four sides. This is certainly preferable to the next-best alternative, which would be:

```
h1 {border-top: thick silver solid;
    border-bottom: thick silver solid;
    border-right: thick silver solid;
    border-left: thick silver solid;}  /* same as previous example */
```

The drawback with border is that you can define only "global" styles, widths, and colors. In other words, the values you supply for border will apply to all four sides equally. If you want the borders to be different for a single element, you'll need to use some of the other border properties. Of course, it's possible to turn the cascade to your advantage:

```
H1 {border: thick silver solid;
    border-left-width: 20px;}
```

The second rule overrides the width value for the left border assigned by the first rule, thus replacing thick with 20px, as you can see in Figure 8-35.

An H1 element with a
silver border

Figure 8-35. Using the cascade to one's advantage

You still need to take the usual precautions with shorthand properties: if you omit a value, the default will be filled in automatically, which can have unintended effects. Consider the following:

```
h4 {border-style: dashed solid double;}
h4 {border: medium green;}
```

Here, you've failed to assign a border-style in the second rule, which means that the default value of none will be used, and no h4 elements will have any border at all.

Borders and Inline Elements

Dealing with borders and inline elements should sound pretty familiar since the rules are largely the same as those for margins and inline elements, as well as for material covered in Chapter 7. Still, I'll briefly touch on the topic again.

First, no matter how thick you make your borders on inline elements, the line height of the element won't change. Let's set top and bottom borders on boldfaced text:

```
strong {border-top: 10px solid gray; border-bottom: 5px solid silver;}
```

Once more, this syntax is allowed in the specification, but it will have absolutely no effect on the line height. However, since borders are visible, they'll be drawn—as you can see for yourself in Figure 8-36.

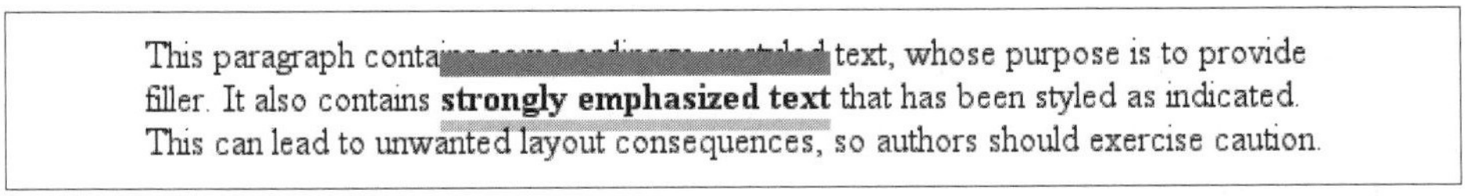

Figure 8-36. Borders on inline nonreplaced elements

The borders had to go somewhere; that's where they went.

Again, all of this is true only for the top and bottom sides of inline elements; the left and right sides are a different story. If you apply a left or right border, not only will it be visible, but it will displace the text around it, as you can see in Figure 8-37:

```
strong {border-left: 25px double gray; background: silver;}
```

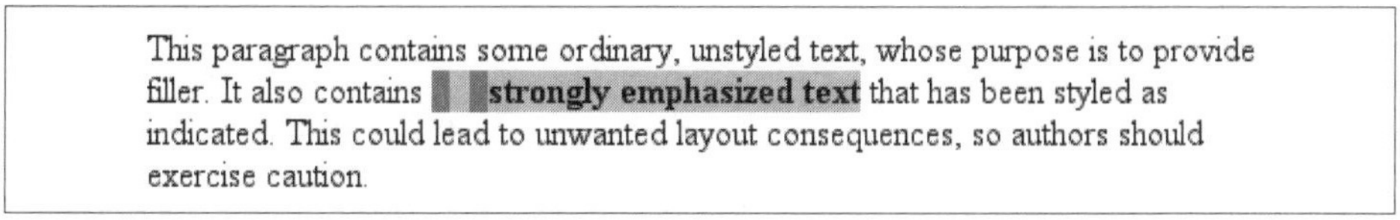

This paragraph contains some ordinary, unstyled text, whose purpose is to provide filler. It also contains **strongly emphasized text** that has been styled as indicated. This could lead to unwanted layout consequences, so authors should exercise caution.

Figure 8-37. An inline nonreplaced element with a left border

With borders, just as with margins, the browser's calculations for line-breaking are not directly affected by any box properties set for inline elements. The only effect is that the space occupied by the borders may shift portions of the line over a bit, which may in turn change which word is at the end of the line.

 There are very few compatibility problems with CSS borders. The most distressing is the fact that Navigator 4.x won't draw a border around the padding area of a block-level element but instead inserts some space between the padding and the border. Speaking of Navigator 4.x, it is extremely dangerous to set borders—or any other box properties—on inline elements. This is as true for borders as it is for margins, and for much the same reasons (which were noted earlier in the chapter).

Padding

Between the borders and the content area, we find the padding of the element box. It is no surprise that the simplest property used to affect this area is called padding.

padding

Values:	[<length> | <percentage>]{1,4} | inherit
Initial value:	Not defined for shorthand elements
Applies to:	All elements
Inherited:	No
Percentages:	Refer to the width of the containing block
Computed value:	See individual properties (padding-top, etc.)
Note:	Padding can never be negative

As you can see, this property accepts any length value or a percentage value. So if you want all h1 elements to have 10 pixels of padding on all sides, it's this easy:

```
h1 {padding: 10px; background-color: silver;}
```

On the other hand, you might want h1 elements to have uneven padding and h2 elements to have regular padding:

```
h1 {padding: 10px 0.25em 3ex 3cm;} /* uneven padding */
h2 {padding: 0.5em 2em;} /* values replicate to the bottom and left sides */
```

It's a little tough to see the padding if that's all you add, though, so let's include a background color, as shown in Figure 8-38:

```
h1 {padding: 10px 0.25em 3ex 3cm; background: gray;}
h2 {padding: 0.5em 2em; background: silver;}
```

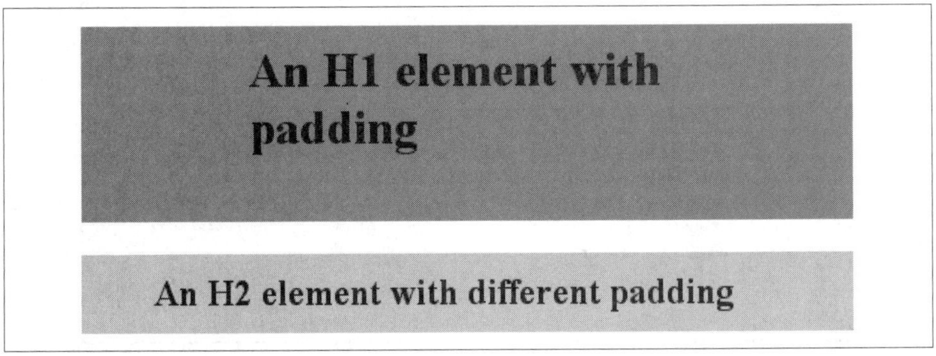

Figure 8-38. Uneven padding with background colors

As Figure 8-38 illustrates, the background of an element extends into the padding. As we discussed before, it also extends to the outer edge of the border, but the background has to go through the padding before it even gets to the border.

By default, elements have no padding. The separation between paragraphs, for example, has traditionally been enforced with margins alone. It's also the case that, without padding, a border on an element will come very close to the content of the element itself. Thus, when putting a border on an element, it's usually a good idea to add some padding as well, as Figure 8-39 illustrates.

Even if you aren't using borders, padding can behave in unique ways. Consider the following rules:

```
p {margin: 1em 0; padding: 1em 0;}
p.one, p.three {background: gray;}
p.two, p.four {background: silver;}
p.three, p.four {margin: 0;}
```

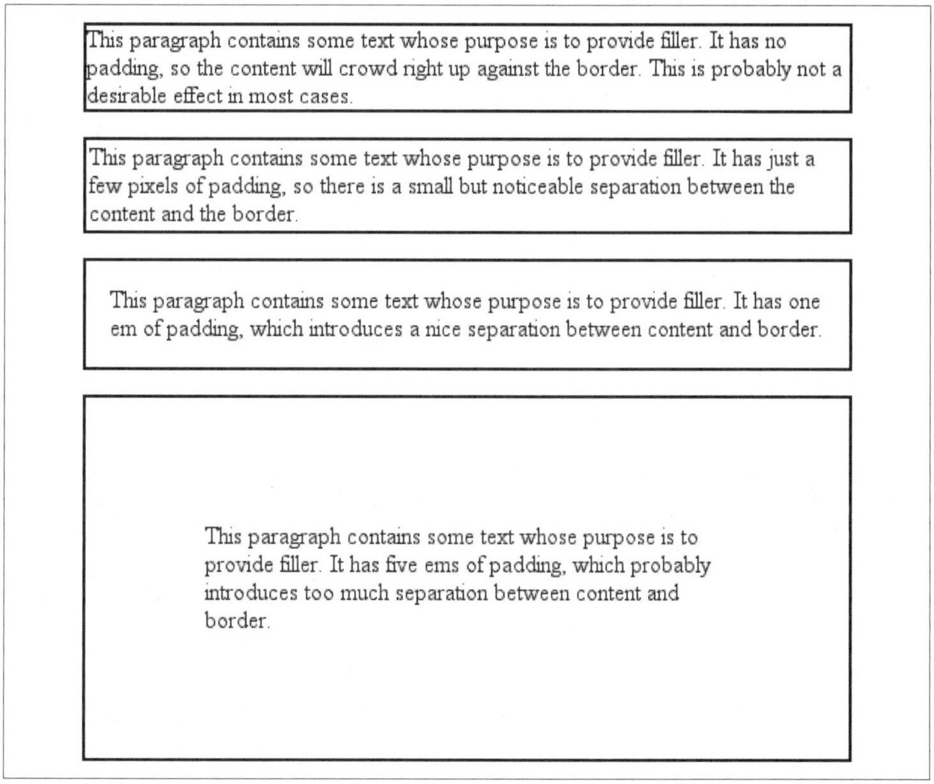

Figure 8-39. The effect of padding on bordered block-level elements

Here we have a situation where all four paragraphs have 1em top and bottom padding, and two out of four have 1em top and bottom margins. The results of this style sheet are shown in Figure 8-40.

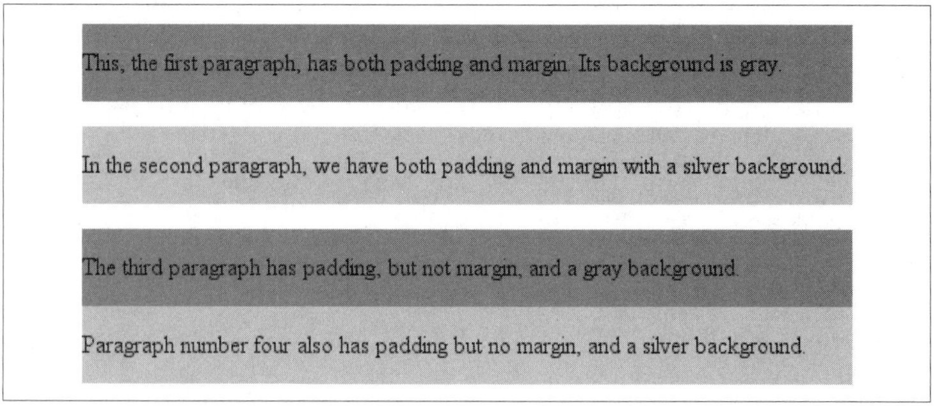

Figure 8-40. Differences between padding and margins

The first two paragraphs have their padding and are separated by one em of space since their margins collapse. The second and third paragraphs are also separated by one em of space because of the bottom margin on the second paragraph. The third and fourth paragraphs are not separated because they have no margins. Note the distance between the content area of the last two paragraphs, however: it's two ems because padding does not collapse. The differing background colors show where one ends and the other begins.

Therefore, using padding to separate the content areas of elements can be trickier than using margins, although it's not without its rewards. For example, to keep paragraphs the traditional "one blank line" apart with padding, you'd have to write:

```
p {margin: 0; padding: 0.5em 0;}
```

The half-em top and bottom padding of each paragraph butt up against each other and total one em of separation. Why would you bother to do this? Because then you could insert separation borders between the paragraphs, should you so choose, and side borders will form the appearance of a solid line. Both of these effects are illustrated in Figure 8-41:

```
p {margin: 0; padding: 0.5em 0; border-bottom: 1px solid gray;
   border-left: 3px double black;}
```

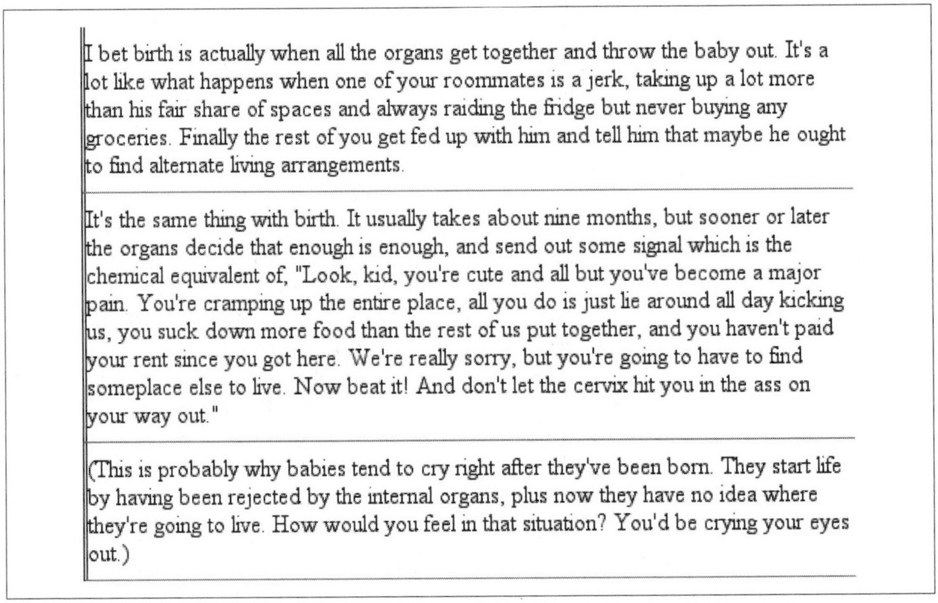

I bet birth is actually when all the organs get together and throw the baby out. It's a lot like what happens when one of your roommates is a jerk, taking up a lot more than his fair share of spaces and always raiding the fridge but never buying any groceries. Finally the rest of you get fed up with him and tell him that maybe he ought to find alternate living arrangements.

It's the same thing with birth. It usually takes about nine months, but sooner or later the organs decide that enough is enough, and send out some signal which is the chemical equivalent of, "Look, kid, you're cute and all but you've become a major pain. You're cramping up the entire place, all you do is just lie around all day kicking us, you suck down more food than the rest of us put together, and you haven't paid your rent since you got here. We're really sorry, but you're going to have to find someplace else to live. Now beat it! And don't let the cervix hit you in the ass on your way out."

(This is probably why babies tend to cry right after they've been born. They start life by having been rejected by the internal organs, plus now they have no idea where they're going to live. How would you feel in that situation? You'd be crying your eyes out.)

Figure 8-41. Using padding instead of margins

Percentage Values and Padding

As I mentioned earlier, it's possible to set percentage values for the padding of an element. As with margins, percentage padding values are computed in relation to the width of the parent element, so they can change if the parent element's width changes. For example, assume the following, which is illustrated in Figure 8-42:

```
p {padding: 10%; background-color: silver;}

<div style="width: 200px;">
<p>This paragraph is contained within a DIV that has a width of 200 pixels,
so its padding will be 10% of the width of the paragraph's parent element.
Given the declared width of 200 pixels, the padding will be 20 pixels on
all sides.</p>
</div>
<div style="width: 100px;">
<p>This paragraph is contained within a DIV with a width of 100 pixels,
so its padding will still be 10% of the width of the paragraph's parent.
There will, therefore, be half as much padding on this paragraph as that
on the first paragraph.</p>
</div>
```

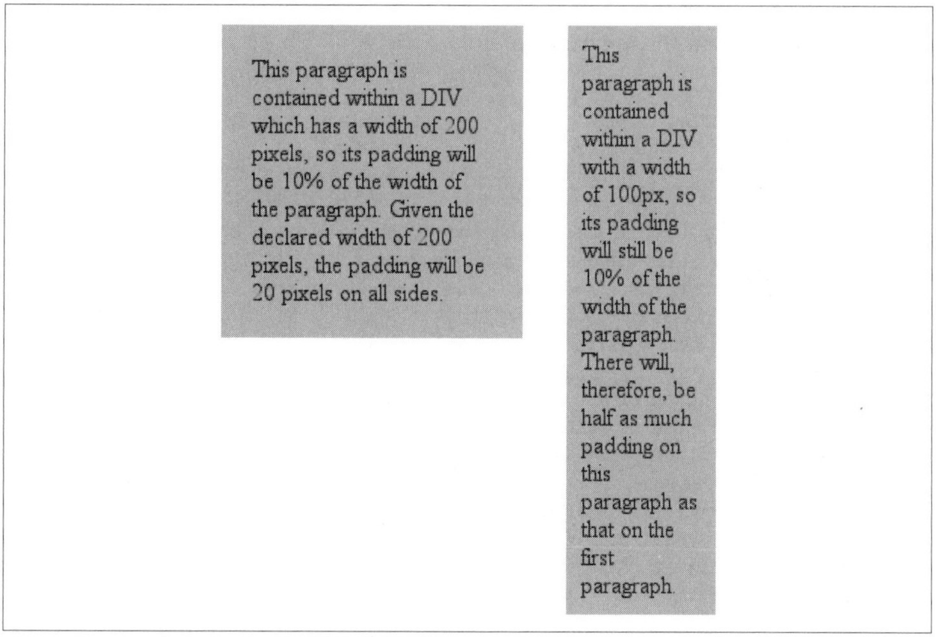

Figure 8-42. Padding, percentages, and the widths of the parent

Note that the top and bottom padding are consistent with the right and left padding; in other words, the percentage of top and bottom padding is calculated with respect to the element's width, not its height. You've seen this before, of course—in the earlier section "Margins," in case you don't remember—but it is worth reviewing again, just to see how it operates.

Single-Side Padding

You guessed it: there are properties that let you set the padding on a single side of the box without affecting the others.

---

padding-top, padding-right, padding-bottom, padding-left

Values:	\<length\> | \<percentage\> | inherit
Initial value:	0
Applies to:	All elements
Inherited:	No
Percentages:	Refer to the width of the containing block
Computed value:	For percentage values, as specified; for length values, the absolute length
Note:	Padding can never be negative

These properties operate as you'd expect. For example, the following two rules will give the same amount of padding:

```
h1 {padding: 0 0 0 0.25in;}
h2 {padding-left: 0.25in;}
```

Padding and Inline Elements

There is one major difference between margins and padding when it comes to inline elements. To illustrate, let's start with right and left padding. Here, if you set values for the left or right padding, they will be visible, as Figure 8-43 demonstrates:

```
strong {padding-left: 10px; padding-right: 10px; background: silver;}
```

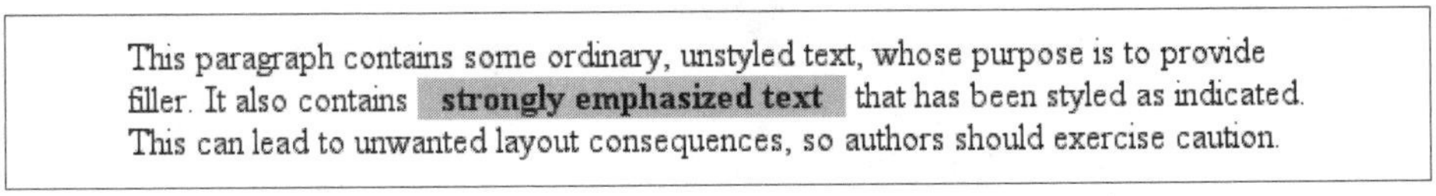

This paragraph contains some ordinary, unstyled text, whose purpose is to provide filler. It also contains strongly emphasized text that has been styled as indicated. This can lead to unwanted layout consequences, so authors should exercise caution.

Figure 8-43. Padding on an inline nonreplaced element

Note the extra space background that appears on either end of the inline nonreplaced element. There's your padding. As with margins, the left padding is applied to the beginning of the element, and the right padding to the end of it; however, padding is *not* applied to the right and left side of each line. The same holds true for replaced elements as well, although of course such elements don't break across lines.

In theory, an inline nonreplaced element with a background color and padding could have a background that extends above and below the element:

```
strong {padding-top: 0.5em; background-color: silver;}
```

Figure 8-44 gives you an idea of what this might look like.

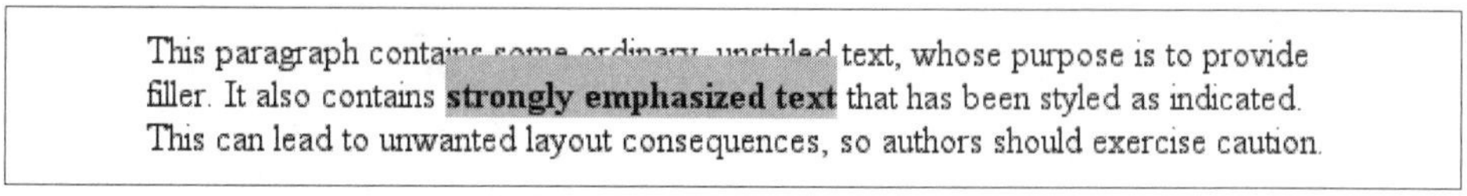

This paragraph contains some ordinary unstyled text, whose purpose is to provide filler. It also contains **strongly emphasized text** that has been styled as indicated. This can lead to unwanted layout consequences, so authors should exercise caution.

Figure 8-44. More padding on an inline nonreplaced element

The line height isn't changed, of course, but since padding does extend the background, it should be visible, right? Right. It is visible, and it overlaps the lines that come before—which is the expected result.

Padding and Replaced Elements

This may come as a surprise, but it is possible to apply padding to replaced elements, although there are still limitations at the time of this writing.

The most surprising case is that you can apply padding to an image, like this:

```
img {background: silver; padding: 1em;}
```

Regardless of whether the replaced element is block-level or inline, the padding will surround its content, and the background color will fill into that padding, as shown in Figure 8-45. You can also see that padding will push an element's border away from its content.

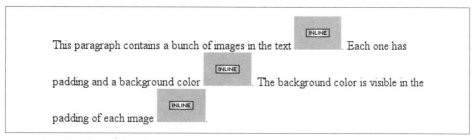

Figure 8-45. Padding replaced elements

As of CSS2.1, however, there was some confusion over what to do about styling form elements such as input. It is not entirely clear where the padding of a checkbox resides, for example. Therefore, as of this writing, some browsers—such as Mozilla—ignore padding (and other forms of styling) for form elements. There is hope that a CSS specification will emerge that describes form-element styling in the future.

The other possible limitation is that many older browsers did not apply padding to images, including IE5 for Windows.

Summary

The ability to apply margins, borders, and padding to any element is one of the things that sets CSS so far above traditional web markup. In the past, enclosing a heading in a colored, bordered box meant wrapping the heading in a table, which is a really bloated and awful way to create such a simple effect. It is this sort of power that makes CSS so compelling.

CHAPTER 9

Colors and Backgrounds

Remember the first time you changed the colors of a web page? Instead of the old black text on a gray background with blue links, all of a sudden you could use any combination of colors you desired—perhaps light blue text on a black background with lime-green hyperlinks. From there, it was just a short hop to colored text and, eventually, even to multiple colors for the text in a page, thanks to <FONT COLOR="...">. Once you could add background images, too, just about anything was possible, or so it seemed. CSS takes color and backgrounds even further, letting you apply many different colors and backgrounds to a single page, and all without a single FONT or TABLE tag.

Colors

When designing a page, you need to plan it out before you start. That's generally true in any case, but with colors, it's even more so. If you're going to make all hyperlinks yellow, will they clash with the background color in any part of your document? If you use too many colors, will it overwhelm the user? (Hint: yes.) If you change the default hyperlink colors, will users still be able to figure out where your links are? (For example, if you make both regular text and hyperlink text the same color, it's much harder to spot links—in fact, almost impossible if the links aren't underlined.)

Despite the added planning, the ability to change the colors of elements is something almost every author will want to use, probably quite often. Used properly, colors can really strengthen the presentation of a document. As an example, let's say you have a design where all h1 elements should be green, most h2 elements should be blue, and all hyperlinks should be dark red. In some cases, however, you want h2 elements to be dark blue because they're associated with different types of information. The simplest way to handle this is to assign a class to each h2 that should be dark blue and declare the following:

```
h1 {color: green;}
h2 {color: blue;}
h2.dkblue {color: navy;}
a {color: maroon;}   /* a good dark red color */
```

 It's actually better to pick class names that describe the type of information contained within, not the visual effect you're trying to achieve. For example, let's say that you want dark blue to be applied to all h2 elements that are subsection headings. It's preferable to pick a class name like subsec or even sub-section, which actually mean something and, more importantly, are independent of any presentational concepts. After all, you might decide later to make all subsection titles dark red instead of dark blue, and the statement h2.dkblue {color: maroon;} is more than a little silly.

From this simple example, you can see that it's generally better to plan ahead when you're using styles, so you can use all of the tools at your disposal. For example, suppose you add a navigational bar to the page in the preceding example. Within this bar, hyperlinks should be yellow, not dark red. If the bar is marked with an ID of navbar, then you only need to add this rule:

```
#navbar a {color: yellow;}
```

This will change the color of hyperlinks within the navigation bar without affecting other hyperlinks throughout the document.

There is really only one type of color in CSS, and that's a plain, solid color. If you set the color of a document to red, the text will be the same shade of red. HTML works the same way, of course. When you declared <BODY LINK="blue" VLINK="blue"> back in the HTML 3.2 days, you expected all hyperlinks to be the same shade of blue, no matter where they were in the document.

Don't change that thinking when using CSS. If you use CSS to set the color of all hyperlinks (both visited and unvisited) to blue, that's what they'll be. In the same way, if you use styles to set the background of the body to green, then the entire body background will be the same shade of green.

In CSS, you can set both the foreground and background colors of any element, from the body down to emphasis and hyperlink elements, and almost everything in between—list items, entire lists, headings, table cells, and even (in a limited fashion) images. To understand how this works, though, it's important to understand what's in the foreground of an element and what isn't.

Let's start with the foreground itself; generally speaking, it's the text of an element, although the foreground also includes the borders around the element. Thus, there are two ways to directly affect the foreground color of an element: by using the color property and by setting the border colors using one of a number of border properties, as discussed in the previous chapter.

Foreground Colors

The easiest way to set the foreground color of an element is with the property color.

<table>
<tr><td colspan="2" align="center">color</td></tr>
<tr><td>Values:</td><td><color> | inherit</td></tr>
<tr><td>Initial value:</td><td>User agent-specific</td></tr>
<tr><td>Applies to:</td><td>All elements</td></tr>
<tr><td>Inherited:</td><td>Yes</td></tr>
<tr><td>Computed value:</td><td>As specified</td></tr>
</table>

As discussed in Chapter 4, this property accepts as a value any valid color type, such as #FFCC00 or rgb(100%,80%,0%), as well as the system-color keywords described in Chapter 13.

For nonreplaced elements, color sets the color of the text in the element, as illustrated in Figure 9-1:

```
<p style="color: gray;">This paragraph has a gray foreground.</p>
<p>This paragraph has the default foreground.</p>
```

This paragraph has a gray foreground.

This paragraph has the default foreground.

Figure 9-1. Declared color versus default color

In Figure 9-1, the default foreground color is black. That isn't always the case since users might have set their browsers (or other user agents) to use a different foreground (text) color. If the default text were set to green, the second paragraph in the preceding example would be green, not black—but the first paragraph would still be gray.

You need not restrict yourself to such simple operations, of course. There are plenty of ways to use color. You might have some paragraphs that contain text warning the user of a potential problem. To make this text stand out, you might decide to color it red. Simply apply a class of warn to each paragraph that contains warning text (<p class="warn">) and the following rule:

```
p.warn {color: red;}
```

In the same document, you might decide that any unvisited links within a warning paragraph should be green:

```
p.warn {color: red;}
p.warn a:link {color: green;}
```

Then you change your mind, deciding that warning text should be dark gray and that links in such text should be medium gray. The preceding rules need only be changed to reflect the new values, as illustrated in Figure 9-2:

```
p.warn {color: #666;}
p.warn a:link {color: #AAA;}
```

> When handling plutonium, care must be taken to avoid the formation of a critical mass.
>
> With plutonium, the possibility of implosion is very real, and must be avoided at all costs. This can be accomplished by keeping the various masses separate.

Figure 9-2. Changing colors

Another use for color is to draw attention to certain types of text. For example, bold-faced text is already fairly obvious, but you could give it a different color to make it stand out even further—let's say, maroon:

```
b, strong {color: maroon;}
```

Then you might decide that you want all table cells with a class of highlight to contain light yellow text:

```
td.highlight {color: #FF9;}
```

Of course, if you don't set a background color for any of your text, you run the risk that a user's setup won't combine well with your own. For example, if a user has set her browser's background to a pale yellow, like #FFC, then the previous rule would generate light yellow text on a pale yellow background. Therefore, it's generally a good idea to set foreground and background colors together. (We'll talk about background colors later in the chapter.)

 Watch out for color usage in Navigator 4, which replaces color values it doesn't recognize. The replacements aren't exactly random, but they're certainly not pretty. For example, invalidValue comes out as a dark blue, and inherit, a valid CSS2 value, will come out as a really awful shade of yellow-green. In other circumstances, transparent backgrounds will come out as black.

Replacing Attributes

There are many uses for color, the most basic of which is to replace the HTML 3.2 BODY attributes TEXT, LINK, ALINK, and VLINK. With the anchor pseudo-classes, color can replace these BODY attributes outright. The first line in the following example can be rewritten with the subsequent CSS, and it will have the result depicted in Figure 9-3:

```
<body text="black" link="#808080" alink="silver" vlink="#333333">

body {color: black;}      /* replacement css */
a:link {color: #808080;}
a:active {color: silver;}
a:visited {color: #333333;}
```

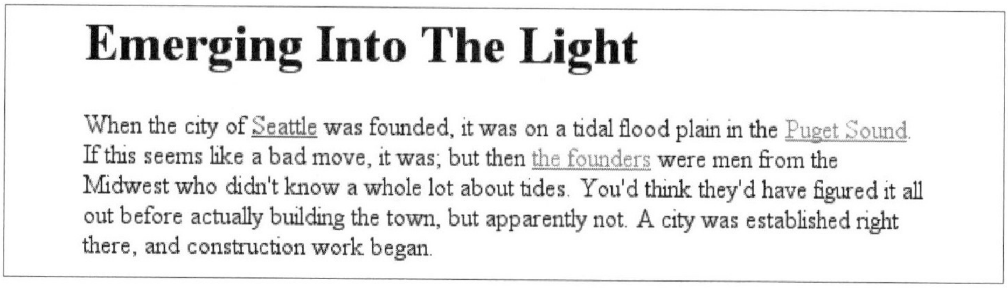

Emerging Into The Light

When the city of Seattle was founded, it was on a tidal flood plain in the Puget Sound. If this seems like a bad move, it was; but then the founders were men from the Midwest who didn't know a whole lot about tides. You'd think they'd have figured it all out before actually building the town, but apparently not. A city was established right there, and construction work began.

Figure 9-3. Replacing BODY attributes with CSS

While this may seem like a lot of extra typing, consider two things. First, this is a major improvement over the old method of BODY attributes, in which you could make changes only at the document level. Back then, if you wanted some links to be medium gray and others to be a relatively dark gray, you couldn't do it with the BODY attributes. Instead, you'd have to use <FONT COLOR="#666666"> on every single anchor that needed to be relatively dark. Not so with CSS; now, you can just add a class to all anchors that need a shade of gray and modify your styles accordingly:

```
body {color: black;}
a:link {color: #808080;}        /* medium gray */
a.external:link {color: silver;}
a:active {color: silver;}
a:visited {color: #333;}    /* a very dark gray */
```

This sets all anchors with a class of external to silver instead of medium gray. They'll still be a dark gray once they're visited, unless you add a special rule for that as well:

```
body {color: black;}
a:link {color: #808080;}        /* medium gray */
a.external:link  {color: #666;}
a:active {color: silver;}
a:visited {color: #333;}    /* a very dark gray */
a.external:visited {color: black;}
```

This will make all external links medium gray before they're visited and black after, while all other links will be dark gray when visited and medium gray when unvisited.

Affecting Borders

The value of color can also affect the borders around an element. Let's assume you've declared these styles, which have the result shown in Figure 9-4:

```
p.aside {color: gray; border-style: solid;}
```

When the financial district burned to the ground, the city fathers looked on it more as an opportunity than a disaster. Here was an opportunity to do things right. Here was their big chance to finally build a city that would be functional, clean, and attractive. Or at least not flooded with sewage every high tide.

> Although the man who started the fire fled town, there's some speculation that he might have been lauded for giving the city an excuse to start over.

A plan was quickly conceived and approved. The fathers got together with the merchants and explained it. "Here's what we'll do," they said, "we'll raise the ground level of the financial district well above the high-tide line. We're going to

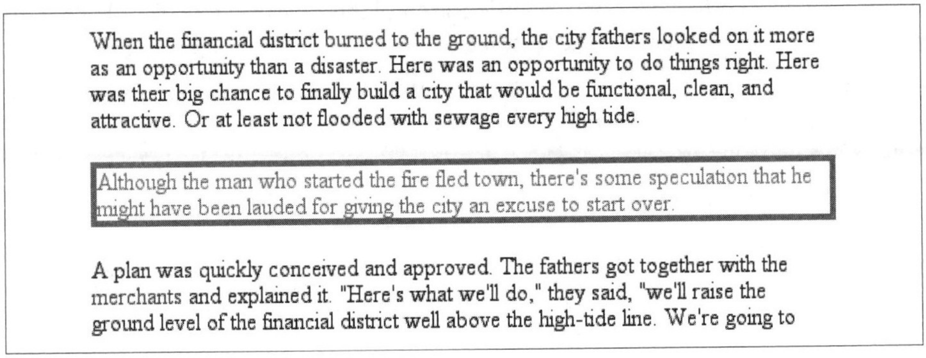

Figure 9-4. Border colors are taken from the content's color

The element `<p class="aside">` has gray text and a gray medium-width solid border. This is because the foreground color is applied to the borders by default. The basic way to override this is with the property `border-color`:

```
p.aside {color: gray; border-style: solid; border-color: black;}
```

This will make the text gray, but the borders will be `black`. Any value set for `border-color` will always override the value of `color`.

The borders, incidentally, allow you to affect the foreground color of images. Since images are already composed of colors, you can't really affect them using `color`, but you can change the color of any border around the image. This can be done using either `color` or `border-color`. Therefore, the following rules will have the same visual effect on images of class `type1` *and* `type2`, as shown in Figure 9-5:

```
img.type1 {color: gray; border-style: solid;}
img.type2 {border-color: gray; border-style: solid;}
```

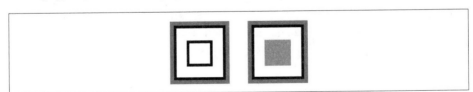

Figure 9-5. Setting the border color for images

Affecting Form Elements

Setting a value for color should (in theory, anyway) apply to form elements. Declaring select elements to have dark gray text should be as simple as this:

```
select {color: rgb(33%,33%,33%);}
```

This might also set the color of the borders around the edge of the select element, or it might not. It all depends on the user agent and its default styles.

You could also set the foreground color of input elements, although, as you can see in Figure 9-6, doing so would apply that color to all inputs, from text to radio button to checkbox inputs:

```
select {color: rgb(33%,33%,33%);}
input {color: gray;}
```

Figure 9-6. Changing form element foregrounds

Note in Figure 9-6 that the text color next to the checkboxes is still black. This is because you've assigned styles only to elements like input and select, not normal paragraph (or other) text.

CSS1 offered no way to distinguish between different types of input elements. So, if you wanted checkboxes to be a different color than radio buttons, you had to assign them classes to get the desired result:

```
input.radio {color: #666;}
input.check {color: #CCC;}

<input type="radio" name="r2" value="a" class="radio" />
<input type="checkbox" name="c3" value="one" class="check" />
```

In CSS2 and later, it's a little easier to distinguish between different elements based on which attributes they have, thanks to attribute selectors:

```
input[type="radio"] {color: #333;}
input[type="checkbox"] {color: #666;}

<input type="radio" name="r2" value="a " />
<input type="checkbox" name="c3" value="one "/>
```

Attribute selectors allow you to dispense with the classes altogether, at least in this instance. Unfortunately, many user agents don't support attribute selectors, so the use of classes may be necessary for a while.

Navigator 4 won't apply colors to form elements, but setting the colors for form elements works in Internet Explorer 4 and up, and Opera 3.5+. However, many versions of other browsers don't allow form-element styling either, due to uncertainty over how they should be styled.

Inheriting Color

As the definition of color indicates, the property is inherited. This makes sense since if you declare p {color: gray;}, you probably expect that any text within that paragraph will also be gray, even if it's emphasized, boldfaced, etc. Of course, if you *want* such elements to be different colors, that's easy enough, as illustrated in Figure 9-7:

```
em {color: gray;}
p {color: black;}
```

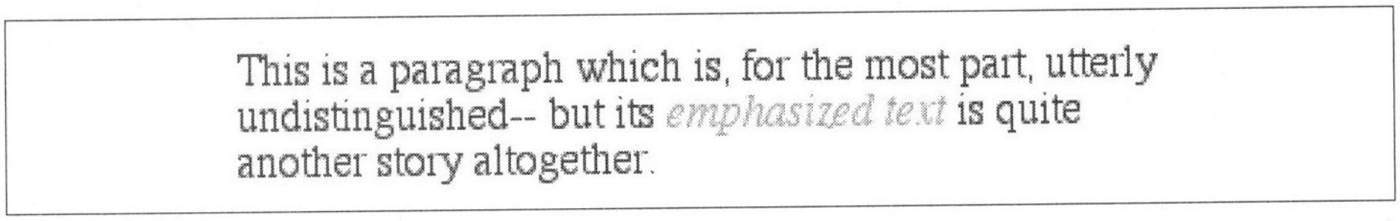

This is a paragraph which is, for the most part, utterly undistinguished-- but its *emphasized text* is quite another story altogether.

Figure 9-7. Different colors for different elements

Since color is inherited, it's theoretically possible to set all of the ordinary text in a document to a color, such as red, by declaring body {color: red;}. This should make red all text that is not otherwise styled (such as anchors, which have their own color styles). However, it's still possible to find browsers that have predefined colors for things like tables, which prevent body colors from inheriting into table cells. In such browsers, since a color value is defined by the browser for table elements, the browser's value will take precedence over the inherited value. This is annoying and unnecessary, but, luckily, it's simple to overcome (usually) by using selectors that list various table elements. For example, to make all of your table content red along with your document's body, try this:

```
body, table, td, th {color: red;}
```

This will generally solve the problem. Note that using such selectors is unnecessary with most modern browsers, which have long since fixed inheritance bugs that plagued them in earlier versions.

Backgrounds

The background area of an element consists of all of the space behind the foreground to the outer edge of the borders; thus, the content box and the padding are all part of an element's background, and the borders are drawn on top of the background.

CSS lets you apply a solid color or create moderately sophisticated effects using background images; its capabilities in this area far outstrip those of HTML.

Background Color

It's possible to declare a color for the background of an element, in a fashion very similar to setting the foreground color. For this, use the property background-color, which accepts (unsurprisingly) any valid color or a keyword that makes the background transparent.

<table>
<tr><th colspan="2" style="text-align:center">background-color</th></tr>
<tr><td>Values:</td><td><color> | transparent | inherit</td></tr>
<tr><td>Initial value:</td><td>transparent</td></tr>
<tr><td>Applies to:</td><td>All elements</td></tr>
<tr><td>Inherited:</td><td>No</td></tr>
<tr><td>Computed value:</td><td>As specified</td></tr>
</table>

If you want the color to extend a little bit from the text in the element, simply add some padding to the mix, as illustrated in Figure 9-8:

```
p {background-color: gray; padding: 10px;}
```

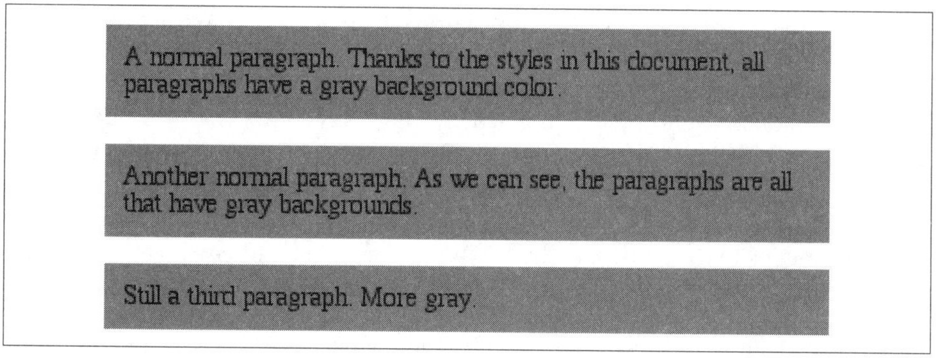

Figure 9-8. Backgrounds and padding

You can set a background color for just about any element, from body all the way down to inline elements such as em and a. background-color is not inherited. Its default value is transparent, which makes sense: if an element doesn't have a defined color, then its background should be transparent so that the background of its ancestor elements will be visible.

One way to picture the inheritance situation is to imagine a clear plastic sign mounted to a textured wall. The wall is still visible through the sign, but this is not the background of the sign, it's the background of the wall (in CSS terms, anyway). Similarly, if you set the canvas to have a background, it can be seen through all of the elements in the document that don't have their own backgrounds. They don't inherit the background; it is visible *through* them. This may seem like an irrelevant distinction, but as you'll see in the section on background images, it's actually a critical difference.

Most of the time, you'll have no reason to use the keyword `transparent` since that's the default value. On occasion, though, it can be useful. Imagine that a user has set his browser to make all links have a white background. When you design your page, you set anchors to have a white foreground, and you don't want a background on those anchors. To make sure your design choice prevails, declare:

```
a {color: white; background-color: transparent;}
```

If you left out the background color, your white foreground would combine with the user's white background to yield totally unreadable links. This is an unlikely example, but it's still possible.

 The potential combination of author and reader styles is the reason why a CSS validator will generate warnings such as, "You have no background-color with your color." It's trying to remind you that author-user color interaction can occur, and your rule has not accounted for this possibility. Warnings do not mean your styles are invalid: only errors prevent validation.

Historical issues

So, setting a background color is a pretty simple thing—except for one small warning: Navigator 4 gets the placement of background colors completely wrong. Instead of applying the background color to the entire content box and padding, the color appears only behind the text itself, as shown in Figure 9-9.

A normal paragraph. Thanks to the styles in this document, all paragraphs have a gray background color.

Another normal paragraph. As we can see, the paragraphs are all that have gray backgrounds, but Navigator 4 is only filling the background in where the text exists.

Still a third paragraph. More gray, but not enough.

Figure 9-9. Navigator 4.x's incorrect behavior

Let me reiterate: *this behavior is totally wrong*. To counteract it, you must set a border on the element, which you can then set to the same color as the background color of your document:

```
body {background: silver;}
p {background-color: gray; padding: 0.1px; border: 1px solid silver;}
```

Note that you must set a `border-style` for this technique to work. It doesn't matter whether you use that specific property or simply a value of the `border` property.

Of course, by doing this, you're setting a border on the element, and that border will show up in other user agents as well. To top things off, Navigator doesn't handle padding very well, so the previous example results in a small amount of blank space between the content box and the borders. Thankfully, newer browsers don't suffer from such problems.

Special effects

Simply by combining `color` and `background-color`, you can create some useful effects:

```
h1 {color: white; background-color: rgb(20%,20%,20%);
    font-family: Arial, sans-serif;}
```

This example is illustrated in Figure 9-10.

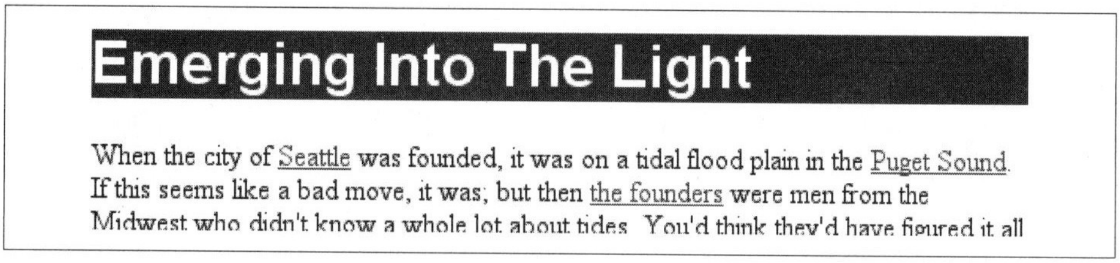

Figure 9-10. A nifty effect for H1 elements

Of course, there are as many color combinations as there are colors, but I can't show all of them here—being stuck in grayscale as we are. Still, I'll try to give you some idea of what you can do.

This style sheet is a little more complicated, as illustrated by Figure 9-11:

```
body {color: black; background-color: white;}
h1, h2 {color: yellow; background-color: rgb(0,51,0);}
p {color: #555;}
a:link {color: black; background-color: silver;}
a:visited {color: gray; background-color: white;}
```

This is just the tiniest beginning of what's possible, of course. By all means, try some examples of your own!

Background Images

Having covered the basics of foreground and background colors, we turn now to the subject of background images. In HTML 3.2, it was possible to associate an image with the background of the document by using the BODY attribute BACKGROUND:

```
<BODY BACKGROUND="bg23.gif">
```

This caused a user agent to load the file *bg23.gif* and then "tile" it in the document background, repeating it in both the horizontal and vertical directions to fill the entire background of the document. This effect can be duplicated in CSS, but CSS

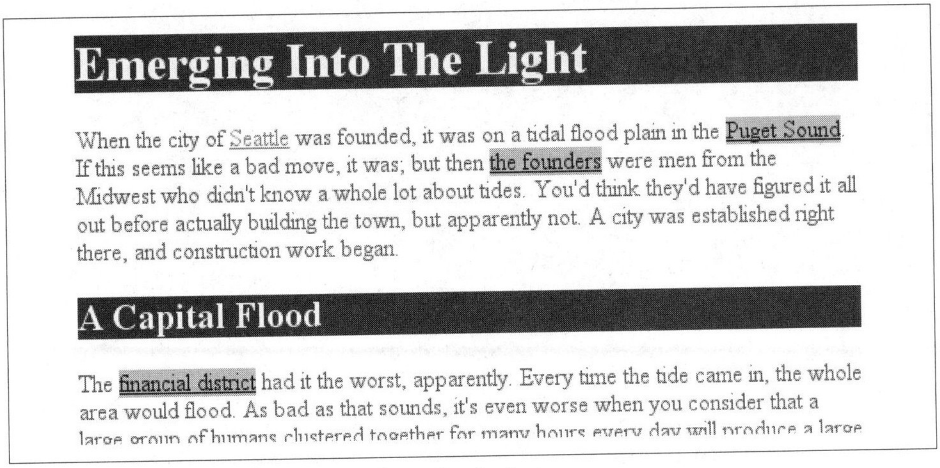

Emerging Into The Light

When the city of Seattle was founded, it was on a tidal flood plain in the Puget Sound. If this seems like a bad move, it was; but then the founders were men from the Midwest who didn't know a whole lot about tides. You'd think they'd have figured it all out before actually building the town, but apparently not. A city was established right there, and construction work began.

A Capital Flood

The financial district had it the worst, apparently. Every time the tide came in, the whole area would flood. As bad as that sounds, it's even worse when you consider that a large group of humans clustered together for many hours every day will produce a large

Figure 9-11. The results of a more complicated style sheet

can do a great deal more than simple tiling of background images. We'll start with the basics and then work our way up.

Using an image

To get an image into the background in the first place, use the property background-image.

---

background-image

Values:	`<uri>` | `none` | `inherit`
Initial value:	`none`
Applies to:	All elements
Inherited:	No
Computed value:	Absolute URI

The default value of none means about what you'd expect: no image is placed in the background. If you want a background image, you must give this property a URL value:

```
body {background-image: url(bg23.gif);}
```

Due to the default values of other background properties, this will tile the image *bg23.gif* in the document's background, as shown in Figure 9-12. As you'll discover shortly, though, tiling isn't the only option.

 It's usually a good idea to specify a background color to go along with your background image; we'll come back to that concept a little later in the chapter.

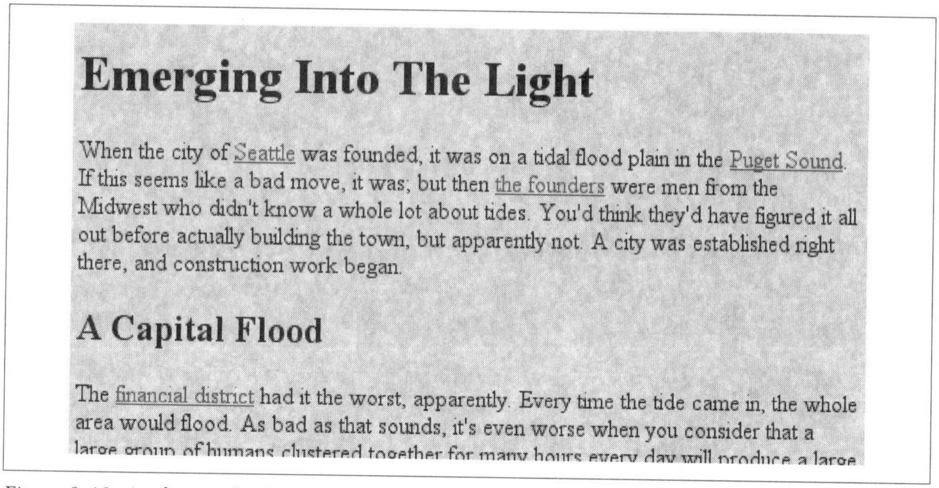

Emerging Into The Light

When the city of Seattle was founded, it was on a tidal flood plain in the Puget Sound. If this seems like a bad move, it was; but then the founders were men from the Midwest who didn't know a whole lot about tides. You'd think they'd have figured it all out before actually building the town, but apparently not. A city was established right there, and construction work began.

A Capital Flood

The financial district had it the worst, apparently. Every time the tide came in, the whole area would flood. As bad as that sounds, it's even worse when you consider that a large group of humans clustered together for many hours every day will produce a large

Figure 9-12. Applying a background image in CSS

You can apply a background image to any element, block-level or inline. Most backgrounds are applied to body elements, of course, but there's no need to stop there:

```
p.starry {background-image: url(http://www.site.web/pix/stars.gif);
   color: white;}
a.grid {background-image: url(smallgrid.gif);}

<p class="starry">It's the end of autumn, which means the stars will be
brighter than ever!  <a href="join.html" class="grid">Join us</a> for
a fabulous evening of planets, stars, nebulae, and more...
```

As you can see in Figure 9-13, you've applied a background to a single paragraph and no other part of the document. You can customize even further, such as placing background images on inline elements like hyperlinks, also depicted in Figure 9-13. Of course, if you want to be able to see the tiling pattern, the image will probably need to be pretty small. After all, individual letters aren't that large!

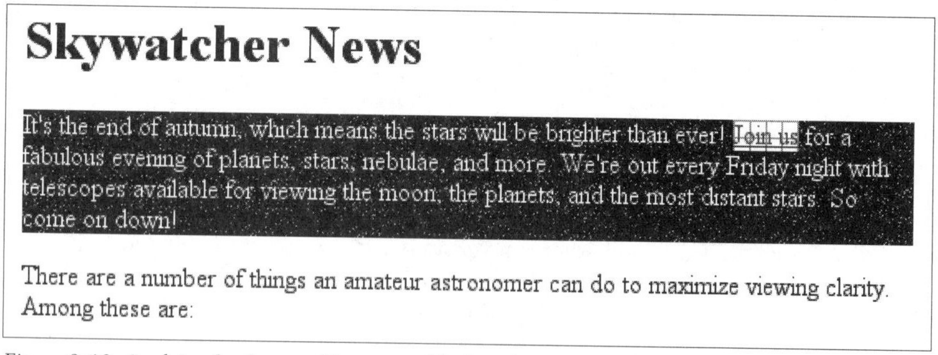

Skywatcher News

It's the end of autumn, which means the stars will be brighter than ever! Join us for a fabulous evening of planets, stars, nebulae, and more. We're out every Friday night with telescopes available for viewing the moon, the planets, and the most distant stars. So come on down!

There are a number of things an amateur astronomer can do to maximize viewing clarity. Among these are:

Figure 9-13. Applying background images to block and inline elements

There are a number of ways to employ specific background images. You might place an image in the background of strong elements to make them stand out more. You could fill in the background of headings with a wavy pattern or with little dots. You can even fill in the cells of tables with patterns to distinguish them from the rest of the page, as shown in Figure 9-14:

```
td.nav {background-image: url(darkgrid.gif);}
```

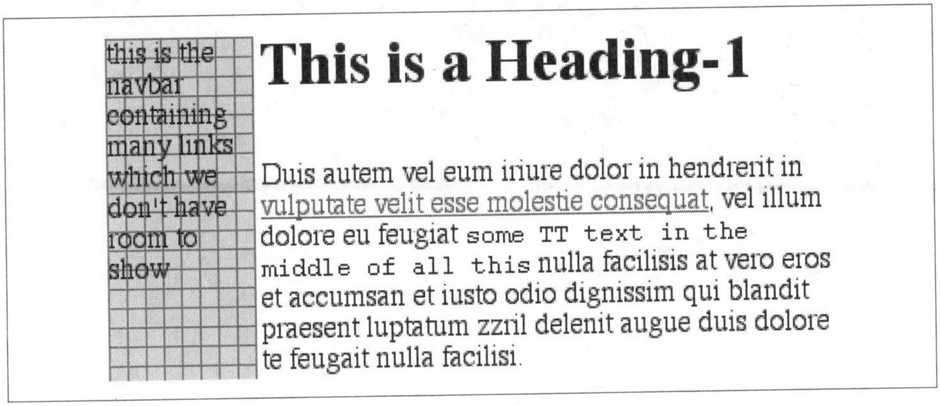

Figure 9-14. Setting a background image for a table cell

You could even, in theory, apply images to the background of replaced elements such as textareas and select lists, although not every user agent is good at handling that sort of thing.

As with background-color, background-image is not inherited—in fact, none of the background properties are inherited. Remember also that specifying the URL of a background image falls under the usual restrictions and caveats for url values: a relative URL should be interpreted with respect to the style sheet, but Navigator 4.x doesn't do this correctly, so absolute URLs may be a better answer.

Why backgrounds aren't inherited

Earlier, I specifically noted that backgrounds are not inherited. Background images demonstrate why inherited backgrounds would be a bad thing. Imagine a situation where backgrounds were inherited, and you applied a background image to the body. That image would be used for the background of every element in the document, with each element doing its own tiling, as shown in Figure 9-15.

Note how the pattern restarted at the top left of every element, including the links. This isn't what most authors would want, so this is why background properties are not inherited. If you *do* want this particular effect for some reason, you can create it with a rule like this:

```
* {background-image: url(yinyang.gif);}
```

Alternatively, you could use the value inherit like this:

```
body {background-image: url(yinyang.gif);}
* {background-image: inherit;}
```

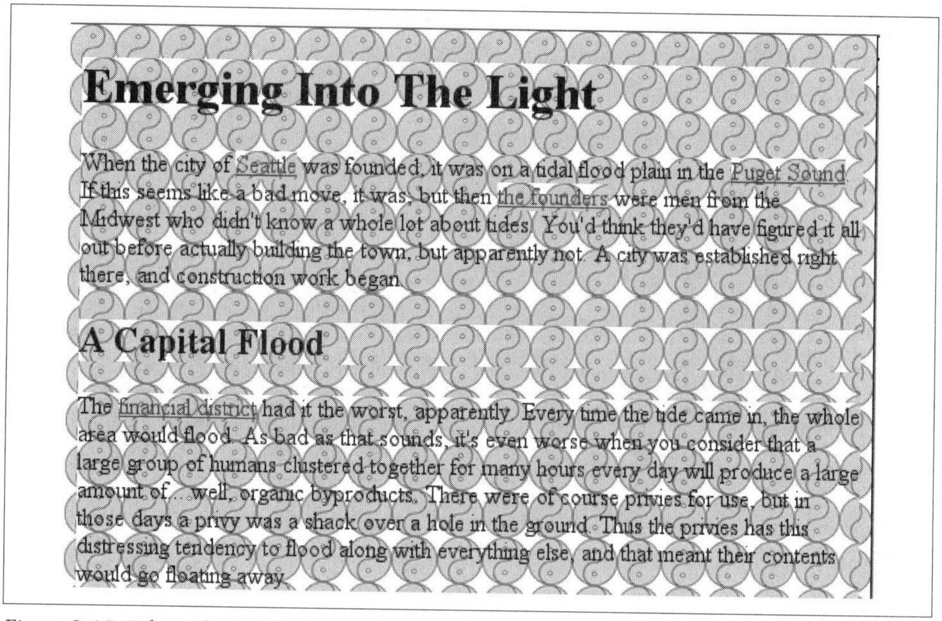

Figure 9-15. What inherited backgrounds would do to layout

Good background practices

Images are laid on top of whatever background color you specify. If you're completely tiling GIF, JPEG, or other opaque image types, this fact doesn't really make a difference, since a fully tiled image will fill up the document background, leaving nowhere for the color to "peek through," so to speak. However, image formats with an alpha channel, such as PNG, can be partially or wholly transparent, and this will cause the image to be combined with the background color. In addition, if the image fails to load for some reason, the user agent will use the specified background color in place of the image. Consider how the "starry paragraph" example would look if the background image failed to load, as in Figure 9-16.

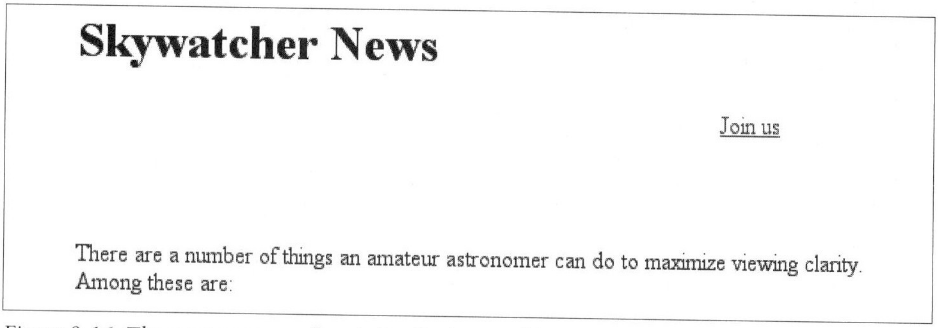

Figure 9-16. The consequences of a missing background image

Figure 9-16 demonstrates why it's always a good idea to specify a background color when using a background image, so that you'll at least get a legible result:

```
p.starry {background-image: url(http://www.site.web/pix/stars.gif);
    background-color: black; color: white;}
a.grid {background-image: url(smallgrid.gif);}

<p class="starry">It's the end of autumn, which means the stars will be
brighter than ever!  <a href="join.html" class="grid">Join us</a> for
a fabulous evening of planets, stars, nebulae, and more...
```

This will fill in a flat black background if the "starry" image can't be rendered for some reason. Besides, if you don't want the image to fully tile across the background of the document, you'll need a color to cover the parts that the image doesn't. Speaking of which....

Repeats with Direction

In the old days, if you wanted some kind of "sidebar" background, you had to create a very short but incredibly wide image to place in the background. At one time, a favorite size for these images was 10 pixels tall by 1,500 pixels wide. Most of that image would be blank space, of course; only the left 100 or so pixels contained the "sidebar" image. The rest of the image was basically wasted.

Wouldn't it be much more efficient to create a sidebar image that's 10 pixels tall and 100 pixels wide, with no wasted blank space, and then repeat it only in the vertical direction? This would certainly make your design job a little easier, and your users' download times a lot faster. Enter background-repeat.

---

background-repeat

Values:	repeat	repeat-x	repeat-y	no-repeat	inherit
Initial value:	repeat
Applies to:	All elements
Inherited:	No
Computed value:	As specified

As you might guess, repeat causes the image to tile in both the horizontal and vertical directions, just as background images have always done in the past. repeat-x and repeat-y cause the image to be repeated in the horizontal or vertical directions, respectively, and no-repeat prevents the image from tiling in any direction.

By default, the background image will start from the top-left corner of an element. (We'll see how to change this later in the chapter.) Therefore, the following rules will have the effect shown in Figure 9-17:

```
body {background-image: url(yinyang.gif);
    background-repeat: repeat-y;}
```

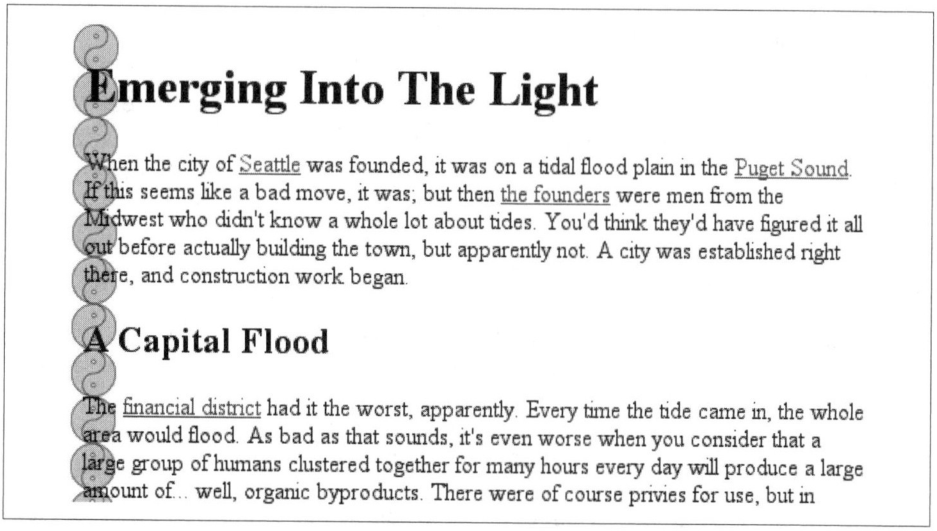

Figure 9-17. Tiling the background image vertically

(I've left out a background color in order to keep the rule short, but remember to include one any time you have a background image.)

Let's assume, though, that you want the image to repeat across the top of the document. Rather than creating a special image with a whole lot of blank space underneath, you can simply make a small change to your rule:

```
body {background-image: url(yinyang.gif);
    background-repeat: repeat-x;}
```

As Figure 9-18 shows, the image is repeated along the *x*-axis (that is, horizontally) from its starting position—in this case, the top-left corner of the browser window.

Finally, you may not want to repeat the background image at all. In this case, you use the value no-repeat:

```
body {background-image: url(yinyang.gif);
    background-repeat: no-repeat;}
```

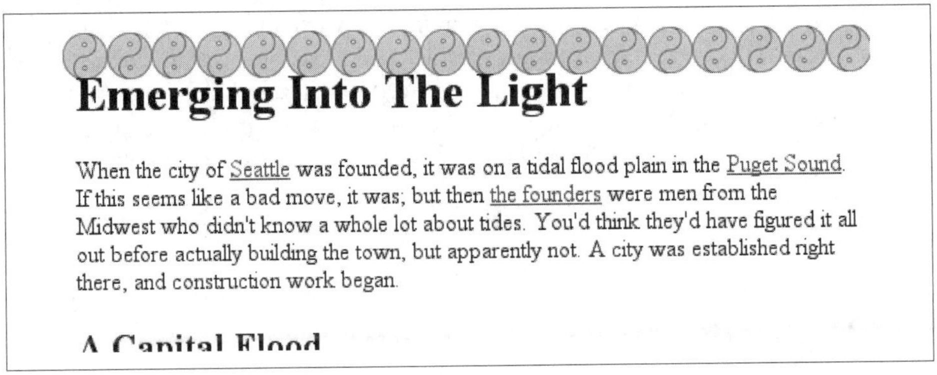

Figure 9-18. Tiling horizontally

This value may not seem terribly useful, given that this declaration would just drop a small image into the top-left corner of the document, but let's try it again with a much bigger symbol, as shown in Figure 9-19:

```
body {background-image: url(bigyinyang.gif);
    background-repeat: no-repeat;}
```

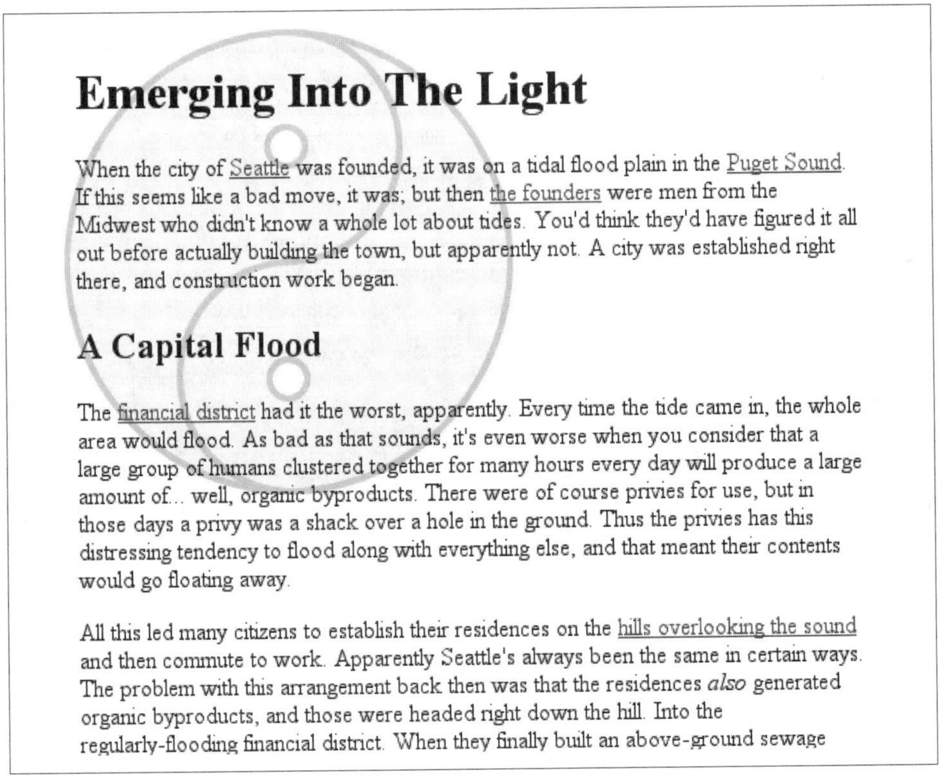

Figure 9-19. Placing a single large background image

The ability to control the repeat direction dramatically expands the range of possible effects. For example, let's say you want a triple border on the left side of each h1 element in your document. You can take that concept further and decide to set a wavy border along the top of each h2 element. The image is colored in such a way that it blends with the background color and produces the wavy effect shown in Figure 9-20:

```
h1 {background-image: url(triplebor.gif); background-repeat: repeat-y;}
h2 {background-image: url(wavybord.gif); background-repeat: repeat-x;
    background-color: #CCC;}
```

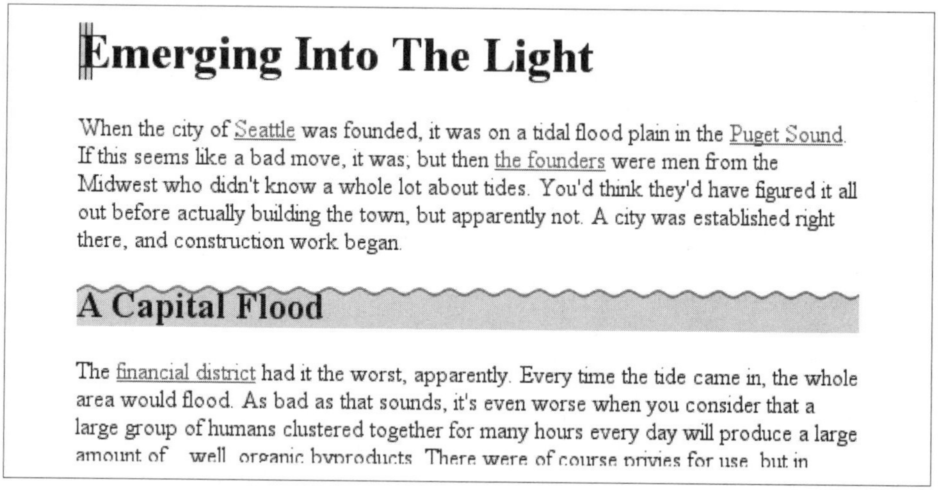

Figure 9-20. Bordering elements with background images

Simply by choosing the appropriate image for the job and employing it in some creative ways, you can set up some very interesting effects. And that isn't all that's possible. Now that you know how to constrain a background image's repetition, how about moving it around in the background area?

Background Positioning

Thanks to background-repeat, it's possible to place a large image in the background of a document and then keep it from repeating. Let's add to that and actually change the image's position in the background.

For example, you could center a background image in the body element, with the result depicted in Figure 9-21:

```
body {background-image: url(bigyinyang.gif);
    background-repeat: no-repeat;
    background-position: center;}
```

You've actually placed a single image in the background and then prevented it from being repeated with the value no-repeat. Every background that includes an image starts with a single image that is then repeated (or not) according to the value of background-repeat. This starting point is called the *origin image*.

Values:	[[<percentage> | <length> | left | center | right] [<percentage>] | <length> | top | center | bottom]?] || [[left | center | right] || [top | center | bottom]] | inherit
Initial value:	0% 0%
Applies to:	Block-level and replaced elements
Inherited:	No
Percentages:	Refer to the corresponding point on both the element and the origin image (see explanation in "Percentage values" later in this chapter)
Computed value:	The absolute length offsets, if <length> is specified; otherwise, percentage values

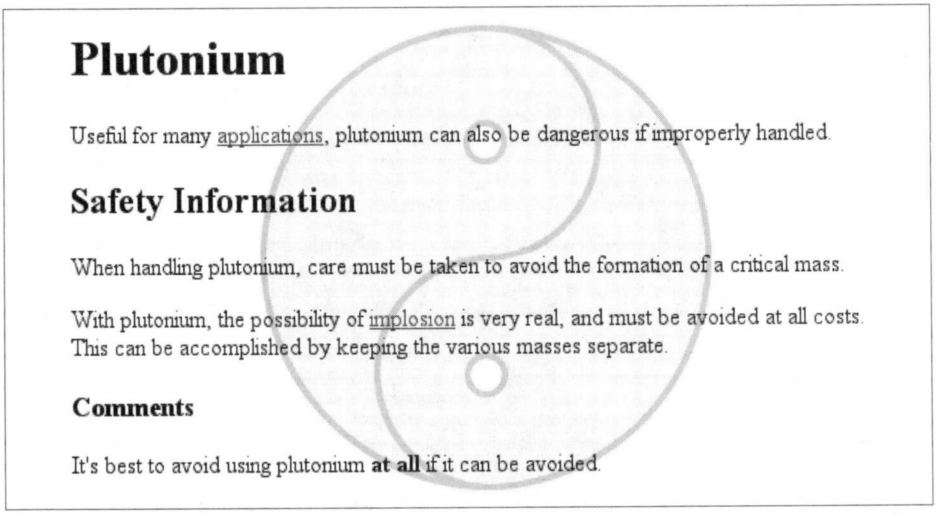

Plutonium

Useful for many applications, plutonium can also be dangerous if improperly handled.

Safety Information

When handling plutonium, care must be taken to avoid the formation of a critical mass.

With plutonium, the possibility of implosion is very real, and must be avoided at all costs. This can be accomplished by keeping the various masses separate.

Comments

It's best to avoid using plutonium **at all** if it can be avoided.

Figure 9-21. Centering a single background image

The placement of the origin image is accomplished with background-position, and there are several ways to supply values for this property. First, there are the keywords top, bottom, left, right, and center. Usually, these appear in pairs, but (as the previous example shows) this is not always true. Then there are length values, such as 50px or 2cm, and finally, percentage values. Each type of value has a slightly different effect on the placement of the background image.

I should mention one more thing: the context in which background images are placed. CSS2 and CSS2.1 state that background-position is used to place the origin image with respect to the padding edge of the element. In other words, the image-placement context is the inner border edge, even though the background area extends to the outer border edge. Not every browser places images properly;

some place the origin image with respect to the outer border edge instead of the inner border edge. In any situation where there is no border, the effect is identical either way.

 For those interested in how CSS has changed over the years, CSS1 defined placement relative to the content area.

Despite image-placement context, a fully tiled background image would indeed fill in the border area's background because a tiled image extends in all four directions. We'll talk about this in more detail later. First, you need to find out how the origin image can be positioned within the element.

Keywords

The image-placement keywords are easiest to understand. They have the effects you'd expect from their names; for example, top right would cause the origin image to be placed in the top-right corner of the element's padding area. Let's go back to the small yin-yang symbol:

```
p {background-image: url(yinyang.gif);
    background-repeat: no-repeat;
    background-position: top right;}
```

This will place a nonrepeated origin image in the top-right corner of each paragraph's padding. Incidentally, the result, shown in Figure 9-22, would be exactly the same if the position were declared as right top. Position keywords can appear in any order (according to the specification), as long as there are no more than two of them—one for the horizontal and one for the vertical.

When the city of Seattle was founded, it was on a tidal flood plain in the Puget Sound. If this seems like a bad move, it was; but then the founders were men from the Midwest who didn't know a whole lot about tides. You'd think they'd have figured it all out before actually building the town, but apparently not. A city was established right there, and construction work began.

A Capital Flood

The financial district had it the worst, apparently. Every time the tide came in, the whole area would flood. As bad as that sounds, it's even worse when you consider that a large group of humans clustered together for many hours every day will produce a large amount of... well, organic byproducts. There were of course privies for use, but in those days a privy was a shack over a hole in the ground. Thus the privies has this distressing tendency to flood along with everything else, and that meant their contents would go floating away.

All this led many citizens to establish their residences on the hills overlooking the sound and then commute to work. Apparently Seattle's always been the same in certain ways. The problem with this arrangement back then was that the residences *also* generated organic

Figure 9-22. Placing the background image in the top right corner of paragraphs

The Netscape 6.x family has a bug that causes it to ignore a rule if the background-position keywords are in a particular order. To avoid tripping the bug, make sure your keywords give the horizontal placement first and then the vertical. Thus, write left center instead of center left.

If only one keyword appears, then the other is assumed to be center. Table 9-1 shows equivalent keyword statements.

Table 9-1. Position keyword equivalents

Single keyword	Equivalent keywords
center	center center
top	top center center top
bottom	bottom center center bottom
right	center right right center
left	center left left center

So if you want an image to appear in the top center of every paragraph, you need only declare:

```
p {background-image: url(yinyang.gif);
   background-repeat: no-repeat;
   background-position: top;}
```

Percentage values

Percentage values are closely related to the keywords, although they behave in a more sophisticated way. Let's say that you want to center an origin image within its element by using percentage values. That's easy enough:

```
p {background-image: url(bigyinyang.gif);
   background-repeat: no-repeat;
   background-position: 50% 50%;}
```

This causes the origin image to be placed such that its center is aligned with the center of its element. In other words, the percentage values apply to both the element and the origin image.

Let's examine the process in closer detail. When you center an origin image in an element, the point in the image that can be described as 50% 50% (the center) is lined up with the point in the element that can be described the same way. If the image is placed at 0% 0%, its top-left corner is placed in the top-left corner of the padding area of the element. 100% 100% causes the origin image's bottom right corner to be placed into the bottom right corner of the padding area:

```
p {background-image: url(oransqr.gif);
   background-repeat: no-repeat;
   padding: 5px;  border: 1px dotted gray;}
p.c1 {background-position: 0% 0%;}
p.c2 {background-position: 50% 50%;}
p.c3 {background-position: 100% 100%;}
p.c4 {background-position: 0% 100%;}
p.c5 {background-position: 100% 0%;}
```

Figure 9-23 illustrates these rules.

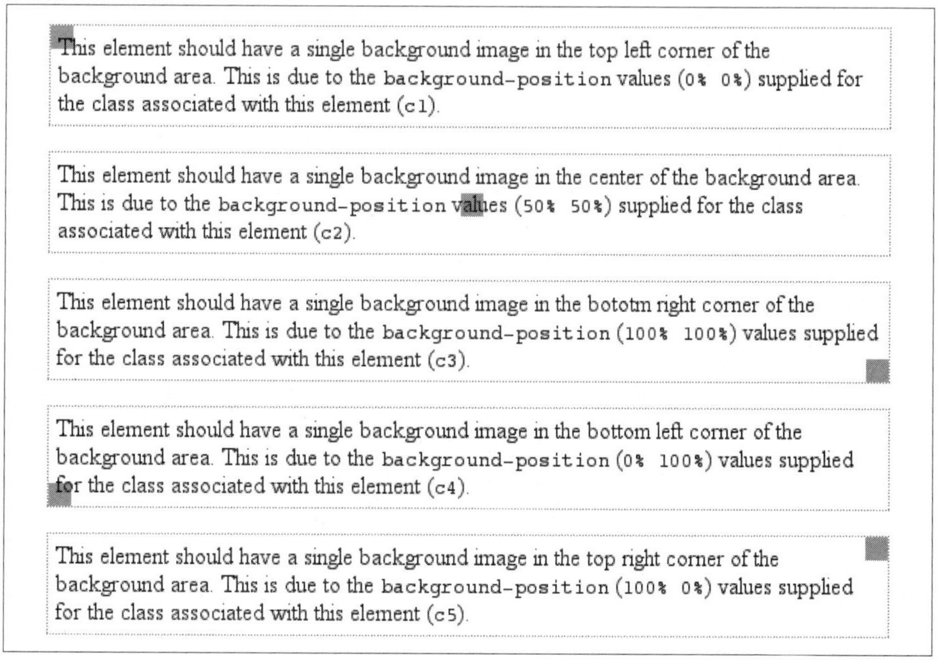

This element should have a single background image in the top left corner of the background area. This is due to the `background-position` values (`0% 0%`) supplied for the class associated with this element (`c1`).

This element should have a single background image in the center of the background area. This is due to the `background-position` values (`50% 50%`) supplied for the class associated with this element (`c2`).

This element should have a single background image in the bototm right corner of the background area. This is due to the `background-position` (`100% 100%`) values supplied for the class associated with this element (`c3`).

This element should have a single background image in the bottom left corner of the background area. This is due to the `background-position` (`0% 100%`) values supplied for the class associated with this element (`c4`).

This element should have a single background image in the top right corner of the background area. This is due to the `background-position` (`100% 0%`) values supplied for the class associated with this element (`c5`).

Figure 9-23. Various percentage positions

Thus, if you want to place a single origin image a third of the way across the element and two-thirds of the way down, your declaration would be:

```
p {background-image: url(bigyinyang.gif);
   background-repeat: no-repeat;
   background-position: 33% 66%;}
```

With these rules, the point in the origin image that is one-third across and two-thirds down from the top-left corner of the image will be aligned with the point that is farthest from the top-left corner of the containing element. Note that the horizontal value *always* comes first with percentage values. If you were to switch the percentages in the preceding example, the image would be placed two-thirds of the way across the element and one-third of the way down.

If you supply only one percentage value, the single value supplied is used as the horizontal value, and the vertical is assumed to be 50%. This is similar to keywords, where if only one keyword is given, the other is assumed to be center. For example:

```
p {background-image: url(yinyang.gif);
   background-repeat: no-repeat;
   background-position: 25%;}
```

The origin image is placed one-quarter of the way across the element's content area and padding area, and halfway down it, as depicted in Figure 9-24.

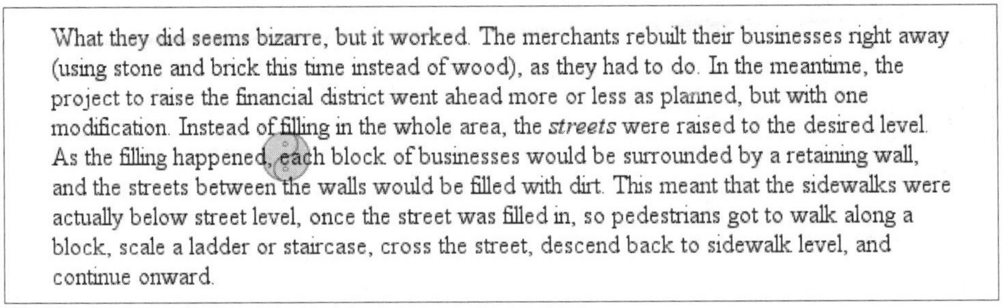

What they did seems bizarre, but it worked. The merchants rebuilt their businesses right away (using stone and brick this time instead of wood), as they had to do. In the meantime, the project to raise the financial district went ahead more or less as planned, but with one modification. Instead of filling in the whole area, the *streets* were raised to the desired level. As the filling happened, each block of businesses would be surrounded by a retaining wall, and the streets between the walls would be filled with dirt. This meant that the sidewalks were actually below street level, once the street was filled in, so pedestrians got to walk along a block, scale a ladder or staircase, cross the street, descend back to sidewalk level, and continue onward.

Figure 9-24. Declaring only one percentage value means the vertical position evaluates to 50%

Table 9-2 gives a breakdown of keyword and percentage equivalencies.

Table 9-2. Positional equivalents

Single keyword	Equivalent keywords	Equivalent percentages
center	center center	50% 50% 50%
top	top center center top	50% 0%
bottom	bottom center center bottom	50% 100%
right	center right right center	100% 50% 100%
left	center left left center	0% 50% 0%
	top left left top	0% 0%
	top right right top	100% 0%
	bottom right right bottom	100% 100%
	bottom left left bottom	0% 100%

In case you're wondering, the default values for `background-position` are 0% 0%, which is functionally the same as `top left`. This is why, unless you set different values for the position, background images always start tiling from the top-left corner of the element's padding area.

Length values

Finally, we turn to length values for positioning. When you supply lengths for the position of the origin image, they are interpreted as offsets from the top-left corner of the element's padding area. The offset point is the top-left corner of the origin image; thus, if you set the values 20px 30px, the top-left corner of the origin image will be 20 pixels to the right of, and 30 pixels below, the top-left corner of the element's padding area, as shown in Figure 9-25:

```
p {background-image: url(yinyang.gif);
   background-repeat: no-repeat;
   background-position: 20px 30px;
   border: 1px dotted gray;}
```

Eventually, of course, they finished the streets and built sidewalks at street level that actually were roofs over the old sidewalks. For some time, there were two levels to the district: street level and the underground. This situation persisted for almost a decade after the project was finished. What finally drove residents to abandon the underground was a rapidly rising rat population, and the attendant joys that come with such a population, like the bubonic plague. The underground was at last shuttered, and now is visited only by tour groups.

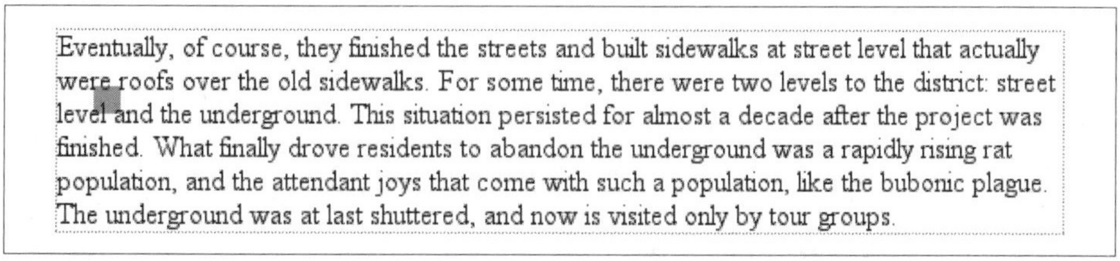

Figure 9-25. Offsetting the background image using length measures

This is quite different from percentage values because the offset is simply from one top-left corner to another. In other words, the top-left corner of the origin image lines up with the point specified in the `background-position` declaration. You can combine length and percentage values, though, to get a "best of both worlds" effect. Let's say you need a background image that extends all the way to the right side of an element and 10 pixels down from the top, as illustrated in Figure 9-26. As always, the horizontal value comes first:

```
p {background-image: url(bg23.gif);
   background-repeat: no-repeat;
   background-position: 100% 10px;
   border: 1px dotted gray;}
```

Eventually, of course, they finished the streets and built sidewalks at street level that actually were roofs over the old sidewalks. For some time, there were two levels to the district: street level and the underground. This situation persisted for almost a decade after the project was finished. What finally drove residents to abandon the underground was a rapidly rising rat population, and the attendant joys that come with such a population, like the bubonic plague. The underground was at last shuttered, and now is visited only by tour groups.

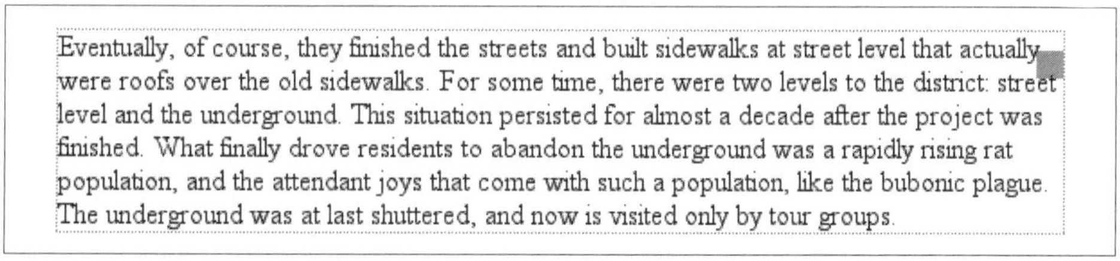

Figure 9-26. Mixing percentages and length values

In versions of CSS prior to 2.1, you could *not* mix keywords with other values. Thus, top 75% was not valid, and if you used a keyword, you were stuck using only keywords. CSS2.1 changed this to make authoring easier and to keep up with other browsers that had already allowed it.

If you're using lengths or percentages, you can use negative values to pull the origin image outside of the element's background area. Consider the example with the very large yin-yang symbol for a background. At one point, you centered it, but what if you only want part of it visible in the top-left corner of the element's padding area? No problem, at least in theory.

First, assume that the origin image is 300 pixels tall by 300 pixels wide. Then, assume that only the bottom right third of it should be visible. You can get the desired effect (shown in Figure 9-27) like this:

```
p {background-image: url(bigyinyang.gif);
   background-repeat: no-repeat;
   background-position: -200px -200px;
   border: 1px dotted gray;}
```

What they did seems bizarre, but it worked. The merchants rebuilt their businesses right away (using stone and brick this time instead of wood), as they had to do. In the meantime, the project to raise the financial district went ahead more or less as planned, but with one modification. Instead of filling in the whole area, the *streets* were raised to the desired level. As the filling happened, each block of businesses would be surrounded by a retaining wall, and the streets between the walls would be filled with dirt. This meant that the sidewalks were actually below street level, once the street was filled in, so pedestrians got to walk along a block, scale a ladder or staircase, cross the street, descend back to sidewalk level, and continue onward.

Figure 9-27. Using negative length values to position the origin image

Or, say you want just the right half of it to be visible and centered within the element:

```
p {background-image: url(bigyinyang.gif);
   background-repeat: no-repeat;
   background-position: -150px 50%;
   border: 1px dotted gray;}
```

Negative percentages are also possible in theory, although there are two issues involved. The first is the limitations of user agents, which may not recognize negative values for background-position. The other is that negative percentages are somewhat interesting to calculate. The origin image and the element are likely to be very different sizes, for one thing, and that can lead to unexpected effects. Consider, for example, the situation created by the following rule and illustrated in Figure 9-28:

```
p {background-image: url(pix/bigyinyang.gif);
   background-repeat: no-repeat;
   background-position: -10% -10%;
   border: 1px dotted gray;
   width: 500px;}
```

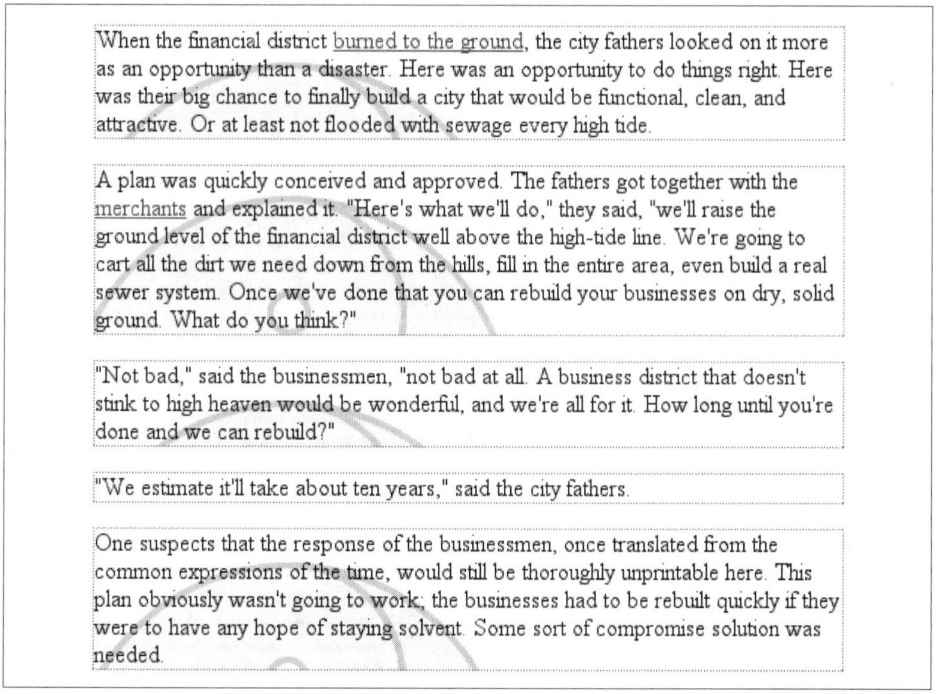

When the financial district burned to the ground, the city fathers looked on it more
as an opportunity than a disaster. Here was an opportunity to do things right. Here
was their big chance to finally build a city that would be functional, clean, and
attractive. Or at least not flooded with sewage every high tide.

A plan was quickly conceived and approved. The fathers got together with the
merchants and explained it. "Here's what we'll do," they said, "we'll raise the
ground level of the financial district well above the high-tide line. We're going to
cart all the dirt we need down from the hills, fill in the entire area, even build a real
sewer system. Once we've done that you can rebuild your businesses on dry, solid
ground. What do you think?"

"Not bad," said the businessmen, "not bad at all. A business district that doesn't
stink to high heaven would be wonderful, and we're all for it. How long until you're
done and we can rebuild?"

"We estimate it'll take about ten years," said the city fathers.

One suspects that the response of the businessmen, once translated from the
common expressions of the time, would still be thoroughly unprintable here. This
plan obviously wasn't going to work; the businesses had to be rebuilt quickly if they
were to have any hope of staying solvent. Some sort of compromise solution was
needed.

Figure 9-28. Varying effects of negative percentage values

The rule calls for the point outside the origin image defined by -10% -10% to be
aligned with a similar point for each paragraph. The image is 300×300 pixels, so we
know its alignment point can be described as 30 pixels above the top of the image,
and 30 pixels to the left of its left edge (effectively -30px and -30px). The paragraph
elements are all the same width (500px), so the horizontal alignment point is 50 pixels to the left of the left edge of their padding areas. This means that each origin
image's left edge will be 20 pixels to the left of the left padding edge of the paragraphs. This is because the -30px alignment point of the images lines up with the -50px
point for the paragraphs. The difference between the two is 20 pixels.

The paragraphs are of differing heights, however, so the vertical alignment point
changes for each paragraph. If a paragraph is 300 pixels high, to pick a semi-random
example, then the top of the origin image will line up exactly with the top of the element's padding area, because both will have vertical alignment points of -30px. If a
paragraph is 50 pixels tall, then its alignment point would be -5px and the top of the
origin image will actually be 25 pixels *below* the top of the padding area.

The same issues can arise with positive percentage values (imagine what would happen if you aligned an origin image to the bottom of an element shorter than the

image), so this isn't to say that you shouldn't use negative values. It's just a reminder that there are, as always, issues to consider.

Throughout this section, every example has had a repeat value of no-repeat. The reason for this is simple: with only a single background image, it's much easier to see how positioning affects the placement of the first background image. You don't have to prevent the background image from repeating, though:

```
p {background-image: url(bigyinyang.gif);
    background-position: -150px 50%;
    border: 1px dotted gray;}
```

So, with the background repeating, you can see from Figure 9-29 that the tiling pattern starts with the position specified by background-position.

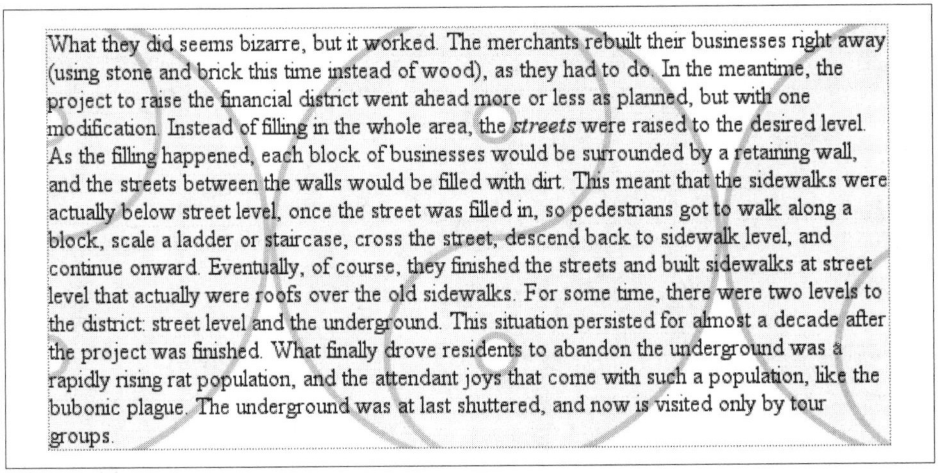

What they did seems bizarre, but it worked. The merchants rebuilt their businesses right away (using stone and brick this time instead of wood), as they had to do. In the meantime, the project to raise the financial district went ahead more or less as planned, but with one modification. Instead of filling in the whole area, the *streets* were raised to the desired level. As the filling happened, each block of businesses would be surrounded by a retaining wall, and the streets between the walls would be filled with dirt. This meant that the sidewalks were actually below street level, once the street was filled in, so pedestrians got to walk along a block, scale a ladder or staircase, cross the street, descend back to sidewalk level, and continue onward. Eventually, of course, they finished the streets and built sidewalks at street level that actually were roofs over the old sidewalks. For some time, there were two levels to the district: street level and the underground. This situation persisted for almost a decade after the project was finished. What finally drove residents to abandon the underground was a rapidly rising rat population, and the attendant joys that come with such a population, like the bubonic plague. The underground was at last shuttered, and now is visited only by tour groups.

Figure 9-29. Use of the background-position property sets the origin of the tiling pattern

This illustrates once more the concept of the origin image, which is very important to understanding the next section.

Repeats with Direction (Revisited)

In the previous section on repetition, we explored the values repeat-x, repeat-y, and repeat, and how they affect the tiling of background images. In each case, however, the tiling pattern always started from the top-left corner of the containing element (e.g., p). This isn't a requirement, of course; as we've seen, the default values for background-position are 0% 0%. So, unless you change the position of the origin image, that's where the tiling starts. Now that you know how to change the position of the origin image, though, you need to figure out how user agents will handle the situation.

It's easiest to show an example and then explain it. Consider the following markup, which is illustrated in Figure 9-30:

```
p {background-image: url(yinyang.gif);
   background-position: center;
   border: 1px dotted gray;}
p.c1 {background-repeat: repeat-y;}
p.c2 {background-repeat: repeat-x;}
```

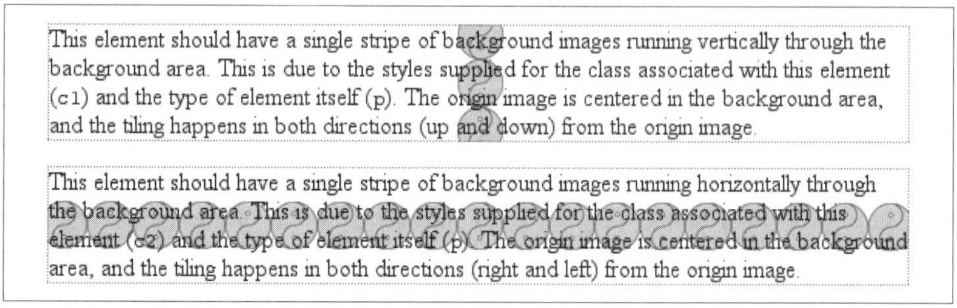

This element should have a single stripe of background images running vertically through the background area. This is due to the styles supplied for the class associated with this element (c1) and the type of element itself (p). The origin image is centered in the background area, and the tiling happens in both directions (up and down) from the origin image.

This element should have a single stripe of background images running horizontally through the background area. This is due to the styles supplied for the class associated with this element (c2) and the type of element itself (p). The origin image is centered in the background area, and the tiling happens in both directions (right and left) from the origin image.

Figure 9-30. Centering the origin image and repeating it

So there you have it: stripes running through the center of the elements. It may look wrong, but it isn't.

The examples shown in Figure 9-30 are correct because the origin image has been placed in the center of the first p element and then tiled along the *y*-axis *in both directions*—in other words, both up *and* down. For the second paragraph, the images are repeated to the right and left.

Therefore, setting a large image in the center of the p and then letting it fully repeat will cause it to tile in all *four* directions: up, down, left, and right. The only difference background-position makes is in determining where the tiling starts. Figure 9-31 shows the difference between tiling from the center of an element and from its top-left corner.

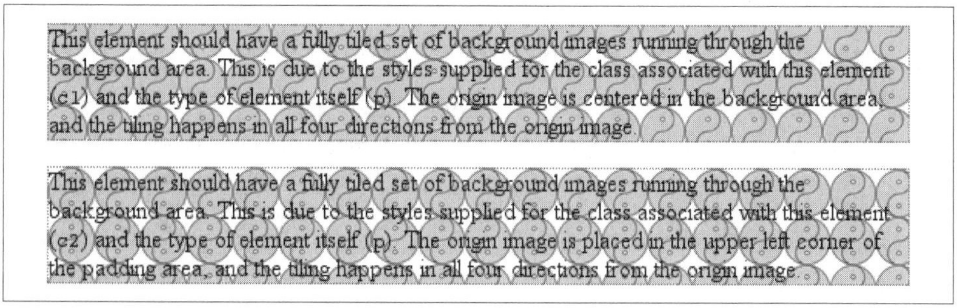

This element should have a fully tiled set of background images running through the background area. This is due to the styles supplied for the class associated with this element (c1) and the type of element itself (p). The origin image is centered in the background area, and the tiling happens in all four directions from the origin image.

This element should have a fully tiled set of background images running through the background area. This is due to the styles supplied for the class associated with this element (c2) and the type of element itself (p). The origin image is placed in the upper left corner of the padding area, and the tiling happens in all four directions from the origin image.

Figure 9-31. The difference between centering a repeat and starting it from the top left

Note the differences along the edges of the element. When the background repeats from the center, as in the first paragraph, the grid of yin-yang symbols is centered within the element, resulting in consistent "clipping" along the edges. In the second paragraph, the tiling begins at the top-left corner of the padding area, so the clipping is not consistent. The variations may seem subtle, but you'll likely need to use both approaches at some point in your design career.

In case you're wondering, there is no way to control the repeat any more than we've already discussed. There is no repeat-left, for example, although such a value could be added in some future version of CSS. For now, you get full tiling, horizontal tiling, vertical tiling, or no tiling at all.

Getting Attached

So, now you can place the origin image for the background anywhere in the background of an element, and you can control (to a degree) how it tiles. As you may already have realized, though, placing an image in the center of the body element may mean, given a sufficiently long document, that the background image won't be initially visible to the reader. After all, a browser provides only a window onto the document. If the document is too long to be displayed in the window, then the user can scroll back and forth through the document. The center could be two or three "screens" below the beginning of the document, or just far enough down to push most of the origin image beyond the bottom of the browser window.

Furthermore, even if you assume that the origin image is initially visible, it always scrolls with the document—it'll vanish every time a user scrolls beyond the image's location. Never fear: there is a way to prevent this scrolling.

---

background-attachment

Values:	scroll | fixed | inherit
Initial value:	scroll
Applies to:	All elements
Inherited:	No
Computed value:	As specified

Using the property background-attachment, you can declare the origin image to be fixed with respect to the viewing area and therefore immune to the effects of scrolling:

```
body {background-image: url(bigyinyang.gif);
   background-repeat: no-repeat;
   background-position: center;
   background-attachment: fixed;}
```

Doing this has two immediate effects, as you can see from Figure 9-32. The first is that the origin image does not scroll along with the document. The second is that the placement of the origin image is determined by the size of the viewing area, not the size (or placement within the viewing area) of the element that contains it.

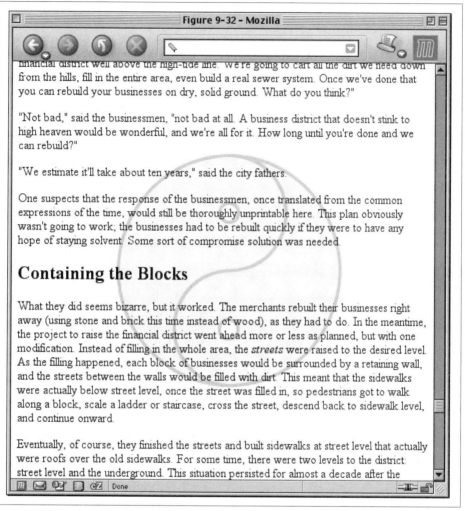

Figure 9-32. Nailing the background in place

In a web browser, the viewing area can change as the user resizes the browser's window. This will cause the background's origin image to shift position as the window changes size. Figure 9-33 depicts several views of the same document. So, in a certain sense, the image isn't fixed in place, but it will remain fixed as long as the viewing area isn't resized.

There is only one other value for background-attachment: the default value scroll. As you'd expect, this causes the background to scroll along with the rest of the

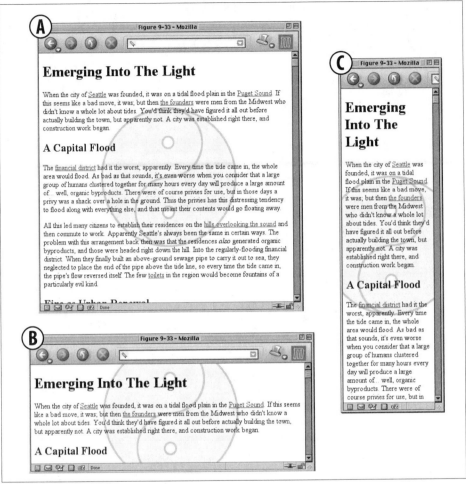

Figure 9-33. The centering continues to hold

document when viewed in a web browser, and it doesn't necessarily change the origin image's position as the window is resized. If the document width is fixed (perhaps by assigning an explicit width to the body element), then resizing the viewing area won't affect the placement of a scroll-attachment origin image at all.

Interesting effects

In technical terms, when a background image has been fixed, it is positioned with respect to the viewing area, not the element that contains it. However, the background will be visible only within its containing element. This has a rather interesting consequence.

Let's say you have a document with a tiled background that actually looks like it's tiled, and an h1 element with the same pattern, only in a different color. Both the body and h1 elements are set to have fixed backgrounds, resulting in something like Figure 9-34:

```
body {background-image: url(grid1.gif); background-repeat: repeat;
    background-attachment: fixed;}
h1 {background-image: url(grid2.gif); background-repeat: repeat;
    background-attachment: fixed;}
```

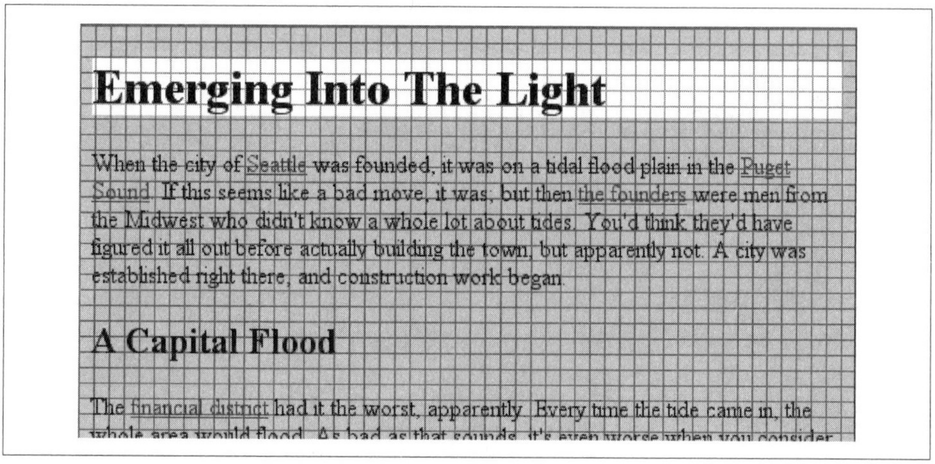

Figure 9-34. Perfect alignment of backgrounds

How is this perfect alignment possible? Remember, when a background is fixed, the origin element is positioned with respect to the viewport. Thus, both background patterns begin tiling from the top-left corner of the viewport, not the individual elements. For the body, you can see the entire repeat pattern. For the h1, however, the only place you can see its background is in the padding and content of the h1 itself. Since both background images are the same size, and they have precisely the same origin, they appear to "line up," as shown in Figure 9-34.

This capability can be used to create some very sophisticated effects. One of the most famous examples is the "complexspiral distorted" demonstration (*http:// www.meyerweb.com/eric/css/edge/complexspiral/glassy.html*), which is illustrated in Figure 9-35.

The visual effects are created by assigning different fixed-attachment background images to non-body elements. The entire demo is driven by one HTML document, four JPEG images, and a style sheet. Because all four images are positioned in the top-left corner of the browser window, but are visible only where they intersect with their elements, the images effectively interleave to create the illusion of translucent rippled glass.

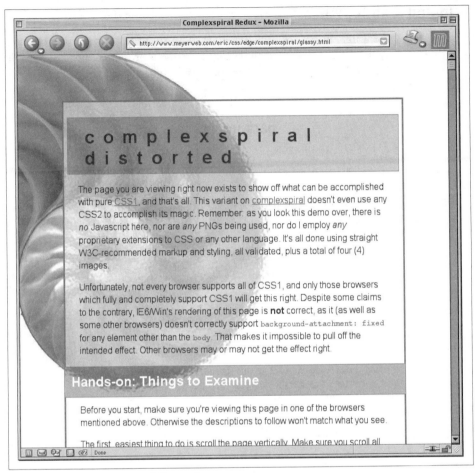

Figure 9-35. The complexspiral distorted

 Internet Explorer for Windows up through IE6 does not properly handle fixed-attachment backgrounds on non-body elements. In other words, you get the expected effect for a fixed body background, but not for other elements. This wrecks the alignment effects seen in Figure 9-34 and Figure 9-35. Internet Explorer 7 supports fixed-attachment backgrounds for all elements.

It is also the case that in paged media, such as printouts, every page generates its own viewport. Therefore, a fixed-attachment background should appear on every page of the printout. This could be used for effects such as watermarking all the pages in a document, for example. The problems are twofold: there is no way to force background images to print with CSS, and not all browsers properly handle the printing of fixed-attachment backgrounds.

Bringing It All Together

Just as with the font properties, the background properties can all be brought together in a single shorthand property: background. This property can take a single value from each of the other background properties, in literally any order.

<table>
<tr><td colspan="2" align="center">background</td></tr>
<tr><td>Values:</td><td>[<background-color> || <background-image> || <background-repeat> || <background-attachment> || <background-position>] | inherit</td></tr>
<tr><td>Initial value:</td><td>Refer to individual properties</td></tr>
<tr><td>Applies to:</td><td>All elements</td></tr>
<tr><td>Inherited:</td><td>No</td></tr>
<tr><td>Percentages:</td><td>Values are allowed for <background-position></td></tr>
<tr><td>Computed value:</td><td>See individual properties</td></tr>
</table>

Therefore, the following statements are all equivalent and will have the effect shown in Figure 9-36:

```
body {background-color: white; background-image: url(yinyang.gif);
    background-position: top left; background-repeat: repeat-y;
    background-attachment: fixed;}
body {background: white url(yinyang.gif) top left repeat-y fixed;}
body {background: fixed url(yinyang.gif) white top left repeat-y;}
body {background: url(yinyang.gif) white repeat-y fixed top left;}
```

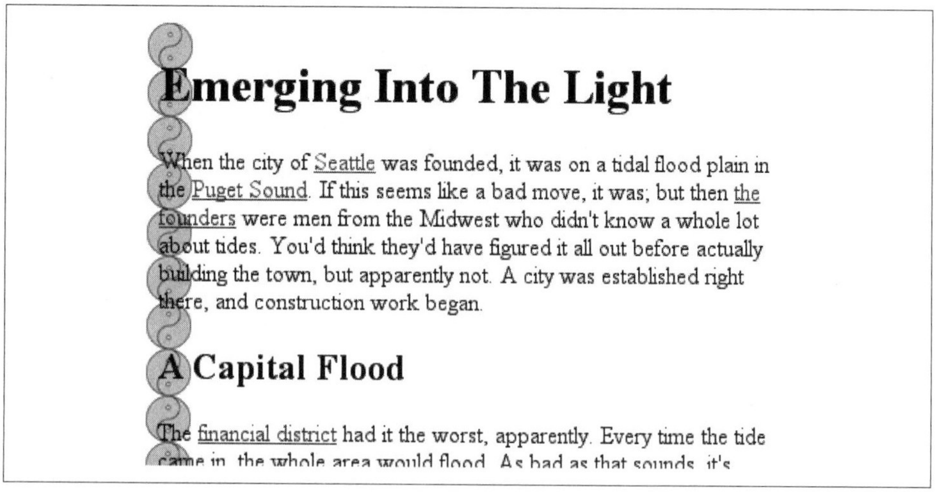

Figure 9-36. Using shorthand

Actually, there is one slight restriction on how the values are ordered in background: if you have two values for background-position, they must appear together and, if they are length or percentage values, they must be ordered horizontal first, then vertical. This probably isn't a surprise, but it is important to remember.

As is the case for shorthand properties, if you leave out any values, the defaults for the relevant properties are filled in automatically. Thus, the following two are equivalent:

```
body {background: white url(yinyang.gif);}
body {background: white url(yinyang.gif) top left repeat scroll;}
```

Even better, there are no required values for background—as long as at least one value is present, you can omit all the rest. Therefore, it's possible to set just the background color using the shorthand property, which is a very common practice:

```
body {background: white;}
```

This is perfectly legal, and in some ways preferred, given the reduced number of keystrokes. In addition, it has the effect of setting all of the other background properties to their defaults, which means that background-image will be set to none. This helps ensure readability by preventing other rules (for example, in the reader style sheet) from setting an image in the background.

Any of the following rules are also legal, as illustrated in Figure 9-37:

```
body {background: url(yinyang.gif) bottom left repeat-y;}
h1 {background: silver;}
h2 {background: url(h2bg.gif) center repeat-x;}
p {background: url(parabg.gif);}
```

One final reminder: background is a shorthand property, and, as such, its default values can obliterate previously assigned values for a given element. For example:

```
h1, h2 {background: gray url(thetrees.jpg) center repeat-x;}
h2 {background: silver;}
```

Given these rules, h1 elements will be styled according to the first rule. h2 elements will be styled according to the second, which means they'll just have a flat silver background. No image will be applied to h2 backgrounds, let alone centered and repeated horizontally. It is more likely that the author meant to do this:

```
h1, h2 {background: gray url(trees.jpg) center repeat-x;}
h2 {background-color: silver;}
```

This lets the background color be changed without wiping out all the other values.

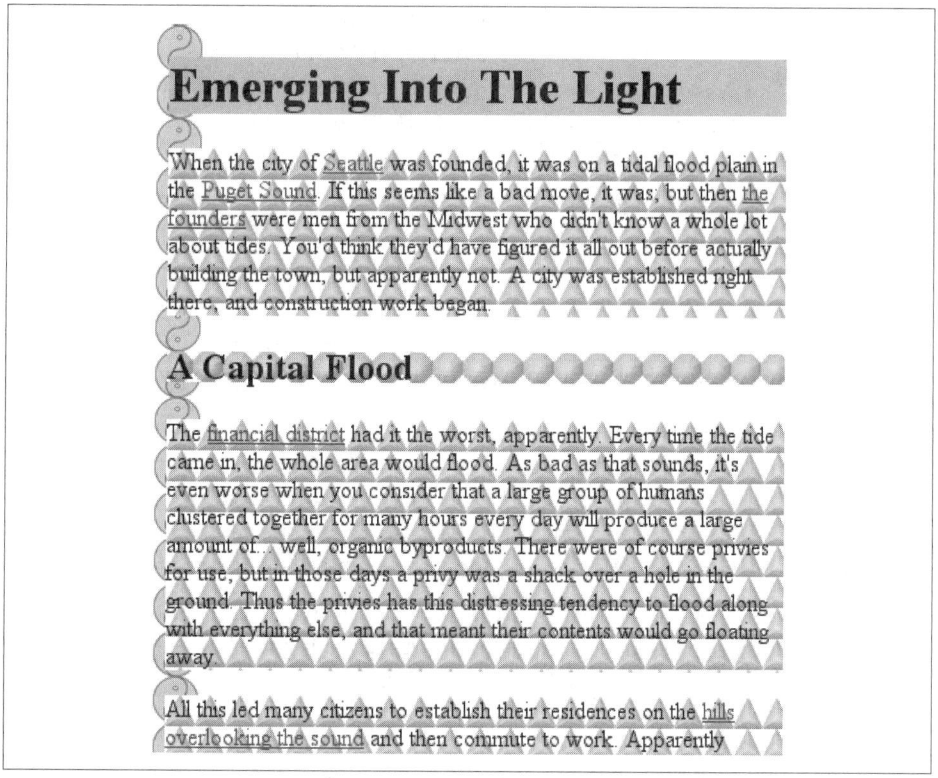

Figure 9-37. Applying many backgrounds to one document

Summary

Setting colors and backgrounds on elements gives authors a great deal of power. The advantage of CSS over traditional methods is that colors and backgrounds can be applied to any element in a document—not just table cells, for example, or anything enclosed in a FONT tag. Despite a few bugs in some implementations, such as Navigator 4's reluctance to apply a background to the entire content area of an element, backgrounds are very widely used properties. Their popularity isn't too hard to understand, either, since color is one easy way to distinguish the look of one page from another.

CSS allows for a great deal more in the way of element styling, however: borders that can be placed on any element, extra margins and padding, and even a way to "float" elements other than images. We'll get into these concepts in the next chapter.

CHAPTER 10

Floating and Positioning

Sure, CSS makes content look good with font changes, backgrounds, and all the rest, but what about accomplishing basic layout tasks? Enter *floating* and *positioning*. These are the tools by which you can set up columnar layout, overlap one piece of layout with another, and generally accomplish everything that so many tables have been used for over the years.

The idea behind positioning is fairly simple. It allows you to define exactly where element boxes will appear relative to where they would ordinarily be—or relative to a parent element, another element, or even to the browser window itself. The power of this feature is both obvious and surprising. It shouldn't shock you to learn that user agents support this element of CSS2 better than many others.

Floating, on the other hand, was first offered in CSS1, based on a capability that had been added by Netscape early in the Web's life. Floating is not exactly positioning, but it certainly isn't normal-flow layout either. We'll see exactly what this means later in the chapter.

Floating

You are almost certainly acquainted with the concept of floated elements. Ever since Netscape 1, it has been possible to float images by declaring, for instance, `<img src="b5.gif" align="right">`. This causes an image to float to the right and allows other content (such as text) to "flow around" the image. The name "floating," in fact, comes from the document "Extensions to HTML 2.0," which stated:

> The additions to your ALIGN options need a lot of explanation. First, the values "left" and "right". Images with those alignments are an entirely new *floating* image type.

In the past, it was only possible to float images and, in some browsers, tables. CSS, on the other hand, lets you float any element, from images to paragraphs to lists. In CSS, this behavior is accomplished using the property `float`.

float

Values:	`left	right	none	inherit`
Initial value:	`none`
Applies to:	All elements
Inherited:	No
Computed value:	As specified

For example, to float an image to the left, you could use this markup:

```
<img src="b4.gif" style="float: left;" alt="b4">
```

As Figure 10-1 makes clear, the image "floats" to the left side of the browser window, and the text flows around it. This is just what you should expect.

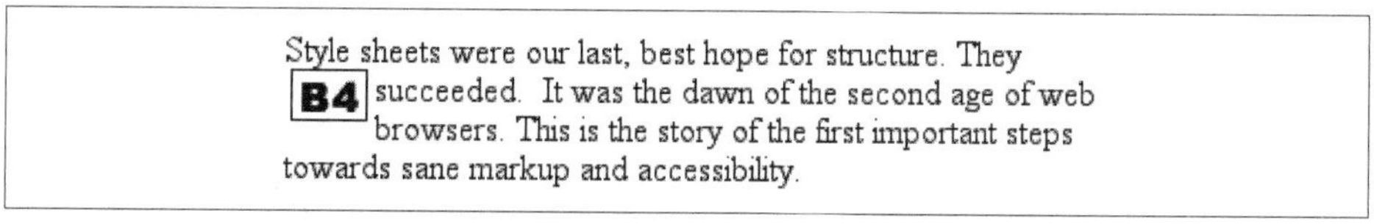

Style sheets were our last, best hope for structure. They **B4** succeeded. It was the dawn of the second age of web browsers. This is the story of the first important steps towards sane markup and accessibility.

Figure 10-1. A floating image

However, when floating elements in CSS, some interesting issues come up.

Floated Elements

Keep a few things in mind with regard to floating elements. First, a floated element is, in some ways, removed from the normal flow of the document, although it still affects the layout. In a manner utterly unique within CSS, floated elements exist almost on their own plane, yet they still have influence over the rest of the document.

This influence derives from the fact that when an element is floated, other content "flows around" it. This is familiar behavior with floated images, but the same is true if you float a paragraph, for example. In Figure 10-2, you can see this effect quite clearly, thanks to the margin added to the floated paragraph:

```
p.aside {float: right; width: 15em; margin: 0 1em 1em; padding: 0.25em;
    border: 1px solid;}
```

One of the first interesting things to notice is that margins around floated elements do not collapse. If you float an image with 20-pixel margins, there will be at least 20 pixels of space around that image. If other elements adjacent to the image—and that means adjacent horizontally *and* vertically—also have margins, those margins will not collapse with the margins on the floated image, as you can see in Figure 10-3:

```
p img {float: left; margin: 25px;}
```

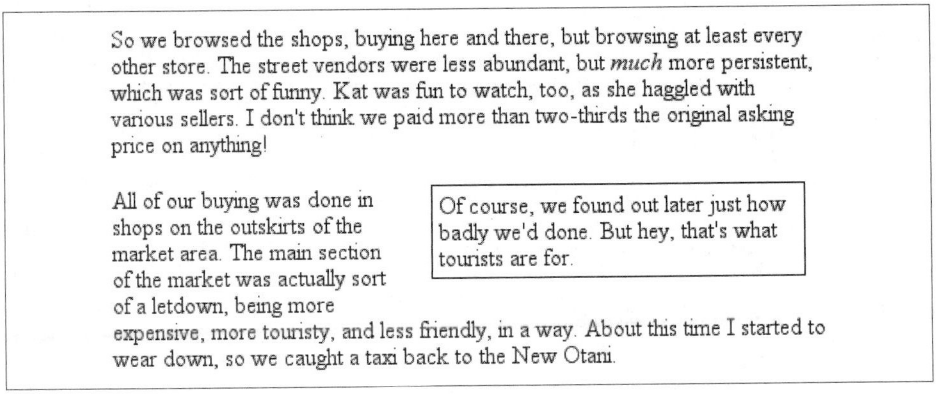

So we browsed the shops, buying here and there, but browsing at least every other store. The street vendors were less abundant, but *much* more persistent, which was sort of funny. Kat was fun to watch, too, as she haggled with various sellers. I don't think we paid more than two-thirds the original asking price on anything!

All of our buying was done in shops on the outskirts of the market area. The main section of the market was actually sort of a letdown, being more expensive, more touristy, and less friendly, in a way. About this time I started to wear down, so we caught a taxi back to the New Otani.

Of course, we found out later just how badly we'd done. But hey, that's what tourists are for.

Figure 10-2. A floating paragraph

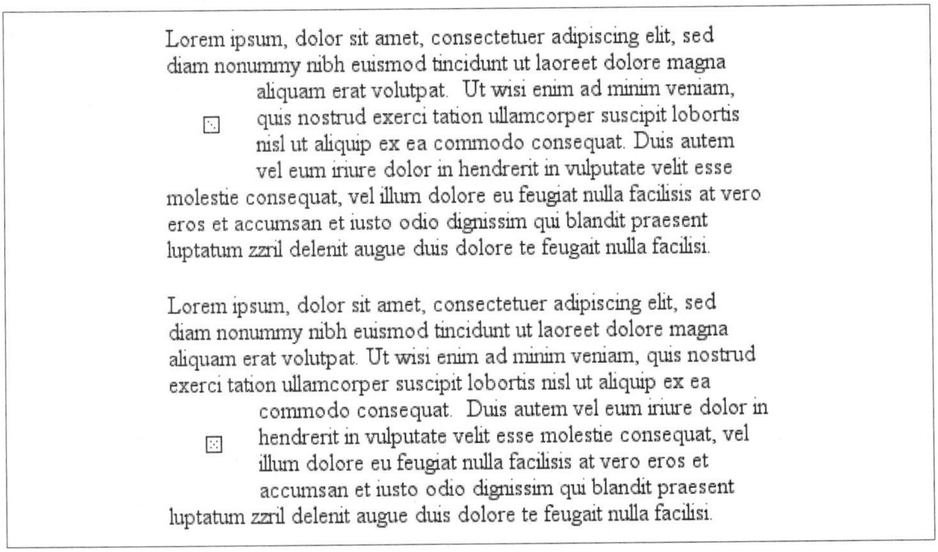

Lorem ipsum, dolor sit amet, consectetuer adipiscing elit, sed diam nonummy nibh euismod tincidunt ut laoreet dolore magna aliquam erat volutpat. Ut wisi enim ad minim veniam, quis nostrud exerci tation ullamcorper suscipit lobortis nisl ut aliquip ex ea commodo consequat. Duis autem vel eum iriure dolor in hendrerit in vulputate velit esse molestie consequat, vel illum dolore eu feugiat nulla facilisis at vero eros et accumsan et iusto odio dignissim qui blandit praesent luptatum zzril delenit augue duis dolore te feugait nulla facilisi.

Lorem ipsum, dolor sit amet, consectetuer adipiscing elit, sed diam nonummy nibh euismod tincidunt ut laoreet dolore magna aliquam erat volutpat. Ut wisi enim ad minim veniam, quis nostrud exerci tation ullamcorper suscipit lobortis nisl ut aliquip ex ea commodo consequat. Duis autem vel eum iriure dolor in hendrerit in vulputate velit esse molestie consequat, vel illum dolore eu feugiat nulla facilisis at vero eros et accumsan et iusto odio dignissim qui blandit praesent luptatum zzril delenit augue duis dolore te feugait nulla facilisi.

Figure 10-3. Floating images with margins

To resurrect the paper-and-plastic analogy from Chapter 7, the plastic margins around an image *never* overlap the plastic surrounding other floated elements.

If you do float a nonreplaced element, you must declare a width for that element. Otherwise, according to the CSS specification, the element's width will tend toward zero. Thus, a floated paragraph could literally be one character wide, assuming one character is the browser's minimum value for width. If you fail to declare a width value for your floated elements, you could end up with something like Figure 10-4. (It's unlikely, granted, but still possible.)

No floating at all

There is one other value for float besides left and right. float: none is used to prevent an element from floating at all.

> So we browsed the shops, buying here and there, but browsing at least every
> other store. The street vendors were less abundant, but *much* more persistent,
> which was sort of funny. Kat was fun to watch, too, as she haggled with
> various sellers. I don't think we paid more than two-thirds the original asking
> price on anything!
>
> All of our buying was done in shops on the outskirts of the | Of
> market area. The main section of the market was actually sort of | course,
> a letdown, being more expensive, more touristy, and less | we
> friendly, in a way. About this time I started to wear down, so we | found
> caught a taxi back to the New Otani. | out
> | later

Figure 10-4. Floated text without an explicit width

This might seem a little silly, since the easiest way to keep an element from floating is to simply avoid declaring a float, right? Well, first of all, the default value of `float` is `none`. In other words, the value has to exist in order for normal, nonfloating behavior to be possible; without it, all elements would float in one way or another.

Second, you might want to override a certain style from an imported style sheet. Imagine that you're using a server-wide style sheet that floats images. On one particular page, you don't want those images to float. Rather than writing a whole new style sheet, you could simply place `img {float: none;}` in your document's embedded style sheet. Beyond this type of circumstance, though, there really isn't much call to actually use `float: none`.

Floating: The Details

Before we start digging into details of floating, it's important to establish the concept of a *containing block*. A floated element's containing block is the nearest block-level ancestor element. Therefore, in the following markup, the floated element's containing block is the paragraph element that contains it:

```
<h1>Test</h1>
<p>
This is paragraph text, but you knew that.  Within the content of this
paragraph is an image that's been floated.
<img src="testy.gif" style="float: right;">
The containing block for the floated image is the paragraph.
</p>
```

 We'll return to the concept of containing blocks when we discuss positioning later in this chapter.

Furthermore, a floated element generates a block box, regardless of the kind of element it is. Thus, if you float a link, even though the element is inline and would ordinarily generate an inline box, it generates a block box when floated. It will be laid out and act as if it were, for example, a div. This is not unlike declaring display: block for the floated element, although it is not necessary to do so.

A series of specific rules govern the placement of a floated element, so let's cover those before digging into applied behavior. These rules are vaguely similar to those that govern the evaluation of margins and widths, and have the same initial appearance of common sense. They are as follows:

1. The left (or right) outer edge of a floated element may not be to the left (or right) of the inner edge of its containing block.

   This is straightforward enough. The outer left edge of a left-floated element can only go as far left as the inner left edge of its containing block; similarly, the furthest right a right-floated element may go is its containing block's inner right edge, as shown in Figure 10-5. (In this and subsequent figures, the circled numbers show the position of the markup element in relation to the source, and the numbered boxes show the position and size of the floated visible element.)

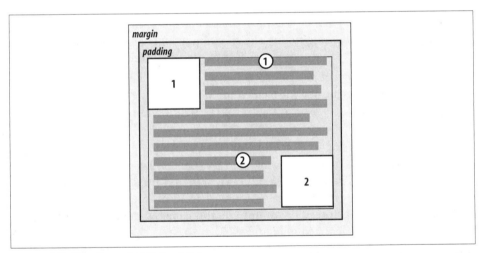

Figure 10-5. Floating to the left (or right)

2. The left (or right) outer edge of a floated element must be to the right (or left) of the right (left) outer edge of a left-floating (or right-floating) element that occurs earlier in the document's source, unless the top of the later element is below the bottom of the former.

   This rule prevents floated elements from "overwriting" one another. If an element is floated to the left, and another floated element is already there, the latter element will be placed against the outer right edge of the previously floated element. If, however, a floated element's top is below the bottom of all earlier floated images, it can float all the way to the inner left edge of the parent. Some examples of this behavior are shown in Figure 10-6.

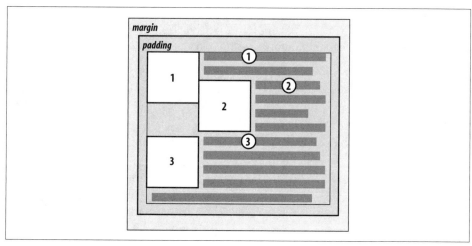

Figure 10-6. Keeping floats from overlapping

The advantage of this rule is that all your floated content will be visible since you don't have to worry about one floated element obscuring another. This makes floating a fairly safe thing to do. The situation is markedly different when using positioning, where you could easily cause elements to overwrite one another.

3. The right outer edge of a left-floating element may not be to the right of the left outer edge of any right-floating element to its right. The left outer edge of a right-floating element may not be to the left of the right outer edge of any left-floating element to its left.

This rule prevents floated elements from overlapping one another. Let's say you have a body that is 500 pixels wide, and its sole content is two images that are 300 pixels wide. The first is floated to the left, and the second is floated to the right. This rule prevents the second image from overlapping the first by 100 pixels. Instead, it is forced down until its top is below the bottom of the right-floating image, as depicted in Figure 10-7.

4. A floating element's top may not be higher than the inner top of its parent. If a floating element is between two collapsing margins, it is placed as though it had a block-level parent element between the two elements.

The first part of this rule is quite simple and keeps floating elements from floating all the way to the top of the document. The correct behavior is illustrated in Figure 10-8. The second part of this rule fine-tunes the alignment in situations— for example, when the middle paragraph of three paragraphs is floated. In that case, the floated paragraph is floated as if it had a block-level parent element (say, a div). This prevents the floated paragraph from moving up to the top of whatever parent the three paragraphs share.

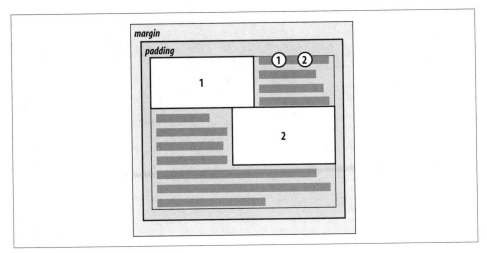

Figure 10-7. More overlap prevention

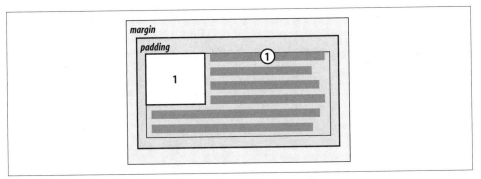

Figure 10-8. Unlike balloons, floated elements can't float upward

5. A floating element's top may not be higher than the top of any earlier floating or block-level element.

   Similar to Rule 4, Rule 5 keeps floated elements from floating all the way to the top of their parent elements. It is also impossible for a floated element's top to be any higher than the top of a floated element that occurs earlier. Figure 10-9 is an example of this; here, you can see that since the second float was forced below the first one, the third float's top is even with the top of the second float, not the first.

6. A floating element's top may not be higher than the top of any line box containing a box generated by an element that comes earlier in the document source.

   Similar to Rules 4 and 5, this rule further limits the upward floating of an element by preventing it from being above the top of a line containing content that precedes the floated element. Let's say that, right in the middle of a paragraph,

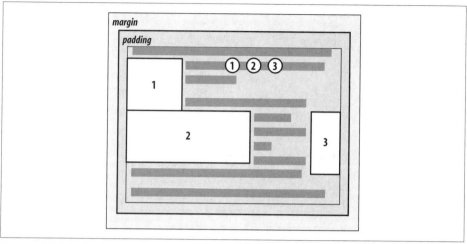

Figure 10-9. Keeping floats below their predecessors

there is a floated image. The highest the top of that image may be placed is the top of the line box from which the image originates. As you can see in Figure 10-10, this keeps images from floating too far upward.

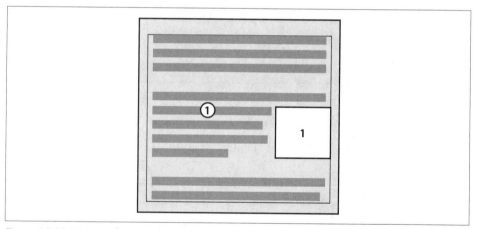

Figure 10-10. Keeping floats level with their context

7. A left (or right) floating element that has another floating element to its left (right) may not have its right outer edge to the right (left) of its containing block's right (left) edge.

In other words, a floating element cannot stick out beyond the edge of its containing element, unless it's too wide to fit on its own. This prevents a situation where a succeeding number of floated elements could appear in a horizontal line and far exceed the edges of the containing block. Instead, a float that would otherwise stick out of its containing block by appearing next to another one will be floated down to a point below any previous floats, as illustrated by Figure 10-11 (the floats start on the next line in the figure to more clearly illustrate the principle at work here). This rule first appeared in CSS2, to correct its omission in CSS1.

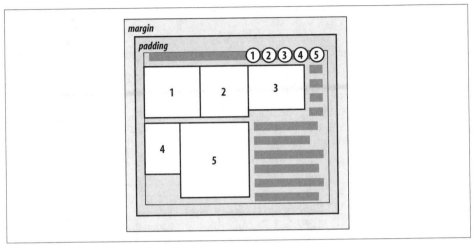

Figure 10-11. If there isn't room, floats get pushed to a new "line"

8. A floating element must be placed as high as possible.

Rule 8 is, of course, subject to the restrictions introduced by the previous seven rules. Historically, browsers aligned the top of a floated element with the top of the line box after the one in which the image's tag appears. Rule 8, however, implies that its top should be even with the top of the same line box as that in which its tag appears, assuming there is enough room. The theoretically correct behaviors are shown in Figure 10-12.

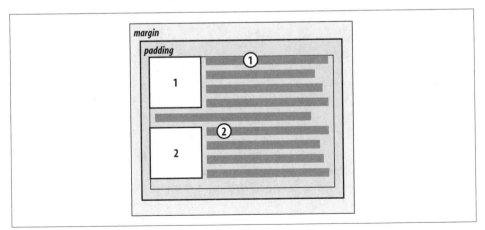

Figure 10-12. Given the other constraints, go as high as possible

Unfortunately, since there is no precisely defined meaning for "as high as possible" (which could mean, and in fact has been argued to mean, "as high as conveniently possible"), you cannot rely on consistent behavior even among browsers that are considered CSS1-conformant. Some browsers will follow historical practice and float the image down into the next line, while others will float the image into the current line if there is room to do so.

9. A left-floating element must be put as far to the left as possible, and a right-floating element as far to the right as possible. A higher position is preferred to one that is further to the right or left.

Again, this rule is subject to restrictions introduced in the preceding rules. There are caveats here similar to those in Rule 8, although they are not quite so fuzzy. As you can see from Figure 10-13, it is pretty easy to tell when an element has gone as far as possible to the right or left.

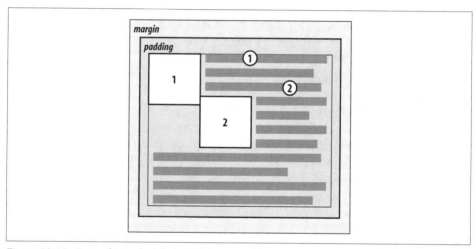

Figure 10-13. Get as far to the left (or right) as possible

Applied Behavior

There are a number of interesting consequences to the rules we've just seen, both because of what the rules say and what they don't say. The first thing to discuss is what happens when the floated element is taller than its parent element.

This happens quite often, as a matter of fact. Take the example of a short document, composed of no more than a few paragraphs and h3 elements, where the first paragraph contains a floated image. Further, this floated image has a margin of five pixels (5px). You would expect the document to be rendered as shown in Figure 10-14.

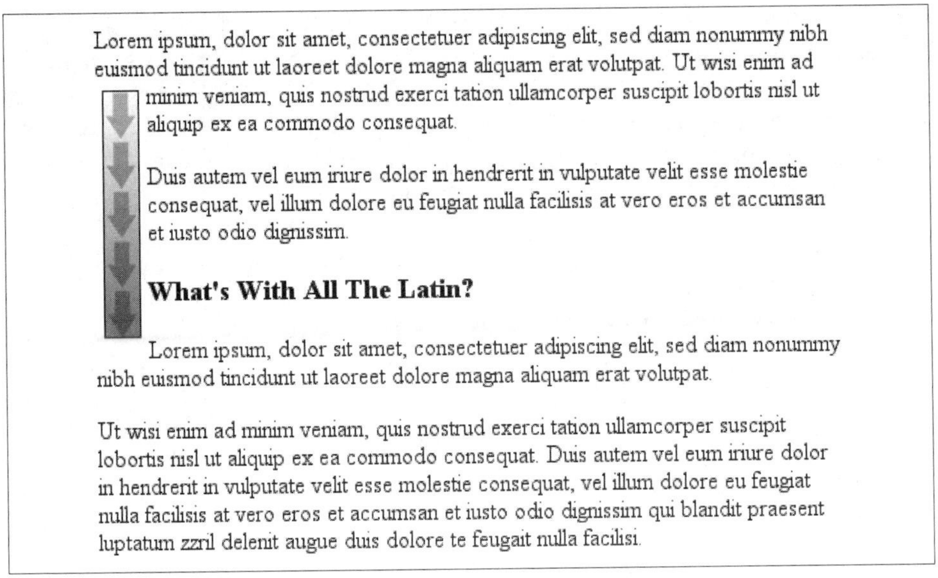

Lorem ipsum, dolor sit amet, consectetuer adipiscing elit, sed diam nonummy nibh euismod tincidunt ut laoreet dolore magna aliquam erat volutpat. Ut wisi enim ad minim veniam, quis nostrud exerci tation ullamcorper suscipit lobortis nisl ut aliquip ex ea commodo consequat.

Duis autem vel eum iriure dolor in hendrerit in vulputate velit esse molestie consequat, vel illum dolore eu feugiat nulla facilisis at vero eros et accumsan et iusto odio dignissim.

What's With All The Latin?

Lorem ipsum, dolor sit amet, consectetuer adipiscing elit, sed diam nonummy nibh euismod tincidunt ut laoreet dolore magna aliquam erat volutpat.

Ut wisi enim ad minim veniam, quis nostrud exerci tation ullamcorper suscipit lobortis nisl ut aliquip ex ea commodo consequat. Duis autem vel eum iriure dolor in hendrerit in vulputate velit esse molestie consequat, vel illum dolore eu feugiat nulla facilisis at vero eros et accumsan et iusto odio dignissim qui blandit praesent luptatum zzril delenit augue duis dolore te feugait nulla facilisi.

Figure 10-14. Expected floating behavior

Nothing there is unusual, of course, but Figure 10-15 shows what happens when you set the first paragraph to have a background.

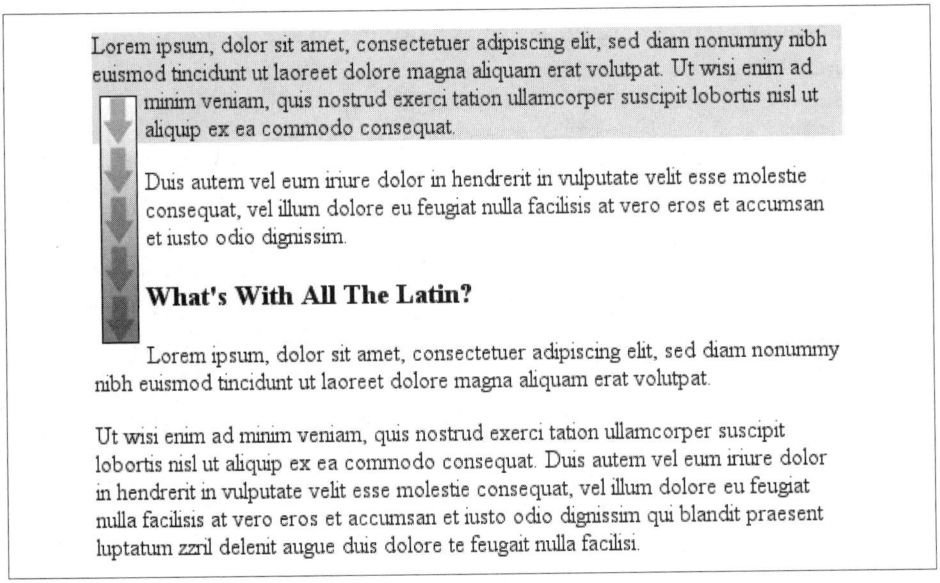

Lorem ipsum, dolor sit amet, consectetuer adipiscing elit, sed diam nonummy nibh euismod tincidunt ut laoreet dolore magna aliquam erat volutpat. Ut wisi enim ad minim veniam, quis nostrud exerci tation ullamcorper suscipit lobortis nisl ut aliquip ex ea commodo consequat.

Duis autem vel eum iriure dolor in hendrerit in vulputate velit esse molestie consequat, vel illum dolore eu feugiat nulla facilisis at vero eros et accumsan et iusto odio dignissim.

What's With All The Latin?

Lorem ipsum, dolor sit amet, consectetuer adipiscing elit, sed diam nonummy nibh euismod tincidunt ut laoreet dolore magna aliquam erat volutpat.

Ut wisi enim ad minim veniam, quis nostrud exerci tation ullamcorper suscipit lobortis nisl ut aliquip ex ea commodo consequat. Duis autem vel eum iriure dolor in hendrerit in vulputate velit esse molestie consequat, vel illum dolore eu feugiat nulla facilisis at vero eros et accumsan et iusto odio dignissim qui blandit praesent luptatum zzril delenit augue duis dolore te feugait nulla facilisi.

Figure 10-15. Backgrounds and floated elements

There is nothing different about the second example, except for the visible background. As you can see, the floated image sticks out of the bottom of its parent element. Of course, it did so in the first example, but it was less obvious there because you couldn't see the background. The floating rules we discussed earlier address only the left, right, and top edges of floats and their parents. The deliberate omission of bottom edges requires the behavior depicted in Figure 10-15.

 In practice, some browsers do not do this correctly. Instead, they will increase the height of a parent element so that the floated element is contained within it, even though this results in a great deal of extra blank space within the parent element.

CSS2.1 clarified one aspect of floated-element behavior: a floated element will expand to contain any floated descendants. (Previous versions of CSS were unclear about what should happen.) Thus, you could contain a float within its parent element by floating the parent, as in this example:

```
<div style="float: left; width: 100%;">
  <img src="hay.gif" style="float: left;">
  The 'div' will stretch around the floated image
  because the 'div' has been floated.
</div>
```

On a related note, consider backgrounds and their relationship to floated elements that occur earlier in the document, which is illustrated in Figure 10-16.

Lorem ipsum, dolor sit amet, consectetuer adipiscing elit, sed diam nonummy nibh euismod tincidunt ut laoreet dolore magna aliquam erat volutpat. Ut wisi enim ad minim veniam, quis nostrud exerci tation ullamcorper suscipit lobortis nisl ut aliquip ex ea commodo consequat.

Duis autem vel eum iriure dolor in hendrerit in vulputate velit esse molestie consequat, vel illum dolore eu feugiat nulla facilisis at vero eros et accumsan et iusto odio dignissim.

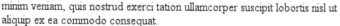

What's With All The Latin?

Lorem ipsum, dolor sit amet, consectetuer adipiscing elit, sed diam nonummy nibh euismod tincidunt ut laoreet dolore magna aliquam erat volutpat.

Ut wisi enim ad minim veniam, quis nostrud exerci tation ullamcorper suscipit lobortis nisl ut aliquip ex ea commodo consequat. Duis autem vel eum iriure dolor in hendrerit in vulputate velit esse molestie consequat, vel illum dolore eu feugiat nulla facilisis at vero eros et accumsan et iusto odio dignissim qui blandit praesent luptatum zzril delenit augue duis dolore te feugait nulla facilisi.

Figure 10-16. Element backgrounds "slide under" floated elements

Because the floated element is both within and outside of the flow, this sort of thing is bound to happen. What's going on? The content of the heading is being "displaced" by the floated element. However, the heading's element width is still as wide as its parent element. Therefore, its content area spans the width of the parent, and so does the background. To avoid being obscured behind the floating element, the actual content doesn't flow all the way across its own content area.

Negative margins

Interestingly, negative margins can cause floated elements to move outside of their parent elements. This seems to be in direct contradiction to the rules explained earlier, but it isn't. In the same way that elements can appear to be wider than their parents through negative margins, floated elements can appear to protrude from their parents.

Let's consider a floated image that is floated to the left, and that has left and top margins of -15px. This image is placed inside a div that has no padding, borders, or margins. The result is shown in Figure 10-17.

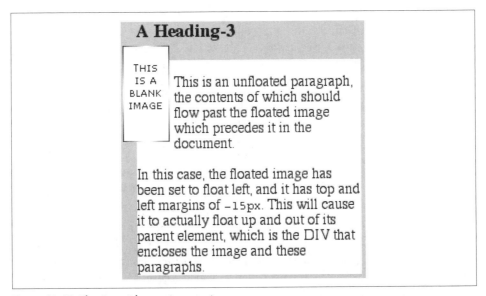

Figure 10-17. Floating with negative margins

Contrary to appearances, this does not violate the restrictions on floated elements being placed outside their parent elements.

A close reading of the rules in the previous section will reveal the technicality that permits this behavior: the outer edges of a floating element must be within the element's parent. However, negative margins can place the floated element's content such that it effectively overlaps its own outer edge, as detailed in Figure 10-18.

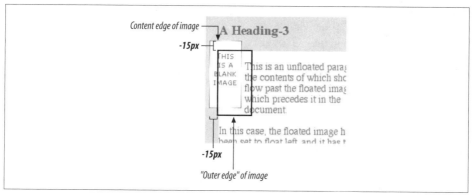

Figure 10-18. The details of floating up and left with negative margins

The math situation works out something like this: assume the top inner edge of the div is at the pixel position 100. To figure out where the top inner edge of the floated element should be, the browser will do this: 100px + (-15px) `margin` + 0 padding = 85px. Thus, the top inner edge of the floated element should be at pixel position 85; even though this is higher than the top inner edge of the float's parent element, the math works out such that the specification isn't violated. A similar line of reasoning explains how the left inner edge of the floated element can be placed to the left of the left inner edge of its parent.

Many of you may have an overwhelming desire to cry "Foul!" right about now. Personally, I don't blame you. It seems completely wrong to allow the top inner edge to be higher than the top outer edge, for example, but with a negative top margin, that's exactly what you get—just as negative margins on normal, nonfloated elements can make them visually wider than their parents. The same is true on all four sides of a floated element's box: if you set the margins to be negative, the content will overrun the outer edge without technically violating the specification.

There is one important question here: when using negative margins, what happens to the document display when an element is floated out of its parent element? For example, an image could be floated so far up that it intrudes into a paragraph that has already been displayed by the user agent. In such a case, it's up to the user agent to decide whether the document should be reflowed. The CSS1 and CSS2 specifications explicitly state that user agents are not required to reflow previous content to accommodate things that happen later in the document. In other words, if an image is floated up into a previous paragraph, it may simply overwrite whatever was already there. On the other hand, the user agent may handle the situation by flowing content around the float. Either way, it's probably a bad idea to count on a particular behavior, which makes the utility of setting negative margins on floats somewhat limited. Hanging floats are probably fairly safe, but trying to push an element upward on the page is generally a bad idea.

There is one other way for a floated element to exceed its parent's inner left and right edges: when the floated element is wider than its parent. In that case, the floated element will simply overflow the right or left inner edge—depending on which way the element is floated—in its best attempt to display correctly. This will lead to a result like that shown in Figure 10-19.

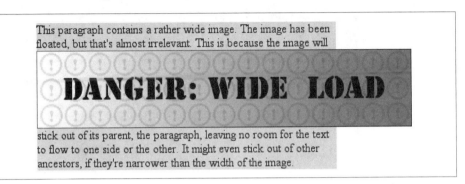

Figure 10-19. Floating an element that is wider than its parent

Floats, Content, and Overlapping

An even more interesting question is this: what happens when a float overlaps content in the normal flow? This can happen if, for example, a float has a negative margin on the side where content is flowing past (e.g., a negative left margin on a right-floating element). You've already seen what happens to the borders and backgrounds of block-level elements. What about inline elements?

CSS1 and CSS2 were not completely clear about the expected behavior in such cases. CSS2.1 clarified the subject with the following explicit rules:

- An inline box that overlaps with a float has its borders, background, and content all rendered "on top" of the float.

- A block box that overlaps with a float has its borders and background rendered "behind" the float, whereas its content is rendered "on top" of the float.

To illustrate these rules, consider the following situation:

```
<img src="testy.gif" class="sideline">
<p class="box">
This paragraph, unremarkable in most ways, does contain an inline element.
This inline contains some <strong>strongly emphasized text, which is
so marked to make an important point</strong>.  The rest of the element's
content is normal anonymous inline content.
</p>
<p>
This is a second paragraph.  There's nothing remarkable about it, really.
Please move along.
</p>
<h2 id="jump-up">A Heading!</h2>
```

Apply the following styles to that markup, with the result shown in Figure 10-20:

```
img.sideline {float: left; margin: 10px -15px 10px 10px;}
p.box {border: 1px solid gray; padding: 0.5em;}
p.box strong {border: 3px double black; background: silver; padding: 2px;}
h2#jump-up {margin-top: -15px; background: silver;}
```

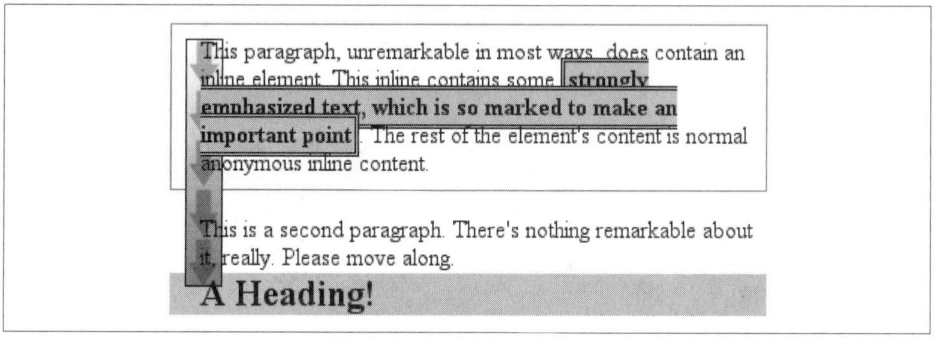

This paragraph, unremarkable in most ways, does contain an inline element. This inline contains some **strongly emphasized text**, which is so marked to make an **important point**. The rest of the element's content is normal anonymous inline content.

This is a second paragraph. There's nothing remarkable about it, really. Please move along.

A Heading!

Figure 10-20. Layout behavior when overlapping floats

The inline element (strong) completely overlaps the floated image—background, border, content, and all. The block elements, on the other hand, have only their content appear on top of the float. Their backgrounds and borders are placed behind the float.

> The overlapping behavior described here is independent of the document source order. It does not matter if an element comes before or after a float; the same behaviors still apply.

Clearing

We've talked quite a bit about floating behavior, so there's only one more thing to discuss before we turn to positioning. You won't always want your content to flow past a floated element—in some cases, you'll specifically want to prevent it. If you have a document that is grouped into sections, you might not want the floated elements from one section hanging down into the next. In that case, you'd want to set the first element of each section to prohibit floating elements from appearing next to it. If the first element might otherwise be placed next to a floated element, it will be pushed down until it appears below the floated image, and all subsequent content will appear after that, as shown in Figure 10-21.

This is accomplished with clear.

For example, to ensure that all h3 elements are not placed to the right of left-floating elements, you would declare h3 {clear: left;}. This can be translated as "make sure that the left side of an h3 is clear of floating images," and it has an effect very similar to the HTML construct <br clear="left">. (Ironically, most browsers'

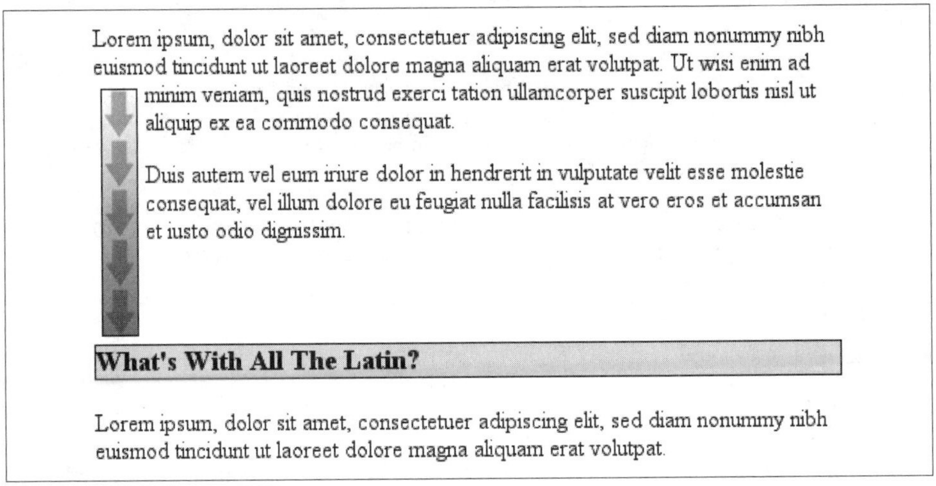

Lorem ipsum, dolor sit amet, consectetuer adipiscing elit, sed diam nonummy nibh euismod tincidunt ut laoreet dolore magna aliquam erat volutpat. Ut wisi enim ad minim veniam, quis nostrud exerci tation ullamcorper suscipit lobortis nisl ut aliquip ex ea commodo consequat.

Duis autem vel eum iriure dolor in hendrerit in vulputate velit esse molestie consequat, vel illum dolore eu feugiat nulla facilisis at vero eros et accumsan et iusto odio dignissim.

What's With All The Latin?

Lorem ipsum, dolor sit amet, consectetuer adipiscing elit, sed diam nonummy nibh euismod tincidunt ut laoreet dolore magna aliquam erat volutpat.

Figure 10-21. Displaying an element in the clear

clear

Values:	left | right | both | none | inherit
Initial value:	none
Applies to:	Block-level elements
Inherited:	No
Computed value:	As specified

default behavior is to have br elements generate inline boxes, so clear doesn't apply to them unless you change their display!) The following rule uses clear to prevent h3 elements from flowing past floated elements to the left side:

```
h3 {clear: left;}
```

While this will push the h3 past any left-floating elements, it will allow floated elements to appear on the right side of h3 elements, as shown in Figure 10-22.

To avoid this sort of thing, and to make sure that h3 elements do not coexist on a line with any floated elements, use the value both:

```
h3 {clear: both;}
```

Understandably enough, this value prevents coexistence with floated elements on both sides of the cleared element, as demonstrated in Figure 10-23.

If, on the other hand, we were only worried about h3 elements being pushed down past floated elements to their right, then you'd use h3 {clear: right;}.

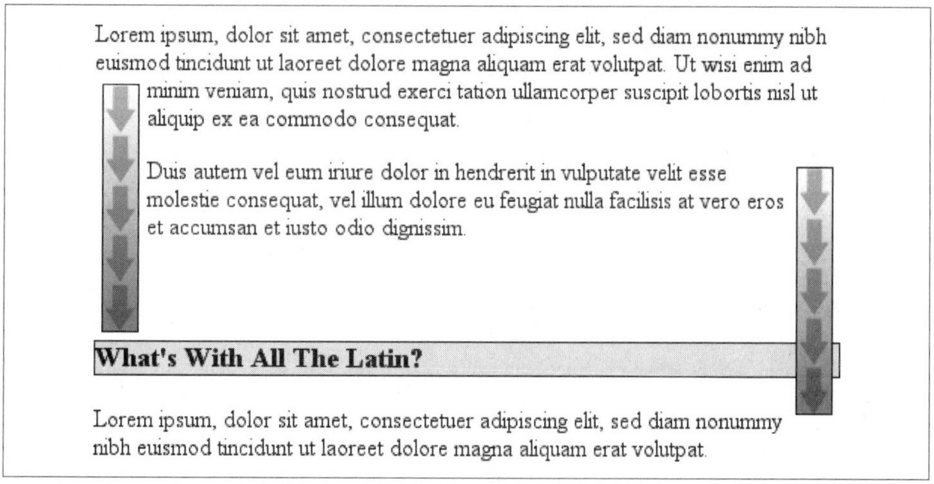

Lorem ipsum, dolor sit amet, consectetuer adipiscing elit, sed diam nonummy nibh euismod tincidunt ut laoreet dolore magna aliquam erat volutpat. Ut wisi enim ad minim veniam, quis nostrud exerci tation ullamcorper suscipit lobortis nisl ut aliquip ex ea commodo consequat.

Duis autem vel eum iriure dolor in hendrerit in vulputate velit esse molestie consequat, vel illum dolore eu feugiat nulla facilisis at vero eros et accumsan et iusto odio dignissim.

What's With All The Latin?

Lorem ipsum, dolor sit amet, consectetuer adipiscing elit, sed diam nonummy nibh euismod tincidunt ut laoreet dolore magna aliquam erat volutpat.

Figure 10-22. Clear to the left, but not the right

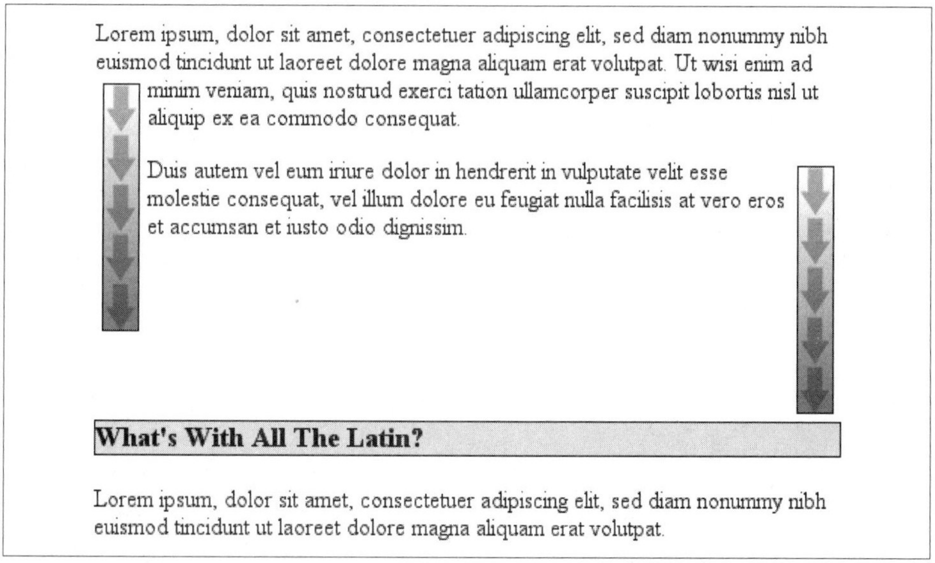

Lorem ipsum, dolor sit amet, consectetuer adipiscing elit, sed diam nonummy nibh euismod tincidunt ut laoreet dolore magna aliquam erat volutpat. Ut wisi enim ad minim veniam, quis nostrud exerci tation ullamcorper suscipit lobortis nisl ut aliquip ex ea commodo consequat.

Duis autem vel eum iriure dolor in hendrerit in vulputate velit esse molestie consequat, vel illum dolore eu feugiat nulla facilisis at vero eros et accumsan et iusto odio dignissim.

What's With All The Latin?

Lorem ipsum, dolor sit amet, consectetuer adipiscing elit, sed diam nonummy nibh euismod tincidunt ut laoreet dolore magna aliquam erat volutpat.

Figure 10-23. Clear on both sides

Finally, there's clear: none, which allows elements to float to either side of an element. As with float: none, this value exists mostly to allow for normal document behavior, in which elements will permit floated elements on both sides. none can be used to override other styles, of course, as shown in Figure 10-24. Despite the document-wide rule that h3 elements will not permit floated elements on either side, one h3 in particular has been set so that it does permit such behavior:

```
h3 {clear: both;}
```

```
<h3 style="clear: none;">What's With All The Latin?</h3>
```

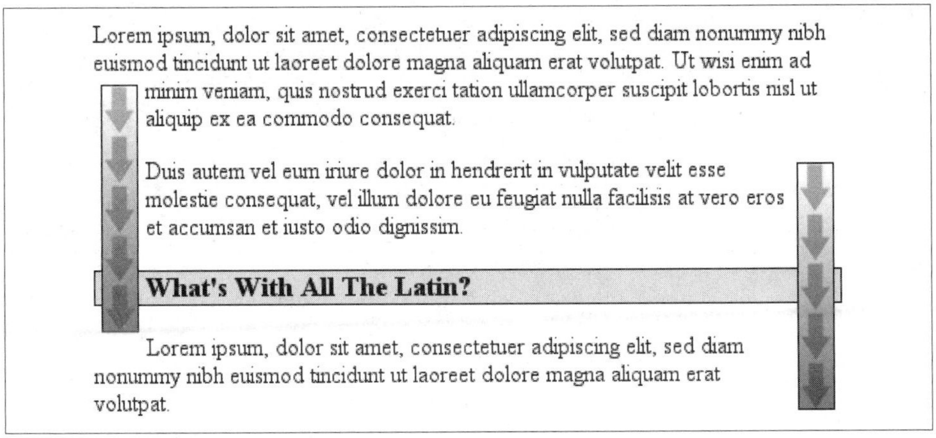

Lorem ipsum, dolor sit amet, consectetuer adipiscing elit, sed diam nonummy nibh euismod tincidunt ut laoreet dolore magna aliquam erat volutpat. Ut wisi enim ad minim veniam, quis nostrud exerci tation ullamcorper suscipit lobortis nisl ut aliquip ex ea commodo consequat.

Duis autem vel eum iriure dolor in hendrerit in vulputate velit esse molestie consequat, vel illum dolore eu feugiat nulla facilisis at vero eros et accumsan et iusto odio dignissim.

What's With All The Latin?

Lorem ipsum, dolor sit amet, consectetuer adipiscing elit, sed diam nonummy nibh euismod tincidunt ut laoreet dolore magna aliquam erat volutpat.

Figure 10-24. Not clear at all

In CSS1 and CSS2, clear worked by increasing the top margin of an element so that it ended up below a floated element, effectively ignoring any margin width set for the top of a cleared element. That is, instead of being 1.5em, for example, it would be increased to 10em, or 25px, or 7.133in, or however much was needed to move the element down far enough so that the content area was below the bottom edge of a floated element.

In CSS2.1, clearance was introduced. *Clearance* is extra spacing added above an element's top margin to push it past any floated elements. This means that the top margin of a cleared element does not change when an element is cleared. Its downward movement is caused by the clearance instead. Pay close attention to the placement of the heading's border in Figure 10-25, which results from the following:

```
img.sider {float: left; margin: 0;}
h3 {border: 1px solid gray; clear: left; margin-top: 15px;}

<img src="boxer.gif" class="sider" height="50" width="50">
<img src="stripe.gif" height="10" width="100">
<h3>Why Doubt Salmon?</h3>
```

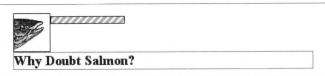

Figure 10-25. Clearing and its effect on margins

There is no separation between the top border of the h3 and the bottom border of the floated image because 25 pixels of clearance were added above the 15-pixel top margin to push the h3's top border edge just past the bottom edge of the float. This will be true unless the h3's top margin calculates to 40 pixels or more, in which case the h3 will naturally place itself below the float and the clear value will be irrelevant.

In most cases, of course, you can't know how far an element needs to be cleared. The way to make sure a cleared element has some space between its top and the bottom of a float is to put a bottom margin on the float itself. So, if you want at least 15 pixels of space below the float in the previous example, you would change the CSS like this:

```
img.sider {float: left; margin: 0 0 15px;}
h3 {border: 1px solid gray; clear: left;}
```

The floated element's bottom margin increases the size of the float box, and thus the point past which cleared elements must be pushed. This is because, as you've seen before, the margin edges of a floated element define the edges of the floated box.

Positioning

The idea behind positioning is fairly simple. It allows you to define exactly where element boxes will appear relative to where they would ordinarily be—or relative to a parent element, another element, or even to the browser window itself.

Basic Concepts

Before we delve into the various kinds of positioning, it's a good idea to look at what types exist and how they differ. We'll also need to define some basic ideas that are fundamental to understanding how positioning works.

Types of positioning

You can choose one of four different types of positioning, which affect how the element's box is generated, by using the position property.

<table>
<tr><td colspan="2" align="center">position</td></tr>
<tr><td>Values:</td><td>static | relative | absolute | fixed | inherit</td></tr>
<tr><td>Initial value:</td><td>static</td></tr>
<tr><td>Applies to:</td><td>All elements</td></tr>
<tr><td>Inherited:</td><td>No</td></tr>
<tr><td>Computed value:</td><td>As specified</td></tr>
</table>

The values of position have the following meanings:

static

> The element's box is generated as normal. Block-level elements generate a rectangular box that is part of the document's flow, and inline-level boxes cause the creation of one or more line boxes that are flowed within their parent element.

relative

> The element's box is offset by some distance. The element retains the shape it would have had were it not positioned, and the space that it would ordinarily have occupied is preserved.

absolute

> The element's box is completely removed from the flow of the document and positioned with respect to its containing block, which may be another element in the document or the initial containing block (described in the next section). Whatever space the element might have occupied in the normal document flow is closed up, as though the element did not exist. The positioned element generates a block-level box, regardless of the type of box it would have generated if it were in the normal flow.

fixed

> The element's box behaves as though it were set to absolute, but its containing block is the viewport itself.

Don't worry so much about the details right now, as we'll look at each of these kinds of positioning later in the chapter. Before we do that, we need to discuss containing blocks.

The containing block

We discussed containing blocks in relation to floats earlier in the chapter. In that case, a float's containing block was defined as the nearest block-level ancestor element. With positioning, the situation is not quite so simple. CSS2.1 defines the following behaviors:

- The containing block of the "root element" (also called the *initial containing block*) is established by the user agent. In HTML, the root element is the html element, although some browsers use body. In most browsers, the initial containing block is a rectangle the size of the viewport.

- For a non-root element whose position value is relative or static, the containing block is formed by the content edge of the nearest block-level, table cell, or inline-block ancestor box.

- For non-root elements that have a position value of absolute, the containing block is set to the nearest ancestor (of any kind) that has a position value other than static. This happens as follows:

  — If the ancestor is block-level, the containing block is set to that element's padding edge; in other words, the area that would be bounded by a border.

  — If the ancestor is inline-level, the containing block is set to the content edge of the ancestor. In left-to-right languages, the top and left of the containing block are the top and left content edges of the first box in the ancestor, and the bottom and right edges are the bottom and right content edges of the last box. In right-to-left languages, the right edge of the containing block corresponds to the right content edge of the first box, and the left is taken from the last box. The top and bottom are the same.

— If there are no ancestors, the element's containing block is defined as the initial containing block.

An important point: elements can be positioned outside of their containing block. This is very similar to the way in which floated elements can use negative margins to float outside of their parent's content area. It also suggests that the term "containing block" should really be "positioning context," but since the specification uses "containing block," so will I. (I do try to minimize confusion. Really!)

Offset properties

Three of the positioning schemes described in the previous section—relative, absolute, and fixed—use four distinct properties to describe the offset of a positioned element's sides with respect to its containing block. These four properties, which we'll refer to as the *offset properties*, are a big part of what makes positioning work.

---

top, right, bottom, left

Values:	<length> | <percentage> | auto | inherit
Initial value:	auto
Applies to:	Positioned elements (that is, elements for which the value of position is something other than static)
Inherited:	No
Percentages:	Refer to the height of the containing block for top and bottom and the width of the containing block for right and left
Computed value:	For relatively positioned elements, see the following Note; for static elements, auto; for length values, the corresponding absolute length; for percentage values, the specified value; otherwise, auto
Note:	The computed values depend on a series of factors; see individual entries in Appendix A for examples

---

These properties describe an offset from the nearest side of the containing block (thus the term *offset*). For example, top describes how far the top margin edge of the positioned element should be placed from the top of its containing block. In the case of top, positive values move the top margin edge of the positioned element *downward*, while negative values move it *above* the top of its containing block. Similarly, left describes how far to the right (for positive values) or left (for negative values) the left margin edge of the positioned element is from the left edge of the containing block. Positive values will shift the margin edge of the positioned element to the right, and negative values will move it to the left.

Another way to look at it is that positive values cause inward offsets, moving the edges toward the center of the containing block, and negative values cause outward offsets.

 The original CSS2 specification actually says that the content edges are offset, not margin edges, but this was inconsistent with other parts of CSS2. The mistake was corrected in later errata and in CSS2.1. The margin edges are used for offset calculations by all actively developed browsers (as of this writing).

The implication of offsetting the margin edges of a positioned element is that everything about an element—margins, borders, padding, and content—is moved in the process of positioning it. Thus, it is possible to set margins, borders, and padding for a positioned element; these will be preserved and kept with the positioned element, and they will be contained within the area defined by the offset properties.

It is important to remember that the offset properties define offset from the analogous side (e.g., left defines the offset from the left side) of the containing block, not from the upper-left corner of the containing block. This is why, for example, one way to fill up the lower-right corner of a containing block is to use these values:

    top: 50%; bottom: 0; left: 50%; right: 0;

In this example, the outer left edge of the positioned element is placed halfway across the containing block. This is its offset from the left edge of the containing block. The outer right edge of the positioned element, however, is not offset from the right edge of the containing block, so the two are coincident. Similar reasoning applies for the top and bottom of the positioned element: the outer top edge is placed halfway down the containing block, but the outer bottom edge is not moved up from the bottom. This creates the result shown in Figure 10-26.

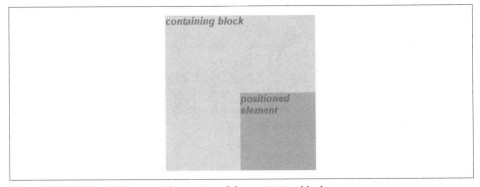

Figure 10-26. Filling the lower-right quarter of the containing block

What's depicted in Figure 10-26, and in most of the examples in this chapter, is based on absolute positioning. Since absolute positioning is the simplest scheme in which to demonstrate how top, right, bottom, and left work, we'll stick to that for now.

Note that the positioned element has a slightly different background color. In Figure 10-26, it has no margins, but if it did, they would create blank space between the borders and the offset edges. This would make the positioned element appear as though it did not completely fill the lower-right quarter of the containing block. In truth, it would fill the area, but it wouldn't be immediately apparent to the eye. Thus, the following two sets of styles would have approximately the same appearance, assuming that the containing block is 100em high by 100em wide:

```
top: 50%; bottom: 0; left: 50%; right: 0; margin: 10em;
top: 60%; bottom: 10%; left: 60%; right: 10%; margin: 0;
```

Again, the similarity would be only visual in nature.

By using negative values, you can position an element outside its containing block. For example, the following values will lead to the result shown in Figure 10-27:

```
top: -5em; bottom: 50%; left: 75%; right: -3em;
```

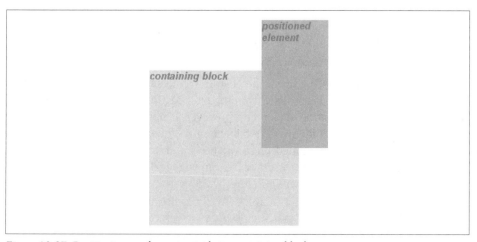

Figure 10-27. Positioning an element outside its containing block

In addition to length and percentage values, the offset properties can also be set to auto, which is the default value. There is no single behavior for auto; it changes based on the type of positioning used. We'll explore how auto works later in the chapter, as we consider each of the positioning types in turn.

Width and Height

There will be many cases when, having determined where you're going to position an element, you'll want to declare how wide and how high that element should be. In addition, there will likely be conditions where you'll want to limit how high or wide a positioned element gets, not to mention cases where you want the browser to go ahead and automatically calculate the width, height, or both.

Setting width and height

If you want to give your positioned element a specific width, then the obvious property to use is width. Similarly, height will let you declare a specific height for a positioned element.

Although it is sometimes important to set the width and height of an element, it is not always necessary when positioning elements. For example, if the placement of the four sides of the element is described using top, right, bottom, and left, then the height and width of the element are implicitly determined by the offsets. Assume that you want an absolutely positioned element to fill the left half of its containing block, from top to bottom. You could use these values, with the result depicted in Figure 10-28:

```
top: 0; bottom: 0; left: 0; right: 50%;
```

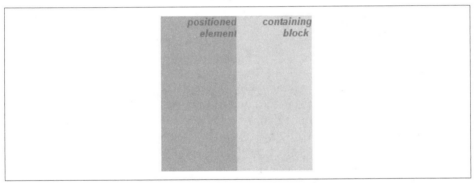

Figure 10-28. Positioning and sizing an element using only the offset properties

Since the default value of both width and height is auto, the result shown in Figure 10-28 is exactly the same as if you had used these values:

```
top: 0; bottom: 0; left: 0; right: 50%; width: 50%; height: 100%;
```

The presence of width and height in this example add nothing to the layout of the element.

Of course, if you were to add padding, a border, or a margin to the element, then the presence of explicit values for height and width do make a difference:

```
top: 0; bottom: 0; left: 0; right: 50%; width: 50%; height: 100%;
    padding: 2em;
```

This will give you a positioned element that extends out of its containing block, as shown in Figure 10-29.

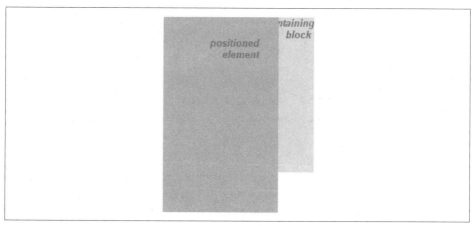

Figure 10-29. Positioning an element partially outside its containing block

This happens because, as we've seen in earlier chapters, the padding is added to the content area, and the content area's size is determined by the values of `height` and `width`. To get the padding you want and still have the element fit into its containing block, you would either remove the `height` and `width` declarations, or else explicitly set them both to auto.

Limiting width and height

Should it become necessary or desirable, you can place limits on an element's width by using the following CSS2 properties, which I'll refer to as the *min-max properties*. An element's content area can be defined to have a minimum dimension using `min-width` and `min-height`.

---

min-width, min-height

Values:	<length> | <percentage> | inherit
Initial value:	0
Applies to:	All elements except nonreplaced inline elements and table elements
Inherited:	No
Percentages:	Refer to the height of the containing block
Computed value:	For percentages, as specified; for length values, the absolute length; otherwise, none

---

Similarly, an element's dimensions can be limited using the properties `max-width` and `max-height`.

The names of these properties make them fairly self-explanatory. What's less obvious at first, but makes sense once you think about it, is that no values for these properties can be negative.

 min-height, min-width, max-height, and max-width were not supported by Internet Explorer for Windows until IE7.

The following styles will force the positioned element to be at least 10em wide by 20em tall, as illustrated in Figure 10-30:

```
top: 10%; bottom: 20%; left: 50%; right: 10%;
    min-width: 10em; min-height: 20em;
```

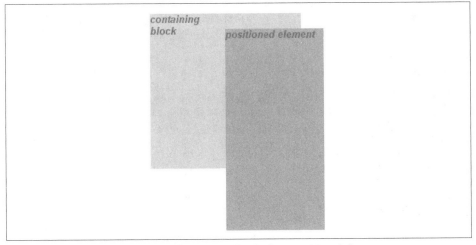

Figure 10-30. Setting a minimum and maximum height for a positioned element

This isn't a very robust solution since it forces the element to be at least a certain size, regardless of the size of its containing block. Here's a better one:

```
top: 10%; bottom: auto; left: 50%; right: 10%; height: auto;
    min-width: 15em;
```

Here you have a case where the element should be 40 percent as wide as the containing block but can never be less than 15em wide. You've also changed the bottom and height so that they're automatically determined. This will let the element be as tall as necessary to display its content, no matter how narrow it gets (never less than 15em, of course!).

We'll look at the role auto plays in the height and width of positioned elements in the next section.

You can turn this around to keep elements from getting too wide or tall by using max-width and max-height. Let's consider a situation where, for some reason, you want an element to have three-quarters the width of its containing block, but to stop getting wider when it hits 400 pixels. The appropriate styles are:

```
left: 0%; right: auto; width: 75%; max-width: 400px;
```

One great advantage of the min-max properties is that they let you mix units with relative safety. You can use percentage-based sizes while setting length-based limits, or vice versa.

It's worth mentioning that these min-max properties can be very useful in conjunction with floated elements as well. For example, you can allow a floated element's width to be relative to the width of its parent element (which is its containing block), while also making sure that the float's width never goes below 10em. The reverse approach is also possible:

```
p.aside {float: left; width: 40em; max-width: 40%;}
```

This will set the float to be 40em wide, unless that would be more than 40 percent of the width of the containing block, in which case the float will be narrowed.

We'll return to the subject of element sizing when discussing each type of positioning.

Content Overflow and Clipping

If the content of an element is too much for the element's size, it's in danger of overflowing the element itself. There are a few alternative solutions in such situations, and CSS2 lets you select among them. It also allows you to define a clipping region to determine the area of the element outside of which these sorts of things become an issue.

Overflow

So let's say that you have, for whatever reason, an element that has been pinned to a specific size, and the content doesn't fit. You can take control of the situation with the overflow property.

<table>
<tr><td colspan="2" align="center">overflow</td></tr>
<tr><td>Values:</td><td>visible | hidden | scroll | auto | inherit</td></tr>
<tr><td>Initial value:</td><td>visible</td></tr>
<tr><td>Applies to:</td><td>Block-level and replaced elements</td></tr>
<tr><td>Inherited:</td><td>No</td></tr>
<tr><td>Computed value:</td><td>As specified</td></tr>
</table>

The default value of visible means that the element's content may be visible outside the element's box. Typically, this would lead to the content simply running outside its own element box but not altering the shape of that box. The following markup results in Figure 10-31:

```
div#sidebar {position: absolute; top: 0; left: 0; width: 25%; height: 7em;
    background: #BBB; overflow: visible;}
```

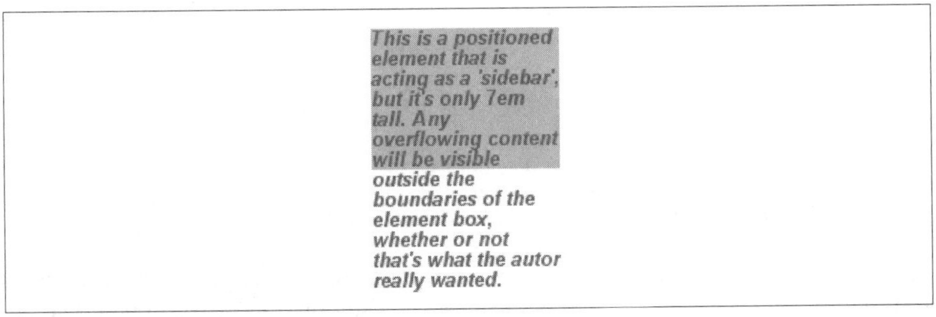

Figure 10-31. Content visibly overflowing the element box

If overflow is set to scroll, the element's content is clipped—that is, cannot be seen—at the edges of the element box, but there is a way to make the extra content available to the user. In a web browser, this could mean a scrollbar (or set of them) or another method of accessing the content without altering the shape of the element itself. One possibility, which could result from the following markup, is depicted in Figure 10-32:

```
div#sidebar {position: absolute; top: 0; left: 0; width: 15%; height: 7em;
    overflow: scroll;}
```

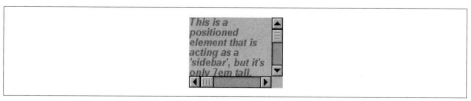

Figure 10-32. Overflowing content made available via a scroll mechanism

If scroll is used, the panning mechanisms (e.g., scrollbars) should always be rendered. To quote the specification, "this avoids any problem with scrollbars appearing or disappearing in a dynamic environment." Thus, even if the element has sufficient space to display all of its content, the scrollbars should still appear. In addition, when printing a page or otherwise displaying the document in a print medium, the content may be displayed as though the value of overflow were declared as visible.

If overflow is set to hidden, the element's content is clipped at the edges of the element box, but no scrolling interface should be provided to make the content outside the clipping region accessible to the user. Consider the following markup:

```
div#sidebar {position: absolute; top: 0; left: 0; width: 15%; height: 7em;
    overflow: hidden;}
```

In such an instance, the clipped content would not be accessible to the user. This would lead to a situation like that illustrated in Figure 10-33.

Figure 10-33. Clipping content at the edges of the content area

Finally, there is overflow: auto. This allows user agents to determine which behavior to use, although they are encouraged to provide a scrolling mechanism when necessary. This is a potentially useful way to use overflow since user agents could interpret it as "provide scrollbars only when needed." (They may not, but they certainly could—and probably should.)

Content clipping

In situations where the content of an absolutely positioned element overflows its element box, and overflow has been set such that the content should be clipped, it is possible to alter the shape of the clipping region by using the property clip.

The default value, auto, means that the contents of the element should not be clipped. The other possibility is to define a clipping shape that is relative to the

clip

Values:	rect(*top*, *right*, *bottom*, *left*) | auto | inherit
Initial value:	auto
Applies to:	Absolutely positioned elements (in CSS2, clip applied to block-level and replaced elements)
Inherited:	No
Computed value:	For a rectangle, a set of four computed lengths representing the edges of the clipping rectangle; otherwise, as specified

element's content area. This does not alter the shape of the content area, but instead alters the area in which content may be rendered.

 While the only clipping shape available in CSS2 is a rectangle, the specification does offer the possibility of other shapes being included in future specifications.

This is accomplished with the shape value rect(*top*, *right*, *bottom*, *left*). You could specify no change in the clipping region like this:

```
clip: rect(0, auto, auto, 0);
```

The syntax of rect is an interesting case. Technically, it can be rect(*top*, *right*, *bottom*, *left*)—note the commas—but the CSS2 specification contains examples both with and without commas and defines rect as accepting both versions. Here, we'll stick to the comma version mostly because it makes things easier to read, and because it's preferred in CSS2.1.

It is extremely important to note that the values for rect(...) are *not* side-offsets. They are, instead, distances from the upper-left corner of the element (or the upper-right, in right-to-left languages). Thus, a clipping rectangle that encloses 20×20-pixel square in the upper-left corner of the element would be defined as:

```
rect(0, 20px, 20px, 0)
```

The only values permitted with rect(...) are length values and auto, which is the same as setting the clipping edge to the appropriate content edge. Thus, the following two statements mean the same thing:

```
clip: rect(auto, auto, 10px, 1em);
clip: rect(0, 0, 10px, 1em);
```

Because all of the offsets in clip are from the top-left corner, and percentages are not permitted, it is practically impossible to create a "centered" clipping area unless you know the dimensions of the element itself. Consider:

```
div#sidebar {position: absolute; top: 0; bottom: 50%; right: 50%; left: 0;
  clip: rect(1em,4em,6em,1em);}
```

Since there is no way to know how many ems tall or wide the element will be, there is no way to define a clipping rectangle—which ends one em to the right, or one em below, the content area of the element. The only way to know this is to set the height and width of the element itself:

```
div#sidebar {position: absolute; top: 0; left: 0; width: 5em; height: 7em;
    clip: rect(1em,4em,6em,1em);}
```

This would cause a result something like that shown in Figure 10-34, where a dashed line has been added to illustrate the edges of the clipping region. This line would not actually appear in a user agent attempting to render the document.

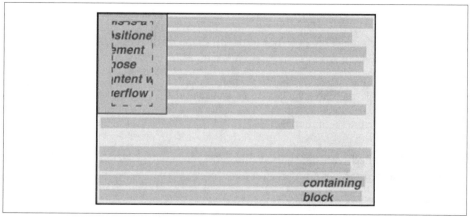

Figure 10-34. Setting the clipping region for overflowing content

It is possible to set negative lengths, though, which will expand the clipping area outside the element's box. If you want to push the clipping area up and left by a quarter-inch, use the following styles (illustrated in Figure 10-35):

```
clip: rect(-0.25in, auto, auto, -0.25in);
```

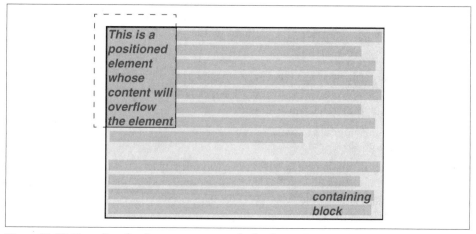

Figure 10-35. Extending the clipping region outside the element box

This doesn't do much good, as you can see. The clipping rectangle extends up and to the left, but since there isn't any content there, it doesn't make much difference.

On the other hand, it might be OK to go beyond the bottom and right edges, but not the top or left. Figure 10-36 shows the results of these styles (and remember, the dashed lines are only for illustrative purposes!):

```
div#sidebar {position: absolute; top: 0; left: 0; width: 5em; height: 7em;
    clip: rect(0,6em,9em,0);}
```

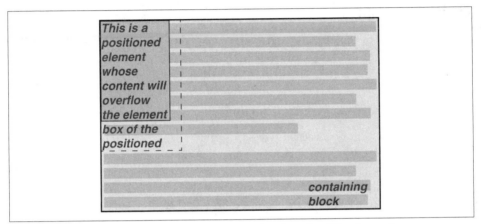

Figure 10-36. Extending the clipping region below and to the right of the element box

This extends the area in which content can be seen. However, it doesn't change the flow of the content, so the only visual effect is that more content is visible below the element. The text does not flow out to the right, because the width of its line boxes is still constrained by the width of the positioned element. If there had been an image wider than the positioned element, or preformatted text with a long line, this might have been visible to the right of the positioned element, up to the point where the clipping rectangle ends.

The syntax of rect(...) is, as you may have already realized, rather unusual when compared to the rest of CSS. It is based on an early draft of the positioning section, which used the top-left-offset scheme. Internet Explorer implemented this syntax before CSS2 was made a full Recommendation, so it conflicted with a last-minute change that made rect(...) use side-offsets, just like the rest of CSS2. This was done, reasonably enough, to make positioning consistent.

By then, however, it was too late: there was an implementation in the marketplace, and rather than force Microsoft to change the browser and thus potentially break existing pages, the standard was changed to reflect implementation. Unfortunately, as we saw before, this means that it is impossible to set a consistent clipping rectangle in situations where the height and width are not precisely defined.

Further compounding the problem is that rect(...) accepts only length units and auto. The addition of percentage units as valid rect(...) values would go a long way toward improving things, and hopefully a future version of CSS will add this capability.

 The long and convoluted history of clip means that, in current browsers, it acts in inconsistent ways and cannot be relied upon in any cross-browser environment.

Element Visibility

In addition to all of the clipping and overflowing, you can also control the visibility of an entire element.

visibility

Values:	visible	hidden	collapse	inherit
Initial value:	visible
Applies to:	All elements
Inherited:	Yes
Computed value:	As specified

This one is pretty easy. If an element is set to have visibility: visible, then it is, of course, visible.

If an element is set to visibility: hidden, it is made "invisible" (to use the wording in the specification). In its invisible state, the element still affects the document's layout as though it were visible. In other words, the element is still there, you just can't see it. Note the difference between this and display: none. In the latter case, the element is not displayed and is also removed from the document altogether so that it doesn't have any effect on document layout. Figure 10-37 shows a document in which a paragraph has been set to hidden, based on the following styles and markup:

```
em.trans {visibility: hidden; border: 3px solid gray; background: silver;
  margin: 2em; padding: 1em;}

<p>
This is a paragraph that should be visible. Lorem ipsum, dolor sit amet,
<em class="trans">consectetuer adipiscing elit, sed diam nonummy nibh </em>
euismod tincidunt ut laoreet dolore magna aliquam erat volutpat.
</p>
```

Everything visible about a hidden element—such as content, background, and borders—will be made invisible. Note that the space is still there because the element is still part of the document's layout. You just can't see it.

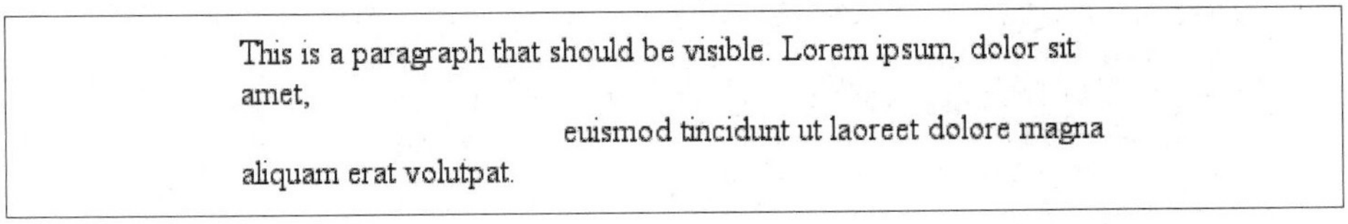

> This is a paragraph that should be visible. Lorem ipsum, dolor sit amet,
>
> euismod tincidunt ut laoreet dolore magna
>
> aliquam erat volutpat.

Figure 10-37. Making elements invisible without suppressing their element boxes

Note too that it's possible to set the descendant element of a hidden element to be visible. This would cause the element to appear wherever it normally would, despite the fact that the ancestor (and possibly its siblings) is invisible. To do so, you must explicitly declare the descendant element visible, since visibility is inherited:

```
p.clear {visibility: hidden;}
p.clear em {visibility: visible;}
```

As for visibility: collapse, this value is used in CSS table rendering, which is covered in the next chapter. According to the CSS2 specification, collapse has the same meaning as hidden if it is used on nontable elements.

Absolute Positioning

Since most of the examples and figures in the previous sections illustrate absolute positioning, you're already halfway to an understanding of how it works. Most of the remaining material covers the details of what happens when absolute positioning is invoked.

Containing blocks and absolutely positioned elements

When an element is positioned absolutely, it is completely removed from the document flow. It is then positioned with respect to its containing block, and its edges are placed using the offset properties (top, left, etc.). The positioned element does not flow around the content of other elements, or vice versa. This implies that an absolutely positioned element may overlap other elements or be overlapped by them. (You'll see how you can affect the overlapping order later in the chapter.)

The containing block for an absolutely positioned element is the nearest ancestor element that has a position value other than static. It is common for an author to pick an element that will serve as the containing block for the absolutely positioned element and give it a position of relative with no offsets:

```
p.contain {position: relative;}
```

Consider the example in Figure 10-38, which is an illustration of the following:

```
p {margin: 2em;}
p.contain {position: relative;}   /* establish a containing block*/
b {position: absolute; top: auto; right: 0; bottom: 0; left: auto;
   width: 8em; height: 5em; border: 1px solid gray;}

<body>
```

```
<p>
This paragraph does <em>not</em> establish a containing block for any of its
descendant elements that are absolutely positioned.  Therefore, the absolutely
positioned <b>boldface </b> element it contains will be positioned with
respect to the initial containing block.
</p>
<p class="contain">
Thanks to 'position: relative', this paragraph establishes a containing
block for any of its descendant elements that are absolutely positioned.
Since there is such an element-- <em>that is to say, <b>a boldfaced element
that is absolutely positioned,</b> placed with respect to its containing
block (the paragraph)</em>, it will appear within the element box generated
by the paragraph.
</p>
</body>
```

This paragraph does *not* establish a containing block for any of its descendant elements that are absolutely positioned. Therefore, the absolutely positioned element it contains will be positioned with respect to the initial containing block.

Thanks to 'position: relative', this paragraph establishes a containing block for any of its descendant elements that are absolutely positioned. Since there is such an element-- *that is to say, placed with respect to its containing block (the paragraph), it will appear within the element box generated by the paragraph.* *a boldfaced element that is absolutely positioned.*

boldface

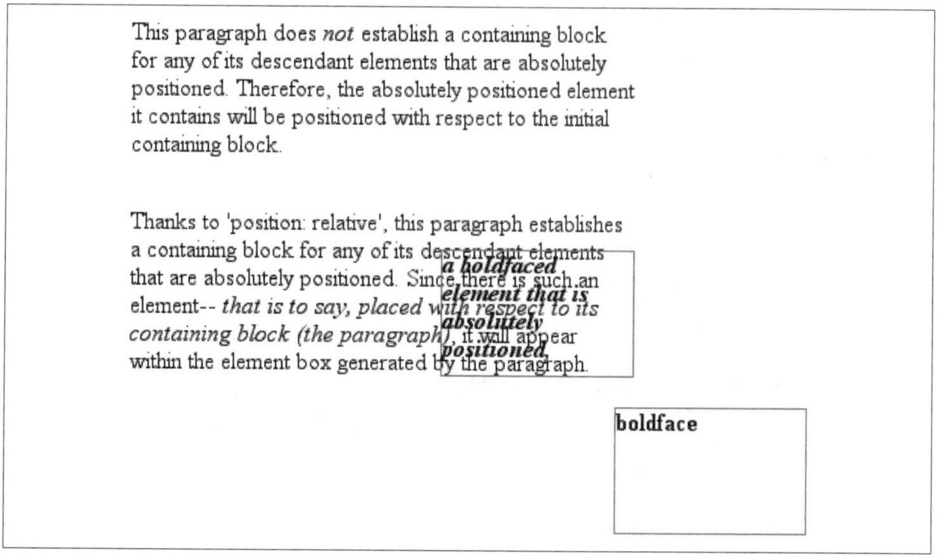

Figure 10-38. Using relative positioning to define containing blocks

The b elements in both paragraphs have been absolutely positioned. The difference is in the containing block used for each one. The b element in the first paragraph is positioned with respect to the initial containing block because all of its ancestor elements have a position of static. The second paragraph, though, has been set to position: relative, so it establishes a containing block for its descendants.

You've probably noted that in the second paragraph, the positioned element overlaps some of the text content of the paragraph. There is no way to avoid this, short of positioning the b element outside of the paragraph (by using a negative value for right or one of the other offset properties) or by specifying a padding for the paragraph that is wide enough to accommodate the positioned element. Also, since the b element has a transparent background, the paragraph's text shows through the positioned element. The only way to avoid this is to set a background for the positioned element, or move it out of the paragraph entirely.

You will sometimes want to ensure that the body element establishes a containing block for all its descendants, rather than allowing the user agent to pick an initial containing block. This is as simple as declaring:

```
body {position: relative;}
```

In such a document, you could drop in an absolutely positioned paragraph, as follows, and get a result like that shown in Figure 10-39:

```
<p style="position: absolute; top: 0; right: 25%; left: 25%; bottom: auto;
    width: 50%; height: auto; background: silver;">...</p>
```

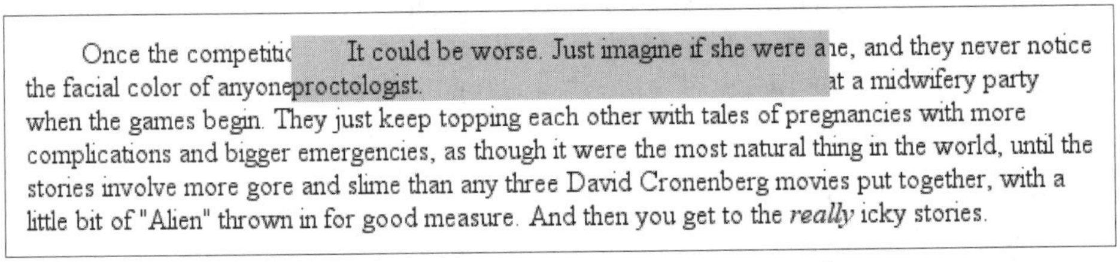

Once the competiti   It could be worse. Just imagine if she were a ne, and they never notice the facial color of anyoneproctologist.   at a midwifery party when the games begin. They just keep topping each other with tales of pregnancies with more complications and bigger emergencies, as though it were the most natural thing in the world, until the stories involve more gore and slime than any three David Cronenberg movies put together, with a little bit of "Alien" thrown in for good measure. And then you get to the *really* icky stories.

Figure 10-39. Positioning an element whose containing block is the root element

The paragraph is now positioned at the very beginning of the document, half as wide as the document's width and overwriting the first few elements.

An important point to highlight is that when an element is absolutely positioned, it also establishes a containing block for its descendant elements. For example, you could absolutely position an element and then absolutely position one of its children, as shown in Figure 10-40, which was generated using the following styles and basic markup:

```
div {position: relative; width: 100%; height: 10em;
    border: 1px solid; background: #EEE;}
div.a {position: absolute; top: 0; right: 0; width: 15em; height: 100%;
    margin-left: auto; background: #CCC;}
div.b {position: absolute; bottom: 0; left: 0; width: 10em; height: 50%;
    margin-top: auto; background: #AAA;}

<div>
  <div class="a">absolutely positioned element A
    <div class="b">absolutely positioned element B</div>
  </div>
  containing block
</div>
```

Remember that if the document is scrolled, the positioned elements will scroll right along with it. This is true of all absolutely positioned elements that are not descendants of fixed-position elements. It happens because, eventually, the elements are

Figure 10-40. Absolutely positioned elements establish containing blocks

positioned in relation to something that's part of the normal flow. For example, if you absolutely position a table whose containing block is the initial containing block, then the table will scroll because the initial containing block is part of the normal flow. Similarly, even if you set up absolutely positioned elements nested four levels deep, the "outermost" of these elements is still positioned with respect to the initial containing block. Thus, it will scroll along with the initial containing block, and all of its descendants will go along for the ride.

 If you want to position elements so that they're placed relative to the viewport and *don't* scroll along with the rest of the document, keep reading. The upcoming section on fixed positioning will tell you how.

Placement and sizing of absolutely positioned elements

It may seem odd to combine the concepts of placement and sizing, but it's necessary with absolutely positioned elements because the specification binds them very closely together. Upon closer inspection, this is not such a strange pairing. Consider what happens if an element is positioned using all four offset properties, like so:

```
#masthead h1 {position: absolute; top: 1em; left: 1em; right: 25%; bottom: 10px;
   margin: 0; padding: 0; background: silver;}
```

Here, the height and width of the h1's element box is determined by the placement of its outer margin edges, as shown in Figure 10-41.

Figure 10-41. Determining the height of an element based on the offset properties

If the containing block were made taller, then the h1 would also become taller; if the containing block is narrowed, then the h1 would become narrower. If you were to add margins or padding to the h1, it would have further effects on the calculated height and width of the h1.

But what if you do all of that and then also try to set an explicit height and width:

```
#masthead h1 {position: absolute; top: 0; left: 1em; right: 10%; bottom: 0;
   margin: 0; padding: 0; height: 1em; width: 50%; background: silver;}
```

Something has to give, because it's incredibly unlikely that all those values will be accurate. In fact, the containing block would have to be exactly two-and-a-half times as wide as the h1's computed value for font-size for all of the shown values to be accurate. Any other width would mean at least one value is wrong and must be ignored. Figuring out which one depends on a number of factors, and the factors change depending on whether an element is replaced or nonreplaced.

For that matter, consider the following:

```
#masthead h1 {position: absolute; top: auto; left: auto;}
```

What should the result be? As it happens, the answer is *not* "reset the values to zero." We'll see the actual answer in the next section.

Auto-edges

When an element is absolutely positioned, a special behavior applies when any of the offset properties other than bottom are set to auto. Let's take top as an example. Consider the following:

```
<p>
When we consider the effect of positioning, it quickly becomes clear that authors
can do a great deal of damage to layout, just as they can do very interesting
things.<span style="position: absolute; top: auto; left: 0;">[4]</span>
This is usually the case with useful technologies: the sword always has
at least two edges, both of them sharp.
</p>
```

What should happen? For left, it's easy: the left edge of the element should be placed against the left edge of its containing block (which you can assume to be the initial containing block). For top, however, something much more interesting happens. The top of the positioned element should line up with the place where its top would have been if it were not positioned at all. In other words, imagine where the span would have been placed if its position value were static; this is its *static position*—where its top edge should be calculated to sit. CSS2.1 elaborates:

> ...the term "static position" (of an element) refers, roughly, to the position an element would have had in the normal flow. More precisely, the static position for "top" is the distance from the top edge of the containing block to the top margin edge of a hypothetical box that would have been the first box of the element if its "position" property had been "static". The value is negative if the hypothetical box is above the containing block.

Therefore, you should get the result shown in Figure 10-42.

> [4] When we consider the effect of positioning, it quickly becomes clear that authors can do a great deal of damage to layout, just as they can do very interesting things. This is usually the case with useful technologies: the sword always has at least two edges, both of them sharp.

Figure 10-42. Absolutely positioning an element consistently with its "static" position

The "[4]" sits just outside the paragraph's content because the initial containing block's left edge is to the left of the paragraph's left edge.

The same basic rules hold true for `left` and `right` being set to auto. In those cases, the left (or right) edge of a positioned element lines up with the spot where the edge would have been placed if the element weren't positioned. Let's modify our previous example so that both `top` and `left` are set to auto:

```
<p>
When we consider the effect of positioning, it quickly becomes clear that authors
can do a great deal of damage to layout, just as they can do very interesting
things.<span style="position: absolute; top: auto; left: auto;">[4]</span>
This is usually the case with useful technologies: the sword always has
at least two edges, both of them sharp.
</p>
```

This would have the result shown in Figure 10-43.

> When we consider the effect of positioning, it quickly becomes clear that authors can do a great deal of damage to layout, just as they can do very interesting things.[4]This is usually the case with useful technologies: the sword always has at least two edges, both of them sharp.

Figure 10-43. Absolutely positioning an element consistently with its "static" position

The "[4]" now sits right where it would have, were it not positioned. Note that, since it is positioned, its normal-flow space is closed up. This causes the positioned element to overlap with the normal-flow content.

 It should be noted that CSS2 and CSS2.1 both state that in cases such as these, "…user agents are free to make a guess at its probable [static] position." Current browsers do a fairly decent job of treating auto values for `top` and `left` as intended and of placing the element consistent with the place it would have been in the normal flow.

This auto-placement works only in certain situations, generally wherever there are few constraints on the other dimensions of a positioned element. Our previous example could be auto-placed because it had no constraints on its height or width, nor any constraints on the placement of the bottom and right edges. But suppose, for some reason, there had been such constraints? Consider:

```
<p>
When we consider the effect of positioning, it quickly becomes clear that authors
can do a great deal of damage to layout, just as they can do very interesting
things.<span style="position: absolute; top: auto; left: auto; right: 0;
bottom: 0; height: 2em; width: 5em;">[4]</span>  This is usually the case with
useful technologies: the sword always has at least two edges, both of them sharp.
</p>
```

It is not possible to satisfy all of those values. Determining what happens is the subject of the next section.

Placing and sizing nonreplaced elements

In general, the size and placement of an element depends on its containing block. The values of its various properties (width, right, padding-left, and so on) affect the situation, but the foundation is the containing block.

Consider the width and horizontal placement of a positioned element. It can be represented as an equation stating that left + margin-left + border-left-width + padding-left + width + padding-right + border-right-width + margin-right + right = the width of the containing block.

This calculation is fairly reasonable. It's basically the equation that determines how block-level elements in the normal flow are sized, except it adds left and right to the mix. So how do all of these interact? There are a series of rules to work through.

First, if left, width, and right are all set to auto, you get the result shown in the previous section: the left edge is placed at its static position, assuming a left-to-right language. In right-to-left languages, the right edge is placed at its static position. The width of the element is set as "shrink to fit," which means the element's content area is made only as wide as necessary to contain the content. This is rather like the way table cells behave. The non-static-position property (right in left-to-right languages, left in right-to-left) is set to take up the remaining distance. For example:

```
<div style="position: relative; width: 25em; border: 1px dotted;">
An absolutely positioned element can have its content
<span style="position: absolute; top: 0; left: 0; right: auto; width: auto;
  background: silver;">shrink-wrapped</span>
thanks to the way positioning rules work.
</div>
```

This yields the result shown in Figure 10-44.

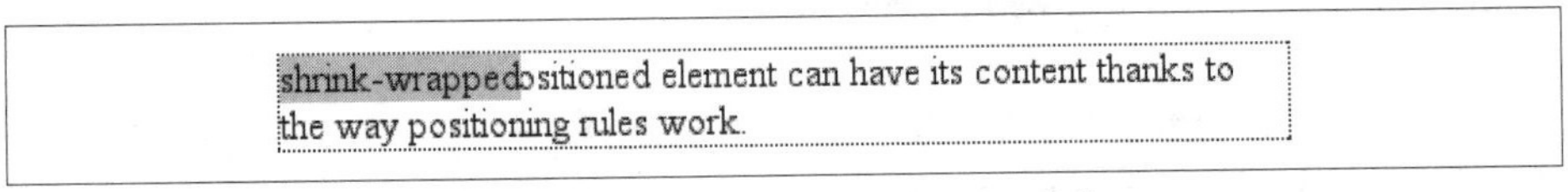

Figure 10-44. The "shrink-to-fit" behavior of absolutely positioned elements

The top of the element is placed against the top of its containing block (the div, in this case) and the width of the element is just as much as is needed to contain the content. The remaining distance from the right edge of the element to the right edge of the containing block becomes the computed value of right.

Now suppose that only the left and right margins are set to auto, not left, width, and right, as in this example:

```
<div style="position: relative; width: 25em; border: 1px dotted;">
An absolutely positioned element can have its content
<span style="position: absolute; top: 0; left: 1em; right: 1em; width: 10em;
  margin: 0 auto; background: silver;">shrink-wrapped</span>
thanks to the way positioning rules work.
</div>
```

What happens here is that the left and right margins, which are both auto, are set to be equal. This will effectively center the element, as shown in Figure 10-45.

An absolutely positi shrink-wrapped   :ontent thanks to the way positioning rules work.

Figure 10-45. Horizontally centering an absolutely positioned element with auto margins

This is basically the same as auto-margin centering in the normal flow. So let's make the margins something other than auto:

```
<div style="position: relative; width: 25em; border: 1px dotted;">
An absolutely positioned element can have its content
<span style="position: absolute; top: 0; left: 1em; right: 1em; width: 10em;
  margin-left: 1em; margin-right: 1em; background: silver;">shrink-wrapped</span>
thanks to the way positioning rules work.
</div>
```

Now you have a problem. The positioned span's properties add up to only 14em, whereas the containing block is 25em wide. That's an 11-em deficit you have to make up somewhere.

 As of this writing, no version of Internet Explorer, including IE7, supports the horizontal-centering behavior of auto top and bottom margins on absolutely positioned elements.

The rules state that, in this case, the user agent ignores the value for right (in left-to-right languages; otherwise, it ignores left) and solves for it. In other words, the result will be the same as if you'd declared:

```
<span style="position: absolute; top: 0; left: 1em; right: 12em; width: 10em;
  margin-left: 1em; margin-right: 1em; background: silver;">shrink-wrapped</span>
```

This has the result shown in Figure 10-46.

If one of the margins had been left as auto, that would have been changed instead. Suppose you change the styles to state:

```
<span style="position: absolute; top: 0; left: 1em; right: 1em; width: 10em;
    margin-left: 1em; margin-right: auto; background: silver;">shrink-wrapped</span>
```

The visual result would be the same as that in Figure 10-46, only it would be attained by computing the right margin to 12em instead of overriding the value assigned to the property right. If, on the other hand, you made the left margin auto, then *it* would be reset, as illustrated in Figure 10-47:

```
<span style="position: absolute; top: 0; left: 1em; right: 1em; width: 10em;
    margin-left: auto; margin-right: 1em; background: silver;">shrink-wrapped</span>
```

An absolutely positioned element cshrink-wrapped   to the way positioning rules work.

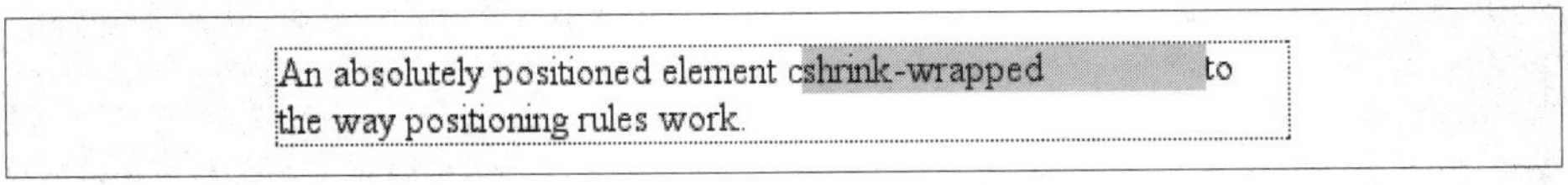

Figure 10-47. Ignoring the value for margin-right in an overconstrained situation

In general, if only one of the properties is set to auto, then it will be modified to satisfy the equation given earlier in the section. Given the following styles, the element's width would expand to whatever size is needed instead of "shrink-wrapping" the content:

```
<span style="position: absolute; top: 0; left: 1em; right: 1em; width: auto;
    margin-left: 1em; margin-right: 1em; background: silver;">shrink-wrapped</span>
```

So far, we've really only examined behavior along the horizontal axis, but very similar rules hold true along the vertical axis. If you take the previous discussion and rotate it 90 degrees, as it were, you get almost the same behavior. For example, the following markup results in Figure 10-48:

```
<div style="position: relative; width: 30em; height: 10em;
    border: 1px solid;">
<div style="position: absolute; left: 0; width: 30%; background: #CCC;
    top: 0;">
element A
</div>
<div style="position: absolute; left: 35%; width: 30%; background: #AAA;
    top: 0; height: 50%;">
element B
</div>
<div style="position: absolute; left: 70%; width: 30%; background: #CCC;
    height: 50%; bottom: 0;">
element C
</div>
</div>
```

In the first case, the height of the element was shrink-wrapped to the content. In the second, the unspecified property (bottom) was set to make up the distance between the bottom of the positioned element and the bottom of its containing block. In the third case, it was top that was unspecified and therefore made up the difference.

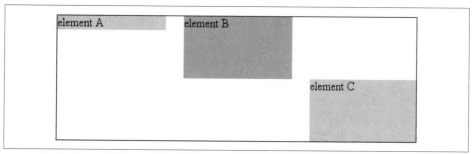

Figure 10-48. Vertical layout behavior for absolutely positioned elements

For that matter, auto-margins can lead to vertical centering. Given the following styles, the absolutely positioned div will be vertically centered within its containing block, as shown in Figure 10-49:

```
<div style="position: relative; width: 10em; height: 10em;
  border: 1px solid;">
<div style="position: absolute; left: 0; width: 100%; background: #CCC;
  top: 0; height: 5em; bottom: 0; margin: auto 0;">
element D
</div>
</div>
```

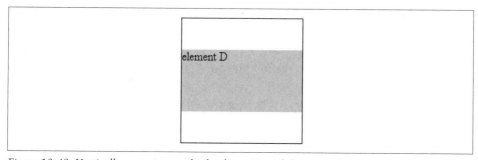

Figure 10-49. Vertically centering an absolutely positioned element with auto margins

There are two small variations to point out. In horizontal layout, either right or left can be placed according to the static position if their values are auto. In vertical layout, only top can take on the static position; bottom, for whatever reason, cannot.

 As of this writing, no version of Internet Explorer, including IE7, supports the vertical-centering behavior of auto top and bottom margins on absolutely positioned elements.

Also, if an absolutely positioned element's size is overconstrained in the vertical direction, bottom is ignored. Thus, in the following situation, the declared value of bottom would be overridden by the calculated value of 5em:

```
<div style="position: relative; width: 10em; height: 10em;
  border: 1px solid;">
<div style="position: absolute; left: 0; width: 100%; background: #CCC;
  top: 0; height: 5em; bottom: 0; margin: 0;">
element D
</div>
</div>
```

There is no provision for top to be ignored if the properties are overconstrained.

Placing and sizing replaced elements

Positioning rules are different for nonreplaced elements than they are for replaced elements. This is because replaced elements have an intrinsic height and width, and therefore are not altered unless explicitly changed by the author. Thus, there is no concept of "shrink to fit" in the positioning of replaced elements.

The behaviors involved in placing and sizing replaced elements are most easily expressed by a series of rules to be followed in order:

1. If width is set to auto, the used value of width is determined by the intrinsic width of the element's content. Thus, if the width of an image is 50 pixels, then the used value is calculated to be 50px. If width is explicitly declared (that is, something like 100px or 50%), then the width is set to that value.

2. If left has the value auto in a left-to-right language, replace auto with the static position. In right-to-left languages, replace an auto value for right with the static position.

3. If either left or right is still auto (in other words, it hasn't been replaced in a previous step), replace any auto on margin-left or margin-right with 0.

4. If, at this point, both margin-left and margin-right are still defined to be auto, set them to be equal, thus centering the element in its containing block.

5. After all that, if there is only one auto value left, change it to equal the remainder of the equation.

This leads to the same basic behaviors we saw with absolutely positioned nonreplaced elements, as long as you assume that there is an explicit width for the nonreplaced element. Therefore, the following two elements will have the same width and placement, assuming the image's intrinsic width is 100 pixels (see Figure 10-50):

```
<div style="width: 200px; height: 50px; border: 1px dotted gray;">
<img src="frown.gif" alt="a frowny face"
  style="position: absolute; top: 0; left: 50px; margin: 0;">
<div style="position: absolute; top: 0; left: 50px;
  width: 100px; height: 100px; margin: 0;">
  it's a div!
</div>
</div>
```

Figure 10-50. Absolutely positioning a replaced element

As with nonreplaced elements, if the values are overconstrained, the user agent is supposed to ignore the value for `right` in left-to-right languages and `left` in right-to-left languages. Thus, in the following example, the declared value for `right` is overridden with a computed value of 50px:

```
<div style="position: relative; width: 300px;">
 <img src="frown.gif" alt="a frowny face"
  style="position: absolute; top: 0; left: 50px; right: 125px; width: 200px;
    margin: 0;">
</div>
```

Similarly, layout along the vertical axis is governed by a series of rules that state:

1. If `height` is set to `auto`, the computed value of `height` is determined by the intrinsic height of the element's content. Thus, the height of an image 50 pixels tall is computed to be 50px. If `height` is explicitly declared (that is, something like 100px or 50%) then the height is set to that value.

2. If `top` has the value `auto`, replace it with the replaced element's static position.

3. If `bottom` has a value of `auto`, replace any `auto` value on `margin-top` or `margin-bottom` with 0.

4. If, at this point, both `margin-top` and `margin-bottom` are still defined to be `auto`, set them to be equal, thus centering the element in its containing block.

5. After all that, if there is only one `auto` value left, change it to equal the remainder of the equation.

As with nonreplaced elements, if the values are overconstrained, the user agent is supposed to ignore the value for `bottom`.

Thus, the following markup would have the results shown in Figure 10-51:

```
<div style="position: relative; height: 200px; width: 200px; border: 1px solid;">
 <img src="one.gif" alt="one" width="25" height="25"
   style="position: absolute;
   top: 0; left: 0; margin: 0;">
 <img src="two.gif" alt="two" width="25" height="25"
   style="position: absolute;
    top: 0; left: 60px; margin: 10px 0; bottom: 4377px;">
 <img src="three.gif" alt=" three" width="25" height="25"
   style="position: absolute;
   left: 0; width: 100px; margin: 10px; bottom: 0;">
```

```
<img src="four.gif" alt=" four" width="25" height="25"
  style="position: absolute;
    top: 0; height: 100px; right: 0; width: 50px;">
<img src="five.gif" alt="five" width="25" height="25"
  style="position: absolute;
    top: 0; left: 0; bottom: 0; right: 0; margin: auto;">
</div>
```

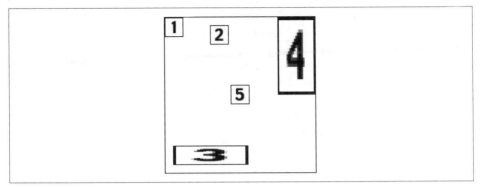

Figure 10-51. Stretching replaced elements through positioning

Placement on the z-axis

With all of the positioning going on, there will inevitably be a situation where two elements try to exist in the same place, visually speaking. Obviously, one of them will have to overlap the other—but how does one control which element comes out "on top"? This is where the property z-index comes in.

z-index	
Values:	<integer>	auto	inherit
Initial value:	auto
Applies to:	Positioned elements
Inherited:	No
Computed value:	As specified

z-index lets you alter the way in which elements overlap one another. It takes its name from the coordinate system in which left-to-right is the *x*-axis and top-to-bottom is the *y*-axis. In such a case, the third axis—that which runs from front to back, or if you prefer, away from the user—is termed the *z*-axis. Thus, elements are given values along this axis and represented using z-index. Figure 10-52 illustrates this system.

In this coordinate system, an element with a high z-index value is closer to the reader than those with lower z-index values. This will cause the high-value element

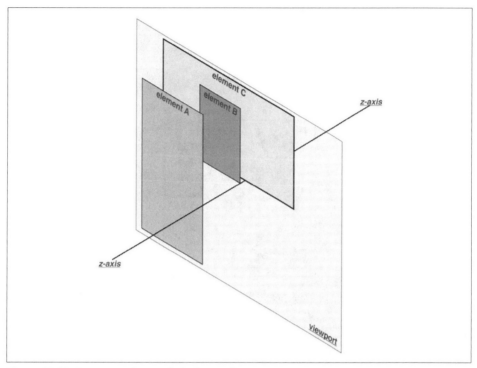

Figure 10-52. A conceptual view of z-index stacking

to overlap the others, as illustrated in Figure 10-53, which is a "head-on" view of Figure 10-52. This is referred to as *stacking*.

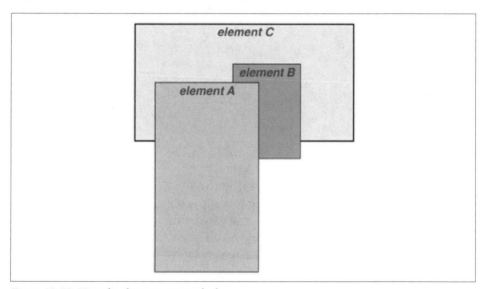

Figure 10-53. How the elements are stacked

Any integer can be used as a value for z-index, including negative numbers. Assigning an element a negative z-index will move it further away from the reader; that is, it will be moved lower in the stack. Consider the following styles, illustrated in Figure 10-54:

```
p#first {position: absolute; top: 0; left: 0;
    width: 20%; height: 10em; z-index: 8;}
p#second {position: absolute; top: 0; left: 10%;
    width: 30%; height: 5em; z-index: 4;}
p#third {position: absolute; top: 15%; left: 5%;
    width: 15%; height: 10em; z-index: 1;}
p#fourth {position: absolute; top: 10%; left: 15%;
    width: 40%; height: 10em; z-index: 0;}
```

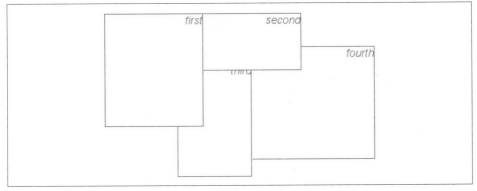

Figure 10-54. Stacked elements can overlap each other

Each of the elements is positioned according to its styles, but the usual order of stacking is altered by the z-index values. Assuming the paragraphs were in numeric order, a reasonable stacking order would have been, from lowest to highest, p#first, p#second, p#third, p#fourth. This would have put p#first behind the other three elements and p#fourth in front of the others. Now, thanks to z-index, the stacking order is under your control.

As the previous example demonstrates, there is no particular need for the z-index values to be contiguous. You can assign any integer of any size. If you want to be fairly certain that an element stayed in front of everything else, you might use a rule such as z-index: 100000. This would work as expected in most cases—although if you ever declared another element's z-index to be 100001 (or higher), it would appear in front.

Once you assign an element a value for z-index (other than auto), that element establishes its own local *stacking context*. This means that all of the element's descendants have their own stacking order, relative to the ancestor element. This is very similar to the way that elements establish new containing blocks. Given the following styles, you would see something like Figure 10-55:

```
p {border: 1px solid; background: #DDD; margin: 0;}
b {background: #808080;}
em {background: #BBB;}
#one {position: absolute; top: 0; left: 0; width: 50%; height: 10em;
  z-index: 10;}
#two {position: absolute; top: 5em; left: 25%; width: 50%; height: 10em;
  z-index: 7;}
#three {position: absolute; top: 11em; left: 0; width: 50%; height: 10em;
  z-index: 1;}
#one b {position: absolute; right: -5em; top: 4em; width: 20em;
  z-index: -404;}
#two b {position: absolute; right: -3em; top: auto;
  z-index: 36;}
#two em {position: absolute; bottom: -0.75em; left: 7em; right: -2em;
  z-index: -42;}
#three b {position: absolute; left: 3em; top: 3.5em; width: 25em;
  z-index: 23;}
```

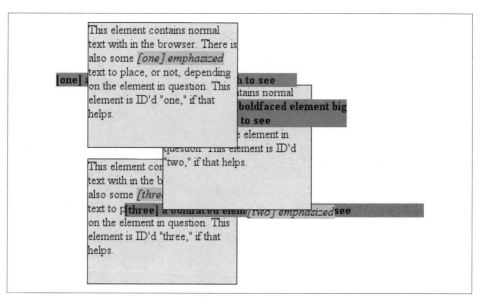

Figure 10-55. Positioned elements establish local stacking contexts

Note where the b and em elements fall in the stacking order. Each of them is correctly positioned with respect to its parent element, of course. However, pay close attention to the children of p#two. While the b element is in front of its parent, and the em is behind, both of them are in front of p#three! This is because the z-index values of 36 and -42 are relative to p#two but not to the document in general. In a sense, p#two and all of its children share a z-index of 7, while having their own mini-z-index within the context of p#two.

Put another way, it's as though the b element has a z-index of 7,36 while the em's value is 7,-42. These are merely implied conceptual values; they don't conform to anything in the specification. However, such a system helps to illustrate how the overall stacking order is determined. Consider:

```
p#one          10
p#one b        10,-404
p#two b        7,36
p#two          7
p#two em       7,-42
p#three b      1,23
p#three        1
```

This conceptual framework precisely describes the order in which these elements would be stacked. While the descendants of an element can be above or below that element in the stacking order, they are all grouped together with their ancestor.

It is also the case that an element that establishes a stacking context for its descendants is placed at the 0 position of that context's z-axis. Thus, you could extend the framework as follows:

```
p#one          10,0
p#one b        10,-404
p#two b        7,36
p#two          7,0
p#two em       7,-42
p#three b      1,23
p#three        1,0
```

There remains one more value to examine. The specification has this to say about the default value, auto:

> The stack level of the generated box in the current stacking context is the same as its parent's box. The box does not establish a new local stacking context. (CSS2.1: 9.9.1)

Thus, any element with z-index: auto can be treated as though it is set to z-index: 0. Now, however, you may wonder what happens to elements with a negative z-index value that are part of the initial containing block's stacking context. For example, ask yourself what should happen given the following:

```
<body>
 <p style="position: absolute; z-index: -1;">Where am I?</p>
</body>
```

Given the rules of stacking, the body element should be at the same stacking context as its parent's box, so that would be 0. It does not establish a new stacking context, so the absolutely positioned p element is placed in the same stacking context as the body element (that of the initial containing block). In other words, the paragraph is placed *behind* the body element. If the body has a nontransparent background, the paragraph will disappear.

That was a possible result in CSS2, at any rate. In CSS2.1, the stacking rules have been changed so that an element can never be stacked below the background of its stacking context. In other words, consider the case where the body element establishes a containing block for its descendants (if it were relatively positioned, for example). An absolutely positioned element that is descended from the body element can never be stacked below the body's background, although it can be stacked below the body's content.

As of this writing, Mozilla and related browsers completely hide the paragraph even if you set both the body and html elements to have transparent backgrounds. This happens in error. Other user agents, like Internet Explorer, place the paragraph above the body's background even if it has one. According to CSS2.1, that's the correct behavior. The upshot is that negative z-index values can lead to unpredictable results, so use them with caution.

Fixed Positioning

As implied in the previous section, fixed positioning is just like absolute positioning, except the containing block of a fixed element is the viewport. In this case, the element is totally removed from the document's flow and does not have a position relative to any part of the document.

Fixed positioning can be exploited in a number of interesting ways. First off, it's possible to create frame-style interfaces using fixed positioning. Consider Figure 10-56, which shows a very common layout scheme.

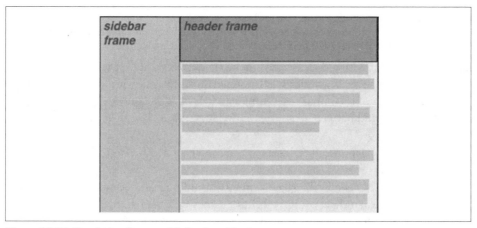

Figure 10-56. Emulating frames with fixed positioning

This could be done using the following styles:

```
div#header {position: fixed; top: 0; bottom: 80%; left: 20%; right: 0;
    background: gray;}
div#sidebar {position: fixed; top: 0; bottom: 0; left: 0; right: 80%;
    background: silver;}
```

This will fix the header and sidebar to the top and side of the viewport, where they will remain regardless of how the document is scrolled. The drawback here, though, is that the rest of the document will be overlapped by the fixed elements. Therefore, the rest of the content should probably be contained in its own div and employ the following:

```
div#main {position: absolute; top: 20%; bottom: 0; left: 20%; right: 0;
    overflow: scroll; background: white;}
```

It would even be possible to create small gaps between the three positioned divs by adding some appropriate margins, demonstrated in Figure 10-57:

```
body {background: black; color: silver;}   /* colors for safety's sake */
div#header {position: fixed; top: 0; bottom: 80%; left: 20%; right: 0;
    background: gray; margin-bottom: 2px; color: yellow;}
div#sidebar {position: fixed; top: 0; bottom: 0; left: 0; right: 80%;
    background: silver; margin-right: 2px; color: maroon;}
div#main {position: absolute; top: 20%; bottom: 0; left: 20%; right: 0;
    overflow: auto; background: white; color: black;}
```

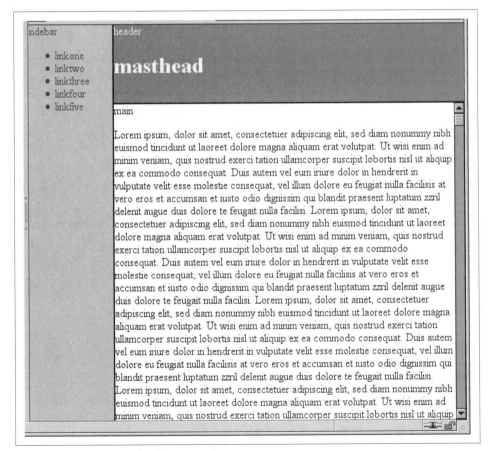

Figure 10-57. Separating the "frames" with margins

Given such a case, a tiled image could be applied to the body background. This image would show through the gaps created by the margins, which could certainly be widened if the author saw fit to do so.

Another use for fixed positioning is to place a "persistent" element on the screen, like a short list of links. You could create a persistent footer with copyright and other information as follows:

```
div#footer {position: fixed; bottom: 0; width: 100%; height: auto;}
```

This would place the footer at the bottom of the viewport and leave it there, no matter how much the document is scrolled.

One drawback of using fixed positioning is that Internet Explorer for Windows didn't support it prior to IE7. There are workarounds that use JavaScript to introduce some support in older versions of IE/Win, but they are not always acceptable to authors because the display is much less smooth than full fixed-position support should be. Another possibility is to absolutely position the element in IE/Win but use fixed positioning in more advanced browsers, although this will not work for all layouts.

 You can also read about emulating fixed positioning in older versions of IE/Win at *http://css-discuss.incutio.com/?page=EmulatingFixedPositioning*.

Relative Positioning

The simplest of the positioning schemes to understand is relative positioning. In this scheme, a positioned element is shifted by use of the offset properties. However, this can have some interesting consequences.

On the surface, it seems simple enough. Suppose you want to shift an image up and to the left. Figure 10-58 shows you the result of these styles:

```
img {position: relative; top: -20px; left: -20px;}
```

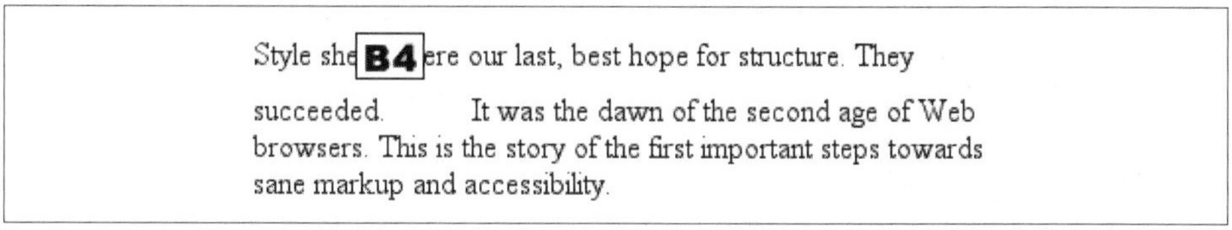

Style she **B4** ere our last, best hope for structure. They
succeeded.   It was the dawn of the second age of Web
browsers. This is the story of the first important steps towards
sane markup and accessibility.

Figure 10-58. A relatively positioned element

---

* Yes, the spelling of "positioning" is incorrect, but that's the way the language crumbles. The page is still a good source of information.

All you've done here is offset the image's top edge 20 pixels upward and offset the left edge 20 pixels to the left. However, notice the blank space where the image would have been, had it not been positioned. This happened because when an element is relatively positioned, it's shifted from its normal place, but the space it would have occupied doesn't disappear. Consider the results of the following styles, which are depicted in Figure 10-59:

```
em {position: relative; top: 8em; color: gray;}
```

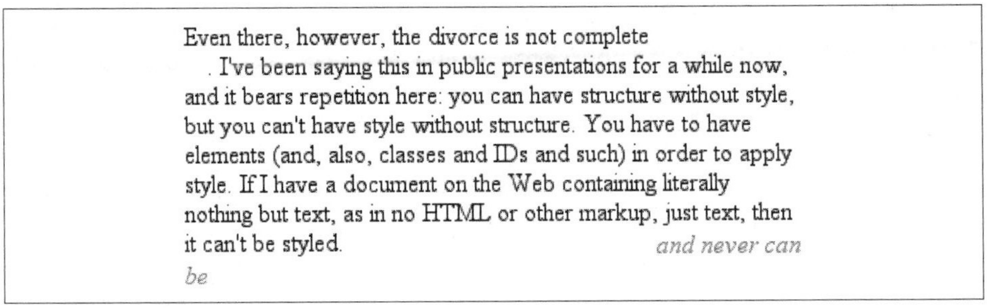

Even there, however, the divorce is not complete
. I've been saying this in public presentations for a while now, and it bears repetition here: you can have structure without style, but you can't have style without structure. You have to have elements (and, also, classes and IDs and such) in order to apply style. If I have a document on the Web containing literally nothing but text, as in no HTML or other markup, just text, then it can't be styled.   *and never can*
be

Figure 10-59. A relatively positioned element

As you can see, the paragraph has some blank space in it. This is where the em element would have been, and the layout of the em element in its new position exactly mirrors the space it left behind.

Of course, it's also possible to shift a relatively positioned element to overlap other content. For example, the following styles and markup are illustrated in Figure 10-60:

```
img.slide {position: relative; left: 30px;}

<p>
In this paragraph, we will find that there is an image that has been pushed to
the right.  It will therefore <img src="star.gif" alt="A star!" class="slide">
overlap content nearby, assuming that it is not the last element in its line box.
</p>
```

In this paragraph, we will find that there is an image that has been

pushed to the right. It will therefore   c🟡lap content nearby, assuming that it is not the last element in its line box.

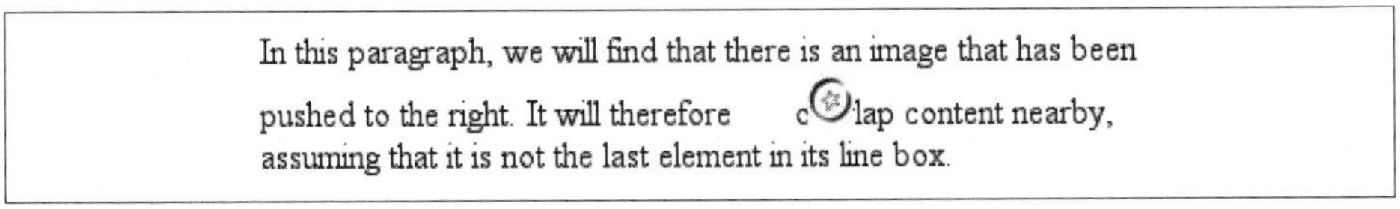

Figure 10-60. Relatively positioned elements can overlap other content

As we saw in previous sections, when you relatively position an element, it immediately establishes a new containing block for any of its children. This containing block corresponds to the place where the element has been positioned.

There is one interesting wrinkle to relative positioning. What happens when a relatively positioned element is overconstrained? For example:

```
strong {position: relative; top: 10px; bottom: 20px;}
```

Here you have values that call for two very different behaviors. If you consider only top: 10px, then the element should be shifted downward 10 pixels, but bottom: 20px clearly calls for the element to be shifted upward 20 pixels.

The original CSS2 specification does not say what should happen in this case. CSS2.1 states that when it comes to overconstrained relative positioning, one value is reset to be the negative of the other. Thus, bottom would always equal -top. This means that the previous example would be treated as though it had been:

```
strong {position: relative; top: 10px; bottom: -10px;}
```

Thus, the strong element will be shifted downward 10 pixels. The specification also makes allowances for writing directions. In relative positioning, right always equals -left in left-to-right languages, but in right-to-left languages, this is reversed: left would always equal -right.

Summary

Floating and positioning are very compelling features of CSS. They're also likely to be an exercise in frustration if you're careless in how you use them. Element overlapping, stacking order, size, and placement all have to be considered carefully when elements are positioned, and floated elements' relation to the normal flow must also be taken into account. Creating layouts using floating and positioning can thus take some adjustment, but the rewards are well worth the price.

While it's true that a great deal of layout can thus be freed of tables, there are still reasons to use tables on the Web, such as presenting stock quotes or sports scores, among others. In the next chapter, we'll examine how CSS has grown to address the question of table layout.

CHAPTER 11

Table Layout

You may have glanced at the title of this chapter and wondered, "Table layout? Isn't that exactly what we're trying to avoid doing?" Indeed so, but this chapter is not about using tables *for* layout. Instead, it's about the ways that tables themselves are laid out within CSS, which is a far more complicated affair than it might first appear. That's why the subject warrants its own chapter.

Tables are unique, compared to the rest of document layout. As of CSS2.1, tables alone possess the ability to associate element sizes with other elements—all the cells in a row have the same height, for example, no matter how much or how little content each individual cell might contain. The same is true for the widths of cells that share a column. There is no other situation in layout where elements from different parts of the document tree influence one another's sizing and layout in such a direct way.

As we'll see, this uniqueness comes at the expense of a great many behaviors and rules that apply to tables, and only tables. In the course of the chapter, we'll look at how tables are visually assembled, two different ways to draw cell borders, and the mechanisms that drive the height and width of tables and their internal elements.

Table Formatting

Before you can start to worry about how cell borders are drawn and tables sized, we need to delve into the fundamental ways in which tables are assembled, and the ways that elements within the table are related to one another. This is referred to as table formatting, and it is quite distinct from table layout: the latter is possible only after the former has been completed.

Visually Arranging a Table

The first thing to understand is how CSS defines the arranging of tables. While this knowledge may seem a bit basic, it's key to understanding how best to style tables.

CSS draws a distinction between table elements and internal table elements. In CSS, internal table elements generate rectangular boxes that have content, padding, and borders, but do not have margins. Therefore, it is *not* possible to define the separation between cells by giving them margins. A CSS-conformant browser will ignore any attempts to apply margins to cells, rows, or any other internal table element (with the exception of captions, which are discussed later in this chapter).

There are six rules for arranging tables. The basis of these rules is a "grid cell," which is one area between the grid lines on which a table is drawn. Consider Figure 11-1, in which two tables are shown along with their grid cells, which are indicated by the dashed lines drawn over the tables.

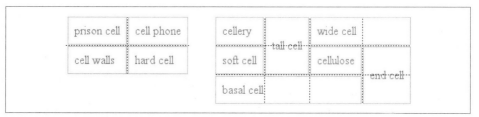

Figure 11-1. Grid cells form the basis of table layout

In a simple two-by-two table, such as the lefthand table shown in Figure 11-1, the grid cells correspond to the cells. In a more complicated table, like the righthand one in Figure 11-1, the edges of the grid cells correspond to the cell borders of all the cells in the table, and cut through those cells that span rows or columns.

These grid cells are largely theoretical constructs, and they cannot be styled or even accessed through the document object model. They simply serve as a way to describe how tables are assembled for styling.

Table arrangement rules

- Each row box encompasses a single row of grid cells. All of the row boxes in a table fill the table from top to bottom in the order they occur in the source document (with the exception of any table header or table footer row boxes, which come at the beginning and end of the table, respectively). Thus, the table contains as many grid rows as there are row elements.

- A row group's box encompasses the same grid cells as the row boxes it contains.

- A column box encompasses one or more columns of grid cells. All of the column boxes are placed next to one another in the order they occur. The first column box is on the left for left-to-right languages, and on the right for right-to-left languages.

- A column group's box encompasses the same grid cells as the column boxes that it contains.

- Although cells may span several rows or columns, CSS does not define how this happens. Instead, the document language defines spanning. Each spanned cell is a rectangular box one or more grid cells wide and high. The top row of this rectangle is in the row that is parent to the cell. The cell's rectangle must be as far to the left as possible in left-to-right languages, but it may not overlap any other cell box. It must also be to the right of all cells in the same row that are earlier in the source document in a left-to-right language. In right-to-left languages, a spanned cell must be as far to the right as possible without overlapping other cells, and must be to the left of all cells in the same row that follow it in the document source.

- A cell's box cannot extend beyond the last row box of a table or row group. If the table structure would create this condition, the cell must be shortened until it fits within the table or row group that encloses it.

> The CSS specification discourages, but does not prohibit, the positioning of table cells and other internal table elements. Positioning a row that contains row-spanning cells, for example, could dramatically alter the layout of the table by removing the row from the table entirely, and thus removing the spanned cells from consideration in the layout of other rows.

By definition, grid cells are rectangular, but they do not all have to be the same size. All the grid cells in a given grid column will be the same width, and all the grid cells in a grid row will be the same height, but the height of one grid row may be different from that of another grid row. Similarly, grid columns may be of different widths.

With those basic rules in mind, you may ask the question: how, exactly, do you know which elements are cells and which are not? We'll find out in the next section.

Table Display Values

In HTML, it's easy to know which elements are parts of tables because the handling of elements like tr and td is built into browsers. In XML, on the other hand, there is no way to intrinsically know which elements might be part of a table. This is where a whole collection of values for display comes into play.

In this chapter, we'll stick to the table-related values, as the others (block, inline, inline-block, run-in, and list-item) are discussed in other chapters. The table-related values can be summarized as follows:

table
> This value specifies that an element defines a block-level table. Thus, it defines a rectangular block that generates a block box. The corresponding HTML element is, not surprisingly, table.

inline-table
> This value specifies that an element defines an inline-level table. This means the element defines a rectangular block that generates an inline box. The closest non-table analog is the value inline-block. The closest HTML element is table, although, by default, HTML tables are not inline.

display

Values: none | inline | block | inline-block | list-item | run-in | table | inline-table | table-row-group | table-header-group | table-footer-group | table-row | table-column-group | table-column | table-cell | table-caption | inherit

Initial value: inline

Applies to: All elements

Inherited: No

Computed value: Varies for floated, positioned, and root elements (see CSS2.1, section 9.7); otherwise, as specified

Note: The values compact and marker appeared in CSS2 but were dropped from CSS2.1 due to a lack of widespread support

table-row

> This value specifies that an element is a row of cells. The corresponding HTML element is the tr element.

table-row-group

> This value specifies that an element groups one or more rows. The corresponding HTML value is tbody.

table-header-group

> This value is very much like table-row-group, except that for visual formatting, the header row group is always displayed before all other rows and row groups and after any top captions. In print, if a table requires multiple pages to print, a user agent may repeat header rows at the top of each page. The specification does not define what happens if you assign table-header-group to multiple elements. A header group can contain multiple rows. The HTML equivalent is thead.

table-footer-group

> This value is very much like table-header-group, except that the footer row group is always displayed after all other rows and row groups and before any bottom captions. In print, if a table requires multiple pages to print, a user agent may repeat footer rows at the bottom of each page. The specification does not define what happens if you assign table-footer-group to multiple elements. This is equivalent to the HTML element tfoot.

table-column

> This value declares that an element describes a column of cells. In CSS terms, elements with this display value are not visually rendered, as if they had the

value none. They exist primarily to help define the presentation of cells within the column. The HTML equivalent is the col element.

table-column-group

This value declares that an element groups one or more columns. Like table-column elements, table-column-group elements are not rendered, but the value is useful for defining presentation for elements within the column group. The HTML equivalent is the colgroup element.

table-cell

This value specifies that an element represents a single cell in a table. The HTML elements th and td are both examples of table-cell elements.

table-caption

This value defines a table's caption. CSS does not define what should happen if multiple elements have the value caption, but it does explicitly warn, "...authors should not put more than one element with 'display: caption' inside a table or inline-table element."

You can get a quick summary of the general effects of these values by taking an excerpt from the example HTML 4.0 style sheet given in Appendix C:

```
table        {display: table;}
tr           {display: table-row;}
thead        {display: table-header-group;}
tbody        {display: table-row-group;}
tfoot        {display: table-footer-group;}
col          {display: table-column;}
colgroup     {display: table-column-group;}
td, th       {display: table-cell;}
caption      {display: table-caption;}
```

In XML, where elements will not have display semantics by default, these values become quite useful. Consider the following markup:

```
<scores>
  <headers>
    <label>Team</label>
    <label>Score</label>
  </headers>
  <game sport="MLB" league="NL">
    <team>
      <name>Reds</name>
      <score>8</score>
    </team>
    <team>
      <name>Cubs</name>
      <score>5</score>
    </team>
  </game>
</scores>
```

This could be formatted in a tabular fashion using the following styles:

```
scores {display: table;}
headers {display: table-header-group;}
game {display: table-row-group;}
team {display: table-row;}
label, name, score {display: table-cell;}
```

The various cells could then be styled as necessary—e.g., boldfacing the label elements and right-aligning the scores.

 While it's theoretically possible to assign table-related display values to any HTML element, Internet Explorer up through IE7 does not support this capability.

Row primacy

CSS defines its table model as "row primacy." In other words, the model assumes that authors will create markup languages where rows are explicitly declared. Columns, on the other hand, are derived from the layout of the rows of cells. Thus, the first column is comprised of all the first cells in each row, the second column of the second cells, and so forth.

Row primacy is not a major issue in HTML, where the markup language is already row-oriented. In XML, it has more of an impact because it constrains the way in which authors can define table markup. Because of the row-oriented nature of the CSS table model, a markup language in which columns are the basis of table layout is not really possible (assuming that the intent is to use CSS to present such documents).

The row primacy of the CSS model will also be evident throughout the rest of the chapter as we explore the details of table presentation.

Columns

Although the CSS table model is row-oriented, columns do still play a part in layout. A cell can belong to both contexts (row and column), even if they are descended from row elements in the document source. In CSS, however, columns and column groups can accept only four styles: border, background, width, and visibility.

In addition, each of these four properties has special rules that apply only in the columnar context:

border

> Borders can be set for columns and column groups only if the property border-collapse has the value collapse. In such circumstances, column and column-group borders participate in the collapsing algorithm that sets the border styles at each cell edge. (See "Collapsing Cell Borders" later in this chapter.)

background

The background of a column or column group will be visible only in cells where both the cell and its row have transparent backgrounds. (See "Table Layers" later in this chapter.)

width

The width property defines the *minimum* width of the column or column group. The content of cells within the column (or group) may force the column to become wider.

visibility

If the value of visibility for a column or column group is collapse, then none of the cells in the column (or group) are rendered. Cells that span from the collapsed column into other columns are clipped, as are cells that span from other columns into the hidden column. Furthermore, the overall width of the table is reduced by the width that the column would have taken up. A declaration of any value for visibility other than collapse for a column or column group is ignored.

Anonymous Table Objects

It's possible that a markup language might not contain enough elements to fully represent tables as they are defined in CSS, or that an author will forget to include all the necessary elements. For example, consider this HTML:

```
<table>
  <td>Name:</td>
  <td><input type="text"></td>
</table>
```

You might glance at this markup and assume that it defines a two-cell table of a single row, but structurally, there is no element defining a row (because the tr is missing).

To cover such possibilities, CSS defines a mechanism for inserting "missing" table components as anonymous objects. To illustrate how this works, let's revisit our missing-row XHTML example. In CSS terms, what effectively happens is that an anonymous table-row object is inserted between the table element and its descendant table cells:

```
<table>
 [anonymous table-row object begins]
  <td>Name:</td>
  <td><input type="text"></td>
 [anonymous table-row object ends]
</table>
```

A visual representation of this process is given in Figure 11-2.

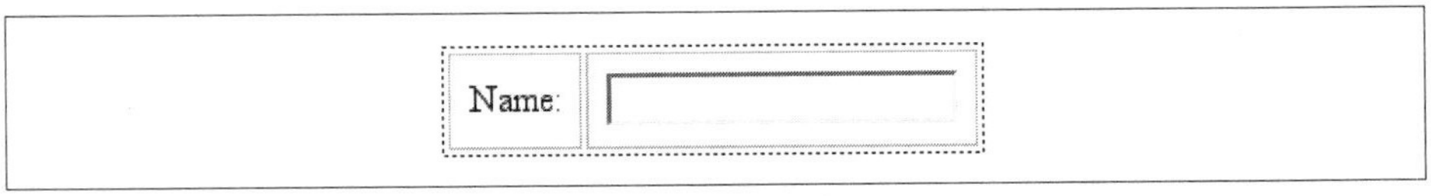

Figure 11-2. Anonymous object generation in table formatting

Seven different kinds of anonymous-object insertions can occur in the CSS table model. Like inheritance and specificity, these seven rules are, an example of a mechanism that attempts to impose intuitive sense on the way CSS behaves.

Object insertion rules

1. If a table-cell element's parent is not a table-row element, then an anonymous table-row object is inserted between the table-cell element and its parent. The inserted object will include all consecutive siblings of the table-cell element. Consider the following styles and markup:

   ```
   system {display: table;}
   name, moons {display: table-cell;}

   <system>
     <name>Mercury</name>
     <moons>0</moons>
   </system>
   ```

   The anonymous table-row object is inserted between the cell elements and the system element, and it encloses both the name and moons elements.

   The same rule holds true even if the parent element is a table-row-group. To extend the example, assume that the following applies:

   ```
   system {display: table;}
   planet {display: table-row-group;}
   name, moons {display: table-cell;}

   <system>
    <planet>
     <name>Mercury</name>
     <moons>0</moons>
    </planet>
    <planet>
     <name>Venus</name>
     <moons>0</moons>
    </planet>
   </system>
   ```

   In this example, both sets of cells will be enclosed in an anonymous table-row object that is inserted between them and the planet elements.

2. If a table-row element's parent is not a table, inline-table, or table-row-group element, then an anonymous table element is inserted between the table-row element and its parent. The inserted object will include all consecutive siblings of the table-row element. Consider the following styles and markup:

   ```
   docbody {display: block;}
   planet {display: table-row;}

   <docbody>
   ```

```
<planet>
 <name>Mercury</name>
 <moons>0</moons>
</planet>
 <planet>
 <name>Venus</name>
 <moons>0</moons>
 </planet>

</docbody>
```

Because the display value of the planet elements' parent is block, the anonymous table object is inserted between the planet elements and the docbody element. This object will enclose both planet elements because they are consecutive siblings.

3. If a table-column element's parent is not a table, inline-table, or table-column-group element, then an anonymous table element is inserted between the table-column element and its parent. This is much the same as the table-row rule just discussed, except for its column-oriented nature.

4. If the parent element of a table-row-group, table-header-group, table-footer-group, table-column-group, or table-caption element is not a table element, then an anonymous table object is inserted between the element and its parent.

5. If a child element of a table or inline-table element is not a table-row-group, table-header-group, table-footer-group, table-row, or table-caption element, then an anonymous table-row object is inserted between the table element and its child element. This anonymous object spans all of the consecutive siblings of the child element that are not table-row-group, table-header-group, table-footer-group, table-row, or table-caption elements. Consider the following markup and styles:

```
system {display: table;}
planet {display: table-row;}
name, moons {display: table-cell;}

<system>
 <planet>
 <name>Mercury</name>
 <moons>0</moons>
 </planet>
 <name>Venus</name>
 <moons>0</moons>
</system>
```

Here, a single anonymous table-row object will be inserted between the system element and the second set of name and moons elements. The planet element is not enclosed by the anonymous object because its display is table-row.

6. If a child element of a table-row-group, table-header-group, or table-footer-group element is not a table-row element, then an anonymous table-row object

is inserted between the element and its child element. This anonymous object spans all consecutive siblings of the child element that are not table-row objects themselves. Consider the following markup and styles:

```
system {display: table;}
planet {display: table-row-group;}
name, moons {display: table-cell;}

<system>
 <planet>
  <name>Mercury</name>
  <moons>0</moons>
 </planet>
  <name>Venus</name>
  <moons>0</moons>
</system>
```

In this case, each set of name and moons elements will be enclosed in an anonymous table-row element. For the second set, the insertion takes place in accord with Rule 5. For the first set, the anonymous object is inserted between the planet element and its children because the planet element is a table-row-group element.

7. If a child element of a table-row element is not a table-cell element, then an anonymous table-cell object is inserted between the element and its child element. This anonymous object encloses all consecutive siblings of the child element that are not table-cell elements themselves. Consider the following markup and styles:

```
system {display: table;}
planet {display: table-row;}
name, moons {display: table-cell;}

<system>
 <planet>
  <name>Mercury</name>
  <num>0</num>
 </planet>
</system>
```

Because the element num does not have a table-related display value, an anonymous table-cell object is inserted between the planet element and the num element.

This behavior also extends to the encapsulation of anonymous inline boxes. Suppose that the num element was not included:

```
<system>
 <planet>
  <name>Mercury</name>
  0
 </planet>
</system>
```

The 0 would still be enclosed in an anonymous `table-cell` object. To further illustrate this point, here is an example adapted from the CSS specification:

```
example {display: table-cell;}
row {display: table-row;}
hi {font-weight: 900;}

<example>
  <row>This is the <hi>top</hi> row.</row>
  <row>This is the <hi>bottom</hi> row.</row>
</example>
```

Within each `row` element, the text fragments and `hi` element are enclosed in an anonymous `table-cell` object.

Table Layers

To assemble a table's presentation, CSS defines six individual "layers" on which the various aspects of a table are placed. Figure 11-3 shows these layers.

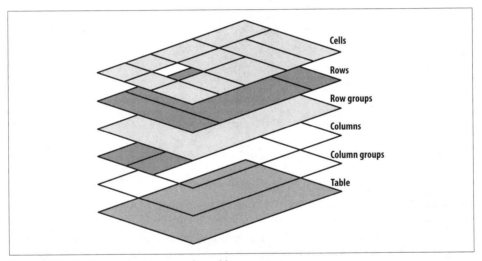

Figure 11-3. The formatting layers used in table presentation

Basically, the styles for each aspect of the table are drawn on their individual layers. Thus, if the `table` element has a green background and a one-pixel black border, then those styles are drawn on the lowest layer. Any styles for the column groups are drawn on the next layer up, the columns themselves on the layer above that, and so on. The top layer, which corresponds to the table cells, is drawn last.

For the most part, this is simply a logical process; after all, if you declare a background color for table cells, you would want that drawn over the background for the `table` element. The most important point revealed by Figure 11-3 is that column styles come below row styles, so a row's background will overwrite a column's background.

It is important to remember that, by default, all elements have transparent backgrounds. Thus, in the following markup, the `table` element's background will be visible "through" cells, rows, columns, and so forth that do not have a background of their own, as illustrated in Figure 11-4:

```
<table style="background: #888;">
 <tr>
  <td>hey</td>
  <td style="background: #CCC;">there</td>
 </tr>
<tr>
  <td>what's</td>
  <td>up?</td>
 </tr>
<tr style="background: #AAA;">
  <td>tiger</td>
  <td style="background: #CCC;">lilly</td>
 </tr>
</table>
```

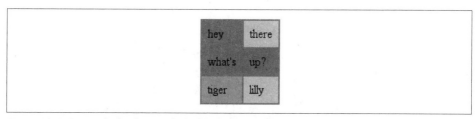

Figure 11-4. Seeing the background of table-formatting layers through other layers

Captions

A table caption is about what you'd expect: a short bit of text that describes the nature of the table's contents. A chart of stock quotes for the fourth quarter of 2003, therefore, might have a caption element whose contents read "Q4 2003 Stock Performance." With the property `caption-side`, you can place this element either above or below the table, regardless of where the caption appears in the table's structure. (In HTML, the `caption` element can appear only after the opening `table` element, but other languages may have different rules.)

Captions are a bit odd, at least in visual terms. The CSS specification states that a caption is formatted as if it were a block box placed immediately before (or after) the table's box, with a couple of exceptions. The first is that the caption can still inherit values from the table, and the second is that a user agent ignores a caption's box when considering what to do with a run-in element that precedes the table. Therefore, a run-in element that comes before a table will not run into a top caption or into the table, but will instead be treated as if its `display` value were `block`.

A simple example should suffice to demonstrate most of the important aspects of caption presentation. Consider the following, illustrated in Figure 11-5:

```
caption {background: gray; margin: 1em 0;
   caption-side: top;}
table {color: white; background: black; margin: 0.5em 0;}
```

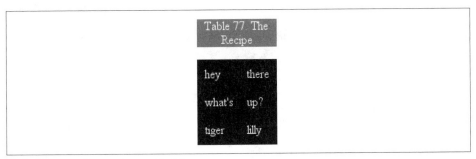

Figure 11-5. Styling captions and tables

The text in the caption element inherits the color value white from the table, while the caption gets its own background. The separation between the table's outer border edge and the caption's outer margin edge is one em because the top margin of the table and bottom margin of the caption have collapsed, as described in Chapter 7. Finally, the width of the caption is based on the content width of the table element, which is considered to be the containing block of the caption. These same results would occur if you changed the value of `caption-side` to `bottom`, except that the caption would be placed after the table's box, and collapsing would occur between the top margin of the caption and the bottom margin of the table.

For the most part, captions are styled just like any block-level element; they can have padding, borders, backgrounds, and so on. For example, if you need to change the horizontal alignment of text within the caption, you use the property `text-align`. Thus, to right-align the caption in the previous example, you would write:

```
caption {background: gray; margin: 1em 0;
   caption-side: top; text-align: right;}
```

As of mid-2006, the styling of captions is still a risky thing. Some browsers honor top and bottom margins on captions, while others do not; some browsers calculate the caption's width in relation to the table's width, while others choose a different path. Listing all the behaviors would be fruitless, since this is an area where rapid change is expected. This note is intended primarily to give readers a heads-up that they may encounter problems.

Table Cell Borders

There are actually two quite distinct border models in CSS. The separated border model takes effect when cells are separated from each other in layout terms. The other option is the collapsed border model, in which there is no visual separation between cells, and cell borders merge, or collapse, with each other. The former is the default model, although in an earlier version of CSS the latter was the default.

An author can choose between the two models with the property `border-collapse`.

---

border-collapse

Values:	`collapse` | `separate` | `inherit`
Initial value:	`separate`
Applies to:	Elements with the `display` value `table` or `inline-table`
Inherited:	Yes
Computed value:	As specified
Note:	In CSS2, the default was `collapse`

The whole point of this property is to offer the author a way to determine which border model the user agent will employ. If the value `collapse` is in effect, then the collapsing borders model is used. If the value is `separate`, then the separated borders model is used. We'll look at the latter model first, since it's actually much simpler to describe.

Separated Cell Borders

In this model, every cell in the table is separated from the other cells by some distance, and the borders of cells do not collapse into each other. Thus, given the following styles and markup, you would see the result shown in Figure 11-6:

```
table {border-collapse: separate;}
td {border: 3px double black; padding: 3px;}

<table cellspacing="0">
```

```
  <tr>
    <td>cell one</td>
    <td>cell two</td>
  </tr>
  <tr>
    <td>cell three</td>
    <td>cell four</td>
  </tr>
</table>
```

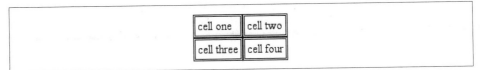

Figure 11-6. Separated (and thus separate) cell borders

Note that the cell borders touch but remain distinct from one another. The three lines between cells are actually the two double borders sitting right next to each other.

The HTML attribute `cellspacing` was included in the previous example to make sure the cells had no separation between them, but its presence is likely a bit troubling. After all, if you can define separate borders, then there ought to be a way to use CSS to alter the spacing between cells. Fortunately, there is.

Border spacing

There may be situations where you want the table cell borders to be separated by some distance. This is easily accomplished with the property `border-spacing`, which provides a more powerful replacement for the HTML attribute `cellspacing`.

---

border-spacing

Values:	\<length\> \<length\>? | inherit
Initial value:	0
Applies to:	Elements with the display value table or inline-table
Inherited:	Yes
Computed value:	Two absolute lengths
Note:	Property is ignored unless border-collapse value is separate

---

Either one or two lengths can be given for the value of this property. If you want all your cells separated by a single pixel, then `border-spacing: 1px;` would suffice. If, on the other hand, you want cells to be separated by one pixel horizontally and five pixels vertically, you'd write `border-spacing: 1px 5px;`. If two lengths are supplied, the first is always the horizontal separation, and the second is always the vertical.

The spacing values are also applied between the borders of cells along the outside of a table and the padding on the table element itself. Given the following styles, you would get the result shown in Figure 11-7:

```
table {border-collapse: separate; border-spacing: 3px 5px;
  padding: 10px; border: 2px solid black;}
td { border: 1px solid gray;}
td#squeeze {border-width: 5px;}
```

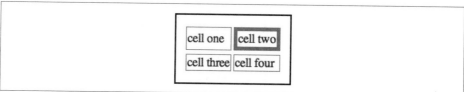

Figure 11-7. Border spacing effects between cells and their enclosing table

In Figure 11-7, there are 3 pixels of space between the borders of any two horizontally adjacent cells, and there are 13 pixels of space between the borders of the right- and left-most cells and the right and left borders of the table element. Similarly, the borders of vertically adjacent cells are 5 pixels apart, and the borders of the cells in the top and bottom rows are 15 pixels from the top and bottom borders of the table, respectively. The separation between cell borders is constant throughout the table, regardless of the border widths of the cells themselves.

Note also that if you're going to declare a border-spacing value, it's executed on the table itself, not on the individual cells. If border-spacing had been declared for the td elements in the previous example, it would have been ignored.

In the separated border model, borders cannot be set for rows, row groups, columns, and column groups. Any border properties declared for such elements must be ignored by a CSS-conformant user agent.

Handling empty cells

Because every cell is, in a visual sense, distinct from all the other cells in the table, what do you do with cells that are empty (i.e., have no content)? You have two choices, which are reflected in the values of the empty-cells property.

If empty-cells is set to show, the borders and background of an empty cell will be drawn, just as with table cells that have content. If the value is hide, then no part of the cell is drawn, just as if the cell were set to visibility: hidden.

If a cell contains any content, it cannot be considered empty. "Content," in this case, includes not only text, images, form elements, and so on, but also the nonbreaking space entity ( ) and any other whitespace *except* the CR (carriage-return), LF (linefeed), tab, and space characters. If all the cells in a row are empty, and all have an empty-cells value of hide, then the entire row is treated as if the row element were set to display: none.

As of this writing, empty-cells is not fully supported by Internet Explorer.

Collapsing Cell Borders

While the collapsing cell model largely describes how HTML tables have always been laid out when they don't have any cell spacing, it is quite a bit more complicated than the separated borders model. There are also some rules that set collapsing cell borders apart from the separated borders model. These are:

- Elements with a display of table or inline-table cannot have any padding, although they can have margins. Thus, there is never any separation between the border around the outside of the table and the edges of its outermost cells.

- Borders can be applied to cells, rows, row groups, columns, and column groups. The table element itself can, as always, have a border.

- There is never any separation between cell borders. In fact, borders collapse into each other where they adjoin, so that only one of the collapsing borders is actually drawn. This is somewhat akin to margin collapsing, where the largest margin wins. When cell borders collapse, the "most interesting" border wins.

- Once they are collapsed, the borders between cells are centered on the hypothetical grid lines between the cells.

We'll explore the last two points in more detail in the next two sections.

Collapsing border layout

To better understand how the collapsing-borders model works, let's look at the layout of a single table row, as shown in Figure 11-8.

For each cell, the padding and content width of the cell is inside the borders, as expected. For the borders between cells, half of the border is to one side of the grid line between two cells, and the other half is to the other side. In each case, only a

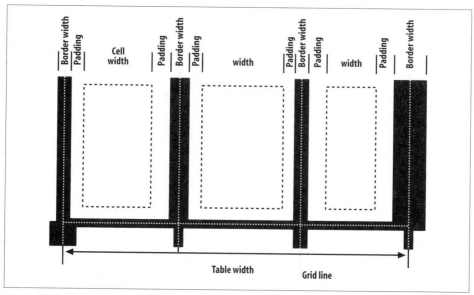

Figure 11-8. The layout of a table row using the collapsing-borders model

single border is drawn along each cell edge. You might think that half of each cell's border is drawn to each side of the grid line, but that's not what happens.

For example, assume that the solid borders on the middle cell are green and the solid borders on the outer two cells are red. The borders on the right and left sides of the middle cell (which collapse with the adjacent borders of the outer cells) will be all green, or all red, depending on which border wins out. We'll discuss how to tell which one wins in the next section.

You may have noticed that the outer borders protrude beyond the table's width. This is because, in this model, *half* the table's borders are included in the width. The other half extends beyond that distance, sitting in the margin itself. This might seem a bit weird, but that's how the model is defined to work.

The specification includes a layout formula that I'll reproduce here for the benefit of those who enjoy such things:

```
row width = (0.5 * border-width₀) + padding-left₁ + width₁ + padding-right₁ +
    border-width1 + padding-left₂ +...+ padding-rightₙ + (0.5 * border-widthₙ)
```

Each $border\text{-}width_i$ refers to the border between cell *i* and the next cell; thus, border-width3 refers to the border between the third and fourth cells. The value n stands for the total number of cells in the row. There is a slight exception to this mechanism. When beginning the layout of a collapsed-border table, the user agent computes an initial left and right border for the table itself. It does this by examining the left border of the first cell in the first row of the table and by taking half of that border's width as the table's initial left border width. The user agent then examines the right border of the last cell in the first row and uses half that width to set the table's initial right border width. For any row after the first, if the left or right border is wider than the initial border widths, it extends into the margin area of the table.

In cases where a border is an odd number of display elements (pixels, printer dots, etc.) wide, the user agent must decide what to do about centering the border on the grid line. It might shift the border so that it is slightly off-center, round up or down to an even number of display elements, or do anything else that seems reasonable.

Border collapsing

When two or more borders are adjacent, they collapse into each other. In fact, they don't collapse so much as fight it out to see which of them will gain supremacy over the others. There are some strict rules governing which borders will win and which will not:

- If one of the collapsing borders has a border-style of hidden, it takes precedence over all other collapsing borders. All borders at this location are hidden.

- If one of the collapsing borders has a border-style of none, it takes the lowest priority. There will be no border drawn at this location unless all of the colliding borders have a value of none. Note that none is the default value for border-style.

- If at least one of the collapsing borders has a value other than none and none of the collapsing borders has a value of hidden, then narrow borders lose out to wider ones. If more than one of the collapsing borders have the same width, then the border style is taken in the following order, from most to least preferred: double, solid, dashed, dotted, ridge, outset, groove, inset. Thus, if two borders with the same width are collapsing, and one is dashed while the other is outset, the border at that location will be dashed.

- If collapsing borders have the same style and width, but differ in color, then the color used is taken from an element in the following list, from most to least preferred: cell, row, row group, column, column group, table. Thus, if the borders of a cell and a column (identical in every way except color) collapse, then the cell's border color (and style and width) will be used. If the collapsing borders come from the same type of element, such as two row borders with the same style and width but different colors, then the color is taken from borders that are the topmost and leftmost (in left-to-right languages; otherwise, topmost and rightmost).

The following styles and markup, presented in Figure 11-9, help illustrate each of the four rules:

```
table {border-collapse: collapse;
    border: 3px outset gray;}
td {border: 1px solid gray; padding: 0.5em;}
```

```
#r2c1, #r2c2 {border-style: hidden;}
#r1c1, #r1c4 {border-width: 5px;}
#r2c4 {border-style: double; border-width: 3px;}
#r3c4 {border-style: dotted; border-width: 2px;}
#r4c1 {border-bottom-style: hidden;}
#r4c3 {border-top: 13px solid silver;}

<table>
<tr>
<td id="r1c1">1-1</td><td id="r1c2">1-2</td>
<td id="r1c3">1-3</td><td id="r1c4">1-4</td>
</tr>
<tr>
<td id="r2c1">2-1</td><td id="r2c2">2-2</td>
<td id="r2c3">2-3</td><td id="r2c4">2-4</td>
</tr>
<tr>
<td id="r3c1">3-1</td><td id="r3c2">3-2</td>
<td id="r3c3">3-3</td><td id="r3c4">3-4</td>
</tr>
<tr>
<td id="r4c1">4-1</td><td id="r4c2">4-2</td>
<td id="r4c3">4-3</td><td id="r4c4">4-4</td>
</tr>
</table>
```

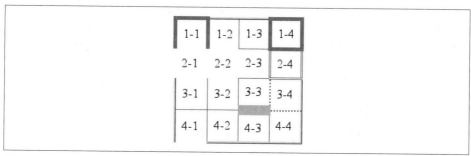

Figure 11-9. Manipulating border widths, styles, and colors leads to some unusual results

Let's consider what happened for each of the cells, in turn:

- For cells 1-1 and 1-4, the five-pixel borders were wider than any of their adjacent borders, so they won out not only over adjoining cell borders, but over the border of the table itself. The only exception is the bottom of cell 1-1, which was suppressed.

- The bottom border on cell 1-1 was suppressed because cells 2-1 and 2-2, with their explicitly hidden borders, completely removed any borders from the edge of the cells. Again, the table's border lost out (on the left edge of cell 2-1) to a cell's border. The bottom border of cell 4-1 was also hidden, so it prevented any border from appearing below the cell.

- The three-pixel double border of cell 2-4 was overridden on top by the five-pixel solid border of cell 1-4. Cell 2-4's border, in turn, overrode the border between itself and cell 2-3 because it was both wider and "more interesting." Cell 2-4 also overrode the border between itself and cell 3-4, even though both are the same width, because 2-4's double style is defined to be "more interesting" than 3-4's dotted border.

- The 13-pixel bottom silver border of cell 3-3 not only overrode the top border of cell 4-3, but it also affected the layout of content within both cells *and* the rows that contain both cells.

- For cells along the outer edge of the table that weren't specially styled, their one-pixel solid borders were overridden by the three-pixel outset border on the `table` element itself.

This is, in fact, about as complicated as it sounds, although the behaviors are largely intuitive and make a little more sense with practice. It's worth noting, though, that the basic Netscape 1-era HTML table presentation can be captured with a fairly simple set of rules, described here and illustrated by Figure 11-10:

```
table {border-collapse: collapse; border: 2px outset gray;}
td {border: 1px inset gray;}
```

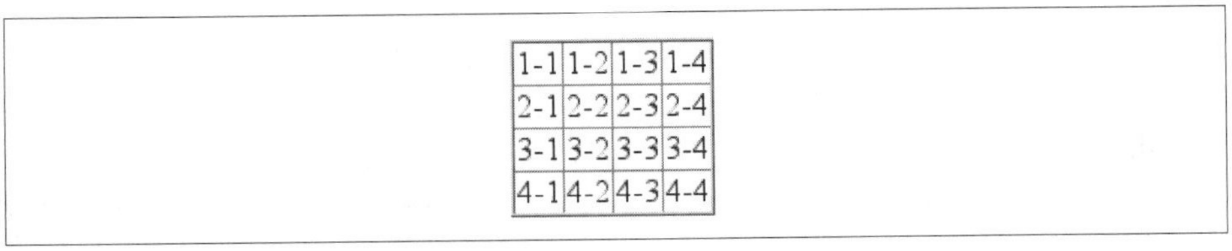

Figure 11-10. Reproducing old-school table presentation

Table Sizing

Now that we've delved into table formatting and cell border appearance, we have the pieces we need to understand the sizing of tables and their internal elements. When it comes to determining table width, there are two different approaches: fixed-width layout and automatic-width layout. Heights are calculated automatically no matter what width algorithms are used.

Width

Since there are two different ways to figure out the width of a table, it's only logical that there be a way to declare which should be used for a given table. Authors can use the property `table-layout` to select between the two kinds of table width calculation.

table-layout

Values:	auto | fixed | inherit
Initial value:	auto
Applies to:	Elements with the display value table or inline-table
Inherited:	Yes
Computed value:	As specified

While the two models can have different results in laying out a specific table, the more fundamental difference between the two is speed. With a fixed-width table layout, the user agent can calculate the layout of the table more quickly than is possible in the automatic-width model.

Fixed layout

The main reason the fixed-layout model is so fast is that its layout does not depend on the contents of table cells. Instead, it's driven by the width values of the table, columns, and cells within that table.

The fixed-layout model works in the following simple steps:

1. Any column element whose width property has a value other than auto sets the width for that column.

2. If a column has an auto width, but the cell in the first row of the table within that column has a width other than auto, then the cell sets the width for that column. If the cell spans multiple columns, the width is divided between the columns.

3. Any columns that are still auto-sized are sized so that their widths are as equal as possible.

At that point, the width of the table is set to either the value of width for the table or the sum of the column widths, whichever is *greater*. If the table turns out to be wider than its columns, then the difference is divided by the number of columns and added to each of them.

This approach is fast because all of the column widths are defined by the first row of the table. The cells in any rows that come after the first are sized according to the column widths that were defined by the first row. The cells in those following rows do not change column widths, which means that any width value assigned to those cells will be ignored. In cases where a cell's content does not fit, the cell's overflow value determines whether the cell contents are clipped, visible, or generate a scrollbar.

Let's consider the following styles and markup, which are illustrated in Figure 11-11:

```
table {table-layout: fixed; width: 400px;
  border-collapse: collapse;}
td {border: 1px solid;}
col#c1 {width: 200px;}
#r1c2 {width: 75px;}
#r2c3 {width: 500px;}

<table>
<colgroup>
<col id="c1"><col id="c2"><col id="c3"><col id="c4">
</colgroup>
<tr>
<td id="r1c1">1-1</td><td id="r1c2">1-2</td>
<td id="r1c3">1-3</td><td id="r1c4">1-4</td>
</tr>
<tr>
<td id="r2c1">2-1</td><td id="r2c2">2-2</td>
<td id="r2c3">2-3</td><td id="r2c4">2-4</td>
</tr>
<tr>
<td id="r3c1">3-1</td><td id="r3c2">3-2</td>
<td id="r3c3">3-3</td><td id="r3c4">3-4</td>
</tr>
<tr>
<td id="r4c1">4-1</td><td id="r4c2">4-2</td>
<td id="r4c3">4-3</td><td id="r4c4">4-4</td>
</tr>
</table>
```

1-1	1-2	1-3	1-4
2-1	2-2	2-3	2-4
3-1	3-2	3-3	3-4
4-1	4-2	4-3	4-4

Figure 11-11. Fixed-width table layout

As you can see in Figure 11-11, the first column is 200 pixels wide, which happens to be half the 400-pixel width of the table. The second column is 75 pixels wide because the first-row cell within that column has been assigned an explicit width. The third and fourth columns are each 61 pixels wide. Why? Because the sum of the column widths for the first and second columns (275px), plus the various borders between columns (3px), equals 278 pixels. 400 minus 278 is 122, and 122 divided in half is 61, so that's how many pixels wide the third and fourth columns will be. What about the 500-pixel width for #r2c3? It's ignored because that cell isn't in the first row of the table.

Note that it is not absolutely necessary for the table to have an explicit width to make use of the fixed-width layout model, although it definitely helps. For example, given the following, a user agent could calculate a width for the table that is 50 pixels narrower than the parent element's width. It would then use that calculated width in the fixed-layout algorithm:

```
table {table-layout: fixed; margin: 0 25px;
    width: auto;}
```

This is not required, however. User agents are also permitted to lay out any table with an auto value for width using the automatic-width layout model.

Automatic layout

The automatic-layout model, while not as fast as fixed layout, is probably much more familiar to you because it's essentially the same model that HTML tables have used for years. In most current user agents, this model's use will be triggered by a table having a width of auto, regardless of the value of table-layout, although this is not assured.

The reason automatic layout is slower is that the table cannot be laid out until the user agent has looked at all of its content. That is, automatic layout requires that the user agent lay out the entire table each time it gets a new cell. This generally requires the user agent to perform some calculations and then go back through the table to perform a second set of calculations. The cells' content has to be fully examined because, as with HTML tables, the table's layout is dependent on it. If there is a 400 pixel-wide image in a cell in the last row, it will force all of the cells above it (those in the same column) to be 400 pixels wide. Thus, the width of every cell has to be calculated, and adjustments must be made (possibly triggering another round of content-width calculations) before the table can be laid out.

The details of the model can be expressed in the following steps:

1. For each cell in a column, calculate both the minimum and maximum cell width.

   a. Determine the minimum width required to display the content. Keep in mind that the content can flow to any number of lines, but it may not stick out of the cell's box. If the cell has a width value that is larger than the minimum possible width, then the minimum cell width is set to the value of width. If the cell's width value is auto, then the minimum cell width is set to the minimum content width.

   b. For the maximum width, determine the width required to display the content without any line breaking other than that forced explicitly (e.g., the <br> element). That value is the maximum cell width.

2. For each column, calculate both the minimum and maximum column width.

   a. The column's minimum width is determined by the largest minimum cell width of the cells within the column. If the column has been given an explicit width value that is larger than any of the minimum cell widths within the column, then the minimum column width is set to the value of width.

b. For the maximum width, take the largest maximum cell width of the cells within the column. If the column has been given an explicit `width` value that is larger than any of the maximum cell widths within the column, then the maximum column width is set to the value of `width`. These two behaviors recreate the traditional HTML table behavior of forcibly expanding any column to be as wide as its widest cell.

3. In cases where a cell spans more than one column, the sum of the minimum column widths must be equal to the minimum cell width for the spanning cell. Similarly, the sum of the maximum column widths must equal the spanning cell's maximum width. User agents should divide any changes in column widths equally among the spanned columns.

In addition, the user agent must take into account that when a column width has a percentage value for its `width`, the percentage is calculated in relation to the width of the table—even though it doesn't yet know what that will be! Instead, it must store the percentage value and use it in the next part of the algorithm.

At this point, the user agent will have determined how wide or narrow each column can be. With that information in hand, it can then proceed to actually figuring out the width of the table. This happens as follows:

1. If the computed width of the table is not `auto`, the computed table width is compared to the sum of all the column widths *plus* any borders and cell spacing. (Columns with percentage widths are likely calculated at this time.) The larger of the two is the final width of the table. If the table's computed width is larger than the sum of the column widths, borders, and cell spacing, then all columns are increased in width by an equal amount until they fit into the table.

2. If the computed width of the table is `auto`, the final width of the table is determined by adding the column widths, borders, and cell spacing. This means that the table will be only as wide as needed to display its content, just as with traditional HTML tables. Any columns with percentage widths use that percentage as a constraint—but one that a user agent does not have to satisfy.

Once the last step is completed, then—and only then—can the user agent actually lay out the table.

The following styles and markup, presented in Figure 11-12, help illustrate how this process works:

```
table {table-layout: auto; width: auto;
  border-collapse: collapse;}
td {border: 1px solid;}
col#c3 {width: 25%;}
#r1c2 {width: 40%;}
#r2c2 {width: 50px;}
#r2c3 {width: 35px;}
#r4c1 {width: 100px;}
#r4c4 {width: 1px;}
```

```
<table>
<colgroup>
<col id="c1"><col id="c2"><col id="c3"><col id="c4">
</colgroup>
<tr>
<td id="r1c1">1-1</td><td id="r1c2">1-2</td>
<td id="r1c3">1-3</td><td id="r1c4">1-4</td>
</tr>
<tr>
<td id="r2c1">2-1</td><td id="r2c2">2-2</td>
<td id="r2c3">2-3</td><td id="r2c4">2-4</td>
</tr>
<tr>
<td id="r3c1">3-1</td><td id="r3c2">3-2</td>
<td id="r3c3">3-3</td><td id="r3c4">3-4</td>
</tr>
<tr>
<td id="r4c1">4-1</td><td id="r4c2">4-2</td>
<td id="r4c3">4-3</td><td id="r4c4">4-4</td>
</tr>
</table>
```

1-1	1-2	1-3	1-4
2-1	2-2	2-3	2-4
3-1	3-2	3-3	3-4
4-1	4-2	4-3	4-4

Figure 11-12. Automatic table layout

Let's consider what happened for each of the columns, in turn:

- For the first column, the only explicit cell or column width is that of cell 4-1, which was given a width of 100px. Because the content is so short, the minimum and maximum column width becomes 100px. (If there were a cell in the column with several sentences of text, it would have increased the maximum column width to whatever width was necessary to display all of the text without line breaking.)

- For the second column, two widths were declared: cell 1-2 was given a width of 40%, and cell 2-2 was given a width of 50px. The minimum width of this column is 50px, and the maximum width is 40 percent of the final table width.

- For the third column, only cell 3-3 had an explicit width (35px), but the column itself was given a width of 25%. Therefore, the minimum column width is 35px, and the maximum width is 25 percent of the final table width.

- For the fourth column, only cell 4-4 was given an explicit width (1px). This is smaller than the minimum content width, so both the minimum and maximum column widths are equal to the minimum content width of the cells. This turns out to be a computed 25 pixels.

The user agent now knows that the four columns have minimum and maximum widths as follows:

1. min 100px / max 100px
2. min 50px / max 40%
3. min 35px / max 25%
4. min 25px / max 25px

Thus, the table's minimum width is the sum of all the column minima plus the borders, which totals 215 pixels. The table's maximum width is 130px + 65 percent, which works out to 371.42857143 pixels (given that 130px represents 35 percent of the overall table width). Let's assume this is, after rounding the fractional number to 371 pixels, the width value user agents will actually use. Thus, the second column will be 148 pixels wide, and the third column will be 93 pixels wide. User agents are not required to actually use the maximum value; they may choose another course of action.

Of course, this was (although it may not seem like it) a very simple and straightforward example: all of the content was basically the same width, and most of the declared widths were pixel lengths. In a situation where a table contains spacer GIFs, paragraphs of text, form elements, and so forth, the process of figuring out the table's layout will likely be a great deal lengthier.

Height

After all of the effort expended in determining the width of the table, you might well wonder how much more complicated height calculation will be. Actually, in CSS terms, it's pretty simple, although browser developers probably don't think so.

The easiest situation to describe is one in which the height is explicitly set via the `height` property. In such cases, the height of the table is defined by the value of `height`. This means that a table may be taller or shorter than the sum of its row heights, although the 11 April 2006 draft of the CSS 2.1 specification states that `height` is treated as a minimum height for table boxes. In such cases, the CSS2.1 specification explicitly refuses to define what should happen, instead noting that the issue may be resolved in future versions of CSS. A user agent could expand or shrink a table's rows to match its height, or leave blank space inside the table's box, or something completely different. It's up to each user agent to decide.

If the height of the table is `auto`, its height is the sum of the heights of all the rows within the table, plus any borders and cell spacing. To determine the height of each row, the user agent goes through a process similar to that used to find the widths of columns. It calculates a minimum and maximum height for the contents of each cell and then uses these to derive a minimum and maximum height for the row. After doing this for all the rows, the user agent figures out what each row's height should be, stacks them all, and uses that calculation to determine the table's height. It's a lot like inline layout, only with less certainty in how things should be done.

In addition to what to do about tables with explicit heights and how to treat row heights within them, you can add the following to the list of things CSS2.1 does not define:

- The effect of a percentage height for table cells
- The effect of a percentage height for table rows and row groups
- How a row-spanning cell affects the heights of the rows that are spanned, except that the rows must contain the spanning cell

As you can see, height calculations in tables are largely left to user agents to determine. Historical evidence suggests that each user agent will likely do something different, so you should probably avoid setting heights as much as possible.

Alignment

In a rather interesting turn of events, alignment of content within cells is much better defined than cell and row heights. This is true even for vertical alignment, which could quite easily affect the height of a row.

Horizontal alignment is the simplest. To align content within a cell, you use the text-align property. In effect, the cell is treated as a block-level box and all of the content within it is aligned as per the text-align value. (For details on text-align, see Chapter 6.)

To vertically align content in a table cell, vertical-align is the relevant property. It uses many of the same values that are used for vertically aligning inline content, but the meanings of those values change when applied to a table cell. To summarize the three simplest cases:

top

    The top of the cell's content is aligned with the top of its row; in the case of row-spanning cells, the top of the cell's content is aligned with the top of the first row it spans.

bottom

    The bottom of the cell's content is aligned with the bottom of its row; in the case of row-spanning cells, the bottom of the cell's content is aligned with the bottom of the last row it spans.

middle

    The middle of the cell's content is aligned with the middle of its row; in the case of row-spanning cells, the middle of the cell's content is aligned with the middle of all the rows it spans.

These are illustrated in Figure 11-13, which uses the following styles and markup:

```
table {table-layout: auto; width: 20em;
  border-collapse: separate; border-spacing: 3px;}
td {border: 1px solid; background: silver;
  padding: 0;}
div {border: 1px dashed gray; background: white;}
#r1c1 {vertical-align: top; height: 10em;}
#r1c2 {vertical-align: middle;}
#r1c3 {vertical-align: bottom;}

<table>
<tr>
<td id="r1c1">
<div>
The contents of this cell are top-aligned.
</div>
</td>
<td id="r1c2">
<div>
The contents of this cell are middle-aligned.
</div>
</td>
<td id="r1c3">
<div>
The contents of this cell are bottom-aligned.
</div>
</td>
</tr>
</table>
```

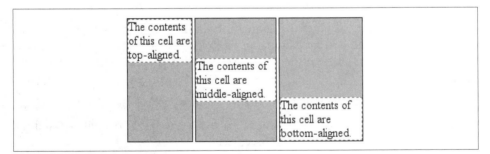

Figure 11-13. Vertical alignment of cell contents

In each case, the alignment is carried out by automatically increasing the padding of the cell itself to achieve the desired effect. In the first cell in Figure 11-13, the bottom padding of the cell has been changed to equal the difference between the height of the cell's box and the height of the content within the cell. For the second cell, the top and bottom padding of the cell have been reset to be equal, thus vertically centering the content of the cell. In the last cell, the cell's top padding has been altered.

The fourth possible value alignment is baseline, and it's a little more complicated than the first three:

baseline

> The baseline of the cell is aligned with the baseline of its row; in the case of row-spanning cells, the baseline of the cell is aligned with the baseline of the first row it spans.

It's easiest to provide an illustration (see Figure 11-14) and then discuss what's happening.

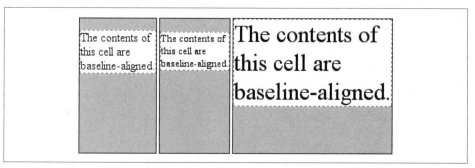

Figure 11-14. Baseline alignment of cell contents

A row's baseline is defined by the lowest initial cell baseline (that is, the baseline of the first line of text) out of all of its cells. Thus, in Figure 11-14, the row's baseline was defined by the third cell, which has the lowest initial baseline. The first two cells then have a baseline of their first line of text aligned with the row's baseline.

As with top, middle, and bottom alignment, baseline-aligned cell content is placed by altering the top and bottom padding of the cells. In cases where none of the cells in a row are baseline-aligned, the row does not even have a baseline—it doesn't really need one.

The detailed process for aligning cell contents within a row is as follows:

1. If any of the cells is baseline-aligned, the row's baseline is determined and the content of the baseline-aligned cells is placed.

2. Any top-aligned cell has its content placed. The row now has a provisional height, which is defined by the lowest cell bottom of the cells that have already had their content placed.

3. If any remaining cells are middle- or bottom-aligned, and the content height is taller than the provisional row height, the height of the row is increased to enclose the tallest of those cells.

4. All remaining cells have their content placed. In any cell whose contents are shorter than the row height, the cell's padding is increased to match the height of the row.

The vertical-align values sub, super, text-top, and text-bottom are ignored when applied to table cells. Thus, the following rule would have the same result as that shown in Figure 11-14:

```
th {vertical-align: text-top;}
```

Summary

Even if you're quite familiar with table layout from years of table-and-spacer design, the mechanisms driving such layout are rather complicated and not at all deterministic. Due to the legacy of HTML table construction, the CSS table model is row-centric, but it does, thankfully, accommodate columns and limited column styling. Thanks to new features that affect cell alignment and table width, you now have even more tools for presenting tables in a pleasing way.

The ability to apply table-related display values to arbitrary elements opens the door to creating table-like layouts using HTML elements such as div, or in XML languages where any element could be used to describe layout components. As of this writing, most browsers other than Internet Explorer support the application of table-related display values to arbitrary elements. Even in its current form, CSS makes presentation more sophisticated, as does the subject of the next chapter: generated content.

CHAPTER 12

Lists and Generated Content

In the realm of CSS layout, lists are an interesting case. The items in a list are simply block boxes, but with an extra bit that doesn't really participate in the document layout hanging off to one side. With an ordered list, that extra bit contains a series of increasing numbers (or letters) that are calculated and mostly formatted by the user agent, not the author. Taking a cue from the document structure, the user agent generates the numbers and their basic presentation.

None of this content generation could be described in CSS1 terms—and, therefore, it couldn't be controlled—but CSS2 introduced features that allow list-item numbering to be described. As a result, CSS now lets you, the author, define your own counting patterns and formats, and associate those counters with *any* element, not just ordered list items. Furthermore, this basic mechanism makes it possible to insert other kinds of content, including text strings, attribute values, or even external resources into a document. Thus, it becomes possible to use CSS to insert link icons, editorial symbols, and more into a design without having to create extra markup.

To see how all these list options fit together, we'll explore basic list styling before moving on to examine the generation of content and counters.

Lists

In a sense, almost anything that isn't narrative text can be considered a list. The U.S. Census, the solar system, my family tree, a restaurant menu, and even all of the friends you've ever had can be represented as a list, or perhaps as a list of lists. These many variations make lists fairly important, which is why it's a shame that list styling in CSS isn't more sophisticated.

The simplest (and best-supported) way to affect a list's styles is to change its marker type. The *marker* of a list item is, for example, the bullet that appears next to each item in an unordered list. In an ordered list, the marker could be a letter, number, or a symbol from some other counting system. You can even replace the markers with images. All of these are accomplished using the different list-style properties.

Types of Lists

To change the type of marker used for a list's items, use the property `list-style-type`.

---

list-style-type

CSS2.1 values:	disc | circle | square | decimal | decimal-leading-zero | lower-roman | upper-roman | lower-greek | lower-latin | upper-latin | armenian | georgian | none | inherit
CSS2 values:	disc | circle | square | decimal | decimal-leading-zero | upper-alpha |lower-alpha | upper-roman | lower-roman | lower-greek | hebrew | armenian | georgian | cjk-ideographic | hiragana | katakana | hiragana-iroha | none | inherit
Initial value:	disc
Applies to:	Elements whose display value is list-item
Inherited:	Yes
Computed value:	As specified

That's quite a few keywords, I know; many of them were introduced in CSS2 but were then dropped in CSS2.1. Table 12-1 lists the keywords that exist in CSS2.1.

Table 12-1. Keywords of the list-style-type property in CSS2.1

Keyword	Effect
disc	Uses a disc (usually a filled circle) for list-item markers
circle	Uses a circle (usually open) for markers
square	Uses a square (filled or open) for markers
decimal	1, 2, 3, 4, 5, …
decimal-leading-zero	01, 02, 03, 04, 05, …
upper-alpha upper-latin	A, B, C, D, E, …
lower-alpha lower-latin	a, b, c, d, e, …
upper-roman	I, II, III, IV, V, …
lower-roman	i, ii, iii, iv, v, …
lower-greek	Lowercase classical Greek symbols
armenian	Traditional Armenian numbering
georgian	Traditional Georgian numbering
none	Uses no marker

Table 12-2 lists those keywords that were introduced in CSS2 but that do not appear in CSS2.1.

Table 12-2. Keywords of the list-style-type property in CSS2

Keyword	Effect
hebrew	Traditional Hebrew numbering
cjk-ideographic	Ideographic numbering
katakana	Japanese numbering (A, I, U, E, O...)
katakana-iroha	Japanese numbering (I, RO, HA, NI, HO...)
hiragana	Japanese numbering (a, i, u, e, o...)
hiragana-iroha	Japanese numbering (i, ro, ha, ni, ho...)

A user agent should treat any value it does not recognize as decimal.

The list-style-type property, as well as all other list-related properties, can be applied only to an element that has a display of list-item, but CSS doesn't distinguish between ordered and unordered list items. Thus, you might be able to set an ordered list to use discs instead of numbers. In fact, the default value of list-style-type is disc, so you might theorize that without explicit declarations to the contrary, all lists (ordered or unordered) will use discs as the marker for each item. This would be logical, but, as it turns out, it's up to the user agent to decide. Even if the user agent doesn't have a predefined rule such as ol {list-style-type: decimal;}, it may prohibit ordered markers from being applied to unordered lists, and vice versa. You can't count on this, so be careful.

For the CSS2 values such as hebrew and georgian, the CSS2 specification doesn't state exactly how these counting systems work, nor how user agents should deal with them. This uncertainty resulted in a lack of widespread implementation, which is why the values in Table 12-2 do not appear in CSS2.1.

If you want to suppress the display of markers altogether, then none is the value you should use. none causes the user agent to refrain from putting anything where the marker would ordinarily be, although it does not interrupt the counting in ordered lists. Thus, the following markup would have the result shown in Figure 12-1:

```
ol li {list-style-type: decimal;}
li.off {list-style-type: none;}

<ol>
<li>Item the first
<li class="off">Item the second
<li>Item the third
<li class="off">Item the fourth
<li>Item the fifth
</ol>
```

list-style-type is inherited, so if you want to have different styles of markers in nested lists, you'll likely need to define them individually. You may also have to

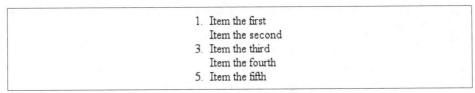

Figure 12-1. Switching off list-item markers

explicitly declare styles for nested lists because the user agent's style sheet may have already defined them. For example, assume that a user agent has the following styles defined:

```
ul {list-style-type: disc;}
ul ul {list-style-type: circle;}
ul ul ul {list-style-type: square;}
```

If this is the case (and it's likely that it will be), you will have to declare your own styles to overcome the user agent's styles—inheritance won't be enough.

List Item Images

Sometimes, a regular marker just won't do. You might prefer to use an image for each marker, which is possible with the property list-style-image.

list-style-image

Values:	<uri> | none | inherit
Initial value:	none
Applies to:	Elements whose display value is list-item
Inherited:	Yes
Computed value:	For <uri> values, the absolute URI; otherwise, none

Here's how it works:

```
ul li {list-style-image: url(ohio.gif);}
```

Yes, it's really that simple. One simple url() value, and you're putting images in for markers, as you can see in Figure 12-2.

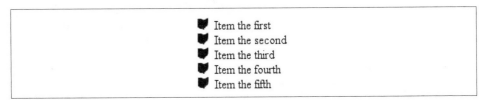

Figure 12-2. Using images as markers

Of course, you should exercise care in the images you use, as the example shown in Figure 12-3 makes painfully clear:

```
ul li {list-style-image: url(big-ohio.gif);}
```

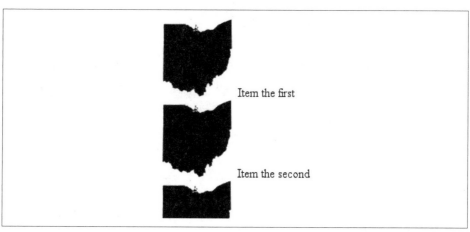

Figure 12-3. Using really big images as markers

It's generally a good idea to provide a fallback marker type in case your image doesn't load, gets corrupted, or is in a format that some user agents can't display. Do this by defining a backup list-style-type for the list:

```
ul li {list-style-image: url(ohio.png); list-style-type: square;}
```

The other thing you can do with list-style-image is set it to the default value of none. This is good practice because list-style-image is inherited, so any nested lists will pick up the image as the marker, unless you prevent that from happening:

```
ul {list-style-image: url(ohio.gif); list-style-type: square;}
ul ul {list-style-image: none;}
```

Since the nested list inherits the item type square but has been set to use no image for its markers, squares are used for the markers in the nested list, as shown in Figure 12-4.

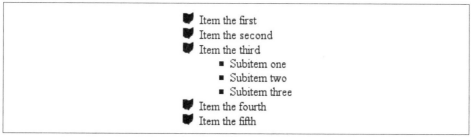

Figure 12-4. Switching off image markers in sublists

Remember that this scenario might not occur in the real world: a user agent may have already defined a list-style-type for ul ul, so the value of square won't be inherited after all. Your browser may vary.

List-Marker Positions

There is one other thing you can do to influence the appearance of list items under CSS2.1: decide whether the marker appears outside or inside the content of the list item. This is accomplished with list-style-position.

---

list-style-position

Values: inside | outside | inherit

Initial value: outside

Applies to: Elements whose display value is list-item

Inherited: Yes

Computed value: As specified

If a marker's position is set to outside (the default), it will appear the way list items always have on the Web. Should you desire a slightly different appearance, though, you can pull the marker in toward the content by setting the value to inside. This causes the marker to be placed "inside" the list item's content. The exact way this happens is undefined, but Figure 12-5 shows one possibility:

```
li.first {list-style-position: inside;}
li.second {list-style-position: outside;}
```

- Item the first; the list marker for this list item is inside the content of the list item.
- Item the second; the list marker for this list item is outside the content of the list item (which is the traditional Web rendering).

Figure 12-5. Placing the markers inside and outside list items

List Styles in Shorthand

For brevity's sake, you can combine the three list-style properties into a convenient single property: list-style.

<table>
<tr><td colspan="2" align="center">**list-style**</td></tr>
<tr><td>Values:</td><td>[<list-style-type> || <list-style-image> || <list-style-position>] | inherit</td></tr>
<tr><td>Initial value:</td><td>Refer to individual properties</td></tr>
<tr><td>Applies to:</td><td>Elements whose display value is list-item</td></tr>
<tr><td>Inherited:</td><td>Yes</td></tr>
<tr><td>Computed value:</td><td>See individual properties</td></tr>
</table>

For example:

```
li {list-style: url(ohio.gif) square inside;}
```

As you can see in Figure 12-6, all three values are applied to the list items.

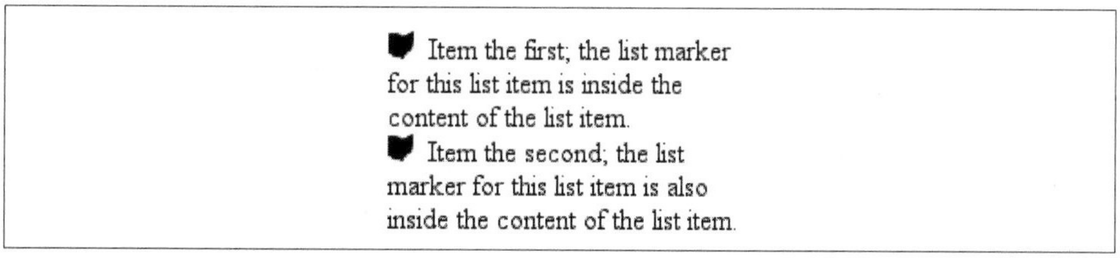

Figure 12-6. Bringing it all together

The values for list-style can be listed in any order, and any of them can be omitted. As long as one is present, the rest will fill in their default values. For instance, the following two rules will have the same visual effect:

```
li.norm {list-style: url(img42.gif);}
li.odd {list-style: url(img42.gif) disc outside;} /* the same thing */
```

They will also override any previous rules in the same way. For example:

```
li {list-style-type: square;}
li.norm {list-style: url(img42.gif);}
li.odd {list-style: url(img42.gif) disc outside;} /* the same thing */
```

The result will be the same as that in Figure 12-6 because the implied list-style-type value of disc for the rule li.norm will override the previous declared value of square, just as the explicit value of disc overrides it in rule li.odd.

List Layout

Now that we've looked at the basics of styling list markers, let's consider how lists are laid out in various browsers. We'll start with a set of three list items devoid of any markers and not yet placed within a list, as shown in Figure 12-7.

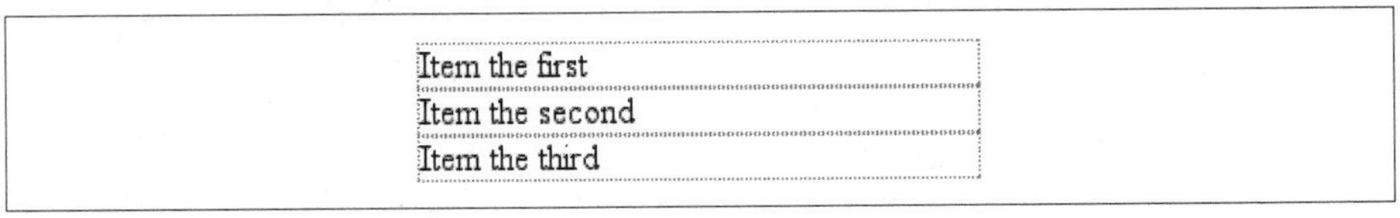

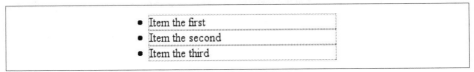

Figure 12-7. Three list items

The border around the list items shows them to be, essentially, like a block-level element. Indeed, the value `list-item` is defined to generate a block box. Now let's add markers, as illustrated in Figure 12-8.

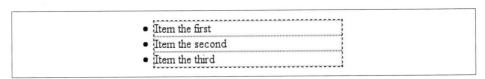

Figure 12-8. Markers are added

The distance between the marker and the list item's content is not defined by CSS, and CSS2.1 does not provide a way to affect that distance. Interestingly, CSS2 does, which is a subject briefly covered in the sidebar "List-Marker Positioning."

With the markers outside the list items' content, they don't affect the layout of other elements, nor do they really even affect the layout of the list items themselves. They just hang a certain distance from the edge of the content, and wherever the content edge goes, the marker will follow. The behavior of the marker works much as though the marker were absolutely positioned in relation to the list-item content, something like `position: absolute; left: -1.5em;`. When the marker is inside, it acts like an inline element at the beginning of the content.

So far, you have yet to add an actual list container; in other words, there is neither a ul nor an ol element represented in the figures. You can add one to the mix, as shown in Figure 12-9 (it's represented by a dashed border).

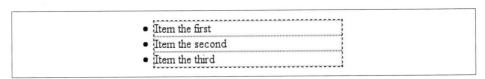

Figure 12-9. Adding a list element

Like the list items, the list element is a block box, one that encompasses its descendant elements. As you can see, however, the markers are not only placed outside the list item contents, but also outside the content area of the list element. The usual "indentation" you expect from lists has not yet been specified.

Most browsers, as of this writing, indent list items by setting either padding or margins for the containing list element. For example, the user agent might apply a rule such as:

```
ul, ol {margin-left: 40px;}
```

This is the rule employed by Internet Explorer and Opera (see Figure 12-9). Most Gecko-based browsers, on the other hand, use a rule like this:

```
ul, ol {padding-left: 40px;}
```

Neither is incorrect, but the discrepancy can lead to problems if you want to eliminate the indentation of the list items. Figure 12-10 shows the difference between the two approaches.

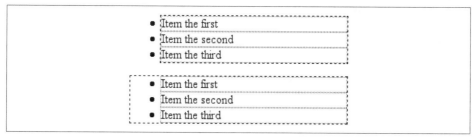

Figure 12-10. Margins and padding as indentation devices

 The distance of 40px is a relic of early web browsers, which indented lists by a pixel amount. A better value would be something like 2.5em, since this scales the indentation along with changes in the text size.

For authors who want to change the indentation distance of lists, I strongly recommend that you specify both padding and margins to ensure cross-browser compatibility. For example, if you want to use padding to indent a list, use this rule:

```
ul {margin-left: 0; padding-left: 1em;}
```

If you prefer margins, write something like this instead:

```
ul {margin-left: 1em; padding-left: 0;}
```

In either case, remember that the markers will be placed relative to the contents of the list items, and may therefore "hang" outside the main text of a document, or even beyond the edge of the browser window.

Generated Content

CSS2 and CSS2.1 include a new feature called *generated content*. This is content created by the browser but not represented either by markup or content.

For example, list markers are generated content. There is nothing in the markup of a list item that directly represents the markers, and you, the author, do not have to write the markers into your document's content. The browser simply generates the appropriate marker automatically. For unordered lists, the marker is a bullet of some kind, such as a circle, disc, or square. In ordered lists, the marker is a counter that increments by one for each successive list item.

List-Marker Positioning

One feature many authors request is the ability to control the space between a marker and the content of a list item. CSS2 defined ways to do this, including a property called `marker-offset` and a `display` value of `marker`. Implementation experience revealed this to be a clumsy approach, and these features were removed in CSS2.1

As of this writing, the current working draft of the CSS3 Lists module defines a new and more compact way to affect marker placement, which is the `::marker` pseudo-element. Assuming that the module does not change before becoming a full Recommendation, you may someday be able to write rules such as `li::marker {margin-right: 0.125em;}` in order to get markers snugly against the content of list items without actually bringing them inside.

To understand how you can affect list markers and customize the counting of ordered lists (or anything else!), you must first look at more basic generated content.

 As of this writing, no version of Internet Explorer supports generated content.

Inserting Generated Content

To insert generated content into the document, use the `:before` and `:after` pseudo-elements. These place generated content before or after the content of an element by way of the content property (described in the next section).

For example, you might want to precede every hyperlink with the text "(link)" to mark them for printing. This is accomplished with a rule like the following, which has the effect shown in Figure 12-11:

```
a[href]:before {content: "(link)";}
```

> (link)Jeffrey seems to be (link)very happy about (link)something, although I can't quite work out whether his happiness is over (link)OS X, (link)Chimera, the ability to run the Dock and (link)DragThing at the same time, the latter half of my (link)journal entry from yesterday, or (link)something else entirely.

Figure 12-11. Generating text content

Note that there isn't a space between the generated content and the element content. This is because the value of content in the previous example doesn't include a space. You could modify the declaration as follows to make sure there's a space between generated and actual content:

```
a[href]:before {content: "(link) ";}
```

It's a small difference but an important one.

In a similar manner, you might choose to insert a small icon at the end of links to PDF documents. The rule to accomplish this would look something like:

```
a.pdf-doc:after {content: url(pdf-doc-icon.gif);}
```

Suppose you want to further style such links by placing a border around them. This is done with a second rule:

```
a.pdf-doc {border: 1px solid gray;}
```

The result of these two rules is illustrated in Figure 12-12.

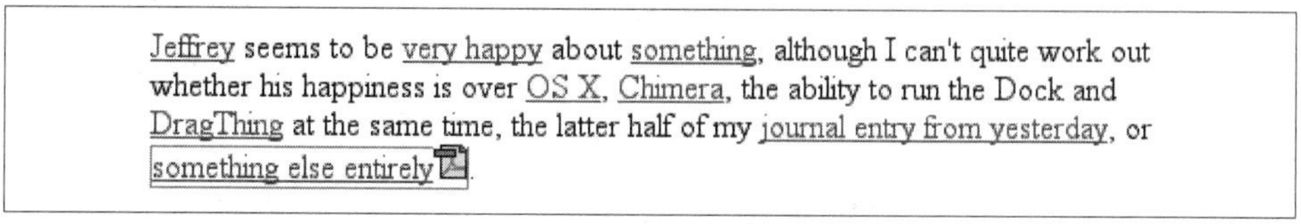

Jeffrey seems to be very happy about something, although I can't quite work out whether his happiness is over OS X, Chimera, the ability to run the Dock and DragThing at the same time, the latter half of my journal entry from yesterday, or something else entirely.

Figure 12-12. Generating icons

Notice how the link border extends around the generated content, just as the link underline extended under the "(link)" text in Figure 12-11. This happens because generated content is placed inside the element box of the element. As of CSS2.1, there isn't a way to place generated content outside the element box, other than list markers.

You might think that positioning would do the trick, except CSS2 and CSS2.1 specifically prohibit the floating or positioning of :before and :after content. List-style properties, along with table properties, are similarly prohibited. In addition, the following restrictions apply:

- If the subject of a :before or :after selector is a block-level element, then the property display can accept only the values none, inline, block, and marker. Any other value is treated as block.

- If the subject of a :before or :after selector is an inline-level element, then the property display can accept only the values none and inline. Any other value is treated as inline.

For example, consider:

```
em:after {content: " (!) "; display: block;}
```

Since em is an inline element, the generated content cannot be made block-level. The value block is therefore reset to inline. In this next example, however, the generated content is made block-level because the target element is also block-level:

```
h1:before {content: "New Section"; display: block; color: gray;}
```

The result is illustrated in Figure 12-13.

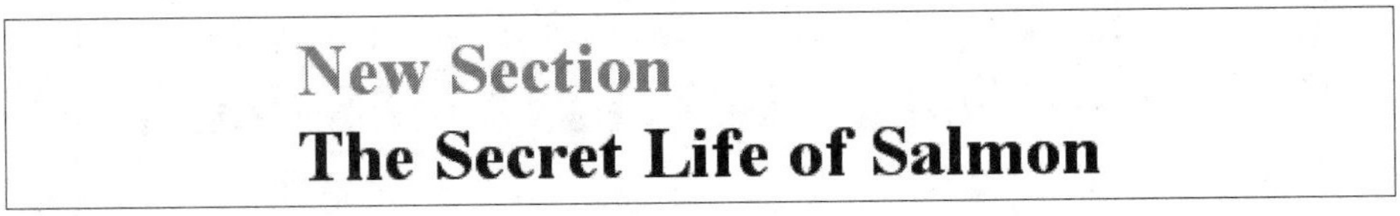

New Section
The Secret Life of Salmon

Figure 12-13. Generating block-level content

One interesting aspect of generated content is that it inherits values from the element to which it's been attached. Thus, given the following rules, the generated text will be green, the same as the content of the paragraphs:

```
p {color: green;}
p:before {content: "::: ";}
```

If you want the generated text to be purple instead, a simple declaration will suffice:

```
p:before {content: "::: "; color: purple;}
```

Such value inheritance happens only with inherited properties, of course. This is worth noting because it influences how certain effects must be approached. Consider:

```
h1 {border-top: 3px solid black; padding-top: 0.25em;}
h1:before {content: "New Section"; display: block; color: gray;
  border-bottom: 1px dotted black; margin-bottom: 0.5em;}
```

Since the generated content is placed inside the element box of the h1, it will be placed under the top border of the element. It would also be placed within any padding, as shown in Figure 12-14.

New Section

The Secret Life of Salmon

Figure 12-14. Taking placement into account

The bottom margin of the generated content, which has been made block-level, pushes the actual content of the element downward by half an em. In every sense, the effect of the generated content in this example is to break up the h1 element into two pieces: the generated-content box and the actual content box. This happens because the generated content has display: block. If you were to change it to display: inline, the effect would be as shown in Figure 12-15:

```
h1 {border-top: 3px solid black; padding-top: 0.25em;}
h1:before {content: "New Section"; display: inline; color: gray;
  border-bottom: 1px dotted black; margin-bottom: 0.5em;}
```

New Section The Secret Life of Salmon

Figure 12-15. Changing the generated content to be inline

Note how the borders are placed and how the top padding is still honored. So is the bottom margin on the generated content, but since the generated content is now inline and margins don't affect line height, the margin has no visible effect.

With the basics of generating content established, let's take a closer look at the way the actual generated content is specified.

Specifying Content

If you're going to generate content, you need a way to describe the content to be generated. As you've already seen, this is handled with the content property, but there's a great deal more to this property than you've seen thus far.

content	
Values:	normal | [<string> | <uri> | <counter> | attr(<identifier>) | open-quote | close-quote | no-open-quote | no-close-quote]+ | inherit
Initial value:	normal
Applies to:	:before and :after pseudo-elements
Inherited:	No
Computed value:	For <uri> values, an absolute URI; for attribute references, the resulting string; otherwise, as specified

You've already seen string and URI values in action, and counters will be covered later in this chapter. Let's talk about strings and URIs in a little more detail before we take a look at the attr( ) and quote values.

String values are presented literally, even if they contain what would otherwise be markup of some kind. Therefore, the following rule would be inserted verbatim into the document, as shown in Figure 12-16:

```
h2:before {content: "<em>&para;</em> "; color: gray;}
```

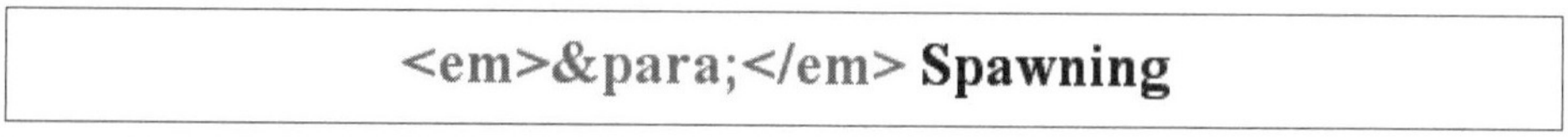

¶ Spawning

Figure 12-16. Strings are displayed verbatim

This means that if you want a newline (return) as part of your generated content, you can't use `<br>`. Instead, you use the string \A, which is the CSS way of representing a newline (based on the Unicode linefeed character, which is hexadecimal position A). Conversely, if you have a long string value and need to break it up over multiple lines, you escape out the linefeeds with the \ character. These are both demonstrated by the following rule and illustrated in Figure 12-17:

```
h2:before {content: "We insert this text before all H2 elements because \
it is a good idea to show how these things work. It may be a bit long \
but the point should be clearly made.  "; color: gray;}
```

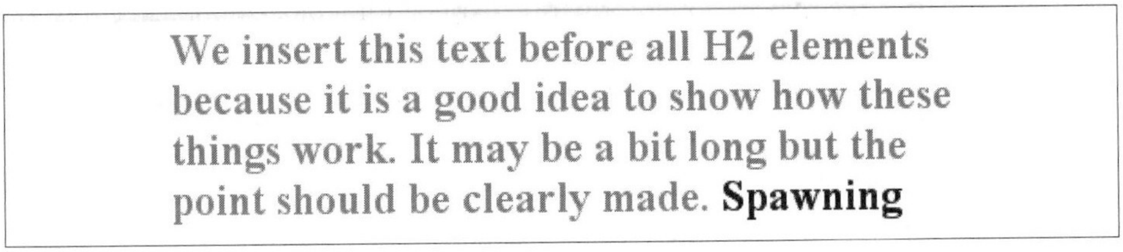

We insert this text before all H2 elements because it is a good idea to show how these things work. It may be a bit long but the point should be clearly made. **Spawning**

Figure 12-17. Inserting and suppressing newlines

You can also use escapes to refer to hexadecimal Unicode values, such as \00AB.

 As of this writing, support for inserting escaped content such as \A and \00AB is not very widespread, even among those browsers that support some generated content.

With URI values, you simply point to an external resource (an image, movie, sound clip, or anything else the user agent supports), which is then inserted into the document in the appropriate place. If the user agent can't support the resource you point it to for any reason—say, you try to insert an SVG image into a browser that doesn't understand SVG, or try to insert a movie into a document when it's being printed—then the user agent is required to ignore the resource completely, and nothing will be inserted.

Inserting attribute values

There are situations where you might want to take the value of an element's attribute and make it a part of the document display. To pick a simple example, you can place the value of every link's `href` attribute immediately after the links, like this:

```
a[href]:after {content: attr(href);}
```

Again, this leads to the problem of the generated content running smack into the actual content. To solve this, add some string values to the declaration, with the result shown in Figure 12-18:

```
a[href]:after {content: " [" attr(href) "]";}
```

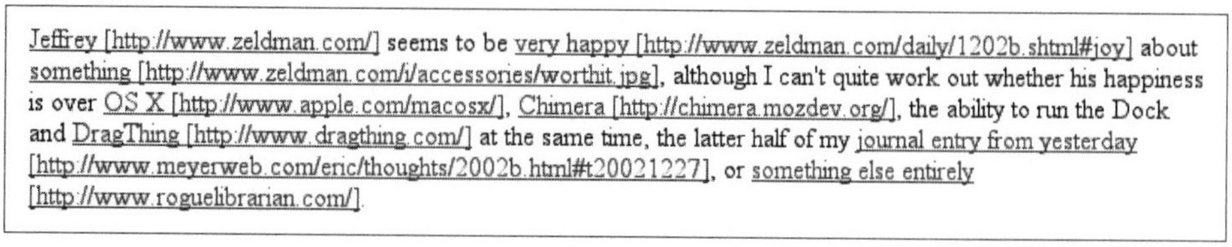

Jeffrey [http://www.zeldman.com/] seems to be very happy [http://www.zeldman.com/daily/1202b.shtml#joy] about something [http://www.zeldman.com/i/accessories/worthit.jpg], although I can't quite work out whether his happiness is over OS X [http://www.apple.com/macosx/], Chimera [http://chimera.mozdev.org/], the ability to run the Dock and DragThing [http://www.dragthing.com/] at the same time, the latter half of my journal entry from yesterday [http://www.meyerweb.com/eric/thoughts/2002b.html#t20021227], or something else entirely [http://www.roguelibrarian.com/].

Figure 12-18. Inserting URLs

This can be useful for print style sheets, as an example. Any attribute value can be inserted as generated content: alt text, class or id values—anything. An author might choose to make the citation information explicit for a block quote, like this:

```
blockquote:after {content: "(" attr(cite) ")"; display: block;
    text-align: right; font-style: italic;}
```

For that matter, a more complicated rule might reveal the text- and link-color values for a legacy document:

```
body:before {content: "Text: " attr(text) " | Link: " attr(link)
    " | Visited: " attr(vlink) " | Active: " attr(alink);
    display: block; padding: 0.33em;
    border: 1px solid black; text-align: center;}
```

Note that if an attribute doesn't exist, an empty string is put in its place. This is what happens in Figure 12-19, in which the previous example is applied to a document whose body element has no alink attribute.

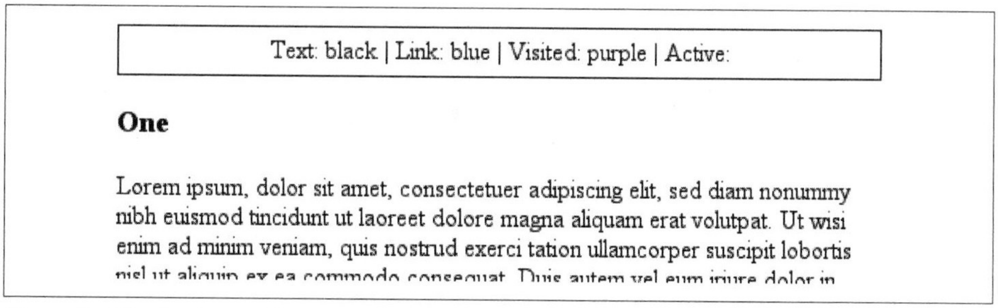

Text: black | Link: blue | Visited: purple | Active:

One

Lorem ipsum, dolor sit amet, consectetuer adipiscing elit, sed diam nonummy nibh euismod tincidunt ut laoreet dolore magna aliquam erat volutpat. Ut wisi enim ad minim veniam, quis nostrud exerci tation ullamcorper suscipit lobortis nisl ut aliquip ex ea commodo consequat. Duis autem vel eum iriure dolor in

Figure 12-19. Missing attributes are skipped

The text "Active: " (including the trailing space) is inserted into the document, as you can see, but there is nothing following it. This is convenient in situations where you want to insert the value of an attribute only when it exists.

> CSS2.x defines the returned value of an attribute reference as an unparsed string. Therefore, if the value of an attribute contains markup or character entities, they will be displayed verbatim.

Generated quotes

A specialized form of generated content is the quotation mark, and CSS2.x provides a powerful way to manage both quotes and their nesting behavior. This is possible due to the pairing of content values like open-quote and the property quotes.

---

quotes

Values:	[<string> <string>]+ | none | inherit
Initial value:	User agent-dependent
Applies to:	All elements
Inherited:	Yes
Computed value:	As specified

Upon studying the value syntax, we find that other than the keywords none and inherit, the only valid value is one or more *pairs* of strings. The first string of the pair defines the open-quote symbol, and the second defines the close-quote symbol. Therefore, of the following two declarations, only the first is valid:

```
quotes: '"' "'";  /* valid */
quotes: '"';  /* NOT VALID */
```

The first rule also illustrates one way to put string quotes around the strings themselves. The double quotation marks are surrounded by single quotation marks, and vice versa.

Let's look at a simple example. Suppose you're creating an XML format to store a list of favorite quotations. Here's one entry in the list:

```
<quotation>
 <quote>I hate quotations.</quote>
 <quotee>Ralph Waldo Emerson</quotee>
</quotation>
```

To present the data in a useful way, you could employ the following rules, with the result shown in Figure 12-20:

```
quotation: {display: block;}
quote {quotes: '"' "'";}
quote:before {content: open-quote;}
quote:after {content: close-quote;}
quotee:before {content: " (";}
quotee:after {content: ")";}
```

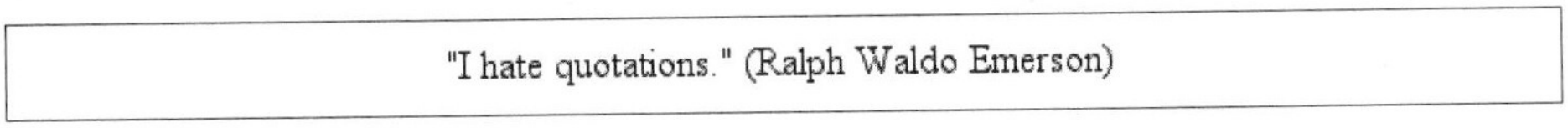

"I hate quotations." (Ralph Waldo Emerson)

Figure 12-20. Inserting quotes and other content

The values open-quote and close-quote are used to insert whatever quoting symbols are appropriate (since different languages have different quotation marks). They use the value of quotes to determine how they should work. Thus, the quotation begins and ends with a double quotation mark.

If you want to use "curly quotes" instead of the plain vertical-line quotation marks, as is common in most print media, the quote rule would read:

```
quote {quotes: '\201C' '\201D';}
```

This uses the hexadecimal Unicode positions for the "curly quote" symbols and, if applied to the previous quotation, would surround Emerson's quote with curly quotes instead of the straight quotes in Figure 12-20.

With quotes, you can define quotation patterns to as many nesting levels as you like. In English, for example, a common practice is to start out with a double quotation mark, and a quotation nested inside the first one gets single quotation marks. This can be recreated with "curly" quotation marks using the following rules:

```
quotation: display: block;}
quote {quotes: '\201C' '\201D' '\2018' '\2019';}
quote:before, q:before{content: open-quote;}
quote:after, q:after {content: close-quote;}
```

When applied to the following markup, these rules will have the effect shown in Figure 12-21:

```
<quotation>
 <quote> In the beginning, there was nothing. And God said: <q>Let there
  be light!</q> And there was still nothing, but you could see it.</quote>
</quotation>
```

"In the beginning, there was nothing. And God said: 'Let there be light!' And there was still nothing, but you could see it."

Figure 12-21. Nested curly quotes

In a case where the nested level of quotation marks is greater than the number of defined pairs, the last pair is reused for the deeper levels. Thus, if you had applied the following rule to the markup shown in Figure 12-21, the inner quote would have had double quotation marks, the same as the outer quote:

```
quote {quotes: '\201C' '\201D';}
```

Generated quotes make possible one other common typographic effect. In situations where there are several paragraphs of quoted text, the close-quote of each paragraph is often omitted; only the opening quote marks are shown, with the exception of the last paragraph. This can be recreated using the no-close-quote value:

```
blockquote {quotes: '"' '"' "'" "'" '"' '"';}
blockquote p:before    {content: open-quote;}
blockquote p:after     {content: no-close-quote;}
```

This will start each paragraph with a double quotation mark but no closing mark. This is true of the last paragraph as well, so if you need to add a closing quote mark, you'd need to class the final paragraph and declare a close-quote for its :after content.

This value is important because it decrements the quotation nesting level without actually generating a symbol. This is why each paragraph starts with a double quotation mark, instead of alternating between double and single marks until the third paragraph is reached. no-close-quote closes the quotation nesting at the end of each paragraph, and thus every paragraph starts at the same nesting level.

This is significant because, as the CSS2.1 specification notes, "Quoting depth is independent of the nesting of the source document or the formatting structure." In other words, when you start a quotation level, it persists across elements until a close-quote is encountered, and the quote nesting level is decremented.

For the sake of completeness, there is a no-open-quote keyword, which has a symmetrical effect to no-close-quote. This keyword increments the quotation nesting level by one but does not generate a symbol.

Counters

We're all familiar with counters; for example, the markers of the list items in ordered lists are counters. In CSS1, there was no way to affect them, largely because there was no need: HTML defined its own counting behaviors for ordered lists, and that was that. With the rise of XML, it's now important to provide a method by which counters can be defined. CSS2 was not content to simply provide for the kind of simple counting found in HTML, however. Two properties and two content values make it possible to define almost any counting format, including subsection counters employing multiple styles, such as "VII.2.c."

Resetting and incrementing

The basis of creating counters is the ability to set both the starting point for a counter and to increment it by some amount. The former is handled by the property counter-reset.

---

counter-reset

Values:	[<identifier> <integer>?]+	none	inherit
Initial value:	User agent-dependent
Applies to:	All elements
Inherited:	No
Computed value:	As specified

A counter identifier is simply a label created by the author. For example, you might name your subsection counter `subsection`, `subsec`, `ss`, or `bob`. The simple act of resetting (or incrementing) an identifier is sufficient to call it into being. In the following rule, the counter `chapter` is defined as it is reset:

```
h1 {counter-reset: chapter;}
```

By default, a counter is reset to zero. If you want to reset to a different number, you can declare the number following the identifier:

```
h1#ch4 {counter-reset: chapter 4;}
```

You can also reset multiple identifiers all at once in identifier-integer pairs. If you leave out an integer, then it defaults to zero:

```
h1 {counter-reset: chapter 4 section -1 subsec figure 1;}
   /* 'subsec' is reset to 0 */
```

As you can see from the previous example, negative values are permitted. It would be perfectly legal to set a counter to -32768 and count up from there.

 CSS does not define what user agents should do with negative counter values in nonnumeric counting styles. For example, there is no defined behavior for what to do if a counter's value is -5 but its display style is `upper-alpha`.

To count up, you'll need a property to indicate that an element increments a counter. Otherwise, the counter would remain at whatever value it was given with a `counter-reset` declaration. The property in question is, not surprisingly, `counter-increment`.

---

counter-increment

Values:	[<identifier> <integer>?]+ | `none` | `inherit`
Initial value:	User agent-dependent
Applies to:	All elements
Inherited:	No
Computed value:	As specified

Like `counter-reset`, `counter-increment` accepts identifier-integer pairs, and the integer portion of these pairs can be zero or negative as well as positive. The difference is that if an integer is omitted from a pair in `counter-increment`, it defaults to 1, not 0.

As an example, here's how a user agent might define counters to recreate the traditional 1, 2, 3 counting of ordered lists:

```
ol {counter-reset: ordered;}  /* defaults to 0 */
ol li {counter-increment: ordered;}  /* defaults to 1 */
```

On the other hand, an author might want to count backward from zero so that the list items use a rising negative system. This would require only a small edit:

```
ol {counter-reset: ordered;}  /* defaults to 0 */
ol li {counter-increment: ordered -1;}
```

The counting of lists would then be -1, -2, -3 and so on. If you replaced the integer -1 with -2, then lists would count -2, -4, -6 and so on.

Using counters

To actually display the counters, though, you need to use the content property in conjunction with one of the counter-related values. To see how this works, let's use an XML-based ordered list like this:

```
<list type="ordered">
 <item>First item</item>
 <item>Item two</item>
 <item>The third item</item>
</list>
```

By applying the following rules to XML employing this structure, you would get the result shown in Figure 12-22:

```
list[type="ordered"] {counter-reset: ordered;}  /* defaults to 0 */
list[type="ordered"] item {display: block;}
list[type="ordered"] item:before {counter-increment: ordered;
 content: counter(ordered) ". "; margin: 0.25em 0;}
```

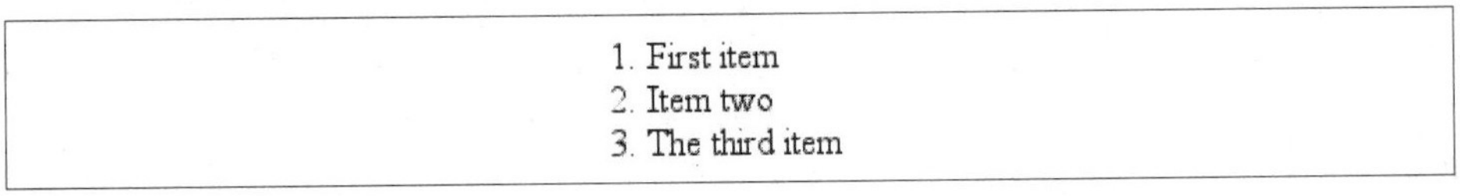

1. First item
2. Item two
3. The third item

Figure 12-22. Counting the items

Note that the generated content is, as usual, placed as inline content at the beginning of the associated element. Thus, the effect is similar to an HTML list with list-style-position: inside; declared.

Note also that the item elements are ordinary elements generating block-level boxes, which means that counters are not restricted only to elements with a display of list-item. In fact, any element can make use of a counter. Consider the following rules:

```
h1:before {counter-reset: section subsec;
   counter-increment: chapter;
   content: counter(chapter) ". ";}
h2:before {counter-reset: subsec;
   counter-increment: section;
   content: counter(chapter )"." counter(section) ". ";}
h3:before {counter-increment: subsec;
   content: counter(chapter) "." counter(section) "." counter(subsec) ". ";}
```

These rules would have the effect shown in Figure 12-23.

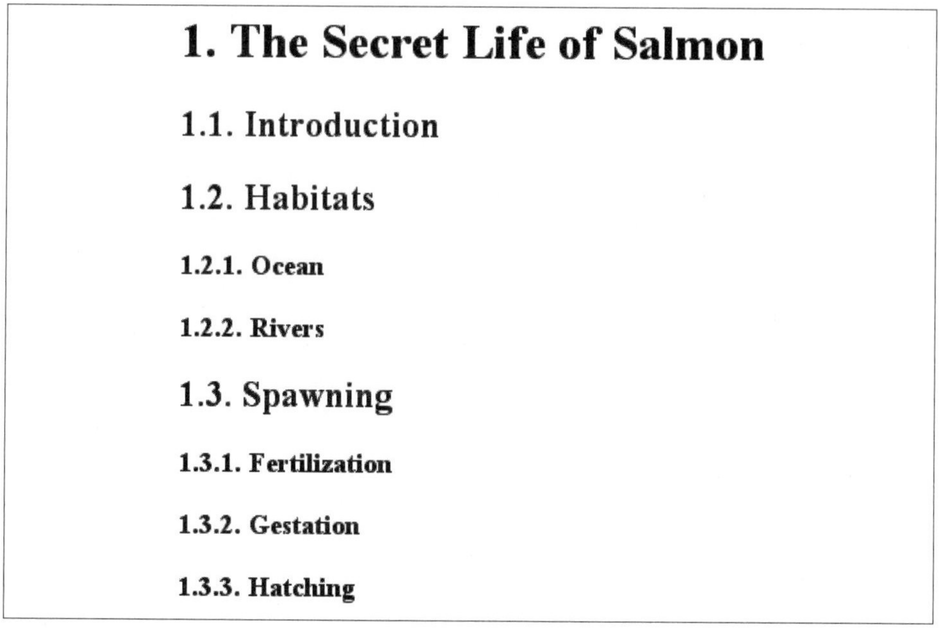

1. The Secret Life of Salmon

1.1. Introduction

1.2. Habitats

1.2.1. Ocean

1.2.2. Rivers

1.3. Spawning

1.3.1. Fertilization

1.3.2. Gestation

1.3.3. Hatching

Figure 12-23. Adding counters to headings

Figure 12-23 illustrates some important points about counter resetting and incrementing. Notice how the h1 element uses the counter chapter, which defaults to zero and has a "1." before the element's text. When a counter is incremented and used by the same element, the incrementation happens *before* the counter is displayed. In a similar way, if a counter is reset and shown in the same element, the reset happens before the counter is displayed. Consider:

```
h1:before, h2:before, h3:before {
  content: counter(chapter) "." counter(section) "." counter(subsec) ". ";}
h1 {counter-reset: section subsec;
  counter-increment: chapter;}
```

The first h1 element in the document would be preceded by the text "1.0.0. " because the counters section and subsec were reset, but not incremented. This means that if you want the first displayed instance of an incremented counter to be 0, then you need to reset that counter to -1, as follows:

```
body {counter-reset: chapter -1;}
h1:before {counter-increment: chapter; content: counter(chapter) ". ";}
```

You can do some interesting things with counters. Consider the following XML:

```
<code type="BASIC">
 <line>PRINT "Hello world!"</line>
 <line>REM This is what the kids are calling a "comment"</line>
 <line>GOTO 10</line>
</code>
```

You can recreate the traditional format of a BASIC program listing with the following rules:

```
code[type="BASIC"] {counter-reset: linenum; font-family: monospace;}
code[type="BASIC"] line {display: block;}
code[type="BASIC"] line:before {counter-increment: linenum;
  content: counter(linenum 10) ": ";}
```

It's also possible to define a list style for each counter as part of the counter( ) format. You can do this by adding a comma-separated list-style-type keyword after the counter's identifier. The following modification of the heading-counter example is illustrated in Figure 12-24:

```
h1:before {counter-reset: section subsec;
  counter-increment: chapter;
  content: counter(chapter,upper-alpha) ". ";}
h2:before {counter-reset: subsec;
  counter-increment: section;
  content: counter(chapter,upper-alpha)"." counter(section) ". ";}
h3:before {counter-increment: subsec;
  content: counter(chapter,upper-alpha) "." counter(section) "."
  counter(subsec,lower-roman) ". ";}
```

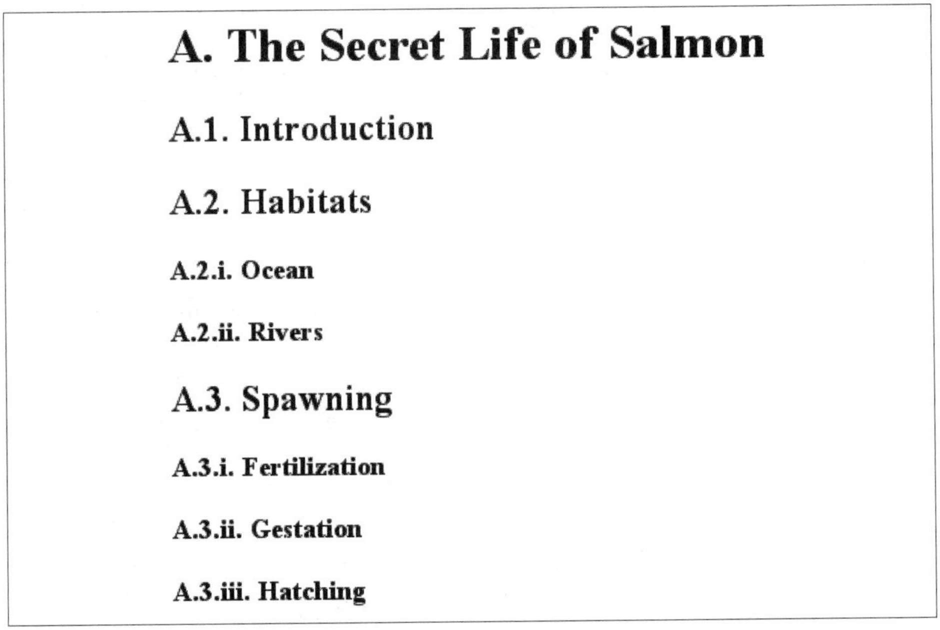

A. The Secret Life of Salmon

A.1. Introduction

A.2. Habitats

A.2.i. Ocean

A.2.ii. Rivers

A.3. Spawning

A.3.i. Fertilization

A.3.ii. Gestation

A.3.iii. Hatching

Figure 12-24. Changing counter styles

Notice that the counter section was not given a style keyword, so it defaulted to the decimal counting style. You can even set counters to use the styles disc, circle, square, and none if you so desire.

One interesting point to note is that elements with a display of none do not increment counters, even if the rule seems to indicate otherwise. In contrast, elements with a visibility of hidden do increment counters:

```
.suppress {counter-increment: cntr; display: none;}
   /* 'cntr' is NOT incremented */
.invisible {counter-increment: cntr; visibility: hidden;}
   /* 'cntr' IS incremented */
```

Counters and scope

So far, we've seen how to string multiple counters together to create section-and-subsection counting. Often, this is something authors desire for nested ordered lists as well, but it would quickly become clumsy to try to create enough counters to cover deep nesting levels. Just to get it working for five-level-deep nested lists would require a bunch of rules like this:

```
ol ol ol ol ol li:before {counter-increment: ord1 ord2 ord3 ord4 ord5;
   content: counter(ord1) "." counter(ord2) "." counter(ord3) "."
   counter(ord4) "." counter(ord5) ".";}
```

Imagine writing enough rules to cover nesting up to 50 levels! (I'm not saying you should nest ordered lists 50 deep. Just follow along for the moment.)

Fortunately, CSS2.x described the concept of *scope* when it comes to counters. Stated simply, every level of nesting creates a new scope for any given counter. Scope is what makes it possible for the following rules to cover nested-list counting in the usual HTML way:

```
ol {counter-reset: ordered;}
ol li:before {counter-increment: ordered;
   content: counter(ordered) ". ";}
```

These rules will all make ordered lists, even those nested inside others, start counting from 1 and increment each item by one—exactly how it's been done in HTML from the beginning.

This works because a new instance of the counter ordered is created at each level of nesting. So, for the first ordered list, an instance of ordered is created. Then, for every list nested inside the first one, another new instance is created, and the counting starts anew with each list.

However, you want ordered lists to count so that each level of nesting creates a new counter appended to the old: 1, 1.1, 1.2, 1.2.1, 1.2.2, 1.3, 2, 2.1, and so on. This can't be done with counter( ), but it *can* be done with counters( ). What a difference an "s" makes.

To create the nested-counter style shown in Figure 12-25, you need these rules:

```
ol {counter-reset: ordered;}
ol li:before {counter-increment: ordered;
   content: counters(ordered,".") " - ";}
```

```
1. - Lists
    1.1. - Types of Lists
    1.2. - List Item Images
    1.3. - List Marker Positions
    1.4. - List Styles in Shorthand
    1.5. - List Layout
2. - Generated Content
    2.1. - Inserting Generated Content
        2.1.1. - Generated Content and Run-In Content
    2.2. - Specifying Content
        2.2.1. - Inserting Attribute Values
        2.2.2. - Generated Quotes
    2.3. - Counters
        2.3.1. - Resetting and Incrementing
        2.3.2. - Using Counters
        2.3.3. - Counters and Scope
3. - Summary
```

Figure 12-25. Nested counters

Basically, the keyword counters(ordered,".") displays the ordered counter from each scope with a period appended, and strings together all of the scoped counters for a given element. Thus, an item in a third-level-nested list would be prefaced with the ordered value for the outermost list's scope, the scope of the list between the outer and current list, and the current list's scope, with each of those followed by a period. The rest of the content value causes a space, hyphen, and space to be added after all of those counters.

As with counter( ), you can define a list style for nested counters, but the same style applies to all of the counters. Thus, if you changed your previous CSS to read as follows, the list items in Figure 12-25 would all use lowercase letters for the counters instead of numbers:

```
ol li:before {counter-increment: ordered;
  content: counters(ordered,".",lower-alpha) ": ";}
```

Summary

Even though list styling isn't as sophisticated as we might like, and browser support for generated content is somewhat spotty (as of this writing, anyway), the ability to style lists is still highly useful. One relatively common use is to take a list of links, remove the markers and indentation, and thus create a navigation sidebar. The combination of simple markup and flexible layout is difficult to resist. With the anticipated enhancements to list styling in CSS3, I expect that lists will become more and more useful.

For now, in situations where a markup language doesn't have intrinsic list elements, generated content can be an enormous help—say, for inserting content such as icons to point to certain types of links (PDF files, Word documents, or even just links to another web site). Generated content also makes it easy to print out link URLs, and its ability to insert and format quotation marks leads to true typographic joy. It's safe to say that the usefulness of generated content is limited only by your imagination. Even better, thanks to counters, you can now associate ordering information to elements that are not typically lists, such as headings or code blocks. Now, if you want to support such features with design that mimics the appearance of the user's operating system, read on. The next chapter will discuss ways to use system colors and fonts in CSS design.

CHAPTER 13

User Interface Styles

The vast majority of CSS is concerned with styling documents, but it offers a passel of useful interface-styling tools for more than just documents. For example, Mozilla's developers created its browser's interface (and that of many Mozilla clones) using a language called XUL. XUL employs CSS and CSS-like declarations to present the navigation buttons, sidebar tabs, dialog boxes, status boxes, and other pieces of the chrome itself.

Similarly, you can reuse aspects of the user's default environment to style a document's fonts and colors; it's even possible to exert influence over focus highlighting and the mouse cursor. CSS2's interface capabilities can make the user's experience more enjoyable—or more confusing, if you aren't careful.

System Fonts and Colors

There may be times when you want your document to mimic the user's computing environment as closely as possible. An obvious example is if you're creating web-based applications, where the goal is to make the web component seem like a part of the user's operating system. While CSS2 doesn't make it possible to reuse every last aspect of the operating system's appearance in your documents, you can choose from a wide variety of colors and a short list of fonts.

System Fonts

Let's say you've created an element that functions as a button (via JavaScript, for example). By making the control look just like a button in the user's computing environment, you meet the user's expectations of how a control should look and thus make it more usable.

To accomplish the given example, simply write a rule like this:

```
a.widget {font: caption;}
```

This will set the font of any a element with a class of widget to use the same font family, size, weight, style, and variant as the text found in captioned controls, such as a button.

CSS2 defines six system font keywords. These are described in the following list:

caption

The font styles used for captioned controls, such as buttons and drop-downs

icon

The font styles used to label operating system icons, such as hard drives, folders, and files

menu

The font styles used for text in drop-down menus and menu lists

message-box

The font styles used to present text in dialog boxes

small-caption

The font styles used for labeling small captioned controls

status-bar

The font styles used for text in window status bars

It's important to realize that these values can be used only with the font property and are their own form of shorthand. For example, let's assume that a user's operating system shows icon labels as 10-pixel Geneva with no boldfacing, italicizing, or small-caps effects. This means that the following three rules are all equivalent, and have the result shown in Figure 13-1:

```
body {font: icon;}
body {font: 10px Geneva;}
body {
  font-weight: normal;
  font-style: normal;
  font-variant: normal;
  font-size: 10px;
  font-family: Geneva;
}
```

So a simple value like icon actually embodies a whole lot of other values. This is fairly unique in CSS, and it makes working with these values just a little more complex than usual.

As an example, suppose you want to use the same font styling as icon labels, but you want the font to be boldfaced even if icon labels are not boldfaced on a user's system. You'd need a rule with the declarations in the order shown:

```
body {font: icon; font-weight: bold;}
```

By writing the declarations in this order, you cause the user agent to set the body element's font to match icon labels with the first declaration, and then modify the

Cascading Style Sheets: The Definitive Guide

By Eric A. Meyer
Published by O'Reilly & Associates
ISBN 1-56592-622-6
456 pages

In many ways, the Cascading Style Sheets (CSS) specification represents a unique development in the history of the World Wide Web. In its inherent ability to allow richly styled structural documents, CSS is both a step forward and a step backward—but it's a good step backward, and a needed one. To see what is meant by this, it is first necessary to understand how the Web got to the point of desperately needing something like CSS, and how CSS makes the web a better place for both page authors and web surfers.

Cascading Style Sheets: The Definitive Guide does exactly that, and then goes on to describe in detail how CSS works, what its properties and values mean, and how authors can use them in the real world. A synthesis of browser support charts, the wisdom of Web design and usability experts, and the author's unique perspective on CSS, this book tells designers how CSS is supposed to work, how browsers treat it, and what paths allow for a safe threading between theory and reality.

Written in a personal style, endeavoring to treat the reader as a peer instead of a student, *Cascading Style Sheets: The Definitive Guide* is the best way to crack open the world of proper style for the Web.

Figure 13-1. Making text look like an icon label

weight of that font with the second. If the order were reversed, then the font declaration's value would override the font-weight value from the second declaration, and the boldfacing would be lost. This is similar to the way shorthand properties (like font itself) must be handled.

You may be wondering about the lack of a generic font family, since it's usually recommended that the author write something like Geneva, sans-serif; (in case a user's browser doesn't support the specified font). CSS won't let you "tack on" a generic font family, but in this case, it isn't needed. If the user agent manages to extract the font family used to display something in the computing environment, then it's a pretty safe bet the same font is available for the browser to use.

If the requested system font style is not available or can't be determined, the user agent is allowed to guess at an appropriate set of font styles. For example, small-caption might be approximated by taking the styles for caption and reducing the font's size. If no such guess can be made, the user agent should use a "user agent default font" instead.

System Colors

As of this writing, the working draft of the CSS3 Color module deprecates the system color keywords in favor of the new property appearance. Similarly, CSS2.1 deprecates these keywords in anticipation of changes in CSS3. Authors are strongly encouraged not to use the system colors, as they are not likely to appear in future versions of CSS. This information is included because some currently available browsers do support system colors.

If you want to reuse the colors specified in the user's operating system, CSS2 defines a series of system color keywords. These are values that can be used in any circumstance where a <color> value is allowed. For example, you could match the background of an element with the user's desktop color by declaring:

```
div#test {background-color: Background;}
```

Thus, for example, you could give a document the system's default text and background color like this:

```
body {color: WindowText; background: Window;}
```

Such customization increases the odds that the user will be able to read the document, since he has presumably configured his operating system to be usable. (If not, he deserves whatever he gets!)

There are 28 system color keywords in total, although CSS does not explicitly define them. Instead, there are some generic (and very short) descriptions of each keyword's meaning. The following list describes all 28 keywords. In cases where there is a direct analog with the options in the "Appearance" tab of the Display control panel in Windows 2000, it is noted parenthetically after the description.

ActiveBorder
> The color applied to the outside border of an active window (the first color in "Active Windows Border").

ActiveCaption
> The background color of the caption of the currently active window (the first color in "Active Title Bar").

AppWorkspace
> The background color used in an application that allows multiple documents—e.g., the background color "behind" the open documents in Microsoft Word (the first color in "Application Background").

Background
> The background color for the desktop (the first color in "Desktop").

ButtonFace
> The color used on the "face" of a three-dimensional button.

ButtonHighlight
> The highlight color found on the edges of three-dimensional display elements that face away from the virtual light source. Thus, if the virtual light source is located in the upper left, this would be the highlight color used on the right and bottom edges of the display element.

ButtonShadow
> The shadow color for three-dimensional display elements.

ButtonText
> The color of text found on push buttons (the font color in "3D Objects").

CaptionText

The color of text found in captions, the size box, and the symbol in a scrollbar arrow box (the font color in "Active Title Bar").

GrayText

The grayed (disabled) text. This keyword is interpreted as #000 if the current display driver does not support a solid gray color.

Highlight

The color of item(s) selected in a control (the first color in "Selected Items").

HighlightText

The text color of item(s) selected in a control (the font color in "Selected Items").

InactiveBorder

The color applied to the outside border of an inactive window (the first color in "Inactive Window Border").

InactiveCaption

The background color of the caption of an inactive window (the first color in "Inactive Title Bar").

InactiveCaptionText

The color of text in an inactive caption (the font color in "Inactive Title Bar").

InfoBackground

The background color in tool tips (the first color in "ToolTip").

InfoText

The text color in tool tips (the font color in "ToolTip").

Menu

The color of a menu's background (the first color in "Menu").

MenuText

The color of text found in menus (the font color in "Menu").

Scrollbar

The "gray area" of a scrollbar.

ThreeDDarkShadow

The same color as a dark shadow found on three-dimensional display elements.

ThreeDFace

The same color as the face of three-dimensional display elements.

ThreeDHighlight

The color of highlights found on three-dimensional display elements.

ThreeDLightShadow

The light color found on three-dimensional display elements (for edges facing the light source).

ThreeDShadow

The dark shadow found on three-dimensional display elements.

Window

> The color in the background of a window (the first color in "Window").

WindowFrame

> The color applied to the frame of a window.

WindowText

> The color of text in windows (the font color in "Window").

CSS2 defines the system color keywords to be case-insensitive but recommends using the mixed capitalization shown in the previous list, which makes the color names more readable. As you can see, ThreeDLightShadow is easier to understand at a glance than threedlightshadow.

An obvious drawback of the vague nature of the system color keywords is that different user agents may interpret the keywords in different ways, even if the user agents are running in the same operating system. Therefore, don't rely absolutely on consistent results when using these keywords. For example, avoid text that reads, "Look for the text whose color matches your desktop", since the user may have placed a desktop graphic (or "wallpaper") over the default desktop color.

Cursors

Another important part of the user interface is the cursor (referred to in the CSS specification as the "pointing device"), which is controlled by a device such as a mouse, trackpad, graphic tablet, or even an optical-reading system. The cursor is useful for providing interaction feedback in most web browsers; an obvious example is that the cursor changes to a small hand with an extended index finger whenever it crosses over a hyperlink.

Changing the Cursor

CSS2 lets you change the cursor icon, which means that it's much easier to create web-based applications that function in a manner similar to desktop applications in the operating system. For example, a link to help files might cause the cursor to turn into a "help" icon such as a question mark, as shown in Figure 13-2.

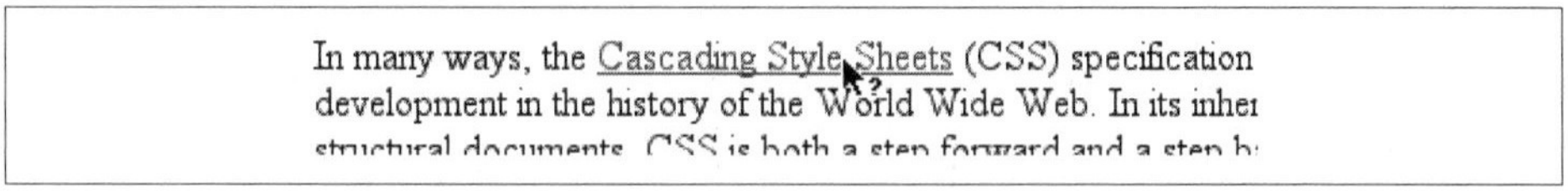

Figure 13-2. Changing the cursor's icon

This is accomplished with the property cursor.

cursor

Values:	[[<uri>,]* [auto | default | pointer | crosshair | move | e-resize | ne-resize | nw-resize | n-resize | se-resize | sw-resize | s-resize | w-resize| text | wait | help | progress]] | inherit
Initial value:	auto
Applies to:	All elements
Inherited:	Yes
Computed value:	For <uri> values, an absolute value; otherwise, as specified

The default value, auto, simply means that the user agent should determine the cursor icon that is most appropriate for the current context. This is not the same as default, which forces the icon to be the operating system's default cursor. The default cursor is usually an arrow, but it does not have to be; it depends on the current computing environment.

Pointing and selection cursors

The value pointer changes the cursor icon to be the same as when the user moves the cursor over a hyperlink. You can even describe this behavior for HTML documents:

```
a[href] {cursor: pointer;}
```

With cursor, any element can be defined to change the icon as though it were a link. This can be very confusing to the user, so I don't recommend doing it often. On the other hand (so to speak), cursor makes it much easier to create interactive, script-driven screen widgets out of non-link elements and then change the icon appropriately, as illustrated by Figure 13-3.

By Eric A. Meyer
Published by O'Reilly & Associates
ISBN 1-56592-622-6

Figure 13-3. Indicating an element's interactivity

Internet Explorer for Windows before IE6 did not recognize pointer, but instead used the value hand to invoke the "pointing hand" icon. IE6 recognizes both values. A common recommendation is to use both values in succession, like this:

```
#example {cursor: pointer; cursor: hand;}
```

This will not validate, but it will get a consistent result in newer browsers and older versions of Explorer. Note that the order is critical: you cannot reverse the values and expect this to work. See *http://developer.mozilla.org/en/docs/Giving_'cursor'_a_Hand* for more details.

The other cursor icon very common to web browsing is the text icon, which appears in situations where the user is able to select text. This is typically an "I-bar" icon, and serves as a visual cue that the user can drag-select the content under the cursor. Figure 13-4 shows a text icon at the end of some already selected text.

> In many ways, the <u>Cascading Style Sheets</u> (CSS) specification represents a unique development in the history of the World Wide Web. In its inherent ability to allow richly styled structural documents, CSS is both a step forward and a step backward—but it's a good step backward, and a needed one. To see what is meant by this, it is first necessary to understand how the Web got to the point of desperately needing something like CSS, and how CSS makes the web a better place for both page authors and web surfers.

Figure 13-4. Selectable text and the text cursor

Another way to indicate interactivity is to use the value crosshair, which changes the cursor icon into, well, a crosshair symbol. This is typically a pair of short lines at a 90-degree angle to each other, one vertical and the other horizontal, looking rather like a plus (+) sign. However, a crosshair could also resemble a multiplication sign (or a lowercase "x") or even an icon similar to the display inside a rifle scope. Crosshairs are usually used with screen-capture programs, and they can be useful in situations where the user is expected to know exactly which pixel is being clicked.

Movement cursors

In many circumstances, the value move will yield a result similar to crosshair. move is used in situations where the author needs to indicate that a screen element can be moved, and it is often rendered like a thick crosshair with arrowheads on the ends of the lines. It may also be rendered as a "gripping hand" whose fingers curl when the user clicks and holds the mouse button. Two possible move renderings are shown in Figure 13-5.

Figure 13-5. Differing icons for move

Then there are the various cursor values related to move: e-resize, ne-resize, and so on. Windows and most graphical Unix-shell users will recognize these as the icons that appear when the mouse cursor is placed over the side or corner edges of a window. For example, placing the cursor over the right side of the window will bring up an e-resize cursor, indicating that the user can drag the right side of the window back and forth to change the window size. Putting the cursor over the lower-left corner invokes the sw-resize cursor icon. There are many different ways to render these icons; Figure 13-6 shows a few of the possibilities.

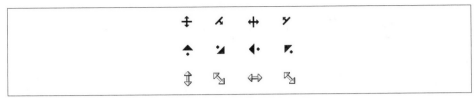

Figure 13-6. A selection of "resize" cursors

Waiting and progressing

Both wait and progress indicate that the program is busy. However, they're not identical: wait means the user should wait until the program isn't as busy, while progress indicates that the user should feel free to continue interacting with the program, even though it's busy. On most operating systems, wait is either a watch (possibly with spinning hands) or an hourglass (possibly turning itself over every so often). progress is typically represented as a spinning "beach ball" or an arrow with a small hourglass off to one side. Figure 13-7 shows some of these icons.

Figure 13-7. Waiting versus progressing

 The value progress was introduced in CSS2.1.

Providing help

In situations where the author wants to indicate that the user can get some form of help, the value help is the answer. Two very common renderings of help are a question mark and an arrow with a small question mark next to it. help can be very useful if you have classed certain links that point to more information or to information that will help the user understand the web page better. For example:

```
a.help {cursor: help;}
```

You can also use help to indicate that an element has "extra" information, such as acronym elements with title attributes. In many user agents, leaving the cursor over a titled acronym will cause the user agent to show the contents of the title attribute in a "tool tip." However, users who move the cursor around quickly, or who have slow computers, may not realize the extra information is there if the cursor didn't change. For such users, the following rule could be useful, and will lead to a result like that shown in Figure 13-8:

```
acronym[title] {cursor: help; border-bottom: 1px dotted gray;}
```

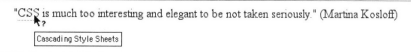

Figure 13-8. Showing that help (in the form of more information) is available

Graphic cursors

Last, but most intriguing, is the ability to call for a customized cursor. This is done using a URL value:

```
a.external {cursor: url(globe.cur), pointer;}
```

With this rule, the user agent is asked to load the file *globe.cur* and use it as the cursor icon, as illustrated in Figure 13-9.

> If you're interested in finding out more, visit the Earth Day Website for more details and schedules.

Figure 13-9. Using a custom graphic cursor

Of course, the user agent has to support the file format used to store *globe.cur*. If it does not, then it will fall back to the value pointer. Note that in the cursor syntax definition, any URL must be followed by a comma and one of the generic keywords. This is different from the property font-family, where you can call for a specific family and not provide any fallbacks. In effect, cursor requires fallbacks for any graphical cursors you might try to employ.

You can even specify multiple cursor files before the fallback keyword. For example, you might create the same basic cursor in several formats and include them all in a rule, hoping a user agent will support at least one of them:

```
a.external {cursor: url(globe.svg#globe), url(globe.cur), url(globe.png),
    url(globe.gif), url(globe.xbm), pointer;}
```

The user agent will go through the different URLs until it finds a file it can use for the cursor icon. If the user agent can't find anything it supports, it will fall back to the keyword.

 You can actually implement animated cursors if a user agent supports animated graphic files for cursor replacements. IE6, for example, supports this ability with *.ani* files.

Outlines

CSS2 introduces one last major piece of user-interface styling: outlines. An outline is sort of like a border, but there are two very important differences. First, outlines do not participate in the flow of the document like borders do, and thus don't trigger document reflow as they appear and disappear. If you give an element a 50-pixel outline, the outline will very likely overlap other elements. Second, outlines can be nonrectangular—but don't start leaping for joy just yet. This does not mean that you can create circular outlines. Instead, it means that an outline on an inline element may not act like a border would on that same element. With an outline, a user agent is allowed to "merge" the pieces of the outline to create a single continuous, but nonrectangular, shape. Figure 13-10 shows an example.

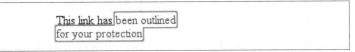

Figure 13-10. Outlines can have irregular shapes

User agents are not required to support nonrectangular outlines. They could instead format outlines on inline nonreplaced elements the same way they do borders. A conforming user agent must, however, make sure that outlines do not take up layout space.

There is one other basic way in which outlines and borders differ: they aren't the same thing, so they can both exist on the same element. This can lead to some interesting effects, such as that illustrated in Figure 13-11.

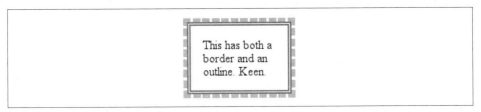

Figure 13-11. The coexistence of borders and outlines

The CSS2 specification states the following: "The outline may be drawn starting just outside the border edge." Note the word *may* in that sentence. User agents are encouraged to do as the sentence suggests, but it isn't a requirement. A user agent could decide to draw outlines inside the inner border edge or at some small distance from the border. As of this writing, all browsers that support outlines draw them just outside the outer border edge, so, thankfully, there is consistency.

Outlines are considered to be part of user-interface styling because they are most often used to indicate the current focus. If a user is using keyboard navigation to jump from link to link, then the link that is currently in focus will usually get an outline. In Internet Explorer for Windows, an outline is applied to any link that has been selected by the user ("clicked," if she's using a mouse), and tends to persist even when it isn't wanted. Other browsers apply outlines to text inputs that have the keyboard focus, thus giving a cue to where input will go if the user starts typing.

As you'll see, outlines are styled a lot like borders, but there are some key differences besides the ones previously mentioned. We'll just skip quickly over the similarities and spend time looking at the differences.

Setting an Outline's Style

As with a border, the most basic aspect of an outline is its style, which is set using outline-style.

<table>
<tr><td colspan="2" align="center">outline-style</td></tr>
<tr><td>Values:</td><td>none | dotted | dashed | solid | double | groove | ridge | inset | outset | inherit</td></tr>
<tr><td>Initial value:</td><td>none</td></tr>
<tr><td>Applies to:</td><td>All elements</td></tr>
<tr><td>Inherited:</td><td>No</td></tr>
<tr><td>Computed value:</td><td>As specified</td></tr>
</table>

The list of style keywords is largely the same as the keywords for border styles, and the visual effects are the same. There is one omission: hidden is not a valid outline style, and user agents are required to effectively treat it as none. This actually makes sense, given that outlines don't affect layout even when they're visible.

The other difference between outlines and borders is that you can specify only one keyword for an outline-style value (compared with up to four keywords for borders). The practical effect is that outlines must have the same outline style all the way around an element, whether they're rectangular or not. This is probably just as well, since trying to figure out how to apply different styles to the same nonrectangular outline would be a pain.

Outline Width

Once you've brought an outline into being by giving it a style, it's a good idea to use outline-width to define (you guessed it) the outline's width.

<table>
<tr><td colspan="2" align="center">outline-width</td></tr>
<tr><td>Values:</td><td>thin | medium | thick | <length> | inherit</td></tr>
<tr><td>Initial value:</td><td>medium</td></tr>
<tr><td>Applies to:</td><td>All elements</td></tr>
<tr><td>Inherited:</td><td>No</td></tr>
<tr><td>Computed value:</td><td>Absolute length; 0 if the style of the border is none or hidden</td></tr>
</table>

The list of keywords should look very familiar to anyone who's set a border width. The only real difference between outline-width and border-width is that, as with the style, you can declare only a single width for the entire outline. Thus, only one keyword is permitted in a value.

Coloring an Outline

Since you can set style and width, it makes sense that outline-color exists to let you give the outline a color.

---

outline-color

Values:	<color> | invert | inherit
Initial value:	invert (or user agent-specific; see text)
Applies to:	All elements
Inherited:	No
Computed value:	As specified

Herein lies the most intriguing difference between borders and outlines: the keyword invert, which is the default value. An inverting outline means that a color inversion is performed for the pixels where the outline exists. See Figure 13-12.

Figure 13-12. Inverting color with an outline

The process of color-inverting pixels "behind" the outline ensures that no matter what appears behind the outline, it will be visible. If a user agent can't support color inversion for some reason, it should use instead the computed value of color for the element.

The ability to invert pixels on screen is very interesting, especially since there's no theoretical limit on the width of an outline. So you could, should you choose, use an outline to invert large portions of your document. This isn't really the purpose of outlines, but Figure 13-13 shows one such result anyway.

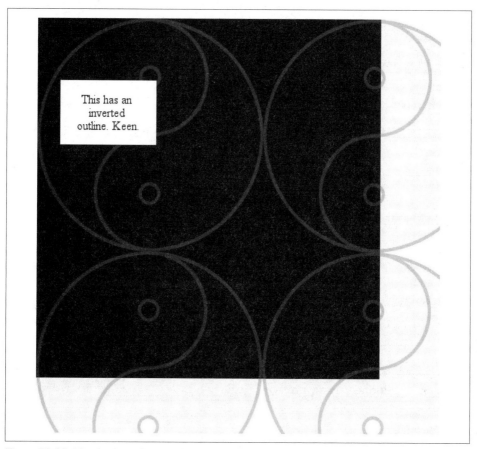

Figure 13-13. Massive inversion

Of course, if you'd rather define a specific color for your outline, just use any valid color value. The results of the following declarations should be obvious enough:

```
outline-color: red;
outline-color: #000;
outline-color: rgb(50%,50%,50%);
```

The potential drawback here is the possibility that an outline color could closely match the colors of the pixels around it, in which case the user won't be able to see it. This is why `invert` was defined.

As with outline styles and widths, you can define only one color for the entire outline.

Bringing It All Together

Like `border` for borders, `outline` is the shorthand property that allows you to set the style, width, and color of an outline all at once.

outline

Values:	[<outline-color> || <outline-style> || <outline-width>] | inherit
Initial value:	Not defined for shorthand properties
Applies to:	All elements
Inherited:	No
Computed value:	See individual properties (outline-color, etc.)

As with other shorthands, outline brings together several properties into a compact notation. It's subject to the same behaviors as other shorthand notations, which override previously defined values. Therefore, in the following example, the outline will use the color keyword invert since it's implied by the second declaration:

```
a:focus {outline-color: red; outline: thick solid;}
```

Because a given outline must be of a uniform style, width, and color, outline is the only shorthand property related to outlines. There are no properties such as outline-top or outline-right.

In cases where you want to simulate an inversion border, you can set an outline with a length value for its width, and set the element's margin to an equal or greater width. Since the outline is drawn "on top" of the margin, it will fill in some of that space, as illustrated in Figure 13-14:

```
div#callbox {outline: 5px solid invert; margin: 5px;}
input:focus {outline: 1em double gray;}
```

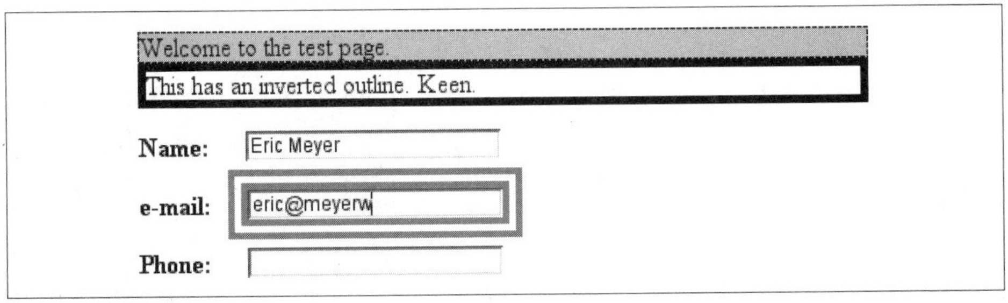

Figure 13-14. Different outlines

As I mentioned earlier, outlines do not participate in the document's flow. This prevents forced reflow in cases like link-focus outlines, which will move from link to link as the focus changes. If an author uses borders to indicate the focus, the document layout may shift or jump around. Outlines can yield the same effects borders allow, but without the jumpiness.

Outlines can accomplish this because they are, by definition, drawn above the rest of the element's box. Since outlines cannot overlap visible portions of their element's box in CSS2, but can overlap only the margins (which are transparent), this is not a big issue. If a future version of CSS allows outlines to move inward to overlap the borders or other visible portions of the element box, then the placement of outlines will become more important.

The one area of unfortunate vagueness in CSS2 is that it explicitly avoids defining the behaviors of two outlines overlapping each other and what happens to outlines on elements that are partially obscured by other elements. You can combine both of these in a single example:

```
div#one {outline: 1em solid invert;}
div#two {outline: 1em solid invert; margin: -2em -2em 0 2em;
  background: white;}
```

Now suppose div#two immediately follows div#one in a document. It will overlap the first div, and its background will overlap portions of the first div's outline. I haven't included a figure to accompany this code block because the CSS2 specification doesn't provide any ideas about what would happen. Should the first div's outline be visible, overlapping the background and contents of the second div? There will also be places where the two inversion outlines intersect; what should happen there? Are the pixels double-inverted, and thus restored to their original state? Or should the pixels be inverted once and then left unchanged? We don't know. Any illustration here would be neither right nor wrong, but simply a possible outcome—and not necessarily the one that user agents end up implementing or that a future version of CSS defines.

Summary

Thanks to user interface styles, it's possible for an author to make a document look more like the user's computing environment, especially with a creative use of system color and fonts. By reusing things with which the user is already familiar, a document can seem more familiar and user-friendly from the outset.

Another way to make users' lives a little easier is to create style sheets that are targeted at media other than their monitors. This would include styles intended specifically for printing, aural (spoken) access of a web page, and even for a projection-screen environment. We'll cover all of those in the next chapter.

CHAPTER 14

Non-Screen Media

Not everyone who accesses the Web can see the effects we've discussed in this book. Some 1.1 million people in the United States are blind, and they have a very different experience of the Web than sighted persons.

Fortunately, CSS is not silent on the matter of non-visual access. CSS2 included the ability to apply styles in non-screen media. While most of the Web's evolution has taken place on monitors—that is to say, in a visual medium—CSS2 can be used in non-visual media, assuming that the user agent has proper support.

The advantages of designing documents that are at once visually and non-visually usable should not be dismissed. If you can take one document and use different, medium-specific style sheets to restyle it for screen, print, and aural rendering, you can save yourself a whole lot of trouble. For example, you wouldn't need to link to "printer-friendly" versions of a page. Instead of creating totally different markup structures, one for screen and another for print, you can make your site more efficient by reusing the same document.

For that matter, it's possible to take a single HTML document that contains the outline of a slideshow and style it for easy reading on a screen, for clean and readable printouts, as a slideshow, and in a manner that a screen reader can translate. In the course of this chapter, we'll look at ways to do the latter three (since the rest of the book concerns itself with screen presentation).

Designating Medium-Specific Style Sheets

You can restrict any kind of style sheet to a specific medium, thanks to the mechanisms defined in HTML and CSS. For HTML-based style sheets, you can impose medium restrictions through the `media` attribute. This works the same for both the `link` and `style` elements:

```
<link rel="stylesheet" type="text/css" media="print"
   href="article-print.css">
```

```
<style type="text/css" media="projection">
body {font-family: sans-serif;}
</style>
```

The media attribute can accept a single medium value or a comma-separated list of values. Thus, to link in a style sheet that should be used in only the screen and projection media, you would write:

```
<link rel="stylesheet" type="text/css" media="screen, projection"
    href="visual.css">
```

In a style sheet itself, you can also impose medium restrictions on @import rules:

```
@import url(visual.css) screen, projection;
@import url(article-print.css) print;
```

Remember that if you don't add medium information to a style sheet, it will be applied in *all* media. Therefore, if you want one set of styles to apply only onscreen, and another to apply only in print, then you need to add medium information to both style sheets. For example:

```
<link rel="stylesheet" type="text/css" media="screen"
    href="article-screen.css">
<link rel="stylesheet" type="text/css" media="print"
    href="article-print.css">
```

If you were to remove the media attribute from the first link element in the preceding example, the rules found in the style sheet *article-screen.css* would be applied in all media, including print, projection, handheld, and everything else.

CSS2 also defines syntax for @media blocks, which lets you define styles for multiple media within the same style sheet. Consider this basic example:

```
<style type="text/css">
body {background: white; color: black;}
@media screen {
    body {font-family: sans-serif;}
    h1 {margin-top: 1em;}
}
@media print {
    body {font-family: serif;}
    h1 {margin-top: 2em; border-bottom: 1px solid silver;}
}
</style>
```

Here you see that in all media, the body element is given a white background and a black foreground. Then a block of rules is provided for the screen medium alone, followed by another block of rules that applies only in the print medium.

@media blocks can be any size and contain any number of rules. In situations where authors may have control over a single style sheet, @media blocks may be the only way to define medium-specific styles. This is also the case in situations where CSS is used to style a document using an XML language that does not contain a media attribute or its equivalent.

Paged Media

In CSS terms, a *paged medium* is any medium where a document's presentation is handled as a series of discrete "pages." This is different from the screen, which is a *continuous medium*: documents are presented as a single, scrollable "page." An analog example of a continuous medium is a papyrus scroll. Printed material, such as books, magazines, and laser printouts, are all paged media. So are slideshows, where a series of slides is shown one at a time. Each slide is a "page" in CSS terms.

Print Styles

Even in the "paperless future," the most commonly encountered paged medium is a printout of some document—a web page, a word-processing document, a spreadsheet, or something else that has been committed to the thin wafers of a dead tree. Authors can do a number of things to make printouts of their documents more pleasing for the user, from affecting page breaking to creating styles meant specifically for print.

Note that print styles would also be applied to document display in a "print preview" mode. Thus, it's possible in some circumstances to see print styles on a monitor.

Differences between screen and print

Beyond the obvious physical differences, there are a number of stylistic differences between screen and print design. The most basic involves font choices. Most designers will tell you that sans-serif fonts are best suited for screen design, but serif fonts are more readable in print. Thus, you might set up a print style sheet that uses Times instead of Verdana for the text in your document.

Another major difference involves font sizing. If you've spent any time at all doing web design, you've probably heard again and again (and again) that points are a horrible choice for font sizing on the Web. This is basically true, especially if you want your text to be consistently sized between browsers and operating systems. However, print design is not web design any more than web design is print design. Using points, or even centimeters or picas, is perfectly OK in print design because printing devices know the physical size of their output area. If a printer has been loaded with 8.5×11 paper, then it knows it has a printing area that will fit within the edges of that piece of paper. It also knows how many dots there are in an inch, since it knows how many dots-per-inch (dpi) it's capable of generating. This means that it can cope with physical-world length units like points.

Therefore, many a print style sheet has started with:

```
body {font: 12pt "Times New Roman", "TimesNR", Times, serif;}
```

It's so traditional, it just might bring a tear of joy to the eye of a graphic designer reading over your shoulder. But make sure he understands that points are acceptable only because of the nature of the print medium—they're still not good for web design.

Alternatively, the lack of backgrounds in most printouts might bring a tear of frustration to that designer's eye. To save users ink, most web browsers are preconfigured not to print background colors and images. If the user wants to see those backgrounds in the printout, she must change an option somewhere in the preferences. CSS can't do anything to force the printing of backgrounds. However, you can use a print style sheet to make backgrounds unnecessary. For example, you might include this rule in your print style sheet:

```
* {color: black !important; background: white !important;}
```

This will ensure that all of your elements will print out as black text and remove any backgrounds you might have assigned in an all-medium style sheet. Since this is how most users' printers will render the page anyway, you're better off setting up your print styles along the same lines. If you have a web design that puts yellow text on a dark gray background, this rule also makes sure that a user with a color printer won't get yellow text on a white piece of paper.

 CSS2.x does not include a mechanism for picking a style sheet based on the user's output device. Thus, all printers will use the print style sheets you define. The CSS3 Media Queries module defines ways to send a different style sheet to color printers than to grayscale printers, but as of this writing, support for media queries is basically nonexistent.

One other difference between paged media and continuous media is that multicolumn layouts are even harder to use in paged media. Suppose you have an article where the text has been formatted as two columns. In a printout, the left side of each page will contain the first column, and the right side the second. This would force the user to read the left side of every page, then go back to the beginning of the printout and read the right side of every page. This is annoying enough on the Web, but on paper it's much worse.

The obvious solution is to use CSS for laying out your two columns (by floating them, perhaps) and then writing a print style sheet that restores the content to a single column. Thus, you might write something like this for the screen style sheet:

```
div#leftcol {float: left; width: 45%;}
div#rightcol {float: right; width: 45%;}
```

Then in your print style sheet, you would write:

```
div#leftcol, div#rightcol {float: none; width: auto;}
```

If CSS had a way to do multicolumn flowed layout, none of this would be necessary. Sadly, although proposals have circulated for years, there is nothing offered as of this writing.

We could spend an entire chapter on the details of print design, but that really isn't the purpose of this book. Let's start exploring the details of paged-media CSS and leave the design discussions for another book.

Defining the page size

In much the same way as it defines the element box, CSS2 defines a *page box* that describes the components of a page. A page box is composed of basically two regions:

- The *page area*, which is the portion of the page where the content is laid out. This is roughly analogous to the content area of a normal element box, to the extent that the edges of the page area act as the initial containing block for layout within a page. (See Chapter 7 for details on containing blocks.)
- The *margin area*, which surrounds the page area.

The page box model is illustrated in Figure 14-1.

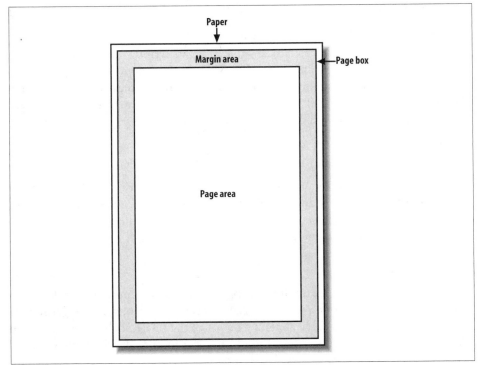

Figure 14-1. The page box

In CSS2, it was possible to define the size of the page box as well as the margins. In CSS2.1, authors can set only the size of the margin area. In both cases, the @page rule is the method by which settings are made. Here's a simple example:

```
@page {size: 7.5in 10in; margin: 0.5in;}
```

This is a CSS2 rule, as it uses the property size, which was not included in CSS2.1 due to a lack of implementation support.

size

Values:	<length>{1,2} | auto | portrait | landscape | inherit
Initial value:	auto
Applies to:	The page area
Inherited:	No

This property is used to define the size of the page area. The value landscape causes the layout to be rotated 90 degrees, whereas portrait is the normal orientation for Western-language printing. Thus, an author could cause a document to be printed "sideways" by declaring:

```
@page {size: landscape;}
```

size is not part of CSS2.1, which means that, as of its writing, no two interoperable implementations of size are known to exist. So, browser support is likely to be poor. CSS2.1 does include the ability to style the margin area of the page box, which is likely to work more reliably. If you want to make sure that only a small bit at the center of every 8.5×11 page would print, you could write:

```
@page {margin: 3.75in;}
```

This would leave a printing area one inch wide by three and a half inches tall.

What's really interesting about the page box is that it doesn't have any relationship to fonts, so you can't use the length units em and ex to describe either the margin area or the page area. Only percentages and "ruler" units like inches, centimeters, or points are permitted in this context.

Selecting page types

CSS2 offers the ability to create different page types using named @page rules. Let's say you have a document on astronomy that is several pages long, and in the middle of it, there is a fairly wide table containing a list of the physical characteristics of all the moons of Saturn. You want to print out the text in portrait mode, but the table needs to be landscape. Here's how you'd start:

```
@page normal {size: portrait; margin: 1in;}
@page rotate {size: landscape; margin: 0.5in;}
```

Now you just need to apply these page types as needed. The table of Saturn's moons has an id of moon-data, so you write the following rules:

```
body {page: normal;}
table#moon-data {page: rotate;}
```

This would cause the table to be printed in landscape mode, but the rest of the document to be printed in portrait orientation. The property page, another outcast in CSS2.1, makes this possible.

Values:	<identifier> | inherit
Initial value:	auto
Applies to:	Block-level elements
Inherited:	Yes

As you can see from looking at the value definition, the whole reason page exists is to let you assign named page types to various elements in your document.

There are more generic page types that you can address through special pseudo-classes, and even better, this is one defined in both CSS2 and CSS2.1. :first lets you apply special styles to the first page in the document. For example, you might want to give the first page a larger top margin than other pages. Here's how:

```
@page {margin: 3cm;}
@page :first {margin-top: 6cm;}
```

This will yield a three-centimeter margin on all pages, with the exception of a six-centimeter top margin on the first page. The effect will be something like that shown in Figure 14-2.

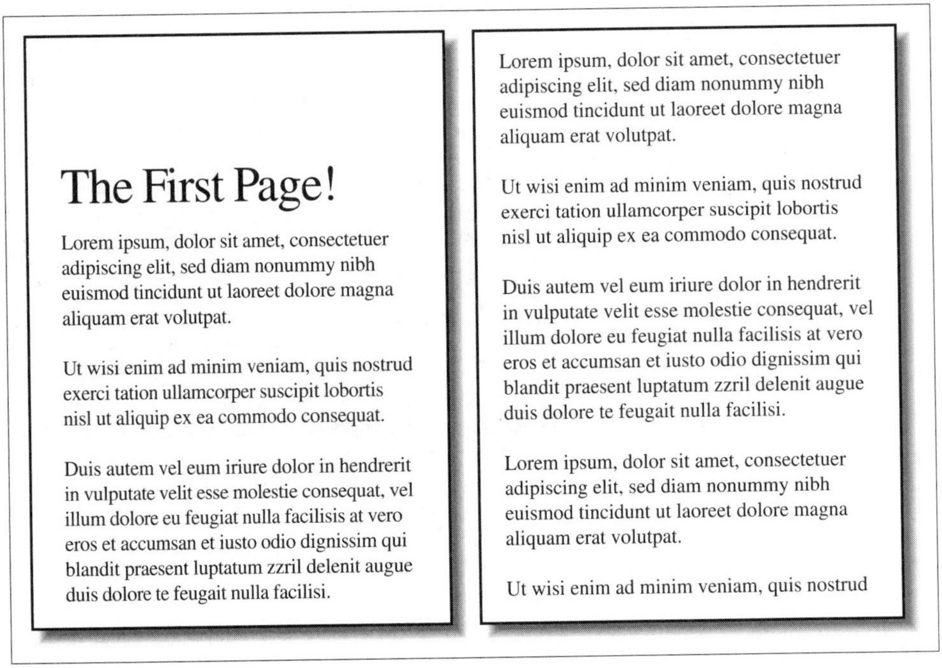

The First Page!

Lorem ipsum, dolor sit amet, consectetuer adipiscing elit, sed diam nonummy nibh euismod tincidunt ut laoreet dolore magna aliquam erat volutpat.

Ut wisi enim ad minim veniam, quis nostrud exerci tation ullamcorper suscipit lobortis nisl ut aliquip ex ea commodo consequat.

Duis autem vel eum iriure dolor in hendrerit in vulputate velit esse molestie consequat, vel illum dolore eu feugiat nulla facilisis at vero eros et accumsan et iusto odio dignissim qui blandit praesent luptatum zzril delenit augue duis dolore te feugait nulla facilisi.

Lorem ipsum, dolor sit amet, consectetuer adipiscing elit, sed diam nonummy nibh euismod tincidunt ut laoreet dolore magna aliquam erat volutpat.

Ut wisi enim ad minim veniam, quis nostrud exerci tation ullamcorper suscipit lobortis nisl ut aliquip ex ea commodo consequat.

Duis autem vel eum iriure dolor in hendrerit in vulputate velit esse molestie consequat, vel illum dolore eu feugiat nulla facilisis at vero eros et accumsan et iusto odio dignissim qui blandit praesent luptatum zzril delenit augue duis dolore te feugait nulla facilisi.

Lorem ipsum, dolor sit amet, consectetuer adipiscing elit, sed diam nonummy nibh euismod tincidunt ut laoreet dolore magna aliquam erat volutpat.

Ut wisi enim ad minim veniam, quis nostrud

Figure 14-2. Specially styling the first page

In addition to styling the first page, you can also style left and right pages, emulating the pages to the left and right of a book's spine. You can style these differently using :left and :right. For example:

```
@page :left {margin-left: 3cm; margin-right: 5cm;}
@page :right {margin-left: 5cm; margin-right: 3cm;}
```

These rules will have the effect of putting larger margins "between" the content of the left and right pages, on the sides where the spine of a book would be. This is a common practice when pages will be bound together into a book of some type. You can see the result of the previous rules in Figure 14-3.

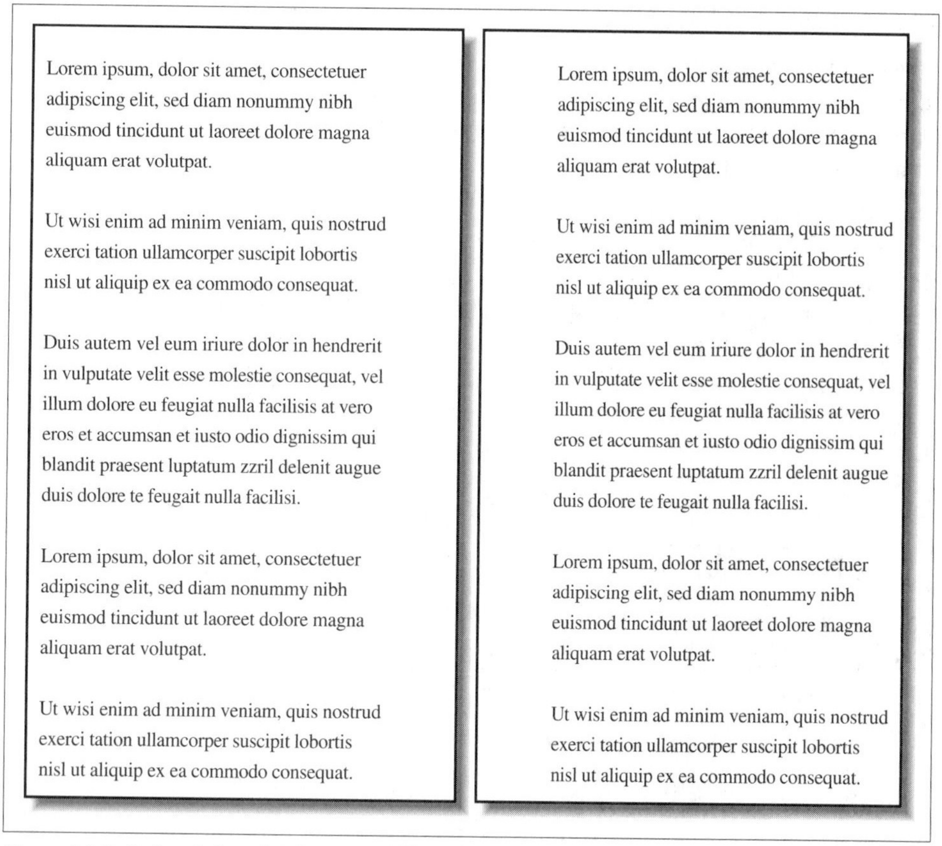

Lorem ipsum, dolor sit amet, consectetuer adipiscing elit, sed diam nonummy nibh euismod tincidunt ut laoreet dolore magna aliquam erat volutpat.

Ut wisi enim ad minim veniam, quis nostrud exerci tation ullamcorper suscipit lobortis nisl ut aliquip ex ea commodo consequat.

Duis autem vel eum iriure dolor in hendrerit in vulputate velit esse molestie consequat, vel illum dolore eu feugiat nulla facilisis at vero eros et accumsan et iusto odio dignissim qui blandit praesent luptatum zzril delenit augue duis dolore te feugait nulla facilisi.

Lorem ipsum, dolor sit amet, consectetuer adipiscing elit, sed diam nonummy nibh euismod tincidunt ut laoreet dolore magna aliquam erat volutpat.

Ut wisi enim ad minim veniam, quis nostrud exerci tation ullamcorper suscipit lobortis nisl ut aliquip ex ea commodo consequat.

Lorem ipsum, dolor sit amet, consectetuer adipiscing elit, sed diam nonummy nibh euismod tincidunt ut laoreet dolore magna aliquam erat volutpat.

Ut wisi enim ad minim veniam, quis nostrud exerci tation ullamcorper suscipit lobortis nisl ut aliquip ex ea commodo consequat.

Duis autem vel eum iriure dolor in hendrerit in vulputate velit esse molestie consequat, vel illum dolore eu feugiat nulla facilisis at vero eros et accumsan et iusto odio dignissim qui blandit praesent luptatum zzril delenit augue duis dolore te feugait nulla facilisi.

Lorem ipsum, dolor sit amet, consectetuer adipiscing elit, sed diam nonummy nibh euismod tincidunt ut laoreet dolore magna aliquam erat volutpat.

Ut wisi enim ad minim veniam, quis nostrud exerci tation ullamcorper suscipit lobortis nisl ut aliquip ex ea commodo consequat.

Figure 14-3. Styling left and right pages differently

Page breaking

In a paged medium, it's a good idea to exert some influence over how page breaks are placed. You can affect page breaking using the properties page-break-before and page-break-after, both of which accept the same set of values.

page-break-before, page-break-after

Values:	auto | always | avoid | left | right | inherit
Initial value:	auto
Applies to:	Nonfloated block-level elements with a position value of relative or static
Inherited:	No
Computed value:	As specified

The default value of auto simply means that a page break is not forced to come before or after an element. This is the same as any normal printout. always causes a page break to be placed before (or after) the styled element.

For example, assume you have a situation where the page title is an h1 element, and the section titles are all h2 elements. You might want a page break right before the beginning of each section of a document and after the document title. This would result in the following rules, illustrated in Figure 14-4:

```
h1 {page-break-after: always;}
h2 {page-break-before: always;}
```

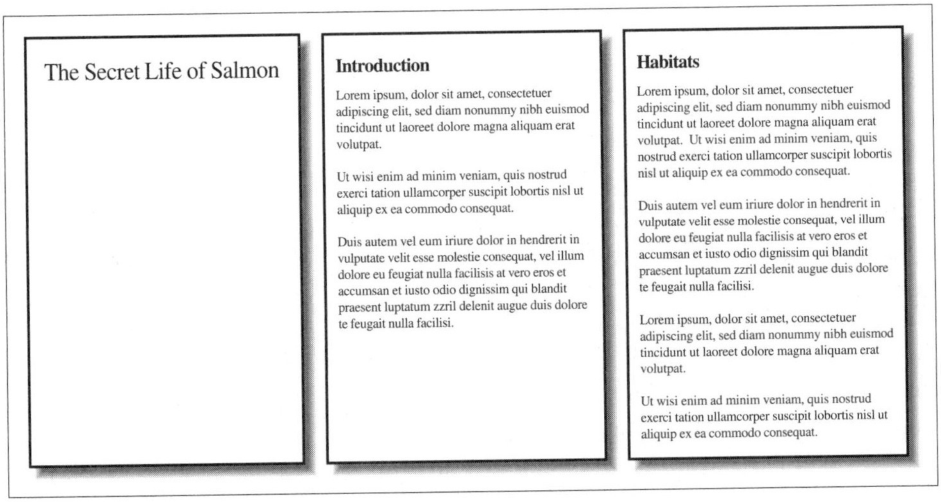

Figure 14-4. Inserting page breaks

If you want the document title to be centered in its page, of course, you would add rules to that effect. Since you don't, you just get a very straightforward rendering of each page.

The values left and right operate in the same manner as always, except they further define the type of page on which printing can resume. Consider the following:

```
h2 {page-break-before: left;}
```

This will force every h2 element to be preceded by enough page breaks so that the h2 will be printed at the top of a left page—that is, a page surface that would appear to the left of a spine if the output were bound. In double-sided printing, this would mean printing on the "back" of a piece of paper.

So let's assume that, in printing, the element just before an h2 is printed on a right page. The previous rule would cause a single page break to be inserted before the h2, thus pushing it to the next page. If the next h2 is preceded by an element on a left page, however, the h2 would be preceded by two page breaks, thus placing it at the top of the next left page. The right page between the two would be intentionally left blank. The value right has the same basic effect, except it forces an element to be printed at the top of a right page, preceded by either one or two page breaks.

The companion to always is avoid, which directs the user agent to do its best to avoid placing a page break either before or after an element. To extend the previous example, suppose you have subsections whose titles are h3 elements. You want to keep these titles together with the text that follows them, so you want to avoid a page break following an h3 whenever possible:

```
h3 {page-break-after: avoid;}
```

Note, though, that the value is called avoid, not never. There is no way to absolutely guarantee that a page break will never be inserted before or after a given element. Consider the following:

```
img {height: 9.5in; width: 8in; page-break-before: avoid;}
h4 {page-break-after: avoid;}
h4 + img {height: 10.5in;}
```

Now, suppose further that you have a situation where an h4 is placed between two images, and its height calculates to half an inch. Each image will have to be printed on a separate page, but there are only two places the h4 can go: at the bottom of the page holding the first element, or on the page after it. If it's placed after the first image, then it must be followed by a page break, since there's no room for the second image to follow it, as shown in Figure 14-5.

On the other hand, if the h4 is placed on a new page following the first image, there won't be room on that same page for the second image. So, again, there will be a page break after the h4. And, in either case, at least one image, if not both, will be preceded by a page break. There's only so much the user agent can do, given a situation like this one.

Obviously, situations such as these are rare, but they can happen—for example, in a case where a document contains nothing but tables preceded by headings. There may be cases where tables print in such a way that they force a heading element to be

Figure 14-5. Necessary page breaking

followed by a page break, even though the author requested that such break placement be avoided.

The same sorts of issues can arise with the other page-break property, `page-break-inside`. Its possible values are more limited than those of its cousins.

---

page-break-inside

Values:	`auto` | `avoid` | `inherit`
Initial value:	`auto`
Applies to:	Nonfloated block-level elements with a `position` value of `relative` or `static`
Inherited:	Yes
Computed value:	As specified

With `page-break-inside`, you pretty much have one option other than the default: you can request that a user agent try to avoid placing page breaks within an element. If you have a series of "aside" divisions, and you don't want them broken across two pages, you could declare:

```
div.aside {page-break-inside: avoid;}
```

Again, this is a suggestion more than an actual rule. If an aside turns out to be longer than a page, obviously the user agent can't help but place a page break inside the element.

Orphans and widows

In an effort to provide finer influence over page breaking, CSS2 defines two properties common to both traditional print typography and desktop publishing: widows and orphans.

---

widows, orphans

Values:	\<integer\> | inherit
Initial value:	2
Applies to:	Block-level elements
Inherited:	Yes
Computed value:	As specified

These properties have similar aims but approach them from different angles. The value of widows defines the minimum number of line boxes found in an element that can be placed at the top of a page without forcing a page break to come before the element. orphans has the same effect in reverse: it gives the minimum number of line boxes that can appear at the bottom of a page without forcing a page break before the element.

Let's take widows as an example. Suppose you declare:

```
p {widows: 4;}
```

This means that any paragraph can have no fewer than four line boxes appear at the top of a page. If the layout of the document would lead to fewer line boxes, then the entire paragraph is placed at the top of the page. Consider the situation shown in Figure 14-6. Cover up the top part of the figure with your hand, so only the second page is visible. Notice that there are two line boxes there, from the end of a paragraph that started on the previous page. Given the default widows value of 2, this is an acceptable rendering. However, if the value were 3 or higher, the entire paragraph would appear at the top of the second page as a single block. This would require that a page break be inserted before the paragraph in question.

Look again at Figure 14-6, but this time cover up the second page with your hand. Notice the four line boxes at the bottom of the page, at the beginning of the last paragraph. This is fine as long as the value of orphans is 4 or less. If it were 5 or higher, the paragraph would again be preceded by a page break and be laid out as a single block at the top of the second page.

Of course, both orphans and widows must be satisfied. If an author declared the following, most paragraphs would be without an interior page break:

```
p {widows: 30; orphans: 30;}
```

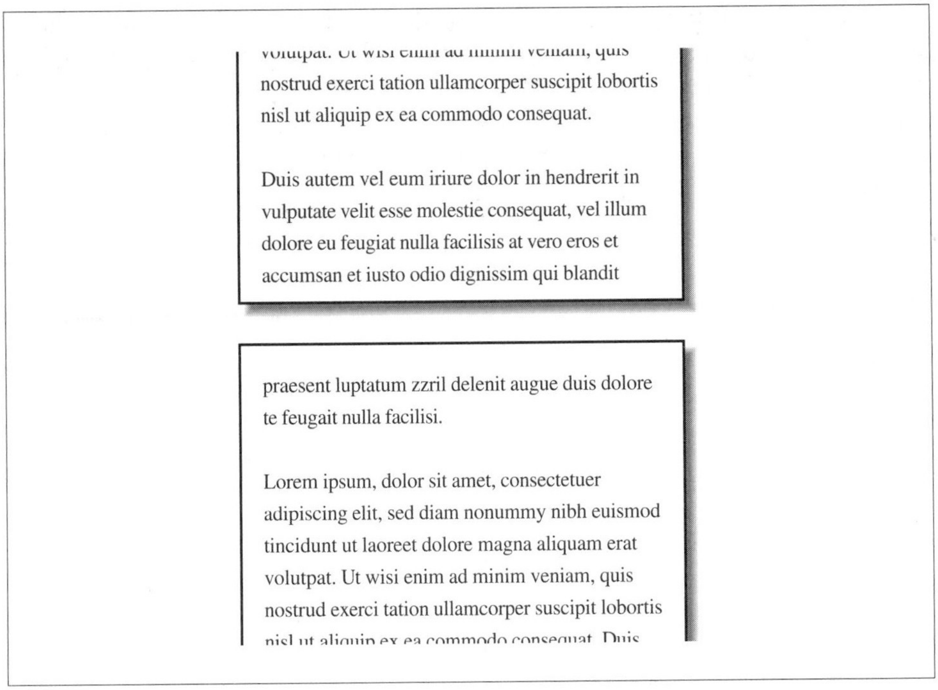

Figure 14-6. Counting the widows

It would take a pretty lengthy paragraph to allow an interior page break given those values. Of course, if the intent is to prevent interior breaking, it would be better expressed as:

```
p {page-break-inside: avoid;}
```

Page-breaking behavior

Because CSS2 allows for some odd page-breaking styles, it defines a set of behaviors regarding allowed page breaks and "best" page breaks. These behaviors guide user agents in how they should handle page breaking in various circumstances.

There are really only two generic places where page breaks are permitted. The first of these is between two block-level boxes. If a page break falls between two block boxes, then the `margin-bottom` value of the element before the page break is reset to 0, as is the `margin-top` of the element following the page break. However, there are two rules that allow a page break to fall between two element boxes:

- If the value of `page-break-after` for the first element—or the value of `page-break-before` for the second element—is always, `left`, or `right`. This is true regardless of the value for theother element, even if it's avoid. (This is a *forced* page break.)
- If the value of the first element's `page-break-after` value is auto, and the same is true for the second element's `page-break-before` value, and if they do not share an ancestor element whose `page-break-inside` value is not avoid.

Figure 14-7 illustrates all of the possible page-break placements between elements in a hypothetical document. Forced page breaks are represented as a filled square, whereas potential (unforced) page breaks are shown as an open square.

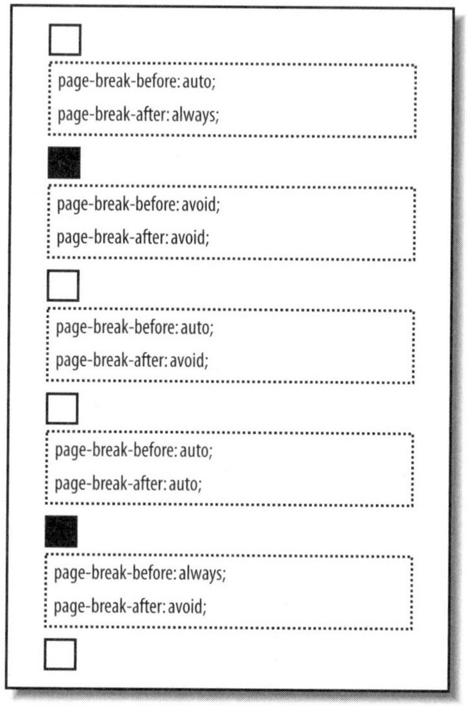

Figure 14-7. Potential page-break placement between block boxes

The second generic place where page breaks are allowed is between two line boxes inside a block-level box. This, too, is governed by a pair of rules:

- A page break may appear between two line boxes only if the number of line boxes between the start of the element and the line box before the page break would be less than the value of orphans for the element. Similarly, a page break can be placed only where the number of line boxes between the line box after the page break and the end of the element is less than the value of widows.

- A page break can be placed between line boxes if the value of page-break-inside for the element is not avoid.

In both cases, the second of the two rules controlling page-break placement is ignored if no page-break placement can satisfy all the rules. Thus, given a situation where an element has been given page-break-inside: avoid but is longer than a full page, a page break is permitted inside the element, between two line boxes. In other words, the second rule regarding page-break placement between line boxes is ignored.

If ignoring the second rule in each pair of rules still does not yield good page-break placement, other rules can also be ignored. In such a situation, the user agent is likely to ignore all page-break property values and proceed as if they were all auto, although this approach is not defined (or required) by the CSS specification.

In addition to the previously explored rules, CSS2 defines a set of "best" page-breaking behaviors:

- Break as few times as possible.
- Make all pages that don't end with a forced break appear to have about the same height.
- Avoid breaking inside a block that has a border.
- Avoid breaking inside a table.
- Avoid breaking inside a floated element.

These recommendations aren't required of user agents, but they offer logical guidance that should promote ideal page-breaking behaviors.

Repeated elements

A very common desire among authors of paged media is the ability to have a *running head*. This is an element that appears on every page, such as the document's title or the author's name. You can specify a running head in CSS2 by using a fixed-position element. For example:

```
div#runhead {position: fixed; top: 0; right: 0;}
```

This will place any div with an id of runhead at the top-right corner of every page box when the document is output to a paged medium. The same rule would place the element in the top-right corner of the viewport in a continuous medium, such as a web browser. Any element positioned in this way will appear on every page. It is not possible to "copy" an element to become a repeated element. Thus, given the following, the h1 element will appear as a running head on every page, including the first one:

```
h1 {position: fixed; top: 0; width: 100%; text-align: center;
    font-size: 80%; border-bottom: 1px solid gray;}
```

The drawback is that the h1 element, being positioned on the first page, cannot be printed as anything except the running head.

Elements outside the page

All of this talk about positioning elements in a paged medium leads to an interesting question: what happens if an element is positioned outside the page box? You don't even need positioning to create such a situation. Think about a pre element that contains a line with 411 characters. This is likely to be wider than any standard piece of paper, so the element will be wider than the page box. What happens then?

As it turns out, CSS2 doesn't say exactly what user agents should do, so it's up to them to come up with a solution. For a very wide pre element, the user agent might simply clip the element to the page box and throw away the rest of the content. It could also generate extra pages to display the "leftover" part of the element.

There are a few general recommendations for handling content outside the page box, two of which are really important. First, content should be allowed to protrude slightly from a page box to allow "bleeding." This implies that no extra page would be generated for the portions of such content that exceed the page box.

Second, user agents are cautioned not to generate large numbers of empty pages for the sole purpose of honoring positioning information. Consider:

```
h1 {position: absolute; top: 1500in;}
```

Assuming that the page boxes are 10 inches high, the user agent would have to precede an h1 with 150 page breaks (and thus 150 blank pages) just to honor that rule. Instead, a user agent might choose to skip the blank pages and only output the last one, which actually contains the h1 element.

The other two recommendations state that user agents should not position elements in strange places just to avoid rendering them, and that content placed outside a page box can be rendered in any number of ways. (Some elements of CSS are useful and intriguing, but some seem to cheerily state the obvious.)

Projection Styles

Aside from printed pages, the other common paged medium is *projection*, which describes information that's being projected onto a large screen, suitable for viewing by a large crowd. Microsoft PowerPoint is one of the best-known projection-medium editors today.

As of this writing, only one user agent supports projection-medium CSS: Opera for Windows. This capability is called "OperaShow," and it allows authors to take any HTML document and turn it into a slideshow. We'll look at the basics of this capability, since it may appear in other user agents in the future, and it provides an interesting view of how CSS can be used in media other than screen or print.

Setting up slides

If you're breaking up a single document into a series of slides, you need a way to define the boundaries between each slide. This is done using the page-break properties. Whether you use page-break-before or page-break-after will depend largely on how your document is constructed.

As an example, consider the HTML document shown in Figure 14-8. There is a series of h2 elements, each followed by an unordered list. This forms the "outline view" for your slideshow.

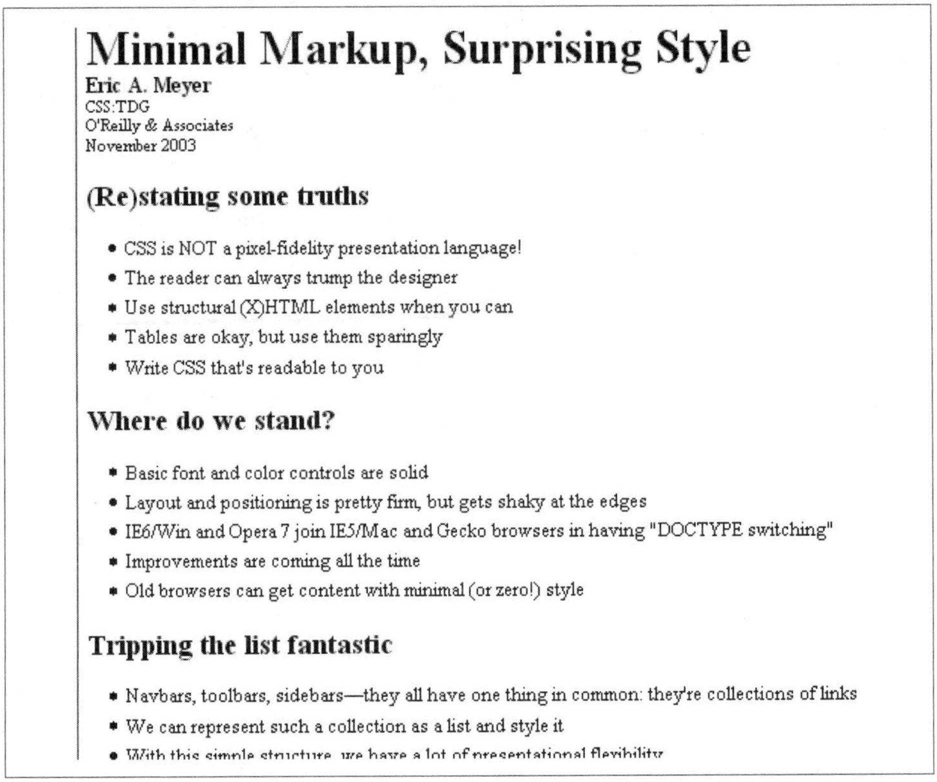

Minimal Markup, Surprising Style

Eric A. Meyer
CSS:TDG
O'Reilly & Associates
November 2003

(Re)stating some truths

- CSS is NOT a pixel-fidelity presentation language!
- The reader can always trump the designer
- Use structural (X)HTML elements when you can
- Tables are okay, but use them sparingly
- Write CSS that's readable to you

Where do we stand?

- Basic font and color controls are solid
- Layout and positioning is pretty firm, but gets shaky at the edges
- IE6/Win and Opera 7 join IE5/Mac and Gecko browsers in having "DOCTYPE switching"
- Improvements are coming all the time
- Old browsers can get content with minimal (or zero!) style

Tripping the list fantastic

- Navbars, toolbars, sidebars—they all have one thing in common: they're collections of links
- We can represent such a collection as a list and style it
- With this simple structure, we have a lot of presentational flexibility

Figure 14-8. A slideshow outline using simple HTML

Now all you need to do is break up the document into slides. Since every slide starts with an h2 element, you can simply declare:

```
h2 {page-break-before: always;}
```

This will ensure that every page (that is, every slide) will start with an h2 element. Since the title of each slide is represented by an h2, this is fine: every slide will have an h2 as its first element. You can see the rendering of a slide in Figure 14-9.

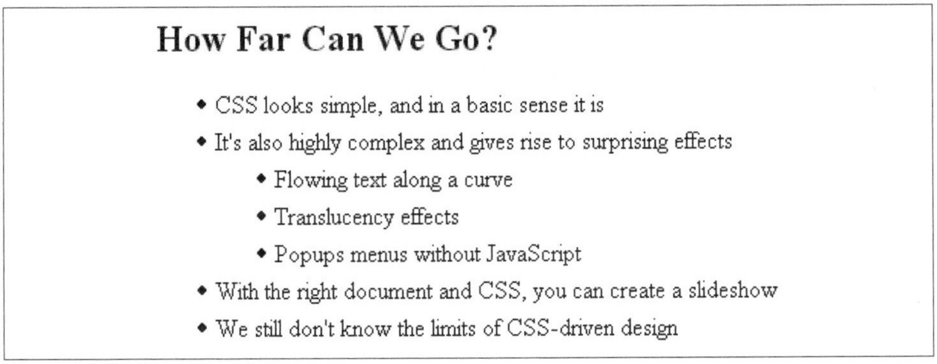

How Far Can We Go?

- CSS looks simple, and in a basic sense it is
- It's also highly complex and gives rise to surprising effects
  - Flowing text along a curve
  - Translucency effects
  - Popups menus without JavaScript
- With the right document and CSS, you can create a slideshow
- We still don't know the limits of CSS-driven design

Figure 14-9. A slide

Of course, the slide looks pretty plain because you've done nothing else to make it look good; you've simply defined where page breaks are to be inserted.

Given the outline as it's currently set up, you could also have defined slide boundaries by inserting page breaks after the lists, instead of before the h2 elements:

```
ul {page-break-after: always;}
```

This method would work well, as long as your outline never includes nested lists. If there is a chance of having unordered lists nested within the "top-level" lists, then you'd either need to go back to putting page breaks before h2 elements, or add a second rule to prevent page-breaking:

```
ul {page-break-after: always;}
ul ul {page-break-after: auto;}
```

Positioning elements

When you position elements, their initial containing block will be the page box in which they are placed. Thus, if you want the title of every slide to actually appear on the bottom of the slide, you would write something like:

```
h2 {page-break-before: always; position: absolute; bottom: 0; right: 0;}
```

This rule would place any h2 element at the bottom-right corner of the page box (slide) in which it appears. Of course, it's possible to position elements with respect to other elements instead of the page box. See Chapter 10 for details on positioning.

A fixed-position element, on the other hand, will appear in every page box in the slideshow, just as in the print medium. This means that you can take a single element, such as the document title, and put it on every slide, like this:

```
h1 {position: fixed; top: 0; right: 0; font-size: 80%;}
```

This technique can be used to create running footers, graphical sidebars for every slide, and so on.

Considerations for projection

It's often said that web designs should be flexible and able to adapt to any resolution—and that's certainly true in most cases. However, projection styling is not web styling, so it often makes sense for a projection style sheet to be created with a specific resolution in mind. As an example, most projectors (as of this writing) default to a resolution of 1024×768. If you know you'll be projecting at that size, it's logical to set up your CSS for that exact size. Font sizing, element placement, and so forth can all be tuned to create the best visual experience for the target resolution.

For that matter, you might create different style sheets for different resolutions: one for 800×600, another for 1024×768, and a third for 1280×1024, just to cover the most common bases. Figure 14-10 shows a slide at 1024×768.

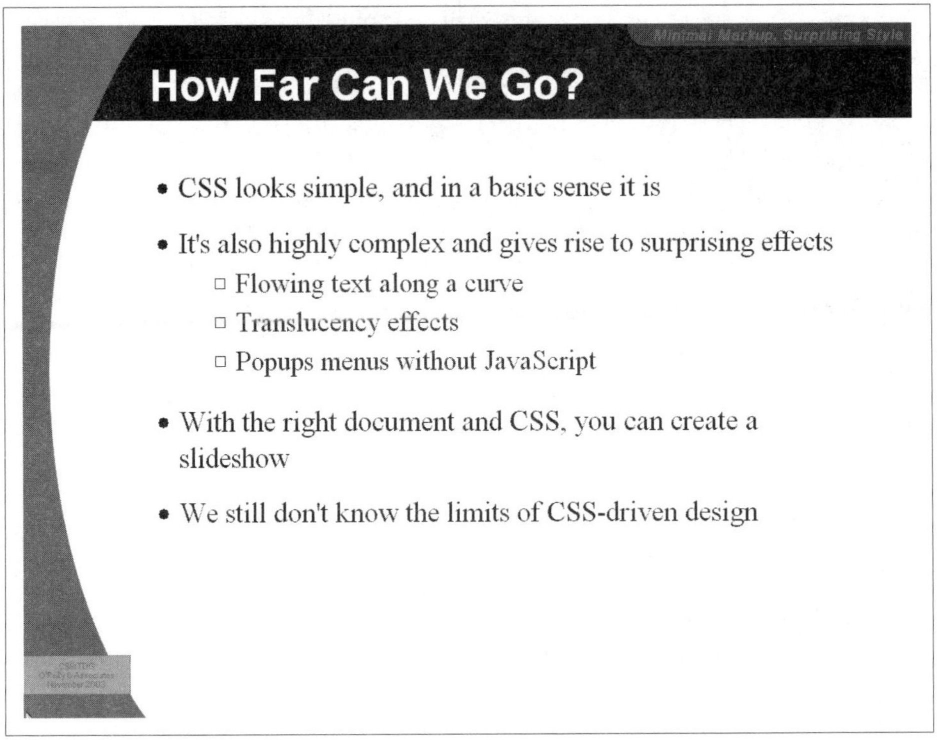

Figure 14-10. A fully styled slide

Another thing to bear in mind is that projected documents are generally more readable for the audience if they employ high-contrast colors. This is particularly true since some projector bulbs aren't as bright as others, and dimmer bulbs call for even higher contrast. This also highlights (no pun intended) the fact that you have even less of a guarantee of color fidelity in projection situations than in normal web design (and that's not saying much).

Aural Styles

Users who cannot see won't benefit from the visual styling that most of CSS enables. For these users, what matters is not the drop shadows or rounded corners, but the actual textual content of the page—which must be rendered audibly if they are to understand it. The blind are not the only user demographic that can benefit from aural rendering of web content. A user agent embedded in a car, for example, might use aural styles to enliven the reading of web content such as driving directions, or even the driver's email.

To meet the needs of these users, CSS2 introduced a section describing aural styles. As of this writing, there are two user agents that support, at least to some degree, aural styles: Emacspeak and Fonix SpeakThis. In spite of this, CSS2.1 effectively deprecates the media type aural and all of the properties associated with it. The current specification includes a note to the effect that future versions of CSS are likely to use the media type speech to represent spoken renderings of documents, but it does not provide any details.

Due to this odd confluence of emerging implementation and deprecation, we will only briefly look at the properties of aural style sheets.

Speaking

At the most basic level, you must determine whether a given element's content should be rendered aurally at all. In aural style sheets, this is handled with the property speak.

<table>
<tr><td colspan="2" align="center">speak</td></tr>
<tr><td>Values:</td><td>normal | none | spell-out | inherit</td></tr>
<tr><td>Initial value:</td><td>normal</td></tr>
<tr><td>Applies to:</td><td>All elements</td></tr>
<tr><td>Inherited:</td><td>Yes</td></tr>
<tr><td>Computed value:</td><td>As specified</td></tr>
</table>

The default value, normal, is used to indicate that an element's content should be spoken. If an element's content should not be spoken for some reason, the value none is used. Even though an element's aural rendering may be suppressed using none, you may override the value on descendant elements, which would thus be rendered. In the following example, the text "Navigation:" would not be rendered aurally, but the text "Home" would be:

```
<div style="speak: none;">
Navigation:
<a href="home.html" style="speak: normal;">Home</a>
</div>
```

If an element and its descendants *must* be prevented from rendering aurally, use display: none instead. In this example, none of the content of the div will be rendered aurally (or in any other medium, for that matter):

```
<div style="display: none;">
Navigation:
<a href="home.html" style="speak: normal;">Home</a>
</div>
```

The third value of speak is spell-out, which will most likely be used in conjunction with acronyms or other content that should be spelled out. For example, the following fragment of markup would be rendered aurally as T-E-D-S, or "tee eee dee ess":

```
<acronym style="speak: spell-out;" title="Technology Evangelism and
    Developer Support">TEDS</acronym>
```

Punctuation and numbers

There are two other properties that affect the way in which element content is rendered aurally. The first affects the rendering of punctuation and is called (appropriately enough) speak-punctuation.

<hr/>

speak-punctuation

Values:	code | none | inherit
Initial value:	none
Applies to:	All elements
Inherited:	Yes
Computed value:	As specified

Given the default value of none, punctuation is rendered aurally as pauses of appropriate lengths, although CSS does not define these lengths. To pick an example, the pause representing a period (and thus the end of a sentence) might be twice as long as the pause representing a comma. Pause lengths are likely to be language-dependent.

With the value code, punctuation is actually rendered aurally. Thus, the following example would be rendered as, "avast comma ye scalawags exclamation point":

```
<p style="speak-punctuation: code;">Avast, ye scalawags!</p>
```

To use another example, the following fragment might be rendered aurally as, "a left bracket href right bracket left curly brace color colon red semicolon right curly brace":

```
<code style="speak-punctuation: code;">a[href] {color: red;}</code>
```

Similar to affecting punctuation rendering, speak-numeral defines the method of speaking numbers.

The default value continuous means that the number is spoken as a whole number, whereas digits causes numbers to be read individually. Consider:

```
<p style="speak-numeral: continuous;">23</p>
<p style="speak-numeral: digits;">23</p>
```

<table>
<tr><td colspan="2" align="center">**speak-numeral**</td></tr>
<tr><td>Values:</td><td>`digits` | `continuous` | `inherit`</td></tr>
<tr><td>Initial value:</td><td>`continuous`</td></tr>
<tr><td>Applies to:</td><td>All elements</td></tr>
<tr><td>Inherited:</td><td>Yes</td></tr>
<tr><td>Computed value:</td><td>As specified</td></tr>
</table>

The aural rendering of the first paragraph would be "twenty-three," whereas the second paragraph would be rendered as "two three." As with punctuation, numeric renderings are language-dependent but undefined.

Speaking table headers

In the aural rendering of a table, it can be easy to lose track of what the cell data actually means. If you're on the 9th row of a 12-row table, and the 6th cell in that row is "21.77," what are the odds you'll remember what the 6th column represents? Will you even remember what the numbers in this row relate to? Table headers provide this information and are easy to check visually. To solve this problem in the aural medium, CSS2 introduced speak-header.

<table>
<tr><td colspan="2" align="center">**speak-header**</td></tr>
<tr><td>Values:</td><td>`once` | `always` | `inherit`</td></tr>
<tr><td>Initial value:</td><td>`once`</td></tr>
<tr><td>Applies to:</td><td>Elements containing table header information</td></tr>
<tr><td>Inherited:</td><td>Yes</td></tr>
<tr><td>Computed value:</td><td>As specified</td></tr>
</table>

By default, a user agent will render the content of a table header only once, when the cell is encountered. The other alternative is to always render the table header information when a cell relating to that header is rendered.

Let's consider the following simple table as an example:

```
<table id="colors">
<caption>Favorite Color</caption>
<tr id="headers">
<th>Jim</th><th>Joe</th><th>Jane</th>
</tr>
```

```
<tr>
<td>red</td><td>green</td><td>blue</td>
<td>
</tr>
</table>
```

Without any styles applied, the aural rendering of this table would be, "Favorite Color Jim Joe Jane red green blue." You can probably figure out what all that means, but imagine a table containing the favorite colors of 10 or 20 people. Now, suppose you apply the following styles to this table:

```
#colors {speak-header: always;}
#headers {speak: none;}
```

The aural rendering of the table should then be, "Favorite Color Jim red Joe green Jane blue." This is much easier to understand, and it will continue to be—no matter how large the table might grow.

 Note that the document language itself defines the method of determining an element's role as a table header. Markup languages may also have ways to associate header information with elements or groups of elements—for example, the attributes scope and axis in HTML4.

Speech rate

In addition to ways to affect the style of speech, CSS also offers speech-rate, which is used to set the speed at which content is aurally rendered.

speech-rate	
Values:	`<number>` | `x-slow` | `slow` | `medium` | `fast` | `x-fast` | `faster` | `slower` | `inherit`
Initial value:	`medium`
Applies to:	All elements
Inherited:	Yes
Computed value:	An absolute number

The values are defined as follows:

<number>
Specifies the speaking rate in words per minute. This is likely to vary by language, since some languages are spoken more quickly than others.

x-slow
Equivalent to 80 words per minute.

slow
> Equivalent to 120 words per minute.

medium
> Equivalent to 180–200 words per minute.

fast
> Equivalent to 300 words per minute.

x-fast
> Equivalent to 500 words per minute.

faster
> Increases the current speech rate by 40 words per minute.

slower
> Decreases the current speech rate by 40 words per minute.

Here are two examples of extreme changes in speech rate:

```
*.duh {speech-rate: x-slow;}
div#disclaimer {speech-rate: x-fast;}
```

CSS does not define how the speech rate is altered. A user agent could draw out each word, stretch out the pauses between words, or both.

Volume

In an aural medium, one of the most important aspects of presentation is the volume of the sound produced by the user agent. Enter the aptly named property, volume.

volume	
Values:	<number> | <percentage> | silent | x-soft | soft | medium | loud | x-loud | inherit
Initial value:	medium
Applies to:	All elements
Inherited:	Yes
Computed value:	An absolute number

The values are defined as follows:

<number>
> Provides a numeric representation of the volume. 0 corresponds to the minimum audible volume, which is *not* the same as being silent; 100 corresponds to the maximum comfortable volume.

<percentage>
> Calculated as a percentage of the inherited value.

silent
:   No sound is produced, which is different from the numeric value 0. This is the aural equivalent of visibility: hidden.

x-soft
:   Equivalent to the numeric value 0.

soft
:   Equivalent to the numeric value 25.

medium
:   Equivalent to the numeric value 50.

loud
:   Equivalent to the numeric value 75.

x-loud
:   Equivalent to the numeric value 100.

It's important to note that the volume value (say that five times fast!) defines the *median* volume, not the precise volume of every sound produced. Thus, the content of an element with volume: 50; may well be rendered with sounds that go above and below that level, especially if the voice is highly inflected or has a dynamic range of sounds.

The numeric range is likely to be user-configured, since only an individual user can determine his minimum audible volume level (0) and maximum comfortable volume level (100). As an example, a user might decide that the minimum audible volume is a 34dB tone, and the maximum comfortable volume is an 84dB tone. This means there is a 50dB range between 0 and 100, and each increase of one in the value will mean a half-dB increase in the median volume. In other words, volume: soft; would translate to a median volume of 46.5dB.

Percentage values have an effect analogous to their effect in font-size: they increase or decrease the value based on the parent element's value. For example:

```
div.marine {volume: 60;}
big {volume: 125%;}

<div class="marine">
When I say jump, I mean <big>rabbit</big>, you maggots!
</div>
```

Given the audio range described before, the content of the div element here would be spoken with a median volume of 64dB. The exception is the big element, which is 125% of the parent's value of 60. This calculates to 75, which is equivalent to 71.5dB.

If a percentage value would place an element's computed numeric value outside the range of 0 through 100, the value is clipped to the nearest value. Suppose you were to change the previous styles to read:

```
div.marine {volume: 60;}
big {volume: 200%;}
```

This would cause the big element's volume value to be computed as 120; that value would then be clipped to 100, which corresponds here to a median volume of 84dB.

The advantage of defining volume in this way is that it permits the same style sheet to serve in different environments. For example, the settings for 0 and 100 will be different in a library than they will be in a car, but the values will effectively correspond to the same intended auditory effects in each setting.

Giving Voice

To this point, we've talked about ways to affect the aural presentation, but what we haven't discussed is a way to choose the voice used to aurally render content. Like font-family, CSS defines a property called voice-family.

---

voice-family

Values:	[[<specific-voice> | <generic-voice>],]* [<specific-voice> | <generic-voice>] | inherit
Initial value:	User agent-dependent
Applies to:	All elements
Inherited:	Yes
Computed value:	As specified

As with font-family, voice-family allows the author to supply a comma-separated list of voices that can be used to render an element's content. The user agent looks for the first voice in the list and uses it if it's available. If not, the user agent looks for the next voice in the list, and so on, until it either finds a specific voice or runs out of specified voices.

Because of the way the value syntax is defined, you can provide a number of specific or generic families in any order. Therefore, you can end your value with a specific family instead of a generic one. For example:

```
h1 {voice-family: Mark, male, Joe;}
```

CSS2.x does not define generic family values, but mentions that male, female, and child are all possible. Therefore, you might style the elements of an XML document as follows:

```
rosen {voice-family:  Gary, Scott, male;}
guild {voice-family: Tim, Jim, male;}
claud {voice-family: Donald, Ian, male;}
gertr {voice-family: Joanna, Susan, female;}
albert {voice-family: Bobby, Paulie, child;}
```

The actual voice chosen to render a given element will affect the way the user perceives that element, since some voices will be pitched higher or lower than others, or may be more or less monotone. CSS provides ways to affect these aspects of a voice as well.

Altering the Voice

Once you've directed the user agent to use a particular voice in the aural rendering of the content, you might want to alter some of its aspects. For example, a voice might sound right, except it's pitched too high for your liking. Another voice might be a little too "dynamic," but otherwise meets your needs. CSS defines properties to affect all of the vocal aspects.

Changing the pitch

Obviously, different voices have different pitches. To pick the most basic of examples, male voices average around 120Hz, whereas female voices average in the vicinity of 210Hz. Thus, every voice family will have its own default pitch, which CSS allows authors to alter using the property pitch.

---

pitch

Values:	\<frequency\> | x-low | low | medium | high | x-high | inherit
Initial value:	medium
Applies to:	All elements
Inherited:	Yes
Computed value:	The absolute frequency value

There is no explicit definition of the keywords x-low through x-high, so all that can be said about them is that each one will be a higher pitch than the one before it. This is similar to the way the font-size keywords xx-small through xx-large are not precisely defined, but each must be larger than the one preceding it.

Frequency values are a different matter. If you define an explicit pitch frequency, the voice will be altered so that its average pitch matches the value you supply. For example:

```
h1 {pitch: 150Hz;}
```

The effects can be dramatic if an unexpected voice is used. Let's consider an example where an element is given two voice-family possibilities and a pitch frequency:

```
h1 {voice-family: Jethro, Susie; pitch: 100Hz;}
```

For the purposes of this example, assume that the default pitch of "Jethro" is 110Hz, and the default pitch for "Susie" is 200Hz. If "Jethro" gets picked, then h1 elements will be read with the voice pitched slightly lower than normal. If "Jethro" isn't available and "Susie" is used instead, there will be an enormous, and potentially bizarre, change from the voice's default.

Regardless of what pitch is used in an element's rendering, you can influence the dynamic range of the pitch by using the property pitch-range.

---

pitch-range

Values:	<number> | inherit
Initial value:	50
Applies to:	All elements
Inherited:	Yes
Computed value:	As specified

The purpose of pitch-range is to raise or lower the inflection in a given voice. The lower the pitch range, the closer all pitches will be to the average, resulting in a monotone voice. The default value, 50, yields "normal" inflections. Values higher than that will increase the degree of "animation" in the voice.

Stress and richness

A companion property to pitch-range is stress, which is intended to help authors minimize or exaggerate the stress patterns in a language.

---

stress

Values:	<number> | inherit
Initial value:	50
Applies to:	All elements
Inherited:	Yes
Computed value:	As specified

Every human language has, to some degree, stress patterns. In English, for example, sentences have different parts that call for different stress. The previous sentence might look something like this:

```
<sentence>
  <primary>In English,</primary>
  <tertiary>for example,</tertiary>
  <secondary>sentences have different parts that call for
different stress.</secondary>
</sentence>
```

A style sheet defining stress levels for each portion of the sentence might say:

```
primary {stress: 65;}
secondary {stress: 50;}
tertiary {stress: 33;}
```

This leads to a decrease in stress for the less important parts of a sentence, and a greater stress on the parts that are considered more important. stress values are language-dependent, so the same value may lead to different stress levels and patterns. CSS does not define such differences (which probably doesn't surprise you by now).

Similar in many ways to stress is richness.

---

richness

Values:	<number> | inherit
Initial value:	50
Applies to:	All elements
Inherited:	Yes
Computed value:	As specified

The higher a voice's richness value, the greater its "brightness" and the more it will "carry" in a room. Lower values will lead to a softer, more "mellifluous" voice (to quote the CSS2 specification). Thus, an actor's soliloquy might be given richness: 80; and a *sotto voce* aside might get richness: 25;.

Pauses and Cues

In visual design, you can draw extra attention to an element by giving it extra margins to separate it from everything else, or by adding borders. This draws the eye toward these elements. In aural presentation, the closest equivalent is the ability to insert pauses and audible cues around an element.

Pauses

All spoken language relies on pauses of some form. The short gaps between words, phrases, and sentences are as critical to understanding the meaning as the words themselves. In a sense, pauses are like the auditory equivalent of margins, in that both serve to separate the element from its surrounding content. In CSS, three properties can be used to insert pauses into a document: pause-before, pause-after, and pause.

---

pause-before, pause-after

Values: <time> | <percentage> | inherit

Initial value: 0

Apply to: All elements

Inherited: No

Computed value: The absolute time value

With the <time> value format, you can express the length of a pause in either seconds or milliseconds. For example, let's say you want a full two-second pause after an h1 element. Either of the following rules have that effect:

```
h1 {pause-after: 2s;}
h1 {pause-after: 2000ms;}  /* the same length of time as '2s' */
```

Percentages are a little trickier, as they are calculated in relation to a measure-implied value of speech-rate. No, really! Let's see how this works. First, consider the following:

```
h1 {speech-rate: 180;}
```

This means any h1 element will be aurally rendered at about three words per second. Now consider:

```
h1 {speech-rate: 180; pause-before: 200%;}
```

The percentage is calculated based on the average word length. In this case, a word will take 333.33 milliseconds to speak, so 200% of that is 666.66 milliseconds. Put another way, there will be a pause before each h1 of about two-thirds of a second. If you alter the rule so the speech-rate value is 120, the pause will be a full second long.

The shorthand pause brings together pause-before and pause-after.

---

pause

Values: [[<time> | <percentage>]{1,2}] | inherit

Initial value: 0

Applies to: All elements

Inherited: No

Computed value: See individual properties (pause-before, etc.)

If you supply only one value, it's taken as the pause value both before and after an element. If you supply two values, the first one is the pause before the element, and the second one is the pause after. Thus, the following rules are all equivalent:

```
pre {pause: 1s;}
pre {pause: 1s 1s;}
pre {pause-before: 1s; pause-after: 1s;}
```

Cues

If pauses aren't enough to call attention to an element, you can insert audio cues before and after it, which are the auditory equivalent of borders. Like the pause properties, there are three cue properties: cue-before, cue-after, and cue.

---

cue-before, cue-after

Values:	<uri> | none | inherit
Initial value:	none
Applies to:	All elements
Inherited:	No
Computed value:	For <uri> values, the absolute URI; otherwise, none

---

By supplying the URI of an audio resource, the user agent is directed to load that resource and play it before (or after) an element. Suppose you want to precede each unvisited hyperlink in a document with a chime, and every visited link with a beep. The rules would look something like this:

```
a:link {cue-before: url(chime.mp3);}
a:visited {cue-before: url(beep.wav);}
```

The shorthand property cue acts as you'd expect.

---

cue

Values:	[<cue-before> || <cue-after>] | inherit
Initial value:	none
Applies to:	All elements
Inherited:	No
Computed value:	See individual properties (cue-before, etc.)

As with pause, supplying a single value for cue means that value will be used for both the before and after cues. Supplying two values means the first is used for the before cue, and the second is used for the after cue. Therefore, the following rules are all equivalent:

```
a[href] {cue: url(ping.mp3);}
a[href] {cue: url(ping.mp3) url(ping.mp3);}
a[href] {cue-before: url(ping.mp3); cue-after: url(ping.mp3);}
```

Pauses, cues, and generated content

Both pauses and cues are played "outside" any generated content. Consider:

```
h1 {cue: url(trumpet.mp3);}
h1:before {content: "Behold! ";}
h1:after {content: ". Verily!";}

<h1>The Beginning</h1>
```

The audio rendering of this element would be, roughly, "(trumpets) Behold! The Beginning. Verily! (trumpets)."

CSS does not specify whether pauses go "outside" cues or vice versa, so the behavior of auditory user agents in this regard cannot be predicted.

Background Sounds

Visual elements can have backgrounds, so it's only fair that audible elements should be able to have them, too. In the aural medium, a background refers to playing a sound while the element is being spoken. The property used to accomplish this is play-during.

---

play-during

Values:	<uri> [mix || repeat]? | auto | none | inherit
Initial value:	auto
Applies to:	All elements
Inherited:	No
Computed value:	For <uri> values, the absolute URI; otherwise, as specified

---

The simplest example is playing a single sound at the beginning of an element's aural rendering:

```
h1 {play-during: url(trumpets.mp3);}
```

Given this rule, any h1 element would be spoken while the sound file *trumpets.mp3* plays. The sound file is played once. If it is shorter than the time it takes to speak the element's contents, it stops before the element is finished. If it's longer than the necessary time, the sound stops once all of the element's content has been spoken.

If you want a sound to repeat throughout the entire speaking of an element, add the keyword repeat. This is the auditory equivalent of background-repeat: repeat:

```
div.ocean {play-during: url(wave.wav) repeat;}
```

Like visible backgrounds, background sounds do not composite by default. Consider the following situation:

```
a:link {play-during: url(chains.mp3) repeat;}
em {play-during: url(bass.mp3) repeat;}
```

```
<a href="http://www.example.com/">This is a <em>really great</em> site!</a>
```

Here, *chains.mp3* will play repetitively behind the text of the link, *except* for the text of the em element. For that text, the chains will not be audible; instead, *bass.mp3* will be heard. The parent's background sound is not heard, just as its background would not be seen behind the em element if both elements had visible backgrounds.

If you want to combine the two, use the keyword mix:

```
a:link {play-during: url(chains.mp3) repeat;}
em {play-during: url(bass.mp3) repeat mix;}
```

Now, *chains.mp3* will be audible behind all of the link text, including the text in the em element. For that element, both *chains.mp3* and *bass.mp3* will be heard mixed together.

The analogy to visible backgrounds breaks down with the value none. This keyword cuts off all background sounds, including any that may belong to ancestor elements. Thus, given the following rules, the em text will have no background sounds at all— neither *bass.mp3* nor *chains.mp3* will be heard:

```
a:link {play-during: url(chains.mp3) repeat;}
em {play-during: none;}
```

```
<a href="http://www.example.com/">This is a <em>really great</em> site!</a>
```

Positioning Sounds

When only one person is speaking, the sound emanates from one point in space, unless of course that person is moving around. In a conversation involving multiple people, the sound of each voice will come from a different point in space.

With the availability of high-end audio systems and 3D sound, it should be possible to position sounds within that space. CSS2.x defines two properties to accomplish this, one of which defines the angle of a sound's source on a horizontal plane, and the second of which defines the source's angle on a vertical plane. The placement of sounds along the horizontal plane is handled using azimuth.

azimuth

Values:	`<angle>` | [[`left-side` | `far-left` | `left` | `center-left` | `center` | `center-right` | `right` | `far-right` | `right-side`] || `behind`] | `leftwards` | `rightwards` | `inherit`
Initial value:	`center`
Applies to:	All elements
Inherited:	Yes
Computed value:	Normalized angle

Angle values can come in three units: deg (degrees), grad (grads), and rad (radians). The possible ranges for these unit types are 0–360deg, 0–400grad, and 0–6.2831853rad. Negative values are permitted, but they are recalculated as positive values. For example, -45deg is equivalent to 315deg (360–45), and -50grad would be the same as 350grad.

Most of the keywords are simply equivalents of angle values. These are shown in Table 14-1, using degrees as the angle value of choice, and illustrated visually in Figure 14-11. The last column of Table 14-1 shows the equivalents of the keywords in the first column being used in conjunction with behind.

Table 14-1. azimuth keyword and angle equivalents

Keyword	Angle		Behind	
center	0		180deg	–180deg
center-right	20deg	–340deg	160deg	–200deg
right	40deg	–320deg	140deg	–220deg
far-right	60deg	–300deg	120deg	–240deg
right-side	90deg	–270deg	90deg	–270deg
center-left	340deg	–20deg	200deg	–160deg
left	320deg	–40deg	220deg	–140deg
far-left	300deg	–60deg	240deg	–120deg
left-side	270deg	–90deg	270deg	–90deg

Note that the keyword behind cannot be combined with an angle value. It can be used only in conjunction with one of the keywords listed in Table 14-1.

There are two keywords in addition to those listed in Table 14-1: leftwards and rightwards. The effect of the former is to subtract 20deg from the current angle value of azimuth, and the latter adds 20deg to the value. For example:

```
body {azimuth: right-side;}   /* equivalent to 90deg */
h1 {azimuth: leftwards;}
```

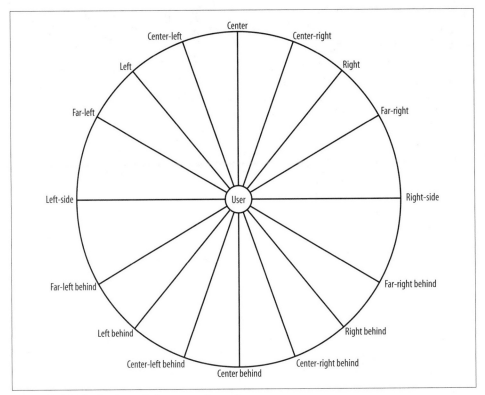

Figure 14-11. The horizontal plane, seen from above

The computed angle value of `azimuth` for the `h1` element is `70deg`. Now consider the following situation:

```
body {azimuth: behind;}   /* equivalent to 180deg */
h1 {azimuth: leftwards;}  /* computes to 160deg */
```

The effect of `leftwards`, given these rules, is to make the sound move to the right, not the left. It's odd, but that's how CSS2 is written. Similarly, using `rightwards` in the previous example would cause the `h1` element's sound source to move 20 degrees to the left.

Much like `azimuth`, only simpler, is `elevation`, which places sounds in the vertical plane.

elevation

Values:	`<angle>` | `below` | `level` | `above` | `higher` | `lower` | `inherit`
Initial value:	`level`
Applies to:	All elements
Inherited:	Yes
Computed value:	Normalized angle

Like azimuth, elevation accepts degree, grad, and radian angles. The three angle-equivalent keywords are above (90 degrees), level (0), and below (–90 degrees). These are illustrated in Figure 14-12.

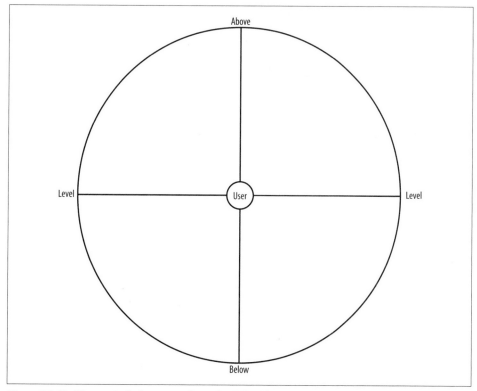

Figure 14-12. The vertical plane, seen from the right side

The relative-placement keywords, higher and lower, either add or subtract 10 degrees from the current elevation angle. Therefore, in the following example, h1 elements that are children of the body will be placed 10 degrees above the horizontal plane:

```
body {elevation: level;}  /* equivalent to 0 */
body > h1 {elevation: higher;}
```

Combining azimuth with elevation

When values for azimuth and elevation are taken together, they define a point in an imaginary sphere whose center is the user. Figure 14-13 illustrates this sphere, along with some cardinal points and the values that would place sounds in those positions.

Imagine a point halfway between straight ahead of you and your immediate right as you sit in a chair, and halfway between the horizon and the zenith. This point could be described as azimuth: 45deg; elevation: 45deg;. Now imagine a sound source at

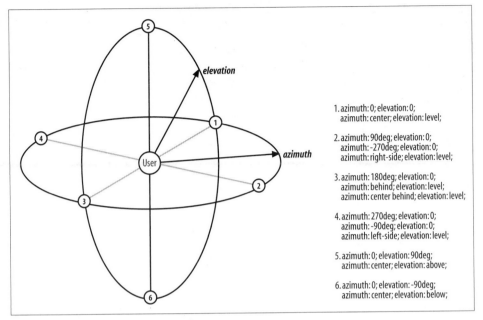

1. azimuth: 0; elevation: 0;
   azimuth: center; elevation: level;

2. azimuth: 90deg; elevation: 0;
   azimuth: -270deg; elevation: 0;
   azimuth: right-side; elevation: level;

3. azimuth: 180deg; elevation: 0;
   azimuth: behind; elevation: level;
   azimuth: center behind; elevation: level;

4. azimuth: 270deg; elevation: 0;
   azimuth: -90deg; elevation: 0;
   azimuth: left-side; elevation: level;

5. azimuth: 0; elevation: 90deg;
   azimuth: center; elevation: above;

6. azimuth: 0; elevation: -90deg;
   azimuth: center; elevation: below;

Figure 14-13. Three-dimensional aural space

the same elevation but located halfway between your immediate left and a point directly behind you. This source could be described in any of the following ways:

```
azimuth: -135deg; elevation: 45deg;
azimuth: 215deg; elevation: 45deg;
azimuth: left behind; elevation: 45deg;
```

It is entirely possible that positioned sounds would assist a user in separating cues from other audio sources, or could help to create positionally separate special material:

```
a[href] {cue: url(ping.wav); azimuth: behind; elevation: 30deg;}
voices.onhigh {play-during: url(choir.mp3); elevation: above;}
```

Summary

Although the first stage of the Web's development was primarily visual in nature, the need to provide web content in other media led to the introduction of medium-specific styling in CSS. The ability to take the same document and customize its presentation in a manner best suited to different output media is deeply powerful. Although its most common application is to create "printer-friendly" styles for documents, we've also seen how projection styles can be used to create slideshows with Opera.

While aural styles would be very useful for blind users, there are only two programs as of this writing that support even a fragment of this portion of CSS, and the media type aural defined in CSS2.x will not be carried forward to future versions of CSS. Instead, the media type speech has been set aside for future work in auditory rendering of documents.

Property Reference

Visual Media

background

This is a shorthand method to express all of the individual background properties within a single declaration. Use of this property is generally encouraged over the individual properties, as it has a slightly better support profile in older browsers and doesn't take as long to type.

Values: [<background-color> || <background-image> || <background-repeat> || <background-attachment> || <background-position>] | inherit

Initial value: Refer to individual properties

Applies to: All elements

Inherited: No

Percentages: Values are allowed for <background-position>

Computed value: See individual properties

background-attachment

This property defines whether the background image scrolls along with the element when the document is scrolled. This can be used to create "aligned" backgrounds; see Chapter 9 for more details.

Values: scroll | fixed | inherit

Initial value: scroll

Applies to: All elements

Inherited: No

Computed value: As specified

background-color

This sets a solid color for the background of the element. This color fills the content, padding, and border areas of the element, extending to the outer edge of the element's border. Borders that have transparent sections, such as dashed borders, will show the background color through the transparent sections.

Values:	<color> | transparent | inherit
Initial value:	transparent
Applies to:	All elements
Inherited:	No
Computed value:	As specified

background-image

This places an image in the background of the element. Depending on the value of background-repeat, the image may tile infinitely, along one axis, or not at all. The initial background image (the origin image) is placed according to the value of background-position.

Values:	<uri> | none | inherit
Initial value:	none
Applies to:	All elements
Inherited:	No
Computed value:	Absolute URI

background-position

This property sets the position of the background's origin image (as defined by background-image); this is the point from which any background repetition will occur.

Values:	[[<percentage> | <length> | left | center | right] [<percentage>] | <length> | top | center | bottom]?] | [[left | center | right] || [top | center | bottom]] | inherit
Initial value:	0% 0%
Applies to:	Block-level and replaced elements
Inherited:	No
Percentages:	Refer to the corresponding point on both the element and the origin image
Computed value:	The absolute length offsets, if <length> is specified; otherwise, percentage values

background-repeat

This defines the tiling pattern for the background image. Note that the axis-related repeat values actually cause repetition in *both* directions along the relevant axis. The repetition begins from the origin image, which is defined as the value of background-image and is placed according to the value of background-position.

Values: repeat | repeat-x | repeat-y | no-repeat | inherit

Initial value: repeat

Applies to: All elements

Inherited: No

Computed value: As specified

border

This is a shorthand property that defines the width, color, and style of an element's border. Note that while none of the values are actually required, omitting a border style will result in no border being applied because the default border style is none.

Values: [<border-width> || <border-style> || <border-color>] | inherit

Initial value: Refer to individual properties

Applies to: All elements

Inherited: No

Computed value: As specified

border-bottom

This shorthand property defines the width, color, and style of the bottom border of an element. As with border, omission of a border style will result in no border appearing.

Values: [<border-width> || <border-style> || <border-color>] | inherit

Initial value: Not defined for shorthand properties

Applies to: All elements

Inherited: No

Computed value: See individual properties (border-width, etc.)

border-bottom-color

This property sets the color for the visible portions of the bottom border of an element. Only a solid color can be defined, and the border's style must be a value other than none or hidden for any border to appear.

Values:	<color> | transparent | inherit
Initial value:	The value of color for the element
Applies to:	All elements
Inherited:	No
Computed value:	If no value is specified, use the computed value of the property color for the same element; otherwise, as specified

border-bottom-style

This defines the style for the bottom border of an element. The value must be something other than none for any border to appear. In CSS1, HTML user agents were only required to support solid and none.

Values:	none | hidden | dotted | dashed | solid | double | groove | ridge | inset | outset | inherit
Initial value:	none
Applies to:	All elements
Inherited:	No
Computed value:	As specified

border-bottom-width

This sets the width for the bottom border of an element, which will take effect only if the border's style is something other than none. If the border style is none, the border width is effectively reset to 0. Negative length values are not permitted.

Values:	thin | medium | thick | <length> | inherit
Initial value:	medium
Applies to:	All elements
Inherited:	No
Computed value:	Absolute length; 0 if the style of the border is none or hidden

border-color

This shorthand property sets the color for the visible portions of the overall border of an element or sets a different color for each of the four sides. Remember that a border's style must be something other than none or hidden for any border to appear.

| Values: | [<color> \| transparent]{1,4} \| inherit |
| Initial value: | Not defined for shorthand properties |

Applies to:	All elements
Inherited:	No
Computed value:	See individual properties (border-top-color, etc.)

border-left

This shorthand property defines the width, color, and style of the left border of an element. As with border, omission of a border style will result in no border appearing.

Values:	[<border-width> || <border-style> || <border-color>]	inherit
Initial value:	Not defined for shorthand properties
Applies to:	All elements
Inherited:	No
Computed value:	See individual properties (border-width, etc.)

border-left-color

This property sets the color for the visible portions of the left border of an element. Only a solid color can be defined, and the border's style must be something other than none or hidden for any border to appear.

Values:	<color>	transparent	inherit
Initial value:	The value of color for the element
Applies to:	All elements
Inherited:	No
Computed value:	If no value is specified, use the computed value of the property color for the same element; otherwise, as specified

border-left-style

This defines the style for the left border of an element. The value must be something other than none for any border to appear. In CSS1, HTML user agents were only required to support solid and none.

Values:	none	hidden	dotted	dashed	solid	double	groove	ridge	inset	outset	inherit
Initial value:	none
Applies to:	All elements
Inherited:	No
Computed value:	As specified

border-left-width

This sets the width for the left border of an element, which will take effect only if the border's style is something other than none. If the border style is none, the border width is effectively reset to 0. Negative length values are not permitted.

Values: thin | medium | thick | <length> | inherit

Initial value: medium

Applies to: All elements

Inherited: No

Computed value: Absolute length; 0 if the style of the border is none or hidden

border-right

This shorthand property defines the width, color, and style of the right border of an element. As with border, omission of a border style will result in no border appearing.

Values: [<border-width> || <border-style> || <border-color>] | inherit

Initial value: Not defined for shorthand properties

Applies to: All elements

Inherited: No

Computed value: See individual properties (border-width, etc.)

border-right-color

This property sets the color for the visible portions of the right border of an element. Only a solid color can be defined, and the border's style must be something other than none or hidden for any border to appear.

Values: <color> | transparent | inherit

Initial value: The value of color for the element

Applies to: All elements

Inherited: No

Computed value: If no value is specified, use the computed value of the property color for the same element; otherwise, as specified

border-right-style

This defines the style for the right border of an element. The value must be something other than none for any border to appear. In CSS1, HTML user agents were only required to support solid and none.

Values:	none | hidden | dotted | dashed | solid | double | groove | ridge | inset | outset | inherit
Initial value:	none
Applies to:	All elements
Inherited:	No
Computed value:	As specified

border-right-width

This sets the width for the right border of an element, which will only take effect if the border's style is something other than none. If the border style is none, the border width is effectively reset to 0. Negative length values are not permitted.

Values:	thin | medium | thick | <length> | inherit
Initial value:	medium
Applies to:	All elements
Inherited:	No
Computed value:	Absolute length; 0 if the style of the border is none or hidden

border-style

This shorthand property can be used to set the styles for the overall border of an element, or for each side individually. The value of any border must be something other than none for the border to appear.

Values:	[none | hidden | dotted | dashed | solid | double | groove | ridge | inset | outset]{1,4} | inherit
Initial value:	Not defined for shorthand properties
Applies to:	All elements
Inherited:	No
Computed value:	See individual properties (border-top-style, etc.)
Note:	In CSS1, HTML user agents were only required to support solid and none; the rest of the values (except for hidden) may be interpreted as solid

border-top

This shorthand property defines the width, color, and style of the top border of an element. As with border, omission of a border style will result in no border appearing.

Values: [<border-width> || <border-style> || <border-color>] | inherit

Initial value: Not defined for shorthand properties

Applies to: All elements

Inherited: No

Computed value: See individual properties (border-width, etc.)

border-top-color

This property sets the color for the visible portions of the top border of an element. Only a solid color can be defined, and the border's style must be something other than none or hidden for any border to appear.

Values: <color> | transparent | inherit

Initial value: The value of color for the element

Applies to: All elements

Inherited: No

Computed value: If no value is specified, use the computed value of the property color for the same element; otherwise, as specified

border-top-style

This defines the style for the top border of an element. The value must be something other than none for any border to appear. In CSS1, HTML user agents were only required to support solid and none.

Values: none | hidden | dotted | dashed | solid | double | groove | ridge | inset | outset | inherit

Initial value: none

Applies to: All elements

Inherited: No

Computed value: As specified

border-top-width

This sets the width for the top border of an element, which will only take effect if the border's style is something other than none. If the style is none, the width is effectively reset to 0. Negative length values are not permitted.

Values: thin | medium | thick | <length> | inherit

Initial value: medium

Applies to: All elements

Inherited: No

Computed value: Absolute length; 0 if the style of the border is none or hidden

border-width

This shorthand property can be used to set the width for the overall border of an element or for each side individually. The width will take effect for a given border only if the border's style is something other than none. If the border style is none, the border width is effectively reset to 0. Negative length values are not permitted.

Values: [thin | medium | thick | <length>]{1,4} | inherit

Initial value: Not defined for shorthand properties

Applies to: All elements

Inherited: No

Computed value: See individual properties (border-top-style, etc.)

bottom

This property defines the offset between the bottom outer margin edge of a positioned element and the bottom edge of its containing block.

Values: <length> | <percentage> | auto | inherit

Initial value: auto

Applies to: Positioned elements (that is, elements for which the value of position is something other than static)

Inherited: No

Percentages: Refer to the height of the containing block

Computed value:	For relatively positioned elements, see Note; for static elements, auto; for length values, the corresponding absolute length; for percentage values, the specified value; otherwise, auto
Note:	For relatively positioned elements, if both bottom and top are auto, their computed values are both 0; if one of them is auto, it becomes the negative of the other; if neither is auto, bottom will become the negative of the value of top

clear

This defines the sides of an element on which no floating elements may appear. In CSS1 and CSS2, this is accomplished by automatically increasing the top margin of the cleared element. In CSS2.1, clearance space is added above the element's top margin, but the margin itself is not altered. In either case, the end result is that the element's top outer border edge is just below the bottom outer margin edge of a floated element on the declared side.

Values:	left	right	both	none	inherit
Initial value:	none
Applies to:	Block-level elements
Inherited:	No
Computed value:	As specified

clip

This is used to define a clipping rectangle inside of which the content of an absolutely positioned element is visible. Content outside this clipping area is treated according to the value of overflow. The clipping area can be smaller or larger than the content area of the element.

Values:	rect(*top*, *right*, *bottom*, *left*)	auto	inherit
Initial value:	auto
Applies to:	Absolutely positioned elements (in CSS2, clip applied to block-level and replaced elements)
Inherited:	No
Computed value:	For a rectangle, a set of four computed lengths representing the edges of the clipping rectangle; otherwise, as specified

color

This property sets the foreground color of an element, which in HTML rendering means the text of an element; raster images are not affected by color. This is also the color applied to any borders of the element, unless overridden by border-color or one of the other border color properties (border-top-color, etc.).

Values: <color> | inherit

Initial value: User agent-specific

Applies to: All elements

Inherited: Yes

Computed value: As specified

content

This is the property used to define the generated content placed before or after an element. By default, this is likely to be inline content, but the type of box the content creates can be controlled using the property display.

Values: normal | [<string> | <uri> | <counter> | attr(<identifier>) | open-quote | close-quote | no-open-quote | no-close-quote]+ | inherit

Initial value: normal

Applies to: :before and :after pseudo-elements

Inherited: No

Computed value: For <uri> values, an absolute URI; for attribute references, the resulting string; otherwise, as specified

counter-increment

With this property, counters can be incremented (or decremented) by any value, positive or negative. If no <integer> is supplied, it defaults to 1.

Values: [<identifier> <integer>?]+ | none | inherit

Initial value: User agent-dependent

Applies to: All elements

Inherited: No

Computed value: As specified

counter-reset

With this property, counters can be set or reset to any value, positive or negative. If no <integer> is supplied, it defaults to 0.

Values: [<identifier> <integer>?]+ | none | inherit

Initial value: User agent-dependent

Applies to: All elements

Inherited: No

Computed value: As specified

cursor

This defines the cursor shape to be used when a mouse pointer is placed within the boundary of an element (although CSS2.1 does not define which edge creates this boundary).

Values: [[<uri>,]* [auto | default | pointer | crosshair | move | e-resize |
                      ne-resize | nw-resize | n-resize | se-resize | sw-resize | s-resize |
                      w-resize| text | wait | help | progress]] | inherit

Initial value: auto

Applies to: All elements

Inherited: Yes

Computed value: For <uri> values, an absolute URI; otherwise, as specified

direction

This property specifies the base writing direction of blocks and the direction of embeddings and overrides for the Unicode bidirectional algorithm. User agents that do not support bidirectional text are permitted to ignore this property.

Values: ltr | rtl | inherit

Initial value: ltr

Applies to: All elements

Inherited: Yes

Computed value: As specified

display

This is used to define the kind of display box an element generates during layout. Gratuitous use of display with a document type such as HTML can be dangerous, as it upsets the display hierarchy already defined in HTML. In the case of XML, which has no such built-in hierarchy, display is indispensable.

Values: none | inline | block | inline-block | list-item | run-in | table | inline-table | table-row-group | table-header-group | table-footer-group | table-row | table-column-group | table-column | table-cell | table-caption | inherit

Initial value: inline

Applies to: All elements

Inherited: No

Computed value: Varies for floated, positioned, and root elements (see CSS2.1, section 9.7); otherwise, as specified

Note: The values compact and marker appeared in CSS2 but were dropped from CSS2.1 due to a lack of widespread support

---

float

This defines the direction in which an element is floated. It has traditionally been applied to images to let text flow around them, but in CSS, any element may be floated. A floated element will generate a block-level box no matter what kind of element it may be. Floated nonreplaced elements should be given an explicit width; otherwise, they may tend to become as narrow as possible.

Values: left | right | none | inherit

Initial value: none

Applies to: All elements

Inherited: No

Computed value: As specified

---

font

This is a shorthand property used to set two or more aspects of an element's font all at once. It can also be used to set the element's font to match an aspect of the user's computing environment using keywords such as icon. Note that if these keywords are not used, the minimum font value must include the font size and family.

Values: [[<font-style> || <font-variant> || <font-weight>]? <font-size> [/ <line-height>]? <font-family>] | caption | icon | menu | message-box | small-caption | status-bar | inherit

Initial value: Refer to individual properties

Applies to: All elements

Inherited:	Yes
Percentages:	Calculated with respect to the parent element for <font-size> and with respect to the element's <font-size> for <line-height>
Computed value:	See individual properties (font-style, etc.)

font-family

This defines a font family to be used in the display of an element's text. Note that use of a specific font family (e.g., Geneva) is wholly dependent on that family being available on a user's machine; no font downloading is implied by this property. Therefore, the use of generic family names as a fallback is strongly encouraged.

Values:	[[<family-name>	<generic-family>],]* [<family-name>	<generic-family>]	inherit
Initial value:	User agent-specific
Applies to:	All elements
Inherited:	Yes
Computed value:	As specified

font-size

This sets the size of the font for an element. Note that it actually sets the height of the character boxes in the font; the actual character glyphs may be taller or shorter than these boxes (usually shorter). Each keyword must be larger than the next smallest keyword and smaller than the next biggest keyword. Negative length and percentage values are not permitted.

Values:	xx-small	x-small	small	medium	large	x-large	xx-large	smaller	larger	<length>	<percentage>	inherit
Initial value:	medium
Applies to:	All elements
Inherited:	Yes
Percentages:	Calculated with respect to the parent element's font size
Computed value:	An absolute length

font-style

This sets the font to use an italic, oblique, or normal font face. Italic text is generally defined as a separate face within the font family. It is theoretically possible for a user agent to compute a slanted font face from the normal face.

Values:	italic | oblique | normal | inherit
Initial value:	normal
Applies to:	All elements
Inherited:	Yes
Computed value:	As specified

font-variant

This property is basically used to define small-caps text. It is theoretically possible for a user agent to compute a small-caps font face from the normal face.

Values:	small-caps | normal | inherit
Initial value:	normal
Applies to:	All elements
Inherited:	Yes
Computed value:	As specified

font-weight

This property sets the font weight used in rendering an element's text. The numeric value 400 is equivalent to the keyword normal, and 700 is equivalent to bold. Each numeric value must be at least as light as the next lowest number and at least as heavy as the next highest number.

Values:	normal | bold | bolder | lighter | 100 | 200 | 300 | 400 | 500 | 600 | 700 | 800 | 900 | inherit
Initial value:	normal
Applies to:	All elements
Inherited:	Yes
Computed value:	One of the numeric values (100, etc.), or one of the numeric values plus one of the relative values (bolder or lighter)

height

This defines the height of an element's content area, outside of which padding, borders, and margins are added. This property is ignored for inline nonreplaced elements. Negative length and percentage values are not permitted.

Values: <length> | <percentage> | auto | inherit

Initial value: auto

Applies to: Block-level and replaced elements

Inherited: No

Percentages: Calculated with respect to the height of the containing block

Computed value: For auto and percentage values, as specified; otherwise, an absolute length, unless the property does not apply to the element (then auto)

left

This property defines the offset between the left outer margin edge of a positioned element and the left edge of its containing block.

Values: <length> | <percentage> | auto | inherit

Initial value: auto

Applies to: Positioned elements (that is, elements for which the value of position is something other than static)

Inherited: No

Percentages: Refer to the width of the containing block

Computed value: For relatively positioned elements, see Note; for static elements, auto; for length values, the corresponding absolute length; for percentage values, the specified value; otherwise, auto

Note: For relatively positioned elements, the computed value of left always equals right

letter-spacing

This defines the amount of whitespace to be inserted between the character boxes of text. Since character glyphs are typically narrower than their character boxes, length values create a modifier to the usual spacing between letters. Thus, normal is synonymous with 0. Negative length values are permitted and will cause letters to bunch closer together.

Values: <length> | normal | inherit

Initial value: normal

Applies to:	All elements
Inherited:	Yes
Computed value:	For length values, the absolute length; otherwise, normal

line-height

This property influences the layout of line boxes. When applied to a block-level element, it defines the minimum distance between baselines within that element, but not the maximum. The difference between the computed values of line-height and font-size (called "leading" in CSS) is split in half and added to the top and bottom of each piece of content in a line of text. The shortest box that can enclose all of those pieces of content is the line box. A raw number value assigns a scaling factor, which is inherited instead of a computed value. Negative values are not permitted.

Values:	<length> | <percentage> | <number> | normal | inherit
Initial value:	normal
Applies to:	All elements (but see text regarding replaced and block-level elements)
Inherited:	Yes
Percentages:	Relative to the font size of the element
Computed value:	For length and percentage values, the absolute value; otherwise, as specified

list-style

This is a shorthand property that condenses all the other list-style properties. Because it applies to any element that has a display of list-item, it will apply only to li elements in ordinary HTML and XHTML, although it can be applied to any element and inherited by list-item elements.

Values:	[<list-style-type> || <list-style-image> || <list-style-position>] | inherit
Initial value:	Refer to individual properties
Applies to:	Elements whose display value is list-item
Inherited:	Yes
Computed value:	See individual properties

list-style-image

This specifies an image to be used as the marker on an ordered or unordered list item. The placement of the image with respect to the content of the list item can be broadly controlled using list-style-position.

Values:	<uri>	none	inherit
Initial value:	none
Applies to:	Elements whose display value is list-item
Inherited:	Yes
Computed value:	For <uri> values, the absolute URI; otherwise, none

list-style-position

This property is used to declare the position of the list marker with respect to the content of the list item. Outside markers are placed some distance from the border edge of the list item, but the distance is not defined in CSS. Inside markers are treated as though they were an inline element inserted at the beginning of the list item's content.

Values:	inside	outside	inherit
Initial value:	outside
Applies to:	Elements whose display value is list-item
Inherited:	Yes
Computed value:	As specified

list-style-type

This is used to declare the type of marker system to be used in the presentation of a list.

CSS2.1 values:	disc	circle	square	decimal	decimal-leading-zero	lower-roman	upper-roman	lower-greek	lower-latin	upper-latin	armenian	georgian	none	inherit
CSS2 values:	disc	circle	square	decimal	decimal-leading-zero	upper-alpha	lower-alpha	upper-roman	lower-roman	lower-greek	hebrew	armenian	georgian	cjk-ideographic	hiragana	katakana	hiragana-iroha	none	inherit
Initial value:	disc
Applies to:	Elements whose display value is list-item
Inherited:	Yes
Computed value:	As specified

margin

This shorthand property sets the width of the overall margin for an element or sets the widths of each individual side margin. Vertically adjacent margins of block-level elements are collapsed, whereas inline elements effectively do not take top and bottom margins. The left and right margins of inline elements do not collapse, nor do margins on floated elements. Negative margin values are permitted, but use them with caution.

Values: [<length> | <percentage> | auto]{1,4} | inherit

Initial value: Not defined

Applies to: All elements

Inherited: No

Percentages: Refer to the width of the containing block

Computed value: See individual properties

margin-bottom

This sets the width of the bottom margin for an element. Negative values are permitted, but use them with caution.

Values: <length> | <percentage> | auto | inherit

Initial value: 0

Applies to: All elements

Inherited: No

Percentages: Refer to the width of the containing block

Computed value: For percentages, as specified; for length values, the absolute length

margin-left

This sets the width of the left margin for an element. Negative values are permitted, but use them with caution.

Values: <length> | <percentage> | auto | inherit

Initial value: 0

Applies to: All elements

Inherited: No

Percentages: Refer to the width of the containing block

Computed value: For percentages, as specified; for length values, the absolute length

margin-right

This sets the width of the right margin for an element. Negative values are permitted, but use them with caution.

Values: <length> | <percentage> | auto | inherit

Initial value: 0

Applies to: All elements

Inherited: No

Percentages: Refer to the width of the containing block

Computed value: For percentages, as specified; for length values, the absolute length

margin-top

This sets the width of the top margin for an element. Negative values are permitted, but use them with caution.

Values: <length> | <percentage> | auto | inherit

Initial value: 0

Applies to: All elements

Inherited: No

Percentages: Refer to the width of the containing block

Computed value: For percentages, as specified; for length values, the absolute length

max-height

The value of this property sets a maximum constraint on the height of the element. Thus, the element can be shorter than the specified value, but not taller. Negative values are not permitted.

Values: <length> | <percentage> | none | inherit

Initial value: none

Applies to: All elements except inline nonreplaced elements and table elements

Inherited: No

Percentages: Refer to the height of the containing block

Computed value: For percentages, as specified; for length values, the absolute length; otherwise, none

max-width

The value of this property sets a maximum constraint on the width of the element. Thus, the element can be narrower than the specified value, but not wider. Negative values are not permitted.

Values: <length> | <percentage> | none | inherit

Initial value: none

Applies to: All elements except inline nonreplaced elements and table elements

Inherited: No

Percentages: Refer to the width of the containing block

Computed value: For percentages, as specified; for length values, the absolute length; otherwise, none

---

min-height

The value of this property sets a minimum constraint on the height of the element. Thus, the element can be taller than the specified value, but not shorter. Negative values are not permitted.

Values: <length> | <percentage> | inherit

Initial value: 0

Applies to: All elements except inline nonreplaced elements and table elements

Inherited: No

Percentages: Refer to the height of the containing block

Computed value: For percentages, as specified; for length values, the absolute length

---

min-width

The value of this property sets a minimum constraint on the width of the element. Thus, the element can be wider than the specified value, but not narrower. Negative values are not permitted.

Values: <length> | <percentage> | inherit

Initial value: 0

Applies to: All elements except inline nonreplaced elements and table elements

Inherited: No

Percentages: refer to the width of the containing block

Computed value: For percentages, as specified; for length values, the absolute length; otherwise, none

outline

This shorthand property is used to set the overall outline for an element. Outlines can be of irregular shape, and they do not change or otherwise affect the placement of elements.

Values: [<outline-color> || <outline-style> || <outline-width>] | inherit

Initial value: Not defined for shorthand properties

Applies to: All elements

Inherited: No

Computed value: See individual properties (outline-color, etc.)

outline-color

This property sets the color for the visible portions of the overall outline of an element. Remember that an outline's style must be something other than none for any border to appear.

Values: <color> | invert | inherit

Initial value: invert (or user agent-specific; see text)

Applies to: All elements

Inherited: No

Computed value: As specified

outline-style

This property is used to set the style for the overall border of an element. The style must be something other than none for any outline to appear.

Values: none | dotted | dashed | solid | double | groove | ridge | inset | outset | inherit

Initial value: none

Applies to: All elements

Inherited: No

Computed value: As specified

outline-width

This property sets the width for the overall outline of an element. The width will take effect only for a given outline if the outline's style is something other than none. If the style is none, the width is effectively reset to 0. Negative length values are not permitted.

Values:	thin	medium	thick	<length>	inherit

Initial value:	medium

Applies to:	All elements

Inherited:	No

Computed value:	Absolute length; 0 if the style of the border is none or hidden

---

overflow

This defines what happens to content that overflows the content area of an element. For the value scroll, user agents are supposed to provide a scrolling mechanism whether or not it is actually needed; thus, for example, scrollbars would appear even if all content can fit within the element box.

Values:	visible	hidden	scroll	auto	inherit

Initial value:	visible

Applies to:	Block-level and replaced elements

Inherited:	No

Computed value:	As specified

---

padding

This shorthand property sets the width of the overall padding for an element or sets the widths of each individual side padding. Padding set on inline nonreplaced elements does not affect line-height calculations; therefore, such an element with both padding and a background may visibly extend into other lines and potentially overlap other content. The background of the element will extend throughout the padding. Negative padding values are not permitted.

Values:	[<length>	<percentage>]{1,4}	inherit

Initial value:	Not defined for shorthand elements

Applies to:	All elements

Inherited:	No

Percentages:	Refer to the width of the containing block

Computed value:	See individual properties (padding-top, etc.)

Note:	Padding can never be negative

padding-bottom

This property sets the width of the bottom padding for an element. Bottom padding set on inline nonreplaced elements does not affect line-height calculations; therefore, such an element with both bottom padding and a background may visibly extend into other lines and potentially overlap other content. Negative padding values are not permitted.

Values:	<length> | <percentage> | inherit
Initial value:	0
Applies to:	All elements
Inherited:	No
Percentages:	Refer to the width of the containing block
Computed value:	For percentage values, as specified; for length values, the absolute length
Note:	Padding can never be negative

padding-left

This property sets the width of the left padding for an element. Left padding set for an inline nonreplaced element will appear only on the left edge of the first inline box generated by the element. Negative padding values are not permitted.

Values:	<length> | <percentage> | inherit
Initial value:	0
Applies to:	All elements
Inherited:	No
Percentages:	Refer to the width of the containing block
Computed value:	For percentage values, as specified; for length values, the absolute length
Note:	Padding can never be negative

padding-right

This property sets the width of the right padding for an element. Right padding set for an inline nonreplaced element will appear only on the right edge of the last inline box generated by the element. Negative padding values are not permitted.

Values:	<length> | <percentage> | inherit
Initial value:	0
Applies to:	All elements
Inherited:	No

Percentages:	Refer to the width of the containing block
Computed value:	For percentage values, as specified; for length values, the absolute length
Note:	Padding can never be negative

padding-top

This property sets the width of the top padding for an element. Top padding set on inline nonreplaced elements does not affect line-height calculations; therefore, such an element with both top padding and a background may visibly extend into other lines and potentially overlap other content. Negative padding values are not permitted.

Values:	<length>	<percentage>	inherit
Initial value:	0
Applies to:	All elements
Inherited:	No
Percentages:	Refer to the width of the containing block
Computed value:	For percentage values, as specified; for length values, the absolute length
Note:	Padding can never be negative

position

This defines the positioning scheme used to lay out an element. Any element may be positioned, although elements positioned with absolute or fixed will generate a block-level box no matter what kind of element they are. An element that is relatively positioned is offset from its default placement in the normal flow.

Values:	static	relative	absolute	fixed	inherit
Initial value:	static
Applies to:	All elements
Inherited:	No
Computed value:	As specified

quotes

This property is used to determine the quotation pattern used with quotes and nested quotes. The actual quote marks are inserted via the property content.

Values:	[<string> <string>]+	none	inherit
Initial value:	User agent-dependent

Applies to:	All elements
Inherited:	Yes
Computed value:	As specified

right

This property defines the offset between the right outer margin edge of a positioned element and the right edge of its containing block.

Values:	<length>	<percentage>	auto	inherit
Initial value:	auto
Applies to:	Positioned elements (that is, elements for which the value of position is something other than static)
Inherited:	No
Percentages:	Refer to the width of the containing block
Computed value:	For relatively positioned elements, see Note; for static elements, auto; for length values, the corresponding absolute length; for percentage values, the specified value; otherwise, auto
Note:	For relatively positioned elements, the computed value of left always equals right

text-align

This property sets the horizontal alignment of text within a block-level element by defining the point with which line boxes are aligned. The value justify is supported by allowing user agents to programmatically adjust the letter and word spacing of the line's content; results may vary by user agent.

CSS2.1 values:	left	center	right	justify	inherit
CSS2 values:	left	center	right	justify	<string>	inherit
Initial value:	User agent-specific; may also depend on writing direction
Applies to:	Block-level elements
Inherited:	Yes
Computed value:	As specified
Note:	CSS2 included a <string> value that was dropped from CSS2.1 due to a lack of widespread support

text-decoration

This property allows certain text effects such as underlining. These decorations will "span" descendant elements that do not have decorations of their own. User agents are not required to support blink.

Values:	none | [underline || overline || line-through || blink] | inherit
Initial value:	none
Applies to:	All elements
Inherited:	No
Computed value:	As specified

text-indent

Used to define the indentation of the first line of content in a block-level element. This is most often used to create a "tab" effect. Negative values are permitted and cause "outdent" (or "hanging indent") effects.

Values:	<length> | <percentage> | inherit
Initial value:	0
Applies to:	Block-level elements
Inherited:	Yes
Percentages:	Refer to the width of the containg block
Computed value:	For percentage values, as specified; for length values, the absolute length

text-transform

This property changes the case of letters in an element, regardless of the case of the text in the document source. The determination of which letters are to be capitalized by the value capitalize is not precisely defined, as it depends on user agents knowing how to recognize a "word."

Values:	uppercase | lowercase | capitalize | none | inherit
Initial value:	none
Applies to:	All elements
Inherited:	Yes
Computed value:	As specified

top

This property defines the offset between the top outer margin edge of a positioned element and the top edge of its containing block.

Values: <length> | <percentage> | auto | inherit

Initial value: auto

Applies to: Positioned elements (that is, elements for which the value of position is something other than static)

Inherited: No

Percentages: Refer to the height of the containing block

Computed value: For relatively positioned elements, see Note; for static elements, auto; for length values, the corresponding absolute length; for percentage values, the specified value; otherwise, auto

Note: For relatively positioned elements, if both top and bottom are auto, their computed values are both 0; if one of them is auto, it becomes the negative of the other; if neither is auto, bottom will become the negative of the value of top

unicode-bidi

This allows the author to generate levels of embedding within the Unicode embedding algorithm. User agents that do not support bidirectional text are permitted to ignore this property.

Values: normal | embed | bidi-override | inherit

Initial value: normal

Applies to: All elements

Inherited: No

Computed value: As specified

vertical-align

This defines the vertical alignment of an inline element's baseline with respect to the baseline of the line in which it resides. Negative length and percentage values are permitted, and they lower the element instead of raising it. In table cells, this property sets the alignment of the content of the cell within the cell box.

Values: baseline | sub | super | top | text-top | middle | bottom | text-bottom | <percentage> | <length> | inherit

Initial value: baseline

Applies to:	Inline elements and table cells
Inherited:	No
Percentages:	Refer to the value of line-height for the element
Computed value:	For percentage and length values, the absolute length; otherwise, as specified
Note:	When applied to table cells, only the values baseline, top, middle, and bottom are recognized

visibility

This specifies whether the element box generated by an element is rendered. This means the element could occupy the space it would ordinarily, but be completely invisible. The value collapse is used in tables to remove columns or rows from the table's layout.

Values:	visible	hidden	collapse	inherit
Initial value:	visible
Applies to:	All elements
Inherited:	Yes
Computed value:	As specified

white-space

This declares how whitespace within an element is handled during layout. The values pre-wrap and pre-line were added in CSS2.1.

Values:	normal	nowrap	pre	pre-wrap	pre-line	inherit
Initial value:	normal
Applies to:	All elements (CSS2.1); block-level elements (CSS1 and CSS2)
Inherited:	No
Computed value:	As specified

width

This defines the width of an element's content area, outside of which padding, borders, and margins are added. This property is ignored for inline nonreplaced elements. Negative length and percentage values are not permitted.

Values:	<length>	<percentage>	auto	inherit
Initial value:	auto

Applies to:	Block-level and replaced elements
Inherited:	No
Percentages:	Refer to the width of the containing block
Computed value:	For auto and percentage values, as specified; otherwise, an absolute length, unless the property does not apply to the element (then auto)

word-spacing

This defines the amount of whitespace to be inserted between words in an element. For the purposes of this property, a "word" is defined as a string of characters surrounded by whitespace. Length values create a modifier to the usual spacing between words; thus, normal is synonymous with 0. Negative length values are permitted and will cause words to bunch closer together.

Values:	<length>	normal	inherit
Initial value:	normal
Applies to:	All elements
Inherited:	Yes
Computed value:	For normal, the absolute length 0; otherwise, the absolute length

z-index

This property sets the placement of a positioned element along the z-axis, which is defined as the axis that extends perpendicular to the display area. Positive numbers are closer to the user, and negative numbers are further away.

Values:	<integer>	auto	inherit
Initial value:	auto
Applies to:	Positioned elements
Inherited:	No
Computed value:	As specified

Tables

border-collapse

This property defines the layout model used in laying out the borders in a table—i.e., those applied to cells, rows, and so forth. Although the property applies only to tables, it is inherited by all the elements within the table.

Values:	collapse	separate	inherit
Initial value:	separate
Applies to:	Elements with the display value table or inline-table
Inherited:	Yes
Computed value:	As specified
Note:	In CSS2, the default value was collapse

border-spacing

This specifies the distance between cell borders in the separated borders model. The first of the two length values is the horizontal separation, and the second is the vertical. This property is ignored unless border-collapse is set to separate. Although the property only applies to tables, it is inherited by all of the elements within the table.

Values:	<length> <length>?	inherit
Initial value:	0
Applies to:	Elements with the display value table or inline-table
Inherited:	Yes
Computed value:	Two absolute lengths
Note:	This property is ignored unless border-collapse value is separate

caption-side

This specifies the placement of a table caption with respect to the table box. The caption is rendered as though it were a block-level element placed just before (or after) the table.

Values:	top	bottom
Initial value:	top
Applies to:	Elements with the display value table-caption
Inherited:	Yes
Computed value:	As specified
Note:	The values left and right appeared in CSS2 but were dropped from CSS2.1 due to a lack of widespread support

empty-cells

This defines the presentation of table cells that contain no content. If shown, the cell's borders and background are drawn. This property is ignored unless border-collapse is set to separate.

Values:	show | hide | inherit
Initial value:	show
Applies to:	Elements with the display value table-cell
Inherited:	Yes
Computed value:	As specified
Note:	This property is ignored unless border-collapse value is separate

table-layout

This property specifies which layout algorithm is used to lay out a table. The fixed layout algorithm is faster but less flexible, while the automatic algorithm is slower but more reflective of traditional HTML tables.

Values:	auto | fixed | inherit
Initial value:	auto
Applies to:	Elements with the display value table or inline-table
Inherited:	Yes
Computed value:	As specified

Paged Media

orphans

This specifies the minimum number of text lines within the element that can be left at the bottom of a page. This can affect the placement of page breaks within the element.

Values:	<integer> | inherit
Initial value:	2
Applies to:	Block-level elements
Inherited:	Yes
Computed value:	As specified

page-break-after

This declares whether page breaks should be placed after an element. While it is possible to force breaks with always, it is not possible to guarantee prevention; the best an author can do is ask the user agent to avoid inserting a page break if possible.

Values:	auto | always | avoid | left | right | inherit
Initial value:	auto
Applies to:	Nonfloated block-level elements with a position value of relative or static
Inherited:	No
Computed value: As specified	

page-break-before

Declares whether page breaks should be placed before an element. While it is possible to force breaks with always, it is not possible to guarantee prevention; the best an author can do is ask the user agent to avoid inserting a page break if possible.

Values:	auto | always | avoid | left | right | inherit
Initial value:	auto
Applies to:	Nonfloated block-level elements with a position value of relative or static
Inherited:	No
Computed value: As specified	

page-break-inside

This declares whether page breaks should be placed inside an element. Because an element might be taller than a page box, it is not possible to guarantee prevention; the best an author can do is ask the user agent to avoid inserting a page break if possible.

Values:	auto | avoid | inherit
Initial value:	auto
Applies to:	Nonfloated block-level elements with a position value of relative or static
Inherited:	Yes
Computed value: As specified	

widows

This specifies the minimum number of text lines within the element that can be left at the top of a page. This can affect the placement of page breaks within the element.

Values:	<integer> | inherit
Initial value:	2

Applies to:	Block-level elements
Inherited:	Yes
Computed value:	As specified

Dropped from CSS2.1

The following properties appeared in CSS2 but were dropped from CSS2.1 due to a lack of widespread support. They do not have computed value information since computed values were first explicitly defined in CSS2.1.

Visual Styles

font-size-adjust

The aim of this property is to allow authors to trigger font scaling such that substitute fonts will not look too different from the font the author intended, even if the substitute font has a different x-height. Note that this property does not appear in CSS2.1.

Values:	<number> | none | inherit
Initial value:	none
Applies to:	All elements
Inherited:	Yes

font-stretch

With this property, the character glyphs in a given font can be made wider or narrower, ideally by selected condensed or expanded faces from the font's family. Note that this property does not appear in CSS2.1.

Values:	normal | wider | narrower | ultra-condensed | extra-condensed | condensed | semi-condensed | semi-expanded | expanded | extra-expanded | ultra-expanded | inherit
Initial value:	normal
Applies to:	All elements
Inherited:	Yes

marker-offset

This property specifies the distance between the nearest border edge of a marker box and its associated element box.

Values: <length> | auto | inherit

Initial value: auto

Applies to: Elements with a display value of marker

Inherited: No

Note: This property is obsolete as of CSS2.1 and will likely not reappear in CSS3, and the same is true for the display value of marker; as of this writing, it appears that other mechanisms will be used to achieve these effects

text-shadow

This permits the assignment of one or more "shadows" to the text in an element. The first two length values in a shadow definition set horizontal and vertical offsets, respectively, from the element's text. The third length defines a blurring radius. Note that this property does not appear in CSS2.1.

Values: none | [<color> || <length> <length> <length>? ,]* [<color> || <length> <length> <length>?] | inherit

Initial value: none

Applies to: All elements

Inherited: No

Paged Media

marks

This property defines whether "cross marks" (otherwise known as register marks or registration marks) should be placed outside the content area but within the printable area of the canvas. The exact placement and rendering of the marks is not defined. Note that this value does not appear in CSS2.1.

Values: [crop || cross] | none | inherit

Initial value: none

Applies to: Page context

Inherited: N/A

page

This property, in conjunction with size, specifies a particular page type to be used in the printing of an element. Note that this property does not appear in CSS2.1.

Values:	<identifier> | inherit
Initial value:	auto
Applies to:	Block-level elements
Inherited:	Yes

size

With this property, authors can declare the size and orientation of the page box used in the printing of an element. It can be used in conjunction with page, although this is not always necessary. Note that this property does not appear in CSS2.1.

Values:	<length>{1,2} | auto | portrait | landscape | inherit
Initial value:	auto
Applies to:	The page area
Inherited:	No

Aural Styles

azimuth

This property sets the angle along the horizontal plane (otherwise known as the horizon) from which a sound should seem to emanate. This is used in conjunction with elevation to place the sound at a point on a hypothetical sphere with the user at its center.

Values:	<angle> | [[left-side | far-left | left | center-left | center | center-right | right | far-right | right-side] || behind] | leftwards | rightwards | inherit
Initial value:	center
Applies to:	All elements
Inherited:	Yes
Computed value:	Normalized angle

cue

This is a shorthand property that allows an author to define cues that precede and follow the audio rendering of an element's content. A "cue" is something like an auditory icon.

Values:	[<cue-before>		<cue-after>]	inherit
Initial value:	none
Applies to:	All elements
Inherited:	No
Computed value:	See individual properties (cue-before, etc.)

cue-after

This property allows an author to define a cue that follows the audio rendering of an element's content.

Values:	<uri>	none	inherit
Initial value:	none
Applies to:	All elements
Inherited:	No
Computed value:	For <uri> values, the absolute URI; otherwise, none

cue-before

This property allows an author to define a cue that precedes the audio rendering of an element's content.

Values:	<uri>	none	inherit
Initial value:	none
Applies to:	All elements
Inherited:	No
Computed value:	For <uri> values, the absolute URI; otherwise, none

elevation

This property sets the angle above or below the horizontal plane (otherwise known as the horizon) from which a sound should seem to emanate. This is used in conjunction with azimuth to place the sound at a point on a hypothetical sphere with the user at its center.

Values:	<angle>	below	level	above	higher	lower	inherit
Initial value:	level
Applies to:	All elements
Inherited:	Yes
Computed value:	Normalized angle

pause

This is a shorthand property that allows an author to define pauses that precede and follow the audio rendering of an element's content. A "pause" is an interval in which no content is audibly rendered, although background sounds may still be audible.

Values:	[[<time> | <percentage>]{1,2}] | inherit
Initial value:	0
Applies to:	All elements
Inherited:	No
Computed value:	See individual properties (pause-before, etc.)

pause-after

This property allows an author to define the length of a pause that follows the audio rendering of an element's content.

Values:	<time> | <percentage> | inherit
Initial value:s:	0
Applies to:	All elements
Inherited:	No
Computed value:	The absolute time value

pause-before

This property allows an author to define the length of a pause that precedes the audio rendering of an element's content.

Values:	<time> | <percentage> | inherit
Initial values:	0
Applies to:	All elements
Inherited:	No
Computed value:	The absolute time value

pitch

Specifies the average pitch (frequency) of the speaking voice used to audibly render the element's content. The average pitch of a voice will depend greatly on the voice family.

Values:	<frequency> | x-low | low | medium | high | x-high | inherit
Initial value:	medium
Applies to:	All elements
Inherited:	Yes
Computed value:	The absolute frequency value

pitch-range

This property specifies the variation in average pitch used by the speaking voice, while audibly rendering the element's content. The higher the variation, the more "animated" the voice will sound.

Values:	<number> | inherit
Initial value:	50
Applies to:	All elements
Inherited:	Yes
Computed value:	As specified

play-during

This provides a sound to be played "in the background" while the element's contents are audibly rendered. The sound can be mixed with other background sounds (set using play-during on an ancestor element), or it can replace other sounds for the duration of the element's audio rendering.

Values:	<uri> | [mix || repeat]? | auto | none | inherit
Initial value:	auto
Applies to:	All elements
Inherited:	No
Computed value:	For <uri> values, the absolute URI; otherwise, as specified

richness

This property sets the "brightness" of the speaking voice used when audibly rendering the element's content. The brighter the voice, the more it will "carry."

Values:	<number> | inherit
Initial value:	50

Applies to: All elements

Inherited: yes

Computed value: As specified

---

speak

This determines how an element's contents will be audibly rendered, or indeed if they will be rendered at all. The value `spell-out` is typically used for acronyms and abbreviations, such as W3C or CSS. If the value is `none`, the element is skipped (it takes no time to be audibly rendered).

Values: `normal | none | spell-out | inherit`

Initial value: `normal`

Applies to: All elements

Inherited: Yes

Computed value: As specified

---

speak-header

This specifies whether the content of table headers is spoken before every cell associated with those headers, or only when the header associated with a cell is different from the header associated with the previously rendered cell.

Values: `once | always | inherit`

Initial value: `once`

Applies to: Elements containing table header information

Inherited: Yes

Computed value: As specified

---

speak-numeral

This property determines how numbers are spoken during audible rendering.

Values: `digits | continuous | inherit`

Initial value: `continuous`

Applies to: All elements

Inherited:	Yes
Computed value:	As specified

speak-punctuation

This property determines how punctuation is spoken during audible rendering. The value code causes punctuation symbols to be rendered literally.

Values:	code | none | inherit
Initial value:	none
Applies to:	All elements
Inherited:	Yes
Computed value:	As specified

speech-rate

This sets the average rate at which words are spoken when an element's content is audibly rendered.

Values:	<number> | x-slow | slow | medium | fast | x-fast | faster | slower | inherit
Initial value:	medium
Applies to:	All elements
Inherited:	Yes
Computed value:	An absolute number

stress

This property affects the height of peaks in the intonation of a speaking voice. These peaks are in turn generated by stress marks within a language.

Values:	<number> | inherit
Initial value:	50
Applies to:	All elements
Inherited:	Yes
Computed value:	As specified

voice-family

This property is used to define a list of voice families that can be used in the audio rendering of an element's content, and is comparable to font-family. The permitted generic voices are male, female, and child.

Values: [[<specific-voice> | <generic-voice>],]* [<specific-voice> | <generic-voice>] | inherit

Initial value: User agent-dependent

Applies to: All elements

Inherited: Yes

Computed value: As specified

volume

This sets the median volume level for the waveform of the audibly rendered content. Thus, a waveform with large peaks and valleys may go well above or below the volume level set with this property. Note that 0 is not the same as silent.

Values: <number> | <percentage> | silent | x-soft | soft | medium | loud | x-loud | inherit

Initial value: medium

Applies to: All elements

Inherited: Yes

Computed value: An absolute number

Selector, Pseudo-Class, and Pseudo-Element Reference

Selectors

Universal Selector

This selector matches any element name in the document's language. If a rule does not have an explicit selector, then the universal selector is inferred.

Pattern: *

Examples:

```
* {color: red;}
div * p {color: blue;}
```

Type Selector

This selector matches the name of an element in the document's language. Every instance of the element name is matched. (CSS1 referred to these as *element selectors*.)

Pattern: element1

Examples:

```
body {background: #FFF;}
p {font-size: 1em;}
```

Descendant Selector

This allows the author to select an element based on its status as a descendant of another element. The matched element can be a child, grandchild, great-grandchild, etc., of the ancestor element. (CSS1 referred to these as contextual selectors.)

Pattern: element1 element2

Examples:

```
body h1 {font-size: 200%;}
table tr td div ul li {color: purple;}
```

Child Selector

This type of selector is used to match an element based on its status as a child of another element. This is more restrictive than a descendant element, since only a child will be matched.

Pattern: element1 > element2

Examples:

```
div > p {color: cyan;}
ul > li {font-weight: bold;}
```

Adjacent Sibling Selector

This allows the author to select an element that is the following adjacent sibling of another element. Any text between the two elements is ignored; only elements and their positions in the document tree are considered.

Pattern: element1 + element2

Examples:

```
table + p {margin-top: 2.5em;}
h1 + * {margin-top: 0;}
```

Class Selector

In languages that permit it, such as HTML, SVG, and MathML, a class selector using "dot notation" can be used to select elements that have a class containing a specific value or values. The name of the class value must immediately follow the dot. Multiple class values can be "chained" together. If no element name precedes the dot, the selector matches all elements containing that class value.

Patterns: element1.classname element1.classname1.classname2

Examples:

```
p.urgent {color: red;}
a.external {font-style: italic;}
.example {background: olive;}
```

ID Selector

In languages that permit it, such as HTML, an ID selector using "hash notation" can be used to select elements that have an ID containing a specific value or values. The name of the ID value must immediately follow the octothorpe (#). If no element name precedes the octothorpe, the selector matches all elements containing that ID value.

Pattern: `element1#idname`

Examples:

```
h1#page-title {font-size: 250%;}
body#home {background: silver;}
#example {background: lime;}
```

Simple Attribute Selector

This allows authors to select any element based on the presence of an attribute, regardless of the attribute's value.

Pattern: `element1[attr]`

Examples:

```
a[rel] {border-bottom: 3px double gray;}
p[class] {border: 1px dotted silver;}
```

Exact Attribute Value Selector

This allows authors to select any element based on the precise complete value of an attribute.

Pattern: `element1[attr="value"]`

Examples:

```
a[rel="Home"] {font-weight: bold;}
p[class="urgent"] {color: red;;}
```

Partial Attribute Value Selector

This allows authors to select any element based on a portion of the space-separated value of an attribute. Note that `[class~="value"]` is equivalent to `.value` (see above).

Pattern: `element1[attr~="value"]`

Examples:

```
a[rel~="friend"] {text-transform: uppercase;}
p[class~="warning"] {background: yellow;}
```

Beginning Substring Attribute Value Selector

This allows authors to select any element based on a substring at the very beginning of an attribute's value.

Pattern: `element1[attr^="substring"]`

Examples:

```
a[href^="/blog"] {text-transform: uppercase;}
p[class^="test-"] {background: yellow;}
```

Ending Substring Attribute Value Selector

This allows authors to select any element based on a substring at the very end of an attribute's value.

Pattern: `element1[attr$="substring"]`

Example:

```
a[href$=".pdf"] {font-style: italic;}
```

Arbitrary Substring Attribute Value Selector

This allows authors to select any element based on a substring found anywhere within an attribute's value.

Pattern: `element1[attr*="substring"]`

Examples:

```
a[href*="oreilly.com"] {font-weight: bold;}
div [class*="port"] {border: 1px solid red;}
```

Language Attribute Selector

This allows authors to select any element with a `lang` attribute whose value is a hyphen-separated list of values, starting with the value provided in the selector.

Pattern: `element1[lang|="lc"]`

Examples:

```
html[lang|="en"] {color: gray;}
```

Pseudo-Classes and Pseudo-Elements

:active

This applies to an element during the period in which it is activated. The most common example of this is clicking on a hyperlink in an HTML document: during the time that the mouse button is held down, the link is active. There are other ways to activate elements, and other elements can in theory be activated, although CSS doesn't define this.

Type: Pseudo-class

Applies to: An element that is being activated

Examples:

```
a:active {color: red;}
*:active {background: blue;}
```

:after

This allows the author to insert generated content at the end of an element's content. By default, the pseudo-element is inline, but this can be changed using the property display.

Type: Pseudo-element

Generates: A pseudo-element containing generated content placed after the content in the element

Examples:

```
a.external:after {content: " " url(/icons/globe.gif);}
p:after {content: " | ";}
```

:before

This allows the author to insert generated content at the beginning of an element's content. By default, the pseudo-element is inline, but this can be changed using the property display.

Type: Pseudo-element

Generates: A pseudo-element containing generated content placed before the content in the element

Examples:

```
a[href]:before {content: "[LINK] ";}
p:before {content: attr(class);}
```

:first-child

With this pseudo-class, an element is matched only when it is the first child of another element. For example, p:first-child will select any p element that is the first child of some other element. It does *not*, as is commonly assumed, select whatever element is the first child of a paragraph; for that, an author would write p > *:first-child.

Type: Pseudo-class

Applies to: Any element that is the first child of another element

Examples:

```
body *:first-child {font-weight: bold;}
p:first-child {font-size: 125%;}
```

:first-letter

This is used to style the first letter of an element. Any leading punctuation should be styled along with the first letter. Some languages have letter combinations that should be treated as a single character, and a user agent may apply the first-letter style to both. Prior to CSS2.1, :first-letter could be attached only to block-level elements. CSS2.1 expands its scope to include all elements. There is a limited set of properties that can apply to a first letter.

Type: Pseudo-element

Generates: A pseudo-element that contains the first letter of an element

Examples:

```
h1:first-letter {font-size: 166%;}
a:first-letter {text-decoration: underline;}
```

:first-line

This is used to style the first line of text in an element, no matter how many or how few words may appear in that line. :first-line can be attached only to block-level elements. There is a limited set of properties that can apply to a first line.

Type: Pseudo-element

Generates: A pseudo-element that contains the first formatted line of an element

Examples:

```
p.lead:first-line {font-weight: bold;}
```

:focus

This applies to an element during the period in which it has focus. One example from HTML is an input box that has the text-input cursor within it; that is, when the user starts typing, text will be entered into that box. Other elements, such as hyperlinks, can also have focus, although CSS does not define which ones.

Type: Pseudo-class

Applies to: An element that has focus

Examples:

```
a:focus {outline: 1px dotted red;}
input:focus {background: yellow;}
```

:hover

This applies to an element during the period in which it is "hovered." Hovering is defined as the user designating an element without activating it. The most common example of this is moving the mouse pointer inside the boundaries of a hyperlink in an HTML document. Other elements can in theory be hovered, although CSS doesn't define which ones.

Type: Pseudo-class

Applies to: An element in a hovered state

Examples:

```
a[href]:hover {text-decoration: underline;}
p:hover {background: yellow;}
```

:lang

This matches elements based on their human language encoding. Such language information must be contained within or otherwise associated with the document; it cannot be assigned from CSS. The handling of :lang is the same as for |= attribute selectors.

Type: Pseudo-class

Applies to: Any element with associated language-encoding information

Examples:

```
html:lang(en) {background: silver;}
*:lang(fr) {quotes: '«  '  ' »';}
```

:link

This applies to a link to a URI that has not been visited; that is, the URI to which the link points does not appear in the user agent's history. This state is mutually exclusive with the :visited state.

Type: Pseudo-class

Applies to: A link to another resource that has not been visited

Examples:

```
a:link {color: blue;}
*:link {text-decoration: underline;}
```

:visited

This applies to a link to a URI that has been visited; that is, the URI to which the link points appears in the user agent's history. This state is mutually exclusive with the :link state.

Type: Pseudo-class

Applies to: A link to another resource that has already been visited

Examples:

```
a:visited {color: purple;}
*:visited {color: gray;}
```

Sample HTML 4 Style Sheet

The following style sheet is adapted from Appendix D of the CSS2.1 specification. There are two important things to note. The first is that while CSS2.1 says that "developers are encouraged to use [this] as a default style sheet in their implementations," this isn't always possible. For example, there is a rule that states:

```
ol, ul, dir, menu, dd
                {margin-left: 40px;}
```

This describes the legacy indenting of lists to a distance of 40 pixels, and it uses a left margin to do it. However, some browsers have used a 40-pixel left padding instead of a margin, believing this to be a better solution. (See Chapter 12 for details.) Therefore, *you cannot rely on this as the exact default style sheet for any given user agent.* It is provided more for illustrative purposes and as a learning tool.

The second thing to note is that not all HTML elements are fully described in this style sheet because CSS is not yet detailed enough to completely and accurately describe them. The classic examples are form elements, such as submit buttons, which are replaced elements but have their own special formatting needs. Submit buttons are replaced elements, and thus the bottom edge of their box should align with the baseline. Authors, however, are likely to expect the text inside the button to align with the baseline of other text in the same line. This is a reasonable expectation, but CSS does not (as of this writing) have the ability to describe such behavior; therefore, all that is said about such elements is the following rule:

```
button, textarea, input, object, select, img {
                display:inline-block;}
```

The rest of the formatting of such elements is left to the user agent.

With these caveats in mind, here is the style sheet (with some slight reformatting) found in the CSS2 specification. Any changes other than reformatting are noted in comments.

```
address, blockquote, body, dd, div, dl, dt, fieldset, form,
frame, frameset, h1, h2, h3, h4, h5, h6, noframes,
ol, p, ul, center, dir, hr, menu, pre {
                   display: block;}
li                 {display: list-item;}
head               {display: none;}
table              {display: table;}
tr                 {display: table-row;}
thead              {display: table-header-group;}
tbody              {display: table-row-group;}
tfoot              {display: table-footer-group;}
col                {display: table-column;}
colgroup           {display: table-column-group;}
td, th             {display: table-cell;}
caption            {display: table-caption;}
th                 {font-weight: bolder; text-align: center;}
caption            {text-align: center;}
body               {padding: 8px; line-height: 1.12em;}
h1                 {font-size: 2em; margin: .67em 0;}
h2                 {font-size: 1.5em; margin: .75em 0;}
h3                 {font-size: 1.17em; margin: .83em 0;}
h4, p, blockquote, ul, fieldset, form, ol, dl, dir, menu {
                   margin: 1.12em 0;}
h5                 {font-size: .83em; margin: 1.5em 0;}
h6                 {font-size: .75em; margin: 1.67em 0;}
h1, h2, h3, h4, h5, h6, b, strong {
                   font-weight: bolder;}
blockquote         {margin-left: 40px; margin-right: 40px;}
i, cite, em, var, address  {
                   font-style: italic;}
pre, tt, code, kbd, samp {
                   font-family: monospace;}
pre                {white-space: pre;}
button, textarea, input, object, select, img {
                   display:inline-block;}
big                {font-size: 1.17em;}
small, sub, sup {font-size: .83em;}
sub                {vertical-align: sub;}
sup                {vertical-align: super;}
s, strike, del {text-decoration: line-through;}
hr                 {border: 1px inset;}
ol, ul, dir, menu, dd  {
                   margin-left: 40px;}
ol                 {list-style-type: decimal;}
ol ul, ul ol, ul ul, ol ol {
                   margin-top: 0; margin-bottom: 0;}
u, ins             {text-decoration: underline;}
br:before          {content: "\A";}
center             {text-align: center;}
abbr, acronym      {font-variant: small-caps; letter-spacing: 0.1em;}
:link,:visited {text-decoration: underline;}
:focus             {outline: thin dotted invert;}
```

```
/* Begin bidirectionality settings (do not change) */
BDO[DIR="ltr"]  {direction: ltr; unicode-bidi: bidi-override;}
BDO[DIR="rtl"]  {direction: rtl; unicode-bidi: bidi-override;}

*[DIR="ltr"]    {direction: ltr; unicode-bidi: embed;}
*[DIR="rtl"]    {direction: rtl; unicode-bidi: embed;}

@media print {
  h1            {page-break-before: always;}
  h1, h2, h3, h4, h5, h6 {
                  page-break-after: avoid;}
  ul, ol, dl    {page-break-before: avoid;}
}
@media aural {  /* changed from 'speech' which was not defined in CSS2 */
  h1, h2, h3, h4, h5, h6 {
                  voice-family: paul, male; stress: 20; richness: 90;}
  h1            {pitch: x-low; pitch-range: 90;}
  h2            {pitch: x-low; pitch-range: 80;}
  h3            {pitch: low; pitch-range: 70;}
  h4            {pitch: medium; pitch-range: 60;}
  h5            {pitch: medium; pitch-range: 50;}
  h6            {pitch: medium; pitch-range: 40;}
  li, dt, dd    {pitch: medium; richness: 60;}
  dt            {stress: 80;}
  pre, code, tt {pitch: medium; pitch-range: 0; stress: 0; richness: 80;}
  em            {pitch: medium; pitch-range: 60; stress: 60; richness: 50;}
  strong        {pitch: medium; pitch-range: 60; stress: 90; richness: 90;}
  dfn           {pitch: high; pitch-range: 60; stress: 60;}
  s, strike     {richness: 0;}
  i             {pitch: medium; pitch-range: 60; stress: 60; richness: 50;}
  b             {pitch: medium; pitch-range: 60; stress: 90; richness: 90;}
  u             {richness: 0;}
  a:link        {voice-family: harry, male;}
  a:visited     {voice-family: betty, female;}
  a:active      {voice-family: betty, female; pitch-range: 80; pitch: x-high;}
}
```

Index

Symbols

+ (plus sign)
  in adjacent-sibling selectors, 49
  in property syntax, xii
<> (angle brackets) in property syntax, xii
> (greater-than symbol) in child selectors, 48
@import directive, 18
| (vertical bar)
  in attribute selector, 43
  in property syntax, xii
|| (vertical double bar) in property syntax, xii
~ (tilde) in attribute selectors, 41

A

a element, 51
absolute length units, 84
absolute positioning, 303, 317
  containing blocks and, 303, 317
  height and width affecting, 320
  nonreplaced elements, 323
  on z-axis, 329
  replaced elements, 327
  scrolling and, 319
  stacking context and order for, 331
absolute URL, 90
ActiveBorder system color, 398
ActiveCaption system color, 398
adjacent-sibling combinator, 49
adjacent-sibling selectors, 49, 492
align attribute, img element, 283

alignment
  justified, 133, 145
  of baseline, 141
  of cell content, 366
  of middle of element, 141
  spacing and, 145
  superscripting and subscripting, 139
  to baseline, 138
  to bottom of line box, 140
  to bottom of text, 140
  vertical, 134
alink attribute, body element
  active pseudo-class and, 54
alt attribute, attribute selectors used with, 39
alternate style sheets, 16
alternate stylesheet attribute, 16
ancestors of elements, 45
angle brackets (<>) in property syntax, xii
angle values, 92
animated cursors, 404
AppWorkspace system color, 398
aspect value of font, 119
asterisk (*)
  as universal selector, 28, 32
  in property syntax, xii
attribute selectors, 38–43, 493, 494
  applying to multiple attributes, 39, 40
  exact-value attribute selectors, 39
  partial-value attribute selectors, 41
  particular attribute selectors, 43
  simple attribute selectors, 38, 493
  specificity of, 63
attribute values, as generated content, 383

specificity, 62–67
    calculating, 63
    cascade rule for, 71, 73
    of attribute selectors, 63, 66
    of class selectors, 63
    of grouped selectors, 64
    of ID selectors, 63
    of inherited values, 69
    of inline styles, 66
    of multiple rules, 64
    of non-CSS presentational hints, 75
    of pseudo-classes, 63
    of pseudo-elements, 63
    of universal selector, 63, 70
    resolving ties between, 71
speech media type, 430
speech-rate property, 433, 489
square brackets ([])
    in attribute selectors, 38
    in property syntax, xii
stacking context, for absolute
        positioning, 331
static position of element, 321
static positioning, 302, 303
status-bar system font, 396
stress property, 438, 489
strikethru text, 148
structural HTML markup, 2
structured documents, 2
style attribute, 21, 73
style element, 17, 20
style rules, 19, 23
    important declarations, 67
    inline, 73
    multiple, specificity of, 64
    order of, in cascade rules, 71, 73
    origin of, 71, 72
    parts of, 24
    weight of, 71, 72
style sheets, 4
    alternate, 16
    alternate style sheets, 16
    embedded, 18
    example of, 499
    external style sheets, 13
    filename extension for, 14
    linking to documents, 18
    linking to multiple documents, 5
    multiple, linking to document, 15
    persistent style sheets, 17
    preferred style sheets, 17
    reader style sheets, 6

styles, 19
styling features of CSS, 3
styling, rich, 3
superscripting, 139
syntax conventions used in this book, xii
system colors, 398
system fonts, 123, 395

T

table captions, 343
table columns, 340
table element, 341
    internal table elements, 339
    layer for, 349
table footers, 342
table headers, 342
table-layout property, 359, 480
tables, 339–369, 478–480
    anonymous table objects, 345
    arrangement rules for, 339
    automatic layout for, 362, 480
    block-level, 341
    captions for, 350
    fixed-layout model for, 360
    headers for, spoken, 432, 488
    height of, 365
    hidden borders and, 224
    inline-level, 341
    layers of, 349
    missing components of, 345
    row primacy model for, 344
    specifying elements for, 341
    width of, 359
tags, 12
tbody element, 342
td element, 343
teletype printers, media type for, 15
television, media type for, 15
text, 128
    aligning horizontally, 474
    aligning vertically, 134
    blinking, 148, 475
    carriage returns in, 154
    centering, 132
    color of, 149, 151
    drop shadows for, 152
    hyphenation of, 133
    indenting, 128, 475
    leading, 134
    letter spacing of, 145
    overlining, 148

shadows for, 483
strikethru, 148
underlining, 148, 150
whitespace between words and lines, 153
wrapping, 154
text attribute, body element, replacing using
color property, 249
text-align property, 131, 474
compared to margin-left and
margin-right, 165
for cell content, 366
for table captions, 351
text-bottom alignment, 140
text-decoration property, 148, 475
text-indent property, 128, 475
text-shadow property, 483
text-transform property, 146, 475
tfoot element, 342
th element, 343
thead element, 342
ThreeDDarkShadow system color, 399
ThreeDFace system color, 399
ThreeDHighlight system color, 399
ThreeDLightShadow system color, 399
ThreeDShadow system color, 399
tilde (~) in attribute selectors, 41
tiling of background images, 256, 257, 451
time values, 92
title attribute
attribute selectors used with, 39
link tag, 16
toolbars, displaying links across
horizontally, 202
tooltips, attribute selectors used with, 39
top alignment, 140
top property, 476
tr element, 342
transparent borders, 233
tty media type, 15
tv media type, 15
type attribute, link tag, 14
type selectors, 491
typographical conventions used in this
book, xi

U

underline keyword, 91
underlined text, 148
unicode-bidi property, 476
Uniform Resource Identifier, 93

units and values, 77–93
units for aural styles, 92
universal selector, 28, 491
in class selectors, 32, 34
in ID selectors, 36
specificity of, 70
URI (Uniform Resource Identifier),
specifying, 93
URL (Uniform Resource Locator)
relative to style sheet, 91
specifying, 90
user agents, 8
as origin of declarations, 71, 72
default styles of, 72
Emacspeak, 93
Fonix SpeakThis, 430
weight of declarations and, 72
user interface
colors for, 398
cursors, 400
fonts for, 395
user interface styles, 395–410

V

value of property, 24, 26
colors as, 78
keywords as, 91
URLs as, 90
values and units, 77–93
vertical alignment
of inline nonreplaced elements, 186
of table cell content, 366
of text, 137
vertical bar (|)
in attribute selector, 43
in property syntax, xii
vertical double bar (||) in property syntax, xii
vertical formatting, of block-level
elements, 170
vertical-align property, 186, 476
for table cell content, 366
text-decoration and, 150
visibility of elements, 316, 477
visibility property, 316, 477
visual styles, 482
vlink attribute, body element, 52, 249
voice used for speaking, 436, 486, 487, 489
voice-family property, 436, 490
volume of speech, 490
volume property, 434, 490

W

W3C, 3
waiting cursor, 403
watch cursor, 403
web sites
    for this book, xiv
    O'Reilly Media, Inc., xiv
Web, history of, 1
web-safe colors, 83
white-space property, 153, 477
whitespace, handling, 477
widows property, 422, 424, 481
width property, 161, 208, 308, 477
    affect of negative margins on, 166
    columns and column groups, 345
    positioned elements and, 307
    replaced elements and, 169
    setting to auto, 163
wildcard, 28
Window system color, 400
WindowFrame system color, 400

WindowText system color, 400
words, spacing between, 143, 144, 478
word-spacing property, 143, 478
World Wide Web, 1
World Wide Web Consortium (W3C),
    HTML elements deprecated by, 3
wrapping text, 154

X

XHTML
    CSS and, 11–21
    deprecated elements in, 7, 21
    specification, 7
XML
    element selectors for, 24
    replacing HTML, 7

Z

z-axis, absolute positioning on, 478
z-index property, 478

About the Author

Eric A. Meyer has been working with the Web since late 1993 and is an internationally recognized expert on the subjects of HTML, CSS, and web standards. A widely read author, he is also the founder of Complex Spiral Consulting (*www.complexspiral.com*), which counts among its clients America Online; Apple Computer, Inc.; Wells Fargo Bank; and Macromedia, which described Eric as "a critical partner in our efforts to transform Macromedia Dreamweaver MX 2004 into a revolutionary tool for CSS-based design."

Beginning in early 1994, Eric was the visual designer and campus web coordinator for the Case Western Reserve University web site, where he also authored a widely acclaimed series of three HTML tutorials and was project coordinator for the online version of the *Encyclopedia of Cleveland History* and the *Dictionary of Cleveland Biography*, the first encyclopedia of urban history published fully and freely on the Web.

Author of *Eric Meyer on CSS* and *More Eric Meyer on CSS* (New Riders), *Cascading Style Sheets: The Definitive Guide* (O'Reilly), and *CSS2.0 Programmer's Reference* (Osborne/McGraw-Hill), as well as numerous articles for the O'Reilly Network, Web Techniques, and Web Review, Eric also created the CSS Browser Compatibility Charts and coordinated the authoring and creation of the W3C's official CSS Test Suite. He has lectured to a wide variety of organizations, including Los Alamos National Laboratory, the New York Public Library, Cornell University, and the University of Northern Iowa. Eric has also delivered addresses and technical presentations at numerous conferences, among them An Event Apart (which he cofounded), the IW3C2 WWW series, Web Design World, CMP, SXSW, the User Interface conference series, and The Other Dreamweaver Conference.

In his personal time, Eric acts as List Chaperone of the highly active css-discuss mailing list (*www.css-discuss.org*), which he cofounded with John Allsopp of Western Civilisation, and which is now supported by *evolt.org*. Eric lives in Cleveland, Ohio, which is a much nicer city than you've been led to believe. For nine years he was the host of "Your Father's Oldsmobile," a Big Band-era radio show heard weekly on WRUW 91.1 FM in Cleveland.

You can find more detailed information on Eric's personal web page at *http://www.meyerweb.com/eric*.

Colophon

Our look is the result of reader comments, our own experimentation, and feedback from distribution channels. Distinctive covers complement our distinctive approach to technical topics, breathing personality and life into potentially dry subjects.

The animals on the cover of *CSS: The Definitive Guide*, Third Edition, are salmon (*salmonidae*), which is a family of fish consisting of many different species. Two of the most common salmon are the Pacific salmon and the Atlantic salmon.

Pacific salmon live in the northern Pacific Ocean off the coasts of North America and Asia. There are five subspecies of Pacific salmon, with an average weight of 10 to 30 pounds. Pacific salmon are born in the fall in freshwater stream gravel beds, where they incubate through the winter and emerge as inch-long fish. They live for a year or two in streams or lakes and then head downstream to the ocean. There they live for a few years, before heading back upstream to their exact place of birth to spawn and then die.

Atlantic salmon live in the northern Atlantic Ocean off the coasts of North America and Europe. There are many subspecies of Atlantic salmon, including the trout and the char. Their average weight is 10 to 20 pounds. The Atlantic salmon family has a life cycle similar to that of its Pacific cousins, and also travels from freshwater gravel beds to the sea. A major difference between the two, however, is that the Atlantic salmon does not die after spawning; it can return to the ocean and then return to the stream to spawn again, usually two or three times.

Salmon, in general, are graceful, silver-colored fish with spots on their backs and fins. Their diet consists of plankton, insect larvae, shrimp, and smaller fish. Their unusually keen sense of smell is thought to help them navigate from the ocean back to the exact spot of their birth, upstream past many obstacles. Some species of salmon remain landlocked, living their entire lives in freshwater.

Salmon are an important part of the ecosystem, as their decaying bodies provide fertilizer for streambeds. Their numbers have been dwindling over the years, however. Factors in the declining salmon population include habitat destruction, fishing, dams that block spawning paths, acid rain, droughts, floods, and pollution.

The cover image is a 19th-century engraving from the Dover Pictorial Archive. The cover font is Adobe ITC Garamond. The text font is Linotype Birka; the heading font is Adobe Myriad Condensed; and the code font is LucasFont's TheSans Mono Condensed.

Better than e-books

Buy *CSS: The Definitive Guide,* 2nd Edition, and access
the digital edition FREE on Safari for 45 days.

Go to www.oreilly.com/go/safarienabled
and type in coupon code TMA5-VZBB-BUKE-FXCI-EA9C

Search
thousands of
top tech books

Download
whole chapters

Cut and Paste
code examples

Find
answers fast

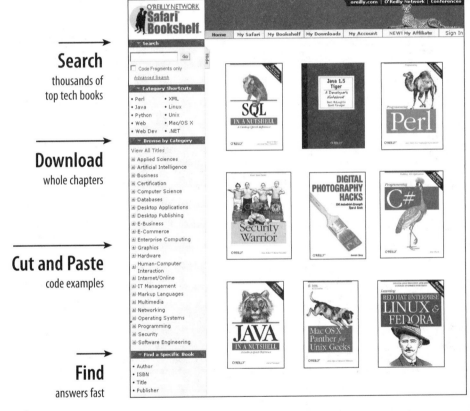

Search Safari! The premier electronic reference
library for programmers and IT professionals.

Related Titles from O'Reilly

Web Programming

ActionScript 3 Cookbook

ActionScript for Flash MX: The Definitive Guide, *2nd Edition*

Ajax Design Patterns

Ajax Hacks

Building Scalable Web Sites

Dynamic HTML: The Definitive Reference, *2nd Edition*

Flash Hacks

Essential PHP Security

Google Advertising Tools

Google Hacks, *2nd Edition*

Google Map Hacks

Google Pocket Guide

Google: The Missing Manual, *2nd Edition*

Head First HTML with CSS & XHTML

Head Rush Ajax

HTTP: The Definitive Guide

JavaScript & DHTML Cookbook

JavaScript Pocket Reference, *2nd Edition*

JavaScript: The Definitive Guide, *4th Edition*

Learning PHP 5

Learning PHP and MySQL

PHP Cookbook

PHP Hacks

PHP in a Nutshell

PHP Pocket Reference, *2nd Edition*

PHPUnit Pocket Guide

Programming ColdFusion MX, *2nd Edition*

Programming PHP, *2nd Edition*

Upgrading to PHP 5

Web Database Applications with PHP and MySQL, *2nd Edition*

Web Site Cookbook

Webmaster in a Nutshell, *3rd Edition*

Web Administration

Apache Cookbook

Apache Pocket Reference

Apache: The Definitive Guide, *3rd Edition*

Perl for Web Site Management

Squid: The Definitive Guide

Web Performance Tuning, *2nd Edition*